ART AND POWER

Europe under the dictators 1930-45

ART AND POWER

Europe under the dictators 1930-45

The XXIII Council of Europe exhibition

Council of Europe
Conseil de l'Europe

Compiled and selected by
Dawn Ades
Tim Benton
David Elliott
Iain Boyd Whyte

Foreword by Eric Hobsbawm
Afterword by Neal Ascherson

Supported by the Foreign and Commonwealth Office
and the Arts Council of England

Sponsored by

⌀BNL
Banca Nazionale del Lavoro

Hayward Gallery

Published on the occasion of the exhibition
Art and Power: Europe under the dictators 1930–45,
organized by the Hayward Gallery, London,
in collaboration with the Centre de Cultura Contemporània
de Barcelona and the Deutsches Historisches Museum, Berlin

Hayward Gallery, London
26 October 1995 – 21 January 1996

Centre de Cultura Contemporània de Barcelona
26 February – 6 May 1996

Deutsches Historisches Museum, Berlin
7 June – 20 August 1996

Catalogue supported by the Embassy of the Federal Republic of Germany

Exhibition organized by Andrew Dempsey
with Martin Caiger-Smith
assisted by Cindy Hubert and Achim Borchardt

Catalogue edited by David Britt
Designed by Herman Lelie
Produced by Oktagon, Stuttgart

Cover: Vera Mukhina, *Industrial Worker and Collective Farm Girl*,
1937; Carlos Sáenz de Tejada, illustration from *Canción de la Falange*,
by Agustín de Foxa, 1939, Biblioteca de Catalunya, Barcelona.

Frontispiece: International Exhibition, Paris 1937. Regatta in
progress on 13 June, with Italian Pavilion in foreground (sculpture by
Giorgio Gori), German Pavilion at right and Soviet Pavilion in the
background (sculpture by Vera Mukhina).

ISBN 1 85332 148 6 (softback)

Hayward Gallery, National Touring Exhibitions and Arts Council
Collection publications are distributed by Cornerhouse Publications,
70 Oxford Street, Manchester M1 5NH (tel. 0161 237 9662;
fax 0161 237 9664)

CONTENTS

COMMITTEE OF HONOUR

Mr Josef Zieleniec
Chairman in office of the Committee of Ministers of the Council of Europe

M Hervé de Charette, Minister for Foreign Affairs
France

Dr Klaus Kinkel, Federal Minister for Foreign Affairs
Federal Republic of Germany

Signora Susanna Agnelli, Minister for Foreign Affairs
Italy

Don Javier Solana Madariaga, Minister for Foreign Affairs
Spain

Rt Hon Malcolm Rifkind QC MP
Secretary of State for Foreign and Commonwealth Affairs
United Kingdom

His Excellency Mr Anatoly Adamishin
Ambassador of the Russian Federation

Eberhard Diepgen
Governing Mayor of Berlin

Signor Francesco Rutelli
Mayor of Rome

EUROPEAN ORGANIZING COMMITTEE

Professor Dr Klaus Gallwitz, Chairman, Consultants on Council of Europe Art Exhibitions

Professor Dr Winfried Nerdinger, Architekturmuseum, Technische Universität München

José Guirao Cabrera, Director, Museo Nacional Centro de Arte Reina Sofía
Madrid

Germain Viatte, Director, Musée National d'Art Moderne, Centre Georges Pompidou
Paris

Dottoressa Augusta Monferini, former Director of the Galleria Nazionale d'Arte Moderna
Rome

Professor Francesco Dal Co, Istituto Universitario di Architettura di Venezia

Olle Granath, Director, Nationalmuseum
Stockholm

Lidia Iovleva, Deputy Director, State Tretyakov Gallery
Moscow

Professor Vladimir Rezvin, Director, A.V. Shchusev State Research Museum of Architecture
Moscow

Evgenia Petrova, Deputy Director, Russian State Museum
St Petersburg

Ryszard Stanislawski

ACKNOWLEDGMENTS

The long and distinguished series of Council of Europe exhibitions began in Brussels in 1955. The subject of that first exhibition was *Humanist Europe*. From the outset, these exhibitions have been a key element in the Council's cultural programme, with the objective of reminding Europeans of their common history and cultural heritage.

There have been two previous exhibitions in this series in this country: *Romanticism* at the Tate Gallery in 1959 and *The Age of Neo-Classicism* at the Royal Academy and the Victoria & Albert Museum in 1972, both of which were organized by the Arts Council of Great Britain, whose exhibitions team have since transferred to the SBC, with continuing responsibility for the programme of exhibitions at the Hayward Gallery.

The invitation to the British Government to stage a third exhibition, this time on a more recent period, was made at the suggestion of the Council of Europe's Consultants on Art Exhibitions, a group which includes the directors of several major European museums. Their Chairman, Professor Dr Klaus Gallwitz, former Director of the Städelsches Kunstinstitut und Städtische Galerie in Frankfurt, further suggested that the exhibition be devoted to art in Europe during the 1930s and 1940s, in succession, as he explains in his preface to this catalogue, to *Tendenzen der zwanziger Jahre*, held in Berlin in 1977. The United Kingdom representatives on the Council of Europe's advisory group, Dr Robert Anderson and Sir David Wilson, the current and former Directors of the British Museum, have both been instrumental in carrying our project forward in its planning stages with the Council of Europe's advisers.

The former Director of Exhibitions at the SBC, Joanna Drew, received and developed the project when it was first mooted by Professor Dr Klaus Gallwitz in 1988. Under her, the project was carefully nurtured by David Sylvester and Nicholas Serota in the early stages, until it took a direction of its own, with the formal appointment of a curatorial team.

An important reason why the invitation to organize an exhibition on art in Europe during the 1930s and 1940s was extended to Her Majesty's Government was that the United Kingdom had resisted totalitarian rule during this period. It is the plight of artists and architects under totalitarian rule which we have chosen to examine. But before the subject of our exhibition came into such focus we consulted widely with European colleagues and specialists. Firstly, we have had the vital guidance throughout of a European Organizing Committee. Secondly, we were able, thanks to the support of the Council of Europe, The Open Society Fund and the United Kingdom embassies of participating European countries, to organize an international symposium at the Courtauld Institute of Art in January 1994, at which an invaluable exchange of views took place with specialists from no fewer than seventeen countries.

Shortly after the Courtauld symposium we invited Professor Dawn Ades of the Art History and Theory Department, University of Essex; Professor Tim Benton, Dean of the Faculty of Humanities of the Open University; Dr Iain Boyd Whyte, Director of the Centre for Architectural History and Theory at the University of Edinburgh; and David Elliott, Director of the Museum of Modern Art in Oxford, to devise and select the exhibition. They were later joined by Lutz Becker, whose special responsibility has been the film element of this exhibition, and by Simonetta Fraquelli, a specialist on the history of twentieth-century Italian art. This core team has formed the present exhibition. We would like to express our particular thanks to them, to Julia Engelhardt, who organized the symposium, and to the following for their assistance in undertaking research and helping us to develop the exhibition: Ester Coen, Emily Braun and Robert Williams, for the Italian section, with additional assistance from Silvia Mollo in Rome; Bernd Nicolai in Berlin; and Marko Daniel, Achim Borchardt and Ines Schlenker in London.

As well as forming the exhibition, our selectors have had the responsibility of helping us to shape this no less complex publication. Here we should like to make special mention of our editor, David Britt, who has co-ordinated the production of a catalogue with distinguished contributors from Spain, Italy, France, Germany, Russia and the United States, as well as from this country. The SBC has collaborated with the publishers Oktagon, in Stuttgart, to produce the catalogue and we should like warmly to acknowledge the help of Oktagon's Director, Uwe Kraus, and of the catalogue designer, Herman Lelie. The architect, Mark Fisher, has played a key part in the conception as well as the presentation of the exhibition. We are grateful to him and to his collaborators, Kate Hepburn and Mark Norton, of the design group 4i, for the imagination they have brought to the challenge of presenting such diverse material in the galleries.

In Strasbourg, the Council of Europe's special adviser on art exhibitions, David Mardell, has provided continuous support, encouragement and advice. We are much indebted to him and to his assistant, Mme Irène Herrenschmidt. In the UK, the Cultural Relations Department of the Foreign and Commonwealth Office has been closely involved since the invitation from the Council of Europe was received by our Government. We are especially grateful to the current and former Heads of the Cultural Relations Department, Mr. Anthony Sprake and Mr. Nicholas Elam (now Ambassador at Luxembourg), and to their colleagues in the Foreign and Commonwealth Office.

Funds for an exhibition which has involved both the assembly of work from many different countries and a complex presentation in the galleries of the Hayward have been most generously provided by the Council of Europe itself and by the Foreign and Commonwealth Office in this country. An additional contribution was kindly made by the International Initiatives Fund of the Arts Council of England. Though exceptionally generous, these funds were not in themselves sufficient and we were, therefore, extremely grateful when the Banca Nazionale del Lavoro S.p.A. stepped in at a timely moment to sponsor the exhibition. We are pleased to acknowledge this help and to convey our thanks to the Bank's top management and their representatives of the London Branch.

Further financial support and much help in kind has been provided by the cultural services of several London embassies, particularly the German Embassy which has made a special grant towards this catalogue, and the Goethe-Institut, which has been supportive throughout. We also acknowledge with gratitude the encouragement and support of the cultural services of the Italian, Spanish and French Embassies, as well as the Italian and French Institutes in London, in addition to the support and advice received from the embassies and cultural representatives in London of the forty-three member states of the European Cultural Convention.

It is rare for Council of Europe exhibitions to be shown in more than one city. Indeed the only precedent is *From Viking to Crusader: The Scandinavians and Europe, 800–1200*, which took place in Berlin, Copenhagen and Paris in 1992–3. Simultaneous expressions of interest in collaboration on the XXIII Council of Europe exhibition were received from the Deutsches Historisches Museum in Berlin and the Centre de Cultura Contemporània in Barcelona. Interest quickly evolved into partnership, thanks to the positive commitment of the directors of both institutions, Professor Dr Christoph Stölzl and Señor Josep Ramoneda, as well as their staff. The exhibition will be shown in both cities in 1996. In this connection we should like to thank M. Jean Dethier of the Centre Georges Pompidou, who helped bring about the collaboration with the CCCB, where his own exhibition *La Ville* was shown after Paris.

We should like to make clear our very deep gratitude to the many museums and private collectors in the United States, continental Europe and Britain which have collaborated with us in making this exhibition possible. Books can be made without objects, but not exhibitions. We should have fallen at the first hurdle, had it not been for the very generous response with which our colleagues in the museums of Russia, Germany, Italy, Spain, the Netherlands and the United States received our requests for loans. We thank them for their generosity, their patience and their interest, much as we wish to thank the Ministries of Culture and respective authorities in those countries for facilitating the often complicated loan procedures.

Within the present Exhibitions Department of the SBC, it has sometimes seemed as if the whole staff was engaged in this project, at one point or another. We owe a particular debt of gratitude to Andrew Dempsey, Assistant Director of the Exhibitions Department from 1987 to 1993 and Associate Curator from 1993 to 1995 with particular responsibility for this exhibition, who has seen this project through from beginning to end. We cannot mention everybody but would like to express particular gratitude to the following colleagues in the Exhibitions Department for their unstinting efforts: Martin Caiger-Smith, who took on joint organizational responsibility for certain aspects of the exhibition in the final months of preparation, and Cindy Hubert, the Assistant Exhibition Organizer who has underpinned the operation throughout; Lise Connellan, Susan Ferleger Brades, Greg Hilty, Mark King, Kate Lloyd, Linda Schofield, Angie Whitbread, Imogen Winter and our former colleague, Leigh Markopoulos; and to many colleagues in other departments of the SBC for their no less essential contributions, notably Joanne Hallgren and Julyn Walker in the Development Department, Alison Rowe in the Marketing Department, and our former Press Officer, Nigel Semmens, and Alison Wright, his successor.

Sir Brian Corby,
Chairman, The South Bank Board

Nicholas Snowman,
Chief Executive, SBC

Henry Meyric Hughes,
Director of Exhibitions, SBC

PREFACE

Klaus Gallwitz

In 1977 the Western part of Berlin witnessed the exhibition *Tendenzen der zwanziger Jahre* (Tendencies of the 1920s). In the divided city, the Neue Nationalgalerie, the Orangerie of Schloss Charlottenburg and the Akademie der Künste housed the work of the avant-garde of one of the great decades of European art.

That was in the middle of the Cold War, and the exhibition, the fifteenth organized by the Council of Europe, was inaccessible to people beyond the Wall: a view of 'Modernism Undivided' without Eastern participation. The exhibition *Westkunst*, shown in Cologne in 1981, was a statement of this political and artistic reality: the postwar aesthetic was defined in Atlantic terms.

And so there has been no sequel to that exhibition in Berlin. The 1930s, the age of totalitarianism and war, have been tabooed, disregarded, or else looked at only from specialized aspects. After all, who was in a position to be unbiased? Memories in postwar Europe differed too widely; the ideological pressures of the present were too strong. The title of our exhibition, *Art and Power*, is a deliberate reference to this continuing dilemma.

In 1930 José Ortega y Gasset gave this diagnosis: 'For good or ill, the decisive factor that governs public life in Europe at present is the rise of the masses to full social power.' This was our starting point. Early in 1988, in discussions within a small group of museum colleagues at the Council of Europe in Strasbourg, the concept took shape: it was that of art in Europe between the Great Depression and the Potsdam Conference, between dictatorship and freedom.

London commended itself to us as the setting for the exhibition. Great Britain had held out against Fascism, and during the Second World War the chimes of Big Ben in Westminster reached us from the BBC. This was the voice of freedom; anyone in our countries who listened to it, or passed it on, was risking his or her life. In itself, this made the island capital seem the appropriate setting for this contradictory, conflict-laden chapter in the history of art.

We were not disappointed in the response. Our colleagues at the Hayward Gallery took up the suggestion and made the project their own. The results of intensive researches on an international scale are now before us; and the opening of the Eastern borders has lent the project an unexpected impulse and a new motivation.

In the exhibition, architecture and film are given the prominence that their historical importance demands – as against the controversial position of painting and sculpture in the service of totalitarian ideologies, which is also represented here. The British capital itself turns out to have been a particular focus for Continental contradictions. Almost in the very style of his adversaries – and as a scornful indictment of them – Oskar Kokoschka (who later moved to London) painted himself in 1937 as a 'Degenerate Artist'. Here, too, Salvador Dalí was introduced to the refugee Sigmund Freud by the writer Stefan Zweig. Dalí, who did not hide his admiration for the movement of the soft flesh of Hitler's back packed tightly into his uniform, sketched, in a state of fascination, two portraits of the Viennese scholar. At the same time, as a riposte to the Munich exhibition in which 'Degenerate Art' was pilloried, the New Burlington Galleries in London held an exhibition of those same artists who were outlawed in Germany. Again, it was here that Elias Canetti, tucked away in Hampstead, was assembling his notes for the book that became *Crowds and Power*. Shortly after the outbreak of war, Henry Moore made his first *Shelter Drawings*: glimpses of a 'human condition' that looked much the same all over Europe. London bears the marks of a European decade.

That the exhibition became possible is to the credit of all the staff of the Hayward Gallery, and of the selectors and specialists who have participated in the enterprise. We are indebted to Henry Meyric Hughes and Andrew Dempsey, but also to Joanna Drew, David Sylvester and Nicholas Serota (who were involved in the early stages). I am grateful to my colleagues at the Council of Europe in Strasbourg for their support over many years – and in particular to David Mardell, who has the responsibility for exhibitions, for his tireless and ever-present support of this, the Twenty-Third Council of Europe Exhibition.

As Europe once more seeks to find its voice, this exhibition seeks to contribute to the regaining of a common memory – in London as well as in Barcelona and in Berlin, where it will subsequently be shown.

Photographies Schall et « L'Illustration ».

LES MOTIFS DE SCULPTURE QUI COURONNENT TROIS DES PRINCIPAUX PAVILLONS ÉTRANGERS

L'Allemagne (Aigle, professeur Schmidt-Ehmen) - L'U.R.S.S. (l'industrie et l'agriculture, groupe en acier de Mme Mouchina)
L'Italie (les diverses corporations, par les sculpteurs Servettaz, Mascherini, Fontana, Minguzzi et Bortolotti).

Page from *L'Illustration*, 1937

FOREWORD

Eric Hobsbawm

Art has been used to reinforce the power of political rulers and states since the ancient Egyptians, though the relationship between power and art has not always been smooth. The present exhibition illustrates probably the least happy episode in this relationship in the twentieth century, in what has been called the 'Europe of the Dictators', between 1930 and 1945.

For a century before the First World War it had been confidently assumed that Europe was moving in the direction of political liberalism, civil rights and constitutional government by elected authorities, though not necessarily republics. Shortly before 1914 even democracy – government by the vote of all adult males, though not yet of females – was making rapid progress. The Great War seemed to accelerate this development dramatically. After it ended Europe consisted of parliamentary regimes of one kind or another, except for war-torn and revolutionary Soviet Russia. However, almost immediately, the direction of political development was reversed. Europe, and indeed most parts of the globe, moved away from political liberalism. By the middle of the Second World War no more than twelve out of the sixty-five sovereign states of the interwar period had anything like constitutional elected governments. The regimes of the political right which took over everywhere except in Russia were hostile to democracy in principle. Communism, still confined to Russia, claimed to be democratic in theory and nomenclature, but was in practice an unlimited dictatorship.

Most of the regimes with which this exhibition is concerned consciously and deliberately broke with the immediate past. Whether this radical break was made from the political right or left – outside Europe, as in Kemal Atatürk's Turkey, these labels were sometimes beside the point – is less important than that such regimes saw their role, not as maintaining or restoring or even improving their society but as transforming and reconstructing it. They were not landlords of old buildings but architects of new ones. Equally to the point, they were ruled, or came to be ruled, by absolute leaders whose command was law. Moreover, although these were the opposite of democratic, they all claimed to derive from and operate through 'the people' and to lead and shape them. These common characteristics distinguished both Fascist and Communist regimes in this period from the older states, in spite of their fundamental differences and mutual hostility. In them, power not only made enormous demands on art, but art found it difficult or even impossible to escape the demands and controls of political authority. Not surprisingly, an exhibition on Art and Power in this period is dominated by the arts in Hitler's Germany (1933–45), Stalin's USSR (*c.* 1930–53) and Mussolini's Italy (1922–45).

However, it cannot overlook the public arts of the states whose governments were being subverted. Appropriately, therefore, this exhibition begins with the one occasion when all states and their arts were in public confrontation: the Paris International Exhibition of 1937, the last before the Second World War of a series of such displays which had begun in London in 1851. They had been perhaps the most characteristic form in which art and power collaborated during the era of bourgeois liberalism. While providing prestige for the countries which organized them, rather as Olympic Games do today, what they had celebrated was not the state but civil society, not political power but economic, technical and cultural achievement, not conflict but the coexistence of nations. Descended from fairs (the American ones were even called 'World Fairs'), they were not designed as permanent structures, though they left some monuments behind, notably the Eiffel Tower.

Small 'national' pavilions had first appeared in 1867, but became increasingly prominent in what developed into public competitions between states. In 1937 they dominated the Exhibition totally. The thirty-eight rival displays – more than in any previous exhibition – represented a higher proportion of the world's sovereign states than ever before or since. All, or almost all, made political statements, if only by advertising the virtues of their 'way of life' and arts. The show itself was designed to bring glory to France, then governed by a Popular Front of the left under its first Socialist prime minister, and its most permanent memorial is probably Picasso's *Guernica*, first shown in the pavilion of the embattled Spanish Republic. Yet the 1937 Exhibition was clearly then, and is still in retrospect, dominated by the German and Soviet pavilions, huge and deliberately symbolic, which confronted each other across the mall.

There are three primary demands which power usually makes on art, and which absolute power makes on a larger scale than more limited authorities. The first is to demonstrate the glory and triumph of power itself, as in the great arches and columns celebrating victories in war ever since the Roman Empire, the major model for public art. Rather than by single constructions, the dimensions and ambitions of power in the age of the great leaders were to be demonstrated by the sheer scale of the structures they planned or realized and, typically, not so much by single buildings and monuments as by giant ensembles – replanned cities or even regions – for example, the motorways pioneered in an Italy with few cars. These could best express the planned reshaping of countries and societies. Pomp and gigantism were the face of power they wished the arts to present.

The second major function of art under power was to organize it as public drama. Ritual and ceremony are essential to the political process, and with the democratization of politics power increasingly became public theatre, with the people as audience and – this was the specific innovation of the era of dictators – as organized participants. The construction of wide rectilinear processional avenues for secular political display belongs essentially to the nineteenth century. The Mall in London (1911) with its vista from the Admiralty Arch to Buckingham Palace is a characteristic if late example. Increasingly, national monuments, built to stimulate or provide expression for mass patriotism, also included planned spaces for special ceremonies. The piazza Venezia in Rome was as essential to the awful Vittorio Emanuele monument as,

International Exhibition, Paris 1937, showing Soviet and German pavilions

later, to Mussolini's harangues. The rise of public mass entertainment, and above all mass sport, provided an additional supply of public terrains and structures custom-built for the expression of mass emotion, notably stadia. These could be and were used for the purposes of power. Hitler both spoke at the Berlin Sportpalast and discovered the political potential of the Olympic Games (1936).

The importance of art for power in this field lay not so much in the buildings and spaces themselves, but in what took place inside or between them. What power required was performance art in the enclosed spaces, elaborate ceremonies (the British became particularly adept at inventing royal rituals of this kind from the late nineteenth century onwards); and, in the open spaces, processions or mass choreography. The leaders' theatre of power combined military and civilian components and preferred open spaces. The contribution to crowd choreography of labour demonstrations, wars, stage spectacles and the new cinema epics pioneered before 1914 by the young Italian cinema remains to be adequately investigated.

A third service that art could render power was educational or propagandist: it could teach, inform and inculcate the state's value system. Before the era of the people's participation in politics these functions had been left mainly to churches and other religious bodies, but in the nineteenth century they were increasingly undertaken by secular governments, most obviously through public elementary education. The dictatorships did not innovate in this field, except by banning dissident voices and making state orthodoxy compulsory.

However, one traditional form of political art requires some comment, if only because it was rapidly on the way to extinction: monumental public statuary. Before the French Revolution, it had been confined to princes and allegorical figures; in the nineteenth century, however, it became a sort of open-air museum of national history as seen through great men. (Unless they were royal or symbolic, women were absent.) Its educational value was patent. Not for nothing did the arts in nineteenth-century France come under the Ministry of Public Instruction. Thus, in order to educate a largely illiterate people after the 1917 revolution, Lenin proposed to put up monuments to suitable persons – Danton, Garibaldi, Marx, Engels, Herzen, assorted poets and others – in conspicuous spots in cities, especially where soldiers could see them.

What has been called 'statuemania' reached its peak between 1870 and 1914, when 150 statues were erected

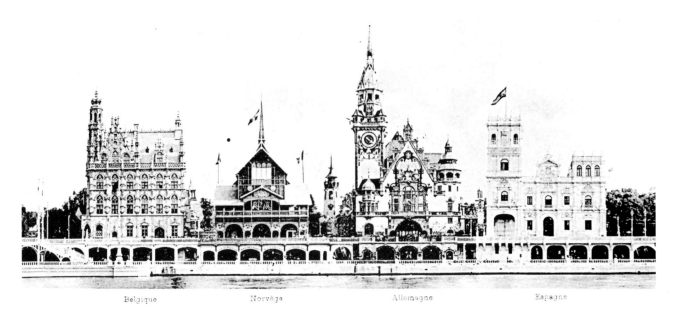

Belgique   Norvège   Allemagne   Espagne

Universal Exhibition, Paris 1900: national pavilions

in Paris, as against only twenty-six from 1815 to 1870 – and those primarily military figures, which had almost all been removed after 1870. (Under the German occupation in 1940–44 a further seventy-five of these glories of Culture, Progress and Republican identity were removed by the Vichy government.) Yet after the Great War, except the now universal war memorials, bronze and marble went distinctly out of fashion. The elaborate visual language of symbolism and allegory became as incomprehensible in the twentieth century as the classical myths now were for most people. In France the Paris municipal council (1937) feared that 'the tyranny of commemorative statuary rests like a heavy weight on projects that might be proposed by gifted artists and administrators with good taste.' Only the USSR, true to Lenin's example, maintained its unqualified attachment to public statuary, including giant symbolic monuments surrounded by workers, peasants, soldiers and arms.

Power clearly needed art. But what kind of art? The major problem arose out of the 'Modernist' revolution in the arts in the last years before the Great War, which produced styles and works designed to be unacceptable to anyone whose tastes were, like most people's, rooted in the nineteenth century. They were therefore unacceptable to conservative and even to conventional liberal governments. One might have expected regimes dedicated to breaking with the past and hailing the future to be more at ease with the avant-garde. However, there were two difficulties which were to prove insurmountable.

The first was that the avant-garde in the arts was not necessarily marching in the same direction as the political radicals of right or left. Probably the Soviet revolution and revulsion against the war attracted many to the radical left, although in literature some of the most talented writers can only be described as men of the extreme right. The German Nazis were not entirely wrong to describe the Modernism of the Weimar Republic as 'cultural Bolshevism'. National Socialism was therefore *a priori* hostile to the avant-garde. In Russia, most of the pre-1917 avant-garde had been non-political or doubtful about the October Revolution which, unlike the 1905 revolution, made no great appeal to Russian intellectuals. However, thanks to a sympathetic minister, Anatoly Lunacharsky, the avant-garde was given its head, so long as artists were not actively hostile to the Revolution, and it dominated the scene for several years, although several of its less politically committed stars gradually drifted westwards. The 1920s in Soviet Russia were desperately poor, but culturally vibrant. Under Stalin this changed dramatically.

The only dictatorship relatively at ease with Modernism was Mussolini's (one of whose mistresses saw herself as a patroness of contemporary art). Important branches of the local avant-garde (for example the Futurists) actually favoured Fascism, while most Italian intellectuals not already strongly committed to the left did not find it unacceptable, at least until the Spanish Civil War and Mussolini's adoption of Hitler's racism. It is true that the Italian avant-garde, like most of the Italian arts at the time, formed a somewhat provincial backwater. Even so, it can hardly be said to have dominated. The brilliance of Italian architecture, later discovered by the rest of the world, had little chance of emerging. As in Hitler's Germany and Stalin's Soviet Union, the mood of official Fascist architecture was not adventure, but pompous rhetoric.

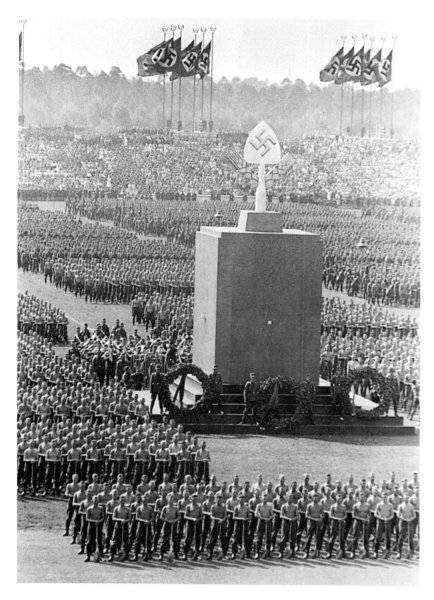

Labour
Convention,
Zeppelinfeld,
Nuremberg,
September 1937

The second difficulty was that Modernism appealed to a minority, whereas the governments were populist. On ideological and practical grounds they preferred arts that would appeal to the public, or at least be readily understood by it. This was rarely a top priority for creative talents who lived by innovation, experiment and quite often by provoking those who admired the art displayed in official Salons and Academies. Power and art disagreed most obviously over painting, since the regimes encouraged works in older academic, or at any rate realistic, styles, preferably blown up to large size and filled with heroic and sentimental clichés – even, in Germany, adding a little male erotic fantasy. Even in broadminded Italy official prizes like the Premio Cremona of 1939 (with seventy-nine contestants) were won by what could almost serve as a photofit portrait of public painting in any dictatorial country. Perhaps not surprisingly, since its subject was 'Listening to a speech by Il Duce on the radio'.

Architecture did not produce equally dramatic conflicts between power and art, since it did not raise the problem of how to represent any reality other than itself. Nevertheless, in one important respect power and Modernist architecture (did not Adolf Loos proclaim that 'Ornament is Crime'?) remained part of the artistic instrumentarium both of populist regimes and commercial producers for the mass market. Consider the London and the Moscow Undergrounds – the Metro being probably the largest artistic enterprise undertaken in Stalin's Soviet Union. The London Tube, thanks to the patronage and decisions of an enlightened manager, became the largest showcase of a stripped, simple lucid and functional Modernism in interwar Britain, running far ahead of public taste. The stations of the Moscow Metro, though initially still sometimes designed by surviving Constructivists, increasingly became subterranean palaces full of marble, malachite and grandiose decoration. They were, in a sense, a far more ambitious counterpart to the gigantic Art Deco and Neo-Baroque movie palaces which went up in Western cities during the 1920s and 1930s with the same object: to give men and women who had no access to individual luxury the experience that, for a collective moment, it was theirs.

One might even argue that the less sophisticated the mass public, the greater the appeal of decoration. It probably reached its peak in the architecture of postwar Stalinism, from which the surviving vestiges of early Soviet Modernism had finally been expunged, to produce a sort of echo of nineteenth-century taste.

How are we to judge the art of the dictators? The years of Stalin's rule in the USSR and of the Third Reich in Germany show a sharp decline in the cultural achievement of these two countries, compared to the Weimar Republic (1919–33) and the Soviet period before 1930. In Italy the contrast is not so great, since the pre-Fascist period had not been one of such creative brilliance – nor, unlike Germany and Russia in the 1920s, had the country been a major international style-setter. Admittedly, unlike Nazi Germany, Stalin's Russia and Franco's Spain, Fascist Italy did not drive out its creative talents *en masse*, force them into silence at home or, as in the worst years of Stalin, kill them. Nevertheless, compared to the cultural achievements and international influence of post-1945 Italy, the Fascist era does not look impressive.

Hence, what power destroyed or stifled in the era of the dictators is more evident than what it achieved. These regimes were better at stopping undesirable artists creating undesirable works than at finding good art to express their aspirations.

They were not the first to want buildings and monuments to celebrate their power and glory, nor did they add much to the traditional ways of achieving these objects. And yet, it does not look as though the era of the dictators produced official buildings, spaces and vistas to compare with, say, the Paris of the two Napoleons, eighteenth-century St Petersburg or that great song of triumph to mid-nineteenth-century bourgeois liberalism, the Vienna Ringstrasse.

It was harder for art to demonstrate the dictators' intention and ability to change the shape of their countries. The antiquity of European civilization deprived them of the most obvious way of doing so: the building of entirely new capital cities like nineteenth-century Washington and twentieth-century Brasilia. (The only dictator who had this opportunity was Kemal Atatürk in Ankara.) Engineers symbolized this better than architects and sculptors. The real symbol of Soviet planned world-change was 'Dneprostroi', the much-photographed great Dnieper dam. The most lasting stone memorial to the Soviet era (unless the distinctly pre-Stalinist Lenin Mausoleum on Red Square manages to survive) is, almost certainly, the Moscow Metro. As for the arts, their most impressive contribution to expressing this aspiration was the (pre-Stalinist) Soviet cinema of the 1920s – the films of Eisenstein and Pudovkin, and V. Turin's unjustly neglected *Turksib*, the epic of railway building.

However, dictators also wanted art to express their ideal of 'the people', preferably at moments of devotion to, or enthusiasm for, the regime. This produced a spectactular quantity of terrible paintings, distinguished from each other chiefly by the face and costume of the national leader. In literature the results were less disastrous, though seldom worth turning back to. However, photography, and above all film, lent itself rather successfully to the aims of power in this respect.

Lastly, the dictators wished to mobilize the national past on their behalf, mythologizing or inventing it where necessary. For Italian Fascism the point of reference was ancient Rome, for Hitler's Germany a combination of the racially pure barbarians of the Teutonic forests and medieval knighthood, for Franco's Spain the age of the triumphant Catholic rulers who expelled unbelievers and resisted Luther. The Soviet Union had more trouble taking up the heritage of the tsars which the Revolution had, after all, been made to destroy, but eventually Stalin also found it convenient to mobilize it, especially against the Germans. However, the appeal to historic continuity across the

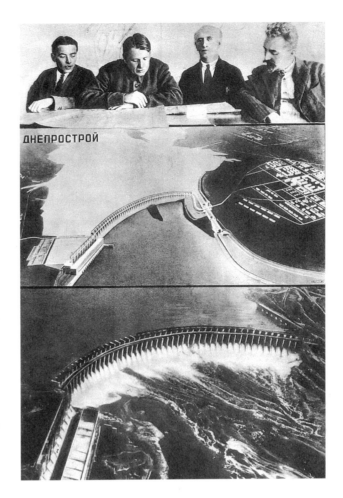

Dneprostroi
(from *USSR in Construction*)

imagined centuries never came as naturally as in the dictatorships of the right.

How much of the art of power has survived in these countries? Surprisingly little in Germany, more in Italy, perhaps most (including the magnificent postwar restoration of St Petersburg) in Russia. Only one thing has gone from all of them: power mobilizing art and people as public theatre. This, the most serious impact of power on art between 1930 and 1945, disappeared with the regimes that had guaranteed its survival through the regular repetition of public ritual. The Nuremberg Rallies, the May Day and Revolution Anniversaries on Red Square, were the heart of what power expected from art. They died forever, along with that power. States which realized themselves as show-politics demonstrated their and its impermanence. If the theatre-state is to live, the show must go on. In the end it did not. The curtain is down and will not be raised again.

SELECTORS' INTRODUCTION

Dawn Ades, Tim Benton, David Elliott, Iain Boyd Whyte

An exhibition that brings together the art and architecture – both official and unofficial – produced under the three major European dictatorships in the 1930s inevitably reveals both similarities and dissimilarities between these regimes. Any list of the similarities would begin with the elevation of power over legality and the systematic use of violence and terror in order to subordinate the individual will to that of the state. To achieve this, traditional class and cultural affinities were destroyed, and the populace was radicalized in support of the new social structures centred on the party. Every source of information and persuasion was mobilized to support this revolutionary shift, with the result that the 1930s were marked in the totalitarian states by the politicization of the arts and mass media, which were recruited to convey the ideological messages of the state.

Typically, official art included visions of heroism and death: of the subjection and sacrifice of the individual for the victory of the party and the nation. In the shaping of these myths, vulgar appeals to national history – authentic or invented – played a central role, as the dictators measured their creations against the triumphs of the past. This reading of history as the struggle and victory of nationhood was enacted by the totalitarian regimes in elaborate parades, rituals and ceremonies in which the ordered masses of the people themselves became the substance of the work of art.

Conscripted into the service of the state, architecture and the other visual arts became an expression and a historical record of a shared totalitarian ideology. At the same time, however, they also registered the differences between the three principal totalitarian regimes. In National Socialist Germany, for example, in line with official policy, women were represented either as passive homemakers or as objects of desire; in the USSR women were assigned a more active role as both mothers and workers. In both Germany and the Soviet Union, individual utterance was eventually subjugated to the imperatives of the state; the situation in Italy was less defined and more fluid. As Umberto Eco recently noted: 'Mussolini did not have any philosophy, only a rhetoric.'[1] Cultural production in Italy reflected this uncertainty, with Modernist and traditionalist imperatives accorded official approval according to the

changing predilections of the leadership. Where a comparable toleration existed in National Socialist Germany – in industrial architecture and design – it was the product of conscious planning rather than opportunism. Equally significant differences mark the German and Soviet experiences, most obviously in their definition of the insider and demonization of the outsider, in terms of 'race' or class.

In the decades immediately following the Second World War, an exhibition like *Art and Power* would have been unthinkable. Nikolaus Pevsner's admonition, that any word devoted to Nazi architecture was a word too many, summarized this view. This understandable hostility was matched by the refusal, imposed by the realities of the Cold War, to see any virtue in Soviet Socialist Realism. Although the opposing poles of Modernism and realism had been established in the critical writing of the 1930s, the hardening of this division into an absolute political and aesthetic imperative was the product of the immediate postwar decades, when the official Soviet art of the Eastern Bloc was regarded solely as the necessary antithesis to the unlimited freedom claimed by the avant-garde in the West. Indeed, painterly abstraction and the cult of novelty became icons of Western democracy. Socialist Realism was everything that radical Western art was not, and was conveniently conflated with the Fascist art of 1930s Germany and Italy as totalitarian art.

Lumped together totalitarian art was consigned to a precarious existence in the West; isolated initially like an infectious bacillus in a series of enclosed exhibitions, it has recently been reintegrated into a broader history of European art. A series of important exhibitions held over two decades[2] have started to confront the complexities of art and cultural politics under the dictators, as have post-*perestroika* exhibitions of Soviet Socialist Realist art and architecture.[3] In addition to the many exhibitions dedicated to the art of the victims of the Holocaust and the Purges,[4] other exhibitions[5] have either focused on the fate of the avant-garde under totalitarian rule or have taken a wider view of tendencies in realism during the 1930s and 1940s as national variants of a much broader historical tendency.

Many have seen dangers here. To quote Igor Golomstock: 'Totalitarian realism, uprooted from its historical context, appeared harmless enough.'[6]

1 Umberto Eco, 'Ur-Fascism', *The New York Review of Books*, 22 June 1995, 13.

2 *Kunst im Dritten Reich – Dokumente der Unterwerfung* (Frankfurt am Main: Kunstverein, 1974). A volume of Reaktionen to the exhibition was published in the following year. *Skulptur und Macht. Figurative Plastik im Deutschland der 30er und 40er Jahre* (Berlin: Akademie der Künste, 1983). *Kunst und Diktatur. Architektur, Bildhauerei und Malerei in Österreich, Deutschland, Italien und der Sowjetunion 1922-1956* (Vienna: Künstlerhaus, 1994).

3 *Engineers of the Human Soul. Soviet Socialist Realist Painting 1930s to 1960s* (Oxford: Museum of Modern Art, 1992). *Agitatsiya za schast'e / Agitation zum Glück. Sowjetische Kunst der Stalinzeit* (Bremen: Edition Temmen, 1994). *Tyrannei des Schönen* (Vienna: Österreichisches Museum für Angewandte Kunst, 1994). *The Aesthetic Arsenal. Socialist Realism under Stalin* (New York: The Institute for Contemporary Art, PS1 Museum, 1994).

Proposals to display Nazi art in public collections stimulated passionate debate in Germany in the mid-1980s, with ultimate victory going to those who argued that the contaminated works should not share the same walls as those by artists who had suffered persecution and even death at the hands of the National Socialist regime. At the same time, the essential similarity (and dissimilarity) between Nazi Germany in 1933-45 and the Soviet Union between 1932 and the death of Stalin in 1953 was the point at issue in the *Historikerstreit* – the Historians' Dispute. In Russia the vast machine of Socialist Realism simply ran out of steam – and from the late 1960s it was rapidly dismantled by a revived avant-garde. In this, such artists as Komar and Melamid, Eric Bulatov and Ilya Kabakov used the languages, forms and thought patterns of Socialist Realism to construct bitter-sweet pastiches which through their anger and absurdity subverted all official meaning and authority. In Italy, the situation was complicated by the fact that most of the Modernist architects who dominated after the war (BBPR, Ponti, Libera, Moretti, Michelucci) had been able to achieve some success on the margins of Fascist patronage. A concerted effort was made to play down the political engagement of these young men in the 1930s, as if the Modernism of their work were itself enough to inoculate it against Fascist contamination.

Behind all these ambiguities lurked the perceived death in the West of the Modernist project. With Postmodernist critics questioning the formalist abstractions that had dominated Western perceptions of high art during the era of the Cold War, the claims of more realist languages that sought direct communication between author and audience gained increased attention. Among the beneficiaries of this new mood of Postmodernist uncertainty have been monumental, neo-classicizing architecture and realist painting. Inevitably, this process of reassessment was boosted by the fall of the Berlin Wall, and the end of the Cold War, which gave new access – both actual and intellectual – to the artistic production of Soviet Russia.

It is impossible to recreate here the political and emotional context of fear, terror and oppression. As Otto Dix once wrote: 'One cannot paint despair.' Yet the cultural context can be illuminated by confronting the official artists of the dictatorships in the 1930s with the critical voices who had been pushed to the margins of society, exiled, or silenced. The exhibition therefore limits itself neither to those affirmative works which glorified the power of the state nor to the art of protest and exile. In this way, the differences as well as the

B. Prokorov, *Fascism is the Enemy of Culture*, 1939

similarities between the extremes of art and power will be revealed, and their ambiguous and fragile relationship exposed. The conventional poles of 'good' and 'bad' have sometimes conspired to conceal the nature of this relationship. Totalitarian culture embraced some aspects of the Modernist movement while it anathematized others. Modernism in its turn had authoritarian tendencies which may have provided a fertile seedbed for the subsequent development of totalitarian art and architecture. And how did individual artists cope with these vast changes in political climate? Were resistance or collaboration the only options for the artist in a repressive regime? How could the rampant individualism of the avant-garde ever be reconciled with the collective force of the nation state?

There are many answers to these questions. Accepting the impossibility of embracing in one exhibition the visual arts in three countries over a whole decade, we focus on the capitals – Rome, Moscow and Berlin – which served as the hubs from which power radiated. These sections are introduced through an event that was dedicated to peace but in fact served to highlight the tensions and the instability of Europe: the Paris International Exhibition of 1937. There the German and Soviet pavilions confronted each other, while the Spanish Republican government, fighting for its life against the Nazi-backed forces of Franco, mobilized Picasso and Miró to supplement the powerful graphic propaganda in its Modernist pavilion.

The exhibition deals with the painful history that has created the Europe in which we live. The spectres of authoritarianism, racism and rampant nationalism which haunted those years are still with us today.

4 Including *Tvorchestvo v lageryakh i ssylkakh – Gulag Art* (Moscow: Union of Artists RSFSR – 'Memorial', 1990) and *Art of the Shoah* (Sheffield: The Mappin Art Gallery, 1995).

5 *Les Réalismes 1919-1939* (Paris: Centre Georges Pompidou, 1981).
'Die Axt hat geblüht . . . 1937. Europäische Konflikte der 30er Jahre in Erinnerung an die frühe Avantgarde' (Düsseldorf: Städtische Kunsthalle, 1987).
'Degenerate Art': The Fate of the Avant-Garde in Nazi Germany (Los Angeles: Los Angeles County Museum of Art, 1991).
Europa, Europa: Das Jahrhundert der Avantgarde in Mittel- und Osteuropa (Bonn: Kunst- und Ausstellungshalle der Bundesrepublik Deutschland, 1994).
Identity and Alterity: Figures of the Body 1895-1995 (Venice: La Biennale di Venezia, 1995).

6 Igor Golomstock, *Totalitarian Art* (London, 1990), x.

CHRONOLOGY

Marko Daniel

ART

1929

- Ludwig Mies van der Rohe designs the German Pavilion, a paradigm of Rationalist architecture, for the Exposición Internacional in Barcelona.
- Alfred Rosenberg, Heinrich Himmler and Gregor Strasser found the Combat League for German Culture (Kampfbund für deutsche Kultur) to promote 'German' (i.e. Nazi) culture.

Inauguration of the Turkmenistan-Siberian Railway, 1930 (Arkady Shaikhet)

1930

- Luis Buñuel's and Salvador Dalí's film *L'Age d'or* opens at Studio 28 in Paris on 28 November. Right-wing protesters storm the cinema after a few performances, and the police react by banning the film.

Unemployed ex-serviceman, Hanover, c. 1930 (Walter Ballhause)

POWER

1929

- On 24 October, Black Thursday, the Great Crash on the New York Stock Exchange signals the start of a worldwide economic crisis.
- In April, the 16th Communist party congress in Moscow confirms Stalin's declaration that the collectivization of agriculture and the rapid development of heavy industry are the only way forward and approves the first Five Year Plan (nominal dates, 1928–33), which calls for an expansion of industry by 180% and of agriculture by 55%.
- Mass expulsions cut total membership of the Soviet Communist party by 11% and continue in subsequent years, eliminating 'unreliable', critical or simply slack members.
- Heinrich Himmler is appointed leader of the SS (*Schutzstaffel*), rival and eventual successor to the SA (*Sturmabteilung*) as the paramilitary arm of the Nazi party.

1930

- Mussolini proclaims that either the Italian Fascist State is corporative or it is not Fascist at all. A new law of 20 March reforms the National Council of Corporations.
- Salaries of Italian government employees are cut by 12%. Other workers suffer similar reductions. Mussolini proudly explains: 'Fortunately the Italian people are not accustomed to eat much, and therefore feel the privations less acutely than others.'
- A law is ratified to stop the drift of the Italian rural population to the cities.
- In Moscow in January, the Central Committee demands the 'liquidation of the Kulak as a class' through enforced collectivization. According to one estimate, some 2 million Kulak families – the wealthier independent peasants – are killed, imprisoned or deported to Siberia.
- By March, over half the independent farmers are collectivized, but the resultant damage forces Stalin to slow down. He accuses 'over-ambitious' local party bosses of being 'dizzy with success' and allows peasants to work and sell from small plots of land.

Election Fever, photomontage of Nazi posters (1932) from Joseph Goebbels, *Das erwachende Berlin* (1934)

1931

- In Rome, the first Quadriennale d'Arte Nazionale exhibition is held by the National Syndicate of Fascist Visual Art at the Palazzo delle Esposizioni, and the first exhibition of Futurist *Aeropittura* takes place.
- In March, Mussolini opens the second national exhibition of the Italian Movement for Rational Architecture (MIAR) at Galleria Bardi in Rome. MIAR promotes Rationalist (Modernist) architecture as the embodiment of Fascist principles, but the group's anti-establishment tone soon loses it public support, and it eventually dissolves.
- In Moscow a competition for the Palace of the Soviets is announced; architects from all over the world, including Le Corbusier and Walter Gropius, submit proposals.
- Rosenberg's *Der Mythos des 20. Jahrhunderts published.*

1932

- The 10th anniversary of the Fascist takeover is celebrated in Rome with the *Mostra della Rivoluzione Fascista*, which establishes the new direction of cultural politics.
- On 18 March, master plan for Rome ratified by the Senate. Clearance for the development of Via dei Fori Imperiali starts on 28 October.

- Aleksei Rykov, a leader of the moderate opposition, is replaced as chairman of the Council of People's Commissars by Stalin's faithful lieutenant Vyacheslav Molotov.
- On 30 March, Heinrich Brüning, a centrist, becomes Chancellor of Germany.
- In June, the last French troops leave German soil.
- The Young Plan, in which German First World War reparations are renegotiated, is adopted on 1 September. Though more lenient than the Dawes Plan of 1924, it is rendered unviable by the economic crisis, and Hitler, who has opposed the plan since its publication in 1929, gains popular support.
- In the September Reichstag elections, the Nazis become the second strongest party behind the Socialists.

1931

- After winning the elections of 14 April, the Spanish Left deposes King Alfonso XIII and declares a Republic. The main changes under the new constitution include religious freedom, disestablishment of the Church, secularization of education and dissolution of the Jesuits.
- On 21 September, Britain abandons the gold standard. Most countries follow suit.
- A decree of 27 May obliges Italian university professors to swear an oath of allegiance to the Fascists. Only 11 refuse to do so, among them the art historian Lionello Venturi.
- In October, the poet and activist A. L. de Bosis drops anti-Fascist manifestos from his aircraft over Rome. Escaping, he dies when his aircraft Pegaso plunges into the sea off Corsica.
- In the USSR, during the enforced collectivization of agriculture, poor harvests are compounded by drought (1932 and 1933), resulting in millions of deaths.
- In October, Hitler builds on his election success by courting representatives of industry, agriculture and the political right at the Harzburg Front.

1932

- On 2 July, Franklin D. Roosevelt is elected President of the USA. In his acceptance speech he coins the phrase of the 'New Deal' for the 'forgotten man', which comes to represent his radical programme of domestic reform between 1933 and 1939.
- As the recession worsens, and unemployment reaches 6 million, Germany stops paying the reparations agreed at Versailles.

- Giuseppe Terragni is commissioned to build the Casa del Fascio in Como. Finished in 1936, this perfect half-cube is the flagship of Rationalist architecture in Italy.
- In Moscow in April, a decree of the Central Committee abolishes all independent literary groupings and replaces them by the single Union of Soviet Writers. In June, former members of the dissolved artists' groups meet in Moscow and establish MOSSKhA as the Moscow branch of the Union of Soviet Artists.
- At the end of the year, a big retrospective of *Artists of the Russian Federation over Fifteen Years* opens at the Russian Museum in Leningrad, with a section devoted to the revolutionary avant-garde. The exhibition later travels to Moscow (June 1933), where the 'formalist' content is cut back in favour of Socialist Realism.
- In Germany, on 21 January, Dessau Council closes the Bauhaus. It is continued by Mies van der Rohe in Berlin until final closure in 1933.
- In his book *Kampf um die Kunst*, Paul Schultze-Naumburg sets out the strategic significance of art for National Socialism.
- Modern sculptures in the Dresden collection are confiscated.

- Hitler stands against the aged President Hindenburg at the elections in April. Hindenburg is re-elected, but Hitler gains a significant vote: 36.8% on the second ballot.
- Hindenburg dismisses Chancellor Brüning on 30 May and appoints Franz von Papen and (in December) Kurt von Schleicher; both are conservatives.

'Action Against the Un-German Spirit': Book burning, Berlin, 10 May 1933

1933

- In Manhattan, work starts on the gigantic Rockefeller Center. Marxist references in Diego Rivera's entrance-hall mural meet with the patron's disapproval, and it is removed (later to be overpainted by José María Sert).
- Le Corbusier assumes the leadership of CIAM (Congrès Internationaux d'Architecture Moderne) at the Athens congress, which sets out Rationalist principles for urban planning and the Functional City.
- In Italy, Giuseppe Pagano, a champion of Rationalism, becomes editor of the architectural journal *Casabella* (founded 1928).
- In 1933–35, the University City in Rome is built by a team of architects under Marcello Piacentini.
- In December Sironi, Funi, Campigli and Carrà publish the *Manifesto della pittura murale*, in which mural painting is proclaimed as the 'ideal patrimony of the Nation'.
- In Moscow, an exhibition is organized to celebrate the fifteenth anniversary of the Red Army.
- Independent art magazines are abolished and replaced by *Iskusstvo* ('Art'), the official journal of the

1933

- In Spain, the excesses of left-wing extremists are followed by a swing to the right and the creation of a Fascist movement, *La Falange*. The right-wing parties win the general election on 19 November.
- In Italy, the Institute for Industrial Reconstruction is set up to provide subsidies for industry and to bail out banks suffering from bad debts.
- Membership of the Italian Fascist party is a requirement for any administrative post.
- The Italian carpenter Primo Carnera becomes world heavyweight champion, and Mussolini declares that boxing is an 'essentially Fascist method of self-expression'.
- In Berlin, after both Papen and Schleicher fail to establish a stable government, Hitler is appointed Chancellor on 30 January. He heads a coalition in which the Nazis are the junior partner.
- The Reichstag in Berlin burns down on 27 February. A young Dutch Communist, van der Lubbe, is arrested; the National Socialists allege a plot and step up their campaign against the Communists, many of whom are arrested.

Union of Soviet Artists. The first leading article calls for a 'merciless battle against formalism'.

• Osip Beskin, head of the art critics' section of MOSSKhA and editor of *Iskusstvo* and *Tvorchestvo* ('Creativity'), leads the campaign against the avant-garde with his fiercely critical book on *Formalism in Painting*.

• In Germany the Ministry of Propaganda is set up in March, placing Joseph Goebbels in overall charge of culture.

• In May, Robert Ley founds the DAF (Deutsche Arbeitsfront, German Labour Front), controlling all trade union activity and industrial relations. One division, KdF (Kraft durch Freude, Strength through Joy), is responsible for mass leisure activities and official cultural events.

• On 10 May, in Berlin and other German cities, the Nazis publicly burn books by authors including Sigmund Freud, Erich Kästner, Heinrich Mann and Kurt Tucholsky.

• At their party congress, the Nazis introduce *rassische Baukunst* ('racial architecture') as official policy.

• The Nazi student organization puts up an exhibition of *German Art* including works by Emil Nolde, Ernst Barlach, Karl Schmidt-Rottluff and others, in order to make a case for Expressionism as official Nazi art.

• In September Goebbels brings all aspects of culture under a new state body, the Reichskulturkammer.

• Schmidt-Rottluff, Otto Dix, Max Liebermann, Käthe Kollwitz and others resign from the Prussian Academy; Paul Klee, Vasily Kandinsky, George Grosz, Gropius and others emigrate. Max Beckmann flees to Paris.

1934

• In Moscow the All-Union Creative Conference of Architects declares: 'Our task is the struggle to embody in the language of architecture the great slogans of our epoch.'

• A project by Boris Iofan, Vladimir Shchuko and Vladimir Gel'freikh is chosen for the Palace of the Soviets. The 315-metre building is to be crowned by a 100-metre statue of Lenin. However, by the outbreak of war in 1941, only part of the metal framework is erected.

• August: at the First All-Union Congress of Soviet Writers in Moscow, Andrei Zhdanov lays down the doctrine of Socialist Realism, explaining that the artist should not only 'depict reality in its revolutionary development' but also educate the worker in the spirit

• Having gained 44% of seats in the 5 March elections, the National Socialists, with Nationalist and Centre party support, pass an Enabling Act. Initially limited to four years, this frees Hitler from all democratic control and grants him dictatorial powers.

• The German government announces its first Four Year Plan, designed to combat unemployment and the agricultural crisis.

• By mid-July the Nazis are the only legal party in Germany; trade unions and strikes have been outlawed; an estimated 27,000 political prisoners are held in concentration camps.

• A company is set up to build the world's first motorways (*Autobahnen*) throughout Germany.

Zhdanov speaking, Moscow 1934

1934

• A strike by coal miners in Asturias is put down by Foreign Legion troops under General Franco.

• At the Italian elections in March, a turnout of 95% results in a paltry 15,000 votes declared for the opposition.

• In May, a new Italian law on the 'Constitution and Function of Corporations' creates 22 corporations with responsibility for all aspects of labour relations and the organization of the economy in agriculture, industry and the service sector.

• June: the first meeting between Mussolini and Hitler takes place in Venice.

• In December there are skirmishes between Italian and Ethiopian troops on the border of Italian Somaliland.

of Communism. In November, the All-Union Congress of Soviet Architects hails Stalin as the 'first architect and builder of our Socialist Motherland.'

• Work starts on the Moscow Métro stations, designed in 'Stalinist baroque'. The first train runs by May 1935.

• 1934–40: The Red Army Theatre is built by Karo Alabyan and Vasily Simbirtsev in Moscow. Its plan in the shape of a five-pointed star symbolizes the Soviet state.

• An *Aeropittura* exhibition opens in Berlin.

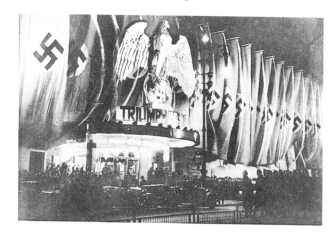

Premiere of Riefenstahl's film *Triumph des Willens*, Berlin 1935

Official Soviet picture of Belomor slave labour camp, 1933

1935

• Near Rome, the Cinecittà studio complex is developed (1935–36) on the site of the bankrupt CINES studios; it operates under government control.

• Gruppo del Milione founded in Milan.

• The General Plan for the Reconstruction of Moscow is approved.

• N. Golossov builds an office block for *Pravda* in Moscow, in a style incorporating Russian Futurist elements.

• Kazimir Malevich dies in Leningrad and is given a municipal, public funeral.

• In Moscow in April, the Executive Committee of the Communist International (Comintern) welcomes the appointment of Hitler as Chancellor, convinced that 'the establishment of an open Fascist dictatorship, which will destroy the democratic illusions of the masses and free them from the influence of the Social Democrats, will speed Germany on the path towards proletarian revolution'.

• The 17th Soviet Communist party congress sees Stalin firmly ensconced as party leader, surrounded by loyal supporters. This 'Congress of Victors' celebrates the alleged successes of collectivization and surpassing of targets under the first Five Year Plan. The programme for the Second Plan continues to emphasize heavy industry and agriculture but also includes support for a Soviet intelligentsia and the promotion of Stakhanovites, or worker-heroes; by its end, the USSR is the third largest industrial power in the world, after the USA and Germany.

• In December, Stalin's associate S. Kirov is assassinated. It is rumoured that he opposed Stalin in the Politburo, and that Stalin himself had him killed. But Stalin takes the event as his cue to launch the Great Purge, with a wave of arrests on charges of treason and counter-revolution.

• The USSR joins the League of Nations.

• Hindenburg dies on 2 August, and Hitler assumes the powers of President. His official title of Führer and Reich Chancellor is approved by plebiscite with a majority of nearly 90%.

• Germany suspends payment of all foreign debt.

• Night of the Long Knives (29 July): Himmler and Hermann Goering send SS squads to purge the SA of leaders doubtfully loyal to Hitler; ex-Chancellor Schleicher also murdered.

1935

• With the invasion of Ethiopia (Abyssinia) on 2 October, Mussolini attempts to 'capture an empire'. The modern Italian army and air force fight defenders armed with rifles and wooden spears.

• The 7th Comintern congress in Moscow endorses alliances with Social Democratic parties against Fascism: the so-called Popular Fronts.

• 'Life has become better, life has become happier.' Following Stalin's encouraging words, the rationing of bread and some other foodstuffs is ended on 1 January.

• French-Soviet mutual aid agreement signed in May.

- The *Blut und Boden (Blood and Soil)* art exhibition opens in Munich. Adolf Hitler gives a speech at the Cultural Session of the party congress in Nuremberg, in which he announces that the eradication of Modernism is one of Nazism's most urgent aims.
- Release of Leni Riefenstahl's film *Triumph des Willens*, celebrating the carefully staged spectacles, mass marches and propaganda events of the 1934 Nuremberg Rally.

Treasures of the Prado loaded for transport to Valencia, 1936

1936

- At the outbreak of the Spanish civil war, Federico García Lorca is shot by Nationalists in Granada.
- Picasso accepts the symbolic directorship of the Museo del Prado in Madrid. Its collections, with other parts of the 'national heritage', are stored in safe locations such as the vaults of the Bank of Spain or transferred to Valencia and eventually to Geneva.
- The Spanish Republic commissions José María Sert to paint murals for the Council Chamber of the League of Nations in Geneva.
- Michelucci's Florence railway station is completed.
- In August, the Olympic Games are held in Werner March's stripped Neoclassical stadium in Berlin.
- On 27 November, Goebbels bans all art criticism and limits 'art reporting' to pure description. The newspaper *Völkischer Beobachter* (29 November) explains that 'The only possible criterion of judgment for a work of art in a National Socialist state is the National Socialist conception of culture. Only the party and the state have the right to define standards in accordance with the National Socialist conception of culture.'
- Adolf Ziegler becomes President of the Reichskulturkammer, now declared free of all Jewish elements.

- In a plebiscite on 13 January, voters in the Saarland (under French mandate since 1919) choose union with Germany.
- In March, conscription is reintroduced in Germany.
- The German-British naval agreement of 18 June enables Hitler substantially to increase the size of his fleet.
- On 15 September the Nuremberg Racial Laws, which deprive Jews of German citizenship and make marriage with other Germans illegal, are approved by the National Socialist party congress.

German troops cross Hohenzollern Bridge, Cologne, March 1936

1936

- On 16 February, a left-wing alliance, the Popular Front, wins the Spanish elections.
- On the pretext of the murder of the Monarchist party leader, General Franco heads an army uprising in the Spanish Moroccan colony on 17 July; it spreads to the mainland the next day. The ensuing three-year civil war pitches Franco's Nationalists, representing most of the army, the Church, industrialists and other conservative elements, against the elected Republican government and its alliance of Basques, Catalans, Socialists, Communists, liberals and anarchists.
- In August, an international non-intervention pact is made worthless when Germany and Italy send troops to Spain; in November, the first volunteer contingents of the International Brigades arrive in besieged Madrid to join the Republican side.
- After international disapproval over Ethiopia, Hitler is alone in supporting Mussolini, and on 25 October Germany and Italy sign a treaty of friendship, thus formalizing the Rome-Berlin Axis.
- In Moscow, the Great Purge gathers speed in August with the first major show trial, in which Lenin's former colleagues Zinoviev and Kamenev and fourteen others are sentenced to death as 'Trotskyites plotting to overthrow and assassinate Stalin'. Imaginary

Procession at opening of Haus der Deutschen Kunst, Munich 1937

Hitler visits *Entartete Kunst*, Munich 1937

conspirators are denounced in all spheres of public life. Stalin appoints Nikolai Yezhov as Commissar for Internal Affairs to speed up the work of the secret police (NKVD). Forced confessions of sabotage, treason, espionage or terrorism are used by secret tribunals (*troiki*) to pass summary death or labour-camp sentences on millions of victims, including whole families, between 1932 and 1938.

• A new Soviet constitution, adopted in December, turns the USSR into a voluntary federation of equal Soviet Socialist Republics, based on a pyramid of soviets and councils from local level upwards. On paper, it provides Soviet citizens with exemplary civil rights.

• Goebbels (17 January) and Goering call for Germany to concentrate on 'guns' rather than 'butter'.

• On 7 March, Hitler denounces the 1925 Locarno Pact and orders the German army into the demilitarized Rhineland zone.

• Goering oversees the introduction of the second Four Year Plan, designed to make German industry and agriculture entirely self-sufficient, especially through the development of synthetic and substitute materials. In a secret memorandum, Hitler specifies that the army and the economy must be ready for war within four years.

Guernica, April 1937

1937

• Picasso paints *Guernica* for the Spanish pavilion at the Paris International Exhibition, where the Soviet pavilion by Iofan and the German pavilion by Speer both obtain gold medals.

• In Republican Valencia in July, the second International Writers' Congress (Congreso de Intelectuales) is attended by, among others, André Malraux, Ernest Hemingway, Pablo Neruda, Stephen Spender, and the Spanish poets Antonio Machado, Rafael Alberti and Miguel Hernández.

1937

• On 26 April, the Basque town of Guernica is bombed by the German Condor Legion on behalf of the Nationalists.

• In June, Hitler and Mussolini withdraw from the non-intervention committee for Spain, and Germany signs a military cooperation treaty with Franco. The USA and Britain continue their policy of neutrality.

• On 6 September, Carlo Rosselli, exiled leader of the Italian anti-Fascist movement Giustizia e Libertà, is murdered at Bagnoles-de-l'Orne in France on the orders of the Italian secret service.

- On 27 April, Antonio Gramsci, the Communist philosopher and politician, dies after nearly nine years in prison.
- On 18 July, Hitler opens the first *Grosse Deutsche Kunstausstellung* (Great German Art Exhibition) in the new Haus der Deutschen Kunst in Munich. The next day, the exhibition *Entartete Kunst* (Degenerate Art) opens in the nearby Hofgarten.
- Albert Speer is appointed General Inspector of Buildings for the remodelling of Berlin. Hitler publishes a directive on the redevelopment of German cities.
- Speer designs the monumental Zeppelinfeld stadium for the Nuremberg Rally.
- The Nazis confiscate 600 paintings by Ernst Ludwig Kirchner as examples of 'degenerate art'. Kirchner commits suicide.
- A Society for the Development of a German People's Car is set up, initially under the DAF. In 1938 a manufacturing company is launched to mass-produce the KdF-Wagen, designed by Ferdinand Porsche and later known as the Volkswagen.

1938

- The *Exposició Trimestral d'Arts Plàstiques* is held in Barcelona, carrying on the propaganda theme of the Republican pavilion at the International Exhibition in Paris.
- Eugenio d'Ors, 'Franco's philosopher', curates the Spanish participation at the 21st Venice Biennale, where the Italian section includes *aeropitture* of Spain and Africa.
- In Italy, *Vita Giovanile*, founded as a Fascist youth journal, is renamed *Corrente (di Vita Giovanile)* and drops Fascist symbolism from its masthead as a sign of its increasingly critical stance.
- In Moscow, artists participating in the first major showing of Socialist Realism, *20 Years of the Workers' and Peasants' Red Army*, have to choose from an official list of approved subjects.
- The poet Osip Mandelstam, arrested in 1937, is shot.
- In Berlin, Speer builds the New Reich Chancellery (Neue Reichskanzlei) for Hitler.

- Taking its cue from the German call for guns before butter, the Gran Consiglio del Fascismo orders the pursuit of *Autarchia* (self-sufficiency) in Italian military production at the expense of civilian needs.
- In the USSR, 17 leading Communists are 'exposed' as 'Trotskyites' and executed. It is later estimated that in related purges approximately 20% of party members are expelled, 20% of army officers are arrested or shot, and all the old guard Bolsheviks disappear.
- Over 93% of peasant households in the USSR are now collectivized, but agriculture has yet to recover from the havoc wrought by the enforced conversion of 26 million individual holdings (1929) into 235,000 collective farms. Livestock figures remain lower than in the late 1920s.
- In Berlin, Soviet envoys start the negotiations that eventually lead to the non-aggression pact of 1939.

'Aryan [Non-Jewish] Business' sign goes up, Italy, December 1938

1938

- On 7 October, the Gran Consiglio del Fascismo adopts Racial Laws along National Socialist lines. Jews are excluded from military service, teaching, banking and the civil service. Their right to own property is severely restricted. Over 90 academics are dismissed; the physicist Enrico Fermi refuses to return home after receiving his Nobel Prize in Oslo and moves to the USA. Marriages between Aryans and non-Aryans are outlawed, and all foreigners require special dispensation to marry Italians.
- Civilian state employees in Italy are obliged to wear uniforms.
- Stalin dismisses Yezhov as head of the NKVD, thus ending the Great Purge, in which the secret police have become established as an unrivalled tool of political control.
- Despite increased use of forced (prison-camp) labour, few gains are made under the Third Five Year Plan, between 1938 and 1942. Though it initially allows for the making of some so-called luxury goods, by 1939 production is shifted entirely to arms manufacture.

Franco at victory parade, Madrid 1939

1939

- A team of historians and illustrators works on the 8-volume *Historia de la Cruzada Española*, a record of the Spanish civil war strictly from the Nationalist point of view.
- Fascist party secretary Roberto Farinacci sets up the Premio Cremona for Fascist art. It calls for set themes, didactic and overtly political content, and propagandistic spirit. In direct opposition, Bottai, the Minister of Education, sets up the Premio Bergamo, which – though equally political – supports more experimental tendencies.
- The USSR participates in the New York World's Fair with a pavilion by Iofan that fails to match the drama of his Paris contribution.
- A major Soviet exhibition, *The Industry of Socialism*, is organized as a showcase of Socialist Realism. Three-quarters of visitors come in organized parties.
- An exhibition of French landscape painting, focusing on the Barbizon School and the works of the Impressionists, takes place at the Museum of New Western Art, Moscow. The works are drawn exclusively from Russian museums, but the exhibition's theme effectively challenges official stylistic prescriptions.
- On 1 August, Molotov opens the All-Union Agricultural Exhibition, on a permanent site, originally planned to open in 1937 as a celebration of the first 20 years of the USSR.
- The creation of the Stalin Prize, worth 100,000 roubles or about 500 monthly salaries, is announced on Stalin's 60th birthday, 21 December. A birthday exhibition, *Comrade Stalin and the Soviet People*, sanctions the Stalin cult with hagiographic representations of scenes from his life.
- Some 5,000 modern paintings are burned at the Feuerwache in Berlin. In Switzerland, the Nazis auction off confiscated works of 'degenerate art'.

- Under threat of German invasion, the Austrian Prime Minister, Kurt Schuschnigg, resigns on 24 February. His successor, Arthur Seyss-Inquart, promptly calls on Hitler for help. German troops cross the border on 11 March, and two days later the *Anschluss* or annexation of Austria is completed.
- In May, the Czechoslovakia crisis develops when Hitler asserts that the German ethnic minority in the Sudetenland is threatened by the Czechs. International negotiations produce the Munich Agreement of 29 September, under which the area is ceded to Germany.
- In the *Kristallnacht* pogrom on the night of 9-10 November, virtually all synagogues in Germany are destroyed, over 100 Jews killed and 20,000 deported to concentration camps.

1939

- On 27 February, two weeks after the end of resistance in Catalonia, France and Great Britain recognize Franco's Nationalist government in Burgos. Madrid falls on 28 March, and on 1 April Franco declares the civil war over. His rule is now unchallenged.
- Germany and Italy sign the Pact of Steel, a military cooperation treaty.
- Italy invades Albania on 7 April.
- On 15 March, German troops invade Czechoslovakia. Hitler breaks up the country into the German Protectorate of Bohemia and Moravia and the state of Slovakia.
- Germany and the USSR sign a commercial agreement.
- On 23 August, Stalin and Hitler sign a non-aggression pact.
- On 1 September, Germany invades Poland. Britain and France issue an ultimatum demanding withdrawal by 3 September. When this expires, they declare war. The USA declares neutrality.
- On 17 September, under a secret clause in the non-aggression pact, the Red Army enters Poland from the east. German troops take Warsaw on 27 September, and Germany and the USSR divide Poland. The USSR attacks Finland.
- Military expenditure in Germany reaches 32.3 billion marks, a 17-fold increase on 1933.

1940

- On 1 April, one year after the end of the civil war, Franco inaugurates the building of his huge monument at the Valley of the Fallen (Valle de los Caídos), in the mountains near the old royal retreat of El Escorial.
- The cultural critic Walter Benjamin commits suicide at the French-Spanish border on 27 October, after the Nationalists threaten to hand him over to the Gestapo.
- Renato Guttuso is awarded the second Premio Bergamo for his *Flight from Etna* (1940).
- Nicolai Trotsky's Palace of Soviets, the centrepiece of the new Leningrad, is completed.

German dead, Moscow, December 1941

1940

- At the beginning of May, Germany attacks Holland, Belgium and Luxembourg. On 10 May, German forces cross into France.
- Between 28 May and 3 June, more than 300,000 British and French troops are evacuated to Britain from Dunkirk.
- On 10 June, Italy declares war on Britain and France.
- On 14 June, German troops enter Paris. On 22 June, Marshal Pétain signs an armistice and sets up the 'French State' in Vichy.
- The Moscow peace agreement ends the Russian war with Finland.
- In June, the USSR seizes Lithuania, Estonia and Latvia.
- After the success of British air defences in the Battle of Britain, the Germans suspend plans for an early invasion.
- On 20 August, the Spaniard Ramón Mercader (allegedly a Stalinist agent) stabs Trotsky to death at his home in Mexico.
- In November, the Germans present the creation of a Jewish ghetto in Warsaw as a 'prophylactic measure'.

1941

- Winter 1941–42: the exhibition *Leningrad in the Days of the Patriotic War* shows works painted under the harsh conditions of the siege of Leningrad.
- Bertolt Brecht and Max Ernst reach the USA.

Inmates in quarry at Flossenbürg concentration camp, Bavaria

1941

- In his message to Congress on 1 June, President Roosevelt pronounces the *Four Freedoms*: freedom of expression and of religion, freedom from suffering and from fear.
- In March, German forces under General Erwin Rommel invade Egypt to support the faltering Italian troops.
- On 22 June the Germans launch Operation Barbarossa, the invasion of the USSR. Stalin's rhetoric promptly transforms what has hitherto been called an 'imperialist war' into a 'peoples' war against Fascism'.
- In September, Reinhard Heydrich, chief of the Gestapo, orders Jews over the age of 6 to wear a yellow Star of David on their clothes.
- By December, the Germans are within 50 kilometres of Moscow, but the Soviet winter campaign forces them back, and Hitler suspends the initiative.
- On 7 December, the Japanese attack Pearl Harbor and sink part of the US Pacific Fleet. The USA declares war on Japan, and Hitler and Mussolini declare war on the USA.

1942

- Work is suspended on EUR or E'42, the Universal Exhibition site in Rome, conceived as the first stage of a new capital city built according to Fascist ideological and architectural principles.
- In Moscow, ambitious exhibitions like *The Great Patriotic War* (and *The Heroic Front and Rear* of 1943) illustrate the major role of art within Soviet wartime society.
- In Munich, the annual *Grosse Deutsche Kunstausstellung* unites war images, Romantic landscapes, female nudes and portraits of Hitler.
- A propaganda exhibition, mockingly entitled *Der sowjetische Paradies* (The Soviet Paradise), opens in Berlin in May. Photos, graphics, models and architectural reconstructions are used to paint a horrific picture of prisons, systematic torture and the hardships of everyday life. This is contrasted with displays of expensive seized arms and military equipment.
- Another exhibition, *Kunst und Technik* (Art and Technology), celebrates German workers' achievements and draws heroic parallels with the deeds of soldiers.

1943

- In Stalingrad, Alabyan and Simbirtsev begin work on a series of major war-related urban reconstruction projects that take the representation of Socialist ideology as a fundamental part of the design process.
- *Casabella* ceases publication on direct orders from the Italian Ministry of Popular Culture, and most Rationalist architects join the Resistance. The architects Giolli, Banfi and Pagano are deported to their deaths in German concentration camps.

1942

- On 21 January, Heydrich maps out the 'Final Solution of the Jewish question' at the Wannsee Conference in Berlin, with his proposals for mass murder and forced labour in concentration camps.
- In July, the first Jews from Warsaw are deported to the Treblinka concentration camp, and the systematic mass murder of Jews starts. An estimated 5.7 million Jews and 400,000 Gypsies are among those murdered by 1945.
- British and American forces under General Dwight D. Eisenhower disembark in North Africa on 8 November and start bombing raids over Italy.

1943

- On 8 February, the entire German 6th Army surrenders outside Stalingrad with 150,000 casualties and 50,000 prisoners of war. On 18 February, in a nation-wide broadcast from a mass rally in Berlin, Goebbels calls for a commitment to 'Total War'.
- In April, an uprising in the Warsaw ghetto is suppressed; 50,000 Jews die. Between July and September more than 300,000 people are deported to Treblinka.
- Rommel's Afrika Korps capitulates on 5 May.
- After British and American troops land in Sicily on 10 July, the Gran Consiglio del Fascismo removes Mussolini from power on 25 July and has him arrested. Marshal Pietro Badoglio becomes Prime Minister; King Vittorio Emanuele III assumes supreme military command. In August, the Fascist party is dissolved.
- On 8 September, Italy and the Allies sign an armistice. Badoglio then declares war on Germany, whereupon German parachutists liberate Mussolini, who proclaims the short-lived Republic of Salò.

Warsaw Ghetto, April 1943

1944

- Sergei Eisenstein films the first part of *Ivan the Terrible*. Commissioned by Stalin – who conceived it as a parable of his own life and political struggles – the film becomes a powerful critique of the Soviet leader.

1944

- On 6 June (D-Day), Allied Forces land in Normandy.
- On 24 July, Soviet troops of the 1st White Russian Army capture Lublin and discover the first death camp at Majdanek, with few surviving prisoners.
- In July, the International Monetary Conference opens at Bretton Woods, New Hampshire. The birth of the International Monetary Fund is announced and the conference ends with an agreement to fund an International Bank for Reconstruction and Development (the World Bank).

1945

- Having worked on official government film projects under Mussolini while secretly participating in and filming the anti-Fascist Resistance, Roberto Rossellini directs *Roma città aperta*. With its documentary footage of life under German occupation, this film plays a seminal role in the development of Italian postwar Neorealism.

Russians at Tempelhof Airport, Berlin 1945 (Yevgeny Khaldei)

1945

- At the Yalta Conference in February, Churchill, Roosevelt and Stalin plan the final stages of war and discuss the conditions for a secure peace. Europe is divided into spheres of influence, in effect the future Eastern and Western blocs.
- By 25 April the Red Army has surrounded Berlin; Soviet and US forces meet at the Elbe.
- On 28 April Italian partisans kill Mussolini, and two days later Hitler and Eva Braun commit suicide in the underground bunker of the Reich Chancellery in Berlin.
- On 7 May representatives of the Allies accept Germany's unconditional surrender.
- After the USA drops atomic bombs on Hiroshima and Nagasaki and the USSR declares war on Japan, the Second World War ends on 15 August.

Final shot of Rossellini's *Roma città aperta*, 1945

Mussolini and
Hitler with
sculpture by Josef
Thorak, 1938

THE BATTLE FOR ART

David Elliott

'Freedom' versus Autonomy

'The [French] Revolution wrote, as it were, the word freedom on its banner but, in truth, it equated freedom with the arbitrary will and licentiousness of the individual . . . This idol of 1789, which [in fact] was the enemy of freedom and individuality, has been destroyed by us and replaced by a monument to true freedom . . . [The German Revolution] has effected a complete change from the concept of "I" to the concept of "we", from the individual to the whole.' (Otto Dietrich, 1939.)[1]

'In October 1917 we overthrew the Tsar, the landlords and capitalists, and the Great Proletarian Revolution has since developed in our country. The great Lenin, our father and educator, proclaimed that from that time forward we would no longer have either rulers or ruled, and that the people would be equal and free. In this way he buried the old bourgeois politics of the Tsarist era and proclaimed the new politics of Bolshevism, the politics of friendship, the politics of the brotherhood of the peoples of our country.' (Joseph Stalin, 1935.)[2]

'To truly understand Fascism, one must first understand this truth: that it is not a reactionary tyrannical movement nor a blind ferocious hatred of change. On the contrary, it is and intends always to grow into an even more democratic aristocracy, governed not by the people but for the people and for their interests, ruled by a hierarchy which is always open, in which all can join, and into which the interests of all have penetrated.' (Margherita Sarfatti, 1934.)[3]

Unconvincing as it may be to hear the representatives of National Socialism, Communism or Fascism speaking about 'freedom', they all, in their different ways, believed that their collective, corporate states had created new forms of living which, because they were ostensibly for the benefit of all their citizens, were implicitly more 'free' than previous, more limited structures which had benefited only despots or bourgeois democrats.

In his speech to the party faithful, Otto Dietrich, Joseph Goebbels's Chief of Press, unwittingly touched on one of the central paradoxes of modern history when he noted that the third annual celebration organized for the Day of Art in the great 'City of Art'

of Munich had coincided with the 150th anniversary of the French Revolution. Here, within the intellectual ferment of the European Enlightenment, he identified the germ of the series of conflicts in which the meaning of 'modernity' may be understood.

Logically, the free expression of the rights of the individual would, by definition, become less free if they were collectivized – a point which had been articulated with extreme passion by the Marquis de Sade. Individual freedoms soon agglomerated into new forms of nationhood, in which the people were governed not by despots but by their own collective will. Only in such states as these, Dietrich argued, could 'true freedom' be found. Yet, when it was analysed, the power of collective will was as confining, as confused and as mystical an entity as the divine right of kings had ever been.

The dictators of the 1930s were the apotheosis of modernity. By looking simultaneously at both the past and the future, they were able to sustain the fantasy of being able to stand outside their own time. They were prepared to draw a line through the past but would then have no compunction in reinvoking and remodelling its culture to suit their own ends.[4] Aggressively modernizing, they were modern but hated Modernism. Their impulse to repudiate both modern art and modern culture, however, has to do with the semantic confusion between the 'modern' and the 'Modernist'.[5]

The aesthetic foundation upon which all 'modern art' has been built – the notion that an artist's individual conscience or sensibility can lead to personal or universal redemption – is in direct opposition to this corporate view of culture, and was violently repudiated both by Stalin and by Hitler. There were similarly repressive tendencies within the Italian Fascist party, though Mussolini long refused to give them a free hand.

The idea of the autonomy of artistic expression was crystallized towards the end of the eighteenth century in the *Critiques* of Immanuel Kant. These set out the notion of a subjective but altruistic form of aesthetics which expressed, symbolically and intuitively, what Kant described as the Absolute – a universal moral consciousness. Art was purely an end in itself; and, if its practice happened to illustrate other forms of reality, this was coincidental to the act of transcendent creation

1 Dr. Otto Dietrich, opening speech at the Third Day of German Art, Munich, 14 July 1939, reported in *Die Münchner Zeitung*, 15-16 July; cited in Robert S. Wistrich, *Weekend in Munich. Art, Propaganda and Terror in the Third Reich* (London, 1995), 74.

2 Joseph Stalin, from a speech made at a conference of elite collective farm workers from Tadzhikistan and Turkmenistan and government and party leaders, Moscow, 4 December 1935, in *SSSR na stroike*, nos. 9-12 (1937), 33.

3 Margherita Sarfatti, from a talk broadcast on the NBC radio network, New York, 2 April 1934, in Philip V. Cannistraro and Brian R. Sullivan, *Il Duce's Other Woman* (New York, 1993), 425.

4 Boris Groys identifies the radicalism of Stalinism as its preparedness to exploit the art and culture of the past; the avant-garde, he claims, was still working within the same cultural continuum as the art of the past although it was careful to repudiate it. Groys, *The Total Art of Stalin* (Princeton, 1992), 41-45.

5 The beginning of Modernism is usually attributed to the formalistic experiments embarked on by visual artists, writers and musicians from the beginning of this century.

whereby art became a paradigm of individual and social freedoms.

Kant's ideas had been influenced by the ferment of opinion about the nature of law, morality and society which had consumed Europe during the previous century. In 1750 Jean-Jacques Rousseau had pointed out in a seminal essay, *Discours sur les Sciences et les Arts*, that science, art and literature – far from representing a universal ideal – had for many years been the agents of servility and corruption:

'Princes always view with pleasure the spread among their subjects of the taste for the arts . . . besides fostering that spiritual pettiness so appropriate to slavery, they know well that the needs that people create for themselves are like chains binding them . . . The sciences, letters and arts . . . wind garlands of flowers around the iron chains that bind [the people and] stifle in them the feeling of that original liberty for which they seemed to have been born, makes them love their slavery and turn them into what are called civilized people.'

And from this point onwards, the idea of a specialized, fragmented and modern world became a pervasive double to that of the romantic, unitary being of the alienated but 'noble savage' – the human being who had not been corrupted by the decadence and idleness of despotism. Rousseau summarized the cause of this corruption as simply 'inequality . . . Wherever men are equal, there will be neither rich nor poor. Wealth inevitably leads to luxury and idleness; luxury permits a cultivation of the arts, and idleness that of the sciences'.[6]

Under despotism, art had reflected and reinforced the immoral power of the state. As an antidote, Rousseau maintained that the search for freedom and equality demanded that a moral sense should pervade all aspects of the new culture. By the end of the eighteenth century, Kant had provided an idealistic framework for such convictions, in which autonomy in the arts represented a field of non-specific, secular, symbolic and intransigent morality.

Kant's mapping out of the field of the aesthetic, as full of potential conflict as it may be, remained important because it constituted a symbolic space through which artists could move and work and in which they represented, as much as depicted, alternative forms of reality.[7] In modern societies, 'Bohemia' and the avant-garde have fulfilled symbolic functions as counter-cultures in which aesthetics was established as an ethical field.

The concept of the avant-garde developed in parallel with that of modern art. The term had originally been taken from military usage by Henri de Saint-Simon in the 1820s to denote those revolutionaries and artists who could sense the future.[8] By the beginning of the twentieth century, however, its meaning had moved away from what was essentially a positivist model of progress to evolve a discourse along Kantian lines, creating a 'politics' and an 'ideology' that were entirely specific to art.

Inevitably, at times, this discourse became both conflated and confused with political ideology as such; when faced by the naked reality of power its fragile autonomy soon crumbled. In the brave new worlds of the dictators, the idea of an avant-garde could seem either like an unwelcome reminder of the past or a rallying point for counter-revolution. It was, accordingly, one of the first manifestations of the old order which had to be obliterated.

As the heirs of the French Revolution, the dictators believed that they had at last fulfilled Rousseau's demand: men were now 'equal', and there were no longer rich nor poor. But the price the people had to pay for this was high: in an inversion of Rousseau's original model, the chains which bound the people were fashioned not by despots but by themselves. The 'noble savage' had lost his autonomy as well as his integrity; the modern, ignoble barbarian was firmly in control.

Art as a Weapon[9]

'A new epoch is moulded not by literary men but by warriors.' (Adolf Hitler, 1937.)[10]

'In our hands we hold a sure weapon, thanks to which we can overcome all the difficulties besetting our path. This weapon is the great and invincible doctrine of Marx-Engels-Lenin-Stalin, a doctrine that has been put into practice by our Party and our Soviets.' (Andrei Zhdanov, 1934.)[11]

'A group of soldiers who at three o'clock on a January afternoon will have to get into a lorry to enter the line of fire at four, or go up in an aeroplane to bomb cities or counter-attack enemy flights, would seek in vain the perfect preparation for these in the grieving kiss of a mother, of a wife, of children or in rereading passionate letters . . . Instead these fighters should sit around a table, where they are served a [meal of] "Drum Roll of Colonial Fish" and some "Raw Meat Torn by Trumpet Blasts".' (Filippo Tommaso Marinetti, 1932.)[12]

6 Jean-Jacques Rousseau, *Observations* (Paris, 1751).

7 Terry Eagleton, *The Ideology of the Aesthetic* (Oxford, 1990), 70–100.

8 See Linda Nochlin, 'The Invention of the Avant-Garde', in Nochlin, *The Politics of Vision* (London, 1991), 1–18.

9 The Leninist slogan 'Art as a weapon of struggle' was taken up in Germany during the late 1920s by the Communist party, but the National Socialist party's leftist origins also led it to share the same cultural attitude. See Adolf Behne, 'Kunst als Waffe', *Die Weltbühne*, no. 34 (1931), 301–04.

10 Adolf Hitler, from speech at opening of Haus der Deutschen Kunst in Munich, 1937, in exh. cat. *Führer durch die Ausstellung Entartete "Kunst"* (Munich, 1937), 26; reprint tr. by David Britt in Stephanie Barron, ed., exh. cat. *'Degenerate Art'* (Los Angeles: Los Angeles County Museum of Art, 1991), 339ff.

11 Andrei Zhdanov, from keynote speech to First All-Union Congress of Soviet Writers, Moscow, 1934, in Zhdanov et al., *Problems of Soviet Literature. Reports and Speeches at the First Soviet Writers' Congress* (New York, 1935).

12 Filippo Tommaso Marinetti, from Marinetti, *La Cucina Futurista* (1932), tr. as Futurist Cookbook, ed. L. Chamberlain (London, 1989), 102.

In the words of Hitler, a failed painter, more successful politician and would-be architect of the Thousand Year Reich; of Zhdanov, a party hack, Stalin's mouthpiece and Soviet cultural supremo; and of Marinetti, a bellicose Futurist, anarchist and strong supporter of Fascist ideals, the rhetoric of war and struggle echoed across the 1930s like a trumpet blast. In Germany, the USSR and Italy, increasingly intense battles for the control of art and culture were an integral part of the establishment of power and prefigured the real war which started in Spain and then spread throughout Europe. These battles for art – or cultural revolutions – were part of the process of purging or cleansing through which each 'threatened' nation could be healed and made whole. Its enemies could be found everywhere; but first they had to be eliminated at home – where they seemed to threaten its very existence. Art was a weapon that could be used for this end. Only when a firm hand had taken control could attention be directed further afield, to those unknown enemies who lurked beyond the frontiers.

Both Hitler and Stalin had departed from Marx in that they believed that the control of culture was as important as that of the economy; both agreed with Lenin that, in a revolutionary society, culture had to be engaged with the party.[13] But party culture did not already exist: it had to be created, and during the 1930s, both in Germany and in Russia, cultural revolutions took place during which all autonomous Modernism was eliminated, to be replaced with a compliant officialdom.

For Stalin and Hitler, cultural purity had to be imposed. Both, in differing degrees, paid homage to the Greek and Roman heritage;[14] but Mussolini had a less defensive attitude. For him, this was already part of a living history; it was firmly rooted in the soil of the first Roman Empire which he now sought to emulate.[15]

These new states, which had all been created out of the chaos of the First World War, were essentially hermetic, self-referential bodies which set out consciously to establish new world orders. They were driven by utopian ideals and shared a common lineage in the traditions of messianic Socialism to which idiosyncratic admixtures of Nietzsche, Nordau and Marx had been added.[16] And all, to a greater or lesser extent, believed in the eugenic theory of the creation of a higher race.[17] The achievement of their programmes was schematized in a process of bureaucratic categorization and pseudo-rational centralized planning, regimented by weighty ministries and fuelled by an obligatory sense of solidarity and enthusiasm. In the religion of dictatorship, facts became fetishes;

unpalatable realities, which denied the onward march of progress, were ignored or obliterated.

In spite of these obvious similarities, however, the ideologies of the dictatorships were distinct. Hitler's book *Mein Kampf* (My Struggle, 1926), the wellspring of the Nazi political programme, advocated the necessity of racial purity as a precondition for the future development of the German peoples according to the destiny which had been ordained for them.[18] Written long before Hitler became a serious political force, it clearly set out the tenets of a totalitarian, racist, military state. The Aryan, Teutonic and Nordic fantasies of the Nazis were based on the desire to establish a *Kultur* which was worthy of a chosen people. This inversion of the Jews' belief in themselves as chosen marked the beginning of the racial policy that culminated in the Holocaust. The Jews were labelled as 'impure': the opposite of all the 'positive' values embedded in the Aryan race.

The ideology of Stalinism was tabulated some time after Stalin had assumed control, as part of the general rewriting of history which resulted from the Central Committee decree of May 1934 *On the Teaching of Civil History in the Schools of the USSR*. This dealt with the issue of Stalin's political legitimacy as the natural and chosen heir of Lenin; the converse was the obliteration and demonization of such enemies as Trotsky and Bukharin. From this Stalin derived his mandate to forge ahead with the construction of heavy industry and the collectivization of agriculture in the Five Year Plans.[19] The *Short Course in the History of the All-Union Communist Party (of Bolsheviks)* finally appeared in 1938 after the Great Purge and provided the correct party line on historical development to date.[20] It was a justification of the increasingly florid Stalin cult, as well as mandatory reading for all painters of historical subjects. Such a version of events was grossly mendacious, but it provided a seamless narrative to support the image of Stalin which had been regularly appearing in propaganda and art since the beginning of the decade. Gustavs Klucis's Five Year Plan poster, *Under the Banner of Lenin for Socialist Construction* (1930; p. 221) shows the face of Lenin as a mask, with that of Stalin emerging behind him; it was one of the first and most telling manifestations of this lie.

The ideology of Marxism-Leninism-Stalinism which supported the Union of Soviet Socialist Republics was non-racial, although racial discrimination undoubtedly existed. As a result, its ethos was imperial rather than national and incorporated many races under a single leader (see p. 239; Shegal: *Leader, Teacher, Friend*). Much

13 See V. I. Lenin, 'Party Organization and Party Literature' (1905) and 'In Memory of Herzen' (1912), in C. Vaughan James, *Soviet Socialist Realism: Origins and Theory* (London, 1973), 101–11.

14 In both Germany and the USSR, Neoclassicism was marked in sculpture (but in Germany it was also an important feature of Nazi architecture and painting). Of Soviet sculptors, the work from the late 1930s by Matvei Manizer is closest to the featureless muscular classicism of the Nazis and was influenced by them.

15 Mussolini was initially contemptuous of Hitler's racism, making the point that if he were correct 'the Lapps must be considered the highest type of humanity', and adding that 'Thirty centuries of history have enabled us to look with majestic pity at certain doctrines taught on the other side of the Alps by the descendants of people who were wholly illiterate in the days when Rome boasted a Caesar, a Virgil and an Augustus.' Speech at Bari, 1934, in Christopher Hibbert, *Benito Mussolini. The Rise and Fall of Il Duce* (Harmondsworth, 1965), 98–99.

16 Friedrich Nietzsche (1844–1900), German classical scholar, philosopher and critic. Wrote *The Birth of Tragedy* (1872), *Thus Spake Zarathustra* (1883–84) and *Beyond Good and Evil* (1886). He analysed the differences between the higher 'Apollonian' and primal 'Dionysian' impulses within culture and developed the idea of a Superman (*Übermensch*), whose Will to Power took him beyond the realms of conventional morality. Nietzsche's ideas established an influential anti-rationalist current in European thought. Max Nordau (1849–1923), German writer, physician and early Jewish nationalist whose popular and widely translated book *Entartung* (*Degeneration*, 1892) first linked this term to the discussion of modern art and literature by suggesting that modern artists had lost the power of accurate observation and reflected instead their own nervous deformities. Nordau's discredited theories were later taken up by both Stalinist and Nazi ideologues.

17 Both the New Soviet Man and the Nazi Aryan Superman can trace their origins back to this source.

stress was laid on the fact that the land area of the USSR covered one-sixth of the earth, from the Pacific Ocean to the White Sea. The history of antisemitism in Russia dates from long before the Revolution, but – since Karl Marx, and some active party functionaries, such as Lazar Kaganovich, were Jewish – it did not become enmeshed in party policy until the Cold War, by which time Stalin's power in the party was unchallenged, and 'cosmopolitanism' rather than 'formalism' became the main enemy of the state.[21]

Italian Fascism, like Nazism, was a nationalist ideology which attracted for a time a much broader range of adherents. A streetwise amalgamation of nationalism and Socialism, forged in the social ferment which followed the First World War, it established its credibility in the image of the fasces – the insignia of the popularly elected lawmakers of ancient Rome. An axe head, projecting from a bundle of elm or birch rods tied together by a red strap, became a symbol not only of strength in unity but also of the penal power of the state – both corporal and capital. Fascist gangs of Blackshirts helped Mussolini to suppress opposition, but beyond a state-sponsored syndicalism there was little coherent ideology to the movement which incorporated many different and conflicting viewpoints which Mussolini manipulated. Thus, during the 1920s he was critical of Nazi racism,[22] but a significant wing of his party did not share this view; it was eventually adopted as party policy in 1938 when, under German influence, the anti-semitic Racial Laws were enacted.

No formal summary of Fascism appeared until 1932, when Mussolini published the 'Dottrina del Fascismo' (Doctrine of Fascism) in the *Enciclopedia Italiana*. Typically, this built an ideology out of pragmatism: 'Our programme is simple. We wish to govern Italy. They ask us for programmes, but there are already too many. It is not programmes that are wanting for the salvation of Italy but men and willpower.'

Equally telling was the showpiece *Mostra della Rivoluzione Fascista* (Exhibition of the Fascist Revolution), which opened in Rome in the same year, to mark the tenth anniversary of the party's advent to power. The most modern and striking display techniques were used, and artists and architects of all tendencies were invited to participate in the design (pp. 39, 140–41).

Victims and Losers

'The triumph was short-lived, of course: triumphs are always short-lived and, as it is written, the Jew's joy ends in fright.' (Primo Levi, 1982.)[23]

Rome's and Berlin's vainglorious dreams of world domination were soon to crumble to dust. The cult of the warrior met its nemesis. By May 1945, the war was drawing to a close; Hitler and Mussolini were dead and Allied troops had swept across Europe. But the battle for art was not yet won. Under the dictatorships non-party artists and writers, along with many others, had been murdered, forced into exile or had to cover their tracks at home.[24] And the new Europe was characterized by a terrible vacuum where once stood people, language and art.

Energy and power had begun to slip across the Atlantic, with those many artists who had gone into exile, to New York, where a new generation of American artists was about to change the scale and ambition of modern painting. In Europe, modern art revived, but haltingly. The Cold War narrowed its social and political horizons, and optimism seemed either foolish or subversive. In Italy, a divide developed between realist, Communist-inspired painters such as Renato Guttuso and abstract artists such as Lucio Fontana (who, during the 1930s, had been a strong supporter of the Fascists). But it was now a world of superpowers, in which America vied with the Soviet Union to dominate the world stage. Italy was firmly rooted within the American camp, as was the German Federal Republic.

Nationalism of the old kind was unthinkable in the empires of either East or West, and new forms of international culture had to be put in its place. For a time, Socialist Realism became the lingua franca of the Eastern bloc. In the West, Modernism had always aspired to be a universal and international movement but increasingly – in economic and political as well as in cultural terms – it was America that called the shots.

Germany was split between the USSR and the West, and started to construct two separate cultures and histories with which to justify its respective positions. In the Federal Republic there was an active debate about the relative merits of abstraction and realism, which had political parallels in the rejigged conflict between the rival doctrines of individual 'freedom' and collective 'democracy'. In the German Democratic Republic there was a continuation of the Moscow party line, but by 1953, after the death of Stalin, this position was modified as a younger

18 The first part of *Mein Kampf* was written in 1923 in Landsberg fortress in Bavaria, where Hitler was imprisoned after the Beer Hall Putsch, and was published in Munich in 1926. A second part of the book was written between 1925 and 1927, after Hitler had reconstructed the Nazi party; this was printed along with a revision of the main text. By 1939 the book had sold 5.2 million copies in Germany.

19 Lenin had warned the Central Committee of the Communist Party about the ambition of Stalin in his will and had suggested that he should be removed from his post, but Stalin suppressed this document during the power struggle with Trotsky and Bukharin which ensued after Lenin's death in 1924. For the text of Lenin's letters, see Mikhail Heller and Aleksandr M. Nekrich, *Utopia in Power: The History of the Soviet Union from 1917 to the Present* (New York, 1986), 159–66.

20 See Matthew Cullerne Bown, *Art under Stalin* (Oxford, 1991), 93–94.

21 See Igor Golomstock, *Totalitarian Art in the Soviet Union, Third Reich, Fascist Italy and the People's Republic of China* (London, 1990), 146–47.

22 See note 15.

23 Primo Levi, *If Not Now, When* (London, 1982), 112.

24 Of the artists shown in the exhibition: in the USSR Aleksandr Drevin, Vera Yermolayeva, Gustavs Klucis, Vasily Kuptsov and Kazimir Malevich were imprisoned by the NKVD – Klucis and Drevin were murdered; in Germany John Heartfield, Max Beckmann, Walter Gropius, Oscar Kokoschka, Paul Klee and Mies van der Rohe went into exile; Hans Grundig and Felix Nussbaum were confined in concentration camps – only Grundig survived; in Italy Corrado Cagli went into exile, and Arturo Nathan was killed in Belsen.

generation of East German artists began to invent a revised form of realism which tried to accommodate leftist traditions within both the history of German art and European Modernism.[25]

In the Darmstadt Dialogues of July 1950, Willi Baumeister passionately and effectively defended abstract art from attack by the realist painter Carl Hofer and right-wing critics such as Hans Sedlmayr who blamed modern art for the 'loss of centre' in our culture.[26] Modernism – but only of an international kind – won the day in the West and received official patronage. And it was not until the 1960s that the generation of painters which included Georg Baselitz, Gerhard Richter, Sigmar Polke, Jörg Immendorff, Anselm Kiefer and Markus Lüpertz was able, authentically and unapologetically, to reintegrate a concern with German cultural history and sensibility in their work.

One dictator – Stalin – had survived, and the purges continued in the USSR as Zhdanov, and latterly Georgi Malenkov, imposed an increasingly constricted concept of art. Opposition was impossible, but after Stalin's death an independent, autonomous art again slowly began to take root within an unpromising, sterile seedbed.[27] Within the system itself, however, deprived of its supreme leader and no longer fuelled by terror, entropy took its toll.[28] Mikhail Gorbachev's *perestroika* and the collapse of the Berlin Wall dealt the *coup de grâce*. Although it had enlisted some talented artists, the dogma of Socialist Realism could now be perceived as a nightmare rather than as a creative method or a style; it is one from which Russia has only recently, haltingly and painfully, begun to awake.

This battle for art has now come to an end, but it has been replaced by other no less vital contests. One paradox is clear: the point at which art becomes a weapon is the very moment when it loses its power. But the converse is also true: when power tries to enlist art for its own purposes, it runs the risk of curtailing other basic freedoms. In this battle there can be no winners, only losers and victims; and being a loser is probably the more convivial fate.

Like all ideals, complete artistic autonomy is impossible, but it is a symbol which should be cherished. For a free society, art is both a reflection of its complexity and an intimation of its capacity for change. As a result, modern art – almost by definition – often has an incompatible or critical relationship with the culture in which it is made. In a politics of totalitarianism (or even of consensus), where democracy is elevated at the expense of freedom, it is easy to overlook its value. But, like a canary down a coalmine, its state, no longer allied to power but dependent on it, may be an indicator of potential disaster.

In the world of metaphor which art resolutely occupies, the health of the canary is of the greatest importance; the essence (and paradox) of the autonomy of modern art is that it should be valued not only for itself but also as a sign and guarantor of other freedoms – particularly when it turns to peck the hand that solicitously tries to feed it.

25 See David Elliott, 'Absent Guests. Art, Truth and Paradox in the Art of the German Democratic Republic', in Irit Rogoff, *The Divided Heritage. Problems in German Modernism* (Cambridge, 1991), 24–49.

26 Willi Baumeister, 'Ansprache in Darmstadt', in Baumeister, *Das Unbekannte in der Kunst* (Cologne, 1974), 200–12.

27 See *'Drugoye iskusstvo'. Moskva 1956–76*, 2 vols (Moscow, 1991).

28 See Aleksandr Sidorov, 'The Thaw', in exh. cat. *Engineers of the Human Soul: Soviet Socialist Realist Painting 1930s to 1960s* (Oxford: Museum of Modern Art, 1992), 30–40.

SPEAKING WITHOUT ADJECTIVES

Architecture in the Service of Totalitarianism *Tim Benton*

1 Ezra Pound, *Jefferson and/or Mussolini* (London, 1933), 17.

2 F. T. Marinetti, 'Risposte alle obiezioni', 11 August, 1912. Response to criticism of the *Manifesto tecnico della letteratura futurista*, 11 May 1912, reprinted in Luciano de Maria, ed., *Marinetti e il Futurismo* (Milan, 1973).

3 *Mussolini ha sempre ragione*. In the later 1930s, it was common for popular demonstrations of loyalty, for example, by schoolchildren, to include this phrase.

4 *Credere, obbedire, combattere*. The slogan was adopted by the Gioventù Italiana del Littorio (GIL), the Fascist youth movement founded in 1937 in succession to the Opera Nazionale Balilla (ONB).

5 Most controversial was the oath of loyalty to King and the Fascist regime imposed on university professors in August 1931; a dozen professors refused to sign and were sacked or resigned their posts, while 1,250 complied. The GIL oath was: 'In the name of God and Italy I swear that I will execute the orders of the DUCE and serve with all my strength and, if necessary, with my blood the Cause of the Fascist Revolution.' Tracy H. Koon, *Believe Obey Fight* (North Carolina, 1985), 149.

6 The shortage of popularly priced radio receivers (the number of licences in Italy passed the million mark only in 1939) meant that most people heard the Duce's transmissions in public gatherings. Koon (as note 5), 156.

7 The name given to the struggle to achieve *Autarchia* or self-sufficiency in food production, in defiance of the sanctions imposed by the League of Nations during and after the Abyssinian campaign.

8 'Closely analysed, Mussolini's lexicon, his idiolect, barely extends beyond 100 words. But if this range is modest . . . it was, by compensation very broad, national in its reach . . . Words and ideas were generic, could be dilated on at will and free of any scientific precision.' Augusto Simonini, *Il linguaggio di Mussolini* (Milan, 1978), 11.

9 In fifteenth-century Florence, the *ringhiera* was attached to the Palazzo dei Priori (or Palazzo Vecchio), in the shadow of the tower.

'I am a flat-chested highbrow. I can "cure" the whole trouble simply by criticism of style. Oh can I? Yes. I have been saying so for some time.'(Ezra Pound, 1933.)[1]

'I believe it necessary to suppress the adjective and the adverb, because they constitute (taken together and individually), the multicoloured festoons, the *trompe-l'oeil* swags, pedestals, parapets and balustrades of the old traditional period.' (F. T. Marinetti, 1912.)[2]

Building for Rhetoric

The natural means of communication, for a totalitarian regime, is propaganda, and it is often by absurd slogans that totalitarian leaders have been judged. 'Mussolini is always right'[3] was as important an element in wearing down a people's common sense and judgment as the slogans of the Fascist party (Believe, Obey, Fight),[4] or the oaths of personal loyalty to the leader sworn by the Fascist militia or youth organizations.[5]

The typical instrument of propaganda in the 1930s, in all regimes, was the microphone. Some successful leaders mastered the artificial intimacy of radio, as Baldwin and Roosevelt did; but the totalitarian regimes of the Soviet Union, Germany and Italy used the microphone mainly as a public address system.[6] These regimes placed great importance on public demonstrations of authority and obedience: rallies, sporting displays, speeches relayed to urban public spaces. And at every site where large numbers of people gathered, buildings, sculptures and paintings were enlisted to transform comradeship into tribalism, pride into a sense of superiority, a sense of belonging into hatred of outsiders, progress into conscription for a Five Year Plan or the 'Battle for Grain'.[7] Buildings played a crucial role in this political process.

Many of the public buildings of the 1930s can best be approached as propaganda, not simply by virtue of the insignia, heroic narratives and inscriptions which cover them inside and out, but of the expressive form of the architecture. Propaganda has its characteristic sounds and syntactic patterns;[8] and so, to an extent, does 'regime architecture'. Much of this follows from the contradictions that establish themselves at the heart

of dictatorial regimes: the need to be familiar as well as autocratic, to be 'of the people' but not of a specific region or class. Some of it is technical: communicating to vast, agitated crowds requires a language which can be broken up into segments, articulated in bold, abstract bursts, placing great stress on single words or groups of words whose staccato rhythms, guttural consonants, rippling Rs and open vowels can carry the violence of the message more emphatically than the lexical meanings of the words. Public art and architecture, too, had to work to a beat, at a gigantic scale, to convey a message at a distance.

The new order had to be demonstrated in city centres, in wide avenues or squares lined with imposing buildings. The new, semi-industrialized building methods allowed huge buildings to be put up at reasonable cost, meeting the needs of burgeoning bureaucracies. These buildings, typically, were short on quality detailing, humanistic scale and proportion. Some of this, too, is technical and not restricted to totalitarian regimes.

To compare buildings and urban interventions with the political harangue does not tell the whole story, but it's a start. Many of them were designed precisely to support and amplify demagoguery. There was a specialized architecture of the public rally. The most famous piece of rally urbanism was the layout of avenues, parks and assembly buildings at Nuremberg, designed to host the annual Nazi party rallies. The Zeppelinfeld, designed by Albert Speer, was the built receptacle for a climax of processions, from home town parades to the arrival in the city, the march along broad parkland avenues to a packed and regimented space where members could be addressed by the Führer and perform party ceremonies. To walk round the Zeppelinfeld (now partly demolished), to stand on Hitler's podium, to see again the images from Leni Riefenstahl's *Triumph of the Will*, is to explore disturbing corners of the uncanny. Here there is no new function, no comforting replacement iconography, to distance us from the personalities and intentions of the National Socialists.

In Italy, the Fascist oratorical pulpit, the *arengo* or *arengario*, had many precedents in medieval and Renaissance urban design: many old Italian cities had a *ringhiera* – a balcony or raised platform attached to the

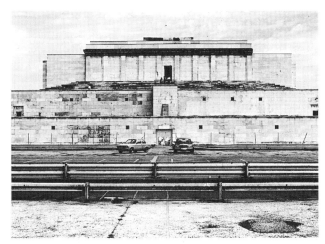

Albert Speer, Zeppelinfeld, Nuremberg, 1934 (as seen in 1979)

Antonio Maraini, *Arengo*, Brescia, 1928–32, showing relief of First World War and emergence of Fascism

government building – where rulers could address the public, proclamations could be made and punishments meted out.[9] In Rome, the most famous Fascist *arengario* was the balcony of the fifteenth-century Palazzo Venezia where, above a piazza carved out of medieval and baroque Rome, Mussolini made his most bombastic speeches, which were simultaneously relayed to piazzas all over Italy. There, on 2 October 1935, he declared the general mobilization before the Ethiopian campaign:

'Revolutionary Blackshirts! Men and women of all Italy! Italians all over the world, beyond the mountains and beyond the seas! Hear this!

'A solemn hour is about to strike in the history of the fatherland. Twenty million men are, at this moment, occupying the piazzas of the whole of Italy. Never in the history of mankind has a more gigantic spectacle been seen. Twenty million men: a single heart, a single will, a single decision.'[10]

Sometimes we find a free-standing *arengario*. An unusual example is the porphyry pulpit that now stands forlornly in the car park of the Piazza della Vittoria, Brescia. Designed by Antonio Maraini, it has a modern,

cantilevered form and is faced with nine reliefs illustrating the history of the city, each in the style of the time, from the Byzantine Exarchate to the first World War and its Fascist aftermath. The *arengario* commemorates the fierce independence and fighting spirit that led the Brescians, after the humiliating defeat of Caporetto in 1917, to the eventual victory of Vittorio Veneto.

The Fascist urban intervention in Brescia, designed by Marcello Piacentini in 1927–28 and built between 1928 and 1932, exemplifies the elements of totalitarian propaganda. At a functional level, the new plan was modern, ruthlessly demolishing the medieval heart of the city in the interests of freeing up traffic circulation. Modern and quintessentially Fascist, too were the buildings defining the piazza: a post office and the organs of the developing corporative state (insurance buildings and banks). Making the post work, and the trains run on time, were central planks of the Fascist campaign against the bourgeois, liberal and democratic order. Most Italian cities still have a Fascist railway station and post office;[11] the efficient, modern style of these buildings, together with their more or less discreet iconography of fasces, shrines to Fascist martyrs and Italian or Latin inscriptions, entrenched the claims of state propaganda.

Rewriting the Song Sheet

To many committed Fascists, the March on Rome (1922) and the gradual absorption of all social functions within a totalitarian regime was a social, economic and political revolution, appropriately represented in terms of youthful, avant-garde enthusiasm. The problem was that there were structural contradictions (to be found in Germany and Russia as well), between the radical roots of the movement and the coercive requirements of authority (which needed stability, an element of respectability and confidence).

The case of propaganda music is revealing. Speaking of the street-fighting days of 1919–22, the compiler of an Italian 'revolutionary' song book asserted: 'Fascism won, because it had more beautiful songs than the opposition.'[12] The 'Fascist hymns' were to evolve in a way that was prophetic for art and architecture.

The fate of what became the anthem of the Fascist party, *Giovinezza*, was characteristic. A lively prewar ode to youth,[13] this was taken over, and given new words, by the *arditi*: the desperadoes who, after

10 *Popolo d'Italia*, 3 October 1935, xxii.

11 Apart from Florence railway station, won in competition amid much public controversy by a group of young Florentine architects led by Giovanni Michelucci (1932–34), Ufficio V (a design department in the Ministry of Communications), and one of its architects Angiolo Mazzoni, built post offices and railway stations all over Italy which were always original and often very striking: A. Forti, exh. cat. *Angiolo Mazzoni (1894–1979): Architetto nell'Italia fra le due guerre* (Bologna, 1994). Competitions led to the appointment of four young modern architects to design the main post offices in Rome (1932) and to the gigantic post office in Naples (1929–31), designed by Giuseppe Vaccaro. Sergio Poretti, *Progetti e costruzione dei palazzi delle poste a Roma 1933–35* (Rome, 1990).

12 A. Gravelli, *I canti della Rivoluzione* (Rome, 1934), 13.

13 Originally composed by Giuseppe Blanc in 1910 while on a ski training exercise with some students from Oxilia, it was adopted as 'The Hymn of the Alpini Skiers'. The *arditi* version was written by Marcello Nanni during the First World War.

Caporetto, added their fanaticism and courage to the Italian military recovery. Organized into volunteer outfits – the *fiamme nere* – whose ranks were swollen by released convicts with nothing to lose, they invented their own uniform. Their shaven heads, fez hats, black shirts and skull-and-crossbones insignia, and their preferred weapons (dagger and grenade), acquired a morbid fascination for the youth of the postwar period. Many of them later joined up as Fascist *squadristi*, in *fasci di combattimento* under local war-lords – or *Ras* – or followed the call of Gabriele d'Annunzio in his freelance seizure of Fiume (Rijeka). The very real violence and intimidation of the *squadristi* underpins the fundamental illegality of Fascism; it erupted during the Matteotti crisis (1925–26), when Fascist gangs saw an opportunity to see off their enemies in the political centre and on the left. Almost all the *gerarchi* (hierarchs) who took leading roles in the Fascist administration had been blooded in *arditismo* or *squadrismo*. The words they sang to *Giovinezza* captured the full flavour of death-or-glory nihilism:

With dagger and grenade / *Col pugnale e con la bomba*
Living with terror / *Nella vita del terrore*
When the shell explodes / *Quando l'obice rimbomba*
Our hearts are steadfast / *Non ci trema in petto il cuore*

Our one true flag / *Nostra unica bandiera*
Has one colour only / *Sei di un unico colore*
A flame that is all black / *Sei una fiamma tutta nera*
Blazing in every heart! / *Che divampa in ogni cuor!*[14]

To the same tune, the official 'Triumphal Hymn of the National Fascist Party', as recorded in the 1930s, had very different words:

Hail, o people of heroes, / *Salve, o Popolo d'Eroi,*
Hail, o immortal fatherland! / *Salve, o Patria*
                                    Immortale!
Thy children are reborn / *Sono rinati i figli tuoi*
With faith in the Ideal / *Con la fè nell'ideale*

The valour of thy warriors / *Il valore dei tuoi guerrieri,*
The virtue of the pioneers / *La virtù dei pionieri*
The vision of Dante Alighieri / *La vision*
                                    dell'Alighieri[15]
Shines today in every heart / *Oggi brilla in tutti i cuor.*[16]

By the 1930s the party had been made subservient to the state, the *squadri* reformed into the Fascist militia, and the image of Fascism tidied up. This created contradictions between the popular roots of Fascism and authority. Thus, the song that most successfully captured the euphoria of the Ethiopian campaign was *Faccetta Nera* (Little Black Face), by the prolific composer Ruccione. The beautiful Abyssinian girl ('slave among slaves') dreams of the Italian soldiers who will set her free and carry her off in triumph to Rome, where she, too, will wear a 'black shirt', become a Roman and march past the King and Mussolini. It is characteristic of the times that *Faccetta Nera* was later censored on the grounds that it might encourage interracial cohabitation. The very expression of aggressive male dominance that had made the song so popular, and matched the mood of imperialism, was considered too rich for the public radio.

The task which faced Mussolini and his balding Blackshirt *gerarchi* was to retain the fervour and charisma of the early days while disciplining the faithful into a compliant party bureaucracy. The manipulators of Fascist culture attempted this by keeping the slogans but changing the emphasis. The slogans of violent *arditismo* and *squadrismo* – '*Eia, eia, eia allala!*',[17] '*A noi!*',[18] '*Me ne frego*',[19] '*Noi tiremo diritto*'[20] – reappear throughout the official culture of the 1930s, but increasingly give way to more pompous slogans evoking the Roman Empire and the Augustan age: *Roma rivendica l'Impero* (Rome reclaims its Empire) or *Civiltà, ordine, autorità* (Civilization, order, authority).

'A Higher Law' and a Modernist Rhetoric

With hindsight, this evolution from Fascist 'revolution' to imperial 'restoration' may seem inevitable. But, on the face of it, Fascism did not require imperial imagery to build its support. What *was* required was a myth of subservience to a higher ideal, a form of civil conscription or religious conversion. The official entry in the Treccani Encyclopedia on 'Fascism', ghost-written for Mussolini by the philosopher Giovanni Gentile, was explicit about this:

'Fascism is a religious concept, in which man is seen in his immanent relationship to a higher law, with an objective will that transcends the individual human being and elevates him to be a conscious member of a spiritual society.'[21]

Modernist architects responded with enthusiasm to the challenge of evoking this 'religious concept' and spiritual allegiance. Modernism or Rationalism in Italian architecture had developed its most coherent

14 A. V. Savona and M. L. Straniero, *Canti dell'Italia fascista* (Rome, 1979), 55.

15 Dante came to play an increasingly important role in Fascist myth-making; see Domenico Venturini, *Dante Alighieri e Benito Mussolini*, 2nd ed. (1932).

16 Savona and Straniero (as note 14), 205.

17 A battle cry which D'Annunzio claimed to have invented in the trenches, though it was current much earlier.

18 D'Annunzio's rallying cry from Fiume, subsequently a street-fighting call to arms

19 Decorously translated as 'I don't give a damn', it expresses disdain for the pain of a wound, as well as contempt for intellectuals. A song based on its initials, *M.N.F, Emme, Enne, Effe*, by Vittorio Mascheroni with words by Angelo Borella, 1929, was a loutish attack on intellectuals ('*filosofesso*') and the bourgeoisie.

20 'We will shoot straight', coined at the time of the Ethiopian War but recalled by Mussolini to characterize the new Racial Laws that followed from Hitler's visit in May 1938. Antisemitic voices had been heard in Italy in the early 1930s, but were not given official sanction until the 'Manifesto of Racial Sciences' in July 1938. This document, probably written by Mussolini, initiated a press and legal campaign which led to the exclusion of Jews from schools, public service, the professions and intermarriage with non-Jewish Italians.

21 Giovanni Gentile, writing under Mussolini's signature, 'Fascismo', in the Treccani *Enciclopedia Italiana* (1935–36).

and enthusiastic groupings in Milan and Como.[22] After a successful exhibition in 1928,[23] the Rationalists went on the offensive in the Second Italian Exhibition of Rationalist Architecture, held at the Galleria Bardi in Rome in 1931. Mussolini himself came to the opening and was handed a pamphlet claiming that the Rationalists were the only true Fascist architects:[24]

'Mussolini wants an art of our times, a Fascist art … The architecture of the era of Mussolini must respond to the character of masculinity, force and pride of the Revolution. The old architects are an emblem of impotence which won't do … Our movement has no other moral mission than that of serving the Revolution in hard times.'[25]

Mussolini gave them some support in a brief speech in Perugia, where he called for 'a new art, an art for our times, a Fascist art'. At first they thought they could take on the architectural establishment and win. P. M. Bardi (editor of the Roman journal *Quadrante*) assembled a photomontage, entitled 'Panel of Horrors', in which the most ludicrous examples of eclectic classicism were contrasted with the work of architects like Enrico del Debbio, Giovanni Muzio and Marcello Piacentini: established architects who were transforming their work in a more Rationalist direction.[26] Henceforth, the attempt to win favour with Mussolini depended on delicate alliances with the architects in power, and especially with Piacentini.[27] A key figure here was Giuseppe Pagano, editor of the magazine *Casabella*.

The Rationalists now proceeded to demonstrate that they could be superbly effective propagandists. Giuseppe Terragni, Adalberto Libera and Mario de Renzi, with the artist Mario Sironi, were given the key task of celebrating the tenth anniversary of Mussolini's March on Rome in 1932. Libera and De Renzi designed a temporary façade for the Palazzo delle Esposizioni on the via Nazionale, consisting of four giant Modernist fasces faced in steel sheeting, adding an aggressive political symbol to the neo-baroque building. Stripped to essentials, Libera's internal decor achieved just the right mixture of symbolism and theatrical effect; and Terragni and his associates produced some of the most spectacular pieces of violent agitprop outside Russia (p. 140). Similarly, at the Triennale in Milan, in 1933, the Italian Rationalists assembled one of the most impressive collections of Modernist pavilions in Europe. None of these young architects was apparently much troubled with scruples about working for the regime; all were members of the Syndicate of Fascist Architects.

Adalberto Libera and Mario de Renzi, Façade of *Mostra della Rivoluzione Fascista*, Rome 1932

Giuseppe Terragni, Sala O, *Mostra della Rivoluzione Fascista*, Rome 1932

22 Gruppo 7 (S. Larco, G. Frette, C. E. Rava, L. Figini, G. Pollini, G. Terragni, Castagnoli [replaced by A. Libera]) formed in 1926 in Como and published manifesto texts in *La Rassegna italiana* from December 1926 to May 1927. Around it gathered a number of Rationalist architects in Turin, Milan and the rest of Lombardy. They exhibited at the Third Triennale, Monza, in 1927. See Giorgio Ciucci and Francesco Dal Co, *Architettura Italiana del '900* (Milan, 1990), 100–01.

23 The exhibition was held at the Galleria Bardi, Rome, in 1928 and included the work of Piero Bottoni, Calza Bini, Piccinato and Matté-Trucco, as well as the Lombard Rationalists.

24 P. M. Bardi, *Rapporto sull'architettura (per Mussolini)* (1931).

25 Manifesto presented to Mussolini at the MIAR exhibition, 30 March 1931, in L. Patetta, *L'architettura in Italia 1919–1943. Le polemiche* (Milan, 1972).

26 The complexity of these relationships is illustrated by the facts that both Muzio and Terragni worked closely with Sironi, that Muzio collaborated with the young Modernists Paniconi and Pediconi on part of the E'42 project, and that Pagano saw similarities of approach in their work: a shared willingness to go for formal external effects rather than an organic, rational unity between plan and elevation. Giuseppe Pagano, 'Tre anni di architettura in Italia', *Casabella*, no. 10 (February 1937), cited in Giorgio Ciucci, *Gli architetti e il Fascismo* (Turin, 1989), 74.

27 Richard A. Etlin, *Modernism in Italian Architecture 1890–1940* (Cambridge Mass., and London, 1991), ch. 10, 'The Rationalist Discovery of Fascism', traces this history.

Adolfo Coppedè, Casa del Fascio, Signa, 1928 (later built)

28 Carlo Cresti, *Architettura e Fascismo* (Florence, 1986), 26–27.

29 Peter Eisenman has devoted a number of articles to analysing Terragni's work: 'Casa del Fascio', *Perspecta*, 13/14 (1971), 62–65; 'Dall'oggetto alla relazionalità: la casa del Fascio di Terragni', *Casabella* (January 1970), 38–41.

30 Some nondescript elevation drawings published in Ada Francesca Marciano, *Giuseppe Terragni, Opera Completa 1925–1943*, 91, are attributed to Terragni's associate Zuccoli and dated 1928. Etlin (as note 27), 452–57, argues that Terragni was himself involved in this deception as late as 1933.

Many new buildings were designed to celebrate the triumph of Fascism in towns and cities of all shapes and sizes. Some, such as the neo-Imperial pastiche by Adolfo Coppedè in Signa (1928),[28] were an absurd attempt to evoke the Imperial past. At the other extreme, Terragni was able to design and build a Fascist headquarters building, the Casa del Fascio in Como (1932–34), which has been generally regarded as one of the very best buildings in Europe of its period.[29]

The circumstances were peculiar. Terragni's brother became mayor of Como in 1934, while the building was being designed. Terragni had just successfully built a Modernist block of flats (1928), by cleverly inducing the building authorities to approve a traditional design, which he adapted in stages until it took on the form of

Giuseppe Terragni, Casa del Fascio, Como, 1934–36

a radical modern building. It seems that he, or one of his associates, tried the same trick with the headquarters of the Como Fascist party.[30]

When the Casa del Fascio was opened in 1936, the building had no representational sculpture on the outside, and only abstract decorations on the inside, apart from icons of Il Duce. But, though the imagery of the building may appear apolitical, this was contradicted by the architect's own explicit statements. It was steeped in rhetoric:

'The moving quality of the work is no longer the rhetorical figure with spade or pick on his shoulder and the sun sinking behind him. It resides rather in acknowledging the thousands and thousands of black-shirted citizens amassed in front of the Casa del Fascio to hear the voice of their leader announce to Italians and foreigners the advent of the Empire.'[31]

A contemporary photograph, in which photomontage seems to be used to swell the crowd, records this definitive image. Terragni made a practice of supplying lengthy theoretical justifications for his buildings, in which designs apparently 'empty' of explicit meaning were associated with the correct political rhetoric. For the Casa del Fascio he took as his text Mussolini's statement that 'Fascism is a glass house.' No secrets, no obfuscating bureaucracy, should separate the Fascist leaders from their people: 'The past and the Fascist faith are the flame and life which cannot, and should not, be forgotten or diminished. The great moral significance is thus linked to the typically functional concepts which must preside in the construction of the Casa del Fascio.'[32]

Pressure was put on Terragni to include more explicit Fascist symbols: a *torre del Littorio* (Tower of the Lictorate, intended to represent Fascist authority) and an *arengario*. Some elevation drawings record variants of a tower. It is not clear whether drawings like these were ever intended for execution, or simply to demonstrate political commitment. In the end, the only vestige of this tower is the section of blank wall on the right of the principle façade. The *arengario* function has been subsumed into the open loggia which occupies the rest of the façade.

At the time, Bardi made a determined effort to promote the Casa del Fascio as a Fascist Parthenon, a celebration of military conquest in a perfect form. Pagano, on the other hand, while admiring Terragni's invention, accused him in *Casabella* of a certain 'rhetoric of unusual forms', of what he calls a 'Mannerism of Functionalism'.[33]

Is the Casa del Fascio a building of political

rhetoric, indelibly marked by its Fascist message? Terragni certainly went to great lengths to say so; and it included some highly charged iconography. The 'Shrine to the Fascist Martyrs', just inside the entrance, incorporated a glass block in which relics of local Fascists killed in street fighting were embedded. Brooding images of Il Duce and slogans (Order, Authority, Justice) by the sculptor Mario Radice decorated the interior, alongside abstract relief sculptures.

However, Terragni's belief that party officials would understand the building proved ill-founded. The secretary general demanded that the blank wall should be decorated with clearly propagandistic imagery. Terragni asked Sironi and then Marcello Nizzoli to devise something. Nizzoli came up with some lightweight frames, on which propagandistic images on enamel panels could be hung. Several photomontage sketches were produced, but the wall was in the end left unmarked.

The Casa del Fascio achieved great acclaim among modern architects, but it also contributed to disunity among Modernist groupings. The rift between Terragni and Pagano was to take an ugly turn when, on the introduction of Mussolini's Racial Laws in 1938, Terragni began to attack Pagano as Jewish (he wasn't) and to describe him and his colleague Gino Levi-Montalcini as 'foreigners'.[34]

Pagano and his journal *Casabella* (co-edited by Edoardo Persico until his early death) remained the main platform for promoting the employment of modern architects for official buildings. The battle was not finally lost until after 1940, when Pagano and four other architects were dismissed from the EUR (E'42) project; but the turning point had occurred much earlier.

The Rhetoric of Empire

By 1934, when the first competitions for Il Duce's new official headquarters, the Palazzo del Littorio, were held in Rome, a number of symbolic elements were coming together in Fascist architecture.[35] Rhetorical forms were becoming codified. A tower, the *torre del Littorio*, sometimes even detailed as a lictor's axe[36], had come to stand for a combination of the medieval civic tower and an abstract symbol of authority. Many quite modest Fascist municipal buildings can be recognized, even today, after the flags and fasces have been stripped off, by the presence of a vertical feature representing

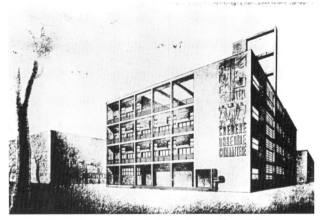

Giuseppe Terragni or associate, design for Como with possible modifications, *c.* 1932

the *torre del Littorio*. To this was attached the typical Fascist *arengario*, usually in the form of a projecting balcony, decorated with relief sculpture and inscriptions based on texts from Mussolini's speeches. These were the necessary substantives of Fascist composition, which required few architectural 'adjectives' to embellish them.

In its definitive form – of which Marinetti certainly approved – the Fascist urban centre must be seen from above, filled with people. Some of the new towns in the newly drained Pontine marshes, beginning with Littoria (Latina) and Sabaudia, showed how all these elements could be deployed within a modern architectural and urban idiom.[37]

By the time Terragni designed another Casa del Fascio in the little Milanese town of Lissone, in 1938–39, it was equipped with a *torre del Littorio*, a demonstrative *arengario* and the motto, 'Believe, Obey, Fight.' Terragni complained in his accompanying text of the 'disorientating, uncalled-for return to the ambiguous antimodern polemics of 1938'.[38] Room for

Inauguration of the new town of Sabaudia

31 Giuseppe Terragni, 'La costruzione della Casa del Fascio di Como', *Quadrante* 35–36 (1936), translated in Thomas L. Schumacher, *Surface and Symbol: Giuseppe Terragni and the Architecture of Italian Rationalism* (New York, 1991) 151.

32 Terragni (as note 31), 153.

33 'Seicentismo del funzionale', 'Tre anni di architettura in Italia', *Casabella*, no. 110 (February 1937).

34 Etlin (as note 27), 580ff.

35 This was self-consciously seen as a search for a *stile fascista* or *stile littorio*: F. Palozzi, *Il nuovo stil littorio: I progetti per il palazzo del Littorio e della MRF in via dell'Impero* (Milan and Rome, 1936).

36 Libera was particularly fond of this device, using a lictor's axe, either alone or in a row, for the façade of the *Mostra della Rivoluzione Fascista*, Rome, 1932, for the *Littorio* Pavilion at the Universal Exhibition, Brussels, 1935, and in a design for the Italian Pavilion in Chicago, 1939. See F. Garofalo, *Adalberto Libera* (Bologna, 1989), 80.

37 For Sabaudia, a competition was held (1933) in which a group of young Roman urbanists, led by Piccinato, was successful. Ricky Burdett, *Sabaudia, Città nuova fascista* (London, 1982).

38 Marciano (as note 30), 234.

Adalberto Libera, Mario de Renzi, Giuseppe Vaccaro, design for Auditorium, Rome 1935

39 Also known as E'42, the *Esposizione Universale di Roma* was launched by Mussolini as the 'Olympiad of Civilization' and promoted as a token of Italian Fascism's peaceful intentions. The huge exhibition site was planned as a satellite town on the road to the coast. The exhibition buildings were to become museums, ministries and office buildings. The project was abandoned after Italy entered the war.

40 'Potremo salvarci dalle falsi tradizioni e dalle ossessioni monumentali?', *Costruzione-Casabella*, no. 157 (January 1941).

41 Gian Luigi Banfi, of the Milanese firm BBPR, was another modern architect murdered in the German camps.

42 At the end of his long autobiography, when Speer admits guilt for 'my active association with events', he tellingly puts this in architectural terms: 'I had assented to having the globe of the world crown that domed hall which was to be the symbol of the new Berlin. Nor was it only symbolically that Hitler dreamed of possessing the globe.' Albert Speer, *Inside the Third Reich* (London, 1975), 696.

43 Pound (as note 1), 34.

invention was being squeezed out. Many architects thought that they could make the unadorned structural forms of Rationalist architecture acceptable by juxtaposing them with classicizing sculptures. This was the tactic adopted by Libera, De Renzi and Vaccaro in their designs for the Auditorium building (1935), intended to replace the concert hall originally in the Mausoleum of Augustus.

Despite the move towards a pompous official *stile littorio* after 1934, Piacentini, the most influential 'official' architect of the regime, maintained open communications with those of the Modernists who would accept him. He invited several young architects onto the editorial board of his journal *Architettura*, which he substantially redesigned and modernized under their influence. He continued to invite architects like Pagano, Gio Ponti (editor of *Domus* and bridge between Modernists and traditionalists) and others to collaborate with him on official commissions, such as the University City in Rome and the huge project of EUR.[39]

But as the decade progressed – and particularly after the Ethiopian war, the international sanctions, the campaign for *Autarchia* (self-sufficiency in food and industrial production) and the declaration of Empire – the mood turned increasingly towards overt allusions to Imperial Rome. Piacentini, who had attacked the critic Ugo Ojetti for suggesting that buildings required columns and arches to acquire the necessary dignity and authority, finished up by imposing classicizing detail on his young collaborators at EUR. A project which began as one of the more adventurous urban projects of Europe ended sadly among half-built carcasses and unused marble columns.

Pagano eventually came off the fence and, in a context of increasingly bitter racist attacks from right and left, wrote a searing attack on Piacentini and all the established architects and critics who had accepted the drift into classicism. The title of his article 'Can we save ourselves from false traditions and monumental obsessions?' indicates his state of mind.[40] After joining his regiment and fighting in the war, Pagano embarked on a campaign of resistance and sabotage which led eventually to his arrest, torture and death in a concentration camp.[41]

In its most ambitious form, the task of representing the totalitarian state in great representative buildings defeated the political will and architectural imagination in the USSR, Germany and Italy. The Palace of the Soviets, for which a series of international competitions was held in the early 1930s, produced little (pp. 51, 203) but some very large drawings and models. The Congress Hall in Nuremberg was begun but left incomplete, and Speer's gigantic hall in Berlin (p. 283) remained a dream.[42] In Italy, after two competitions for the Palazzo del Littorio (pp. 124, 142), a much impoverished building was begun and abandoned in 1942. Representing the collective will in the person of a single dictator turned out to be easier than building an architectural symbol for it.

If we take Ezra Pound's view of Mussolini seriously, part of the dictator's failure will have been that of devising an appropriate physical form for his political ambition:

'I don't believe any estimate of Mussolini will be valid unless it starts from his passion for construction. Treat him as artifex and all the details fall into place. Take him as anything save the artist and you will get muddled with contradictions. Or you will waste a lot of time finding that he don't fit your particular preconceptions or your particular theories.'[43]

BERLIN, 1 MAY 1936

Iain Boyd Whyte

On 2 May 1936 *The Times* carried a long article under the heading 'Herr Hitler's May Day', an account of the celebrations held the day before in Berlin. As *The Times* correspondent reported: 'Central Berlin was entirely given over today to the "disciplined enjoyment of the workers' holiday" which the National Socialist régime had ordained . . . In the morning the chief event was a speech by Herr Hitler delivered in the Lustgarten, in which a large Maypole had been erected and decorated with swastikas and fir branches. Herr Hitler drove to the Lustgarten along some miles of broad thoroughfare, where large crowds of workers were marshalled behind lines of SA men. Many wandered away as soon as the Führer had passed, but most waited to hear his speech through loud-speakers and to join afterwards in singing Deutschland über Alles and the Horst Wessel Lied.'[1]

The focus of this celebration was the Lustgarten in central Berlin, a rectangular city square flanked on three sides by public buildings – Royal Palace, Cathedral, and Altes Museum – and on the fourth by the River Spree. This site, set on the small island on which the settlement of Berlin had been founded in the fourteenth century, represented the absolute epicentre of Prussia and thus, after the unification of the German states in 1871, of all Germany. As its name suggests, the Lustgarten was originally conceived as a small urban park, with avenues of trees offering an area of shade and repose in the city centre. In 1936, however, in preparation for the Olympic Games, the trees were felled, the square was paved, and viewing stands were erected on two sides. The city garden was turned into a parade ground, which was inaugurated on 1 May 1936.

The stage management of this event offers clear insights into the conscription of architecture, urban form, scenographic decorations, and painting as essential tools in the construction of the myths on which the National Socialist ideology was based. In forging this make-believe world of the National Socialist spirit, the visual arts played a central role both as a provider of symbolic images and as a record of party triumphs. Every possible medium was exploited, from medievalizing frescos in Luftwaffe messes to the instant reportage of the newsreel. Both were essential to the delivery of the National Socialist message, but functioned in quite different ways. Conventional

painting put traditional iconographic systems and quasi-humanistic references at the disposal of the new regime; film and radio offered apparently coherent alternative realities. A revealing intersection of these two mythologies can be seen in the representations of the 1936 May Day parade in Berlin, of which two paintings are illustrated here (p. 44), by Rudolf Hengstenberg and August Blunck.

A large version of the Hengstenberg painting was exhibited in the German pavilion at the 1937 Universal Exhibition in Paris, suggesting that it represented mainstream party ideology.[2] In its appeal to the emotional engagement of the viewer it is very direct: the essential information is layered in three blocks, a classical building forming the distant background, a maypole at centre stage, and a Baroque configuration of flags and bodies in the foreground. Between these layers, the extras in the drama perform their prescribed roles.

The essential backdrop for the whole spectacle is formed by the Altes Museum, built by Karl Friedrich Schinkel in the 1820s. It is Neoclassical in style and indebted to Hellenistic models. Following the defeat of the French at the Battle of Leipzig in 1813, the victorious state of Prussia emerged with greatly expanded territories as the dominant power between the Rhine and the Oder. In its new-found confidence it measured itself against Periclean Athens and found in Schinkel an architect equal to this almost impossible

1 'Herr Hitler's May Day', *The Times*, 2 May 1936, p. 14.

2 This official connection and the painting of 1 May 1936 was cited in December 1994 as a reason to ban an exhibition of Hengstenberg's paintings planned for Potsdam. See 'Politikerzensur für einen Künstler', *Der Tagesspiegel*, Berlin, 16 December 1994.

The Lustgarten decorated for the Olympic Games, Berlin 1936

August Blunck, *Parade in the Lustgarten*, 1 May 1936

Rudolf Hengstenberg, *May Day Celebration*, Berlin 1936. US Army Center for Military History, Washington DC

3 Moeller van den Bruck, *Der preussische Stil* (Munich, 1916); further editions 1922, 1931, 1934, 1935. Citation from third edition (Breslau, 1931), 151.

4 Jakob Graf, *Familienkunde und Rassenbiologie für Schulen*, 2nd ed. (Munich, 1935), 107. Translation from George L. Mosse, *Nazi Culture: A Documentary History* (New York, 1981), 79.

5 Hans Weigert, *Die Kunst von Heute als Spiegel der Zeit* (Leipzig, 1934), 143.

6 Saul Friedländer, *Kitsch und Tod: Der Widerschein des Nazismus* (Munich, 1986), 119.

task. The new Prussian capital was conceived in the 1820s as 'Athens on the Spree', and applauded as such a century later by nationalistic critics: Moeller van den Bruck, for example, in his very influential book *Der preussische Stil* (The Prussian Style), first published in 1916, insisted that 'the unity of Berlin, of Prussia, of all Prussians was the unity of Classicism'.[3] Following the defeat of 1918 and the humiliation of Versailles, the golden age of Prussian Classicism presented an especially beguiling resonance. Images of classical nobility and racial purity were central to National Socialist party ideology. As a school textbook explained in 1935:

'In the second millennium BC, the Aryans (the Nordic race) invaded India and established Aryan culture there. A branch related to the Aryans created the foundations of power and the flowering of the Persian empire. Ancient Hellenic culture, likewise, is traceable to the blood of Nordic immigrants. Paintings that have come down to us, as well as descriptions dating from that period, attest to the fact that the Hellenes, as long as they kept their race pure, were tall, light-skinned, light-eyed, blond people . . . Nordic boldness not only is a precondition for the martial exploits of nations of Nordic origin, but it is also a prerequisite for the courageous profession of new, great ideas.'[4]

While Aryan purity was alluded to by the architectural backdrop, a second racial narrative is introduced by the maypole set at the centre of the Lustgarten on the axis of the museum. Festooned with garlands and banners, and topped by a swastika, the maypole invoked the images of the German soil and the German peasant on which National Socialist hopes were pinned. The art historian Hans Weigert wrote in 1934:

'The Germans wish to renew themselves from the deepest maternal foundations of blood and soil. Thanks to the forces that have been awakened by our revolution, Germany now stands in the front line of the struggle with which the human spirit is charged today. This is the struggle to restore sense to the ever-more chaotic economy by the introduction of discipline and order, the struggle to tie the anarchic masses once again into a hierarchy, the struggle to give new impulses and substance to spiritual life in general and to art in particular.'[5]

What better symbol of these desires than the maypole, the traditional symbol throughout Northern Europe of the end of winter and of the reawakening of nature, and the focus of the communal games and feasts celebrating the arrival of the new spring? While it may well have made sense in rural Germany to select the biggest tree in the woods and bring it into the village, festooned in ribbons, cakes and even sausages, it made absolutely no sense in Berlin in 1936, where it took on the form of the purest and most potent kitsch. Its potency lay in the suggestion of order, immutability, and harmony so close to the heart of the petit bourgeois. The world should be just as it always was: the great industrial metropolis was really a village; communal and family values had been revived and reasserted by the party. As Saul Friedländer has noted in his essay on kitsch, death, and National Socialism: 'The kitsch vision favours the aesthetic criteria of a submissive mass, joyously receptive in its quest for harmony and sentimentality.' Kitsch, in this instance, is the aesthetic device that forms the potentially anarchic masses into orderly rows, and, as Friedländer points out, promotes the Nazi leader in the role of Everyman, 'intimately joined to the world of cosy cottages and to the hearts of the simple folk.'[6]

These images of timeless ritual, rebirth and regeneration are reinforced by the group of journeymen, in their traditional outfits, marching in the May Day parade. According to a surviving medieval practice, apprentices who had passed an initial test were obliged to wander through the German states as itinerant craftsmen, preparing for the final test that would lead them to the status of master of their chosen trade. By including a group of these wandering journeymen, Hengstenberg deftly unites medieval customs, a conservative appeal to traditional values in the arts and crafts, and an unspoken commentary on organized labour.

The very first May Day parade staged by the Nazis in Berlin in 1933 had been organized as a massive rally, with marching columns representing the various trades, skills, and groups of industrial workers, converging into a single body on the Tempelhofer Feld: a 'Volks-gemeinschaft' or community of the People.[7] A day later, on 2 May 1933, the existing trades unions were banned and replaced by the German Workers' Front (DAF), under the total control of the party. All this is neatly paraphrased by Hengstenberg's four journeymen, marching in step in the great parade.

The theme of the 'anarchic masses' given order, hierarchy and form is the theme of the Baroque heap of humanity in the foreground of Hengstenberg's canvas. The group is made up mainly of mothers and children, some in Hitler Youth uniform, who are pulled inexorably into the canvas towards the focus of Party and Leader. Motherhood and mobilized youth are, of course, themes absolutely central to the National Socialist enterprise. According to Joseph Goebbels' novel *Michael*, 'The mission of woman is to be beautiful and to bring children into the world.'[8]

Not any old children, moreover, but racially pure children, since the German mother was the bastion of Nazi eugenic theory. As the party ideologue Alfred Rosenberg insisted in a chilling passage published in 1930, this purity was under threat from emancipated women – the product of 'democracy and Marxism' – who claimed for themselves the final word in questions of morality: 'From the right to absolute personal freedom follows necessarily the denial of racial barriers. The "emancipated" woman claims for herself the right to sexual intercourse with Niggers, Jews, and Chinamen. And the woman who should be the appointed preserver of the race turns – thanks to the advocates of emancipation – into the destroyer of every foundation of the people.'[9]

Racial purity was linked directly to artistic purity. Rosenberg continued: 'And if the women of a nation give birth to Nigger or Jewish bastards, then the slimy torrent of Nigger "art" will continue to spread unhindered across Europe as it does today.'[10] If

'degenerate' sex produces 'degenerate' art, then the converse of Rosenberg's arguments – one might hazard – would also be the case, with thoughts of 'pure' sexuality stimulating 'pure' art.

In the case of Hengstenberg, the iconography of purity is based on straightforward Christian symbolism. The pure mother becomes the party, and the only-begotten son becomes fodder for the Hitler Youth. A comparison between Hengstenberg's group and a sketch by Rubens of the *Mystic Marriage of St Catherine*, now in the Städel Gallery in Frankfurt, makes this general point very clearly. Where Rubens has the Holy Child leaning forward yet restrained firmly by the embrace of the Madonna, Hengstenberg has the baby held in front of the reassuring embrace of the swastika flag. Further comparisons might also be drawn between the compositions of the two paintings, the flags, armour, gestures, and swirling Baroque sky. Academic art expertise, formerly devoted to the service of the Church, is here put to the use of the party.

Religious faith is rarely separable from images of obedience and death. Rubens summons St George in his suit of armour to create this nexus. Hengstenberg, more insidiously, does it with the two little drummer boys in the left foreground. These paragons of alert obedience, proud of their Hitler Youth uniforms, drums and banners, have been educated to their task by a propaganda machine which taught that 'The National Socialist philosophical revolution has replaced the illusory image of a cultivated personality with the reality of the true German man, whose stature is determined by blood and historical fate. It has substituted for the humanistic concept of culture, which had continued in vogue up to very recently, a system of

7 For a detailed account, see: 'Von der proletarischen Masse zum Kriegsvolk. Massenaufmarsch und Öffentlichkeit im deutschen Faschismus am Beispiel des 1. Mai 1933', in Klaus Benken and Frank Wagner, eds., *Inszenierung der Macht* (Berlin, 1987), 17–51.

8 Joseph Goebbels, *Michael: Ein deutsches Schicksal in Tagebuchblättern* (Munich, 1929), 41.

9 Alfred Rosenberg, *Der Mythos des 20. Jahrhunderts* (Munich, 1930), 505. On the role of women in National Socialist ideology see Renate Bridenthal, Atina Grossmann and Marion Kaplan, eds., *When Biology Became Destiny: Women in Weimar and Nazi Germany* (New York, 1984).

10 Rosenberg (as note 9), 510.

Peter Paul Rubens, *Study for Mystic Marriage of St Catherine*

11 Anon., *Erziehung und Unterricht in der höheren Schule, Amtliche Ausgabe des Reichs- und Preussischen Ministeriums für Wissenschaft, Erziehung und Volksbildung* (Berlin, 1938), 12. Quoted in Mosse (as note 4), 283.

12 Friedländer (as note 6), 130.

13 Joseph Goebbels, diary entry of 28 April 1933, in Goebbels, *Die Tagebücher: Sämtliche Fragmente*, 4 vols. (Munich, 1987). For Speer's own account of this early Party commission, see Albert Speer, *Inside the Third Reich* (London, 1970), 26–27.

14 See Heinz Weidner, *Berlin im Festschmuck vom 15. Jahrhundert bis zur Gegenwart* (Berlin, 1940).

education which developed out of the fellowship of actual battle.'[11]

The martial drum, in line with the journeymen and the maypole, launches the axis of kitsch and death, which Friedländer proposes as the hermeneutic pairing that enable us to understand not only Nazi culture but also the lasting fascination exerted by this perversion of the Western humanist tradition: 'Facing the kitsch aesthetic is the unfathomable world of myths; on one side the visions of harmony, on the other the summer-lightning of the apocalypse; on one side flower-garlanded girls and the snow-capped peaks of the Bavarian Alps, on the other the call to the dead of the Feldherrnhalle, the ecstasy of the Götterdämmerung, the visions of the end of the world . . . On one side are invoked the tranquil forces of moral values, while on the other side are flickering the fires of extermination.'[12]

Where were these sturdy youths nine years later? Thrown into the battle for Berlin, armed with a 1918 rifle and the Führer's assurance that Berlin would never fall to the Soviet army.

Hengstenberg's painting only gives a slice, albeit a revealing one, of the action in Berlin on May Day 1936. For a wider view we should turn to August Blunck's representation. Taken high above the crowds from the roof of the Royal Palace (Berliner Schloss), Blunck's image approaches the view from an aeroplane or an airship, the quintessentially Modernist conception of the city (p. 44). From Blunck's canvas one gains a better impression of the festive decorations installed by the architect Albert Speer, consisting of tall swastika banners, echoing the colonnade of the Altes Museum. Speer had first made his name within the party

hierarchy with his rapid redesign for the decorations on Tempelhofer Feld for the May Day celebrations in 1933. On that occasion, Goebbels had noted in his diary: 'Gigantic structures built on Tempelfhofer Feld. They present a grandiose image of the National Socialist will to build.'[13]

Speer thus found himself in a long line of distinguished architects who had designed festival decorations to mark special occasions or military victories; a line that goes back to Memling's design for gates of honour for the Great Elector in the 1670s, to Gentz's amphitheatre for Friedrich Wilhelm III, built in the Lustgarten in 1798, and to the decorative columns that Schinkel placed at the Brandenburg Gate to celebrate the defeat of the French in 1814.[14] Yet while the decorations of Gentz and Schinkel were conceived as additions and adornments to the existing city fabric, Speer's banners denied and masked the architectural realities of the city. This tells us much about the 'National Socialist will to build'. As Blunck's painting shows, the banners installed by Speer create an anonymous, pure, cubic space in the centre of the city and of the Reich, a space that denies the Cathedral and the topography of the river, and turns its back on the former Royal Palace in order to concentrate attention on the speaker's tribune in front of the Altes Museum, which itself is reduced to an anonymous screen. In Speer's own drawing of this space this cold emptiness is even more striking. An anonymous space was thus created that had freed itself from the immediate history of Berlin, the church and the monarchy, yet was still associated with Schinkel and with the distant aura of an Hellenic past. Within this space, the party could present itself as unfettered, dynamic, and innovatory: in short, as modern.

Modern, too, is the iconoclastic relationship with the existing city fabric, which reached its apogee in Speer's plan for a North-South Axis for Berlin. The idea of demolishing large tracts of an existing city to make way for a new, supra-historical and thus ahistorical architectural imperative did not begin with Speer. It was a standard polemical gesture of the Modernist movement, given its most powerful expression in Le Corbusier's Voisin Plan for Paris, dated 1925, or, closer to home, in Ludwig Hilberseimer's 'Skyscraper City' of 1924, proposed as a renewal scheme for Berlin. While Speer's lumpish Mega-Classicism and Hilberseimer's Modernist blocks speak quite different architectural languages, the basic syntactic rules are the same. This raises difficult questions about the relationship between Modernism

Albert Speer, *Decorations for Lustgarten Parade, 1 May 1936*

and Fascism, questions already articulated in 1988 in a controversial article by Boris Groys, which proposed that, in both the Nazi and Soviet contexts, 'totalitarian art was so unyielding towards the avant garde, because it itself was inspired by an avant-garde impulse'.[15] This avant-garde impulse, according to Groys, manifested itself in the manipulation of the masses as a medium for spectacle and artistic creation, in an infatuation with technology, and in the promise of a new world and a new social order utterly different from any that had gone before. Defined strictly in these terms, there is clearly a continuum running between the avant-garde art of the 1920s and the totalitarian art of the 1930s.

The aesthetic reassertion of totality is the great dynamo that links many of the Modernist manifestos of the 1920s with the National Socialist spectacles of the 1930s. Among the most extreme statements of the early 1920s are the architectural utopias produced by the Berlin avant-garde. Hans Scharoun, for example, writing to the Crystal Chain group of architects and utopians in 1920, insisted that the 'ardent will' of the architects 'should rage feverishly towards this night of unification with the primeval urge of the People. Then once again will building have its foundation in the sensuality of Mankind and its crown in the purity of the Beyond. And once again we shall be rooted in reality.'[16]

This ecstatic search for unity in multiplicity led the avant-garde to the formal device of the crystal as the ultimate expression of a vast diversity of form regulated by a small set of immutable structural laws. These laws, according to the avant-garde orthodoxies of the period, would be established by the artistic elite; in this case by the architect. Society was to be united and ordered under the aegis of the artistic revolution, with the architect as the messianic leader of the whole enterprise. These ambitions are neatly summed up in Lyonel Feininger's celebrated image of a crystalline cathedral, used on the cover of the founding manifesto of the Bauhaus in April 1919, or in Wassili Luckhardt's fantasy drawing *Ode to Joy*, in which the ecstatic masses gather around the vast crystalline symbol of hope for social regeneration and unity (p. 49).

In the traditional post-1945 historiography, images such as this were summoned as proof of the essential link between the artistic avant-garde and the politics of the left. And this was substantially true, for the dominant tone in the radical architectural debate in Germany around 1920 was anarcho-socialist, left of centre but unfettered by party loyalties. Later in that decade the same architects did, indeed, improve the lot of the common man with their great housing estates,

built at the behest of the Socialist city councils in Berlin, Frankfurt and elsewhere.

But what is one to think when the same architects offer their skills to the new regime in the early period of National Socialist government? Walter Gropius and Wassili Luckhardt, for example, both produced schemes for the DAF, which replaced the banned trades unions. Clearly, hopes of regeneration and social unity by design were rekindled by the National Socialist revolution, a point confirmed most strikingly by Luckhardt's 1934 proposal to locate one of his 1919-model crystals beside the Wannsee in Berlin as a House of the DAF (p. 49). While the Socialist revolution of 1918/19 and the National Socialist takeover of 1933 inspired Luckhardt to the same crystalline forms, the attraction was not mutual, and the hopes of the avant-garde for patronage by the National Socialist authorities flickered only briefly.

If, as Groys suggests, the aesthetics of totality lay behind the avant-garde project of the 1920s and the totalitarian art of the 1930s, why were the dictators so disinclined to adopt the avant-garde manners as their own? There clearly is an essential difference between the two, which resides somewhere in the gap between form and content, kitsch and art.

Something of this difference can be seen in the comparison of the crystal – the great symbol of regeneration in 1920 – and the swastika. Both functioned as symbols of totality and of an all-embracing order, yet while the crystal was rich in meaning and association, the swastika was dependent for its power on the apparatus of persuasion and propaganda. As a symbol of purity, of divinity, and of unity in multiplicity, the crystal stretches back through history, from the avant-garde gesture of the 1920s to the biblical New Jerusalem. It is laden with associations. The masses gathered around the

15 Boris Groys, 'Die totalitäre Kunst der 30er Jahre: Antiavantgardistisch in der Form und avantgardistisch im Inhalt', in Jürgen Harten, Hans-Werner Schmidt and Marie Luise Syring, eds., exh. cat. *'Die Axt hat geblüht . . .' Europäische Konflikte der 30er Jahre in Erinnerung an die frühe Avantgarde* (Düsseldorf: Städtische Kunsthalle, 1987), 35.

16 Hans Scharoun, letter to the Crystal Chain, no date, in Iain Boyd Whyte, *The Crystal Chain Letter* (Cambridge, Mass., 1985), 61.

Ludwig Hilberseimer, *Project for a Slab Block City*, 1924

Artur Brusenbach,
*Small German
Village Celebrating
Hitler's Fiftieth
Birthday*, 1939

17 Theodor W. Adorno,
Ästhetische Theorie
(Frankfurt am Main,
1970), 355.

18 Hermann Broch,
'The Tower of Babel', in:
*Hugo Hofmannsthal and
His Time*, tr. Michael P.
Steinberg (Chicago,
1984), 170–171.

19 Walter Benjamin,
'The Work of Art in the
Age of Mechanical
Reproduction', in
Benjamin, *Illuminations*
(New York, 1969), 241.

20 Dieter Bartetzko,
*Illusionen in Stein:
Stimmungsarchitektur im
deutschen Faschismus*
(Reinbek bei Hamburg,
1985), 13.

Expressionist crystal were joining this historical continuum. In contrast, the crystal put in the service of National Socialism could not function in a state that predicated its existence – as did the Soviet Union – on the abandonment of history in favour of selective historical invention, and the destruction of the old social order. To express the new ambition for social unity and totality an apparently ahistorical symbol was found: the swastika.

In the images of Berlin in May 1936 it is the swastika flag that bonds the heady mixture of Schinkel, the maypole, and the ordered masses. In saluting the flag one saluted Hitler; in accepting the visual order of the flag one fell into line with the party. This absolute identification of swastika symbol with the leader of the party can be seen very clearly in a painting by Artur Brusenbach, alluringly entitled *Small German Village Celebrating Hitler's Fiftieth Birthday*, in which one looks in vain for smiling faces or mugs of beer raised in honour of the Führer. Instead, there are flags everywhere, on posts, poles, in windows and on walls. The potency of the swastika flag lay in its total lack of cultural reference. It recalled nothing in the past, referred to no social class or historical grouping. And for this reason it could symbolize the strategic breakdown of all the social orders and groupings that had marked previous versions of German society.

The relationship between the culturally rich symbol of the crystal and the empty symbol of the swastika offers insights into the relationship between kitsch and art. As Theodor Adorno perceptively noted, 'Contrary to the conventional wisdom concerning culture, kitsch is not simply the waste product of art . . . for lurking within it are constantly recurring opportunities to bound free from art.'[17] The notion of kitsch as a potentially powerful, independent force working to its own agenda is the theme of Hermann Broch's analysis of kitsch, which deserves to be quoted at length:

'Kitsch is the confusion of the ethical with the aesthetic, and therein lies its relation to the radically evil. Every value system must produce – from dialectical foundations – its countersystem or, rather, its imitative system, in which the infinite value goal – God in religion, truth in science, beauty in art – is reduced to the finite and the earthly, and is hence made "value-less": this is the essence of the Antichrist. The ethical attitude with which a man is charged within the framework of these systems, and which he must manifest through the "good works" of action, thought, and creation, is an immediate function of the infinite value goal, and for that reason its earthly residue acquires an aesthetic effect, an aesthetic value – this is particularly visible in artistic creation. If, on the other hand, infinite systems are made finite through imitation, the relevant value goal is likewise pushed back into the finite and the earthly: God becomes an idol, truth dogma, beauty effect; an infinite system becomes a closed one. The imitative system that emerges from art is that of kitsch, and kitsch, accordingly, is not bad art but anti-art, and hence simply occupies the place of evil vis-à-vis the primal system.'[18]

In his celebrated essay 'The Work of Art in the Age of Mechanical Reproduction', Walter Benjamin concludes that the introduction of aesthetics into political life is the 'logical result' of Fascism.[19] The aesthetic criteria, however, were those that Broch has characterized as 'value-less', proposing merely the superficial appeal to order or to sentimentality, unsupported by any corresponding value system that could link the visual or intellectual pattern to a transcendent system of ethical values, thereby transforming it into a work of art. The paintings of Hengstenberg and Blunck are bad, not in terms of mere technique, but in their bland acceptance that Schinkel's colonnade, the maypole, and the serried ranks of swastika banners somehow offered symbols of a coherent value system to the masses gathered in their shadows.

With the advent of the technologies of mass communication, the radio and the newsreel, the masses – as Dieter Bartetzko has noted – became 'at the same time both subject and object of the spectacles, both victims and sustainers of the new order'.[20] This tendency was remarked upon as early as 1934 by Ernst

48

Wassili Luckhardt, Monument to Labour: *Ode to Joy, c.* 1920

Jünger, who noted in an essay on photography: 'Today any event worthy of notice is surrounded by a circle of lenses and microphones and lit up by the flaming explosion of flashbulbs. In many cases, the event itself is completely subordinated to its transmission; to a great degree, it has been turned into an object. Thus we have already experienced political trials, parliamentary meetings, and contests whose whole purpose is to be the object of a planetary broadcast. The event is bound neither to its particular space nor to its particular time, since it can be mirrored anywhere and repeated any number of times.'[21]

Needless to say, the Lustgarten on 1 May 1936 was bristling with cameras and microphones, capturing and broadcasting the events in Berlin via the newsreel and the *Volksempfänger*, the inexpensive people's radio that insinuated the thoughts of the Führer into every household in the nation. And what thoughts these were, setting the rosy vision of the new, harmonious Germany against the threat of the enemy within. The new Germany had been forged, said Hitler on 1 May 1936, by the refocusing of the disparate ambitions of the masses towards a common goal, with the result that 'in the framework of the community of the nation there arose out of the weak wills of 60 million individuals a gigantically powerful clenched will of all.' And this 'clenched will' would destroy any questioning or oppositional voice. 'The lie goes forth again,' Hitler continued , 'that Germany will tomorrow or the day after fall upon Austria or Czechoslovakia. I ask myself always: Who can these elements be – (Shouts of "The Jews") – who will have no peace, who incite continually, who must sow distrust, and want no understanding? Who are they? (Renewed shouts of "The Jews").'[22]

These messages from the assembled masses were brought to the even greater masses of the nation not by the paintings of Hengstenberg or of Blunck, but by the newsreel and the radio. The new National Socialist community and the triumph of the will over morality or legality were constructed by scenic devices derived from the traditional art forms and imposed by the new technologies. The harmony of the village, the small town, and the small state, which had been lost with the advent of industrial technology and a mobile labour market, was to be restored through the intervention of technology itself. Through technology and mass communications, the division between life and art was to be erased, with the result that moral judgment was replaced by a judgment of aesthetic 'effect': the good replaced by the spectacular.

21 Ernst Jünger, 'On Pain' (1934), quoted in Kaes (as note 21), 110.

22 *The Times* (as note 1).

Wassili Luckhardt, Proposed building for the DAF, 1934

ART AS MONUMENT

Dawn Ades

1 Rivera's mural was dismantled and stored; it was installed in its present location, the Theater of the City College, San Francisco, in 1961.

2 Serge Guilbaut, *How New York Stole the Idea of Modern Art* (Chicago and London, 1983), 41.

3 Ibid.

4 Clement Greenberg, 'Avant-Garde and Kitsch', *Partisan Review* (Fall 1939); Greenberg's 'Towards a Newer Laocoön', *Partisan Review* (July–August 1940), in defence of abstract art, marked a shift away from the 1939 text which maintained that a living, avant-garde culture depended for its survival on Socialism. See Greenberg, *The Collected Essays and Criticism 1939–1944*, ed. John O'Brian (Chicago, 1988).

In 1940, Diego Rivera painted a mural over 22 metres long and 6 metres high at the Golden Gate Fair in San Francisco. It was part of the 'Art in Action' section of the exhibition, and the public paid fifty cents to watch the famous Mexican artist at work. The mural's theme, immediate context and subsequent history open up some of the problems and debates that surround monumental art in the twentieth century.

Its theme was the politically hot topic of 'Pan-American Unity', which was being actively canvassed at the time, most strongly by those anxious to keep the United States out of the Second World War. Most of the giant mural compares the creative and scientific achievements through history of 'the North and South of this continent': i.e. Canada, the USA and Mexico, but one panel is dedicated to the European dictators. A twisted scene of carnage, barbed wire and bodies, with the busts of the dictators – Stalin clasping the bloody ice pick that had killed Trotsky earlier that year, Hitler saluting and Mussolini clasping the fasces – emerging from a cloud of poison gas. At the centre, however, is the figure of Charlie Chaplin, whose satire *The Great Dictator* had just been released, gesticulating towards a scene from the film, with 'Hitler' holding the world-balloon.

The difficulty of judging the tone of this scene, which seems compounded of both outrage and mockery, is partly explained by attitudes in the USA to the European War, which seemed to mark the end of the Old World and the collapse of its civilization. The Golden Gate Fair itself was a frank celebration of the New World, a little regretful at the absence of some of the countries that had been swallowed up by Hitler since the Fair the previous year, but on the whole optimistic. Another factor may be Rivera's own sense of the contradictions of making monumental art in a site of ephemeral entertainment, and even perhaps of rivalry with the medium of film.[1]

This mural and its setting have been construed as the final straw for artists long suspicious of politically committed art, fearful of its descent into frank propaganda and confused by the numerous changes in the official cultural policy of the Communist party and the left since 1935. Meyer Schapiro's group, the Federation of Modern Painters and Sculptors, whose position was loosely based on the André Breton-Leon Trotsky manifesto of 1938, 'Towards a Revolutionary Independent Art', 'rejected the politicization of art which led to such absurdities as posters advertising the Golden Gate Park exhibition in 1940, which combined Diego Rivera with strippers from the Folies-Bergère'.[2] Political art seemed to be reduced to the fairground, to pure entertainment rather than serious criticism; and, 'if this was the price of democratization in art, then democratization was unthinkable'.[3]

The ground was thus laid for Clement Greenberg's idea of an avant-garde art, essentially opposed to kitsch, to develop into the highly influential theory of an art whose critical function was to investigate its own medium and form.[4] The history of modern art has largely been written according to Greenberg; and monumental art, Rivera's along with that of the totalitarian regimes, has become an embarrassing footnote. It is not a question here of re-evaluating this position, but rather of attempting to shake loose the tight knot of rejection that has bound all monumental art together, whether of the Fascist or Communist regimes, of the Spanish Republic, of revolutionary Mexico or of the bourgeois democracies.

A monument in the classic sense of the term commemorates a person, event or action; it can refer to a written record, a sepulchre, a boundary, or the remains or remnant of something. 'Monumental art', on the other hand, can be taken simply to mean sculpture or painting that is huge or stupendous; in other words, the term's significance as *reminder* – celebration or memorial – may be emptied out. This essay considers works of art, made in the period roughly covered by the *Art and Power* exhibition, which laid claim to be monumental in more than sheer size. An examination of these claims, how they interlocked with questions of style, function or ideology and what shifts occurred in the deployment of the word *monumental* may help to outline changes in the relations between art and its publics, public art and its patrons.

Built monuments – sculpture or combinations of architecture and sculpture – are for public spaces. Visible signs of authority, they have constituted complex and various messages to the present. They assert power in various ways : through a particular idea of history, or of nationhood, or the celebration of superior individual achievements. The shift to the frankly didactic or agitational that has occurred this century was a natural extension of the power of exhortation that was already implicit or explicit; but this has raised an important question for twentieth-century monumental art: who is being addressed and by whom? Can there be such a thing as a genuinely demotic monumental art – that is, a monumental art not addressed to, but rather of, the people?[5] Certainly, such claims were made in some quarters. Was it possible for monumental art to reinvent itself? Monumental art tried to come to terms with a newly defined 'popular', and this process had inbuilt contradictions.

Following the revolutions in both Mexico (1910–20) and the USSR (1917), plans were swiftly elaborated for programmes of public art. One of Lenin's first legislative acts in April 1918 was to decree the removal of the monuments erected in honour of the Tsars ('monstrous idols'), and 'organize a broad competition in designing monuments to commemorate the great days of the Russian Socialist Revolution'.[6] In August 1918 he drew up a list of persons to whom monuments were to be erected, which included 66 names of revolutionaries, writers, philosophers, scientists, artists and composers.[7] Sergei Eisenstein opens his filmic celebration of the October Revolution of 1917 with the dismembering of the enormous statue of Tsar Alexander III, which finally, roped and mutilated, topples ignominiously together with its chair from the high pedestal. It is notable, however, that he intercuts this scene with revolutionary groups and masses, including some 'spotlit' anonymous heroic figures, ancestors of Vera Mukhina's peacetime peasant and industrial worker, rather than with individual heroes of the Revolution.

In the early years of the Soviet Union, notwithstanding Lenin's decree, the right to determine what the new monuments and monumental art should be was strongly contested, and the irrelevance of monumental figurative sculpture was argued from the Constructivist side. Nikolai Punin, writing about Tatlin's *Monument to the Third International* in 1920, favourably compared its dynamic creative design and use of materials with the limitations and static quality of figurative monuments: 'The agitational action of such monuments is extraordinarily weak amidst the noise, movements and dimensions of the streets.'[8] For Punin, moreover, a monument without a practical function – which Tatlin's (ideally) had – was pointless.

Punin objected to figurative monuments on the grounds that, beside their static and feeble effect, they cultivated individual heroism and conflicted with

Diego Rivera, *Pan-American Unity*, mural, 1940, City College, San Francisco

history: 'At best they express the character, feelings and thought of the hero, but who expresses the tension of the emotions and thoughts of the collective thousand?'[9] They conflict with history, because – as Einstein demonstrates so vividly in *October* – it is the people and not the individual hero whose acts are history.

Attacks on figurative monuments also came from very different quarters: at the end of the 1920s, Robert Desnos, the Surrealist poet, distinguishing between stone allegories and portraits, wrote: 'To erect the effigy of a being, who once lived, on a pedestal, is equivalent to raising him to the rank of a god, and in our times such an enterprise is less legitimate than ever.'[10] Statues, he suggests, should be only the accessories to life, 'with its procession of strange manifestations, miracles, deep looks, insults and warm embraces'. Desnos' proposal was to take the statue off its pedestal, and have a bronze Baudelaire strolling among the crowds or leaning on the parapet of a bridge. What both these arguments have in common is the underlying idea that the genre of the monumental figure portrait cannot hold its own in the modern

5 During the war in Britain, propaganda posters appeared calling on the people to 'defend your country and your homes'; all over the land the 'y' was swiftly scratched out to give 'our country and our homes'. This relatively trivial incident reveals a profound shift in popular political perceptions and attitudes to authority.
6 V. I. Lenin, 'Decree: On the Monuments of the Republic, 12 April 1918', in Lenin, *On Literature and Art* (London, 1967), 245.
7 Lenin (as note 6), 247. These included Karl Marx, Mikhail Bakunin, Henri de Saint-Simon, Robert Owen, Aleksandr Pushkin, Andrei Rublëv, Mikhail Vrubel' and Frédéric Chopin.
8 N. N. Punin, 'The Monument to the Third International', 1920, tr. Christina Lodder, in 'Modern Art and Modernism, Supplementary Documents (Blocks VIII–IX)' (The Open University, 1983), 6.
9 Ibid.
10 Robert Desnos, 'Pygmalion et le Sphinx' *Documents*, vol. 2, no. 1 (1930), 36.

Model of proposed Palace of the Soviets, Soviet Pavilion, International Exhibition, Paris 1937

11 Witness the furore provoked in Britain by the statue of Churchill in Parliament Square, which offended because it had swung too far towards naturalism and away from dignity, and more recently by the statue of Air Chief Marshal 'Bomber' Harris in the Strand, which was seen as a remarkably insensitive way of marking D-Day. This sculpture, interestingly, does what Desnos recommended, standing on the ground without a pedestal.

12 Craig Owens, 'The Allegorical Impulse: Towards a Theory of Postmodernism', October, no. 12 (Spring 1980), reprinted in C. Harrison and P. Wood, eds., Art in Theory 1900–1990, 1052.

13 See Hanne Bergius, Norbert Miller und Karl Riha, eds., Johannes Baader (Lahn-Giessen, 1977), 187, and Kate Winskell, 'Dada, Russia and Modernity, 1915–1922', doctoral dissertation, Courtauld Institute of Art, London, April 1995, 67.

14 Christian Zervos 'Réflexions sur la tentative d'Esthétique dirigée du IIIe Reich ', Cahiers d'Art, vol. 11, nos 8–10 (1936), 212.

age: that it is either ineffectual, illegitimate, unnatural or offensive.[11]

Although the Constructivist monument (arguably a completely new form, rather than a hybrid of sculpture and architecture) championed by Punin, Tatlin and others soon lost official support in favour of precisely the kind of figurative monument it sought to replace, the questions that Punin raised were among those that continued to be debated in relation to twentieth-century monumental art in general: the leader vs. the masses, modernity vs. tradition, national vs. universal. In the decades that followed the Revolution, the Soviet leadership went on to plan fantastic edifices topped with the giant figure of Lenin or Stalin. (The competition for the Palace of the Soviets produced perhaps the supreme examples; see pp. 51, 203.) In these the monument ceases to represent the ideal fusion of architecture and sculpture: the building, vast as it is, becomes the pedestal for the figure. There is a strange disjunction of scale that fails to resolve itself, except in the idea ridiculed by Desnos of a superhuman mortal. To an extent, subjects such as Stalin or Lenin as 'Leader, Teacher, Friend' (p. 239) can be seen as attempts to defuse and conciliate the tension between the cult of the hero and the rights of the collective.

The populist rhetoric of the totalitarian regimes thus sometimes offers revealing contradictions in the context of monumental art. Perhaps surprisingly, there were no monumental figures in bronze or stone of Hitler, although his image was ubiquitous in paintings (p. 295) and smaller portrait busts. (Mussolini, however, did not stint in presenting himself and the King-Emperor on all scales; see p. 127.)

If portrait monuments were the natural expression of the cult of the Leader, another major genre of monumental sculpture and painting, allegory, was intended to form the symbolic order that constructed a sense of nationhood, especially for those regimes seeking to authenticate and legitimize themselves through history and tradition.

At least since Hegel, allegory – the appropriation of an existing image to make a present point – has been regarded as a debased device, icy, remote and inauthentic, an 'aesthetic aberration, the antithesis of art'.[12] Walter Benjamin restored interest to the term, if not to the type of official art that continued to be produced under its name. Normally banished from the Modernist canon, allegory posited a relationship between modernity and history, which Benjamin as a Marxist recognized as an urgent issue. For him, though, it was not monuments but their ruins that constituted

'allegory'. This had a disjunctive, atomizing character – not being whole, essential or organic – and could thus be extended to refer to collage and photomontage as well, which recycle and juxtapose materials in unexpected but significant combinations. In this light, George Grosz's montage of a bourgeois constructed of newspaper clippings, coloured lithograph and hair could be read as an allegory of capitalism.

The type of art that interested Benjamin, usually in a Dada or Surrealist context – montage, photography, film, the city street that was also the Surrealists' natural hunting ground – was as remote from Greenberg's Modernism as was kitsch or propaganda. At the first International Dada Fair in Berlin in 1920, Johannes Baader erected a large conglomeration of material, objects, photographs, slogans, newspapers, in a heap that was described as 'Dadaist monumental architecture in five floors, three parks, a tunnel, two lifts and a cylinder end.' It has been suggested that this was an ironic comment on Oswald Spengler's The Decline of the West;[13] certainly it revels in the appropriation of imagery that is part of the 'allegorical impulse', as later defined in Postmodernist theory. From this perspective, Dada's disruptive iconoclasm is seen as a 'truer' face of the twentieth century than its faded monuments. Dada's techniques of disjunction and appropriation seem the opposite of the binding and controlling impulses of monumental art, but 'allegory' presides at the heart of each.

Both Germany and Italy laid claim to the classical tradition. Sironi represented Italy as a female version of Emperor Augustus, while Giorgio Gori's equestrian statue The Spirit of Fascist Italy, which fronted the Italian Pavilion at the Paris 1937 exhibition (p. 2), drew upon many layers of equestrian imagery from Rome onwards. For Germany and Italy, the monument had a classical aura that reinforced its message of longevity and a continuity that was intended to legitimize the illegitimate dictatorship. By contrast with Italy, though, there was little in Germany that mediated between the classical and the modern: between the pastiche antique and the great machines and autobahns. It is significant that Cahiers d'Art, while attacking the aesthetic of the Third Reich, reproduced photographs of German machinery – the diesel motor and the Mannesmann tube – among its photographs of modern buildings and their interiors at the Paris Exhibition. Its editor, Christian Zervos, commented on the sculpture of the Third Reich as consisting of 'beings carved out for sport, struggle, violence; depth is missing'.[14] Virtually interchangeable male nudes represent things such as

Comradeship, Youth, Sport, Victory, even the *Ostmark* ('Eastern Frontier'). These lack depth in the sense in which Zervos understood it: that is, signs of human sensibility or specific individual being, but also signs of the elaborate culture required by allegory. The only attributes tend to be helmets and cloaks, unlike the giant nudish figures in the Foro Mussolini in Rome, who are carefully identified via the signs of the modern sports they represent. Would both these cases be condemned under the one label of 'Alexandrianism', as Greenberg dubbed it, a late version of the academicism 'in which the really important issues are left untouched because they involve controversy, and in which creative activity dwindles to virtuosity in the small details of form'?[15]

These instances of monumental sculpture attempting to authenticate themselves and the idea of history they represent are in fact quite different, and both, though probably unintentionally, offend against virtuoso academicism. In the case of the Nazi sculptures, there is a clue in the *Ostmark* sculpture. This archaic term is resonant not of classical Rome but of medieval Germany, and it reminds us that the past had to incorporate Wagnerian Nordic mythology and the Teutonic Knights as much as classical antiquity. Thus these native/classical bodies had to compromise and lose specificity in order to retain both their aesthetic and their ideological character. In the Roman sculptures, by contrast, the modernized versions of allegorical attributes, which deliberately display familiarity with and capacity to ring changes on their ancient sources, become dissonant and ludicrous because what is being sought is a non-allegorical identity with the ludic nudes of the past. (Tennis is not played in the nude.)

A much more elegant response to allegory's 'conviction of the remoteness of the past, and desire to redeem it for the present'[16] is Arturo Martini's great bronze *Winged Victory* or *Victory in the Air*. This celebrated the crossing of the Atlantic by an Italian air squadron led by Marshal Italo Balbo, and dominated the *Cour d'Honneur* of the Italian Pavilion at the Paris International Exhibition of 1937. Fully three-dimensional, the huge female figure is suspended from the wall so that she appears to be in flight, attended by eagles flying in formation like the pilots. She honours as much the national exploit as the conquest of the Atlantic, and therefore combines the idea of the Italian nation – so often, as in Sironi's murals, represented by a draped female figure – with a modernized version of the antique figure of Winged Victory.

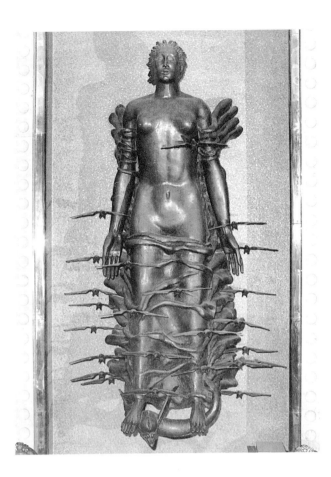

Arturo Martini, *Victory in the Air*, Commando della Zona Aerea Territoriale di Milano, Milan

15 Greenberg 'Avant-Garde and Kitsch', in Greenberg, *Collected Essays and Criticism* (as note 4), 6.

Italy was not alone, of course, in rooting much of its monumental art in nationalist allegories, centred on the classicized female figure, which were then elaborated to suit the particular context (Industry, Transport, Justice or whatever). Versions of this had long been part of the official rhetoric of many nations, including France and Britain. Marianne, the Revolutionary symbol of the French Republic, reappears at the heart of the Popular Front's 'Peoples' Fair', the Paris 1937 exhibition. Antoine Bourdelle's bronze *La France*, complete with spear, stood on the top terrace at the centre of the colonnades of the Palais de Tokyo, the new Musées d'Art moderne, above bas-relief allegories elaborating on the idea of France's geographical extensions by sea and air (Imperial France).

16 Owens (as note 12).

Germany chose as its national sign the eagle, usually publicly displayed in conjunction with the swastika. Architectural decoration in the Third Reich was almost exclusively limited to these two forms. The USSR obviously needed a universal symbol of revolution; it is a matter of debate whether figures carrying the hammer and sickle could be described as allegorical. The sculptures topping the German and the Soviet Pavilions at the Paris International Exhibition make an interesting comparison (p. 10). The inevitable eagle faced Vera Mukhina's colossal steel-clad statue, *Industrial Worker and Collective Farm Girl*. These figures are anonymous but not abstract; they are not 'allegories' of an abstract concept or virtue, but the young heroes of a new world order. Unlike images of specific heroes, martyrs or leaders, though, they do not stand out from the crowd as individuals, for they are simultaneously of it. It is important to note that the two figures, striding and dynamic man and woman, are treated equally in terms of gender, for this is one of the many features that distinguishes Soviet imagery from that of Nazi Germany. The tendency of the latter in monumental statues, and indeed in all plastic arts, was to a ludicrous exaggeration of male and female difference, as in the towering Thorak triads (p. 336) that flanked the entrance to the German pavilion.

What modernity should constitute in the context of monumental art was also of course inflected by the political context. For Léger, the ideal modern monument was Radio City in New York. For Punin: 'A monument must live the social and political life of the city and the city must live in it. It must be necessary and dynamic; then it will be modern. The forms of contemporary, agitational plastic arts lie beyond the depiction of man as an individual. They are found by the artist who is not crippled by the feudal and bourgeois traditions of the Renaissance, but who has laboured like a worker on the three unities of contemporary plastic consciousness: material, construction, volume.'[17] Mural painting in this century,

secular offspring of religious frescoes, has taken on a more elaborate didactic function than statuary was capable of, especially in the hands of its greatest exponents, the Mexican muralists.

In Mexico, a programme of monumental art to decorate public buildings was inaugurated shortly after the Revolution of 1910–20, by José María Vasconcelos, the new Minister of Education. However, his plan for harmoniously vague and elevating humanist allegories was rudely overtaken by the artists he had gathered together. In 1923 the newly formed Union of Mexican Workers, Technicians, Painters and Sculptors issued their Manifesto repudiating easel painting and asserting their commitment to a didactic and national mural art. Although this is not directly part of our story, it is important both as precursor and comparison in relation to the claims and practice of mural painting as a monumental art. Signed by, among others, José Clemente Orozco and Diego Rivera, but largely composed by David Alfaro Siqueiros, the Manifesto claimed that the art of the Mexican people was directly linked to their Indian traditions, was 'of the people and therefore collective . . . We reject so-called salon painting and all the ultra-intellectual salon art of the aristocracy and exalt the manifestations of monumental art because they are useful. We believe that any work of art which is alien or contrary to popular taste is bourgeois and should disappear because it perverts the aesthetic of our race.'[18]

What would have seemed a natural alliance, though, between the Soviet Union and the Mexican muralists came to little; plans for Rivera to paint a mural in Moscow during his visit there in 1927–28 never materialized, and official art there remained largely concentrated in the production of posters, statues and easel painting – admittedly often on a large scale – rather than murals.[19]

Appreciation of Rivera in Europe came from an unlikely quarter: the Surrealist leader André Breton, who visited Mexico in 1938, and wrote enthusiastically of Rivera's work, not only in his essay 'Souvenir du Mexique' but in letters to Surrealist friends and colleagues. André Masson wrote in response: 'I have often thought of his [Rivera's] lot (to be a great monumental painter), which has always seemed to me the best career there is for someone who wants to reveal the conception he has of the world, of life, his *raison d'être* – "by means of painting".'[20] For Masson himself, a painter who, through Surrealism, was committed to the idea of revolution but lived in a bourgeois democracy, this was impossible: 'Long live

17 Punin (as note 8), 6.

18 'Manifesto of the Union of Mexican Workers, Technicians, Painters and Sculptors', *El Machete*, Mexico City 1923, tr. Polyglossia, in Dawn Ades, exh. cat. *Art in Latin America* (London, 1989), 324.

19 Siqueiros, who remained a member of the Communist Party, was an influential figure in Eastern Europe after the war. Among those who collaborated with him in the 1930s on mural projects such as the Electricians' Union in Mexico City was Josep Renau, who was responsible for the graphic material of the Spanish Pavilion at the 1937 Paris International Exhibition.

20 André Masson, letter to André Breton, 29 June 1938, in exh. cat. *André Breton: la beauté convulsive* (Paris: Centre Georges Pompidou, 1991), 239.

View of Soviet Pavilion, International Exhibition, Paris 1937

Mexico which is in harmony with Diego Rivera, and long live Diego Rivera who puts his genius at the service of an entire people.'[21]

How did Breton, whose resistance to propaganda in art, and to the very idea of a 'proletarian' art or literature, had been thoroughly honed and articulated in a series of confrontations with the French Communist party earlier in the 1930s, justify his response to Rivera?[22] In 'Souvenir du Mexique' he talks not of the grand political vision of Rivera's murals but of their direct, story-telling character, like a popular picture-book, and their link to the Pre-Columbian past.[23]

Breton refuses to relate Rivera to the issues of Socialist Realism, but his companion in Mexico, Leon Trotsky, does precisely that in a letter to the editors of *Partisan Review* in 1938. Trotsky contrasts Rivera's work with Stalinist Socialist Realism, whose anachronistic photographic naturalism and historical falsifications express the 'profound decline of the proletarian revolution': 'Incredible as it seemed at first sight, there was no place for the art of Diego Rivera, either in Moscow, or in Leningrad, or in any other section of the USSR where the bureaucracy born of the revolution was erecting grandiose palaces and monuments to itself. And how could the Kremlin clique tolerate in its kingdom an artist who paints neither icons representing the 'leader' nor life-size portraits of Voroshilov's horse?'[24]

The 'Manifesto for an Independent Revolutionary Art', signed by Breton and Rivera, though drawn up by Breton in collaboration with Trotsky, was published in 1938. While drawing a clear distinction between Fascism and Communism, this robust assertion of the artist's need and right to complete creative independence outlines the degradation of conditions in Germany and the USSR. The Soviet Union represents 'not Communism but its most dangerous and treacherous enemy'.[25] The Manifesto is an appeal to find a common ground for all the scattered and isolated revolutionary artists. Although the movement it represented, FIARI, was short-lived and utopian, the Manifesto sought to address in simple terms the conflict between the individual artist and hostile social forms, without reviving 'a so-called pure art which generally serves the extremely impure ends of reaction',[26] or losing a belief in the capacity of art to influence the fate of society.

The International Exhibition of 1937 in Paris was the last showcase in Europe before the Second World War for the display of art that was 'monumental' in a variety of different senses: that is, monuments in the classic sense of commemorative sculpture, allegorical and symbolic figures, and work in two or three dimensions that was simply on a massive scale. The works of mural painting, mosaic, stained glass and tapestry fell into both didactic and decorative categories.

The most prominent two-dimensional monumental works were those of Sironi, Picasso, Dufy, Léger and the Delaunays. Those who had publicly entered the debate – Sironi and Léger – claimed their *raison d'être* to lie in the popular, collective character of the mural. Le Corbusier, however, raised some awkward questions about the character of the spectator-public. He noted that few paused to look at Picasso's *Guernica* (p. 77), while Dufy's vast mural on the history of electricity (p. 118), which was simply a panoramic view of individual inventors with a few illustrative anecdotes but with very little concern for structure, drew crowds who amused themselves identifying the various characters.

Both Sironi and Léger wrote about monumental mural painting, but from very different perspectives. Sironi's Manifesto of Mural Painting, which was also signed by Achille Funi, Massimo Campigli and Carlo Carrà, argued that art had a social function, and that mural painting was 'social painting par excellence', because it 'acts on the popular imagination more directly than any other form of painting'.[27] The Manifesto is haughtily vague, however, about what exactly the social, civic, didactic function of Fascist mural painting constituted. The impression that mural painting should leave on the public would not be by virtue of the subject matter – which was, Sironi argues, the error of the Communists. It should rather be by the 'style'. The mural 'must give a unity of style and grandeur of contour to common life. Thus art will once again become what it was in the greatest of times and at the heart of the greatest civilizations: a perfect instrument of spiritual direction.' Through mural painting, order, control and the authority of antiquity would become the 'Fascist style'.

Far from Rivera's rousing and polemical populism, Sironi dreamed of the unforced superiority of muralism, which would synthesize tradition and contemporary life. His own compositions, such as the mosaic for the Italian Pavilion of 1937 (pp. 154, 157), or the great stained-glass window for the Palazzo dell'Industria in Rome, avoid specific subject matter in favour of an 'ideal tension', to apply Mussolini's phrase, between grand abstractions embodied in allegorical figures and 'typical' scenes from contemporary Italian society exemplifying work and sport, home and the battlefield, etc. His images are thus intended structurally to represent Italy: 'the juridical and ideal

21 Ibid.

22 See, e.g., André Breton, 'Position Politique du Surréalisme', *La Bibliothèque Volante*, no. 2 (1971), and Breton, *What is Surrealism? Selected Writings*, ed. F. Rosemont (London, 1978).

23 André Breton, 'Souvenir du Mexique', *Minotaure*, vol. 6, nos. 12–13, (May 1939), 30–52.

24 Leon Trotsky, 'Art and Politics: a Letter to the Editors of *Partisan Review*', *Partisan Review* (1938), 8.

25 'Manifesto for an Independent Revolutionary Art', in André Breton, *What is Surrealism?* (as note 22), 184.

26 Ibid., 186.

27 Mario Sironi, 'Manifesto of Mural Painting' (1933), in Harrison and Woods (as note 12), 408.

structure of Italy today. This structure draws its strength from age-old tradition . . . and from the perpetual capacity of the Latin race for work and renewal. "Believe, Obey, Fight": that is the inscription placed between the large silhouettes of the mosaic in which Mario Sironi represents Italy today. The manly figure of the Duce, beside that of the King-Emperor, opposite the stained glass where one sees the mystical faces of St Ambrose, St Martin and the Archangel Michael, seems to warn us that in the life of the people, what is of value is not just material riches, but above all the ideal forces of faith, discipline and sacrifice.'[28]

28 P. Sacerdoti, in *Le Pavillon Italien, Exposition de Paris* (Paris, 1937), 77.

Fernand Léger, whose huge mural *Transport of Forces* was housed in the Palace of Discovery in Paris in 1937, believed no less in the triumph of the mural as 'modern monument', but from a diametrically opposite position to that of Sironi. He regarded mural painting as a necessary response to the exigencies of modern architecture (the 'new pitiless reality' of the architect's white wall) and to public needs of a practical and psychological kind. The monument is or should be a 'popular work', which needs the collaboration of architect, painter and sculptor; but this is not a matter of 'demagogical concessions' or lowering standards to meet popular desires: 'It is a human necessity which demands that, in works or realizations that touch people, crowds, the men who direct or command them must listen to hearts beating.'[29]

Mural painting is artisanal and collective. The problem, as Léger saw it, was to forge a work that was monumental – in the sense that it was public, collective, and a hybrid of painting, sculpture and architecture – and would act as directly on the crowd through 'pure plastic values' as did the advertisements, shop windows and modern forms of spectacle to which people were already accustomed. Both Léger and Rivera keep to the ideal of an art that will be comprehensible to the people. But while Rivera structured his giant, multi-figure canvases to present strong arguments about the evils of capitalism, the importance of its specific historical past to present-day Mexico, contrasting the oppression of the colonial period with the harmony of Pre-Columbian Mexico, and revelling somewhat contradictorily in the power and magic of the machine, Léger avoided the didactic and the distracting character of figurative narrative in favour of the free use of colour on large surfaces. Wary of coercive claims, Léger saw the 'social function' of his murals in terms of a loosening of habits of thought chaining 'the ordinary man' to a subservient past. His revolution was 'not only of a plastic order, but also of a psychological

29 Fernand Léger, 'Le Mur, l'architecte, le peintre' (1933), in Léger, *Fonctions de la peinture* (Utrecht, 1965), 120.

30 Fernand Léger, 'De la peinture murale' (1952), in Léger (as note 29), 111.

31 Carlos Monsivais, 'La hora cívica: de monumentos cívicos y sus espectadores', in Monsivais, *Los rituales del caos* (Mexico City, 1995), 149.

32 See exh. cat. *Kunst und Diktatur* (Vienna: Künstlerhaus, 1994), 2:842–45.

order'[30]: a statement which raises intriguing connections with Surrealism.

The fact that, outside the totalitarian regimes, the ephemeral International Exhibitions or World Fairs proved the most viable venue for monumental art is paradoxical. That which was conceived as embodying an idea of permanency and the constant and vital interpenetration of past and present proved even more vulnerable than portable works of art. Little of the monumental art from the Paris 1937 exhibition found a permanent home, and much, like Léger's *Transport of Forces* and Joan Miró's *Catalan Peasant in Revolt* (*The Harvester*, p. 80), disappeared. Robert and Sonia Delaunay's large paintings from the Railway and Aeronautical Pavilions (pp. 116, 119) were rolled up and forgotten for decades – as indeed was Rivera's huge mural for the 1940 Golden Gate Fair.

Commemorative figurative monuments in their imperishable materials of stone, bronze or steel appear to guarantee eternal fame, while reminding the spectator of mortality. 'Civic sculpture,' Carlos Monsivais wrote, 'is the homage of the lasting to that which will never return.' Statues both '*are*, and *represent*'.[31] Perhaps this is one of the reasons for the violence of the reaction against them when power changes hands. As fetishes of the symbolic order that constructed them, they arouse a kind of primitive animistic awe. At least since the destruction of the idol of Baal, or the disfigurement of the stone heads of the Olmec in America over two thousand years ago, one of the first acts of a liberated people has been the overthrow of the monuments of the previous rulership, which overnight has become illegitimate. When the Soviet Union and other Eastern Bloc regimes crumbled at the end of the 1980s some of the most memorable images were of the dismantling of the stone effigies of the leaders and heroes; the violent destruction of the statue of the police chief – and the careful dismantling with saws, ropes, and cranes of Dolezal's double statue of Lenin and Stalin[32]; photographs show Stalin almost covered with autumn leaves, and graveyards of disgraced monuments in forgotten corners of the cities.

Plan of International Exhibition, Paris 1937, from special number of *L'Illustration*

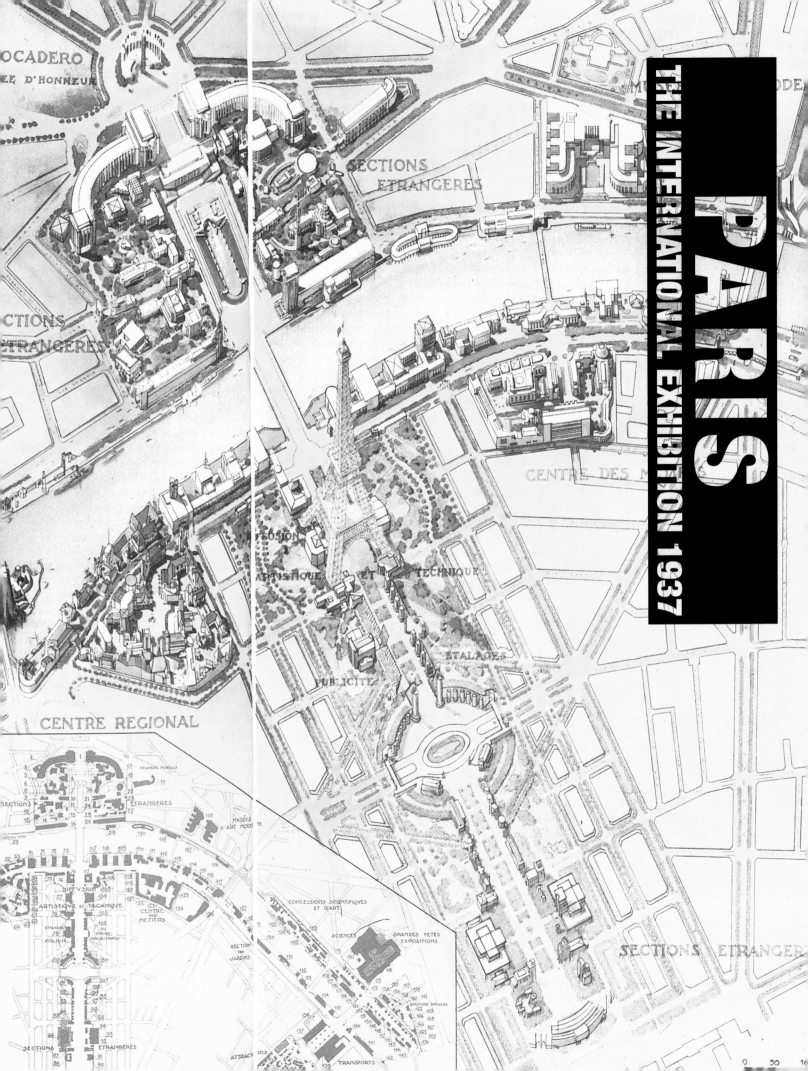

PARIS

THE INTERNATIONAL EXHIBITION 1937

PARIS 1937

Art and the Power of Nations   *Dawn Ades*

The International Exhibition (*Exposition internationale des Arts et des Techniques dans la Vie moderne*), which opened in Paris in May 1937, was a massive spectacle, presented as a celebration of human achievement but exposing the tensions and contradictions of the gloomy decade that ended with the outbreak of the Second World War.[1] Two features stood out in contemporary accounts of this exhibition and lodged in the memory of most of its visitors: the notorious confrontation between the German and Soviet Pavilions, facing each other on the right bank of the Seine, and the Modernist Pavilion, housing Picasso's *Guernica*, of the Spanish government, then fighting for its life against the Nazi-backed rebellion of Franco. These images of aggression and resistance, each in its way a symbol of power, seemed to challenge the fact that the exhibition was dedicated to peace. An express purpose of the 1937 Exhibition was to shore up Europe's faith in civilization (the question of whose civilization could not be looked at too closely). In the introduction to the Exhibition's *Livre d'Or officiel*, Edmond Labbé, its chief commissioner, wrote:

'In a world on which the menace of the future weighs heavily, it has seemed for some time that civilization had begun to lose faith in itself, in its values, energies and duties. A kind of discouragement and lassitude has overrun people's spirits, undermining the very basis of hope. And now here is the Exhibition, springing up suddenly, with a supreme will and momentum, rising to the sky like a great cry of confidence and ardour from the whole of humanity.'[2]

The fact that the countries whose art and architecture form the subject of our exhibition were such important presences at Paris in 1937, and that the Pavilions and their contents offer significant and usefully condensed samples of the official art and propaganda of their regimes, were obviously important factors in choosing the Paris 1937 International Exhibition as our starting point. The German, Soviet and Italian Pavilions all constituted important cultural statements by their respective governments – as did that of Spain – and their diverse architectural styles point in interesting ways to the values they invested in appearance and display.

The Spanish Pavilion occupies a special position. The civil war then raging in Spain seemed to many, in so far as it was a battle between a democratically elected government and Fascism, to be the prelude of another full-scale European war. Eric Hobsbawm has argued that, 'inasmuch as Fascism and war were identified with particular foreign states, Germany and Italy, what was at stake in this struggle was . . . the defence of the British and French nations against the Germans'.[3]

This pavilion therefore had both national and international dimensions, as a focus of anti-Fascist support. Moreover, only in a world fair on this scale would it have been possible for the Spanish Republicans and Nationalists to be present simultaneously. The Pontifical Pavilion, where twelve countries were invited to provide altarpieces for the chapel, included one (p. 101) by the painter and newly converted Franco supporter Jose María Sert, grand-uncle of the Spanish Pavilion's architect.

The foreign pavilions that concern us are not just isolated pockets of interest but have to be situated and understood within the context of the exhibition as a whole, whose physical space and theoretical schema were elaborately and carefully controlled. Paris, after all, was still the artistic capital of the 'world' and a universal focus of attention. It was still the liveliest centre for debate about the pressing issues of the time: autonomy versus commitment, nationalism versus internationalism, tradition versus the new, the problem of state control, the role of propaganda, man and machine, 'exotic' and 'European' – and the question of realism, which was as much a matter of politics as of style. It is not too farfetched to suggest that the Exhibition was intended as an expression of international solidarity, made possible by a peculiarly French spirit of civilized co-operation.

Conceived long before, the Exhibition opened in May 1937 under the auspices of the Popular Front government, led by France's first Socialist premier, Léon Blum. It was a people's festival, educational tool and expression of national pride.[4] The cultural goal of the Popular Front, as Jacques Soustelle put it, was to 'open the gates of culture'.[5] The Communists (PCF) in the Popular Front must be credited with 'greatly and permanently enhancing the state's administrative and financial responsibility for cultural life',[6] but their view of culture was extremely conservative: it was high French culture, as the Surrealists found during their brief alliance with the PCF.

1 The exhibition has been extensively researched. See for instance Sarah Wilson, 'Art and the Politics of the Left in France c. 1935–1955', unpublished PhD thesis, Courtauld Institute of Art, London, 1992; exh. cat. *Paris 1937: Cinquantenaire de l'Exposition internationale des Arts et des Techniques dans la Vie moderne* (Paris: Musée de la ville de Paris, 1987); exh. cat. *Paris-Paris, Créations en France 1937–1957* (Paris: Centre Georges Pompidou, 1981); exh. cat. *1937 Exposition des arts et des techniques* (Paris: Centre Georges Pompidou, 1979); exh. cat. *Paris 1937: L'Art indépendant* (Paris: Musée d'Art moderne de la Ville de Paris, 1987).

2 Edmond Labbé, 'Introduction', *Le Livre d'Or officiel de l'Exposition internationale des Arts et des Techniques* (Paris, 1937), 24.

3 E. J. Hobsbawm, *Nations and Nationalism since 1780: Programme, Myth, Reality* (London, 1992), 147.

4 Reactionary sentiment compared it unfavourably with the 1931 Colonial Exhibition: see the report by Amédée Ozenfant, cited below.

5 Herman Lebovics, *True France: The Wars over Cultural identity 1900–1945* (Ithaca, 1992), 157.

6 Ibid.

7 *Paris 1937: L'Art indépendant* (as note 1), 18.

8 Hobsbawm (as note 3), 146.

9 Louis Aragon, Speech at the Comédie des Champs-Elysées, 5 October 1937.

10 No world fair or international exhibition, strictly so called, had been held in Paris since 1900; but the 1937 Exhibition was presented and frequently discussed in relation to its two immediate predecessors, the 1925 *Exposition des Arts décoratifs* and the huge *Exposition coloniale* of 1931.

The opening show at the new Musées d'Art Moderne at the Palais de Tokyo, at one end of the Exhibition site, *Chefs-d'oeuvre d'art français*, for which Léon Blum wrote the preface, was as much a Popular Front manifestation as was the Maison du Travail, which commemorated the international trades union movement. *Chefs-d'oeuvre d'art français* followed French art through its masterpieces from the fourteenth to the nineteenth century, ending with Cézanne and Monet; the story was then picked up by *L'Art indépendant*, at the Petit Palais. In this, 1,500 works were shown, with the focus on ten artists including Matisse, Braque, Rouault and Picasso. (The criterion for inclusion was that one must either be French or have lived in France for a long time.) This exhibition was savagely attacked from the right, for its 'character of hideous obscenity',[7] and from the left and the international avant-garde for its omission of foreign artists.

The exhibition at the Jeu de Paume, *Origines et développement de l'art international indépendant*, aimed to counteract the nationalist spirit of these exhibitions. It emphasized the individual artistic experience, the role of primitivism in the development of modern art, and structured its rooms round the modern movements: Fauvism, Cubism, Dada, Surrealism, Constructivism and Abstraction.

Under the Popular Front, 'the remarriage of social revolution and patriotic sentiment was an extremely complex phenomenon'.[8] The right had to an extent forfeited its nationalist claims by expressing sympathy with Fascism: there was a French phrase, 'better Hitler than Léon Blum', which certainly had its parallels in Britain. The Stalin-Laval mutual aid pact, moreover, had directly contributed to the change of policy on the part of the PCF, and to the ex-Surrealist Louis Aragon's new-found, nationalist enthusiasm for '*Réalisme socialiste, Réalisme français*'.[9]

The international exhibitions in Paris since the first French Olympiad of 1855 had contributed dramatically to the face of Paris, above all with the construction of the Trocadéro and its museums in 1878 and the Eiffel Tower in 1889. The 1937 exhibition was partly erected on the same site (p. 117), a grand sweep from the Invalides to the Trocadéro, crossing the Seine at the Pont d'Iéna and incorporating the Eiffel Tower at the centre.[10] Within its four-and-a-half-mile circumference, including the Grand Palais, were nearly three hundred palaces and pavilions.

Successive views of the Trocadéro site, Paris 1936–37

A new underpass was constructed on the north bank of the Seine, and above this rose the Soviet and German Pavilions. At the head of the Foreign Section, these faced each other across the great pedestrian avenue that formed the main axis of the exhibition. Albert Speer described the circumstances of this staged confrontation: 'Hitler . . . abruptly threatened withdrawal from the Paris World's Fair of 1937, although the invitation had already been accepted and the site for the German Pavilion fixed. He strongly disliked all the sketches he was shown. The Ministry of Economics thereupon asked me for a design. The Soviet Russian and the German Pavilions were to be placed directly opposite one another on the fairground; the French directors of the Fair had deliberately arranged this confrontation. While looking over the site in Paris, I by chance stumbled into a room containing the secret sketch of the Soviet Pavilion. A sculpted pair of figures thirty-three [metres] tall, on a high platform, were striding triumphantly towards the German Pavilion. I therefore designed a cubic mass, also elevated on stout pillars, which seemed to be checking this onslaught, while from the cornice of my tower an eagle with a swastika in its claws looked down on the Russian sculptures. I received a gold medal for the building; so did my Soviet colleague.'[11]

Dramatic and photogenic as these constructions were,[12] flanking the avenue which led from the Trocadéro to the Eiffel Tower and Invalides, it is clear that they were intended to be framed and controlled within the overall plan. The grand scheme of the exhibition, fuelled by a 'desperate optimism' and desire for peace, was symbolically to override the tensions and the belligerence of the European nations. At the northern head of the avenue, in the Place du Trocadéro, was the Peace Tower, or Monument to Peace, designed by Bazin and Laprade. The view through to it was unimpeded, because the Trocadéro Museum (erected for the 1878 Paris World Fair) had been demolished in the early stages of construction work for the 1937 Exhibition. Situated at the top of the slope that rose from the banks of the Seine, and framed by the remodelled museum wings of the Palais de Tokyo, the Peace Tower thus dominated the rival pavilions. It was based on Trajan's column, transforming a symbol of military victory to one of peace; in green bronze, it had the names of the great Apostles of Peace listed in letters of gold. Behind the monument, a semicircular edifice created a sanctuary above which hung the flags of the forty-two participating nations.

The international pavilions in the Foreign Section formed a relatively small proportion of the exhibition as a whole. France and Greater France took up the majority of the site. First, there were the fifty-three French pavilions, devoted to the theme of the exhibition, arts and techniques; second, France d'Outre-Mer, the eleven colonies of 'Greater France', which occupied the Ile des Cygnes in mid-Seine; third, the seventeen Centres Régionaux.

The double theme of the exhibition was the arts and technology, which had once been united in the Greek word *techne*. The material was classified in fourteen different 'groups', which started with 'Expressions of Thought', or 'Manifestations of Thought', and included such headings as 'Urbanism and Architecture', 'Graphic and Plastic Arts' and 'Advertising'.[13] These groups were then subdivided into classes.

Each of the foreign pavilions presented its wares under the same classifications, though not all succeeded in preparing their material in time for publication in the *Rapport général*, let alone for the official general catalogue. Under Spain, for instance, the entry simply read: 'The pavilion is occupied in its entirety by the Spanish state.' The German Pavilion was fully documented under the proper groups and classes, its painters, sculptors, architects and numerous other categories of artists, designers and craftsmen listed in their places. Italy, too, was well organized and documented. Both countries, as well as their ideological rival, the Soviet Union, took full advantage of the opportunities offered by the stress on communication and culture both to present visual propaganda (images of the 'leader', for instance, in a variety of media) and to construct a mythical narrative of national identity.

The Palace of Discovery (Palais de la Découverte) belonged to the first group, the 'Expression of Thought', as did an exhibition devoted to libraries. Separate pavilions were devoted to French Crafts, Artist Decorators and Decorative Arts. The Wood pavilion had a spectacular interior, with inlaid marquetry murals of pastoral scenes and woodcutters.[14] There were large numbers of decorative murals in a faintly classical, naturalist style. By contrast the Aeronautical Palace (Palais de l'Aéronautique, also called Palais de l'Air and Palais de l'Aviation; see p. 118) was decorated with large abstract murals, with motifs of circles or spirals loosely based on propellers, by Sonia and Robert Delaunay, who also made the murals for the Railway Pavilion (p. 116). Léger's great mural *Le Transport des Forces* was housed in the Palace of Discovery, the most successful of the pavilions that

11 Albert Speer, *Inside the Third Reich* (London, 1970), 81. (See below, p. 193.)

12 See ' L'Exposition 1937', special number of *L'Illustration*, 14 August 1937.

13 *Exposition internationale des Arts et des Techniques dans la Vie moderne, 1937: Catalogue général officiel* (Paris, 1937); Paul Valéry, who was responsible for Group 1, described the problems of exhibiting the intangible products of thought: 'Un Problème d'exposition', in Valéry, *Oeuvres complètes* 1150.

14 Whether or not urban, industrial France could be incorporated into the regionalist vision of a 'true France' was disputed; see Lebovics (as note 5).

held to traditional media. At the far southern end of the avenue, beyond the Eiffel Tower – and in fact marking the southern culmination of the exhibition as the Tower of Peace did to the north – was the Palace of Light and Electricity (p. 118), which contained Raoul Dufy's vast but feeble mural on the history of electricity. Among the topics of other French pavilions were Elegance and Adornment (situated next to the Italian Pavilion), Cold, Gas, Toys, Fashion, Peace, Labour, 'photo cine fono' (tucked right under the foot of the Eiffel Tower), Press, Advertising and Radio. In spite of the mammoth effort to rationalize the Exhibition's contents and the theme of the pavilions, an element of the arbitrary and irrational inevitably accompanies such classifications.

Several of the foreign pavilions – notably the Spanish and the Soviet – had special cinemas constructed as part of their installations. A number of pavilions followed the trend established by Russia at international trade fairs in the late 1920s and early 1930s, of using photomontages or blown-up photographs for didactic or publicity displays. The Spanish Pavilion was the most extreme instance of the incorporation of photomontage into architectural panels, supporting the critic Joseph Ney's view that the best modern buildings in the exhibition were little more than three-dimensional propaganda. In the Italian Pavilion, the section on the graphic arts included all the literary and publicity material. Above the displays of books, reviews, posters and photographs, suspended on huge transparent panels, were photographs of the declaiming head of Mussolini.

The spirit of compromise, whose goal was to pursue peace and avoid extremism at any cost, could be seen working through most of the official publications and architecture. *Cahiers d'Art*, in its number devoted to 'Souvenirs de l'Exposition', found only five pavilions worthy of individual mention: Czechoslovakia (Jaromir Krejcar), Finland (Alvar Aalto), Spain (Luis Lacasa and Josep Lluis Sert), Sweden (Sven Ivar Lind), and Japan (Sakahura).[15] Ney lamented the absence of any good modern architecture; what there was, he felt, was an eclectic, picturesque and fairly amusing collection of the errors of the last twenty years.[16]

However, a world fair, where the pavilions need distinctive identities, could never really have been compatible with the spare, international Modernism that Ney admired.[17] The Palais de Tokyo, home of the new Museums of Modern Art, with its tall, slim columns and Neoclassical relief sculptures by Despiau, represented the triumph of the old over architects like Le Corbusier and Mallet-Stevens. Albert Speer,

architect of the German Pavilion, noted with apparent surprise that 'France also favoured Neoclassicism for her public buildings. It has often been asserted that this style is characteristic of the architecture of totalitarian states. That is not at all true. Rather, it was characteristic of the era and left its impress upon Washington, London and Paris as well as Rome, Moscow and our plans for Berlin.'[18]

Fernand Léger's radical conceptions for the exhibition make a striking contrast with the final spectacle. One of his proposals was for a Paris scraped white and clean: 'Imagine Paris all white; that is to say all the façades scraped and cleaned, employing all the unemployed to do this work.'[19] The other was an even more conceptual project, to transform Paris according to the principles of De Stijl by painting it in primary colours, yellow, red and blue, with the outline of the ageing Eiffel Tower camouflaged. By night the whole city would be transformed with multicoloured lines of electric lights, and in addition there would be cinematic projections in the sky (an echo of the utopian dreams of the Russian Constructivists in the 1920s). The idea of using the large numbers of unemployed, the consequence of the depression following the 1929 Wall Street crash, was precisely what the organizers did.[20]

There were scandals connected to the awards of concessions (for example the Amusement Park), and costs had been vastly in excess of those initially voted and approved by the government in 1934–5, rising from 300 million francs to 1,500 million.[21] To an extent, though, Léger's concept was realized, for the Exhibition was at its most brilliant at night, when illuminations and fireworks transformed the Eiffel Tower, and the pavilions were floodlit.

Although the art and architecture of the Nazi and Soviet regimes was often at the time described as being 'cut from the same cloth', they were in fact very different, just as the heroic figurative sculpture that characterized official art in both states had its basis in a different concept of the human body – a coerced body, in both cases, but in Germany one stripped for war rather than work, producing glib gladiators whose references to ancient Greece were irrationally made to stand in for Hitler's Aryan ideal. Speer's elongated columns and classical entablature supporting the Nazi eagle had a conventional relationship with the two massive sculptural groups by Josef Thorak; but Boris Iofan's Soviet Pavilion was anything but classical in its design or traditional in its relationship with sculpture. Its façade, for one thing, does not prepare one for the startling, rising thrust of the building seen from the

15 'Souvenirs de l'Exposition', *Cahiers d'Art*, nos. 8–9 (1937).

16 Joseph Ney, 'Réflexions sur l'architecture à propos de l'Exposition 1937', *Cahiers d'Art*, nos. 8–9 (1937), 248.

17 At the first postwar world fair, in Brussels in 1958, during the Cold War, the confrontation between the Nazi and Soviet Pavilions was depressingly replayed, but with the US Pavilion in place of the German. The need to assert national identities reached ludicrous proportions in that Brussels Expo, where the British Pavilion managed to combine a 'vernacular' aura of cosy thatch and beam, and the occasional turret ('every man's home is his castle'), with a massive industrial shed behind to show technological products.

18 Speer (as note 11), 81.

19 Fernand Léger, 'Réponse à une enquête: que feriez-vous si vous aviez à organiser l'Exposition de 1937?' *VU*, no. 387 (1935), quoted in *1937 Exposition internationale* (as note 1).

20 'The World's Fair was actually constructed by vast armies of the hitherto unemployed, and had partly been conceived to absorb and conceal that unemployment.' Wilson (as note 1).

21 Eugen Weber, *The Hollow Years: France in the 1930s* (London, 1995), 170. The costs of the foreign Pavilions were of course born by the governments in question. The British Pavilion was in fact funded by a Maharajah.

side. From this angle (p. 12) it looks like a pedestal for Mukhina's sculpture, in scale with the huge figures of the worker and the farm girl, while from the front the stacked rectangles make an unmistakable reference to the skyscraper rather than the classical temple. Mukhina's steel-clad sculpture of the boy and girl united in their forward march has its roots not in some eternal Greek past but in the Social Realism that sprang from the Russian Wanderers movement, and in such Constructivist images as El Lissitzky's photomontage posters of the 1920s.

Official publications tried to keep politics out of it, adopting a carefully bland and even admiring tone for the rival pavilions: the English guide described Speer's building as 'no less imposing' than the Soviet one.[22] In reviews and newspapers, however, there was bitter dispute and disagreement about the architecture and the ideologies of the respective regimes. Christian Zervos, the editor of *Cahiers d'Art*, wrote two blistering articles on the aesthetic eclipse represented by the oppression of state-organized institutions.[23] In the sculpture of the Third Reich, wrote Zervos, 'The influence of antique statuary is visible throughout. "We believe," one artist says, "in the encounter between the German genius and the Greek genius." Other sculptors have specialized in carving eagles.'[24]

No *Cahiers d'Art* artist, Zervos pointed out, had had anything to do with the exhibition of modern French art that had opened in Berlin on 1 June 1937 (*Art français moderne* at the Prussian Academy of Fine Art). To emphasize his belief in the absolute autonomy of art and the irrelevance of national considerations, Zervos dedicated *Cahiers d'Art*, no. 1/2 of 1938, to contemporary art in Germany, England and the USA, including Georg Kolbe (who worked for the Nazis) as well as artists branded as degenerate by the regime, such as E. L. Kirchner, Paul Klee and Oskar Kokoschka.

The Italian Pavilion sought a balance between the traditional and the new, and its eclecticism is evident in the works on show. Giorgio Gori's equestrian statue *The Genius of Fascism* (p. 2) confronted abstract sculptures by Fontana suspended on the rigging of the flagpoles that lined the banks of the Seine, and made a striking contrast too with Arturo Martini's impressive bronze *Victory in the Air* (p. 53).

The Italian Pavilion was a triumph of well-honed propaganda, which succeeded in integrating the given themes of the Exhibition not only with the historical narrative that was so important a part of Mussolini's rhetoric (from the founding of Rome by Romulus to Il Duce himself, via the great moments of Italian genius)

but also with the notion of social organization. The French-language guide quoted the pavilion's commissioner, Piccio: 'We have been at pains to give the visitors a sufficient notion of all that Fascist Italy has done for the development of the arts, the sciences, technology and social organization.'[25] This last was the theme of Mario Sironi's vast mosaic (see p. 154), representing the figure of contemporary Fascist Italy, classically draped and seated like an allegory of justice, surrounded by allegorical figures of the more important corporative bodies in the state. Sironi also designed the hall devoted to Greater Italy (Italie d'Outre-Mer), which contained both photographic blowups of Italy's colonial activities and a heavy bas-relief, with Italy again represented as an allegorical figure presiding over workers, 'illustrating the civilizing mission that Italy today, as the heir to Rome, is pursuing in its African territories.'[26]

Such works have a massive immobility that contradicts the abstract idea of struggle – 'maintain that high ideal tension', said Mussolini – which underlay the Fascist aesthetic, and which was a perversion of the Futurists' claim that there was no beauty except in conflict. In his critique of Fascism, Walter Benjamin used the Fascists' own slogans to define the predicament that the Paris Exhibition of 1937 so energetically sought to deny: 'Mankind's . . . self-alienation has reached such a degree that it can experience its own destruction as an aesthetic pleasure of the first order. This is the situation of politics which Fascism is rendering aesthetic. Communism responds by politicizing art.'[27]

22 *Arts and Crafts in Modern Life* (Paris, 1937), official guide (English edition).

23 Christian Zervos, 'Réflexions sur la tentative d'esthétique dirigée du IIIe Reich', *Cahiers d'Art* (1936) nos. 8–10; (1937) nos. 1–2.

24 Zervos listed five tendencies in official painting in the Third Reich: portrait, propaganda, war, 'return to the native land' and decorative art. Zervos (as note 23), nos. 8–10, 209–12.

25 *L'Exposition de Paris 1937: Le pavillon italien* (Paris, 1937), 14.

26 Ibid., 38 (?).

27 Walter Benjamin, 'The Work of Art in the Age of Mechanical Reproduction' (1936), in Benjamin, *Illuminations*, ed. Hannah Arendt, tr. Harry Zohn (London, 1970), 244.

SPAIN: CULTURE AT WAR

Marko Daniel

In the Holy Name of Spain

'Since the first moments of the civil war, the fate of the historical and artistic heritage of Spain has had a profound effect on worldwide public opinion.'[1] With these words, Josep Renau, the Director General of Fine Arts, introduced a detailed review of the Spanish Republic's efforts to safeguard the artistic heritage of the nation. From the very beginning of the Spanish civil war, art was seen by Republicans and Nationalists alike as an essential part of the larger battle. And this was nowhere more neatly shown than in the International Exhibition in Paris in 1937, where the famous pavilion of the Spanish Republic vied with the rival contribution of Franco's Nationalists for the attention of visitors from all over the world.

How had this come about? On 17 July 1936, General Francisco Franco took charge of troops in Spain's North African colony and started an armed insurrection against the Popular Front government of the Spanish Republic. The rebels accused the democratically elected rulers of being tools of Moscow, intent on destroying Spain, and proclaimed their intention of reestablishing order and protecting the unity and integrity of the nation. Specifically, the Republicans had introduced dramatic social changes to transform the essentially feudal social structures that the Nationalists wanted to see preserved.

Notwithstanding an international non-intervention treaty, Germany and Italy openly supported Franco's Nationalists; the Soviet Union and international left-wing organizations came to the aid of the Republic, though in a far less substantial manner. Interestingly, each side drew attention to these foreign supporters of its adversary and represented itself as defending Spain against foreign aggression.

The Nationalists' value system was based on tradition, and in particular on the link between State and Church. They presented themselves as the spiritual heirs of Ferdinand and Isabella, the *Reyes Católicos* who first united Spain in the fifteenth century in the name of Christianity.[2] Shadowing the Italian Fascist fascination with the Roman empire and similar mythologizing by the Nazis, they drew on the symbolic insignia of the former Spanish empire for their own corporate identity.

The very manifesto with which Franco launched the military uprising in the 'Holy Name of Spain' aimed to justify armed intervention by accusing the Republican government of supporting attacks on 'monuments and artistic treasures'.[3] This set the tone for the most sustained strand of the Nationalists' propaganda effort. The Republicans, on the other hand, saw art as part of a programme of social-political change informed by the theories of the progressive and political left in Europe and Latin America; they eagerly espoused the revolutionary art and culture of the Weimar Republic, Mexico and the Soviet Union, on the clear understanding that aesthetic and political concerns were part of the same package.

An early cultural clash came at the beginning of the civil war, with the siege of the Alcázar in Toledo. This medieval citadel was used as an academy for elite officers, who all supported Franco's side; a group of Nationalist soldiers and some civilians took refuge there and successfully sustained a protracted Republican siege during which the famous national monument was subjected to heavy bombardment and shelling. By a historical fluke, the supporters of a military coup, the insurrectionists, could thus be depicted as engaged in heroic resistance, and the Republican/Nationalist opposition appeared in terms of destruction/protection. In the official history of the war, written immediately after Franco's victory, the Alcázar incident features not just as a chapter of military history but with special emphasis on the 'destruction of the artistic treasure of Toledo'.[4] In a sumptuously illustrated book in honour of Nationalist recipients of the *Cruz Laureada de San Fernando* for heroism,[5] slightly surreal imagery is used for its capacity to mythologize through visual associations (p. 102). In *The Generalísimo* José Caballero depicts Franco striding across the Straits of Gibraltar in the guise of a young, handsome warrior. But Viladomat's image for *The Heroes of the Alcázar* again focuses on the destruction of the monument by the Republicans; an accusing El-Greco-like Madonna floats over the ruins.

1 Josep Renau, 'L'organisation de la défense du patrimoine artistique et historique espagnol pendant la guerre civile', *Mouseion* 39–40 (1937), 7.

2 'The Spanish soul is Christian by nature . . . one can hardly distinguish between what makes us Spanish and what Christian.' I. G. Menéndez Reigada, quoted in Manuel Tuñón de Lara, *La guerra civil española. 50 años después* (Barcelona, 1985), 289.

3 See Fernando Díaz-Plaja, *La guerra de España en sus documentos* (Esplugas de Llobregat, 1969), 11.

4 Joaquín Arrarás Iribarren and Carlos Sáenz de Tejada, eds., *Historia de la Cruzada Española* (Madrid, 1939–44); contains a separate chapter on the 'Destrucción del tesoro artístico de Toledo', vol. 7, t. 29, 1943, 198–236.

5 Fermina de Bonilla, Domingo Viladomat et al., *Laureados de España* (Madrid, 1940).

At the Universal Exhibition, Paris 1937

Officially, the Republic was the sole representative of the Spanish people at the Universal Exhibition, as the Nationalists' rival government was not recognized by the international community. Given the Nationalists' fusion of politics and religion, it comes as no surprise that the Vatican provided Franco's side with an opportunity to participate. The Pontifical Pavilion in the Foreign Section, just behind the Spanish Pavilion, included votive altarpieces offered by various countries.[6] Among them, in the centre of the apse, was José María Sert's painting *St Teresa, Ambassadress of Divine Love to Spain, Offers to Our Lord the Spanish Martyrs of 1936* (p. 101). Though identified as a national contribution, it was commissioned by Cardinal Isidro Gomá y Tomás, the Archbishop of Toledo and a famous supporter of the Nationalist movement.[7]

The political-historical references of the painting are made clear by its original setting. Sert's huge canvas (6 x 3 metres), painted in brownish glazes on a bright gilt ground, was topped by a golden moulded plaster curtain and flanked by two semi-ruined columns in red fake marble, which bore the motto 'PLUS ULTRA' in *trompe-l'oeil* carving: an obvious allusion to the Pillars of Hercules (see p. 26), an emblem of Spanish monarchy ever since the *Reyes Católicos*. The colour scheme of bands of gold and red strikingly recalled the traditional Spanish flag flown by the Nationalists, and at the insistence of the French government the columns had to be changed to a neutral black.[8]

With outstretched arms St Teresa, patron saint of Spain, offers to the crucified Christ the souls of the Nationalist martyrs beneath her. Swooping down from heaven head first, Christ appears to be flying his Cross like a precision bomber; he has freed his right hand to embrace the raised arm of St Teresa, thus forming a strong vertical axis. A circular aureole surrounding Christ floats over a triangle formed by the saint, the bishops at her feet, the angled crucifix and the huddled masses at the bottom of the canvas. Inscribed in this composition there is a representation, sanctioned by the conventions of religious iconography, of the stable social order that was promoted by the Nationalists. St Teresa's intercession endorses a hierarchy in which the Church occupies a privileged position: the bishops appear in close proximity to St Teresa's express lift to heaven, above the ranks of the victims, mediating between them and the higher levels.

While the painting laments death, it glorifies dying for the Nationalists. In official statements, the Church did not hesitate to endorse Nationalist attacks on the Republic: 'Communists and anarchists are the sons of Cain . . . incapable of getting rid of God or Christ, they satisfy their hatred on His images, temples and ministers . . . Martyrdom is the supreme category of love. And how have the red flowers of martyrdom flourished in our Spain!'[9] In the dramatically foreshortened swirls of the composition and the spiralling dynamics of the upward movement, St Teresa ensures that those who die in the Nationalist cause go straight to heaven; the Republicans are shown as enemies of all the values represented by the Church.

This point is emphasized by the image of a burning church in the middleground on the right. In general, the destruction of churches by 'Reds' was one of the most frequent accusations levelled against the Republicans. Here the pictorial reference is quite specific. We are looking at a representation of Vic cathedral,[10] which was severely damaged on 21 July 1936 when a band of Republican sympathizers vented their anger at the Church's role in the Nationalist uprising by going on a rampage. Over many years, José María Sert himself had decorated the interior of the church with mural paintings, which went up in flames during the attack. Despite its minor role within the painting, the incident was extremely important to Sert. Though never deeply committed, he had previously supported liberal politics, and in 1936 the Republic commissioned him to execute a mural scheme for the Council Chamber of the League of Nations in Geneva (p. 100). Yet in mid-1937 he presented himself at the Nationalist headquarters in Burgos offering his services. The only explanation ever proposed for this dramatic change of heart[11] is Sert's outrage at the destruction of his lifelong project; he went back to Vic to repaint the cathedral as soon as that became possible and spent the final years of his life until 1945 on this task. Sert's case epitomizes the efficacy with which the Nationalists had assumed the mantle of protectors of art and culture, parallel to their accusations of left-wing attacks on the Church.

The Spanish Pavilion

The Spanish Republic participated in the Paris International Exhibition with a national pavilion entirely devoted to propaganda. In itself that would not have been unusual. But, instead of displays of industrial and commercial achievements, the Republic chose to represent itself entirely through art and culture. The

6 The *Guide du pavillon pontifical* stated on p. 32: 'All around the church, votive altars have been donated by a number of foreign countries.' It is significant that these altars are said to have been offered by countries, and not by Church institutions or individuals.

7 On 1 July 1937, Cardinal Gomá, the Primate of Spain, wrote an open letter to Catholics worldwide legitimizing the Nationalists' insurrection as a battle against an atheist revolution.

8 According to Alberto del Castillo, *José María Sert. Su vida y su obra* (Barcelona and Buenos Aires, 1947), 264. (The Republican flag was red, yellow and purple.)

9 From a pastoral letter by Pla i Deniel, Bishop of Salamanca, 30 September 1936, quoted by Angel Viñas, 'Los condicionantes internacionales', in Tuñón de Lara (as note 2), 288.

10 I am grateful to María del Mar Arnús for pointing this out to me.

11 It is said that he was arrested as a 'Red' and sentenced to death, only to be saved by Ramón Serrano Súñer, the Nationalist Foreign Minister, who recognized the propaganda potential of the fact that a well-known painter had crossed the lines as a consequence of the destruction of art. Cf. Francisco de Sert, 'Contradicciones de un pintor. Apunte biográfico', in exh. cat. *José María Sert, 1874–1945* (Madrid: Palacio de Velázquez), 1987, 64.

fact that Spain was in the midst of a civil war, with severe disruptions to commerce, must to some degree be responsible for this. The organizers made every effort to show that the government was in control, and to counter Nationalist claims that Spain had become dangerously destabilized by the left. Successful participation in such an international event as the Paris Exhibition would, it was felt, raise the standing of the Republican government[12] and bring tangible benefits in its train. It was the purpose of the Spanish Pavilion to draw attention to the ravages of civil war in Spain and to elicit direct support for the Republic: 'The architecture of the Pavilion must always be subordinate to the programme of the central government.'[13]

Designed by Josep Lluis Sert (José María Sert's grandnephew, who was a disciple of Le Corbusier and a founder-member of the Spanish Rationalist GATCPAC[14] group) in conjunction with Luis Lacasa, who had previously worked for the Republican government on Madrid's University City project, the Spanish Pavilion (p. 71) was a light, unostentatious, elegant exercise in Rationalist architecture. It stood on the main avenue linking the Trocadéro with the Eiffel Tower, in the centre of the Foreign Section, where it occupied a highly visible though relatively small site. Its simply structured exterior was almost self-effacing, in marked contrast to the attention-seeking German and Soviet Pavilions that glared at each other across the approach to the Pont d'Iéna. The Pavilion was built in dry construction and consisted of standard, mass-produced items including steel beams, various types of insulating panel and glass.

Conceived as a flexible, accessible container in which a sequence of spaces defined a system of circulation,[15] the design openly revealed its structure from the moment the visitor stepped into the covered entrance area, which sat on steel pillars underneath the two main floors. As the building was explored – across the courtyard, up the external ramp that led to the second floor, or looking down the open gallery between the two upper floors – there were constant reminders of the internal structure. The clarity of the architecture drew attention to the Pavilion's contents and the narrative they created; it could be understood as the setting for a tour which elaborated the same propaganda issues at various stages in terms of avant-garde art, popular art and documentary displays.

A fanfare of avant-garde sculpture greeted the visitor. Slightly taller than the building itself, Alberto Sánchez Pérez's totemic *The Spanish People Have a Path That Leads to a Star* (see p. 73) presided over one side of the entrance area; Picasso's *Woman's Head*, one of five sculptures he showed in the Pavilion, stood on the other, with González's *Montserrat* (p. 75) between them, just to the left of the steps leading up the main entrance. This impressive display was continued inside the open ground floor, where Alexander Calder's *Mercury Fountain* stood opposite the unquestionable highlight of the Pavilion, if not of the whole Exhibition: the mural painting *Guernica*, which Picasso had produced especially for this location.

The next stage of the tour was the second-floor gallery, reached only by an outside ramp from the courtyard. It started with the Fine Arts section, which included a changing rota of internationally lesser-known Spanish artists, and continued with displays of popular arts and crafts, together with information on the various autonomous regions of Spain. Visitors then descended a flight of stairs, past Joan Miró's large mural of a *Catalan Peasant in Revolt* (p. 80) to the Documentary Section on the first floor, before leaving the Pavilion by another outside staircase that led down to the main front entrance.

Rather than describe all the individual exhibits, I shall analyse, by way of a few examples, how they fitted into the overall concept and constructed a story about Spain that filled the cool, restrained space of the Pavilion with dramatic content. No object existed solely in its own right: its content, iconography or message was informed or transformed by others in a different medium and in a different part of the building.

When Picasso accepted the commission to provide a large mural for the Spanish Pavilion, he was unsure what to paint. The government considered that anything he might contribute represented the most

12 'It would seem expedient to participate in the Exhibition, and we should immediately take all necessary steps to give an impression of security [by showing] that our government continues to pursue such matters. In the worst case, if the participation of private, commercial and industrial exhibitors etc. proved difficult . . . it would always be possible to make a cheap but decorative pavilion and to exhibit works of art, propaganda etc.' Letter from Araquistain to Alvarez del Vayo, quoted in J. Alix, exh. cat. *Pabellón Español. Exposición Internacional de Paris, 1937* (Madrid: Centro de Arte Reina Sofía, 1987), 25.

13 Letter from the architect Torres Clavé to Josep Lluis Sert, 27 December 1936. Quoted in Fernando Martín Martín, *El pabellón español en la Exposición Universal de Paris en 1937* (Seville, 1982), 36.

14 Grupo de Arquitectos y Técnicos Catalanes para el Progreso de la Arquitectura Contemporánea, founded in Barcelona in 1931(?).

15 Cf. .i.Bozal Fernández, Valeriano et al., *España. Vanguardia artística y realidad social, 1936–1976* (Barcelona, 1976), 33.

Spanish Pavilion, 1937: Picasso's *Guernica* and Calder's *Mercury Fountain*

prestigious artistic support imaginable; as the Finance Minister, Juan Negrín, commented, 'In terms of propaganda for the Republic, the presence of the mural painted by Picasso is equal to a military victory on the front.'[16] Then, on 26 April 1937, the Basque town of Guernica was bombed by German planes of the Condor Legion, which operated in Spain on behalf of the Nationalists. As reports of the virtual annihilation of a whole town filtered through, Picasso transformed the event into a painting whose sweepingly grand political and artistic conception ensured instant fame. With its classical tripartite composition, monochrome colouring and shallow, stagy, slightly cubistic space, *Guernica* (p. 77) avoids any journalistic depiction of specific circumstances and focuses instead on the suffering caused by the attack. It is a measure of the extraordinary success of *Guernica* that its symbolic value as a general anti-war statement has transformed our understanding of the historical event.

This was the third time since the beginning of the civil war that Picasso had given unequivocal public support to the Republic. In September 1936 he had accepted the honorary directorship of the Museo del Prado,[17] and in January 1937 he had started a series of etchings, *Dream and Lie of Franco*, in which he lampooned the Fascist leader with savage irony (p. 76). These prints were exhibited in the Pavilion, where copies were also on sale to the public to raise funds for the government.

Joan Miró's great mural *The Catalan Peasant in Revolt* (p. 80), on the flight of stairs that provided the only access down to the first floor, was tied into its political context by two captions that exhorted spectators, in the words of *Don Quixote*, to 'expose their lives for liberty'.[18] The mural itself covered all the available wall space (5.50 x 3.65 metres), which gave extreme impact to the simple profile of a peasant's head wearing the typical Catalan red beret. Holding a sickle in his raised right hand, Miró's peasant shares a common iconographical context with Julio González's welded iron sculpture *Montserrat* (p. 75), which represents a peasant mother with an infant on one arm and a sickle in the other hand.

According to Fernando Martín Martín, the significance of these figures was made absolutely clear to the public by the placing of the words of *Els Segadors* (The Harvesters), the unofficial anthem of radical Catalan supporters of the Republic, underneath Miró's mural.[19] The political message was reinforced by Miró's poster *Aidez l'Espagne* (p. 82). The outcome of an abortive commission to design a French stamp whose proceeds would go to support the Spanish Republic, the poster depicts another figure in the Catalan red beret, with a dramatically foreshortened raised fist. Underneath the very simplified design in red, white, yellow and black on a blue ground, Miró wrote: 'In the present struggle I see, on the Fascist side, spent forces; on the opposite side, the people, whose boundless creative will gives Spain an impetus which will astonish the world.'[20]

As visitors walked up the ramp from the courtyard to the second-floor entrance, they first glimpsed larger-than-life portrait photos of the sculptors Emiliano Barral and Francisco Pérez Mateo, surrounded by examples of their work. With the inscription 'Two Artists, Two Heroes of the Defence of Madrid' and biographical panels, this section paid homage to the two artists who had died on the Madrid front in 1936. Along the second floor, there followed a line of sculptures, juxtaposing two heads by Barral and Pérez Mateo with Picasso's *Bather*. Like the inclusion of Pérez Mateo's *Bear* (p. 89) in the garden and his *Bather* at the foot of the ramp, this amounted to something more than the simple interweaving of local talent among internationally renowned Spanish artists. The latter demonstrated the political commitment of the leaders of the historic avant-garde; the inclusion of Barral and Pérez Mateo, who had died for their beliefs, deepened and extended the suggested link between art and politics. Their political conviction and the artistic quality of the avant-garde mutually reinforced each other.

The documentary sections on the first floor were also, to varying degrees, part of the overall mix of art and propaganda. The montage exhibit dealing with the mercury mines at Almadén – still one of the world's most important producers – illustrates the diversity of points that such displays could make. First, it

16 Martín Martín (as note 13), 125.

17 The decree was signed by Manuel Azaña on 19 September and published in the *Gaceta de Madrid*, no. 264, on 20 September.

18 Quoted in French, it read: ON DOIT EXPOSER SA VIE POUR LA LIBERTÉ, DON QUICHOTTE II 58; Alix (as note 12), 132.

19 This hymn to harvesters included the lines: 'The enemy is going to run when the arms of freedom are raised. Just as we harvest wheat, so we shall harvest ears of gold, we're going to break the chains.' Martín Martín (as note 13), 172, 184 n.29. (Other sources state only that it was 'an inspiration', not that the text was shown under the painting.)

20 Translated by Peter Watson, 'Joan Miró', *Horizon*, 4, no. 20 (August 1941), 132–33.

Spanish Pavilion, 1937: commemoration of Barral and Pérez Mateo

highlighted the commercial importance of the product, which was virtually all exported and thus represented an valuable source of income. Second, a historical panel showed the social advances in the working conditions of miners; third, together with photographic material and a sample of cinnabar, a row of special mercury flasks stood at the bottom of the panels. The row of bottles, whose shape was repeated in the graphics of export statistics, also provided a physical link to the famous *Mercury Fountain* (p. 65), which Alexander Calder had made for a prime site in the entrance foyer opposite *Guernica.* This piece was a large construction of tarred iron in which mercury ran along grooves and channels, activating mobile elements at the end of which a dancing copper wire was bent to form the word ALMADEN. The mercury flowing through the fountain had been shipped from Spain in the bottles displayed in the upstairs gallery. The intensely visual experience of quicksilver splashing over black tar onto the gently swaying mobile is an essential part of the Pavilion's propaganda discourse. The mercury first acquires a value through art; then, in the documentary section, this is translated into commercial and political significance.

The use of photomontage throughout the Pavilion, inside and out, ensured high visual impact for cultural, social and economic information. Made under the supervision of Josep Renau, the photomontage artist from Valencia who found himself in Paris on official business as the Director General of Fine Arts, the panels covered such topics as literacy programmes, the provision of schools and hospitals, and help for infants and war widows, as well as the roles of industry and agriculture in the war effort and the effects of warfare on Spanish cities.

In one of the most striking examples, the role of women in the new society is represented in a photomontage that juxtaposes two life-size images on a 'before and after' double panel (p. 69). On the left is a woman wearing the traditional costume of Salamanca. Her face looks gloomily out from underneath a scarf covering her head and shoulders. The right-hand panel is in striking contrast. A young militiawoman in uniform strides forward. Her face is brightly lit, and her mouth opens as if caught in mid-speech. This dynamism seems a direct challenge to the rigidity and the still, symmetrical pose of the other woman, swaddled as she is by her costume. Whereas she is photographed roughly from head height, the soldier's picture is taken from the level of her feet upwards: these countermovements of perspective subtly determine our attitude to the two figures. The woman from

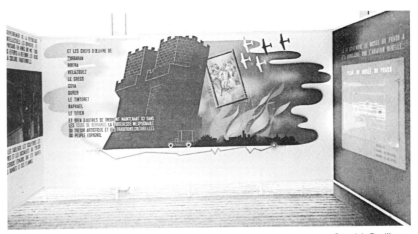

Spanish Pavilion, 1937: safeguarding the Prado treasures (photomontage)

Salamanca stands in front of a plain background – a whitewashed house and doorway with a high step – which flattens and immobilizes its subject. The militiawoman, by contrast, is represented on a transparent glass panel. Thus, not only is she integrated with the rest of the exhibition, as the viewer looks through the glass onto the other displays on aspects of modern life surrounding her; but, importantly, as the visitor moves through the exhibition so does she, relative to the background. A caption leaves no room for doubt about the changing role of women: 'Freeing herself from her wrapping of superstition and misery, from the immemorial slave is born THE WOMAN, capable of taking an active part in the development of the future.'

Cultural heritage

Virtually all the propaganda in the Spanish Pavilion, no matter how political or militant its aim, was based on or related to art. This employment of art can be seen as an engagement with Nationalist propaganda: while the latter concentrated on attacking an alleged lack of concern for culture on the Republican side, the government responded by couching every single political statement in terms of (modern) art and presenting themselves as unsurpassed patrons of the avant-garde: 'The strengthening and development of culture, like the problems of public education, today occupy the Spanish government no less than the war itself.'[21]

But weren't the Republicans sidestepping the specific accusations of the Nationalists, who did not talk about contemporary art but about the destruction of Spain's cultural heritage? In fact, the Pavilion contained a direct rebuttal of that accusation. A whole section was devoted to the protection of the works of art from the Prado, organized by Renau while Picasso

21 Angel Ossorio y Gallardo, quoted in Martín Martín (as note 13), 37.

was honorary director of the museum. Starting on the right, the first panel dealt with a Nationalist air raid on 16 November 1936 clearly directed against the Prado Museum. It showed a blueprint plan indicating the location of hits from incendiary and blast bombs on the museum, after Bengal lights or flares had been dropped around it to mark the target. The centre panel depicted two ghost-like arms rising out of the flames of a burning Madrid skyline, holding aloft El Greco's *Trinity* from the Prado, while an outline lorry travelled along the road to the protection of the Torres de Serrano in Valencia. A caption explained that the masterpieces of the collection were safely stored in these two medieval towers, which represented 'the impregnable fortress of the artistic treasure and cultural traditions of the Spanish people' (p. 67). The final panel, directly facing the plan of the Prado, showed three armed militiamen gazing intently at a wall covered with paintings: the products of traditional culture had been saved from bombs and flames only through the concerted efforts of government, intellectuals, workers and peasants in arms.

As I mentioned at the beginning, Renau had written a comprehensive illustrated report on the steps taken by the government to prevent war damage to the national heritage. As the magazine in which it appeared was published by the League of Nations (which could not be seen to take sides in the war), all remarks that identified the Nationalists as the perpetrators of destruction had to be removed.[22] However, the prime audience of conservators and other museum staff was well aware of the situation in Spain and had already been targeted by an open letter written by the former director of Madrid's Biblioteca Nacional, who had joined the Nationalist side and criticized the Republicans. Renau presented the main points of his article in an open lecture, which was organized and widely publicized by the French art review *Beaux-Arts*.[23] This two-pronged approach illustrates again how concerned the Republicans were by Nationalist accusations of cultural vandalism.

In the entrance foyer of the Spanish Pavilion, next to the display of Picasso's *Dream and Lie of Franco*, hung posters for a major exhibition of Catalan medieval art in the Jeu de Paume in Paris. The works in that show, from the National Museum of Catalan Art in Barcelona, had been transported to Paris to protect them against possible war damage; any such evidence of Republican concern for culture contributed to their propaganda battle with the Nationalists. As Christian Zervos pointed out in his polemical introduction to the

catalogue, the French public was overwhelmed by flagrantly contradictory press reports on the Spanish situation. Seeing these pieces in all their glory served as evidence that they had not been destroyed, as the Nationalists alleged, but formed an essential, valued part of the Republic's creation of a political-cultural identity.

Towards the end of the war, as the Republican government, by now on the brink of collapse, withdrew from one temporary headquarters after another, the fate of the treasures of the Prado became progressively more precarious. In the Figueras Agreement of 3 February 1937, the government bowed to increasing international pressure and ceded control of the works to an International Committee, which had been set up specifically for the Salvation of the Spanish Artistic Treasures. This was not organized by the League of Nations or another neutral body, as one might assume, but on the initiative of the ubiquitous José María Sert, who brokered the negotiations semi-independently, though ultimately on behalf of his friends in the Nationalist government.[24] As a mass exodus of Spanish refugees trekked across the border into France, the Republican government sent the Prado treasures on their way to Geneva, where they finally relinquished all control over them to the International Committee, which deposited the works with the League of Nations. In June 1939, two months after the end of the civil war, the new Spanish government opened an exhibition of 'Masterpieces of the Prado Museum' in Geneva. Thus the Nationalists were able to reap the rewards of the extraordinary protection campaign that the Republicans had conducted as a direct consequence of the Nationalists' very own attacks.[25]

After the closure of the 1937 Paris International Exhibition, Picasso's *Guernica* embarked on a money-raising tour round Britain and the USA. In what is perhaps one of the great ironies of the whole conflict, when this icon of twentieth-century art went on show at London's New Burlington Galleries it failed to attract the same attention as Ignacio Zuloaga's *Toledo in Flames*, which was exhibited there immediately afterwards on behalf of Nationalist supporters. (A second London showing, at the Whitechapel Art Gallery, was more successful.) As *Guernica* continued on its way to fame and exile in The Museum of Modern Art in New York, and Franco prepared to send prisoners of war to build a giant monument (the monstrous *Holy Cross of the Valley of the Fallen*; see p. 107), it was evident that culture had been instrumental in shaping the ideological battleground on which the Second World War and the Cold War were to be enacted.[26]

22 The Spanish reprint in Renau (as note 1), 45–118, reinstates these sections.

23 'La protection des oeuvres d'art en Espagne, par M. Renau, Directeur des Beaux-Arts en Espagne', *Beaux-Arts*, no. 239 (30 July 1937), 1, 3.

24 J. M. Sert discussed every move with the Duke of Alba, who was the Nationalist representative in London. The International Committee itself was presided over by D. David-Weill, President of the Conseil des Musées Nationaux (Palais du Louvre), and included prominent French, British, Swiss, Dutch and US museum administrators.

25 The exhibition was not organized by the Spanish government, which was still negotiating the return of the works to the Prado; the catalogue simply expressed gratitude to 'the Spanish government', blithely ignoring the ambiguities which that term implied.

26 If this signalled the end of the civil war, the end of Franco's dictatorship and the return of democracy culminated in *Guernica's* arrival at the Casón of the Prado in 1981.

SE DEGAGEANT DE SON ENVELOPPE DE SUPERSTITION ET DE MISE-
RE DE L'ESCLAVE INMEMORIALE EST NEE **LA FEMME**
CAPABLE DE PRENDRE UNE PART ACTIVE A L'ELABORTION DE L'AVENIR

Spanish Pavilion, 1937: the new woman (photomontage)

Josep Lluis Sert and Luis Lacasa
Spanish Pavilion at the 1937 Paris Exhibition.
(photo Kollar)

Josep Lluis Sert and Luis Lacasa
model of the Spanish Pavilion. Museo Nacional
Centro de Arte Reina Sofía, Madrid

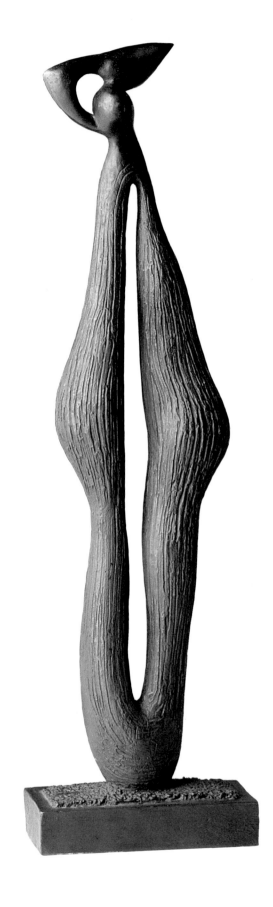

Alberto Sánchez Pérez
*Sign of a Country Woman, on a
Road, in the Rain*, 1927–30.
Eduardo Capa Collection,
Madrid

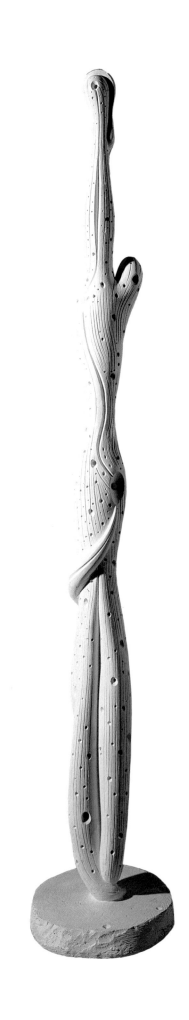

Alberto Sánchez Pérez
The Spanish People Have a Path that Leads to
a Star, 1937 (maquette).
Museo Nacional Centro de Arte Reina Sofía,
Madrid
[Not exhibited]

Julio González
Woman Before a Mirror, c. 1936–37.
IVAM. Instituto Valenciano de Arte Moderno,
Valencia

Julio González
La Montserrat,
1937.
Stedelijk Museum,
Amsterdam

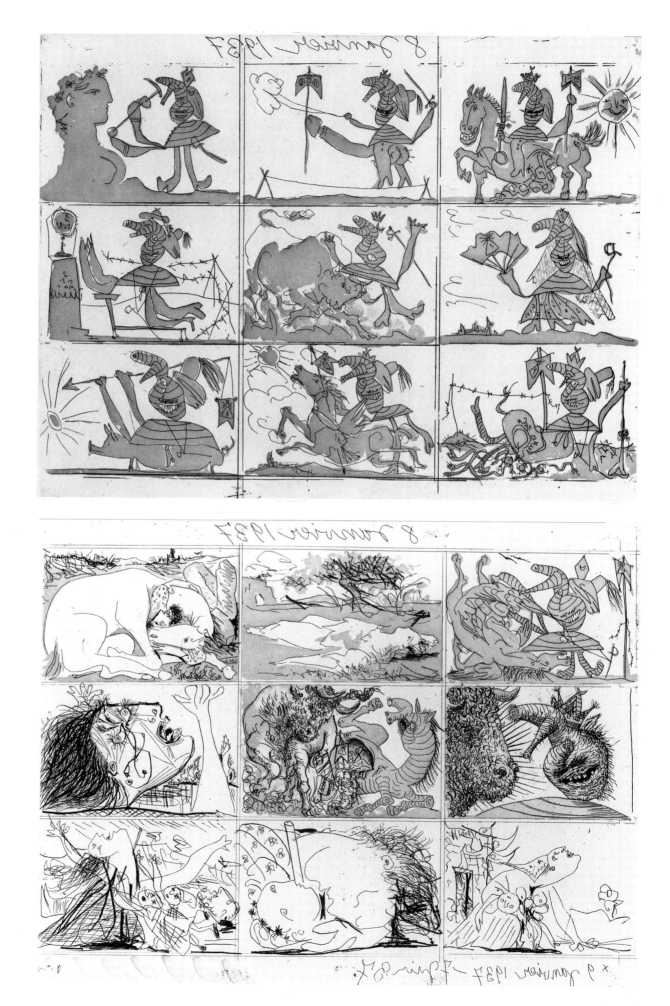

Pablo Picasso
The Dream and Lie of Franco 1 & 2, 1937.
British Museum, London

Pablo Picasso
Guernica, 1937
(photo Kollar)

Pablo Picasso
Head of Crying Woman with Handkerchief III,
1937.
Museo Nacional Centro de Arte Reina Sofía,
Madrid

Pablo Picasso
Mother with Dead Child II, 1937.
Museo Nacional Centro de Arte Reina Sofía,
Madrid

Joan Miró
*The Catalan
Peasant in Revolt*
(Spanish Pavilion,
Paris Exhibition,
1937)

Joan Miró
Still Life with Old Shoe, 1937.
The Museum of Modern Art, New York, Gift of
James Thrall Soby

Joan Miró
Aidez l'Espagne, 1937.
Imperial War Museum, London

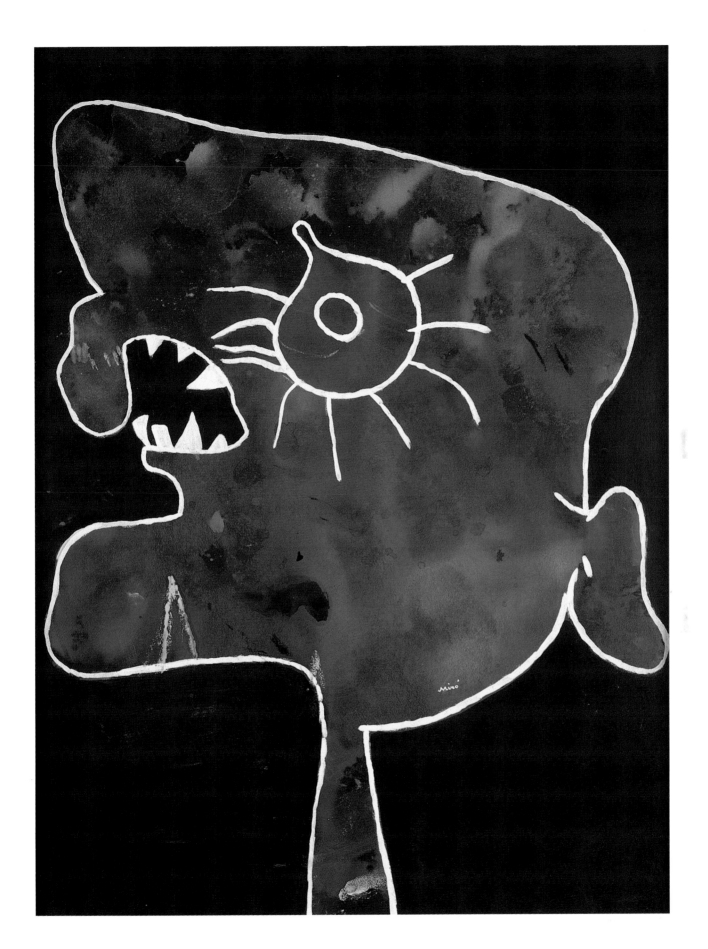

Joan Miró
Head of a Man, 1937.
Richard S. Zeisler Collection, New York

Santiago Pelegrín
Bomb in Tetuán, 1937.
Museu Nacional d'Art de Catalunya, Barcelona

Horacio Ferrer
Madrid 1937 (Black Aeroplanes)
Carmen Ferrer, Adán Ferrer, Horacio Ferrer,
Madrid

Juan Borrás Casanova
Old Spain, 1937.
Museu Nacional d'Art de Catalunya, Barcelona

José Gutiérrez Solana
The Procession of Death, 1930.
Museo Nacional Centro de Arte Reina Sofía,
Madrid

José Antonio
Soldier, 1937.
Museu Nacional d'Art de Catalunya, Barcelona

Emiliano Barral
Portrait of Luis Quintanilla, 1925. Museu
Nacional d'Art de Catalunya, Barcelona

Francisco Pérez Mateo
Bear, 1931.
Museo Nacional Centro de Arte Reina Sofía,
Madrid

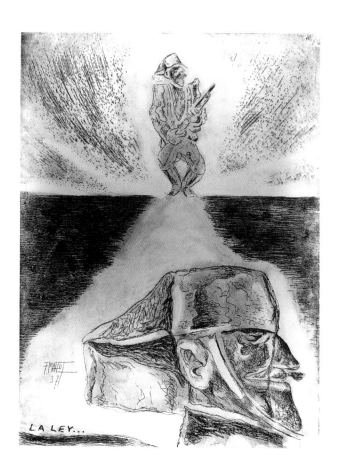

Francisco Mateos
from the series *Salamanca* and *El Sitio de Madrid*, 1937.
Museu Nacional d'Art de Catalunya, Barcelona:

Hope to God that Franco Wins
The Generalísimo is Receiving Today
The Law

Legionaires
Prussian Chiefs
The Vaticanists
Italian Music

El sitio de Madrid — Los legionarios

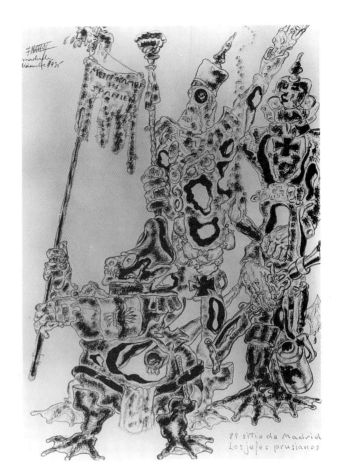

El sitio de Madrid
Los jefes prusianos

El sitio de Madrid
Los vaticanistas

El sitio de Madrid
música italiana

Josep Renau
Covers for *Nueva Cultura*,
1935–36.
IVAM, Instituto Valenciano de Arte Moderno, Valencia.

Josep Renau
The Path of Bourgeois Democracy, 1932.
IVAM, Instituto Valenciano de Arte Moderno, Valencia

Josep Renau
*The Commissioner at the Nerve Centre of our
Popular Army*, 1936.
IVAM, Instituto Valenciano de Arte Moderno,
Valencia

Josep Renau
Industry of War, 1936.
IVAM, Instituto Valenciano de Arte Moderno,
Valencia

Josep Renau
Happy New Year 1943. IVAM, Instituto
Valenciano de Arte Moderno, Valencia

Josep Renau
Stalingrad. The New Star of Freedom, 1942.
IVAM, Instituto Valenciano de Arte Moderno,
Valencia

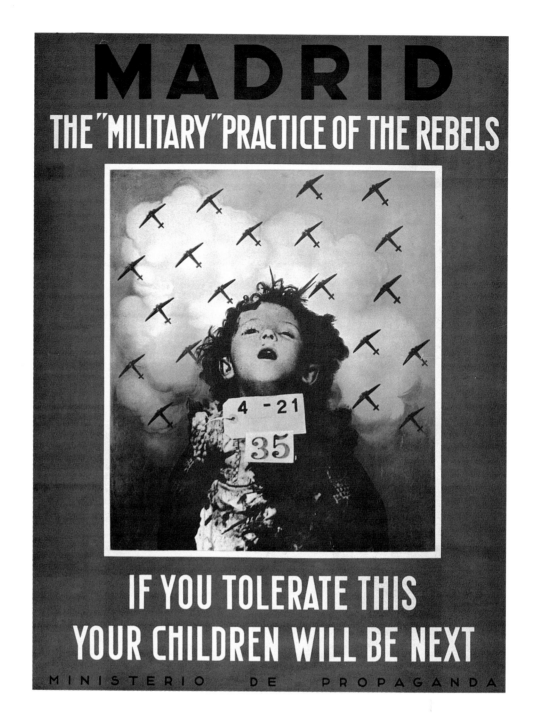

Anonymous
Madrid. The 'Military' Practice of the Rebels.
Imperial War Museum, London

Pere Català i Pic
Let's Squash Fascism, 1936. IVAM, Instituto
Valenciano de Arte Moderno, Valencia

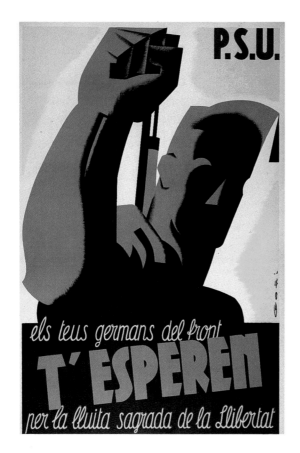

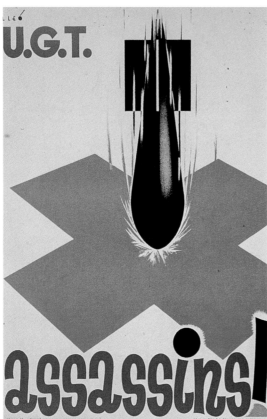

L. Goni
Your Brothers at the Front Await You.
Imperial War Museum, London

Lleó
Assassins!
Biblioteca Nacional, Madrid

Josep Renau
19 Years of the Soviet Union and of Fighting for Liberty and World-Wide Peace, 1936. Biblioteca Nacional, Madrid

Coves
We Shall Win for the Good of the World's Proletariat, 1936.
Biblioteca Nacional, Madrid

Moneny
Homage to the USSR, 1937.
Biblioteca Nacional, Madrid

José María Sert
The Lesson at Salamanca (The Solidarity of Peoples), 1935–6.
Palais des Nations, Geneva

José Maria Sert
St Teresa, Ambassadress of Divine Love to
Spain, Offers to Our Lord the Spanish Martyrs
of 1936, 1937.
Museu Nacional d'Art de Catalunya, Barcelona

Illustrations from *Laureados de España*

Domingo Viladomat
The Heroes of the Alcazar

José Caballero
The Generalisimo
Biblioteca de Catalunya, Barcelona

Salvador Dalí
*Soft Construction with Boiled Beans –
Premonition of Civil War*, 1936.
Philadelphia Museum of Art, The Louise and
Walter Arensberg Collection

Anonymous
Spain Resurrects, 1939. Biblioteca Nacional, Madrid

Anonymous
Franco, 1939. Biblioteca Nacional, Madrid

Morell
Spain Has Arrived, 1939. Biblioteca Nacional, Madrid

Anonymous
Spain is the Spiritual Leader of the World, c. 1939.
Biblioteca Nacional, Madrid

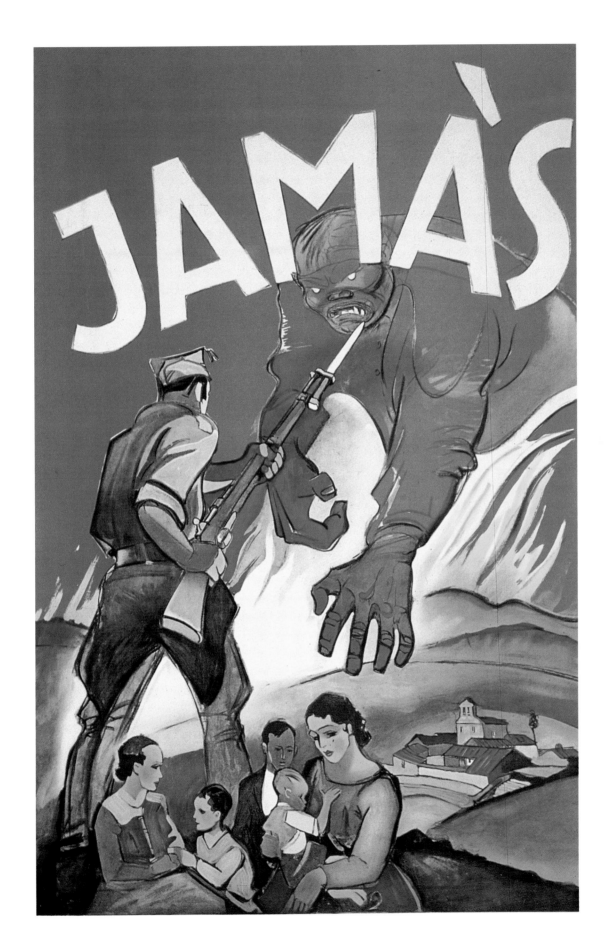

Anonymous
Never Again, c. 1939.
Biblioteca Nacional, Madrid

Francisco
Cabrero Torres-
Quevedo
*Design for a
monumental cross
for the Valley of
the Fallen,*
1941–2.
Private Collection,
Madrid

106

Aerial view of Franco's Holy Cross of the Valley
of the Fallen (under construction)

The Basilica, Valley of the Fallen

THE GERMAN PAVILION

Karen A. Fiss

1 Wilhelm Lotz, 'The German Pavilion', in *Ausstellung Paris 1937 für Kunst und Technik. Deutsche Abteilung* (Berlin, 1937), 14.

2 Speech given by German Economics Minister Hjalmar Schacht at the inauguration of the Deutsches Haus, quoted in *L'Oeuvre*, 27 May 1937. The German pavilion was at least five times more costly than any other foreign structure at the fair; see Edmond Labbé, *Exposition internationale des arts et des techniques dans la vie moderne, Paris 1937: Rapport général*, Ministère du Commerce et de l'Industrie (Paris, 1940), vol. 2, annex D, 81.

3 Jeffrey T. Schnapp, 'Epic Demonstrations: Fascist Modernity and the 1932 Exhibition of the Fascist Revolution', in *Fascism, Aesthetics, and Culture*, ed. Richard J. Golsan (Hanover, N.H., and London, 1992), 3. Schnapp's article specifically analyses an Italian Fascist exhibition that differed substantially in form and context from that of the Nazis in Paris. I have modified his term 'aesthetic overproduction' to describe the static fusion of styles in the creation of pastiche, whereas Schnapp applied it to the dynamic collage of visual effects featured in the Italian 'multimedia museum in motion'.

4 Albert Speer, *Inside the Third Reich*, tr. Richard and Clara Winston (New York, 1970), 96.

5 Alex Scobie, *Hitler's State Architecture. The Impact of Classical Antiquity*, (University Park, Pa., 1990), 5.

6 Lotz (as note 1), 19.

7 Dieter Bartetzko, 'Tödliches Lächeln – Der deutsche Ausstellungspavillon von Albert Speer', in exh. cat. '*Die Axt hat geblüht . . .* ' *Europäische Konflikte der 30er Jahre in Erinnerung an die frühe Avantgarde* (Düsseldorf: Städtische Kunsthalle, 1987), 337–43. The Egyptian monument shown in this catalogue is not the Temple of Horus at Edfu but the entrance wall to the complex of King Djoser at Saqqara. Thanks to Jan Assmann and Louise Hitchcock for clarifying this matter.

According to the official German catalogue, the 'Deutsches Haus' – the German pavilion – was 'meant to be an ambassador of its country, bearing witness of its artistic endeavour, and reflecting the strength and personality of the entire nation'.[1] The National Socialist regime's agenda for the 1937 Paris International Exhibition was twofold: the government was striving to demonstrate the revitalization of the German 'national spirit', while also trying to persuade other countries to reopen or expand their trade relations with Germany. The Third Reich was thus attempting to market itself in Paris both as a technologically advanced nation and as a people rooted in timeless tradition. Nazi propaganda also emphasized the grandeur and expense of the pavilion as evidence of Germany's commitment to 'world peace' and to the 'reconstruction of a healthy and solid world economy'.[2] To substantiate Germany's economic viability, a wide range of merchandise was exhibited, including television and film technology, medical equipment, a Mercedes racing car, children's toys and fine china.

The pursuit of international trade opportunities, however, produced an ideological double bind for the Third Reich. The Nazis claimed to have lifted Germany above the decadence and alienation of bourgeois capitalist societies. Prominent Nazi ideologues denigrated international commerce, associating it with the so-called Jewish preoccupation with finance. Despite Hitler's declared policy of self-sufficiency, the demands of economic reorganization and the extensive rearmament programme required an increased flow of foreign currency and raw materials into the country. This contradiction between Nazi mythology and economic reality was just one of a series of paradoxes the Third Reich attempted to harmonize in projecting a totalized image of Nazi Germany. Through what has been termed a strategy of 'aesthetic overproduction', the unstable and inconsistent foundations of National Socialism were cloaked in a mystifying web of rhetorical and artistic signifiers. A plethora of overdetermined representations and symbols enabled Nazism 'to make of paradox a productive principle' – to sustain the oxymoronic tensions essential to its survival and propagation.[3]

This compensatory strategy of overproduction manifested itself visually in the montage of architectural styles that made up the design of the pavilion. The principal aim of its architect, Albert Speer, was to create an imperial, quasi-religious monument that would counter the forward thrust of the Soviet pavilion and dominate it in height.[4] In opposition to Boris Iofan's dynamic, multiplanar structure, the fortress-like façade of the Deutsches Haus appeared stoic and immutable. To achieve this austere monumentality, Speer's monolithic building made simultaneous references to a number of historical antecedents. The pavilion was at once a classical temple, a medieval church, and a huge, ancient sarcophagus, while still drawing upon modern design and construction methods. Its exterior shared with functionalist architecture the renunciation of superfluous ornament and the use of a steel supporting structure. Yet, overlaid on that steel construction was a façade of native German limestone, with swastika-patterned gold and red mosaic tile applied in the recesses between the fluted piers.

German Pavilion, 1937 (Hans Hoffmann)

The large-cut stone, the fluted piers and the ceremonial entrance steps were all intended to recall the solemn dignity of ancient Rome.[5] The incorporation into the monumental architectural programme of Josef Thorak's bronze figural groups, which flanked the pavilion's entrance, also derived from this identification with the antique. The pavilion guidebook, written by prominent Nazi art critics and officials, denied that its revived classicism was an act of 'mere slavish copying'. On the contrary, the text claimed, the similarities stemmed from a world view shared with the ancients:

'[The] reason for the fundamental harmony of our buildings with those of the Ancient World is a similar attitude towards building as such . . . Building is the powerful display of the forces of a nation, which expresses therein its vital energy. Today, peaceful work and the proud joy of doing things and of giving form to ideas cause the erection of buildings that personify our endeavour and ability.'[6]

The German pavilion also recalled medieval ecclesiastical architecture, with its (bell) tower, its long central nave and its chancel. A large stained-glass window and matching mosaic composition graced the opposing podium and entrance walls respectively. The expected Christian motif, however, was replaced by an image of the German eagle grasping a swastika. On the podium-altar was an architectural model of the Haus der Deutschen Kunst, in Munich, the art gallery designed by Paul Ludwig Troost, which opened the same summer as the 1937 Paris Exhibition – though Troost, who had been Hitler's favoured architect before Speer, had died three years before its completion. The honoured place accorded to the museum model served to accentuate the quasi-religious significance bestowed on art and architecture by the Nazis, and also to commemorate Troost's death.

Finally, Speer's design owed much of its cultic power to its evocation of funerary architecture. The model of the museum built by the recently deceased Troost was displayed on the podium much like a body lying in state. As Dieter Bartetzko has noted, the Deutsches Haus exemplified the 'architectural death cult' of National Socialism. The long hall suggested an immense, hermetically sealed sarcophagus, while the frontal tower was like a gigantic funerary monument. Bartetzko likens Speer's façade to the entrance of an ancient Egyptian burial complex.[7] In addition, he draws formal comparisons between the Deutsches Haus and the Munich Ehrentempel (Temple of Honour), built by Troost to house the graves of Nazi party members killed in the premature putsch of 1923. This Ehrentempel was one of the earliest realizations of Nazi architecture, and represented an important memorial in the Nazi symbolic system of sacrifice and death.

As Speer himself proclaimed on the occasion of the 1937 Exhibition, Troost's Munich buildings, as well as his own Paris pavilion and Nuremberg Rally Ground, were envisioned as 'guide(s) for future construction in Germany'.[8] The significance of these monuments was made clear in the arrangement of the pavilion: while Troost's museum model marked the far end of the exhibition hall, a large maquette of the Nuremberg complex and a painting of the Ehrentempel dominated its entrance way. Moreover, the Third Reich intended to reconstruct the pavilion tower at the Nuremberg Rally Ground after the closing of the Exhibition.[9] The building and models, then, literally framed each other in a self-referential circle of homage.

In contrast to the stark monumentality of Speer's façade, the architect Woldemar Brinkmann created a luxurious interior in order to make the disparate clusters of commercial goods look more glamorous. He rejected the modern trend towards white walls and sleek exhibition spaces in favour of dense, swastika-patterned wallpaper and a hall filled with heavy, wooden vitrines. Elaborate chandeliers and wall sconces illuminated the space at night. Asserting the primacy of the state over private financial ambition, the official guidebook maintained that the exhibit had 'nothing to do with selfish individual interests'. The pavilion, it said, did not 'lure the people into some cheap show' but rather revealed to them the strength of German communal unity: 'The great hall creates the effect of a unit . . . the individual

departments are not in competition with each other . . . [but] are all housed under the same roof, organized according to the will of one man, united in the ideal of the community of the German people – witnesses of the new Germany and its Führer. This will and this spirit accompany the visitor as long as he is in the pavilion. It is as though they were inscribed above every showcase, on every table, on every column.'[10]

Despite the catalogue's insistence on the pantheistic presence of the Führer, representations of Hitler himself were consciously excluded from the artistic programme.[11] The Deutsches Haus also lacked the didactic charts, oversized slogans and wall texts that characterized its Soviet counterpart. The German organizers' choice of more static and traditional art forms for its visual propaganda was intended to shift attention away from the militarism of National Socialism towards the cultural and scientific achievements of the regime. The effectiveness of this representational strategy was reflected in the French press; for example, the mainstream newspaper L'Oeuvre proclaimed the Deutsches Haus to be 'an imposing manifestation of the civilizing energies of Germany, of a Germany which has cast off its warrior gear and is speaking to the world through the voices of its scholars, engineers and artists'.[12]

This shift in emphasis relied on a broader ideological transformation of the cultural categories of technology, labour and production under National Socialism. German advocates of 'conservative revolution' attempted to separate technology from the rationalized world of Zivilisation and joined it to the organic realm of völkische Kultur.[13] Through its incorporation into the transcendental language of Race, Blood and Spirit (Geist), technology was elevated from the status of commodity to become the embodiment of the German ethos. State control of the visual arts provided the Nazi regime with the representational means necessary to sustain the contradictions inherent in its fusion of völkisch community and technological optimism. The deliberate juxtaposition in the German pavilion of advanced industrial machines, displaying a distinctly Modernist aesthetic, with stylistically regressive examples of Nazi art gave an impression of National Socialism as simultaneously eternal and avant-garde.

German Pavilion, 1937: model of Haus der Deutschen Kunst and stained-glass window

In an age of industrial sophistication, the anti-modern artwork served as a kind of guarantee of the purity and immutability of the German soul. Writing on the Paris Exhibition in 1937, Gisèle Freund said that the Germans were simply too 'material'-minded for the ephemeral, physically insubstantial medium of photography: rather, the Third Reich needed the prestige and auratic presence of traditional media and handcrafted objects in the Deutsches Haus to produce what Freund termed its 'symbolic cocoon'.[14]

When compared to the Soviet pavilion, which combined Social Realist works of art with photo-murals and Modernistic architectural accents, the formal, Victorian-looking decor of the German building seems elegant but antiquated. On the other hand, Soviet machinery, as exemplified by the car at the centre of the hall, appeared aesthetically and technologically backward in relation to the aerodynamic lines of the German racing car. Thus, while Nazism

German Pavilion, 1937: interior

8 Dedication page written by Albert Speer for Deutschland in Paris: Ein Bild-Buch von Heinrich Hoffmann (Munich, 1937), 5.
9 Report dated Oct. 1936, Politisches Archiv des Auswärtigen Amtes, Bonn.
10 Robert Kain, 'The Interior of The German Pavilion', in Deutsche Abteilung (as note 1), 23–27.
11 Hitler appeared only once, a small figure in a painting of a Nuremberg Rally at night.
12 'L'inauguration du pavillon de l'Allemagne: une imposante manifestation', L'Oeuvre, 27 May 1937.
13 Jeffrey Herf, Reactionary Modernism. Technology, Culture, and Politics in Weimar and the Third Reich (Cambridge, 1984).
14 Gisèle Freund, 'La photographie à l'Exposition', Art et métiers graphiques, no. 62 (1937), 38. Though Freund neglects the extensive use of photography and montage by the Nazis in other propagandistic endeavours, she correctly discerns their desire to create an insular iconographic system.

German Pavilion, 1937: Rudolf Hengstenberg, *Comradeship*

15 See *Bauhaus-Moderne im Nationalsozialismus*, ed. Winfried Nerdinger (Munich, 1993); Barbara Miller Lane, *Architecture and Politics in Germany, 1918–1945* (Cambridge, Mass., 1968); *Faschistische Architekturen*, ed. Hartmut Frank (Hamburg, 1985).
16 Schacht quoted in *L'Oeuvre* (as note 12).
17 Berthold Hinz, *Art in the Third Reich* (New York, 1979), 111.
18 *Die Entstehung der Mosaiken und des Glasfensters im Deutschen Haus* (Berlin, 1937).
19 Stefanie Poley, 'Die Frau als "Lebensquell"', in Poley, *Rollenbilder im Nationalsozialismus* (Bad Honnef, 1991), 33–34.
20 Anson Rabinbach, 'The Aesthetics of Production in the Third Reich', in *International Fascism*, ed. George Mosse (London, 1979), 195.
21 Kain (as note 10), 29.

German Pavilion, 1937: *Work*; *Strength Through Joy*, mosaics

attacked Modernist painting and sculpture as degenerate, it fully embraced Modernist aesthetics and methods in the technological sphere, as well as in other areas of production.[15]

Concurrent with the importance placed on technological advance was the celebration of the 'noble German worker' and the improvement or 'beautification' of worker life. At the inauguration of the Deutsches Haus, Hjalmar Schacht, the German Minister of Economics, announced that one of the main objectives of the pavilion was to demonstrate Germany's 'love of work'.[16] Yet the numerous paintings in the pavilion which depicted technological subjects – factories, railways, the construction of new highways and ships – deliberately excluded representations of the actual human labour involved in contemporary industry. Industrial scenes were portrayed as sites of 'anonymous

production', devoid of human presence. The depicted buildings 'seemed to spring up by themselves as if "at the Führer's command".[17] For example, in the paintings of the Krupp steel plant at Rheinhausen and the building of the Mangfall Bridge, the factory or construction site functioned as the heroic subject of the artwork.

The only representations of work in the pavilion were iconic depictions of idealized workers and allegorical conceits on the theme of labour. The stained-glass window above the podium illustrated those types of work that 'symbolize the German People':[18] industry was symbolized by a man holding a sledgehammer, an image of manual rather than technical production; intellectual work by the honoured Nazi architect holding a blueprint; agriculture by the shovel; and artistic work by a female figure holding a violin. The abstraction of labour was further elaborated in the two mosaics entitled *Work* and *Strength Through Joy*, the latter a reference to the Nazi leisure organization bearing the same name. The personification of work in the form of four isolated male icons (more than three times life size) elided any reference to the class context and political agency of the German proletariat. The companion mosaic illustrating leisure, which recalled allegories of the four seasons, reinforced the utopian image of nonalienated community. Exploiting the woman/nature paradigm, this mosaic also emphasized the gender division of labour and the unadulterated robustness expected of the Aryan female.[19] The static poses of the idealized racial types also reveal the Nazi desire to suspend time and obliterate the dynamic flux of social change. In reality, the Nazi government had viciously suppressed trade unions, frozen wages and pushed the worker to increased levels of production and efficiency.[20] The aestheticization of labour served to mask the condition of industrial production under National Socialism by submerging it in a discourse of *völkisch* tradition and lofty ideals.

Accordingly, the only painting in the pavilion which depicted men at work, Rudolf Hengstenberg's *Comradeship*, was intended as an allegory of class harmony. This canvas, which hung above the Podium of Honour, portrays the building of a house by an architect and his workshop – a common metaphor for

collective production. All references to modern construction methods and equipment have been eliminated. The didactic title emphasizes that the members of the team have been brought together by a shared dedication both to their project and to their leader. Yet it is clear in this painting that a peaceful hierarchy is nevertheless in place. The architect, framed by the repetitive triangular roof beams and distinguished by his more elegant attire, is unquestionably the figure of authority. The plain-clothed workers await directions from the central group of engineers, who bear the professional markers of jacket and tie. The painting's simple facture and schematic backdrop make its polemical message easily comprehensible.

The canvas can also be read as a commentary on the development of the new Nazi architecture and, in particular, on the building of the Deutsches Haus. The official guidebook, which refers to Hengstenberg's painting as 'the allegory, *Law of National Work*', stresses that comradeship is crucial for the successful synthesis of the arts into one totalizing vision: 'The architect does not claim a monopoly in the further development of this art. The painter, the sculptor and the craftsman work with him; for there is no question of imitation here, but rather of going ahead in one spirit, the spirit of high artistic will, of an unshakeable sense of responsibility and of technical mastery.'[21]

The semblance of unity in stylistic, spiritual and political terms was effected in the pavilion through the overproduction and synthesis of redundant visual codes. The manufacturing of a National Socialist identity for a world audience required an artistic veneer to mask the fundamental discrepancies between party rhetoric and political reality. Simultaneously, the orchestration of imagery also served to sustain the paradoxes that were essential to maintain the viability of Nazi ideology itself. National Socialism generated its affective force and mobilizing energy by fusing such oppositions as romantic anticapitalism and technological progress, historical continuity and revolutionary rupture. These tensions coalesced in the 'symbolic cocoon' of the Deutsches Haus, which couched National Socialist economic and political ambitions in the ersatz discourse of global peace, *völkisch* utopia and heroic servitude.

ALBERTO SÁNCHEZ

An Artist at the Crossroads *Josefina Alix Trueba*

It is almost impossible to define, in a few pages, the personality and the work of an artist of extraordinary distinction who is nevertheless virtually unknown. Hitherto a neglected figure, Alberto Sánchez Pérez deserves mention alongside the most important sculptors of the historical avant-garde. In this I find myself in agreement with Pablo Picasso, who wrote: 'Alberto's work has considerably influenced many artists of our time, many important artists. His theories and his work stimulated a creative restlessness and provided impetus for those avant-garde art movements in Spain which broke with academicism and reactionary conformism.'[1]

Alberto emerges as one of the most interesting of the creative figures produced by the early twentieth-century revolution in sculpture. His unique contribution lay in the forging of a new kind of sculptural feeling; its effects are still with us today. And yet his work has remained little known, for reasons that are entirely extra-artistic. One was the general difficulty that faced all those Spanish artists who stayed at home at a time when anyone who sought an audience for his work was expected to go to Paris. Another was Alberto's enforced exile in Moscow in 1938, and his consistent refusal thereafter to overcome his artistic isolation by leaving the USSR and settling in Western Europe. His work remained virtually forgotten until, in the 1970s, a series of exhibitions in Spain began to restore his reputation.

Alberto's work can be approached from more than one viewpoint. On the one hand, he created works that deserve to be appreciated as a fundamental contribution to twentieth-century European sculpture; on the other, he succeeded, where many of his contemporaries failed, in synthesizing the theory and practice of a totally modern art – involving no aesthetic concessions – with the ideology and thought of the revolutionary left. Alberto succeeded in fusing Surrealist and abstract techniques with meanings akin to realism, thus transcending that famous controversy of the 1930s, the *Querelle du Réalisme*.[2]

Finally, in the context of 'Art and Power', Alberto presents himself as a figure at the crossroads, exiled to the Soviet Union and therefore involved in one of the regions highlighted by this exhibition.

Sculptor of the Land

There is no space here to trace Alberto's life or career in detail; suffice it to say that, by his own almost unaided efforts, he developed from an almost illiterate baker into an artist of genius, recognized as such by the ablest contemporary critics. Born into a poor family in Toledo in 1895, he worked in several occupations as a child and arrived in Madrid in 1907. In 1915 he became a baker and learned to read and write. The rest was inspired intuition, work without rest and almost without sleep, solitary study, conscientious hours spent visiting museums.

In 1922 a chance meeting with the Uruguayan painter Rafael Barradas – the same artist who was to be so influential on the early development of Salvador Dalí – was the start of a close friendship that was crucial to the emergence of the sculptor's vocation. From then on, thanks to the art magazines, and *Cahiers d'Art* in particular, Alberto knew what was happening in Paris; and he seems to have had an limitless capacity to absorb what was said in café debates (*tertulias*).

At first he produced drawings based on popular tradition – children, figures, carnival masks, popular characters – which reflected a thoroughly progressive commitment to his roots in the people. In the 1925 *Exposición de Artistas Ibéricos*[3] he exhibited a series of totally figurative sculptures, constructed out of geometrical planes in a neo-Cubist manner. With these he achieved considerable success, which – had it not been for his highly self-critical personality and his constant desire to transcend himself – might have led him to become a maker of quite unremarkable figurative sculpture.

Two years later, however, we detect a fundamental transformation that points to the Alberto of genius. During those two years he probably deepened his knowledge of Picasso through magazines; he certainly learned about the Surrealist movement, whose revolutionary character must have attracted him at once. A drawing dated 1927 represents a sort of animal skeleton, sectioned to show another, similar figure inside. These are stony, fossilized, geological forms, as though straight from an archaeological dig. Alberto had now developed a fully defined visual language, within the realm of what I have called 'Telluric Surrealism'.[4] At that time, he was in fact the most advanced of all Surrealist sculptors: this drawing, with its clear rocky forms and its similarity to Picasso's stony and organic Surrealist phase, predates by one year Picasso's famous Cannes and Dinard drawings of 1928–29.

We know that Alberto had access to foreign influences; but the true source of this extraordinary burst of creativity was his intuitive and sometimes mystical passion for fusion with nature. This meant that, instead of allowing himself to be drawn along the path of the merely 'poetic' and 'automatic', he was encouraged to meditate on geology and cosmology; he was probably attending lectures at the Residencia de Estudiantes in Madrid on such topics as 'Inorganic Evolution', 'The Atom and its Mysteries', 'Geology and Landscape', 'The Art of Fossil Man' and 'The Formation of the New Age'.

It was Alberto's sense of total communion with telluric forces that underlay the work of what became known

1 Pablo Picasso, 'Presentación', in Peter Martin (pseud. of Luis Lacasa), *Alberto* (Budapest, 1964).

2 In the 1930s, the controversy over the need to produce realist art in response to social issues, and over the validity of Socialist Realism in the West, was especially intense in France and in Spain, especially after the triumph of Popular Fronts in both countries – as can be seen from the 1936 *Querelle du Réalisme* (see note 14) and the 1937 Congreso de Intelectuales de Valencia.

3 The *I. Exposición de Artistas Ibéricos* took place in the Palacio de Velázquez in the Parque del Retiro, Madrid, in 1925. It presented a highly diverse selection of Spain's budding *arte nuevo*. Its overall quality was unexceptional, but it became a landmark in the evolution of the Spanish avant-garde.

4 I use the term Telluric Surrealism to refer to a group of Madrid-based artists who took a fresh view of the earth and landscape of Castile; it includes Alberto Sánchez, Benjamín Palencia, Antonio Rodríguez Luna, and, to some extent, Maruja Mallo.

Alberto Sánchez Pérez, *Untitled (Two Animal Figures)*, 1927

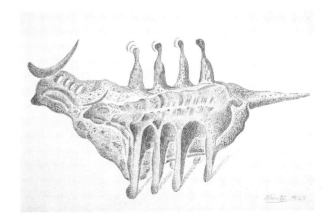

5 Now a suburb of Madrid, Vallecas was then a typically dry and arid village of the Castilian meseta.

6 Most of Alberto's pre-civil-war works were destroyed in his Madrid studio by bombing. Others disappeared at the end of the war.

7 Alberto Sánchez, *Palabras de un escultor* (Valencia, 1975), originally published in Arte magazine (Madrid, 1933).

8 Alberto Sánchez, 'Sobre la escuela de Vallecas', in Sánchez (as note 7).

9 Almost all of Alberto's works between 1927 and 1937 had descriptive titles to aid comprehension. Sometimes these titles were explained by the artist himself: 'Once I was on the Cerro Testigo when I heard an explosion on the plain towards Cinchón. I saw some rocks fly up. I went down the mountain to find the source of the explosion and I found some beautiful pieces of rock which seemed to contain trapped water. Gradually I took these rocks home . . . Following my idea of making works based on observation, I decided to make a sculpture with all the stones I had taken. I called this work *Bird of my Invention Made of Stones Created by a Blast.* One Sunday afternoon, on the way to Vallecas, I saw a perfectly twisted cloud with the Cerro Testigo at its base. This was the source of the sculpture called *Horizon Sculpture: Sign of the Wind.* As I followed the course of the Jarama to Vallecas late one night, a bird shot through space, and I could not make it out. Another night, at the same time, I saw the same bird again. This suggested the sculpture *Unknown Volume which Flies in the Silence of the Night.'* Alberto Sánchez, 'Sobre la Escuela de Vallecas', in Sánchez (as note 7).

10 Letter from Alberto to Luis Lacasa, September 1958.

as the School of Vallecas.[5] Accompanied by the painter Benjamín Palencia, Alberto would walk over the parched hills and fields round the village of Vallecas, generally in the high summer sun, following the tracks of the railway line to Madrid and searching for the essence of Castilian nature. He collected objects from the ground – sand, stones, pebbles and the like – which sometimes served to create or suggest sculptural forms. These walks in the environs of Madrid strengthened the 'visual faith' that Alberto derived, in his own words, from his admiration of Picasso above all, but also of Eisenstein, El Greco, Zurbarán, Cervantes and Velázquez. The experience was the cornerstone of his passionate love for nature: Vallecas, Toledo, the arid lands of Castile, ploughed furrows, mud, stones, pebbles, nocturnal colours, the sounds of the rural silence. His passion was not for landscape alone but for geological forces; it was a fusion of mysticism with the conscientious study of form, colour and material qualities.

Alberto harnessed this inner force to create a sculptural oeuvre that is among the most distinctive and imaginative of the twentieth century. His work holds its place alongside that of Jacques Lipchitz, Alexandre Archipenko, Alberto Giacometti, Constantin Brancusi, Hans Arp, Henry Moore – or it would, had he not been dogged by ill-fortune. He was always short of money; and – aside from his stubborn reluctance to seek fame by leaving the relative isolation of Madrid and, later, of his Moscow exile – the greater part of his sculptural work was destroyed during the Spanish civil war.[6]

In Alberto's article 'Words of a Sculptor', published in 1933, we can trace all the artist's important ideas. This passionate, vividly poetic declaration of faith reveals how his involvement with nature led him to extract its forms, colours and textures at source, from the roots, without any need to allude to a specific object:

'They say The City. I respond . . . The Countryside. With the emotions that clay, sand and quartz give me . . .

'May my amazement make me fall into the ditches; from rising and falling, may my body turn into mud . . . May the impression be so strong that I turn into a newly ploughed, wet lump of earth . . .

'Sculptures made of tree trunks scraped bare by bulls, among bodies of

Alberto Sánchez Pérez, *Bird of my Invention Made of Stones Created by a Blast*, 1929-30 (lost)

white wood like the bones of antediluvian animals . . .

'I want to put into my forms what is there to be seen at five o'clock in the morning . . .

'Forms made by water and wind on the rocks which were left balanced, alone, on mountain ridges, striped by the excrement and the beaks and talons of large birds.'[7]

All in all, Alberto's great contribution to contemporary sculpture was his proposal to make the whole earth into a sculptural object:

'I had no problem in going to look for these forms in the countryside, forms that I often found to have been drawn by men

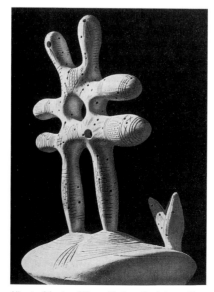

Alberto Sánchez Pérez, *Horizon Sculpture, Sign of the Wind*, 1930 (lost)

as they worked the land. All that I did was to lift these forms from the ground.'[8]

Alberto's ideas are significant in the context of Spain; they also surprisingly anticipate the concerns of contemporary Land Art. The result is a succession of extraordinary works in which natural forms are reinterpreted in an abstract language, with powerful poetic connotations that make them difficult to situate precisely within any specific movement. We can certainly trace an affinity with Surrealism, though their extraordinary attachment to the reality of earth and matter introduces a strongly realist element. Such works as *Horizon Sculpture, Sign of the Wind, Monument to the Birds, Three Feminine Forms for a Reedy River, Unknown Volume which Flies in the Silence of the Night, Bird of my Invention Made of Stones Created by a Blast* and *Animal Frightened by Its Solitude*[9] are readily comparable – and indeed almost contemporary – with Giacometti's works of the 1930s, or Arp's experiments with organic sculpture.

Alberto's insistence on explaining the content of his works through highly descriptive and poetic titles should be seen against the background of the tension between two factors: on one side his imaginative power, abundant creativity and avant-garde commitment; on the other his working-class origins and the revolutionary thinking that made him a man of the left. 'It was never my habit to separate art from social life,' he was to write from Moscow to the architect Luis Lacasa, 'and you know very well that there can be no social life without its political life. Right or wrong, this attitude has always been part of me, and it is the reason I am where I am.'[10]

Alberto and the Dispute over Realism

Alberto's attitude to the issue of realism was the cause of much controversy. Generally speaking, his contemporaries – or rather those dedicated to the cause of *arte nuevo*, new art – greatly respected and admired Alberto's work and personality. Nonetheless, dissonant voices began to arise, urging him to lean towards an art with clearly defined realist connotations. He was accused of producing an elitist art, when there never was an artist less elitist than Alberto.

His social commitment never wavered, but it never confined his artistic vision. In the most natural way, his work was a perfect representation of reality, and yet quite distinct from it. As he explained in his statement, 'On the Vallecas School': 'This led me to the conclusion that anything I could make in visual form already existed; so I saw very clearly that, as far as I was concerned, I could never create non-existent things. I calmed down. I tried to make simpler sculptures. And now I had no problem in seeking out these forms in the countryside.'[11]

Alberto was not the only artist at that time to confront the problem of reconciling his ideas with his artistic practice. A crucial debate took place in 1935 in the magazine *Nueva Cultura*,[12] which came out clearly in favour of placing art at the service of the people and the revolution. Issue 2 carried a lengthy open letter to Alberto himself, headed 'Situation and Perspectives of Spanish Art'. This was a harsh attack on the elitist attitudes of those artists who contributed to the creation of a bourgeois, anti-revolutionary and reactionary art; it had a considerable impact on young and committed artists. The letter advocated a militant realism, and demanded that Alberto make a clear and unequivocal commitment to revolutionary art. Issue 5 of *Nueva Cultura* carried a laconic reply from Alberto in which he affirmed his desire to help the artistic cause, while hinting between the lines that revolutionary art did not necessarily have to be realist.

In the same issue of the magazine, the Villecas School painter Antonio Rodríguez Luna replied as follows: 'Our works interest very few people: we have been involved in visual speculation devoid of human content . . . We must make a social art (note that I do not use the word "political") out of the bitterness, the struggles and the illusions borne every day by those in the countryside, mines and factories.'[13]

This debate was an anticipation of the one that was to take place in France in the following year: the famous *Querelle du Réalisme*,[14] which involved some of the major contemporary French artists committed to the victory of the Popular Front. In Spain, under the Second Republic of 1931, the brutal suppression of the 1934 miners' revolt in Asturias had forced a polarization of opinion in all

spheres – including, of course, the arts. Alberto was always fully committed to left-wing ideology; his position was clear, but he was not willing to do what was demanded of him: to abandon the artistic practice which he believed to be right in favour of figurative and militant realism.

For Alberto, this issue had come to a head two years earlier, in 1933, when he faced the stark prospect of abandoning art for as long as social and political conditions did not allow him absolute expressive freedom. In that year he gave a lecture called 'Art as Personal Transcendence'.[15] By transcendence he meant the overcoming of realism and of the figurative tradition, and the creation of completely new forms, in the broadest creative sense. However, he told his audience:

'The art of personal transcendence is not for the present. Now there are things that interest me far more than individual art: the remedy for hunger in Spain, and work for all, i.e. economic revolution. Until the triumph of the revolution is in perfect running order, the revolution of the spirit is not possible. In other words, to enter fully into the spiritual revolution, men and women must first be set free. This is possible if we all set to work on useful things, and by useful I mean work in laboratories, workshops, factories, fields. All else is self-indulgence.'

Overcoming Contradictions

This problem, which tormented Alberto for a considerable time, found a resolution when he published some hard-hitting political drawings in *Nueva Cultura*. This silenced the barrage of criticism. With the outbreak of the Spanish Civil War soon afterwards, ideological positions became clearer, as most artists almost instinctively put their art at the service of the anti-Fascist cause.

Alberto's was one of the most unusual cases. With the situation at its most critical, he was invited to contribute to the Spanish Pavilion at the 1937 Paris International Exhibition.[16] He lived there for a few frenetic months, working on the Pavilion and achieving one of his most treasured goals: that of meeting Picasso. The rapport between the two was immediate. Alberto admired Picasso, and Picasso admired Alberto, especially his

sculpture *The Spanish People Have a Path that Leads to a Star*.[17] It must have been one of the supreme moments of Alberto's life. At last he could work freely alongside those artists whom he admired, and with whom he could debate as an equal. He also met Fernand Léger, Lipchitz and Giacometti, with all of whom he had much in common.

In his magnificent and densely evocative concrete sculpture, 13 metres high, Alberto succeeded in transcending the contradiction between realism and abstraction as no one had done before. The great shaft, which appears to be made of something neither wholly mineral nor wholly vegetable, is in fact the plant closest to a rock, a kind of giant cactus, rich in symbolism: an apparently dry object, yet full of moisture; seemingly defenceless in its forced stillness, and yet able to defend itself against attack: all in all, a living being that grows and gathers strength under the most adverse conditions. The work appears to belong somewhere between abstraction and Surrealism; and yet, for all its symbolic complexity, the viewer readily grasps its meaning. The cactus spirals up from the ground towards the sky like a snake, which can simultaneously be read as a feminine form, as a mother and child – all these are symbols of life – or even as a powerful arm lifting a clenched fist up to the sky. Alberto reaffirmed his love for the earth by carving and etching wavy lines like furrows into the surface, or small dots, like the marks on pebbles or insects, creating a cosmic and stellar feeling.

In 1938, having finished work at the Spanish Pavilion in Paris, Alberto returned to Spain and spent several months in Valencia, the seat of the Republican government, where he produced some extremely interesting stage sets. In these he maintained his Modernist commitment, transforming landscapes into quasi-Surrealist forms. The sets were for a militant propaganda play called *Las Germanías de Valencia* (Valencia Slang). The play itself was a failure, but the audience applauded Alberto's decor. This, along with the sculpture in the Spanish Pavilion in Paris, was proof that it was possible to produce an art for the people without falling into coarse realism and bad taste.

11 See note 9.

12 *Nueva Cultura* was published in Valencia between January 1935 and October 1937. Its editorial committee consisted of José (Josep) Renau, the poster designer, photomontage artist and Director General of Fine Arts during the civil war; the author Angel Gaos; Antonio Deltoro; and Francisco Carreño Prieto, a draughtsman.

13 'Los artistas y Nueva Cultura', *Nueva Cultura*, no. 5 (June–July 1935), 13–14.

14 The interesting arguments on realism put forward by French artists during meetings in 1936 have been republished in Serge Fauchereau, ed., *La Querelle du Réalisme* (Paris, 1987). This book includes statements by Léger, Marcel Gromaire, Le Corbusier, Jean Lurçat, Louis Aragon, André Lhote, Max Ernst, Jean Cassou, Delaunay, Goerg, and others.

15 Alberto Sánchez, 'El arte como superación personal', in *C.N.T.* (Madrid), 7 February 1933.

16 For more on this subject see Josefina Alix Trueba, exh. cat. *Pabellón Español: Exposición Internacional de Paris, 1937* (Madrid: Centro de Arte Reina Sofía, 1987).

17 After the Exhibition closed, Alberto's sculpture and Miró's mural were packed for return to Spain, but at some point they disappeared; nonetheless, we have not lost the utopian hope of finding them some day. In 1986, the plaster model that Alberto made in Paris, to be enlarged and cast in cement, was found in store at the Palacio Nacional de Montjuic, Barcelona. It is now in the Museo Nacional Centro de Arte Reina Sofía in Madrid.

18 Unpublished text written in 1948. Property of Alberto's family.

Alberto Sánchez Pérez, *Caucasian Partridge*, 1956–58

Exile, and a New Beginning

At the end of 1938, the Republican government sent Alberto to the Soviet Union to teach drawing to some of the thousands of Spanish children who had been sent there as refugees. What was intended to be a temporary visit ended in permanent exile, following the defeat of the Republic by General Franco's forces.

Alberto's time in Moscow, until his death in 1962, was not easy. He left Spain with the dream of participating in a project in which he firmly believed, and in Moscow he was well received. He did not find it especially hard to adapt, though till the day he died he longed to return to Spain. Alberto's roots in the soil of Spain went so deep that in exile an important part of himself was missing. Interestingly, he never learned Russian. He lived and worked in Russia, was in touch with Russian artists and made many friends among them, taught drawing, designed some important stage sets; his work is represented in the Pushkin Museum in Moscow and in the Theatre Museum; he was a design consultant for Gregori Kozintsev's famous film *Don Quixote*, and an adviser to the Gitano Theatre in Moscow – and all this without speaking Russian!

However, it was many years before he could once again become the Alberto of *The Spanish People Have a Path that Leads to a Star*. The historical situation was one that favoured and indeed imposed

'Socialist Realism'. In this he seems to have acquiesced. Circumstances demanded it, and he was not about to make works that flouted the party line. Respecting his principles, and in accordance with the stand he had taken in 1933, he therefore chose to abandon his creative work almost entirely.

From 1939 to 1956 he did little more than paint still-lifes and landscapes on his own, at home. In these he learned to master oil paint and brushes, materials he had not used in Spain. His skills improved significantly, in a period that he treated as a sort of apprenticeship. Around 1948, he even produced a kind of self-criticism, in an interesting unpublished text in which he attacked all so-called bourgeois painting from the Barbizon School to Cézanne:

'A clear case of the dehumanization of art is that of a Frenchman [Cézanne], solitary in life and thought, fiercely rural. For him, life was leisure: to contemplate the landscapes produced for him by facile dreams, landscapes that he believed to be born in his mind; to collect good fruit to smell, eat, and then paint. Man's inner condition, the life of thoughts and feelings, means nothing to him; it does not exist . . .

'He, Cézanne, considers . . . that a human being is the same as a bit of brass piping from an old stove. This is the attitude of a slave-driver to his slaves, only interested in the money he can make from a sale; this is the Fascist idea of Man . . .

'I do acknowledge, albeit in small doses, that the Barbizon School was a milestone in the development of a new visual light; but this light did not shine with the brightness needed to help mankind to build a better world: it developed from

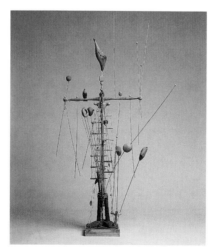

Alberto Sánchez Pérez, *Signpost on the Belaya River*, 1957–58

the bourgeois mentality and led to confusing abstract worlds . . . in vice, in idle, visual contemplation, in the corrosive and degenerate sensuality of monstrously cultured and moneyed ex-humans, in the absurd and criminal anarcho-bourgeois imperial-fascist metaphysics. This is what led us to collections of human lampshades, tearing the skin from the corpses of anti-Fascist prisoners in the hideous German death camps.'[18]

It is fascinating to see how, in this psychological situation, Alberto never falsified his own artistic impulse: he merely conducted his explorations in private rather than in public. He was often visited by Spanish friends, and occasionally by his great friend Pablo Neruda, who encouraged him to continue on the path he had followed in Spain and in Paris. They urged him to leave the USSR and move to France, where he would find more outlets for his abilities. But he refused to go: he would leave only if it were to return to Spain with uncompromised freedom and integrity.

From 1956 onwards, the situation in the USSR changed drastically. Alberto recovered his previous spirit and set to work with a will. In the remaining six years of his life, he was able to recreate the rich and magical world he had left behind in 1937. He made a series of masterly works directly inspired by his Spanish period, but with renewed energy and with all the skill and control over materials that he had gained through his solitary years of apprenticeship.

Works like *Signpost on the Belaya River*, *Skylark Song*, *Caucasian Partridge* and *Bull* represent a magnificent synthesis of his many years in the USSR and his deeply Spanish spirit. In what were still sombre circumstances, he advanced and reaffirmed himself as an artist of boundless courage.

We are left with the figure of Alberto as an artist of integrity, a genius of forceful principles who could survive and be reborn amid the ashes to which Power had tried to reduce him.

Translated by Gabriel Pérez-Barreiro

CONTEMPORARY VOICES *Compiled by John Willett*

Notes of a Tourist at the Exhibition, 1937 *Amédée Ozenfant*

Paris wore its tinge of crystal and pearl, reflecting the spring periwinkles.

I confess. I came to Paris because I had to. I would take the opportunity to look round the Exhibition; not that I am particularly keen on trampling through the rubble; it's all unfinished, they tell me.

As I had to see Monsieur X on business I rang him from Le Bourget. Meet in two hours' time. To which he added: 'So you're coming to see our ridiculous exhibition. When I think back to that wonderful Colonial Exhibition, and how it displayed the whole grandeur of the French Empire before the eyes of the world, then I have to blush for France. To think how those criminals of the Popular Front have dragged our poor country downhill!'

This made me want to go to the Exhibition right away, since X is one of those complacent idiots. You only have to follow the exact opposite of their judgments to get close to the truth.

The Porte Monumentale. Monstrous gewgaws dangling from the belly of the Place de la Concorde. This gate is as hideous as what they called the 'Art Nouveau Salamander' of 1900, whose absurd belly opened at the same point. In childhood I was shocked; the gate is pure Lalique.

But then: as soon as I could see the huge spectacle of the Exhibition it bowled me over, and how! Staggering: talk of grandeur! It is huge, varied, orderly, majestic and absolutely natural, relaxed, young. What a shock . . .

I spent the whole afternoon walking round it.

At an outdoor café, with the Seine at my feet, I jotted down my initial reactions:

From the first instant I was so swept away that I forgot my appointment with the idiot. I called him to say I had been held up and he should come and join me at the Exhibition; instead, as I had hoped, he preferred to put our meeting off till another day.

Swept off my feet, that's me.

And yet I have lived half my life in Paris. I have been lucky enough to see the most beautifully built-up places in the world: the Bosphorus, the Kremlin, the banks of the Neva, the Grand Canal, the Roman Forum,

and so many other poems composed of stone and natural features. And here, before my eyes, was the Exhibition. Deliberately I evoke the images of these cities; I bring them up one after the other; I superimpose them on reality like transparencies. And the reality supports these dream pictures enhanced by my memory; what my eyes are seeing is in no way ridiculous when tested against such famous places.

If this temporary city had been built of materials that last, it would remain as one of the most beautiful groups of buildings in the world. If we still had the Forum in its original state, you can be sure that it would be the Forum that would look a shambles, disorganized and in bad taste.

TUESDAY. The plan of this exhibition is admirable, the circulation of crowds and visual impressions perfect. And even this huge city, at the heart of a great capital, barely interferes with its permanent traffic, so attractively ingenious is the network of walkways and underpasses provided by the town planners. Paris and London could learn from their example.

I came for an hour; I'm still here at midnight, captivated by the often excellent architecture of the various buildings, nearly all of them gay or witty.

In architecture, as with all the other arts and techniques, it is our advances that are being shown, advances definitely gained, consolidated. Not many radical innovations. [The Arts Déco exhibition of] 1925 brought novelty; 1938 shows its integration, the general acceptance of a sane new architecture.

New materials? General use of those tried out and proposed twelve years back, now used as a matter of course: in 1925 their trials were clumsy, didactic, awkward, showy, stunning, prophetic, aggressive; made acceptable now by relaxation, sometimes too much of it, leading to an indifferent competence however successful. A purity too sure of its methods to be the point of departure for any radically new advance: in short, a point of arrival. Hence, in a certain sense, a socialization of past temerities. And thereby a certain very satisfying coherence, which in reality only

Spanish Pavilion, 1937

arises from similarity of conceptions, general acceptance of solutions, community of taste and other factors – and not too much individual genius.

Each period seems to have its particular task: in architecture, broadly speaking, the period 1900–14, a period of preliminaries and contradictions: Jugendstil, Hennebique, Loos, the Perrets; Gropius in 1914, anticipating the vacuum-cleaner period from 1918 to about 1922. Then the period of practical aesthetic functionalism from 1923 to 1925, and the return of decoration with the exhibition of 1925. And from then on a whole intensely active sequence of mutual osmosis and endosmosis between all these different trends.

1937 is the moment at which, all these forces having sorted themselves out (and to some extent become neutralized), a dominant style, free of prickles, could flower and flourish. An exquisite style, as in the Swiss Pavilion, with its rationally constructive elegance and healthily breathing volumes, or the Austrian Pavilion etc. . . . It is perhaps in the timber structures (Japan, Finland above all) that the most ingenious constructive ideas are to be found. For the architects and engineers handle steel with an easy boldness that shows a perfect familiarity with the limits of what is possible, achieving the elegance earned by all extreme solutions. The mastery of wood and steel shown by these architects and engineers is on a level with that of their Gothic precursors in the Sainte-Chapelle, who mastered their materials so as to conquer light.

'There's no spiritual element here!' yell the reactionaries.

Need I describe all the palaces, objects,

Railway Pavilion, 1937: façade and interior with mural by Robert and Sonia Delaunay

machines, sculptures, paintings? There is such an invention as photography.

Indeed photography plays an important part. Its discovery was largely due to painters. The early photographers started by creating those admirable works that have barely been surpassed since; then the technique was monopolized by halfwits blinded by the automatism of the darkroom, and there was an undignified exploitation of the medium by commercial bulb-squeezers, amateurs, pseudo-artists, who used it to make mock paintings or documents fit for short–sighted process-servers. The exhibition shows that the artists have recaptured control of photography, that this medium is neither more nor less than a means of pictorial construction, like glazes and colours, which serves the creative imagination – once it is at the service of a great artist.

There are here a great many objects, of all sorts, where the employment of machines, those systems of natural forces controlled by the intelligence, has rendered them visually and intellectually perfect.

Once again the spirit has found a kind of incarnation in the materials. The materials give body to the spiritual element.

WEDNESDAY. I am on the Trocadéro bridge looking at the Seine.

Oh, what a bore these little youths in berets can be! Here come three more of them who point at the monstrous German pavilion and say: 'Smashing! You can see those people have got a Chief!'

Here is another lot: 'Why can't we do the same? What are we waiting for? Heil Hitler!'

But the Exhibition is not the work of such simpletons. It is the work of that aristocracy drawn from the world's best,

those skilled workers of every class and speciality, starting with the higher mathematicians and their incomprehensible doctorates, the engineers with their daring experiments, boffins of all sorts, the most qualified workmen: all those whose contribution was 'in the spirit' of the Exhibition: the desire to do a good job, the will of the French Popular Front, a moment delegated by the International of ideas, art and labour. That International which is so menaced by the International of money and lovers of the past, in their alliance against the forces of evolution.

Some people, I know, would like to have seen a radical demonstration of ultra-modern building. Such as the Eiffel Tower provided in 1889. The fact is that, as I said, we are not in a moment of innovation, but one of taking stock.

Today, I take the facts as they present themselves to my view. When reality makes so good a case for itself it is only right to accept it. Confronted with such an expenditure of effort and its high degree of success, I have neither the wit nor the heart to be critical.

After all, when did the state last have the courage to tackle such an immense enterprise (550 metres)? A period that can be resumed in sonnets is not terribly reassuring. When it ventures into books of a thousand pages, buildings measured in hundreds of metres, then we have some hope.

So what about the USSR, Germany? Are we to applaud?

It is not size that worries me: size suggests strength, courage, power. And without courage, what are we to hope for? There are cases where size becomes a kind

International Exhibition, 1937: views northward and southward from the Eiffel Tower

of beauty. But I don't want to say more, having undertaken not to run anybody down. The overall effort is admirable, though I had better look away from the German pavilion if I am to keep my promise.

SATURDAY. Today I went round the Museums and Exhibitions, a rapid visit to get an overall view. *Chefs-d'oeuvre de l'Art français* in the galleries of the future museum of living artists; *Maîtres de l'Art indépendant* in the Petit Palais, where a lot of space is given to the great generation of our elders; finally that perfect show at the Jeu de Paume with its lucid presentation of *Origines et Développements de l'Art international indépendant*.

In a sense, the French School is at one and the same time the curator of the permanent conditions, the *sine qua non*, without which a work of art has no reason to exist, and the eternal liberator from tradition. The revolutionary spirit endemic in France serves art, by continually influencing it against parasites and in favour of new departures.

Given the state of our tame democracy and its habit of shielding the second-rate, the public authorities have gone as far as

they could towards the relegation or burial of the worst pillars of artistic reaction (though without being able to eliminate those who consider themselves to be among the 'moderns'). Indeed the 'left wing' of the arts, for better or worse, has never been so firmly and officially supported as now.

One of France's scandals, finally, is about to end: French art, that great visual poem which needs no translation, one of the best ambassadors of our culture – modern art is at last to get its museum in Paris.

Modern art (along with beauty products) is one of the last French exports to represent the country abroad: living abroad as I now do, I can testify to that. It will be possible to see French painting *in France*! A government prepared to take risks, a well-disposed Director of the Beaux-Arts, have found that the Exhibition provides a way of putting a stop to an ancient and idiotic situation.

SUNDAY. I am writing at a little table in the Spanish Pavilion's Catalan tavern. Painful. A show of Spanish suffering. The caption to a moving photograph of orphaned children reads: 'All they had in the world was their parents, and their misfortunes have left them with the worn features of men.'

The huge *Guernica* of the great Spanish artist stands before me.

This man is always up to the situation. We have known times when the world was at ease; everyone was diminished. Our present period is great, dramatic, dangerous. *Guernica* is worthy of it. Worthy without showing off, without hidden meanings or word-games that only thirty-four initiates can understand. Making no concessions to the dangerous tendency of parties of the left to overrate the 'subject' and promote platitudes so long as these are 'on the right lines'; often underrating the poetry and music of the visual in favour of the most banal themes; and thus neglecting the powerful social effect of truly beautiful things, which always are in some sense revolutionary in themselves. For what is so special about the power of a beautiful work, if not the ability of certain forms to move the senses, and so bring intellectual and moral conviction?

Guernica makes one *feel* the terrible drama of a great people abandoned to medieval tyrants, and makes one *think* about it. The master has used only such means as are proper to the visual arts, and yet he brings the whole world to grasp the great Spanish tragedy, if they have eyes to see. The proof:

A little bourgeois woman passed by my table and went down to the first floor, where the photographs of the Spanish war are displayed: you see children who have been massacred by Franco's Christians and Moors. The woman said to her daughter: 'How dreadful all that is! It makes my back tickle, as if a spider had been put down my neck.' Then, looking at *Guernica*, she told her child: 'I don't know what that's meant to be,

but it gives me a very queer feeling. Queer, it makes me, just as if somebody's cutting me in pieces. Come on, let's go! War is terrible . . . Poor Spain!'

And off she went, dragging her child by the hand, in the vague direction of the crowds.

The idiots proclaim that 'the Exhibition lacks spiritual values; they've been banned by the materialists of the Popular Front'.

But what heartfelt passion and commitment were needed to bring off this Exhibition! So much is called for to make even the smallest enterprise come off properly; and this one was not small. And it has come off really well. The Exhibition offers a whole lesson in ethics.

Some names? After these few days, I give up. It would be as shocking as having generals put their name to a battle.

What is great here, and emerges strongly from this strongpoint, is the fact that the victory is the work of thousands of beings who contributed to its conception, to the construction of all its elements, from the biggest to the most basic; and that all these people were more or less creators. Consciously or not, they were obeying that deep and generous movement, that impetus of youth, gaiety, enthusiasm which inspired France on the emergence of the Popular Front and, by rousing foreigners and Frenchmen alike in one single movement of the heart, wits and muscles, brought them

to contribute to this vast display of the state of human progress at a moment of tragedy for the world.

Amédée Ozenfant, 'Notes d'un touriste à l'Exposition', *Cahiers d'Art* 12 (1937): 242ff. (slightly abridged).

Translated by John Willett

The magazine also reviewed the three painting exhibitions mentioned in the article; Christian Zervos, its editor, wrote some blistering 'Réflexions sur la tentative d'esthétique dirigée du IIIe Reich' in the previous number (12:51ff.).

The painter Amédée Ozenfant (1886-1966) had been associated with Charles-Edouard Jeanneret (Le Corbusier) in the launching of the Purist movement after the First World War, and their book *Après le Cubisme* linked this to the increasingly monumental Cubism of Fernand Léger. From 1920 to 1924 they edited the magazine *L'Esprit Nouveau*; then, in 1929 Ozenfant published his principal book, *L'Art*, a wide-ranging study of the origins and philosophy of modern art. His paintings figured in the 1970 Tate Gallery exhibition *Léger and Purist Paris*.

Ozenfant was an international figure, who in 1937 was teaching at the French Lycée in London. He married a Russian, painted murals for Erich Mendelsohn's house in Berlin before 1933, and taught at the New School in New York during the Second World War, when he did some broadcasting to France, including a children's programme called 'Ozenfant aux enfants'.

Palace of Light, 1937; interior with mural by Raoul Dufy

Palace of the Air, 1937: interior

Poster for EUR, *c.* 1941 (detail)

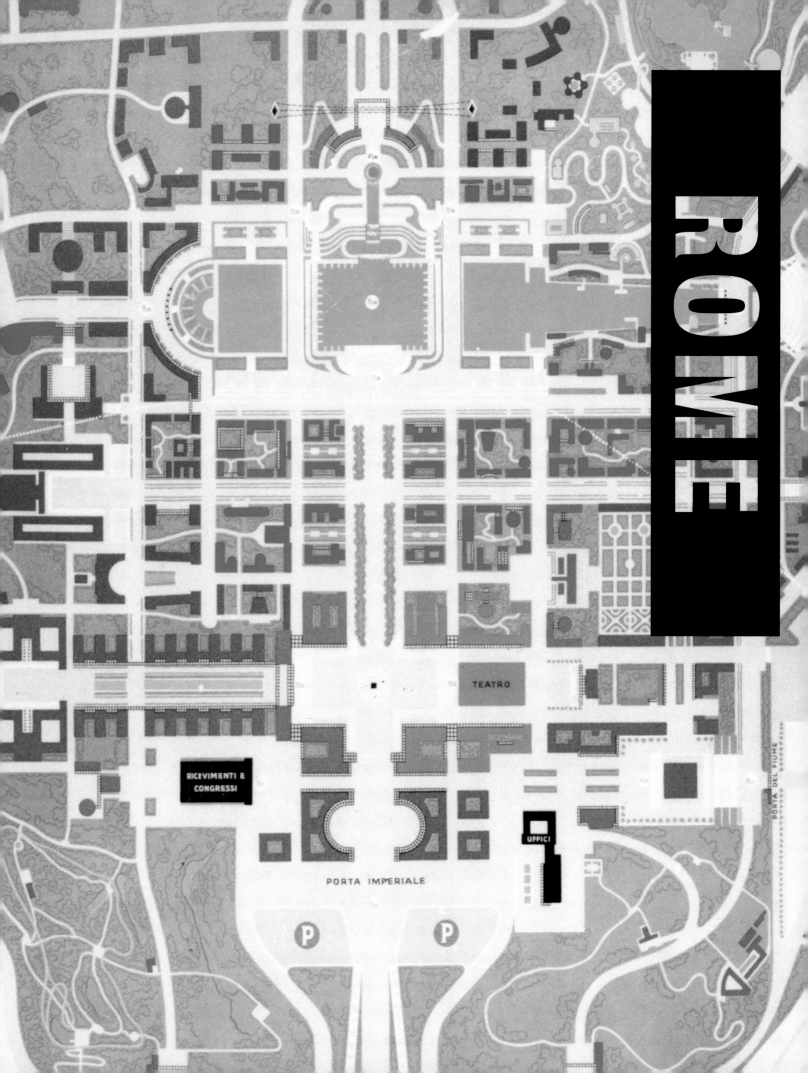

ROME

RICEVIMENTI E CONGRESSI

TEATRO

UFFICI

PORTA IMPERIALE

PORTA DEL FIUME

P   P

ROME RECLAIMS ITS EMPIRE

Architecture   *Tim Benton*

1 Text by V. Emanuele Bravetta, music by Giuseppe Blanc, 1925; the music carries a dedication to 'Benito Mussolini, standard-bearer of Rome'. Reprinted in A. V. Savona and M. L. Straniero, *Canti dell'Italia Fascista (1919–1945)* (Rome, 1979).

2 Mussolini, speech proclaiming the Empire, 10 May 1936, reproduced as a lapidary inscription in the *Mostra Augustea della Romanità*, 1937–38.

3 As the decade progressed, a distinction was made between 'internationalism' (Jewish, Bolshevik, un-Italian) and 'universality' (based on Rome's claim to primacy); see Giorgio Pini, 'Difesa della Razza', in Paolo Orano, *Inchiesta sulla razza* (Rome, 1939), 190.

4 This was not resolved until the Lateran Pacts of 1929, when the Papacy accepted the Italian state with its capital in Rome. Mussolini allowed the Church a central role in education, much to the disgust of some of the most ardent Fascists.

5 Some fifteen churches were destroyed, and a large number of historic buildings were dismantled and rebuilt elsewhere. See Spiro Kostoff, *The Third Rome: Traffic and Glory* (Berkeley, 1973).

6 In 1925, Mussolini established the Governatorato of Rome with great new powers. Governors were mostly drawn from old Roman aristocracy, but Giuseppe Bottai was also Governor for a period.

7 Margherita Sarfatti, *Segni, colori e luci* (Bologna, 1925), 238.

8 Giorgio Ciucci, *Gli Architetti e il Fascismo* (Turin, 1989), 81.

9 In 1929, the GUR (Group of Roman Urbanists) designed garden cities for workers and for new business quarters, leaving the centre free to 'glow in all its beauty, while the new city should proclaim the national rebirth'. Ciucci (as note 8), 97–98.

Rome reclaims its Empire / *Roma rivendica l'Impero*
The hour of the Eagle has struck / *L'ora dell'Aquil sonò*
Trumpet blasts salute the flight / *Squilli di trombe
                                              salutano il vol*
From Capitol to Quirinal / *Dal Campidoglio al Quirinal*
Earth, we want to dominate you / *Terra ti vogliamo
                                              dominar*
Sea, we want to navigate you / *Mare ti vogliamo navigar*
The Lictorate returns as the signal / *Il Littorio ritorna
                                              segnal*
Of power and civilization / *Di forza, di civiltà!*
    (March of the Legions, 1926.)[1]

'The Italian people has created the Empire with its blood, will make it fertile with its labour and defend it against whomsoever with its arms. In this certain hope, raise high, legionaries, the standards, the steel and your hearts, and salute, after fifteen centuries, the reappearance of the Empire on the fated hills of Rome.'[2]

From the moment when it was decided to locate the capital of unified Italy in Rome (1870), Italian politicians and urbanists were faced with contradictory pressures. The city offered two claims for universal authority: the Roman Empire and the Papacy.[3] Any attempt to recruit these two great authorities in support of the regime inevitably pointed up deficiencies: initial efforts to develop colonies led to the humiliating defeat of Adowa in Ethiopia, while the Papacy at first refused even to recognize Rome as the capital of the new state.[4] Furthermore, any attempt to modernize a city whose population grew from 244,000 in 1871 to over a million in 1931, to provide offices, wide thoroughfares, public transport and utilities, meant destroying the churches and disturbing the archaeological sites on which this reflected authority depended.[5] To make matters worse, Mussolini and successive Governors of Rome,[6] not to say the whole Chamber of Deputies and the nation's press, felt it necessary to interfere at every stage in any proposed change to the nation's heritage. Some excellent architects and urbanists contributed to the architectural discourse in Rome in the 1930s. Many of their best ideas were dashed on the rocks of these fearsome circumstances. As Margherita Sarfatti wrote in 1925: 'In Rome architecture is made and unmade rather more than elsewhere.'[7]

As Giorgio Ciucci has observed,[8] the key issues of planning in the 1930s had been well established before the Fascist era. From the outset, it seemed to be very difficult to find a middle way between conservation and demolition; the monument to Vittorio Emanuele II and its associated clearances and road widening (1884–1910) had already involved cutting a swathe through medieval and Renaissance Rome.

The Plan of 1931, produced under Mussolini's eye by a committee representing divergent views, was necessarily a compromise. Nevertheless, certain assumptions gradually won general acceptance. First, archaeological sites (especially those of the Augustan era) were central to the presentation of Fascism as a revival of Empire. Second, a triumphal way (the via dell'Impero) would have to be created to link the piazza Venezia (where Il Duce had installed his state apartments in 1929) with a new road to Ostia and the sea (via del Mare). Third, a monumental development to the north (housing, sports arenas, new roads and bridges) should form a gateway to the modern city; this became the Foro Mussolini. Fourth, the southern approaches along the via del Mare would need a great feature, which turned out to be the exhibition city of EUR. Fifth, the working class should be moved out of the centre into new districts on the west, east and south.[9] Though the demolition envisaged was little more than in earlier plans, this amounted to a dramatic reshaping of the urban landscape.

Mussolini was keenly interested in monumental interventions in the city centre.[10] In a speech in 1925, inaugurating the Roman Governatorato, he declared, somewhat wildly:

'In five years Rome must be seen to be marvellous to all the people of the world: vast, ordered, powerful, as it was in the first Augustan Empire. You must continue to liberate the trunk of the great oak from everything which still smothers it. Open up spaces around the Augusteo [Mausoleum of Augustus], the Theatre of Marcellus, the Campidoglio, the Pantheon. Everything which has grown up in the centuries of decadence must be swept away. In five years, from piazza Colonna, across a great area, should be visible the mass of the Pantheon.'[11]

In the event, the first three of these great demolition jobs had been achieved by 1943.

Demolishing buildings to expose antique ruins ran counter to the tradition known as the *barocchetto*, based on detailed study of Roman building traditions, to which many of the most influential academic architects were committed. For example, Gustavo Giovannoni (for many years head of the School of Architecture) was bold enough to protest at the plan (1934) to carve a slice through the Borgo (the Renaissance quarter between the Vatican and the Tiber) to make the via della Conciliazione.[12] But this broad avenue lined with obelisks was a typical example of urbanism celebrating political achievements: too important to be allowed to fail. Its completion allowed Mussolini to claim for his regime the reflected authority of the Church, and to stamp the relationship with his own authority.

In any investigation of Fascist interventions in Rome, it is important to realize that the debate between young and old, traditionalists and Modernists, 'ins' and 'outs', remained open until the last years of the 1930s. Nevertheless, there was a drift towards Neoclassical and imperial imagery. The key dates are 1936, with the capture of Addis Ababa and the declaration of the new Italian Empire, and 1937–38, when Mussolini's visit to Germany and Hitler's visit to Italy sealed the Axis alliance.[13]

Mussolini, the new Augustus

Long before the declaration of Empire on 9 May 1936, Mussolini had begun his programme to celebrate Rome's first Emperor, and to bring every site associated with him to the surface of the city.[14] In 1926, the archaeologist G. Q. Giglioli began work on the Mausoleum of Augustus (known as the Augusteo), a huge circular ruin in a rather rundown area near the river. The latest use found for this building had been in 1907 when, equipped with a steel roof, it became the Auditorium (the largest assembly hall in the city). In June 1927, Enrico del Debbio and a group from the Federazione Fascista dell'Urbe proposed a plan for the site; despite the clearing of 1,000 square metres of land, the stated aim, in line with Del Debbio's *barocchetto* interests, was to create picturesque vistas through old buildings and not to build 'pompous and inexpressive new palaces'.[15] The 1931 Plan swept away these subtleties and framed the Augusteo with a huge rectangular piazza lined with new buildings. On 22 October 1934, Mussolini made a speech outlining the project and, seizing a pickaxe, cried 'And now let the pickaxe speak!' The image (in film, photograph and painting) of Mussolini energetically wielding a pickaxe proved an effective means of projecting the demolition of the old Rome as a 'revolutionary' Fascist act. The iconography of the pickaxe and the pneumatic drill became almost as strong as that of the dagger and machine gun in monumental art of the period.

As the project developed, new ingredients were added: a Latin inscription recording part of the testament of Augustus (the *Res gestae*), copied from the Temple of Augustus in Ankara, and, most important, the reconstruction of the Ara Pacis,[16] at Mussolini's urgent behest, on a site between the Augusteo and the river (p. 122). This was completed in 1938, and a glazed protective building designed to present it to the public. A copy of the *Res gestae* was attached to the forward face of the raised podium.

The architect Vittorio Ballio Morpurgo was given the task of building the piazza, lined with precisely the 'pompous and inexpressive palaces' which Del Debbio had resisted. The buildings were decorated with inscriptions, reliefs and mosaics linking Imperial Roman achievements with Fascist ones. One of the largest squares in Rome, the piazzale Augusto Imperatore represents an enormous effort of archaeology, demolition and new construction. It fails to make the desired propaganda impact, largely because Morpurgo's buildings deaden rather than fire the imagination.

More successful was the *Mostra Augustea della Romanità*, opened on 23 September 1937 (in the same Palazzo delle Esposizioni where the youthful exuberance of the young Modernists had celebrated the tenth anniversary of the March on Rome in the *Mostra della Rivoluzione Fascista* of 1932). It ran for a year, being visited in May 1938 by Hitler and his retinue.

10 Mussolini, speech of 31 December 1925 at the Campidoglio, in *Opera Omnia* 22:47–48.

11 The idea of blasting through a space between piazza Colonna (the business centre of the city) and the Pantheon was taken up by a number of planners but fortunately abandoned. The liberation of the Theatre of Marcellus from the houses which surrounded and engulfed it (1926–28) formed part of the general clearance of churches, houses and palaces required to make way for the proposed via del Mare, which would connect piazza Venezia to Ostia and the sea. D. Manacorda and R. Tamassia, *Il piccone del Regime* (Rome, 1985), 171–81.

12 Giovannoni had adopted the *barocchetto* style to dignify two suburban workers' housing projects, at Monte Sacro and Garbatella. Ciucci (as note 8), 85–86.

13 Alex Scobie, *Hitler's State Architecture* (Pennsylvania and London, 1990), 26–31.

14 Giuseppe Bottai, *L'Italia d'Augusto e l'Italia d'oggi* (Rome, 1937), stresses the similarity of purpose of Augustus and Mussolini; E. Balbo, *Protagonisti dell'Impero di Roma, Augusto e Mussolini* (Rome, 1941; written 1937) was more explicit, comparing Mussolini's achievements with those of Augustus one by one. (Cited in Kostoff, as note 5, 302.)

Mussolini starts demolition work for via dell'Impero, 1928–32

Piazza di Augusto Imperatore after clearance and rebuilding in 1934–38

The restored *Ara Pacis* in its pavilion by Morpurgo

The theme of imperial renewal was emblazoned over the portico in the words of Il Duce: 'Italians, let the glories of the past be superseded by the glories of the future!'[17]

Two hundred fragments of sculpture and two thousand plaster casts, made from original pieces scattered all over Europe, were used to reconstruct the Rome of Julius Caesar and Augustus. The second large room in the exhibition was entitled the Sala dell'Impero and included a full-size reconstruction of the pronaos of the temple of Augustus at Ankara, with copies and explanations of the *Res gestae*. Room XXVI was entitled 'The immortality of the idea of Rome. The rebirth of Empire in Fascist Italy'. The catalogue insists: 'With

Fascism, by the will of Il Duce, every ideal, every institution, every Roman building, has once more come to be celebrated in the new Italy; and, after the epic undertaking of the soldiers on African soil, on the ruins of a barbaric empire is reborn the Roman Empire.'[18]

Inscriptions from Mussolini, Dante and ancient Roman authors lined the hall, alongside images of recent Fascist rallies and new constructions. Three triumphal arches illustrated the supposed continuity of the Roman ideal: the Arch of Constantine (celebrating victory over Maxentius and the beginnings of official Christianity), the Arch of Bolzano (a war memorial designed by Marcello Piacentini, celebrating the victory over Austria) and another Fascist monument, the Arch of the Fileni in Cyrenaica, designed by F. di Fausto, recording Il Duce's visit to Libya and the inauguration of the Libyan coast road (Strada Litoranea). The regime's new towns (Littoria, Sabaudia and others) were illustrated as 'truly Roman works of Fascism', followed by illustrations of the Foro Mussolini ('a truly classical centre of physical instruction').[19] As a permanent reminder, marble relief maps of the growth of ancient Rome from its humble origins to world Empire, and of its modern Fascist resurgence, were affixed to the wall of the Basilica of Maxentius (they're still there). The collection of sculptures and casts became the core of the Museo della Civiltà Romana, which still exists in EUR.

The via dell'Impero (now via dei Fori Imperiali) presented the most awkward consequences of Mussolini's cultural policy.[20] To make a wide, level avenue (700 metres long and 30 metres wide) linking the Colosseum and the Arch of Constantine with the piazza Venezia, involved not only covering over large tracts of the recently excavated Imperial Fora, but also levelling a hill (Collina della Velia) to open up a view of the Colosseum. Mussolini was clear about his motives: 'Rome now has in the centre a street truly designed for its great military parades, which until now have been restricted to the periphery or the countryside.'[21]

It was originally named via dei Monti; Mussolini impulsively renamed it via dell'Impero on the night of 27–28 October 1932, anticipating the declaration of Empire by three and a half years. Inaugurated on 28 October 1932 with a parade of 17,000 wounded Blackshirt veterans, the via dell'Impero was a platform from which to view the ruins of Imperial Rome, but also a brutal act of destruction of those same ruins. More importantly, it constituted a significant act of delusion: an attempt magically to attract the powers of ancient Rome to the fledgling Fascist Empire.

Palazzo del Littorio

The next step was to have been the construction of the symbolic and actual heart of the regime, on the via dell'Impero, facing the Basilica of Maxentius. The Palazzo del Littorio was to incorporate the headquarters of the Fascist party, a suite for Mussolini, a permanent Museum of Fascism (based on the *Mostra della Rivoluzione Fascista* and including a shrine to the Fascist martyrs), and a podium for speeches (*arengario*) facing onto the new via dell'Impero. Some designs also found a place for the reconstructed Ara Pacis.[22] The effect would have been to move the spiritual centre of Fascism from piazza Venezia to a midpoint on the via dell'Impero.

When the architectural competition was announced in December 1933, it seemed as if Mussolini meant to balance the heavily retrospective context of the via dell'Impero with a bold, new building in a modern style. Only twelve months before, describing the façade of the *Mostra della Rivoluzione Fascista* (p. 39), the exhibition organizer had declared: 'There was a need in Rome of such a gesture of salutary violence . . . And thus the Duce called it "superb and typically Fascist", then adding that the permanent seat for the future Museum of the Fascist Revolution that will rise on the via dell'Impero should be "a modern monumental construction".'[23]

Mussolini was still prepared to defend the Modernists in May 1934, when they were attacked in the Chamber of Deputies by a chorus of ageing and mostly ignorant *gerarchi*,[24] led on by Roberto Farinacci. In a tumultuous debate, disparaging references were made to the two recent competitions won by modern architects (Florence railway station and the new town of Sabaudia);[25] but both these projects were dear to Mussolini, representing his modernizing drive to put Italy back on its feet. He made a point of inviting the architects concerned to the Palazzo Venezia and mentioned this fact in a press release (10 June). This was taken by both P. M. Bardi (of the Quadrante group) and Giuseppe Pagano (of *Casabella*) as a sign that modern architecture would be accepted as the official Fascist style.

The jury for the Palazzo del Littorio competition was chaired by Achille Starace, secretary general of the Fascist party, with Piacentini as secretary and rapporteur. There were two other architects (both reactionary classicists), two archaeologists, the Governor of Rome and other political figures. Pagano welcomed the initiative at first, writing in *Casabella* in January 1934:

'It will be a great struggle. Once again two worlds will be up against each other: on the one hand a static world, in love with formalism and rhetoric, which defines itself as defender of *Romanitas*, of the supreme laws of the spirit and of the Italian tradition, and on the other hand the world of life and progress which will draw health from the raw and eternal purity of simple things and which will try to express the ideal of Italian modernity by means of the proportions and rhythms of today without recourse to the dimensions of the dinosaurs, the rhetoric of the Spanish baroque or the formulae of Vitruvius.'[26]

Significantly, after studying the brief and the site in detail, Pagano subsequently refused to enter the competition himself, arguing that it was impossible for modern architects to compete with the Imperial Fora, the Basilica of Maxentius and the Colosseum.[27]

Several modern architects did submit designs, however, and this competition did indeed turn out to be a watershed in the struggle to find a monumental style for the regime. Over a hundred groups submitted designs, and 71 were selected for a major exhibition on 23 September 1934. Pagano was unimpressed: 'an isolated nucleus of modern life . . . cannot possibly be . . . realized without undermining the archaeological integrity of the area'.[28] Piacentini, however, writing in his journal *Architettura*, declared that at last Italian architecture had found its 'character' (one combining tradition and innovation), thanks to the unifying spirit of Fascism.[29]

The jury reported to Mussolini in December, and it seems that he himself played a role in the final decision.[30] The result was a compromise, listing fourteen projects by both modern and traditional architects. Among the younger architects there was a team including Terragni, Lingeri, Sironi and Nizzoli, and there were projects by Giuseppe Samonà, Luigi Moretti, Adalberto Libera, Mario de Renzi and La Padula, Ridolfi and Rossi. Among the academic architects were Del Debbio, Foschini and Morpurgo.

The problem of combining revolutionary Modernism with classicizing monumentality taxed all the architects. Libera tried to repeat his success at the *Mostra della Rivoluzione Fascista* of 1932, using the Fascist tower and pulpit motifs (*Torre del Littorio* in the form of a fasces; projecting *arengario*). The façade was deployed in a huge curve around this central dominant feature. His *Sacrario dei Martiri* would have reproduced exactly the *Sacrario* in the *Mostra*. A number of the competing groups offered two solutions to the problem, an uncompromisingly modern one and one more symbolic and monumental in character. One

18 Speech by Professor Giulio Quirino Giglioli, in Roberto Vighi, *Mostra Augustea della Romanità* (Rome, 1937), viii.19 Ibid, 363.

19 Ibid, 365.

20 Begun in 1928, it was inaugurated by Mussolini in 1932. The road was meant to continue south towards San Giovanni but was never completed. Manacorda and Tamassia (as note 12), 181–94.

21 Ibid, 181.

22 For example, Moretti's Project A and Gio Ponti's unpremiated design. S. Danesi and L. Patetta, *Il razionalismo e l'architettura in Italia durante il Fascismo* (Venice, 1976), 156.

23 Dino Alfieri, catalogue of the *Mostra della Rivoluzione Fascista*, January 1933, cited in Richard Etlin, *Modernism in Italian Architecture, 1890–1940* (Cambridge, Mass., and London, 1991), 413–14 (Etlin's translation).

24 Literally 'hierarchs', these were Mussolini's most trusted colleagues, almost all of whom had shared his experience of the trenches and street warfare. Those hostile to Modernism were Farinacci, Giunta and Teruzzi; see F. Brunetti, *Architettura e Fascismo* (Florence, 1993), 257.

25 Etlin (as note 24), 429–30. In this heated exchange, the most reactionary party activists attacked not only the Rationalists but also the modernizing academic architecture of Piacentini, helping to cement the working alliance between Piacentini and the young Rationalists.

26 G. Pagano, 'Per il palazzo del Littorio, l'opinione di "Casabella"', *Casabella*, no. 73 (January 1934).

27 G. Pagano, 'Palazzo del Littorio, atto prima, scena prima', *Casabella*, no. 79 (July 1934).

28 G. Pagano, 'Il concorso per il palazzo del Littorio', *Casabella*, no. 82 (October 1934).

29 M. Piacentini, 'Il concorso nazionale per il progetto del Palazzo del Littorio e della Mostra della Rivoluzione Fascista in via dell'Impero', *Architettura*, special number, 1934.

30 *Popolo d'Italia*, 30 December 1934, cited in Brunetti (as note 25), 259.

31 Carminati, Lingeri, Saliva, Terragni, Vietti, Nizzoli, Sironi.

Milanese group (including Terragni)[31] entered a 'Project B' which in its uncompromising modernity matched that of the Quadrante group including the Milanese architects Banfi, Belgiojoso, Danusso, Figini, Peressutti, Pollini and Rogers (BBPR). In their report, this latter group wrote: 'The acceptance by Il Duce of the best realizations of the regime – Sabaudia and Florence railway station – has closed the latest debates on the relationship between Fascism and modern architecture. It is the last nail in the coffin of all those stylistic pyrotechnics, resulting either from well-intentioned backwardness or from opportunism.' [32]

Of great interest was the Terragni group's 'Project A'.[33] In their report, they wrote: 'We have not forgotten that a great historic era of architecture was before us in "superb archaeological parade". The discourse of the wall from Imperial Rome might have made us compromise, had not our certainty of being sincere in dignified construction, independent of servile imitations, promoted in us a faith to find a spiritual continuity with that which venerable marbles and ponderous carcasses of temples and basilicas express so eloquently.'[34]

The Terragni group's approach to the problem of the Roman ruins and the demands of Modernism was to take the Roman theme of the wall, and an 'antique' material (red porphyry), and transcend structure and material in a modern idiom (p. 142). The façade to the via dell'Impero was treated as a curved sounding board, 80 metres long and pierced in the middle to create an *arengario*. But the properties of wall and material were reversed. Instead of providing a massive support, the wall was suspended from two gigantic reinforced concrete trusses, leaving the ground floor largely clear apart from four 'reinforced granite' piers. The stone

blocks of the façade were held in tension by bands of steel which fanned out from the ends of the supporting trusses along the lines of isostatic tension. The report illustrates experimental tests using a 'Fenolite' model under tension and seen by polarized light. The visual effect is rather like a complex spider's web of lines of force, as if reflecting the waves of energy from the leader's oratory. Ciucci's comment is revealing:

'The abstraction is total, and the myth which the building can transmit (the power accumulated in Mussolini, the transparency of the Fascist idea, the order reconstructed by Fascism) exists in the way artifice refers to real values: the lines of isostatic force, transparent walls, golden section rectangles are devices which take on these values only when they communicate with myth.'[35]

The growing rift between Pagano and the Quadrante group was sharpened by this competition. Pagano's call for a 'moral' architecture of coherent, anti-rhetorical social purpose was apparently undermined by the more extreme Modernists, whose work could easily look just as obsequious and unworldly as that of the compromised Neoclassicists.

It was decided that a second competition should be held, to which these winning groups alone should be invited. But by the time this was held, the brief had changed completely.[36] It was decided to move the building to a less central site, next to the Pyramid of Cestius on the Aventine, where it would have framed the southern approach to the city. By now, Mussolini must have decided that his state apartments must remain in piazza Venezia, the site of so many glorious speeches. The building was now simply to be the party headquarters, and the party secretary was left to select the architects, with help from a committee (including two traditional architects, Giovannoni and Muzio and Pietro Aschieri, who had a foot in both camps).

A decision was announced, in October 1937, in favour of Del Debbio, Foschini and Morpurgo. Of six other schemes deemed worthy of praise, only Moretti and Ridolfi were among the moderns, and both had adapted their style to make a massive, monumental effect. Terragni's group and that of Libera, De Renzi and Vaccaro (who had teamed up) were not mentioned. In three years, the consensus had moved dramatically away from Modernism. After some revision, the Del Debbio project was eventually built on the Foro Mussolini site on the northern outskirts, where its ponderous monumentality forms a poignant contrast with the graceful earlier work by the same architect. In the second competition, all the projects include a *torre*

32 'Concorso per il Palazzo del Littorio e della Mostra della Rivoluzione Fascista in Roma, Relazione', 1934, (printed version of the typescript report submitted with the competition project).
33 The prime authorship in the two projects by this group has been contested. Relying on the memoirs of Terragni's associate Luigi Zuccoli, Giorgio Ciucci accepts that Terragni put more effort into Project B, while Project A was worked up by Luigi Vietti. Ciucci (as note 8), 147.
34 Ibid.
35 Ibid, 148. See also M. Tafuri, 'The Subject and the Mask. An Introduction to Terragni', *Lotus International* (September 1978), 5–31.

A. Carminati, P. Ligeri, M. Nizzoli, E. Saliva, M. Sironi, L. Vietti, G. Terragni, Project A for first Palazzo de Littorio competition, Rome 1934

del Littorio, monumental sculpture and mural art, and all are roughly symmetrical.

Despite the general trend towards bombastic monumentality, one Fascist intervention in the heart of Rome remained refreshingly original. In the long grassed hollow that marked the Roman Circus Maximus (behind the Palatine hill), Libera, De Renzi and Guerrini were commissioned to design a semi-permanent exhibition space in June 1937. The Fascist party used these buildings to house a succession of extremely important propaganda exhibitions, dealing with the key themes of motherhood, childhood, state-organized workers' leisure and autonomous Italian industries (textiles and minerals).[37] The exhibitions were extremely popular and were well served by a building style as lightweight, airy and modern as anything in Europe. Other architects, including Luigi Moretti, contributed pavilions to the site.

Terragni and Lingeri returned to the via dell' Impero site in 1938, when a Milanese friend and patron proposed to sponsor a 'Danteum' which would both commemorate and symbolically represent the *Divine Comedy*.[38] The architects made some designs, and on 10 November 1938 they were received by Il Duce, who told them to develop the scheme in a model. Although nothing came of this, the designs are of great interest in showing Terragni's approach to monumental symbolic architecture. The whole building can be seen as an architectural metaphor of Dante's journey through Hell, Purgatory and Paradise, the latter represented in a golden section room with glass columns. The Fascist message is underscored by subtle reminders of Dante's obsession with revival of Empire: leading off Paradise is a long corridor with, at the end, the Imperial eagle. Terragni's fervent enthusiasm for Fascism allowed him to remain within the bounds of political acceptance, while the extreme abstraction of his design methodology has allowed his work to escape the political context in which it was formed.

Terragni, more than most, was able to reconcile the apparently unbridgeable conflicts of the Fascist era between modern and classical, spiritual and material, political and apolitical; but those able to make any sense of his intentions were extremely rare. By contrast, the simple metaphor of reviving the Roman Empire had a popular appeal which could be easily transmitted through popular culture:

> Columns and arches return / *Tornan colonne ed archi*
> To the glorious ruins, just as one day . . . /
> *I ruderi gloriosi, come un giorno . . .*

From the Capitol, proudly spread her wings /
> *Dal Campidoglio, fiera, libera l'ale*
The august bronze eagle / *L'aquila augusta e bronzea*
Of Imperial Rome / *Della Roma imperiale!*
They shake, the ancient walls / *Fremon le vecchie mura*
Of the Colosseum, pock-marked and black /
> *Del Colosseo, screpolate e nere*
They let out a Hosanna of ardour / *Un osanna levano*
> *di ardore:*
Rise up again, eternal Rome / *risorgi, o Roma eterna,*
The Lictor returns. / *Torna il littore.*
(Popular song, *Torna il littore.*)[39]

The Foro Mussolini

The story of the attempts to turn the centre of Rome into a dramatization of Fascist values is one of an ultimate loss of nerve by the authorities, a failure of the architects to resolve the almost irreconcilable tensions in the situation, and a gradual drift towards heavy, oppressive classicism as a metaphorical celebration of the new Roman Empire. In the story of the Foro Mussolini, the shift towards monumentality took a different form.

The Foro Mussolini occupies a large site on the right bank of the Tiber, to the north of the city, near the antique Roman Ponte Milvio. Apart from a rifle range, and army and youth summer camps, this beautiful site at the foot of Monte Mario had been relatively little exploited, since there were substantial drainage problems and annual flooding from the river. Monte Mario had acquired sentimental value for the party faithful because

36 One thing that contributed to the changed atmosphere was a publication of all 71 winning designs for the first project, *Il nuovo stil littorio: I progetti per il Palazzo del Littorio e della Mostra della Rivoluzione Fascista* (Milan, 1936). Piacentini and the artist Cipriano Oppo contributed articles. In different ways, both authors identified the future trend with a compromise between classicizing eclecticism and outright Modernism.

37 *Mostra delle Colonie estive e dell' Assistenza all' Infanzia* (1937), *Mostra del Tessile Nazionale* (1937–8), *Mostra del Dopolavoro* (1938) *Mostra Autarchia del Minerale Italiano* (1938–39). Maria Luisa Neri, *Mario de Renzi* (Rome, 1993), 124–27.

38 Thomas L. Schumacher, *The Danteum* (Princeton, 19##), 36ff.

39 Words by Giuseppina Zei, in Savona and Straniero (as note 1), 185.

40 Mussolini laid the foundation stone on 5 February 1928. Antonella Greco and Salvatore Santuccio, *Foro Italico* (Rome, 1991), 7.

41 As president of the Marble Consortium of Carrara, Ricci was thought to have an interest in these commissions.

Mario de Renzi, Adalberto Libera, G. Guerrini, exhibition buildings in the Circus Maximus, Rome 1937

42 Giuseppe Pagano, *Casabella* (December 1933).

43 By 1936 Del Debbio had designed, in addition to the Academy of Physical Education and the Stadio dei Marmi, the Stadio dei Cipressi and the first variant of the Olympic stadium which replaced it, the Casa della Balilla Madre, the southern youth hostel, designs for the Duca d'Aosta bridge, a building of storerooms, a Heliotherapeutic Colony, variants of the Museum of Fascism and the Colossus, the Music Academy and a theatre for classical dance, an open air theatre.

44 At first this was referred to as the 'Casa Balilla sperimentale'; see Ricci's report to Mussolini, 22 May 1935 (Santucci and Greco, p. 12). This title appears on Moretti's drawings now conserved in the Archivio Centrale di Stato and dated March 1935. Moretti, then fresh out of architecture school, had played a role in drafting the Rationalist RAMI manifesto of 1931.

45 The Arengo Nazionale would have held 400,000 people, on the parade ground and in the stands. Moretti's drawings study the seating arrangements in terms of a tension between the laws of acoustics, which would have provided a heart-shaped plan, and the requirements of regimented men on parade. The result was a stand with raised 'wings' to amplify and direct the sound.

46 A 'Programma dell'Esposizione Universale e Mondiale di Roma XX Annuale' was drawn up and promoted by Giuseppe Bottai; see *E'42: Utopia e Scenario del Regime* (Rome, 1987), 1:19.

Enrico del Debbio, Accademia fascista di Educazione fisica, 1926–32

the Blackshirts had camped out here during the March on Rome. The Opera Nazionale Balilla (ONB) had been set up in 1926 to organize the leisure time of boys and girls from the age of six to fourteen, and the Foro Mussolini was conceived as a headquarters and training ground for the whole movement.[40]

One of Mussolini's close followers, Renato Ricci, had been placed in charge of the ONB, despite his youth (he was still only thirty-five when the Foro Mussolini was inaugurated in 1932). Ricci came from Carrara, and his passion for marble statues led to a profusion of life-size or over-life-size statues throughout the complex.[41] In particular, the Stadio dei Marmi (seating 20,000 people) was lined with 60 statues, 4 metres high, donated by different cities in Italy (p. 147). A monolithic obelisk, designed by Costantini and inscribed with the legend MUSSOLINI DUX, marked the entrance to the site. Regular newspaper articles and film bulletins charted the progress of this stone, the largest single piece of marble ever quarried in Carrara, to the reinforced concrete scaffolding ramp where, amid much excitement, it was dragged into the vertical and finally set free. Similarly, when Paniconi and Pediconi designed a fountain with a large marble sphere representing the Universe, the monolith was tracked all the way to the site in the popular press. These were not simply wonders of engineering and transportation, but evocations of the achievements of the Roman Empire and the Popes, who had resited obelisks around the city.

Ricci was an enlightened patron of architecture, at the head of an organization which built schools and sporting establishments all over Italy: 'If you see the letters ONB lording it over a building, you can cheerfully assume that building to be the most modern in town, the most up-to-date, the one which, at least in international terms, would be seen to represent a real step on the road to progress. And in fact, in 80 per cent of the cases, you would be right.'[42]

Del Debbio was chosen to design the overall scheme and its key structures. He seems to have played a key role in selecting this beautiful site, as opposed to one near the University City. It was to contain a Royal Fascist Academy of Physical and Youth Education (to train PE instructors for schools all over Italy), a Musical Academy and a range of sporting facilities, including two stadia, banks of tennis courts, rugby and football pitches, swimming pools and a fencing academy. In addition, lodgings for visiting athletes and a large space for a camp site had to be found. Del Debbio brought to his buildings traces of his *barocchetto* style: red rendered walls, set off by rather Mannerist tabernacle windows and niches enclosing statues in white marble. Del Debbio insisted on keeping his buildings as low as possible, to recreate the classical effect of an organic unity with nature. Both stadia were to be hollowed out of the ground. In the Stadio dei Marmi only the ring of statues breaks ground level, while the first design of the Stadio dei Cipressi uses the natural slope of the ground to create additional seating on one side only.

When the first phase was inaugurated by Mussolini in 1932, with a gymnastic display, the Foro Mussolini presented itself as a centre for youthful sporting endeavour.[43] In the next four years, however, its character began to change substantially; this change was partly a cause and partly an effect of a change in the artistic leadership of the project. Luigi Moretti, a young Roman architect, had been given the task of designing the fencing academy at the western end of the site.[44] He changed the southern approach completely, challenging the modest, vernacular quality of Del Debbio's Foresteria Sud with the majestic, marble faced mass of the new building. Moretti's interpretation of the demands of monumental architecture was to plan his buildings in a very modern way, using the latest structural methods to create incredible interior spaces flooded with hidden sources of light, while presenting to the outside world a smooth, closed exterior. The so-called Palestra del Duce (Mussolini's private gymnasium. located above the covered swimming pool) glistens with translucent marble polished to a mirror-like surface and minutely detailed (pp. 127, 146). In his redesign of the piazzale Imperiale, an avenue lined with mosaics and a guard of honour of marble plinths which leads the visitor into the site from the obelisk to the fountain of the marble sphere, Moretti injected an element of elegant monumentality.

More dramatic still was the scheme for a statue 100 metres tall (including plinth), representing Mussolini as

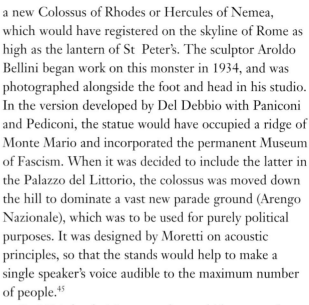

a new Colossus of Rhodes or Hercules of Nemea, which would have registered on the skyline of Rome as high as the lantern of St Peter's. The sculptor Aroldo Bellini began work on this monster in 1934, and was photographed alongside the foot and head in his studio. In the version developed by Del Debbio with Paniconi and Pediconi, the statue would have occupied a ridge of Monte Mario and incorporated the permanent Museum of Fascism. When it was decided to include the latter in the Palazzo del Littorio, the colossus was moved down the hill to dominate a vast new parade ground (Arengo Nazionale), which was to be used for purely political purposes. It was designed by Moretti on acoustic principles, so that the stands would help to make a single speaker's voice audible to the maximum number of people.[45]

In 1936 the decision was taken to bid to stage the 1944 Olympics in Rome, and Moretti was commissioned to provide an even more ambitious plan, covering an area twice as large as the original. In addition to the Arengo Nazionale, Moretti also added a 'Cella Commemorativa' – a little chapel dedicated to the Fascist martyrs – and a house of Italian-German friendship. This whole project was coming to signify much more than the education of Fascist youth.

In 1937, after a long power struggle, Ricci was sacked and the ONB replaced by the GIL (Gioventù Italiano del Littorio), under the direction of the party and its secretary, Starace. The GIL never captured the imagination as the Balilla Youth had done, substituting bureaucratic state control for enthusiastic leadership. Most of the ambitious plans for the Foro Mussolini, from 1937 to 1943, came to nothing, although in 1938 a hurried redecoration of the 'Olympic Stadium' with pylons and eagles was arranged for Hitler's visit.

When the decision was taken to build the Palazzo del Littorio here, in 1937, the final twist in the saga had been completed. Del Debbio himself objected to the new site, knowing that his large palace would fit badly into the Foro Mussolini. The building was redesignated Ministry of Foreign Affairs in 1940 and left unfinished until after the War.

EUR

The attempt to hold the Olympic Games in Rome in 1944 was closely linked to the even more ambitious project to hold an 'Olympics of Civilization' in a new city, EUR, to the south of Rome. The origins of the idea date back to November 1935.[46] Even before the site, on

Aroldo Bellini, head of the bronze statue of *Fascism*, 1934

Luigi Moretti, Mussolini's gymnasium, Foro Mussolini, 1936–37

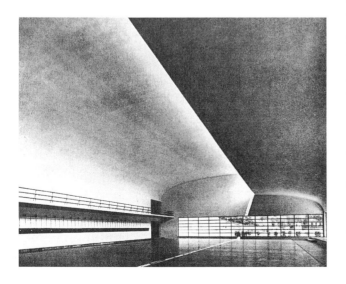

Luigi Moretti, fencing hall, Foro Mussolini, 1934–36

127

a plateau above the Magliana plain, was selected, a project for a *Mostra della Civiltà Italica* had been proposed by BBPR and found considerable support. In December 1936, Vittorio Cini was placed in charge of the project.

In January 1937, Pagano, Piacentini, Piccinato,[47] Rossi and Vietti were commissioned to produce a plan for a new city which would host a Universal Exhibition. Buildings built for the exhibition would then remain as museums, ministries, business centres and housing. The project brought together the GUR group's earlier plan to decentralize Rome and Piacentini's master plan to provide a monumental feature on the southern approaches from Ostia. At first, the group worked together in a spirit of great optimism and innovation – or at least so Pagano reported in *Casabella* in June 1937. Some of the early drawings show a modern city with glass-fronted office blocks and a thoroughly modern approach to circulation, comparable with the most advanced planning in Europe. As time passed, however, Piacentini managed to take an increasingly tight hold on the project, until the others were finally dismissed in 1940. Cini evolved a clear distinction between the permanent buildings, designed to display a durable monumentality (and classicism) which would not go out of fashion in fifty or a hundred years, and the temporary exhibition buildings, where the young architects could experiment with a more modern style.[48] The final version of the model was rigorously symmetrical, aligned along an axis culminating in a great reinforced concrete arch designed by Libera.

As competitions were announced for the major buildings, it became clear that the young architects were going to have to adapt their style if they were to get the work. A violent polemic in the press, aimed at 'liquidating once and for all the subverters of Italian architecture, contaminated by intrigue by the word from Moscow',[49] softened up the public. Even when architects like Moretti, Quaroni, Libera, La Padula,

Figini and Pollini or Pediconi and Paniconi won competitions, they thought it prudent to adapt to the new climate; if they didn't, their designs were changed by Piacentini and his technical office. Moretti, for example, designed a theatre for the piazza Imperiale which grew more and more austerely Neoclassical as the design developed.

All this was too much for Pagano. In a violent outburst, in the course of which he damns most of the recent official architecture of the regime (the 'massacre of the quarter of the Mausoleum of Augustus, the immoral gutting of piazza S. Pietro'), he finally turned on Piacentini:

'But the most abundant wrongdoing is that of Marcello Piacentini, who, with a critical stance based on ancient Rome and with infantile library references is managing to "monumentalize" the future exhibition of Rome . . . In the hands of this artificial Vitruvius, architectural criticism has resolved itself into such a mindless exaltation of the grossest formalisms that one fears for the death of good Italian traditions. Good taste, moderation, harmony, clarity, simplicity and honesty have had to commit Hara Kiri on the altar of the most grotesque exhibitionism.'[50]

In the end, EUR is by no means without interest. Marble columns (often gigantic monoliths) and endlessly repeated arches characterize the surfaces of the buildings, but the scale and sense of harmonious spatial development are still striking. When the debacle of the War put an end to all plans for a Universal Exhibition in 1942, the site was left littered with cut marble and unused columns. Libera's Palazzo dei Ricevimenti e Congressi and the Palazzo della Civiltà Italiana were more or less complete, along with half a dozen other buildings. There is enough here to imagine what an architecture of Roman gravity and modern imagination might have looked like.

48 Report of June 1937, in *E'42* (as note 48), 1:45.

49 'Vampa', writing in *Perseo*, 1 July 1937; in *E'42* (as note 48), 1:49.

50 Giuseppe Pagano, 'Potremo salvarci dalle false tradizioni e dalle ossessioni monumentali?', *Costruzione-Casabella*, no. 157 (January 1941).

EUR planning office, perspective of intermediary project, December 1937

Adalberto Libera, Palazzo dei Ricevimenti e Congressi, EUR, modern detailing and granite columns

'Mussolini is always right': façade of the *Autarchia* exhibition, Rome

ALL ROADS LEAD TO ROME

Simonetta Fraquelli

All Roads Lead to Rome is the title of the central panel of Achille Funi's monumental mural, commissioned for the atrium of Adalberto Libera's conference hall, the Palazzo dei Ricevimenti e Congressi, at EUR (p. 136). The EUR was the new quarter built for the planned World's Fair, the Esposizione Universale di Roma of 1942. Flanked by three Roman emperors on her left and by three popes on her right, the goddess Roma presides enthroned, with the Tiber god at her feet, representing the city, in a mythological continuum, as the centre of all cultures. The subject of Funi's fresco, painted in an academic classical style, perfectly summarizes the intended apotheosis of the Fascist regime, which was doing everything in its power to earn a secure place in Rome's glorious history.[1] The proverbial title of Funi's mural can also be read today as an ironic metaphor for the regime's attempt to dominate and centralize cultural activities during the second decade of its rule, a period during which *romanità*, the cult of Ancient Rome, became dominant.

The mythical status of the city and its symbolic resonance had been part of the Italian, indeed the European, psyche since the time of the Roman Empire. When Italy was unified in 1861, the new state was soon identified with the Roman past, representing as it did a period of Italian unity and cultural supremacy. It was not long before Rome's colonial and imperial traditions were also emulated by the new nation – during the Libyan campaigns of 1911–12, which coincided with the fiftieth anniversary of Italian unification.

The early years of Fascist rule were not characterized by colonial aspirations but by an incitement to political action, to internal revolt and an aggressive and violent rejection of Italy's recent Liberal and democratic past. After Mussolini's accession to power in 1922, references to ancient Rome and Roman imagery, such as the party symbol of the fasces or *fasci littori*, a bundle of rods with an axe, which symbolized the power of the Roman consuls and magistrates – together with eagles, Roman standards and she-wolves – gradually infiltrated many aspects of everyday life in Italy from advertising to school textbooks, even to SPQR inscriptions on drain covers.

The initial, revolutionary phase of Fascism ended with the proclamation of the dictatorship in 1925, which marked the establishment of the totalitarian,

tyrannical regime. At this time a centralized party machine was set up in Rome, and the Fascist symbiosis with the Eternal City became more substantial. Until the Lateran Treaties of 1929 the Church resisted Fascist authoritarianism. However, Mussolini then made a financial pact with the Papacy, whereby its temporal sovereignty was restricted to the Vatican, and Catholicism was confirmed as the religion of the state.

By 1932, when his 'Dottrina del Fascismo' was published in the *Enciclopedia Italiana*,[2] Mussolini was drawing on ancient Rome as a model for his nationalistic and imperialistic aims. With himself, a 'condottiero-like' figure, at Italy's helm, he envisaged the Fascist nation asserting its power and dominating the Mediterranean world; he began by proclaiming the Adriatic Sea as *Mare Nostro* (Our Sea). The image of Il Duce as the 'Saviour of Italy' who was 'always right' (*Mussolini ha sempre ragione*), was primarily imposed through the propaganda machine of the Ufficio Stampa (later the Ministry of Press and Propaganda). Apart from the obvious allure of his oratory, endless photographs, films, busts and equestrian monuments of Il Duce were used to seduce the Italian people.

And yet the regime's policy regarding high culture remained ambivalent. At no time did Mussolini set out a clearly defined state art. During the 1930s, led by what seems to have been a mixture of heightened opportunism and ineptitude, he supported a pluralistic approach towards the fine arts largely defined by the 'enlightened' Fascist Giuseppe Bottai, who became Minister of National Education.[3] An intelligent and cultivated man, Bottai expressed his views on culture early on. In 1927, his review *Critica Fascista* launched a debate on the notion of a possible Fascist art, and Bottai summarized the results: with an emphasis on *italianità* or 'Italianness', a Fascist art should represent the continuation of the grand Italian tradition; it should not simply imitate the styles of the past but should infuse Italy's abiding characteristics of order, solidity and clarity with a modern sensibility. The state should not attempt to influence individual creativity by imposing formulaic or stylistic preferences. Instead, it should provide a framework that would secure the livelihood of artists while supervising the quality of production.

Although Bottai's directives afforded artists a certain creative freedom, the state's gradual establishment of

1 Much of the general discussion of the relationship between artists and the Fascist regime contained herein is indebted to the seminal works on the period including Rossana Bossaglia, *Il 'Novecento italiano': Storia, Documenti, iconografia* (Milan, 1979); Philip V. Cannistraro, *La fabbrica del consenso* (Bari, 1975); Laura Malvano, *Fascismo e politica dell'immagine* (Turin, 1988) and Fernando Tempesti, *Arte dell'Italia fascista* (Milan, 1976); also articles in the exhibition catalogues *Anni trenta arte e cultura in Italia* (Milan, 1982) and *Italian Art in the 20th Century* (London: Royal Academy of Arts, 1989).
    See Simonetta Lux, 'Oppo: La Committenza' in exh. cat. *E 42 L'Esposizione Universale di Roma. Utopia e Scenario del Regime* (Rome: Archivio di Stato; Venice, 1987), 2:218–20, and Monica Pignatti Morano, 'Il Palazzo dei Ricevimenti e Congressi', in *E 42: L'immagine ritrovata* (Rome: Archivio di Stato, 1990), 18–41.

2 *The Enciclopedia italiana* was begun in 1925. The project was supervised by Giovanni Gentile, a philosopher and minister of public instruction. See Philip V. Cannistraro, 'Fascism and Culture in Italy, 1919–1945', in *Italian Art in the Twentieth Century* (as note 1), 149–54.

3 See Ester Coen's essay on Giuseppe Bottai in this catalogue, p. 178.

rigid formal structures ensured a covert and insidious form of control. As part of the Fascist corporative system of 'syndicates', the Federazione dei Sindacati Intellettuali (changed to Confederazione dei Professionisti e degli Artisti in 1931) incorporated organizations for painters and sculptors. In order to work or participate in any exhibitions organized by the regime, an artist had to register with a syndicate and be in possession of a Fascist party membership card. The level of control depended on the individuals in authority. It appears that many artists passively colluded with the regime so as to be allowed to continue their work. This system stifled any free associations of artists;[4] with a few notable exceptions (such as the Galleria di Milano and Il Milione in Milan, and the Galleria della Cometa in Rome), it all but destroyed the nascent art market and gallery system.

From Novecento Italiano to Mural Art

The first group of artists to seek official recognition from the Fascist Party was the Milan-based group, Novecento Italiano. Led by the art critic and intimate friend of Mussolini, Margherita Sarfatti, the group aimed to produce an art that would express the ideals of the new Fascist state.[5] By 1932, its work – as represented by one prominent member, the painter Mario Sironi – did correspond to the ideals of a Fascist art as expressed earlier by Bottai. It combined elements of tradition and modernity; it embodied a fundamental earthy quality and an urbane sophistication aware of industrial and technological innovations; and it was monumental, with an innate sense of form combining both archaic and classical elements (*The Builders* and *The Shepherd*, p. 156). Despite this seeming appropriateness, by the early 1930s Sironi and the group were being attacked by the intransigent factions within the Party, led by Roberto Farinacci, the Party Secretary, who criticized their 'deformed' and exaggerated figures, using these as evidence of foreign and cosmopolitan sympathies.[6] These attacks were aggravated by the breakdown of Sarfatti's personal relationship with Mussolini.

Another factor that contributed to the waning position of the Novecento during early 1930s was its connection to Milan and the industrial north. By the late 1920s the regime had begun to centralize artistic activities in Rome. In 1928 it set up the national Quadriennale exhibition which, beginning in 1931, was

to take place in the capital every four years. Sarfatti's attempts to institute a national art movement, with the Novecento exhibitions (comprising some 100 artists) that she organized in Milan in 1926 and 1929, were thus thwarted.

In addition, her emphasis on modernity began to sit uncomfortably with certain members of the expanded Novecento itself. These included the Tuscan artists Ardengo Soffici and Ottone Rosai, who, with their naturalistic and impressionistic landscapes, were fundamentally opposed to the values promoted by the Milanese artists. Both belonged to the grass-roots movement Strapaese and called for a truly Fascist art that would highlight the rural and regional side of Italian life, with its inherent order, serenity and sobriety.

Modernity was the key word to describe the *Mostra della Rivoluzione fascista*, a monumental exhibition held in 1932 which through documents and special installations celebrated the tenth anniversary of Mussolini's March on Rome and accession to power. Although held at the Palazzo delle Esposizioni in Rome, it can be interpreted as a triumph of the 'Milan school', as it was largely conceived by Sironi together with the Rationalist (i.e Modernist) architect Giuseppe Terragni and the Futurist artists Fortunato Depero and Enrico Prampolini.[7] Painters, sculptors and architects were encouraged by Il Duce himself to 'create a contemporary style, very modern and audacious, without melancholic references to the decorative styles of the past'. And indeed, the architectural interiors of the exhibition, heavily influenced by Futurism and Russian Constructivism, matched its revolutionary theme. Through modern design and the ingenious use of photomontage and reliefs, especially in Terragni's *Sala O* dedicated to the year 1922 (p. 39), the artists responded to the organizers' call for 'an architectonic . . . scenographic style, which evokes the atmosphere of our times'.[8]

The sequence of the exhibition situated the history of Fascism in the historical context of Italian civilization. The ideological message, and the identification with Italy's and Rome's former grandeur, were implicit if not explicit. Despite its international avant-garde inspiration, the design of the exhibition was co-opted by Fascism as a representation of 'the expressive vigour of the most felicitous periods of Italian art'.[9]

The subsequent disintegration of the Novecento movement coincided with Sironi's rejection of easel painting in favour of large-scale mural art.[10] Influenced by the experience of the *Mostra della Rivoluzione* and by the propaganda efficacy of modern Mexican mural

4 For example the group known as the *Sei di Torino*, an anti-Fascist group who worked in the more liberal climate of Turin and who rejected any form of ideological representations in their art. See Pia Vivarelli, 'Personalities and Styles in Figurative Art of the Thirties', in *Italian Art in the Twentieth Century* (as note 1), 181–86.

5 Bossaglia (as note 1); on Sarfatti's influential role in the 1920s and her relationship with Mussolini see Philip V. Cannistraro and Brian S. Sullivan, *Il Duce's Other Woman* (New York, 1993).

6 The pivotal role of Mario Sironi is discussed in several articles by Emily Braun including 'Illustrations of Propaganda: The Political Drawings of Mario Sironi' in *The Journal of Decorative and Propaganda Arts*, no. 3 (Winter 1987), 84–107; 'Mario Sironi and a Fascist Art', in *Italian Art in the 20th Century* (as note 1), 173–180.

7 Rossana Bossaglia, 'Artisti tra Roma e Milano', in *E 42 L'Esposizione* (as note 1), 2:234–38.

8 Exh. cat. *Mostra della Rivoluzione fascista: Guida storica*, ed. Dino Alfieri and Luigi Freddi (Rome: Partito Nazionale Fascista, 1933 - XI; reprint, Bergamo, 1982) (this and previous quotation).

9 Libero Andreotti, 'The Aesthetics of War: The Exhibition of the Fascist Revolution', *Journal of Architectural Education*, no. 45 (February 1992); Jeffrey T. Schnapp, 'Epic Demonstrations: Fascist Modernity and the 1932 Exhibition of the Fascist Revolution', in *Fascism, Aesthetics and Culture*, ed. R. J. Goslan (Hanover and London, 1992), 1–37.

10 Sironi was not the first artist to endorse mural art during the Fascist period. In response to the debate about a state art initiated by Bottai, already mentioned, Severini had pronounced his views in two articles of 1927: 'L'idolatria dell'arte e la decadenza del quadro', and 'Peinture murale'. He argued for a new humanism based on a social function for art, but one that did not contradict intrinsic formal values, See E. Braun, 'Gleanings of Gold. Sironi's Mosaic in the Palazzo dell'Informazione' in *Racemi d'Oro* (Milan, 1992), 115–42.

painting, Sironi now held that the ultimate function of painting was social and didactic.[11] Without promoting any one particular style, he called for mural art to convey the Fascist ideology through suggestive and evocative allegories, which would allude to such universal themes as *italianità*, nation, work and the family. Sironi proposed a re-evaluation of traditional techniques, such as stained glass, fresco and mosaic; with these the modern artist could communicate to the masses without compromising his artistic integrity.

To perform this social function, painting and sculpture needed to be elevated to the same level as architecture. In a vein reminiscent of the tenets of the Bauhaus and De Stijl, the three arts could then be combined to create a new visual style. Sironi reiterated these ideas in the *Manifesto della pittura murale* which he signed in 1933 with Carlo Carrà, Massimo Campigli and Achille Funi, who had all, like him, been members of the Novecento Italiano.[12]

Sironi saw a chance to make his ideas a reality at the Fifth Milan Triennale in 1933. A section of the exhibition was devoted to mural painting and monumental sculpture and reliefs, and Sironi invited some thirty artists – including Giorgio de Chirico, Alberto Savinio, Gino Severini, Carrà, Campigli, Funi, Corrado Cagli, Prampolini and Depero, Arturo Martini and Marino Marini – to decorate the walls of Giovanni Muzio's Palazzo dell'Arte. The artists were given no precise subjects but either left to their own devices or asked to show 'Italy in her various manifestations of work, sport, study and family life'.[13] Sironi's objective was to convey the heroism of Italian civilization through what he called a 'rediscovery of the classical'.

The 1933 Triennale proved highly controversial. The Rationalist architects denounced it as anachronistic, failing to integrate the three arts,[14] while hard-line critics like Farinacci accused the artists of being foreign and Bolshevik. Even the more moderate reviewers criticized the clashing variety of styles and the inclusion of too many minor artists ill-equipped to carry out Sironi's intentions. The Triennale was accused of being anti-Rome, of wilfully excluding 'any object or any decoration of a classic Roman style', so that even the *fasci littori* seemed modified into a Novecento style.[15] Sironi's grand mural, *The Works and Days*, decorated the main Salone d'Onore alongside Funi's *Italian Athletic Games*, De Chirico's *Italian Culture* and Campigli's *Mothers, Countrywomen and Women Workers*, while Carrà's *Roman Italy* and Cagli's *Omens of War* were placed in the vestibule of the Palazzo. Given the

controversy and the ephemeral nature of the exhibition all the murals, except for Severini's mosaic *The Three Arts*, were destroyed or painted over. Of Sironi's own mural, all that remains are evocative studies: distillations of the mythical reality he sought to express (p. 155).

The Fascists' policy of tolerance allowed all the artists involved in the Triennale to continue working. Moreover, the relationship between artists and the regime was made closer by the introduction of the Two Per Cent Law. Part of the regime's vast rebuilding strategy, the law was effectively in force from the mid-1930s onwards, although enacted only in 1942. It stipulated that for each public edifice at least two per cent of overall construction costs had to be devoted to works of art.[16] Most artists accepted this law as a positive move intended to guarantee their livelihood.

By the time of the war in Ethiopia (1935–6) and the creation of the new Italian Empire, the concept of *romanità* had became central to Fascist propaganda. In retrospect, perhaps one positive aspect of this was that it fostered interest in the archaeology of Italy and especially of the capital. In unison with the literal unearthing of Italy's past,[17] the regime set about constructing the new Italy, both practically and metaphorically.

Romanità found direct expression in the pared-down columns and triumphal arches of such monumental Neoclassical edifices as Marcello Piacentini's Palazzo delle Corporazioni (now Palazzo dell'Industria) in Rome. The paintings and sculpture of these years reflected the influence of *romanità* when they formed an integral part of architectural public commissions, such as the heroic statuary around the Foro Mussolini (p. 147), or in the large-scale murals of public buildings, such as ministries, post-offices and railway stations.[18]

Sironi's vast mural *Italy Between the Arts and the Sciences* for the Great Hall of Rome University, and the allegorical mosaic *L'Italia corporativa* (see p. 154), conceived for the Sixth Triennale in 1936 and shown in the Italian pavilion at the Exposition Internationale in Paris in 1937, both allude to Italy's recent victory in Ethiopia (the winged Victory in the Rome mural and the triumphant, all-embracing image of Italy in the mosaic) and the symbolic union of contemporary Italy with its imperial past.

Allegories of *romanità* and *latinità* are also evident in the decorations on the walls of Piacentini's vast Palazzo della Giustizia in Milan. Piacentini stipulated that all the murals or reliefs had to refer to the theme of Justice, either directly or through biblical or historical

11 On Sarfatti's attitude towards Rivera and Mexican murals, see Cannistraro and Sullivan (as note 6), 435–38.

12 The complete text is published in R. Bossaglia (as note 1), 155–56.

13 The contents of the fifth Triennale in 1933 are recorded in Anty Pansera, *Storia e cronaca della Triennale* (Milan, 1978).

14 It was in fact the Rationalists who most successfully achieved the integration of architecture, painting and sculpture in the Sala della Vittoria at the sixth Triennale in 1936. Dominated by Fontana's *Victory* sculpture, which made a direct reference to Italy's recent success in the Ethiopian war, this 'environment' was a synthesis of the Rationalist interpretation of *romanità*.

15 Guido Sommi Picenardi, 'Triennale contro Roma' in *Il Regime Fascista*, 11 May 1933, reprinted in Fabrizio Brunetti, *Architetti e Fascismo* (Florence, 1993).

16 For a brief history of this law, see Simonetta Lux and Ester Coen, exh. cat. *1935: Gli Artisti nell'Università e la questione della pittura murale* (Rome: La Sapienza, 1985), 138.

17 Endowments for archaeology were supervised by the Ministry of Education, under Bottai.

18 Emily Braun, 'Political Rhetoric and Poetic Irony: The Uses of Classicism in the Art of Fascist Italy', in exh. cat. *On Classic Ground: Picasso, Léger, De Chirico and the New Classicism 1910–1930* (London: Tate Gallery, 1990), 345–58.

subject matter. The regime's desire to establish continuity between biblical and Fascist justice, mediated by the influence of Roman justice, was ideally represented in the three monumental reliefs by Arturo Dazzi, Romano Romanelli and Arturo Martini (p. 161) which were placed on the balcony over the central stairway of the Palazzo. The building seems to epitomize Fascist imperial rhetoric, and yet it too was subject to attack. In 1939, soon after many of the murals were completed, the biblical subjects were accused of reflecting Judaism and, to the dismay of Piacentini and Bottai, many of reflecting the murals were covered.[19]

Second Futurism and 'Aeropittura'

The heroic, warmongering, machine-obsessed initial phase of Futurism ended with Italy's entry into the First World War in 1915, and the period of so-called Second Futurism began with Giacomo Balla and Fortunato Depero's *Ricostruzione dell'universo futurista* in 1915; during the 1920s Second Futurism was heavily influenced by a machine aesthetic. By the early 1930s a large contingent of Futurist painters had began to refer to their work as *Aeropittura*. Their early interest in the motor car was replaced by a fascination with aircraft, with flight and with extraterrestrial fantasy. In the *Manifesto dell'Aeropittura* published in 1929, the artists Giacomo Balla, Benedetta, Depero, Gherardo Dottori, Fillia (Luigi Colombo), Filippo Tommaso Marinetti, Prampolini, Mino Somenzi and Tato (Guglielmo Sansoni) launched the idea of an art linked to the most exciting aspect of contemporary life. The establishment of the Air Ministry in 1923 and Italian achievements in the air of the 1920s and 1930s (such as the transatlantic flights of Italo Balbo) had made into a reality what in 1914 Umberto Boccioni had described as 'man's aspiration to speed and the future conquest of the air'.

The themes of speed and flight were depicted by the Aeropainters in two ways: as cosmic analogy, or simply by vertiginous aerial views of planes swooping down over the landscape. The first of these can be seen in the works of Prampolini and Fillia, in which biomorphic and non-objective forms are used to create a 'cosmic and spiritual reality'. The images of Tullio Crali, Alfredo Ambrosi and Tato (pp. 152–53) are more literal. During the 1930s the Aeropainters, supported by the poet and cultural impresario Marinetti, sought to align themselves with the Fascist regime. Rather like the Novecento, they sought official sanction for their

own version of mural art, such as Prampolini's aerodynamic designs for a civil airport included in the Fifth Triennale. The close relationship between the conquest of the air and warfare was not lost on the Futurists, and the wars in Ethiopia and Spain provided them with up-to-date subject matter.[20]

Despite Marinetti's long-standing connection with Mussolini, which dated from the pre-war years, the regime never endorsed the Futurist movement. No doubt it was attracted by the Futurist insistence on technology and military aggression, but by the 1930s Fascism was more concerned with consolidating its image of discipline and order. Marinetti reiterated the fundamental *italianità* of Futurism and strove to dissociate it from foreign movements, but the regime could never let itself be identified with any group that had its roots in anarchism, in internationalism or the Modernist avant-garde.[21]

Abstract Art

Among the more progressive and modern artists working in the 1930s in Italy were the abstract artists of the Milan and Como schools, many of whom belonged to the Parisian movement *Abstraction-Création*. The Galleria del Milione in Milan was the focal point of their activities during the mid-1930s, but their positions and stylistic practices were by no means all the same.[22] The work of the 'Rationalist' abstract painters, Mauro Reggiani, Atanasio Soldati and the Como artists Mario Radice, Carla Badiali, Manlio Rho and sculptors Aldo Galli, Giovanni Prini and Cesare Cattaneo recalled the purist forms of Rationalist architecture. On a more intimate scale, the sculpture of Lucio Fontana, Fausto Melotti and the painter Osvaldo Licini in the mid-1930s can be described as a form of lyrical geometric abstraction (pp. 170–73). Luigi Veronesi, by contrast, crossed the boundaries between disciplines, combining elements of graphics, scenography, photography and painting.

Like other groups working in Italy in the 1930s, some of the abstract artists were not immune to the allure of Fascism, though they never desired or sought official recognition for their art. Their critical mouthpiece, Carlo Belli, equated the formal order and purity of their works with the political order of Fascism, affirming his faith in the new classical age, and some of the artists themselves took a similar line: 'Today we believe in a certain Mediterranean climate

19 'Palazzo della Giustizia di Milano, Le opere decorative' in exh. cat. *Anni trenta* (as note 1), 53–55.

20 At the 1938 Venice Biennale, the Futurists held an exhibition of 'Aeropainters of Spain and Africa'.

21 The relationship between the Futurists and Fascism came to a head in 1937, when a polemic exploded between the Milanese bimonthly *Il Perseo* and the review *Artecrazia* run by the Futurist critic, Mino Somenzi. The anarchic, modern and arbitrary nature of Futurism was attacked for being fundamentally un-Italian and anti-Fascist.

22 A group exhibition of the abstract artists' work was also held in Turin in 1935 in Felice Casorati's studio.

made up of order and equilibrium . . . We are therefore favourably disposed towards the classical. But clearly this does not mean arches or columns.'[23] In the preface to his one-man exhibition in 1935, Melotti proclaimed: 'When the last Greek chisel ceased to resound, night settled on the Mediterranean. It was a long night, illuminated only by the half-moon (the reflected light) of the Renaissance. Now we feel the breeze again on the Mediterranean. And we dare to think it is the dawn of a new era.'

Throughout the decade, these artists, together with Alberto Magnelli, who lived in Paris at the time, were able to work freely, and their paintings were included in the national Quadriennale exhibitions of 1935 and 1939; but they had little critical or commercial success. This may have been why Melotti worked on official propaganda commissions for figurative, academic sculptures – although there may be a correlation between the purity, order and 'musical' rhythm of Melotti's abstract pieces and the simplicity of the classical sculptures he produced for the Palazzo degli Uffici in Esposizione Universale di Roma. Throughout the 1930s, Fontana worked contemporaneously in figurative and abstract styles, switching from one to the other with apparent ease (figurative work includes the *Victory* for the Sala della Vittoria at the Sixth Triennale and the Fountain for the Palazzo dell'Acqua e della Luce in EUR). And yet, whatever style or medium Fontana employed, his art always seemed to elude the categories of order and clarity. Rather like Sironi, with whom he collaborated on architectural projects during the period, his art transcended formal connotations or explanations. Of all the abstract artists, it was perhaps Licini who most subscribed to the idea of art for art's sake. Even his most geometric abstractions – the *archipitture* of around 1936 – are never static or expressionless. In an open letter to the Galleria del Milione in 1935, he asserted 'Painting is the art of colours and forms freely conceived . . . an act of will and of creation, an irrational art, in which fantasy and imagination, that is poetry, predominate'.

The Quadriennale

The artistic pluralism favoured by the moderates within the regime was most clearly visible in the national Quadriennale exhibitions held in the Palazzo delle Esposizioni in Rome from 1931 on.[24] From the outset, it was clear that the regime wanted the event to have a national impact (train fares were lowered to permit more people to attend). The organization was entrusted to a loyal party member, the painter and critic Cipriano Efisio Oppo, who worked in close consultation with Mussolini on all aspects of the exhibition, from the choice of the juries to the most suitable day for the openings.[25] No one group or tendency dominated at the 1931 Quadriennale, but it was slightly weighted towards naturalism and a form of late-Impressionism, as in the landscapes of Ardengo Soffici and the Lombard artist, Arturo Tosi.[26]

Oppo's moment of glory came with the 1935 Quadriennale. On that occasion he incorporated both the work of younger artists and a number of one-man shows devoted to the work of established painters and sculptors such as Severini, Martini, Carrà, De Pisis and De Chirico. The Fascist regime's capacity to absorb seemingly dissonant 'voices' is exemplified by the inclusion of the enigmatic works of De Chirico and his brother, Alberto Savinio, which stressed the interrogative tensions and contradictions that can exist where tradition allies itself with modernity (p. 166).[27] The 1935 Quadriennale also included rooms dedicated to *Aeropittura* and to abstraction, both the subject of little favourable comment at the time.

Perhaps betraying Oppo's own stylistic preferences, emphasis seems to have been on painters of what is loosely termed the Roman school, such as Fausto Pirandello, Mario Mafai, Cagli and Scipione (Gino Bonichi). These works do not celebrate the moment; instead, they seem to allude to an underlying disquiet, a troubled existential condition (pp. 168–69). Scipione had died in 1933, and in the preface to his retrospective, Oppo refers to him as 'a fantastic and tragic apparition', singling out his sublime and hallucinatory views of Rome.[28]

Apart from the mural works of Cagli, which recall his experience at the Fifth Triennale and to which he referred as 'the creation of new myths', the general tone of the work at the 1935 Quadriennale was rather intimate and personal, with echoes of the Metaphysical Painting of the early De Chirico and Carrà, and of Expressionism. In the statements accompanying their showings, most artists stressed the *italianità* of their artistic contributions.[29] Though the spirit of modern classicism was not a purely Italian phenomenon in the 1930s, this constant emphasis on *italianità* relates to Fascist dogma. Nevertheless, the inherent regionalism of the Italian state remained a prominent feature throughout the period, as the Quadriennale exhibitions also showed.[30]

By 1939 the climate in Italy had become more

23 This quotation is taken from the 'Dichiarazioni degli espositori' by O. Bogliardi, G. Ghiringhelli, M. Reggiani published in the *Bollettino* no. 32 of the Galleria del Milione. It can be read as the manifesto of the abstract artists.

24 Four Quadriennale exhibitions were organized during the Fascist period: 1931, 1935, 1939, 1943.

25 Throughout the 1930s, there was an implicit rivalry between the Quadriennale and the international Biennale held in Venice to attract the best artists of the day. Even though the Second Futurists were substantially represented in the 1930s Biennale exhibitions, the nature of the works included generally tended towards academic, classical sculpture or painting. As specific subject competitions were introduced in the Biennale in the early 1930s (long before the Premio Cremona), many of the works included made references to *romanità*.

26 Licini rather scathingly referred to the first Quadriennale as follows: 'It does not seem to me that in Italy at the moment there is any danger of a Picassoesque academicism. In Italy, Cézannian academicism is still going strong, as is low Impressionism and – even worse – an inflated, banal, lurid naturalism.' Osvaldo Licini, letter to the critic Giuseppe Marchiorin Licini, *Errante, erotico, eretico: Gli Scritti letterari e tutte le lettere* (Milan, 1974), 205.

27 De Chirico and Savinio lived in Paris during much of the Fascist period. They were associated with the group known as the *Italiani di Parigi*, who were supported by the critic Waldemar George. The paintings of both could almost be interpreted as anti-Fascist in mood, yet interestingly the regime was able to accommodate even dissonant voices. In the author's opinion Licini also falls into this category.

repressive. With the recently introduced Racial Laws,[31] Jewish artists such as Cagli and Carlo Levi could, no longer participate, while others held aloof, including Sironi, who considered easel painting bourgeois and archaic and did not hold with the pluralism of the Quadriennale. There was, however, a large exhibition of the work of Giorgio Morandi. Through the 1920s and 1930s, Morandi was associated with Strapaese, whose journals, *Il Selvaggio* and *L'italiano* often included his etchings and drawings. The purity and simplicity of his still-lifes and the tranquillity of his landscapes could readily be identified with the movement's love of Italy's regional and rustic traditions (p. 167).[32]

Apart from artists such as Pirandello, Guttuso, Martini, the Futurists and the abstract painters, much of the work seemed to fall into two major categories – either allusive, academic sculptures redolent of Fascist rhetoric, or conventional (conformist) images of mothers and children, still-lifes, landscapes, in a late-Impressionist style: a formalism emptied of meaning.[33]

The Premio Cremona and the Premio Bergamo

The implementation of the Racial Laws in 1938–39 coincided with a polemical debate on the relationship between art and race. All forms of modern art, from Novecento to Futurism and Abstraction – together with those critics who had publicized them, including Oppo and Antonio Maraini, the organizer of the Venice Biennale – were attacked for being un-Italian, for being 'Jewish' and 'Bolshevik' in the racist Roman weekly, *Quadrivio*.[34] Another antisemitic publication, *Il Tevere*, edited by Telesio Interlandi, published a list of 'degenerate' Italian artists which included Marinetti, Carrà, De Chirico, Cagli, Renato Birolli, Reggiani, Fontana, Gino Ghiringhelli, Atanasio Soldati and the architects Pietro Lingeri and Terragni. Marinetti and Somenzi counter-attacked with an opinion survey that came out in favour of modern art, indicating clearly that anti-modern sentiment in Italy was not all-pervasive.[35]

At this time, a small but vocal faction of the Fascist party, led by Farinacci, proposed a form of illustrative propaganda art on the lines advocated by the National Socialists in Germany. An annual prize, the Premio Cremona, was set up in 1938, and its first exhibition was first held in 1939 in Farinacci's native Cremona. Farinacci intended to promote an Italian figurative art that was easily understandable (clearly attacking the more cerebral approach of Sironi). Participants were required to portray themes related to Fascist propaganda: such as *Listening to a Speech by Il Duce on the Radio* or *States of Mind Created by Fascism*. The competitors submitted their work anonymously,[36] and in his opening speech Ugo Ojetti, the conservative critic of the newspaper *Corriere della Sera*, enjoined them to paint 'the joyful, springlike beauty of Italy today and the Italy of the future, that is to say Mussolini's Italy'. The set themes for 1940 and 1941 included *The Battle for Grain* (see p. 174) and *Italian Youth of the Fascist Movement*.[37] The winning works in the Premio Cremona affirmed the conservative Fascist emphasis on the land and the 'health' of the nation; they did not celebrate the more grandiose aspects of Italian civilization.

The Premio Bergamo was set up by Bottai in 1939 in direct opposition to the Premio Cremona. The Premio Bergamo exhibitions set great store in creative freedom, and the choice of themes were in open contrast the rhetorical ones stipulated by the Premio Cremona: in 1939 it was landscape, in 1940 two figures, and the third and fourth (1941 and 1942) were left to the choice of the artist. The exhibition was criticized by *Il Tevere* and *Il Regime Fascista*, but the Prize continued to attract increasing numbers of younger artists.

Among these was Renato Guttuso, who, along with the sculptor Giacomo Manzù and others, belonged to the Milan-based movement Corrente, founded in 1938 with Ernesto Treccani's cultural review, *Vita giovanile*. Influenced by Picasso, especially *Guernica*, Corrente represented a revolt of the younger generation against Fascism. It advocated a figurative art that was neither academic nor escapist but impassioned and expressive, communicating the direct relationship between the artist and the 'drama' of the real world. Works such as Guttuso's *Flight from Etna* and Manzù's bas-relief, *The Crucifixion*, symbolize a unanimous call for resistance to the brutalities of the regime (pp. 176–77).

The inclusion of these artists' work in official prizes and exhibitions such as the Premio Bergamo seems to represent another anomaly of Fascist cultural policy. In addition, there appears to a certain interaction between the Bergamo and Cremona prizes; both can be read – either in competition or in dialectic – as wilful attempts to monopolize culture on the part of the state.[38] Bottai almost betrayed this when at the opening of the Biennale in 1940 he stated 'Art which is directly controlled by the State, as an instrument of propaganda, not only results in illustration or documentation; but, owing to its lack of expression, loses all its efficacy as propaganda'. Perhaps the Minister had in mind that

28 For an evaluation of the Scuola Romana see E. Braun, 'The Scuola Romana: Fact or Fiction?', in *Art in America*, 76, no. 3 (March 1988), 128–37.

29 De Pisis in the preface to his works emphasizes 'My Italian character – even in the historical sense'; see exh. cat. *Il Quadriennale*, (Rome, 1935), 63 (Sala XII).

30 Fabrizio D'Amico, 'Cipriano Efisio Oppo tra due Quadriennali (1935–1939): alla vigilia dell'E 42', in *E 42 L'Esposizione* (as note 1), 2:244–79.

31 Introduction of *Manifesto del razzismo italiano*, 14 July 1938; *Carta della Razza*, 6–7 October 1938. In that November the racial laws were passed. Fernando Tempesti (as note 1), 217.

32 Licini on Morandi: 'Can you see, Marchiori, how low Morandi has fallen, the champion of Italian artistic and bureaucratic mediocrity, the creation of Oppo, Soffici, Cardarelli, Longanesi, Bartolini, of all the nostalgic and reactionary, crablike regressives [*gamberi*] of Strapaese?' Licini (as note 26), 143.

33 This style seemed to characterize the majority of work shown in the regional syndicates exhibitions as well. Laura Malvano (as note 1), 38.

34 The Roman weekly *Il Tevere*, together with reviews such *Il Regime Fascista*, *La Vita Italiano* and perhaps worst of all *La Difesa della Razza*, all attacked modern art at some time. Tempesti (as note 1), 217.

35 The issues surrounding the campaign and the responses to it are contained in E. Crispolti, *Il mito della macchina e altri temi del Futurismo* (Turin, 1969).

36 Tempesti (as note 1, 229) thinks that many of the artists were local art teachers from Cremona.

efficacia propagandistica could be achieved through other, less obvious means.

Bottai's last important cultural initiative was his proposal to create the Ufficio per l'Arte Contemporanea in 1940. Acting as an instrument of state tutelage, information and promotion, which would contain archival, photographic and bibliographic material on all contemporary artists and artistic manifestations, the Ufficio was to be realized after the war in a different form.

Esposizione Universale di Roma

The most prestigious and ambitious attempt of the regime to embrace *romanità* was the Esposizione Universale di Roma, or E'42. It was scheduled to mark the twentieth anniversary of Fascist rule in 1942, and was to be the ultimate showcase for Italy's imperial past and future. Bottai referred to the exhibition as 'the contemporary, concrete and – in a word – Fascist expression of the eternal idea of Rome'.[39]

Through the union of architecture, painting and sculpture, E'42 attempted to synthesize and celebrate the values expressed by the Fascist leader; Melotti received a commission to transform two of Il Duce's famous phrases, 'The Land is Redeemed' and 'Cities are Founded' into sculptural monuments for the Palazzo dell'Autarchia. The legacy of Italian civilization, the *stirpe* (lineage), which had so dominated the language of Fascism throughout the 1930s, was officially replaced at E'42 by that of 'race'. The supremacy of the Italian people, implicit in Fascism's use of *romanità*, had brought with it the most dire implications. The Second World War meant that E'42, or E Quarantamai (E Forty Never) as it was known locally, never took place. With its demise, Fascism's fanciful and tragic

identification with ancient Rome finally collapsed.[40]

Fascism in Italy during the 1920s and 1930s has been referred to as a form of 'imperfect totalitarianism', primarily owing to the continued presence of the monarchy and the Church, both of which exerted some influence (albeit minimal) in the affairs of the state. Nevertheless, it must not be forgotten that it was a tyranny. Opponents to the regime, including a number of intellectuals, were forced to leave Italy or suffered internal exile or imprisonment – sometimes leading to death, as in the case of the politician and philosopher Antonio Gramsci.

Against this background of oppression and intolerance, the regime sought to consolidate and legitimize its existence. Its pluralistic cultural policy created a form of consensus,[41] though ultimately it underscored the disunity and diverging factions that existed within the Fascist regime. Ultimately, the emphasis lay on forms of art that were anti-avant-garde and anti-experimental.

Whereas Mussolini was concerned with his own 'triumphant' image and the means by which this could be imposed, Bottai had believed in the value of art and culture, and the intrinsic quality of the work of art. By the late 1930s he was becoming aware of the failings of his policies.[42] They had served to divide and rule, to foster competitiveness and opportunism, creating conflict and tension both within and beyond the realms of Fascism, though little overt political opposition among the artists.

In 1938, Bottai wrote: 'The revival of the grandeur of Rome is the highest aspiration of Italian poets, who, from Dante, to Leopardi, and D'Annunzio, have prophesied the triumphal events of the Empire, in which – thanks to Il Duce – our generation can play a leading role'.[43] But the roads that were to lead that generation to Rome ended in death not glory.

37 A Premio Cremona exhibition was held in Hanover in September 1940. Farinacci was present; the tone of the event was heavily antisemitic. A representative of Goebbels's ministry was present to make the necessary arrangements for the fourth exhibition which was going to be a sort of Axis Biennale also open to the artists of the Third Reich with the themes *Dal sangue la nuova Europa* ('From Blood, the New Europe') for painting and *Ritratto di personalità rappresentative dell'Asse* ('Portrait of Representative Axis Personalities') for sculpture; it never took place. See Chiara Tellini Perina, 'Il Premio Cremona: "questo novecentismo fascista: forte, vigoroso, epico, romano"', in *Gli anni del Premio Bergamo;: Arte in Italia intorno agli anni Trenta* (Bergamo, 1993), 51–58.

38 Marco Lorandi, 'Il Premio Bergamo 1939–42; le estetiche neoromantiche e le metamorfosi di Novecento' in *Gli Anni* (as note 37), 58–73.

Achille Funi, *All Roads Lead to Rome*, Mural at Palazzo dei Congressi, EUR, 1942

BLACK SHIRTS AND WHITE TELEPHONES

Cinema *Lutz Becker*

The success of Italian Neorealism after the Second World War took the world by surprise and had a profound and lasting effect on film-makers and critics. Due to isolation during the 1930s and the war years, new developments in Italian cinema had gone unnoticed. Outside Italy Neorealism started in 1945, with Roberto Rossellini's *Roma città aperta* (see p. 29); but its rise already existed within Fascist cinema. Structures and methods developed during the 1930s remained in place after the war, and a cadre of well-trained film technicians, directors, screen writers, cameramen and editors were ready to tackle the themes and ideas of the post-war world.[1]

Mussolini, who originally had had little regard for the cinema, found his interest aroused by the sound film revolution. He recognized that there were new opportunities for film to be used as a powerful cultural and propaganda instrument which would replace the antiquated product of the silent film era. Mussolini's first experience of sound film dated back to May 1927, when a team from the American newsreel Fox-Movietone came to Rome to record a statement by the dictator. Very satisfied with the outcome, he is reported to have said: 'Your talking newsreel has tremendous possibilities. Let me speak through it in twenty cities in Italy once a week and I need no other power.'[2] Nevertheless, it took five years more before an Italian sound newsreel was available. *Cinegiornale LUCE* converted to sound production in June 1932, when most Italian cinemas had finally been equipped for sound film projection.

While the press and radio were highly politicized under Fascism, and all aspects of public life were subordinated to Fascist party organizations, Mussolini initially allowed the cinema to develop in relative independence, virtually free from political interference. In 1934, the Ministry of Popular Culture set up a film directorate, Direzione Generale per la Cinematografia, under the directorship of Luigi Freddi.[2] He realized that the introduction of sound film, and the renewal of the film industry, required better professional training than had previously been available in directing, scripting, acting, cinematography and all other areas of film production. In 1935, he founded the Centro Sperimentale di Cinematografia in Rome for the education and training of young film personnel. It soon became one of the two most important film schools in Europe, alongside that of Moscow. Its head was the director, Luigi Chiarini, editor of the influential film journal *Bianco e Nero*. Centro Sperimentale combined practical and theoretical film study; students were taught by experienced directors, designers and critics. Some members of the first generation of students were to become exponents of Neorealism: Michelangelo Antonioni, Roberto Rossellini, Luciano Emmer, Pietro Germi, Luigi Zampa, Giuseppe de Santis.[3]

Being a student at Centro Sperimentale offered opportunities to contribute to *Bianco e Nero*, the journal that became the cradle of a new experimental and realistic approach to film. It even explored, at the height of Fascism, the theories of Eisenstein, Pudovkin and Bela Balasz. Essential works by foreign Socialist writers and film-makers were translated for this widely disseminated periodical by Umberto Barbaro.[4]

A journal devoted to the 'Modernist' mainstream film was *Cinema*, founded in 1935 by Il Duce's son, Vittorio Mussolini, still in his twenties. In contrast to Nazi Germany, the Fascist government of Italy valued the commercial successes of the film industry more highly than propagandistic expediency.[5] In its first years, *Cinema* expressed the official views of Giuseppe Bottai, the Minister of Culture, and of Luigi Freddi, and promoted a strong commercial cinema organized along Hollywood lines with a policy that favoured entertainment above propaganda. Later, from 1940 onwards, *Cinema* would also support the Neorealist tendency, based not so much on the leftist perspective of *Bianco e Nero* as on the 'Reform Fascist' convictions of its young editor-in-chief.

Fascism was concerned with achieving a largely independent film industry, one that could exist without state subsidies. Freddi's aspiration for the Italian film industry was of competitiveness, international standards of professionalism and popular appeal. The films that won prizes at the Venice Film Festival were chosen less for their political tendencies than in recognition of their box-office potential.[6]

To kick-start the film industry towards prosperity, tax rebates were given and loans were provided from Sezione Cinematografica at the Banca del Lavoro to draw in private finance. The control of film imports via ENAIPE, a state-owned body for the importation of

Notes to Fraquelli, *All Roads*, continued.

39 Giuseppe Bottai, *La politica delle arti: Scritti 1918–1943*, ed. Alessandro Masi (Rome, 1992), 156.

40 Several artists, including Sironi and Fontana, were called to participate in the E'42 project. The war prevented the completion of many commissions. Those buildings that were finished subsequently became part of the new quarter of Rome developed after the War and still known as EUR. An analysis of the decorations planned for the Palazzo delle Corporazioni in EUR is contained in Ester Coen, *Il Palazzo delle Corporazioni: Una decorazione mai eseguita* (Rome, 1993).

41 Cannistraro (as note 1), and *E 42 L'Esposizione* (as note 1), 1:30.

42 As note 3.

43 Giuseppe Bottai, 'Il rinnovamento di Roma', *Nouvelles Littéraires*, 12 February 1938, reprinted in Bottai (as note 39), 122.

1 Georges Sadoul, 'Introduction', in, Carlo Lizzani, *Le Cinéma italien* (Paris, 1955), 7.

2 Gian Pietro Brunetta, *Storia del cinema italiano 1895–1945* (Rome, 1979), 317–19.

3 Patrice G. Hovald, *Le Néo-réalisme italien* (Paris, 1959), 31.

4 George A. Huaco, *The Sociology of Film Art* (New York, 1965), 158.

5 Conversation with Vittorio Mussolini in Rome in November 1982.

6 Marcia Landy, *Fascism in Film: The Italian Commercial Cinema, 1931–1943* (Princeton, 1986), 12–13.

foreign films, made sure that the market remained skewed in favour of Italian productions. Large private enterprises such as Cines and Scalera, along with numerous small production companies, prospered in this climate. In 1937 Cinecittà, the largest studio complex in Europe, was established in Rome. This government-supported company became Italy's most effective studio and has continued until the present day. Cinecittà had 16 sound stages and a vast back lot. During the war years, Vittorio Mussolini was put in charge of it.

Evidence of the effectiveness of the regime's supportive film policy can be seen from the rising production figures: from 1932 to 1938 Italy produced an average of 30 feature films per year; in 1939 production rose to 84 films; in 1940 the figure was 68; in 1941 it was 90, reaching its height in 1942 with 119 films.[7]

The rapid industrialization of Italy and the ideological mobilization of the population were traumatic for sections of a largely rural society. The cinema, after a short period of independence, was obliged to play its part in supporting Mussolini's regenerative programme. The 'new order' was summarized in the popular motto *civiltà, ordine e autorità* (civilization, order and authority). The desire of Fascist Italy to project a modern image of itself, at home and abroad, idealized social and technological progress and provided the underlying ideology for most of the feature film production of the 1930s. Melodramas set in hotels and department stores or within the milieu of racing drivers and pilots were particularly popular, replicating the earlier genre of 'society' drama.

The new affluence and modern attitudes were symbolized by the frequent use of the white telephone, which became the popular term for the whole category of films. It not only celebrated the belated arrival of telecommunications in Italy, but encouraged the pretence that Fascist Italy was a Grand Hotel carefree world, to the exclusion of social reality.[8] Some of the most successful films of this genre were directed by Mario Camerini: *Il Signor Max* (1937), *Una donna tra due mondi* (1938) and *Batticuore* (1939).

In the hands of the Fascist regime, the cinema became a dream factory similar to the Hollywood of the period and provided social alibis as well as escapism. It was also a great social leveller, reconciling the traditional with the modern, harmonizing regional and rural values with those of the modern city and its international dimensions. The cinema's political function was to assert and defend Fascist cultural ideals and ambitions; it was seen to have a major role to play in claiming Fascist Italy's place in the world and its position on the international stage.

Freddi articulated these goals in 1937: 'A nation that is able to avoid the harsher realities that involve all the world will be one where all the citizens, even the so-called private citizens, know how to think and act, not merely out of self-interest, but out of regard for the collective group – the nation . . . The most powerful force, over the last three years, which has hastened the development of this attitude has been our film production . . . The new national film production is acquiring an international reputation and meaning because it expresses our time in history, which is truly Italian and Fascist.'[9]

The imperialistic ambitions of the regime were fulfilled in the conquest of Ethiopia in 1935–36. As a 'reconstruction' of the Roman Empire, this was the high point of Fascism's popularity in Italy. Within a few months of the campaign, large sections of Italian society that had been politically indifferent, or even anti-Fascist, joined the jubilant crowds on the piazza Venezia when the victory bells rang. Thanks to Italy's material superiority over Haile Selassie's forces, the war had been fought with little Italian loss of life.

This spectacular re-enactment of past history was reflected on Italian cinema screens through a number of prestigious propaganda productions, which captured an artificial heroic vision. *Scipione l'Africano* (1937), directed by Carmine Gallone, anchored the imperialistic dream in Roman history, and suggested that the Fascists were the rightful inheritors of past greatness. Three war films in particular encapsulated

7 Vernon Jarratt, *The Italian Cinema* (London, 1951), 43.

8 James Hay, *Popular Film Culture in Fascist Italy* (Indianapolis, 1987), 47–54.

9 Luigi Freddi, 'Produzione italiana 1935–XIII – 1937–XV', in *Lo schermo*, June 1937, 14.

'Film is the strongest weapon': Mussolini lays the foundation stone of Istituto LUCE, Rome 1937

the ethos of this campaign: *Lo squadrone bianco* (1936), directed by Auguste Genina, *Sentile di bronzo* (1937), directed by Romolo Marcellini, and *Sotto la croce del sud* (1938), directed by Guido Brignone. Greater realism was achieved in *Luciano Serra pilota* (1938), directed by Goffredo Alessandrini, which was the story of a bomber pilot set in a strong documentary context, produced by Vittorio Mussolini's company, Europa.

The official newsreel of the Istituto Nazionale LUCE had accompanied the development of the Fascist regime from its beginning, but the war in Ethiopia had awakened the full propagandistic potential of its newsreel *Cinegiornale*. Established in 1924 as a producer of documentaries and educational films, LUCE had been transferred into state ownership in the early 1930s. Appreciative of its supportive role in his African triumph, Mussolini laid the foundation stone of a new LUCE building near the Cinecittà complex in 1937. Thanks to the lavish financial support given to the company, and the great technical skill of its cameramen and editors, *Cinegiornale* became a strikingly effective, modern looking, dynamic propaganda tool. LUCE supported all of Mussolini's political and military actions until the demise of the regime in September 1943.[11]

The productions of LUCE were the core of the regime's propaganda drive. By contrast, when war started, feature film production was encouraged to stay out of politics, only occasionally reflecting on political affairs. The omission of topicality was intended to anaesthetize audiences against the consequences of war.[12]

Italian Fascism was particularly full of contradictions and ambiguities. At times the cultural climate allowed dissent; it even encouraged experimentation and sustained a degree of co-existence of differing attitudes. The Direzione Generale tolerated films that departed from the party line, in the hope that their artistic values and formal innovations would eventually enliven official productions. These films were mostly unassuming, often low-budget productions. Their directors, Vittorio de Sica, Alessandro Blasetti, Roberto Rossellini, Luigi Chiarini, Alberto Lattuada and Renato Castellani, had distanced themselves from Fascist stereotypes and intuitively cultivated a feeling of reality and a psychological dimension missing from the works of most of their contemporaries.

Many of the younger generation around *Bianco e Nero* and *Cinema* had studied the realistic developments in French cinema in particular in the films of Jacques Prévert and Marcel Carné. Luchino Visconti's *Ossessione* (1942), co-authored by Giuseppe de Santis and again produced by Vittorio Mussolini, was the first fully realized Neorealist film. It became the emblem and the manifesto for a radical renewal and was the turning point which determined the re-positioning of Italian cinema.

In Germany at the same time, most directors were compromised by National Socialism. With their sense of reality eroded and their sensitivities dulled, film-makers arrived at the end of the war burnt out and deeply disoriented. Their Italian counterparts had maintained their critical discourse throughout the years of Fascism and had preserved their integrity, their energy and the creative urge which enabled them to look beyond it. The fall of Mussolini, the end of the German occupation and the experience of liberation provided the young film generation with the opportunity to take advantage of all they had learned, and to employ it in creating a new film experience, reflecting on authentic social and political problems in Italian society.

10 The war in Ethiopia was the prelude to the Second World War. The only complete film record of this campaign is *Lion of Judah*, produced by the author in 1981.

11 Guido Quazza, ed., *Vincere, Vinceremo. La Guerra Fascista 1940–1943* (Rome, 1975).

12 As a whole, the official production of the Italian film industry was trivial. Carlo Lizzani dismissed the films completely: 'Dutiful camp followers such as Bragaglia, Mattoli, Brignone, Gallone and so on blurred the direct onslaught of the out-and-out propaganda films with a smoke-screen of white telephones and mawkish romance . . . It seems unbelievable today that at a time of worldwide suffering there was such a proliferation of films as non-existent, as empty and as alien to the national mentality as our "commercial" films of those years . . . They were full of gesticulating, soulless shadows speaking a language which would be quite incomprehensible today. These shadows regularly dressed up in evening dress, fed on costly dishes and bellowed opera or whispered sweet nothings, depending on whether they featured famous singers or those gallant, pomaded juvenile leads made to measure at Cinecittà for the Italian provinces.' Quoted in Pierre Leprohon, *The Italian Cinema* (London 1966), 72.

Colossal head of Mussolini built by Italian troops in Ethiopia, 1936, as shown in a LUCE newsreel

Giuseppe Terragni
Mostra della Rivoluzione Fascista, Sala O,
Palazzo delle Esposizioni, 1932

Mostra della Rivoluzione Fascista,
cover of catalogue

**Giuseppe Terragni, A. Carminati, P. Lingeri,
E. Saliva, L. Vietti**
Project A, first Palazzo del Littorio competition
for via dell'Impero, 1934

Luigi Moretti
Project B, first Palazzo del Littorio competition
for via dell'Impero, 1934.
Moretti archive, Archivio Centrale di Stato, Rome

Luigi Moretti
Project B, first Palazzo del Littorio competition
for via dell'Impero, 1934, grand staircase to
Mussolini's apartment.
Archivio Moretti, Archivio Centrale di Stato, Rome

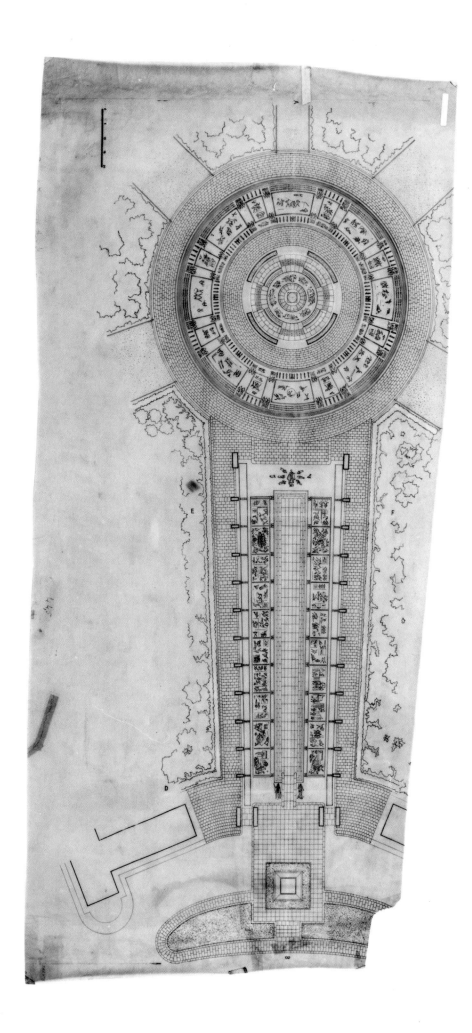

Luigi Moretti
Piazzale
dell'Impero, Foro
Mussolini, plan,
1937.
Archivio Moretti,
Archivio Centrale
di Stato, Rome

Luigi Moretti with A. Capizzano
two studies for mosaic pavement fo the
Fontana dello Sfero, Foro Mussolini, 1937.
Archivio Moretti, Archivio Centrale di Stato, Rome

Luigi Moretti
Il Duce's Gymnasium, Foro Mussolini, 1937
(mosaics by Gino Severini, statue by A. Canevari).
Archivio Moretti, Archivio Centrale di Stato, Rome

Enrico del Debbio
Stadio dei Marmi, Foro Mussolini, 1928–32
(sculptures t.r. Bernardo Morescalchi, b.l. Carlo
de Veroli)

Ernesto Lapadula
two preliminary sketches for Palazzo della
Civiltà Italiana, EUR, 1938.
Archivio Lapadula

F. Guerrini, E. Lapadula, G. Romano
Palazzo della Civiltà Italiana, EUR

Mario de Renzi, L. Figini and G. Pollini
final project for the Palazzi delle
Communicazioni e Trasporti, EUR, 1939–40

Mario de Renzi, L. Figini and G. Pollini
preliminary project for the Palazzi delle
Communicazioni e Trasporti, EUR, 1938.
Archivio De Renzi, Accademia di San Luca

Adalberto Libera
Palazzo dei Ricevimenti e Congressi, EUR,
1938–42

Gerardo Dottori
Portrait of the Duce, 1933.
Civiche Raccolte d'Arte, Milan

Tullio Crali
Nose-Diving on the City, 1939.
Private Collection, Milan

Mario Sironi
study for the mosaic *L'Italia Corporativa*, 1936.
Arco Farnese, Rome

Mario Sironi
Works and Days, 1932.
Private Collection
(not exhibited)

Mario Sironi
Shepherd, 1932.
Civico Museo Revoltella, Trieste

Mario Sironi
Hospitality (Woman with Dog), 1936.
Arco Farnese, Rome

Lucio Fontana
The Harpoonist, 1933–4.
Civico Museo d'Arte Contemporanea, Milano

Marino Marini
Boxer, 1933.
Museo d'Arte Moderna e Contemporanea di
Trento e Rovereto

Arturo Martini
The She-Wolf, 1930–1.
Courtesy Gian Ferrari Arte Moderna, Milan

Arturo Martini
Athena, 1934–5.
Galleria Nazionale d'Arte Moderna, Rome

Arturo Martini
Model for the Palazzo della Giustizia Relief,
Milan, c. 1935.
Collection Daniela Balzaretti, Milan

Corrado Cagli
View of Rome, 1937.
Private Collection, Rome

Corrado Cagli
View of Rome, 1937.
Private Collection, Rome

Alberto Savinio
The God of Armies, 1931–2.
Courtesy Gian Ferrari Arte Moderna, Milan

Giorgio Morandi
Large Still Life, 1935.
Private Collection

Giorgio de Chirico
Visit to the Mysterious Baths, 1935.
Private Collection, courtesy Galleria dello
Scudo, Verona

Giorgio de Chirico
Gladiators, 1928–9.
Civico Museo d'Arte Contemporanea, Milan

Scipione (Gino Bonichi)
Piazza Navona, 1929.
Private Collection, Rome

Fausto Pirandello
The Bath, 1935.
Private Collection, Rome

Lucio Fontana
Relief, 1934.
Instituto Valenciano de Arte Moderno, Valencia

Lucio Fontana
Abstract Sculpture, 1934.
Galleria Civica d'Arte Moderna e
Contemporanea, Turin

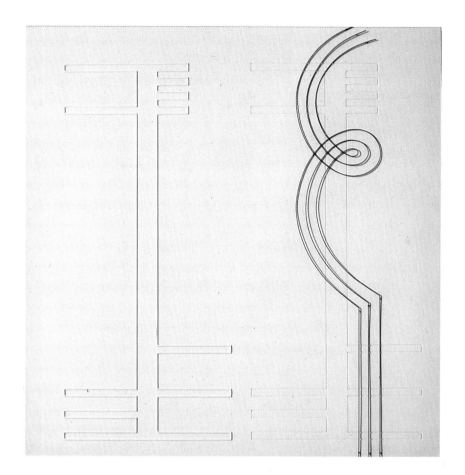

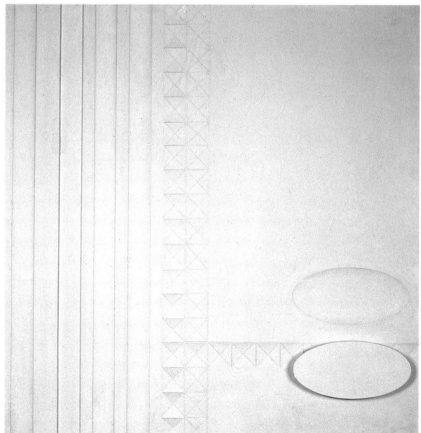

Fausto Melotti
Sculpture No. 24, 1935.
Fondo Rivetti per l'Arte, Turin

Fausto Melotti
Sculpture No. 23.
Museo d'Arte Moderna e Contemporanea di
Trento e Rovereto

Osvaldo Licini
Joke, 1933.
Museo d'Arte Contemporanea di Villa Croce,
Genoa

Osvaldo Licini
Rhythm, 1933.
Museo d'Arte Contemporanea di Villa Croce,
Genoa

Baldassarre Longoni
The Golden Lands of Italy, 1940
Banca Popolare di Cremona

Alberto Ziveri
The Fight, 1937–38.
Galleria Nazionale d'Arte Moderna, Rome

Renato Guttuso
Flight from Mount Etna, 1940.
Galleria Nazionale d'Arte Moderna, Rome

Giacomo Manzù
Crucifixion, 1939.
Galleria Nazionale d'Arte Moderna, Rome

'AGAINST DREARY CONFORMISM'

Giuseppe Bottai and Culture During the Fascist Period *Ester Coen*

1 This essay is not intended to be an exhaustive investigation of Bottai's complicated relationship with Fascism; in it I hope to chart the most important stages of the relations between this complex personality and the culture and institutions of the period, and to demonstrate the important role he played in preserving a measure of freedom and scope for individuality in the arts. For more detailed analysis of Bottai and the period see the following: G. B. Guerri, *Giuseppe Bottai, un fascista critica* (Milan, 1976); A.J. De Grand, *Bottai e la cultura fascista* (Bari, 1978); G. Bottai, *La politica delle arti: Scritte 1918–1943*, ed. A. Masi (Rome, 1992).

2 G. Bottai, *Diario 1944–48*, ed. G. B. Guerri (Milan, 1982; 2nd ed. 1992), 67.

3 Following the parliamentary ballot for the new electoral laws in January 1924, won by the strongest opponents of Fascism, the Socialist deputy Giacomo Matteotti made a violent speech denouncing the crimes of the regime. He was seized on his way to the House on the morning of 10 June by members of the Fascist action squad, and his body was not found until two months later. Public reaction was so violent that Mussolini was obliged to suspend anyone directly implicated in the assassination, thus distancing himself from any responsibility for the death warrant.

4 G. Bottai, *Vent'anni e un giorno (24 luglio 1943)* (Milan, 1949), 30.

Some understanding of the extraordinary state of mind of a man who lived through the diversity and contradictions of the twenty years of Fascism, from its euphoric rise to its tragic and inexorable downfall, and who saw everything from a position of close involvement, can be gained from the autobiographical writings of one of the most complex personalities on the political stage at the time, Giuseppe Bottai.[1] Notwithstanding an unwavering belief in the ideals of Fascism, Bottai continued to defend the rights and freedoms of culture, which he regarded as the highest expression of the dignity of the individual. His actions, and the testimony of those who knew him, depict an upright and honest man, highly cultivated, with a clear but tormented intellect.

'There was constant opposition within Fascist ranks', Bottai was to note on 16 March 1944 in his diaries, written in exile, 'and it was opposition of the democratic, libertarian, popular brand. It was mounted by people who, as well as fighting "revisionism", were battling against feudal overlords who readily resorted to violence and political crime; people who were defending "electionism" against the awarding of benefices by patronage from above. These people championed corporatism against the bureaucratization of economic and social structures, preferring internal criticism, rich in checks and balances, as against the dreary conformism of "blind discipline".'[2]

Although in the early days, after the march on Rome, Fascism had been tainted by an appalling political crime,[3] and had managed to stifle all opposition in the years that followed, by the 1930s a rapid process of normalization was taking place, aimed at reaching the fundamental consensus upon which Mussolini's new state would be built. Within the party, however, even now, the various tendencies that would so dramatically collide at the end of its twenty years in power were beginning to emerge. Bottai's position, as expressed in the columns of *Critica Fascista*, the periodical founded by him in 1923, was a moderate one – in opposition to the extremist wing of the party

personified by the intransigent Roberto Farinacci. His vision of an ethical state, with a qualified return to revolutionary policies designed to create sound economic structures by means of a new legislative body and new institutions, betrays the influence of the idealist philosopher, Giovanni Gentile. When it became clear that the idea of Fascist doctrine that Bottai retained to the end no longer corresponded to the idea entertained by his leader, it was almost too late to renounce a political belief of twenty years' standing. 'I had a clear presentiment of the destructive consequences of such duplicity and double-dealing,' wrote Bottai after the end of the Second World War; 'the seeds of the "double game", later to acquire a far more corrupting significance, were already there. Mussolini was accepted, but his system, in its harshest manifestations and in its strictest logical consequences, was rejected; and the point was reached, by this aberrant route, where anyone who appealed to the pure doctrine against corruption seemed to be playing a double game.'[4]

In November 1926, Bottai was appointed under-secretary at the Ministry of Corporations, and in 1929 was made Minister. He held the position until 1932, when Mussolini, who had come to regard the corporative system as threatening his own authority, dismissed him. While in office, Bottai conducted an important political campaign to promote the new state organization. His *Carta del Lavoro* or Labour Charter contained a series of ethical principles aimed at guaranteeing labour relations. Capital and labour represented the two (reconciled) halves of a 'living organism' – such was Bottai's vision of the Fascist state. He based himself, however, on the idea that state intervention should be limited to the organization and monitoring of systems, and that it should never go beyond the limits defined by a legislation that was set up to impose discipline on the social system. It was during this period, and with these convictions, that he played an active part in cultural debate, maintaining the same libertarian position that had

driven him to give a legal framework to his ideas on the political development of the new state.

It is difficult for us to comprehend today how a man who had lived through the violence of Fascism from the outset, when its activities already contained the seeds of dictatorship, could have believed that the regime would ever turn into a liberal institution. Bottai's was an act of faith. Was it the utopian dream of an insecure revolutionary, or the dubious conviction that he would be able to oppose from within a system whose dangers he already suspected? To put it differently: was his silent complicity designed merely to save his own skin, or did he imagine that his revisionist longings could prevail over Il Duce's despotic logic? Probably these alternatives coexisted in Bottai's mind, evidence of an intellectual conflict that had certainly not escaped the wily Mussolini. Hence his removal from politically powerful positions (though he was never totally marginalized) to posts in which his critical intelligence could be exploited without risk to Mussolini's totalitarian aspirations.

It may now seem difficult to understand the moral hold that Fascist ideology and the Fascist leader had over Bottai, but the power of seduction exerted by Mussolini over the Italian people, especially after the early 1930s, should never be underestimated. Combined with a series of reforms that appeared to be helping the country to find its way out of a difficult economic situation, Mussolini's electrifying rallying calls to the Italian people seemed to bear a message that many wanted to hear. They wanted to be convinced, by the rhetoric, that history could be on their side. 'Leader and followers understood each other at once', wrote Bottai in 1946, 'but it stopped there. The regime, not wishing to be "representative", stopped short at "representation". It ceased to be a regime and became a monopoly. The man's spontaneous language of mime became limited to a narrow range of gestures that the crowds particularly loved. They would call for these gestures and go into raptures over them. "Mussolinism" had become a ritual.'[5]

Until the mid-1930s intellectuals were allowed freedom; in fact they were actively encouraged in their work. At least, so it appeared. Mussolini thought, perhaps, that an image of Fascism could be created through him alone, and that the choreography focused on his own person had no need of further endorsement from elsewhere. Although he had declared that 'there is no civilization without art', immediately encouraging the creation of 'a new art, the art of our time, the art of Fascism',[6] Mussolini (initially) imposed no directives or precise regulations. He may have considered that the spirit of Fascism alone was strong enough to inspire the works of the future.

As an intellectual, one of the few holding high office in the party, Bottai felt it his duty to make his views known. As early as the autumn of 1926 he launched a debate in the pages of his magazine, a 'survey on Fascist art',[7] inviting the views of writers, architects, artists and critics. The results[8] showed that the time was not yet ripe for the formulation of a true Fascist aesthetic; Bottai's view was, however, that 'if some statement had to be made with regard to Fascist art at this time, it could be said to have manifested itself in a *tendency*, stemming from the same tendency that operated in politics, towards sturdier, more spacious, stronger constructions, in the grand tradition of indigenous Italian art, which is still to be found alive and well beneath the encrustations of foreign influences'.[9]

At the same time he showed his distaste for the art of mere apologetics, which gave a platitudinous or grotesque impression of Fascism. Bottai was still in favour of state subsidies that would guarantee to 'the choicest artists', through the corporative organizations of which he was always an ardent advocate, 'artistic, moral and spiritual protection'.

An art of the regime had been under discussion since just after Mussolini came to power in 1922, but not in the way that Bottai would have wanted. On one hand, Filippo Tommaso Marinetti, with a group of the young and not-so-young (including some new members), had fought to keep the banner of Futurism flying. Harking back to the 'Interventionist' battles (for Italy's entry into the First World War) that he had fought alongside Mussolini in

1914, Marinetti maintained that a combination of the emerging forms of Futurism, and the mechanistic ideals of Fascism, could be used to consecrate the rise and rapid forward progress of the 'Fascist revolution'. In fact, until the *Mostra della Rivoluzione fascista*, held in 1932 in celebration of the tenth anniversary of the Fascist March on Rome,[10] the 'lines of force' and 'dynamic simultaneism' of Futurism did indeed represent the celebratory symbolism of the new era. The synthetic, simple forms in gleaming metal, and the idea of an avant garde projected into the future could be seen as corresponding to the urgency and swift action of a government that was already developing a recognizable ideological stance.

On the other hand, Margherita Sarfatti, the art critic, well-known in Fascist circles and on intimate terms with Mussolini, had campaigned for her 'Novecento' group, which included artists from a very broad spectrum of styles, to represent contemporary Italian art abroad as well as at home, in order to show that it was based on historical and traditional sources.

It was Bottai's cultural line that prevailed, however; he was already trying to create the structures and systems for state intervention. Besides being a means of monitoring the quality of the artists' work, this political move was later to turn into a providential source of government support.[11]

Rome became the cultural as well as the administrative centre of the new scenario that was Fascist Italy; and this was taking shape fast. While archaeological excavations brought forth the vestiges of a Rome that had been strong and powerful, and urban restructuring at ground level resuscitated something of a former grandeur, the city also played host to contemporary art exhibitions. The talk was now of a Fascist civilization, though it was evident that any 'new' culture would have to lead to 'a community of thought and doctrine, system and method'.[12] In a speech delivered at the end of 1928,[13] Bottai stated that 'only unitary thinking and an organized culture can establish the relationships and connections that are necessary to give the politics of a ruling class a national quality. A grand political scheme is, fundamentally, simply a method of thinking through, devising,

prearranging and organizing the relationship between the values, tangible and intangible, that affect the life of a nation; an energy that brings the particular back to the universal, determines the underlying qualities of a historical process and creates, in one all-embracing movement, a political style and the character of an era.'

The continuity of a distinguished and highly cultured tradition, and of the technical skills that went with it,[14] was to be the inspiration for a new intellectual flowering and restructuring in which artists were invited to collaborate, directly or indirectly. With the passing of the years, as centralizing policies began to bite, this nationalistic fervour and 'Italian' character, which had lulled even the most educated sections of society into the illusion of belonging to a unified nation at last, took on another aspect: *romanità*. The cult of Rome and being Roman, one of the values enshrined in Fascist rhetoric from the start, grew to astonishing proportions, assuming external signs and rituals that were increasingly formal: 'Rome', pronounced Mussolini, 'is our point of departure and our point of reference; it is our symbol and, if you like, our myth. We dream of a Roman Italy, an Italy that is wise and strong, disciplined and imperial. Much of the spirit of Ancient Rome is being born again in Fascism; the Lictorian fasces are Roman, our war machine is Roman, our pride and our courage are Roman too.'[15]

Bottai was appointed Governor of Rome at the beginning of 1935 and appeared increasingly ready to comply fully with Mussolini's directives;[16] he was responsible for initiating a series of public works aimed at giving Rome an aura of eternity plus, simultaneously, the orderliness of a modern city. His official responsibilities put him in a position where he could extol the greatness of Mussolini's Rome by comparing it favourably, in ideological terms, with the glories of ancient Rome.

Mussolini, who was by now enjoying great public approval, decided to try his luck abroad as well. Defying the opposition that had grown even at high levels within the regime, he embarked on the successful conquest of Ethiopia. Bottai was also a participant in this expansionist campaign,[17] and on his return he was rewarded with the post of Minister of National Education;[18] he was to remain

5 In Bottai (as note 2), 317, entry dated 15 March 1946. The same sentence is repeated by Bottai, with minimal alterations, in Bottai (as note 5), 28.

6 The sentence quoted is from a lecture given by Mussolini in the Accademia di Belle Arti in Perugia on 5 October 1926.

7 In *Critica Fascista*, vol. 4, no. 20 (15 October 1926).

8 *Resultanze dell'inchiesta sull'arte fascista*, in *Critica Fascista*, vol. 5, no. 4 (15 February 1927).

9 See preceding note.

10 The big *Mostra della Rivoluzione Fascista* was held in the Palazzo delle Esposizioni in Rome in 1932. It was under the curatorship of Dino Alfieri and Luigi Freddi and was intended as a historical exhibition, with a section documenting acts of heroism and front line combat by Fascist militants. The personal and public biography of Mussolini was given ample coverage, as was the social and economic organization of Fascism. The contribution made by Italian Fascists abroad and the achievements of the regime in ten years in power were also featured. The façade of the palace was decorated by the architects Libera and De Renzi with four vast, almost abstract Roman fasces and, in the words of the catalogue, the 'geometrical purity' of the volume of the building thus garlanded symbolized 'the synthesis of the totalitarian, all-embracing ideals of the Fascist regime'.

11 During the difficult period of the late 1930s, the Two Per Cent Law (see note 23) made it possible for many artists to survive; the problems they faced were compounded by the closure of the few remaining private galleries and by the absence of any private buyers at the time.

12 G. Bottai, 'Fascismo e cultura', *Critica Fascista*, vol. 6, no. 23 (1 December 1928).

13 See note 12.

14 These ideas had already been expressed on paper in the review *Valori Plastici*, published by Mario Broglio in Rome between 1918 and 1922. The participants were artists interested in affirming the quality of Italian art as against the better known, more widely recognized art of France; included were Giorgio de Chirico, Alberto Savinio, Carlo Carrà, Giorgio Morandi and Ardengo Soffici.

15 Speech by Mussolini quoted by A. Munoz in *Roma di Mussolini* (Milan, 1935), 481–82.

16 'The Capitoline Administration and its Governors loyally bow to Il Duce's command, with unity and continuity of purpose', wrote Bottai in an essay published in *Nuova Antologia* on 1 January 1937 and reprinted in Bottai, *Politica fascista delle arti* (Rome, 1940), 5.

17 Bottai was appointed civil governor of Addis Ababa in May 1936.

18 On 22 November 1936.

19 Bottai (as note 5), 63.

20 The Premio Bergamo was the clear antithesis of the Premio Cremona, the prize established by Roberto Farinacci to display the images and iconography of Fascist propaganda.

21 This phrase is from Bottai's article 'Esposizione del 42', published in *L'illustrazione italiana*, 18 December 1938.

22 Bottai, letter to his family, spring 1944, in Guerri (as note 1), 248.

for more than six years in this position, in which his abilities and intelligence were at last used to the full.

In this new role, which posed no obvious threat to Il Duce's omnipotence, Bottai succeeded in carving out a path that was to deviate from Mussolini's policy of 'Believe, Obey, Fight', and which allowed some scope for the expression of individual opinions: 'It is true that in twenty years of Fascism the new concepts dug deeper and deeper into the life of the country, effecting a radical transformation', wrote Bottai later,[19] 'yet as far as culture is concerned there was an ever-deepening conflict which had frozen intellectuals into sterile conservatism.'

Bottai was becoming increasingly aware of the anti-democratic, dictatorial direction in which politics were moving, particularly since the treaty with Germany; his response was to devise and promote a series of directives for schools, and also some legislation for the protection of the national heritage and in defence of contemporary artistic movements.[20] Amongst actions worth recording was the institution in February 1939 of the School Charter which heralded a fundamental reform of the entire school system. In the same year Bottai created his Central Institute for the Restoration of Works of Art and promulgated the Two Per Cent Law whereby this proportion of the cost of public construction work would be used for decoration. He also set up an arts administration department with an office devoted to contemporary art within the Ministry of Public Education. At the same time he founded two reviews, *Le Arti* and *Primato*, both receptive to the discussion of contemporary art and accessible to writers who had never joined the Fascist party. In 1940 Bottai established the Premio Bergamo, a prize competed for by the least conservative and least traditional artists of the period.

By now, however, times had changed so radically that these political actions, while they protected the various cultural sectors concerned, exacerbated the contradictions inherent in Fascism and exposed the difficult relationship that had been developing between Bottai and the regime over the past few years. On the one hand these demonstrated that he was fundamentally an enlightened and liberal man; on the other he nevertheless acquiesced in such appalling decisions of

Mussolini's as the promulgation of the execrable Race Laws in 1938. Bottai's campaign for a reconstruction of the Fascist state through strength of intellect was condemned from the outset by the cruel reality of current political alliances, which he had neither the opportunity nor the ability to oppose. Liberty as a moral value, upheld unswervingly by Bottai in spite of a thousand contradictions, was insufficient to permit the artists to express the dramatic tensions of the moment. Creative stress was succeeded by an unnerving calm that seemed to suffocate all inspiration, reducing their output to stereotyped images with little or no content.

Empty formalism was the general reaction of most intellectuals of the period to the fierce repression and the onset of war. Paradoxically, their freedom of expression imposed its own restrictions on action. The regime was later to intervene to stamp out individuality of style or experiment, as if to compress personal consciousness into a single, coherent whole. The result of this can be observed in the buildings and decoration put up for EUR, the world fair of 1942, intended to celebrate twenty years of Fascism and to extend Rome towards the sea in memory of the deeds of yore. In 1938, Bottai had declared that 'we shall avoid the superfluous and the grandiose, pomp, opulence, and the ephemeral, and strive for an organic effect, a synthesis'.[21] The government did the exact opposite, seeking by means of the superfluous and the grandiose, by ephemeral pomp and opulence, to draw a veil over the dramatic compromises that had been made, the dangerous political and economic situation that had ensued and that was later magnified out of all proportion by the huge cost of the war.

Bottai's dismissal from the Ministry in February 1943 coincided with his distancing himself from Il Duce's crazy schemes, which were to bring Italy to the brink of the abyss. To stop him, Bottai appended his signature to the decree of 25 July 1943 that provoked the dictator's downfall. For Bottai this was a painful decision, but one that had been brewing through the years of deception and betrayal of the ideals which he had loyally maintained for more than twenty years, and in which he continued to believe. Bottai's signature gave Italy the chance to turn the page on one of the saddest, most tragic periods of her history.

Bottai himself was arrested by the new government of Marshal Badoglio. Released in September 1943, he decided to enrol in the Foreign Legion, to expiate 'the defect of critical and moral strength that has prevented my opposing the degeneration of Fascism to any effect'.[22] He returned to Italy in the summer of 1948, when his term of service came to an end; he had already learned that his conviction for Fascist crimes had been overturned.

Translated by Caroline Beamish

CONTEMPORARY VOICES *Compiled by John Willett*

In Defence of Modern Art, 1938 *Giuseppe Bottai*

Is the present controversy about modern art such a bad thing? We believe not, firstly because there are matters that do not create argument without good reason, and secondly because it is likely that ideas will in due course be clarified to some useful effect. Nor do we find it regrettable that the controversy has taken a political turn, or that this is prompted by the measures taken for the defence of our race. Countering the threat to our culture seems perfectly reasonable, and in line with the Fascist way of doing things. Aside from their obvious political implications, the measures taken with respect to education have a spiritual value: any defence of the race must start where young minds are formed. The same goes for art, where – though here any such 'measures' might seem difficult, if not inappropriate – it is after all reasonable enough to discuss matters calmly, with a view to reassessing the principles and intuitions of modern art in the light of racism.

Leaving aside the remarks of certain obviously ill-informed commentators, the overriding concern for the chief enemies of contemporary art is their suspicion that our race policy will stop short at 'measures', and will fail to address the spiritual values of Italian man. They therefore think fit to make a clean sweep of contemporary art – and especially, it would seem, architecture and the figurative arts – in order to remove any possible obstacle to the emergence of a pure art: that is, an art that is wholly and (let us presume) worthily Italian. We might subscribe to this laudable aspiration, if only it came to us couched in honest and rational terms.

Honesty means not confounding the bad with the good, and not throwing everything too high-handedly into the dustbin. To condemn all modern architecture as Jewish – simply because ugly housing has been built on the outskirts of our cities, large and small – seems gratuitous, to say the least. Attached to such evidence, the name of international Jewry holds no terrors for us. Even the best informed of the hostile critics has not been able to show convincingly that Tirrenia, Sabaudia or Guidonia (to name but a few *cities*) have been designed or built in the Jewish manner.

A rational approach would mean making a properly argued indictment of the contamination of Italian art over the last thirty years, and identifying the sources of that contamination as precisely as possible. After such a scrutiny – which must of course be carried out by someone with the right critical qualifications – would come the time for naming names and demonstrating, again in earnest, that certain artists have succumbed to the Jewish bacillus. But we venture to predict that such a scrutiny will be largely fruitless, for we cannot accept that the intelligence and good taste of the Italian people have been fatally compromised by a passing interest in *dadaismo*, *surrealismo* and those other futile exercises that condemn themselves as soon their names acquire an Italian ending. Let us name only the true artists. Is it worth mentioning the others? Cagli and his like have never seriously engaged the critical faculties of reputable people.

Such widespread and hasty denunciations have led to a suspicion that racism is being used as a cloak for some obscurely reactionary intentions: the references to 'tradition' begin to seem vague and irrelevant to the aims of serious criticism. At times this overtly reactionary attitude (a term that has particularly incensed certain writers) has been dismissed as petty, quasi-political speculation; or even as the malice of elderly pundits, or the bitterness and gall of the unsuccessful. In our view such accusations, too, are almost entirely groundless, since the charges of internationalism levelled against contemporary Italian art are not always unjustified or totally absurd.

The tendency of Italian artists to seek intellectual refreshment in Paris has long been polemically called the 'Paris disease'. We need to establish exactly how much and what these artists of ours have derived from their Parisian experience: has it been a mere motive for artistic exercises, or so strong an impression as to alter the Italian nature of their character for good? This is something for our critics to establish: dispassionate critics who review what needs reviewing. No easy task, this, since the sickness can lurk within the fold, undetected. The supposed connection between the 'Paris disease' and international Jewry may be significant – particularly in reference to certain pseudo-artistic experiments, the turbid Parisian cuisine of émigré brains. This connection collapses, however, when people leap to the wild conclusion that all modern Italian art has the French disease, therefore it is all Jewish, therefore it is not Italian, it is internationalist, anti-traditional, and so on and so forth. It seems naive, to say the least, to imagine that our entire intelligentsia has done nothing but rework foreign or Jewish models, without effort or misgivings, without any trace of sincerity or good faith, and with just one overriding concern: fashion, supposedly the be-all and end-all of most contemporary art. If that were the case, we could safely assert that, if art has any meaning, there are no artists in Italy at all. Or else let us have the names of those other artists, the true ones, who have remained loyal to 'tradition'! On the other hand, if the accusation is directed at anyone who has built ugly houses or clumsy furniture, or who has painted or sculpted in the so-called Novecento 'manner', we may as well ignore it: Italian good taste and intelligence have already passed judgment on that, as they have done for two thousand years.

If anyone argues that this debate is purely marginal, that really it is not worth while for so many people to get so worked up over such questions, we might reply that this is no ordinary controversy. This time, the confrontation takes place on political terrain. What is at stake is not only 'traditional' versus 'modern' (an antithesis more apparent than real), but the very principles of our racist campaign and of our civilization. If we are not careful – and it must be said that the defence has been unanimous – we may end up with an apotheosis of the interior decorator, a colossal reversion to the finest traditions of the international *pompier* style.

Giuseppe Bottai 'L'arte moderna',
Critica Fascista, 1 December 1938.

Translated by Caroline Beamish

Bottai's article is plainly a response to the Racial Laws of 1938 and the closer relations with the Third Reich of which they were an expression. What this could mean for the German artists who had chosen to work in Italy can be seen from the following extracts.

Some German Italophils, 1940–1945   *Kurt Craemer*

1940

Rudolf Levy was a rarity among German painters. Examples of his great talent are to be found in a few German museums, though not nearly enough. To judge from what I have seen of his poems, he also had a remarkable gift for expressing himself in literature. He was then living in Rome in a depressing pensione. But no sooner had we looked over our new quarters [in Florence] and assured him that he would have all the space he needed, than there he was. Of course such changes of residence were not allowed, and it was only the amiability of an official in the Aliens' Department that saved him from being sent back. But Karli Sohn-Rethel also came to join us, and at last our life returned to normal.

We worked all day and met in the evenings round the fire; it was a cold winter. Levy in particular, after many years, found a certain measure of security. Our communal life protected him, and the presence of trusted friends helped him resolve accidents and problems, not least financial ones. And so our rooms, which had long resembled a doss-house, once again started to look like studios.

I had done no work at all for over a year. Levy for more like two. It was a long time since any of us had been able to go from one room to another and judge, with a certain detachment, what had been achieved. When Werner Gilles turned up from Palinuro, with vast rolls of paintings, watercolours and drawings, and we also found a gifted Italian painter living in the top attic, after years of isolation the ensuing set-up was just about perfect . . .

1941

Amongst our regular visitors were Professor Dr Klaus Schilling and his wife. We greatly enjoyed his company, since in him the many talents to which he owed his success were combined with a very human geniality. We found there was so much to be learned from him, not merely about music and painting but in the field of literature too. This man who had made such a mark in his own profession as a bacteriologist did nothing by halves.

As is common with great achievers, he organized his time precisely. Morning and early afternoon were devoted to his bacteriological experiments; for on reaching the age of retirement as Director of the Robert Koch Institute – he specialized in tropical diseases – he had been invited to Italy by Mussolini, whose government gave him every facility for continuing his work. The laboratories of the biggest Florence hospital were put at his disposal. There he would work until four o'clock every day before systematically visiting various art exhibitions, or if these were not available – all the museums having shut by that hour – then private collections or other shows.

In those days when he used to spend his evenings at our fireside, he was – most understandably – fascinated by the work and personality of Giorgione, and his obsessive urge to get to the bottom of these things led him to pass the last hours of the afternoon in the library of the German Art Historical Institute, one floor beneath our flat. We often talked about this painter, who so enchanted both of us and made us wish to know more about the man himself.

Schilling's attitude to modern art was lively and shrewd; it was never dogmatic or restricted to his youthful experiences in Munich. Discussing painting with him was always fruitful and rewarding. What moved him most, however, was his love of music. He told me that at times he was torn between Bach and Beethoven, that Beethoven would at one moment strike him as the root of all evil and Bach as a fount of holiness, while there were other phases of his life where the exact opposite applied.

As for National Socialism, his attitude (as will already have been gathered) was one of total rejection, indeed more than that: he loathed the vulgarity of that so-called 'Movement' just as he loathed all preconceived opinions. He had applied himself far too radically to real problems to take such a crude religious substitute seriously. Race prejudice was unknown to him, and the campaign against the Jews had given him a conspicuous concern about them from the first.

Around then I heard from my mother – Schilling himself told us nothing about it –

that he was having difficulties with his work. The obvious conclusion was that his experiments on people were going badly. He was barred from doing further work at Careggi. Subsequently he left Florence, much against his will, to carry on his activities at the asylum in Volterra. I can remember our listening one evening to a BBC report of a destroyer being sunk with the loss of a few hundred lives, and hearing Schilling say something which later struck me as significant in the light of his eventual fate. It was to the effect that 'if only they would allow us to sacrifice the same number of people as have just died for nothing, there would soon be no more incurable diseases'.

Years later my mother got a letter from his wife; it came from Dachau. Volterra had ended disagreeably; it was impossible to collaborate seriously with Italian doctors. They themselves were now based in Dachau, where they had a delightful house; going off to paint there at weekends took her back to her student days at the Academy. All the same, a lot had altered. Dachau was no longer what it used to be. But of course this might be partly due to herself.

Her husband was happy and interested in his work; he sent affectionate greetings . . .

1945

One evening in early 1945, after northern and southern Italy had joined up one more, we were terribly shaken to hear the first radio reports of the liberation of the concentration camps by British and American troops. Tuning in a bit later on my crackling portable, I heard something about a director of the Robert Koch Institute and experiments that cost six hundred lives; then at the end they repeated his name: Professor Klaus Schilling. The site of his experiments was given as Dachau.

It sent shivers down our spine. We thought of Giorgione, Bach and Beethoven; of songs to the lute; of his wholly civilized attitude to Rudolf Levy, to Pegrim, my black language teacher, to a Jewish couple, the Baers.

He was executed. Hanged. Later I read a more detailed account in the New York

German-language paper *Aufbau*. According to this he had accepted his sentence, but asked for the execution to be postponed so that the results of his dreadful researches should not be lost to humanity. This request was refused.

According to the *Aufbau* report, he gave the Nazi salute and shouted 'Heil Hitler!' as the noose was put round his neck.

That year a letter came from Florence, from a young sculptor who told me our friend Pegrim had become paranoiac when the American troops entered the city, and was now in the Volterra asylum. There was, alas, little or no hope of his getting cured. A postscript added, almost by the way, that there was no news of Rudolf Levy, who had supposedly been shipped off to Germany.

It was only gradually that I learned the story of his last days.

Visiting his flat after a long interval, he is said to have found a letter from a Florence gallery inviting him to send some of his pictures and asking him to appear there himself at a given hour to discuss sales and prices. He told his friends, who warned strongly against this. They even spoke of raising the prospective total themselves; he refused their offer and presented himself at the gallery to keep the appointment . . .

His name is not listed in the records of the concentration camp at Dachau. It has however been found among those of a group of people who left the goods yard at Rifredi in cattle trucks on 24 December 1944. The train in question had, it seems, been held up by troop movements at the junction at Carpi.

It was a particularly cold winter, and around the end of December temperatures remained well below zero. Though there is no documentary record, there is a report saying that a mass grave was uncovered near the sidings, containing an unspecified number of bodies, among which presumably was that of Rudolf Levy. At the time of his summons to that Florentine gallery he had just recovered from a bad bout of consumption. Initiates knew the place as a Gestapo outfit. Why did he go there when he was not even hard up for the money?

It must have been in 1938, when we were living on Ischia, that Rudolf was summoned to report at the German consulate in Naples. Troubled by the look of uncertainty which this provoked in his face, I offered to go there with him. He gladly accepted, and we went off together. Opposite the entrance to the consulate, in the via dei Mille, he asked me to wait at a café.

Rudolf Levy, *Still-Life*, 1923

About a hour later he returned and showed me his passport. A large J had been stamped on the first page, covering everything else, and a new name had been added to his: 'Israel'.

We left the café and followed the crowded street back to the centre of the city. At a particular spot, where the via dei Mille gives into the via Filangeri, he suddenly said: 'Stop here till I am ten or twelve metres from you, then call out 'Israel!' I want to see if I react.'

That was a joke, said in irony, a bitter, deeply felt wisecrack.

But one day he must have got fed up with all that clever camouflage, the permanent flight, the incessant evasions, the eternal self-denials. And that is what his friends in Florence never quite understood. He no longer wished to disclaim the name of Israel.

He had reacted to the call.

From Kurt Craemer, *Mein Panoptikum*, ed. Rudolf Hagelstange (Hamburg: Hoffmann und Campe, 1965), 124–25, 128–32, 132–34, 233–36.

Translated by John Willett

Kurt Craemer (1912–1961) gives this account of Rudolf Levy (1875-1943), one of Matisse's German pupils before the First World War. An appreciation of Italy's artistic heritage was not enough to prevent crimes against humanity, and the group's cultivated friend Professor Schilling, who found the Florentine doctors too uncooperative in his malaria research, was later invited by Himmler to experiment on Polish Catholic priests. He was tried by the US Third Army as one of the first batch of German war criminals in 1945.

Overleaf
Mossoviet studios, General Plan for the Reconstruction of Moscow, 1935. Shchusev Architecture Museum, Moscow

МОСКВА

ПОГОНО-ЛОСИНЫЙ ОСТРОВ

ЧЕРКИЗОВСКОЕ ШОССЕ

ИЗМАЙЛОВО

СОКОЛЬНИЧЕСКИЙ ПАРК

Р. ЯУЗА

СТРОМЫНКА

ИЗМАЙЛОВСКИЙ ПАРК ИМ. СТАЛИНА

БАЯ МАГИСТРАЛЬ

УЛ. КИРОВА

НОВАЯ МАГИСТРАЛЬ

ШОССЕ ЭНТУЗИАСТОВ

НОВОЕ БУЛЬВАРНОЕ КОЛЬЦО

Б. ОРДЫНКА

КУСЦОВСКИЙ ПАРК

НОВАЯ МАГИСТРАЛЬ

ПАРКОВОЕ КОЛЬЦО

ВОСТОЧНЫЙ КАНАЛ

ТЕКСТИЛЬЩИКИ

ПАРК КУЗЬМИНКИ

ЛЮБЛИНО

MOSCOW

INTRODUCTION

David Elliott

1 Mikhail Heller and Aleksandr M. Nekrich, *Utopia in Power. The History of the Soviet Union from 1917 to the Present* (New York, 1986), 289. Pyatakov, originally head of the Ukrainian Bolsheviks and a member of the United Opposition against Stalin in 1926, was executed for 'Trotskyism' in 1938 after his show trial with Radek of the previous year.

2 A group of artists headed by Ilya Repin, known as the *Wanderers* or *Itinerants* on account of the fact that they, and exhibitions of their work, travelled around Russia.

3 An acronym based on the Russian words for proletarian culture.

4 See Lynn Mally, *Culture of the Future. The Proletkult Movement in Revolutionary Russia* (Oxford 1990).

5 Lunacharsky was dismissed from Narkompros in 1929.

6 See J. Arch Getty and Roberta T. Manning, eds., *Stalinist Terror. New Perspectives* (Cambridge, 1993).

7 Sheila Fitzpatrick, *The Cultural Front. Power and Culture in Revolutionary Russia* (Ithaca, 1992), 115–148.

'Since you believe that people's convictions cannot change in a short period of time, you conclude that our statements . . . are insincere . . . that they are lies . . . I agree that people who are not Bolsheviks, the category of ordinary people in general, cannot make an instant change, a U-turn, amputating their own convictions . . . We are a party of people who make the impossible possible . . . and if the party demands it . . . we will be able by an act of will to expel from our brains in twenty-four hours ideas that we have held for years. Yes, I will see black where I thought I saw white, because for me there is no life outside the party.' (Yuri Pyatakov, 1928)[1]

Stalin's cultural revolution started in 1928 with the first Five Year Plan and was, in the first instance, orchestrated through the natural rivalries of existing groups of artists, architects, photographers, film-makers, musicians and writers. The October Revolution of 1917 had failed to answer the question of what the new culture of the Soviet state should be and, throughout the 1920s, a large number of different tendencies were encouraged. Anatoly Lunacharsky, head of NarKomPros (the Ministry of Public Enlightenment), was the main provider of state patronage.

Leningrad, the former Imperial capital of St Petersburg, was as important a cultural centre as Moscow, the new capital, and the fate of its avant-garde pressaged developments in the rest of the country. At one pole of the complicated Soviet art world were the ultra-realist members of AKhRR (Association of Artists of Revolutionary Russia), who worked in the traditions of nineteenth-century genre and history painting. At the other, in enmity and defiance, were the non-objective Suprematists who orbited around Kazimir Malevich at the Leningrad GInKhuK (State Institute of Artistic Culture) and the committed neo-Futurist LEF (Left Front of the Arts) artists and writers who were led by Vladimir Mayakovsky, Aleksandr Rodchenko and Sergei Tretyakov in Moscow. Everyone could see that the dictatorship of the proletariat was at hand, but there was no agreement about what form its culture should take.

Deference to the taste of Lenin, who had died in 1924, did little to clarify the problem. Certainly he disliked Futurism and non-objective art of any kind (and criticized Lunacharsky for supporting it); like Stalin he favoured the realist paintings of the late nineteenth-century *Peredvizhniki* (Wanderers) some of which had addressed social issues;[2] there were many artists within AKhRR who were still working in this pre-Revolutionary style. From the mid-1920s an increasingly strong sentiment became manifest that the Revolution had still to create a popular culture and that the art of the avant-garde was neither intelligible nor acceptable to the broad mass of the people.

Aleksandr Bogdanov, a former close associate of Lenin, had formulated a theory about a new form of proletarian culture which after the Revolution became institutionalized into regional organizations called Proletkults.[3] As well as encouraging artistic production by artists and peasants, these campaigned for the destruction of monuments and the art of the past to make way for the growth of the new. Lenin and Lunacharsky were appalled by their desecration of the national patrimony, as well as by the possibilities this offered to enemies abroad to dismiss the gains of the Revolution. Accordingly, the Proletkults were quickly disbanded, in October 1920, and the whole question of what constituted proletarian culture remained unresolved.[4]

After Lenin's death there was a hiatus in the party leadership, and a conflict ensued between Stalin, Trotsky and Bukharin for the succession. By 1928 Stalin was established as general secretary of the party; Trotsky, who represented the left, was in internal exile (he was deported in the following year); and Bukharin was beginning to be marginalized, with Lunacharsky, on the right as a bourgeois intellectual.[5] At this point, Stalin's position was not yet unassailable and the spectres of 'Leftism' and 'Rightism' provided him with convenient enemies. This started with the campaign against 'bourgeois specialists' in the Shakhty Trial of the same year – the first of a series of show trials that were to recur throughout the next decade with a terrifying regularity.[6]

As part of this political, social and economic upheaval, a revolution in culture took place, in which party activists used the doctrine of class war to seize control of the universities, the media and professions.[7] In both art and literature they referred back to the Bolshevik victories of the Civil War ten years previously. Out of this maelstrom a new, upwardly mobile proletarian party intelligentsia was created which owed its position to Stalin's initiative and found work within the rapidly expanding bureaucracy and newly created industries.

Trotsky had argued against the possibility of a strongly committed, proletarian culture,[8] but Stalin now resurrected the idea and found active support amongst a younger generation of artists, writers, musicians and architects, many of whom were members of the Komsomol, the activist Young Communists' League. The intelligibility of the arts was one of the key issues in this debate, and in March 1928 the first All Union Party Conference on Film Questions cast its lot in favour of populism when it called for fictional films to be 'made in a way that can be appreciated by millions'. By the summer, the All Union Conference on Propaganda and Agitation bolstered the growing hysteria against, 'bourgeois formalism' and 'reactionary jugglers', without giving any clear guidelines as to what kind of art was acceptable.

In this polemic, each art form soon had its own proletarian pressure group which received tacit encouragment from the state.[9] The members of RAPP (Russian Association of Proletarian Writers)[10], took the lead by criticizing established writers such as Vladimir Mayakovsky, Yuri Olesha, Mikhail Bulgakov, Boris Pilniak, Isaak Babel and Evgeny Zamyatin for individualist, formalist or negative attitudes. Mayakovsky's poetry and satirical plays, as well as the work of other members of the LEF group, were among the first targets and in the January 1928 issue of *Novyi LEF*, the poet answered back in an article sarcastically entitled 'You are not understood by the Workers and Peasants'. But there was little respite. Entering what was described in contemporary slogans as 'the Storm of the Five Year Plan', the climate of criticism became increasingly hysterical. The cultural crime of 'formalism' became a sure sign not only of bourgeois and therefore anti-proletarian origins, but also of implacable enmity to the new society which was then being built.

In the frenzied activity of the first Five Year Plan, which by the end of 1932 had been completed ahead of schedule in four years, the cultural revolution began to consume many of those who had been its earliest advocates. At this stage Stalin most probably had no clearly thought out cultural policy but was more concerned with the problems of building up party membership, consolidating power and achieving the plan.[11]

By April 1932 the cultural revolution seemed as though it was in danger of spiralling out of control, and

Stalin with the Central Committee decided that the party should take a firm hand. A resolution *On the Reformation of Literary-Artistic Organizations* accordingly decreed that all artistic groups, with their magazines and journals, should be disbanded and that artists who supported 'the platform of Soviet power' should come together in a single union.

This brought the proletarian arts movement to an end and replaced it with party art. Yet, just as the identification of enemies had tended to be imprecise, based on personal rivalries as well as on the backgrounds, friends and associates of the victim, so the establishment of positive standards for official art was also vague.[12] The doctrine of Socialist Realism was officially announced at the First All Union Congress of Soviet Writers in 1934 where Andrei Zhdanov mouthed Stalin's words by exhorting writers to become 'engineers of human souls' and to use the method of 'revolutionary romanticism' to stand with 'both feet on the ground of real life.' It was left to the artists' unions to decide what this meant in the stylistic terms which related to each discipline. In painting and sculpture, artists who had previously been associated with the ultra-conservative AKhRR during the 1920s were the most favoured.[13]

Because Socialist Realism was a method of creation rather than a style or an aesthetic system, its theorists concentrated on abstract definitions of the kind of political consciousness that all the arts had to reflect and through which their success or failure could be judged. The first of these rules of thumb was *narodnost'* (based on the word for 'people' and 'nation') which was centred around the relationship of the work to popular ideas and sentiments as well as to the ethnic origins of the people it depicted. *Klassovost'* related to the class awareness of the artist which had been heightened during the Cultural Revolution and to how he or she depicted such concerns. *Partiinost'* was the expression of the central and leading role of the Communist party in all aspects of Soviet life as well as membership of the party; and *ideinost'* was the introduction of new thinking and attitudes, of course first approved by the party, as the central content of the artwork. This method of orchestrating culture by command was, in theory, able to incorporate a multiplicity of styles; yet, as the political climate became increasingly harsh, the aesthetic dislikes of party hacks became more capricious. Any trace of foreign influence in painting became suspect and was virulently denounced for closet 'cosmopolitanism'; such relatively biddable artists as Aleksandr Deineka were to suffer this fate in the 1940s.

8 Lev Trotsky, *Literature and Revolution* (1923) (Ann Arbor, 1960).

9 As well as RAPP there were VOPRA (the All Union Association of Proletarian Architects), RAPKh (the Russian Association of Proletarian Artists), ROPF (the Russian Assocation of Proletarian Photographers), RAPM (the Russian Association of Proletarian Musicians), and others. See David Elliott, *New Worlds. Russian Art and Society 1900–1937* (London, 1986), 23–26; 118–45.

10 From the early 1920s until 1927 known as VAPP (the All Union Association of Proletarian Writers) when it was renamed as RAPP.

11 Fitzpatrick (as note 7), 145.

12 See David Elliott, 'Painting of the Stalin Period', in exh. cat. *'Engineers of the Human Soul'. Soviet Socialist Realist Painting 1930s to 1960s* (Oxford: Museum of Modern Art, 1992), 10–17.

13 As early as 1926 members of AKhRR had argued for a new form of 'Heroic Realism'. See V. H. Perelman, 'Ot peredvizhnichestva k geroicheskomu realizmu', and N. G. Kotov, 'Chto takye geroicheskii realizm?' in V. H. Perelman, ed., *4 goda AKhRR 1922–1926* (Moscow, 1926), 102–25, 126–35. In the Stalinist hagiography, Socialist Realism was 'born' at a secret meeting of writers in Maksim Gorky's flat in the early hours of 26 October 1932 which Stalin attended. At this Stalin is on record as saying: 'If the artist is going to depict life correctly, he cannot fail to observe and point out what is leading towards Socialism. So this will be socialist art. It will be Socialist Realism.' 'O politike partii v oblasti literatury i iskusstva', in *Osnovy Marksistsko-Leninskoi Estetiki* (Moscow, 1958), 111. The term 'Socialist Realism' first appears to have been used in an article in the *Literaturnaya Gazeta* for 25 May 1932.

14 Matthew Cullerne Bown, *Art under Stalin* (Oxford, 1991), 40–41.

15 A fascinating transcription of the examination of a painting by Solomon Nikritin by the Art Commission of VseKoKhudozhnik is printed in Kurt London, *The Seven Soviet Arts* (London, 1937), 223–30.

16 For a full translation of the *Pravda* article 'O khudozhnikakh-pachkunakh', see below, p. 255.

17 Nikolai Ivanovich Yezhov (1895–1940) was General Commissar of State Security (NKVD) from 1936 to 1938, when he himself was purged. See Igor Golomstock, *Totalitarian Art* (London, 1990), 112–13.

Official art, mirroring closely the personal taste of Stalin, became more narrow, academic and backward-looking.

Artists, who were accepted as members of the newly created union were required by VseKoKhudozhnik (All-Union Co-operative of Workers in Representational Art) to produce an agreed number of works on specific themes.[14] The choice of themes was orchestrated by the party, and the political and social attitudes shown within them were openly criticized by critics and artists who were members of the board of VseKoKhudozhnik. In the face of strong criticism from his peers the artist had to apologize for his 'mistakes' and refashion his work in a more 'positive' manner.[15] In this way, under the umbrella of party activism, fellow artists acted as a kind of self-regulating aesthetic police force which instructed, guided and even punished intransigent fellows; humiliation was usually followed by compliance, and those who could stomach neither chose to work quietly and privately on their own.

In January 1936 the party's grip on culture became even tighter: the KPDI (Committee for Art Affairs) was formed and made directly responsible to the Central Committee of the Communist party. This supervised the visual arts, music, theatre, and cinema and superseded the previous more educational role of NarKomPros.

1936 was a critical year in the elimination not only of modernism but also of other enemies; the show trials of the Great Purge began against the backdrop of an escalating number of arrests of 'foreign agents' and 'enemies of the people'. From January to March a series of hysterical articles appeared in *Pravda*, the party newspaper, which denounced the enemy of formalism in music, painting, theatre and dance. The unfortunate painter who attracted Zhdanov's attention was Vladimir Lebedev, an old revolutionary from Leningrad, who was working as an illustrator of children's nursery rhymes. His drawings were joyful, impressionistic, funny, but the *Pravda* critic did not see them in this way: in a violent tract entitled 'The Artist-Daubers', a simple horse was likened to 'flayed carrion' and the artist himself was dismissed as a corrupter of children (p. 233).[16]

The party had now assumed total control over all the arts, to such an extent that by 1938 Aleksandr Gerasimov, Stalin's court painter and head of the Union of Soviet Artists, could triumphantly report: 'Enemies of the people, Trotskyist-Bukharinite rabble, Fascist agents who have been active in the art front and have attempted in every way to brake and hinder the development of Soviet art, have been unmasked and neutralized by our Soviet intelligence service under the leadership of Stalin People's Commissar Comrade Yezhov. This has made the creative atmosphere of enthusiasm among the entire mass of artists.'[17]

As Stalin himself had clearly stated, 'Life becomes better, comrades. When life is jollier you work better.'

THE GREAT ILLUSION

Architecture   *Igor A. Kazus*

Building Socialism

By 1933 the USSR had passed through the worst of the economic troubles caused by Stalin's forced collectivization and industrialization of the country. In the Stalinist 'neo-NEP' period of 1934–36, through incredible efforts, the country achieved economic independence, established itself as a great power with a centrally planned command economy and state-controlled social life, and, in terms of some of the most important economic indicators, began to catch up with the leading capitalist countries. Stalin felt significantly stronger, both within the country and in the international arena: he was reaching the apogee of his power.

The rapid development of industrial production in most regions of the country triggered an avalanche of urbanization, highlighting the problems of creating urban structures. However, the new 'super-empire', although capable of tremendous effort in the short-term realization of fantastic aims ('the building of Communism', the establishment of a military-industrial complex, etc.), had very limited general economic resources and was unable to provide a standard of living that was even minimally acceptable to its people.

The evident utopianism of the idea of building Socialism in one country – together with the anti-Bolshevist coup mounted by Stalin under cover of pseudo-Marxist phraseology, manipulated quotations from Lenin, and endless protestations of loyalty to Lenin's vision – gave rise to a significant opposition movement and began to discredit Bolshevism in the minds of millions of people. To retain power, Stalin and his associates needed to deceive the people by systematically creating illusory 'activity' designed to demonstrate the final 'victory of Socialism' in the USSR. In this period in the USSR, architecture and urban planning were assigned a special role in underpinning state power, and the building and rebuilding of cities was given more attention than in any other totalitarian country of the period. By abolishing design groups, by establishing a unified (and single) Union of Soviet Architects, organizing major unitary planning institutes (Giprogor, Gorstroiproyekt, Promstroiproyekt, etc.) and centralized architectural practices within government bodies (People's Commissariats, Soviets of Deputies), by special

competitions, and by other means, Stalin's regime was able to gain the support of the architectural elite of outstanding practitioners, who could be relied on to participate in the attainment of the specified objectives.

Architects, like writers, painters and other artists, were ordered by the state to use the method of 'Socialist Realism' in order 'to demonstrate that there is no country in the world as blessed as the Soviet Union'.[1] The people's faith in this was to be clearly and visibly strengthened by the 'wonders' of tomorrow created today – palaces rising above the clouds, cities springing up in the deserts, gigantic canals linking rivers and seas, gigantic factories. Sometimes the mere decision to build some huge structure, published through official propaganda channels, was in itself enough to generate mass euphoria, 'a dizziness born of success', a mood of optimism. In the 1930s, the USSR became one enormous 'theatre of mass spectacle', and the Soviet architecture of those years, employed to give form to the myths implanted in the mass consciousness, became one of the most effective psychological mechanisms for manipulating the people.

The effects of architectural transformation were felt above all in Moscow, the capital of the USSR, where the historic city centre remained practically unchanged until the mid-1930s. To bring about the fastest possible transformation, a unique urban development document was drawn up, the 'General Plan for the Reconstruction of Moscow'. This took the form of a special joint resolution of the Council of People's Commissars of the USSR and of the Central Committee of the All-Union Communist Party (Bolshevik), dated 10 July 1935, signed by V. M. Molotov and J. V. Stalin respectively. During the period of implementation of the plan (in two stages of five and ten years), a 'truly Socialist city'[2] was to be created.

The guiding principle of the General Plan was the value and practicality of the historic radial and annular layout of the city. The plan, drawn up after a competition in which the famous European architects Ernst May and Hannes Meyer took part, ignored radical proposals from Le Corbusier, Nikolai Ladovsky and Moisei Ginzburg for the transformation of the structure of Moscow. It proposed to retain the existing structure, while radically remodelling it by rearranging the network of streets and squares and embanking the

1 V. Kaverin, 'Iz vospominanii' [Selected memoirs], in *Vest'* (Moscow, 1989), 38.

2 *Stroitel'stvo Moskvy*, (1935) no. 7-8, 1.

3 'On the urban economy of Moscow and the development of the urban economy of the USSR', Resolution of the Plenary Session of the Central Committee of the All-Union Communist Party (Bolshevik), 15 June 1931, in *KPSS v rezolyutsiyakh i resheniyakh s'yezdov, konferentsii i plenumov TsK* (Moscow, 1970), 4:544-58.

4 As note 2.

5 *Arkhitekturnaya gazeta*, 23 March 1935.

6 *Stroitel'stvo Moskvy* (1935), no. 4, 36.

7 *Sovetskoye iskusstvo*, 3 March 1932.

river Moskva. This overall plan, which described itself as definitive, was drawn up painstakingly and in detail, down to the individual sites of the most important representative buildings, under the leadership of two of Russia's most distinguished theoretical and practical urban planners, V. N. Semënov and S. E. Chernyshev. This 'serious, scientifically based plan'[3] was intended to give rise to a spectacular bout of reconstruction that would amount to nothing less than the transformation of the whole country. For its implementation, Moscow city council had set up, by 1933, twenty architectural design and planning studios under the leadership of well-known architects, including such masters of the historicist or 'retrospective' tendency as I. V. Zholtovsky, A. V. Shchusev and I. A. Fomin. Their designs were exhibited in shop windows on the main street of Moscow every year during the May Day and October Revolution celebrations.

As approved, the General Plan presented the rebuilt Moscow as an ideal garden city, surrounded by a broad belt of forests and parks, from which green wedges followed the river banks into the heart of the city. The resolution specially emphasized that 'throughout the work of replanning the city, an integrated architectural design of squares, main thoroughfares, embankments and parks must be achieved, with the use of the best examples of classical and modern architecture, and all the achievements of architectural and building technology, for the construction of residential and public buildings'.[4] The implementation of the General Plan inaugurated the reshaping of the city, as a whole and in its parts, in terms of integrated architectural ensembles. Given that a new architectural language had yet to be evolved – and even in the absence of any unequivocal definition of the term 'classical' – the architects of the 1930s were able to make use of the most varied historical material; it was a historicist approach that relied primarily on the urban development models of classicism, which could be applied immediately and enabled the city to be developed within a dialogue between old and new.

The major practical problems were to be resolved in 1935. After the experience of wholesale collectivization and industrialization, Soviet architects attempted to deploy the same massive efforts to create a new architectural style in a short period. Shchusev was convinced: 'Having mastered the complex practice and theory of architecture, Soviet architects will create works not inferior to the immortal works of the great ages of Greece, Rome and the Italian Renaissance.'[5] All the available resources – engineering, financial and human – were mobilized for the construction of the largest buildings. Working on this scale, it was possible not only to imagine extensive complexes but to build them without delay. In these years, G. B. Piranesi's impressive phantasmagorias were the inspiration for the design of buildings that reflected, in their gigantic masses and overbearing dimensions, the grandeur of the Stalinist age. As the architect V. Shcherbakov said, 'Much that he [Piranesi] could only dream of has been made a reality by us.'[6]

The Palace of the Soviets and the City Centre

The supreme construction project of the Land of the Soviets, the primary architectural ensemble of the capital and its architectural centre, was to be the monumental Palace of the Soviets, designed to be the highest building in the world (415 metres). Built on the site of the demolished nineteenth-century Grand Temple of Christ the Saviour, the Palace of the Soviets was to be the culmination and centre of the multiple-level hierarchical system of Moscow, capital of Russia and the USSR, centre of the progressive world. The centralizing tendency of the General Plan for Moscow thus corresponded to the structure of the utopian model of society that was being built by Stalin.

In the second design competition for the Palace of the Soviets (1932), the highest prizes were awarded to designs that recalled a Romantic version of classicism (I. Zholtovsky) and the Art Deco style (B. Iofan and G. Gamil'ton). Rejecting a Rationalism that would not have permitted the symbolic embodiment of the concept of a public forum, in 1932 the Committee for the Construction of the Palace, headed officially by Molotov but in reality by Stalin, passed a resolution on the organization of the subsequent design process, in which it instructed its architects to make use of 'both new designs and the best designs of classical architecture'.[7] Ultimately, Stalin opted for the design by Iofan, V. Shchuko and V. Gel'freikh (pp. 51, 203), stylistically based on a plan using the artistic resources of classicism combined with an arsenal of Art Deco elements, and thus launching the 'retrospectivist' movement in Soviet architecture.

A broad central avenue was to link the Palace of the Soviets with Red Square; and there – in the initial version of the plan – would stand another building on an equally grandiose scale: the People's Commissariat for Heavy Industry (Narkomtyazhprom). Here, however, the preliminary design competition (1934) proved inconclusive – though two of the entries, those of K. Mel'nikov and I. Leonidov, were among the outstanding designs of the twentieth century. Retaining the spirit of the avant-garde utopias, both Mel'nikov and Leonidov proposed variants on Expressionist symbolic architecture, with no specific prototypes but bearing strong expressive analogies to classical buildings. At this point, the siting of the Heavy Industry building in Red Square itself was recognized to be a mistake, and a new site was found for it in the Zaryad'e district; however, the work that had been done on this monument appeared to some contemporaries as 'the most important stage of the creative growth of Soviet architecture'.[8]

The reconstruction of Gor'ky Street (Tver' Street), traditionally regarded as the city's main thoroughfare, took on a special significance for Moscow in the 1930s. Its transformation took place over two to three years, by rapid methods: old buildings were moved or added to, and new buildings were constructed using the rapid industrial methods devised by the architect A. Mordvinov. Assigned to create a triumphal way, the architects treated the multiple façades of its buildings primarily as a setting for a parade route, a celebratory backdrop for national festivals.

The Moscow Metro

In the emergence of a new form of architecture in the 1930s, one particularly strong influence was that of the architecture of the Moscow Metro, which was created not only as a utilitarian means of transport but as an architectural ensemble of palatial stations. The planning department of Moscow city council expressly linked the architecture of the Metro with the evolution of architecture as a whole: 'Our Metropolitan Railway is a prototype of the general Socialist organization of public services, and this is its great historical significance. The construction of the Metro inaugurates a new and higher phase of Soviet architecture, which will be manifested in the reconstruction of Moscow.'[9]

The first section of the Metro, from Park of Culture and Recreation to Sokolniki, was opened as early as 1935, and this was in fact the first Soviet attempt to use natural stone, works of decorative and applied art, and the 'architecture of light' in a building for public use. It made a great impression on the imagination of the user, who naturally began to view all aspects of life through

this new 'prism'. The life-affirming magnificence of these underground palaces, creating a joyful, major-key mood, was transferred to other spheres of social, productive and state life.

The architecture of the Metro stations was based on a freely varied use of themes from historical architecture, and the result was a number of brilliant compositions. The engineering and design of the stations varied with structural factors and the depth of the site. Among the most spectacular stations are Palace of the Soviets (A. Dushkin and Ya. Likhtenberg, 1935), where the architects made use of classical archetypes; Mayakovsky (A. Dushkin, 1938), where a new spatial solution for the concourse was achieved by using a new design of steel support, and Krasnye Vorota (I. Fomin, 1934–35), where the massive scale of the piers was visually offset by their division into separate vertical elements.

Heroic Architecture

Most representative of the power of the regime were the military buildings, with their clear, expressive imagery: the I. M. Frunze Military Academy (p. 206, 1932–37), the People's Commissariat for Defence on Arbat Square (p. 192, 1933–39) and the Red Army Theatre (p. 192, 1934–40). L. V. Rudnev, who designed the Academy (with his associate V. O. Munts), noted that military buildings must 'play a particularly important part in the great task of creating a monumental architecture in the Land of the Soviets'.[10] His work was characterized by a Romantic vision and use of visual symbolism; he succeeded in combining Constructivist design and sculptural development of form with the use

8 *Arkhitektura SSSR* (1936), no. 6, 1.

9 *Raboty arkhitekturnykh masterskikh* (Moscow, 1936), 1:21.

10 *Zodchiye Moskvy. XX vek* (Moscow, 1988), 170.

A. Dushkin and Ya. Likhtenberg, Palace of the Soviets Metro station, 1935 (built)

of historical styles. The Frunze Academy building is his masterpiece. It creates the heroic image by powerfully and laconically concentrating on the basic idea of the building: the majesty and might of the Red Army, its readiness to resist any who might attack the freedom of the Motherland. The emotional mood of the building, its sense of strength and calm, preparedness and self-possession, are created by the combination of the single, strictly rectilinear, unbroken mass of the main block with a projecting, massive podium.

In designing the People's Commissariat for Defence building on Arbat Square, the same architects achieved 'joyfulness, boldness, a major key' in the image of the building, 'without entirely rejecting classicism, Western tendencies, or even Eastern influences', and by synthesizing these elements attempted to emphasize the international character of the USSR and of its Red Army. Without concentrating on any one historical form, Rudnev produced an image intended to instil 'joy of living and a feeling of boldness' in the onlooker.

The Red Army's ownership of the Academy and Defence buildings was primarily conveyed through relief representations of military attributes and equipment. The light wall contrasted with the massive rustication of the plinth and with the huge bulk of the tower, infusing the whole composition with a sensation of drama. Like many buildings of the period, the Defence Commissariat building was created in the form of a simple volume, without a grandiose main façade in the form of a triumphal arch.

K. S. Alabyan and V. N. Simbirtsev, the architects of the Red Army Theatre building on Commune Square, were told to base their plan on the predetermined form of a five-pointed star. The whole three-dimensional structure of the building, down to the cross-section of the portico columns, was subordinated to this pattern. Unlike the Palace of the Soviets, which symbolized the triumph of Socialist society, the Red Army Theatre embodied the defence of that society, expressing the image of a workers' and peasants' army defending humanistic ideals. The principal virtue of the building, to contemporary eyes, was the way in which it infused the arbitrary form of a star with its own, new social content. Such was the authorities' need for a new iconography that questions of functional convenience became secondary. The theatre was designed primarily as a monument, and consequently, while mastering the star form, its architects positioned a number of auditoria one above another. This gave the building the necessary height – a quality that was interpreted at that time as an expression of the ideological aspirations of the Red Army. In the same vein, the design incorporated a sculpture of a Red Army soldier holding a star, to be mounted on the upper part of the theatre.

Perhaps the closest approach to a possible sense of the method of 'Socialist Realism' was made by Iofan in the Soviet Pavilion at the International Exhibition in Paris. Crystallizing the architectural ideas of pre-war Soviet architecture, this essentially experimental, temporary exhibition building earned a place among those works of contemporary architecture that possessed permanent artistic value. Contemporaries were quick to perceive its exceptional significance. A noted art historian, D. Arkin, wrote: 'It is now clear that the strongest image left by the Paris Exhibition of 1937 will be that of the Soviet Pavilion, crowned with the steel figures of a youth and girl with a hammer and sickle in their raised hands. This image will be associated forever with the 1937 Exhibition, just as the image of the Crystal Palace is associated with the 1851 Exhibition, the vanished Trocadéro with that of 1878 and the Eiffel Tower with that of 1889.'[11]

Indeed, the pavilion itself, with its fusion of architecture and sculpture, was the main representative of the Land of the Soviets at this exhibition. The whole structure had a terse, monumental appearance, as

11 *Pavil'on SSSR na Mezhdunarodnoi vystavke v Parizhe* (Moscow, 1938), 3.

K. S. Alabyan and V. N. Simbirtsev, Red Army Theatre, Moscow, 1934-40 (built)

L. V. Rudnev and others, People's Commissariat for Defence, 1933-39 (built)

telling as a poster but artistically far removed from the spirit of advertising. It was an image of the spiritual strength of Soviet man and Soviet society as a whole, its achievements, its present and its future.

The ideological acuteness and vivid iconography of the pavilion's design, and its bright emotional tone, were a deliberate embodiment of a clear programme. They also determined the artistic details of the decor. Iofan himself stated that the pavilion 'was designed as a triumphal building, reflecting in its dynamics the rapid and powerful growth of the achievements of the world's first Socialist state, and the enthusiasm and joy of this great age of ours, that of the building of Socialism, when work is a matter of honour, valour and heroism'.[12]

Iofan, the winner of the architectural competition, was also responsible for the idea of surmounting the architectural structure with a giant sculpture, half as high as the building itself (i.e. 24.5 metres). He aimed at an architecture of maximum clarity, as open as possible in its general imagery, which would immediately grip the onlooker. 'For the first time,' said the sculptor V. Mukhina, 'an architect proposed to round off an architectural composition with a massive sculpture, which was to continue the idea inherent in the building, and this sculpture was to be an inseparable part of the whole structure.'[13] Taking as her prototypes the ancient *Harmodius and Aristogeiton*, the *Winged Nike* of Samothrace, Rude's *Marseillaise*, and other classical images, Mukhina was able to achieve a synthesis of sculpture and architecture which left no room for excessive expressiveness, academicism or naturalism. Her image of the citizens of the Land of Socialism, filled with strength and faith in the future, precisely captured the spirit that Stalinist propaganda succeeded in instilling into the Soviet people. This is a realist work of art, in the sense that it was an authentic symbol of the new world (p. 240).

On the Exhibition site in Paris, directly opposite the German Pavilion, the Soviet Pavilion symbolized power and faith in the future, set against the growing military potential of Nazi Germany (pp. 2, 10, 12).

The Agricultural Exhibition

The All-Union Agricultural Exhibition, which opened in Moscow on 1 August 1935, had its own function of demonstrating 'the magnificence of the victory of Socialist construction as a whole, and particularly in the agriculture of the USSR'.[14] For the preliminary

competition early in 1935, a number of interesting and varied outlines for the general plan of the exhibition were submitted; varying from structures with symmetrical, compact and star-shaped plans, as in the design by L. S. Teplitsky, to fully developed, highly complex arrangements (as in G. B. Barkhin's design). The general plan of the exhibition as built was based on the design by V. K. Oltarzhevsky (of the exhibition committee's design group), which won the competition against entries from Moscow city council's studios, led by I. V. Zholtovsky, and from A. V. Shchusev, G. B. Barkhin, and research students from the All-Union Academy of Architecture.

The Agricultural Exhibition became a special kind of experimental site: it was both a model of an ideal garden city of the 1930s, dramatically representing the whole country in one place, and a place where architects were given free rein to explore national forms in architecture. Overall, it was a colourful spectacle that impressed visitors with its decorative quality and the symbolism of the pavilion designs. The broad acres of the exhibition complex (136 hectares, 230 pavilions) were divided into a composition of axially orientated main spaces. The exhibition plan was strikingly bold, combining plain geometrical structures with asymmetrical designs; the axial perspectives shifted direction at each of the main focal points of the composition. The main pavilions of the Union Republics lined the main exhibition plaza, the Square of the Friendship of Peoples, designed for festivals, celebrations and meetings. A broad exhibition avenue led to the octagonal plaza where the pavilions for the different branches of agriculture were sited.

Though essentially temporary, the exhibition pavilions were given the appearance of monumental,

12 Ibid., 13.

13 *Arkhitekturnaya gazeta*, 28 February 1938.

14 *Stroitel'stvo Moskvy* (1936), no. 2, 3.

Yu. P. Zenkevich, design for forecourt, All-Union Agricultural Exhibition, 1939

permanent structures. The theatricality and emphatic decoration which gave each building and the complex as a whole the appearance of a festive spectacle were also reflected in the main entrance of the exhibition (L. M. Polyakov, sculptor G. Motovilov). Its lightness and graphic, decorative quality were achieved by a composition of powerful pylons framing a graceful, apparently weightless white arch. The main pavilion (Shchuko and Gel'freikh) was distinguished by its purity and clarity of form. Rectangular in plan, it drew its monumentality from the huge, majestic colonnades of the façades, with a projecting entrance porch. A detached fifty-metre tower supporting a sculptural group, imparting asymmetry and dynamism to the building, replicated Iofan's USSR pavilions in Paris and New York.

The outstanding national pavilions were those of Uzbekistan (S. Polupanov, p. 208) with its graceful pergola (with motifs from the Pompeii frescoes); Armenia (K. S. Alabyan, S. Safaryan), a severely monumental evocation of classical Armenian architecture; and Azerbaidzhan (S. A. Dadashev, M. A. Useinov), again with clear quotations from national tradition. These pavilions were subsequently adopted as models of a valid approach to the use of national traditions in modern Soviet architecture.

Commemoration and Reconstruction

For the evolution of Soviet architecture, the 1930s represented a self-contained artistic process, cut short by the war of 1941–45 and prevented from realizing most of its potential. The General Plan for the Reconstruction of Moscow became a model for all cities of the USSR, and in the postwar period its principles were successfully applied by major British planners, among them Sir Patrick Abercrombie in his plan for London, a valuable element of which was the same principle of an organic combination of old and new in the urban system.

Stalin's regime had made effective use of the professionalism of architects; by the end of the 1930s, Soviet architecture had been accepted by the masses and was perceived by society as an element of its culture. Stalin's great illusion had largely attained its purpose. Opposition to the regime was eliminated. Inspired by the false slogans of the 1936 Constitution and deceived by splendid architectural apparitions – some actually built, but most only on paper – people responded to a climate of uplift and idealism. Despite all the hardship and disorganization of everyday life, people were content with their lives, and looked forward to a bright and happy Socialist future.

As in the 1930s, the extreme situation of the war period led to some inflated designs. As A. Vesnin, President of the Academy of Architecture, pointed out, this was mainly due to the understandable desire to restore devastated cities, urban ensembles and individual buildings in even more beautiful and majestic form. On the other hand, in those years the search for new visual forms appropriate for a situation of national tragedy was particularly difficult, since these were expected to evoke a wide range of historical associations. Memory and heroism, eternal life and triumph, grief and fortitude – these different modulations of the theme of Victory found expression through architectural elements deliberately chosen to convey a timeless quality.

In the designs for the Pantheons for the heroes of the Patriotic War, and for the defenders of Moscow, Leningrad and other cities in 1942–43 (pp. 208–09), architects turned to the canonical forms of the burial mound, the pyramid, the ziggurat, the obelisk, the fortress wall and the triumphal arch. At the end of the war, these designs, together with the designs for reconstruction of the cities, formed a qualitatively new and integrated programme of architectural revival that set its mark on the whole phase of post-Victory construction, determining its stylistic details and defining the expression of the new nature of state power, as transformed by the experience of the war years.

Translated by Roderick Riesco

V. A. Shchuko, V. G. Gel'freikh and others, main pavilion, All-Union Agricultural Exhibition, 1936–39 (built)

THE END OF THE AVANT-GARDE

Painting and Sculpture   *David Elliott*

'The setting up of the People's Commissariat of Education [NarKomPros] began in the midst of the revolutionary battles. The Department of Fine Arts [IZO] was also being organized at that time. It was set up by the representatives of the new art and was the HQ of new trends. These had taken over power in art, and this was a great victory over the critics and collectors who had [previously] been deciding the fate of both art and artists. Only the strongest artists had been able to withstand the struggle against them to establish a new movement, and they were [now] rightfully entitled to the control of IZO NarKomPros.' (Kazimir Malevich, 1923.)[1]

It was in Leningrad, the second city of the USSR, that serious criticism of the avant-garde began. In June 1926, an article entitled 'A Monastery on a State Subsidy', which criticized Malevich and his colleagues in GInKhuK (State Institute of Artistic Culture) had appeared in the city's party newspaper; soon after, the Institute was closed down.[2] Malevich was subsequently arrested and imprisoned for almost three months by the NKVD (People's Commissariat for Internal Affairs) on suspicion of being a German spy.[3]

In Moscow the campaign against the avant-garde did not gain a head of steam until April 1928, when, in the journal *Sovetskoye Foto*, an open letter from the proletarian critic Boris Kushner was published which attacked Rodchenko for plagiarizing the work of such foreign, non-Soviet photographers as Albert Renger-Patzsch and Lászlo Moholy-Nagy.[4]

Faced by such a concerted series of attacks, the avant-garde in both Moscow and Leningrad attempted to adapt to the new cultural climate by choosing subject matter which reflected the transformed political and social realities. Malevich began a series of pastiches of his earlier realist paintings of peasants working in the fields of 1911 to 1912, but their context and meaning was now transformed. Rodchenko searched for more heroic subjects, and Vladimir Mayakovsky joined RAPP, 'because it is the precise channel of the Soviet and party line, and because it must be such.'[5] This was to little avail; increasingly, these artists found themselves isolated and marginalized.

In February 1930 Mayakovsky opened an exhibition called *Twenty Years of Work*, which was intended to prove to RAPP and the party not only his revolutionary and proletarian credentials but also the extent to which his work was intelligible to the masses: letters from satisfied and engaged readers all over Russia were presented as evidence. The exhibition, shown in both Moscow and Leningrad, was ignored by both the party and the press, and further criticisms of his work were published. Severely depressed by this, as well as by a failed love affair, he shot himself on 14 April 1930.

After the funeral, which many thousands of people attended, Mayakovsky's name disappeared from the public gaze. In 1934 his Collected Works began to appear on the initiative of Lily Brik, a close associate and former lover. In the following year he was officially rehabilitated, after Brik had directly approached Stalin for his blessing. The note written in Stalin's hand on her letter simply proclaimed: 'Indifference to his memory and his works is a crime'. It was to be one of many, in those perilous years.

In Leningrad, Malevich, Vera Yermolayeva, Nikolai Suyetin, Pavel Basmanov and Konstantin Rozhdestvensky also became increasingly isolated. The subject of their paintings (pp. 210–13), at a time when agriculture was being savagely collectivized under the first Five Year Plan, was an ambiguously blank-faced peasantry set in flat and depopulated landscapes. Evoking the skulls and crosses of Golgotha, Malevich elevated the redemptive image of the suffering peasant into a kind of Passion that seemed to symbolize the fate of Russia; he also

1 Kazimir Malevich, 'K muzei khudozhestvennoi kultury', 15 August 1923. LGAORSS [State Archives of the October Revolution and Socialist Construction], St Petersburg, fund 4340, inv. 1, file 25. ff. 30–31.

2 G. Sery, 'Monastyr na Gosnabzhenii,' *Leningradskaya Pravda*, 10 June 1926.

3 This probably happened in 1930 and related to Malevich's visit to Poland and Germany in 1927. See Pavel Filonov, diary entry for 4 November 1932. Manuscript department, State Russian Museum, St Petersburg, fund 156, file 28, f.

4 *Sovetskoye Foto*, no. 4, Moscow, April 1928, 176.

5 Vladimir Mayakovsky, speech to a plenary session of RAPP, September 1929; Milena Kalinovska, 'Biography', in *Vladimir Mayakovsky, Three Views* (Oxford, 1982), 26.

Malevich at work, 1930s

made portraits – some of them conventional, others not – of his friends and family. But, in spite of his expulsion from the State Institute of the History of Art in Leningrad at the end of 1929, and his brush with the NKVD, a retrospective exhibition was opened at the Tretyakov Gallery in Moscow in November, which travelled to Kiev at the beginning of 1930.

Unlike many of his colleagues, Malevich was able to continue exhibiting his work until the beginning of 1935. In May of that year, he died of cancer. The Leningrad city council paid for a large public funeral. The Russian Museum not only purchased several works but also, with the state, awarded a pension to his family. Although he and his circle had been severely criticized, and some of them had been arrested, it was still recognized that Malevich had made a substantial contribution to Soviet culture; his death could not be completely ignored. His funeral was that of the avant-garde itself.

After the assassination of Kirov, the Leningrad party boss, in 1934, a large number of intellectuals and artists were arrested, some of whom belonged to the avant-garde circles around Malevich and Pavel Filonov. In December 1934 Yermolayeva, Basmanov and other close associates of Malevich were interrogated. Yermolayeva, like Vladimir Lebedev, had been working as a children's book illustrator, and a cycle of her gouaches for Goethe's story *Reynard the Fox* was suspected of being an encoded criticism of the actions of the NKVD. Although disabled from childhood, she was regarded as a serious enemy of the state and was consigned to a camp near Karaganda where she was to die a few years later.

Filonov, alongside Malevich the leading light of the Leningrad avant-garde, had ever since pre-revolutionary times derived energy not from the modern art of the West but from the traditions of Russian archaic and folk art. A group of followers known as the Masters of Analytical Art had coalesced around him (including Nikolai Yevgrafov and Vasily Kuptsov) and collaborated on illustrating the Finnish epic *Kalevala*. In 1929, the State Russian Museum in Leningrad had offered to organize a one-man show of Filonov's work, but the cultural climate was changing at such a rapid pace that no administrator would take responsibility for the exhibition: the paintings were hung, the catalogue was written, and for two years the exhibition remained on the walls of the Museum; but it was never opened to the public. Groups of interested parties, however, did visit the closed exhibition, and their reactions became a mirror image of the broader polemic in the press.[6] Filonov became a test case and

the closed exhibition a battle ground between conflicting tendencies. In an article entitled 'The Class Essence of Filonovism', one critic felt that, 'devoid of living ties with the working class . . . Filonovism, which seemed previously to have died, is now showing signs of febrile activity at the very moment when the class struggle within the country is reaching its peak. An exhibition of Filonov's work with no Marxist frame around it would be a mistake.'[7]

Yet the battle lines were not yet altogether clearly drawn: the arch-conservative Izaak Brodsky, a devoted member of AKhRR and a leading proponent of Socialist Realism (see pp. 241, 249), spoke out in favour of Filonov as an artist of whom 'our country can be rightfully and legitimately proud'.[8]

Filonov was defeated, yet he continued to work; some of his followers were less fortunate. From 1932 they were summoned for interrogation by the NKVD. Both Yevgrafov and Kuptsov were picked up and questioned about Filonov, his politics and the contents of his and their own bookshelves; under this pressure Kuptsov committed suicide. In 1938 both of Filonov's stepsons were arrested and soon died in camps, and his wife Ekaterina was severely harassed.

Yet, though his work was not favoured and his friends and family were arrested, Filonov's faith in the radical cause did not falter. This was not out of stupidity but out of faith. He had always led an ascetic and monk-like existence, and the apocalyptic and hermetic imagery of his paintings of the late 1930s clearly reveals that, for him, it was the party not the artist which had lost its way. With many others, Filonov starved to death in the wartime siege of Leningrad.

Rodchenko also met with a barrage of criticism in the early 1930s. In 1928 he had written a reply to Kushner's critical open letter: '*Sovetskoye Foto* talks about a "photo-picture" as if it were something closed and eternal. Quite the reverse. One should give a number of different views of an object . . . as if one were examining it and not peeping at it through a keyhole. One should not make photo-pictures but photo-moments, of documentary not artistic value.'[9]

The argument boiled down to what aspects of reality photography should usefully depict. In 1930 Rodchenko took a series of photographs of *Pioneers of the Third Decisive Year of the Five Year Plan* (pp. 214–15), but the politically correct title did not deflect criticism. These young people, snapped in close-up on a May Day parade, had been taken from a low viewpoint; and it was the element of distortion which, for proletarian critics, was a sure sign of 'formalism'. This was the

6 M. N. Grigoreva, ed., *Avangard, octanovlenni na begu* (Leningrad, 1989), 11–13.

7 N. Bogoraz, *Krasnaya gazeta* (Leningrad), 9 January 1931, evening ed.

8 *Krasnaya Gazeta* (Leningrad), 25 November 1930, evening ed.

9 Aleksandr Rodchenko, ['Trends in Contemporary Photography'], *Novyi LEF* (Moscow), no. 9 (September 1928), 33ff.

worst of all cultural 'crimes'; and yet, until Osip Beskin's book on the subject appeared in 1933,[10] it was not clear exactly what formalism specifically constituted. Nevertheless, as a member of LEF, Rodchenko was automatically suspect.[11]

The level of criticism against him was low. A student asked: 'Why does the pioneer look upwards? It is not ideologically correct. Pioneers and the youth of the Komsomol must look ahead.' The same commentator discussed a photograph of a swimming instructor: 'Anyone looking at it would like to see a fine and fit body. In Rodchenko's photograph the image is destroyed by the biological detail. The photograph is an unequivocal confirmation that even formalist artists may resort to naturalistic criteria.'[12]

In January 1932, Rodchenko was expelled from the photo-reporting section of Oktyabr' (the October Group), with which he had been affiliated since 1928. He travelled north as a photo-reporter to the building site of the Stalin White Sea Canal, where convicts, at great loss of human life, were constructing a useless monument to stupidity. With his partner Varvara Stepanova, he was also able to find limited work as a designer of official albums commemorating the exploits of Budënny's First Cavalry in the Civil War, or lauding the achievements of Soviet Uzbekistan.

In 1935, in the privacy of his studio, he began to paint again – an activity which he had rejected fourteen years before, when he had exhibited the three monochrome canvases that he then considered to be his final statement in the medium. His new subjects were clowns and performers at the circus (p. 231).

A similar bathos characterized the work of Vladimir Tatlin during the 1930s. In 1929, in response to the party slogan, 'technology will solve all our problems', and researching a problem which had fascinated him for some time, Tatlin set up a studio – appropriately in the bell tower of Moscow's Novodevichy Monastery – to develop a means for unassisted man-powered flight. He called this project *Letatlin*, a word–play on the Russian verb *letat'*, to fly. He approached the problem not from the viewpoint of the engineer but from that of the artist, seeking to extend the ideas of Constructivism more effectively into society.

On one level, this choice of subject may be interpreted as a critique of the impotence of avant-garde Modernism or Productivism during the mid-1920s – and as a new, ambitious and practical initiative, motivated by previous failures. On another level, Tatlin, who must have been aware of the consequences of failure in an increasingly critical climate, was making a

deeply felt point about the autonomy of art and its relationship to the natural world, through a contemporary reworking of the myth of Icarus. The most precious gift of Constructivism to humanity would be to allow every man or woman the possibility of flying like an angel.

The group researched the flight mechanisms and patterns of birds and insects, looking for ways in which an articulated wing structure could be designed for the human frame. The project continued – with inconclusive flight tests on the Lenin Hills – until 1932, when all artistic groups were dissolved by order of the party. The project, like that of his *Monument for the Third International* (1919), was never fully realized. Subsequently, Tatlin was able to find limited work as a theatre designer, but the great technological dream was over. From the mid-1930s, like Rodchenko, he reverted to painting and drawing portraits and still-lifes, in a series of dark, private, unexhibitable works.

In the ferment of the Cultural Revolution and first Five Year Plan, there were also realist artists of many tendencies who occupied the middle ground between the old non-objective avant-gardes and the literal realism of AKhRR and the party artists; some of these coalesced around groups or magazines. OSt (The Society of Easel Painters), formed in Moscow in 1925, was a focus for young, committed and innovatory painters and included such artists as Aleksandr Deineka (pp. 236–37), Aleksandr Labas, Yuri Pimenov, Aleksandr Tyshler and Konstantin Vialov. The group known as The Circle in Leningrad was a kind of opposite number to this and included such artists as Aleksandr Samokhvalov (p. 235). Much of this work was radical in its depiction of reality and made no attempt at a quasi-photographic documentation of society.

There were also a number of unaffiliated artists who tried to respond to the challenge of depicting new

10 Critic Osip Beskin became editor of *Tvorchestvo* ('Creativity') and *Iskusstvo* ('Art'), two new magazines which both started in 1933. In the same year he also published a book, *Formalizm v zhivopisi* ('Formalism in Painting') which identified a number of the 'enemies' who would be continually harried throughout the rest of the decade.

11 Formalism was an influential avant-garde literary movement, which had developed out of Futurism; it emphasized the importance of studying the structure of the literary text rather than the biography or psychology of the author who had produced it. By the time of the Cultural Revolution, the slur of formalism in visual art denoted an undue emphasis on formal concerns above questions of subject matter or politics.

12 *Sovetskoye Foto*, nos. 5–6 (1936), 6. For peer-group criticism of a painter's work, see the debate on *The Old and the New* by Solomon Nikritin, published in Kurt London, *The Seven Soviet Arts* (London, 1937), 223–32.

Vladimir Tatlin, *Letatlin*, c. 1930

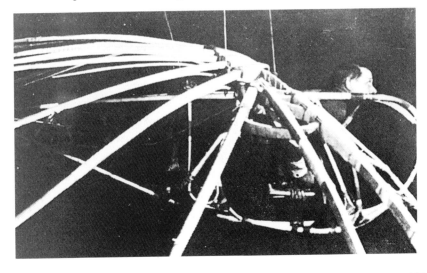

13 Osip Beskin, speaking at a meeting of VseKoKhudozhnik on 10 April 1935 which was considering a painting entitled *The Old and the New* by Nikritin; London (as note 12), 227.

forms of life whilst retaining an individual style. A form of primitive or naive painting characterizes much of the most interesting work of the early 1930s: Georgi Rublëv's *Portrait of Stalin*, of 1935 (p. 228), is a uniquely informal record of the Great Leader; when compared with the photographic *gravitas* of Brodsky's image of Stalin as the architect of the Soviet Union (p. 241), its survival through a time when the possession of such an image could have led to arrest is a cause of surprise.

All human activity led ultimately to the Plan, and artists were sent out into the field to make a record of the process of Socialist Reconstruction. Nikolai Denisovsky visited the gold mines of central Siberia (p. 225), and A.V. Lobanov (p. 223) recorded the interminable cadre meetings that accompanied the building of the new industrial complex at Magnitogorsk. Samuil Adlivankin obediently chronicled the expulsion of Kulaks from collective farms and of wreckers from factories (p. 224). But large academic paintings of the new life in the countryside – as in Taras Gaponenko's *To Mother for the Next Feed* – did not appear until the mid-1930s (p. 234), by which time the worst effects of famine and of the slaughter of the Kulaks had begun to be dissipated. No feat of the imagination could have made a rural idyll out of such devastation.

Gustavs Klucis, who remained a member of the October Group until it was disbanded, but who was also criticized for formalism, toned down the dynamism of his montages and, with Suyetin, was commissioned to decorate Boris Iofan's pavilion for the 1937 Paris Exhibition. In spite of his observance of the party line, his past was against him: he had been a rifleman in the 9th Latvian Infantry Regiment, which, in 1917, had played a decisive role in the establishment of the new Bolshevik regime. In Stalin's paranoic struggle for power, old Bolsheviks of any description seemed to be suspect, and most of the survivors of this regiment were arrested and shot. The Expressionist painter Aleksandr Drevin (p. 232), also from Latvia, and with Rodchenko and Tatlin a teacher at the Moscow VKhuTeIn (All Union Artistic and Technical Institute), shared the same background and met the same fate.

Solomon Nikritin, one of the unacknowledged masters of Russian painting, and like Drevin an Expressionist, decided to develop a large painting of the new Soviet system of justice entitled *The People's Court* (p. 230). The sombre expressions and colours of the figures invest it with dignity, yet the mood is one of sadness and loss. *The People's Court* looks more like a *Last Supper*. Such a lack of optimism could not for long go unremarked:

'I have a feeling that a man who has come to such a pass must feel lonely in the present age. What a dreadful nightmare! Such a thing can only be endured by a lonely being who does not perceive the young man of the present, does not perceive anything at all, and only lives in his own ideas . . . This picture should not be accepted; we should protest against it. After looking at such a work one finds it dreadful to be alive for a month, in spite of all the gaiety of our life. (Applause.)'[13]

OPTIMISTIC REALISM

Cinema *Lutz Becker*

Under Lenin's famous dictum, 'The art of film is for us the most important of all arts', the men and women of the October Revolution embraced film with enthusiasm and developed it into a tool of the revolution. During the early years of the establishment of Communism in Russia and of the Civil War, film became the eyewitness to the great changes that were taking place. All film activities were coordinated by the People's Commissariat for Enlightenment under the chairmanship of Anatoly Lunacharsky. His vision and intellectual scope helped to define the nature of the young Soviet cinema which, from very humble beginnings, grew throughout the 1920s into the most innovative film industry in Europe. Lenin's 1919 Decree on the Nationalization of the Film Industry provided Soviet cinema with the operational and financial basis for this development.[1]

The dynamism of the Revolution and the struggle for its survival produced a strong, enthusiastic generation of film-makers, who created work of high intensity and originality: Dziga Vertov, Esfir Shub, Vsevolod Pudovkin, Sergei Eisenstein, Aleksandr Dovzhenko and others. They worked in the field of the documentary and of feature film, motivated by a personal commitment to the political and cultural aims of the Communist party. A new type of cine-photographer was born at the war front, one who fought alongside the Red Army or travelled with the Agitprop trains to the remotest regions of the Soviet Union. He produced the prototypes for the newsreels which were the backbone of Soviet film propaganda throughout the existence of the USSR, starting with *Kino Nedelya* in 1917 and continuing in 1922 with *Kino Pravda*.

In 1922 the first state-owned film company was set up: this was Goskino, renamed Sovkino in 1924. When in 1928 the first Five Year Plan was inaugurated, the Soviet film industry was given increased financial backing. In 1930 Sovkino was dissolved and a new organization, Soyuzkino, was established linking the industry more closely to the Finance Ministry, but devolving the ideological control to the educational committees of the various Soviet Republics. With increasing centralization in the 1930s, the film industry gradually lost its creative independence and energy. In 1933 the State Directorate for the Film and Photo Industry (GUKF) took over. Its head until 1937 was the ruthless Boris Shumyatsky, who controlled the industry with the powers of a Minister of State.[2] His great achievement was to reorganize the industry for sound film production, establishing an extensive network of cinemas and travelling film units equipped with sound apparatus. This was accompanied by a drastic decline in productivity, with the number of feature films produced falling from 111 films in 1930 to 35 in 1937. Shumyatsky was made the scapegoat for this temporary setback and lost his job in 1938; his successors reaped the long-term result of his reforms. Film output doubled, and the number of cinemas increased from 9,000 in 1930 to 26,000 in 1941.[3] In 1938 an effective propaganda machine replaced all previous organizations. This was the State Committee for Cinema Affairs, directly responsible to the Councils of Peoples' Commissars; from 1939 to the end of the Second World War its chairman was Ivan Bolshakov.[4]

The introduction of sound film coincided with another profound upheaval, the decision of the Central Committee of the Communist party in April 1932 to force the doctrine of Socialist Realism on all the arts. This doctrine gave voice to Stalin's desire to create a Socialist state art, brutally extinguishing the experimentation and the distinguished avant-garde work of the 1920s. Where the silent film era had been marked by works which explored the poetics of the cinema and found new visual metaphors, while also looking for new narrative structures, the new principle above all exploited social stereotypes and introduced regressive or traditionalist, even academic assumptions.

Still from Sergei Eisenstein's *Alexander Nevsky*, 1938

1 G. Dahlke and L. Kaufmann, eds., *Lenin über den Film* (Berlin 1970), 58.

2 Richard Taylor, 'Boris Shumyatsky and the Soviet Cinema in the 1930s', *Historical Journal of Film, Radio and Television*, vol. 6 (1986), no.1.

3 Film production figures taken from *Sovetskiye khudozhestvennye filmy: Annotirovannyi katalog* (Moscow, 1961). Sound film production rose from 2.7 per cent in 1930 to 100 per cent in 1936.

4 Richard Taylor and Ian Christie, eds., *The Film Factory. Russian and Soviet Cinema in Documents* (Cambridge, Mass., 1988), 371.

Maxim Gorky, whose prestige and influence was exploited by Stalin, suggested that labour itself, and its working processes, which are organized by man for man, should be elevated to become the central theme of Socialist literature.[5] The intrinsic propagandistic purpose of Socialist Realism was fully revealed at the first All Union Congress of Soviet Writers, in 1934, by Andrei Zhdanov, Stalin's cultural adviser:

'Comrade Stalin has described our writers as engineers of the human soul . . . What are our obligations, when we adopt this role? First of all, it is necessary to explore life as it is, to be able to reproduce it truthfully in works of art. To represent real life in its revolutionary progression, we must not coldly and pedantically pursue "objective reality". Truthfulness and historical correctness . . . has to be combined with our task of ideologically transforming and re-educating working people in the spirit of Socialism. This method of creative writing and literary criticism we call Socialist Realism.'[6]

Between the two poles – that of Gorky's search for a new type of man defined by work, social condition and attitude and that of Zhdanov's call for a sycophantic revolutionary romanticism and an unreflective praise of Socialist ideals – a few of the film-makers of the 1930s were still able to find space for individual expression.[7]

Some productions, vetted and controlled at script stage by the party, achieved artistic standards which satisfied the home market and were highly regarded abroad. In the early years at least, Socialist Realism, when not over-dogmatically applied, was a real artistic stimulus to some directors. Increasingly, however, films idealized conditions that would have benefited from a more critical treatment; instead of analysing, disclosing and uncovering shortcomings in the system, they became uncritically affirmative.

Some of the most important directors of the 1930s were adroit and brave enough to circumvent bureaucratic pressures and preserve their integrity. Some were even acceptable to Stalin: Friedrich Ermler, Mark Donskoi, the 'brothers' Georgi and Sergei Vasiliev, Leonid Trauberg and Grigori Kozintsev, Sergei Yutkevitch and Mikhail Romm. Unfortunately the future of Soviet cinema was determined by lesser talents who applied the doctrine blindly and opportunistically and led the way to empty didacticism, tedium and official conformity.

In 1935 Stalin congratulated the Soviet cinema on its fifteenth anniversary: 'In the hands of Soviet power, cinema constitutes an enormous and invaluable force. With unique opportunities for spiritual influence over the masses at its command, cinema helps the working class and its party to educate the workers in the spirit of Socialism, to organize the masses for the struggle for Socialism, to raise their cultural level and their political fighting capacity. Soviet power expects new successes from you, new films that . . . will glorify the greatness of the historical deeds in the struggle for workers' and peasants' power in the Soviet Union, mobilize us to fulfil our new tasks and remind us of both the achievements and the difficulties of Socialist construction.'[8]

Shumyatsky observed that, after the successful introduction of Socialist Realism, Stalin regarded film as a collective creation of himself and the film-makers: 'The leader of our party and our country, the leader of World Revolution, Comrade Stalin, devotes much time to film. He finds the time to see films and correct their faults; he finds time to meet the film-makers and to suggest to them ways in which they can develop.'[9]

Stalin interfered in the scripting and casting of films and changed their titles and their endings. Stalin took charge of the personality cult which surrounded him. Without his permission, no film could reach the cinemas. He selected the actors who would be allowed to represent him, he chose the costumes, suggested the *mise-en-scène*, invented ceremonies, hierarchies and mythologies.[10] He is quoted as having said, as early as 1924: 'Film is an illusion which dictates its own law upon life.'[11]

Nikita Khrushchev, in his report to the 20th Congress of the Communist party in 1956, denounced Stalin's policies, and hinted that Stalin knew life only from watching films. Khrushchev accurately identified the dependence of the Soviet leadership on the illusion of the cinema, which had to promote faith and compensate for the shortcomings of life under Stalin's version of Socialism.

5 H. Gunther, *Der sozialistische Übermensch: Maxim Gorki und der sowjetische Heldenmythos* (Stuttgart, 1993).

6 H. J. Schmitt and G. Schramm, eds., *Realismuskonzeptionen: Dokumente zum 1. Allunionskongreß der Sowjetschriftsteller* (Frankfurt am Main, 1974).

7 Ullrich Gregor and Enno Patalas, *Geschichte des Films* (Gütersloh, 1962), 193.

8 Joseph Stalin, 'Congratulations to the Soviet Cinema on its Fifteenth Anniversary', in *Pravda*, 11 January 1935; tr. in Taylor and Christie (as note 4).

9 Boris Shumyatsky, *Kinematografiya millionov* (Moscow, 1935), 33–34.

10 Oksana Bulgakova, 'Herr der Bilder. Stalin und der Film', in H. Gassner, I. Schleier, K. Stengel, eds., *Agitation zum Glück. Sowjetische Kunst der Stalinzeit* (Bremen, 1994), 65–69.

11 D. Volkogonov, 'Stalin', in *Oktjabr*, no. 2 (1988), 97.

Still from Sergei Eisenstein's *Alexander Nevsky*, 1938

K. S. Mel'nikov
competition project for Commissariat of Heavy
Industry, Red Square, 1934.
Shchusev Architecture Museum, Moscow

I. A Fomin, P. V. Abrosimov and M. A. Minkus
competition project for Commissariat of Heavy Industry, Red Square, 1934.
Shchusev Architecture Museum, Moscow

A. and V. Vesnin
competition project for Commissariat of Heavy Industry, Red Square, 1934.
Shchusev Architecture Museum, Moscow

B. M. Iofan, V. A. Shchuko, V. G. Gel'freikh
project for the Palace of the Soviets.
Shchusev Architecture Museum, Moscow

**B. M. Iofan, Yu. P. Zenkevich, V. V. Pelevin,
Ing. B. V. Greits, B. M. Prikot**
design for façade of Spartakovskaya Metro
station, 1938–44.
Shchusev Architecture Museum, Moscow

B. S. Vilensky, L. D. Fishbein
interior of Izmailovskaya Metro station,
1938–44.
Shchusev Architecture Museum, Moscow
(sculpture by M. G. Manizer)

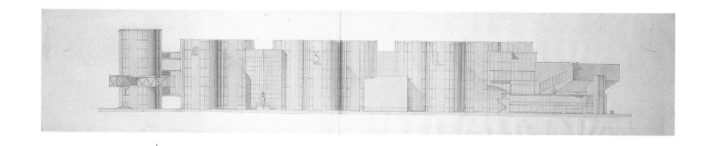

K. S. Mel'nikov
competition project for Frunze Military
Academy, 1931.
Shchusev Architectural Museum, Moscow

L. Rudnev, V. Munts
Frunze Military Academy, rendering, 1932–37.
Shchusev Architecture Museum, Moscow

D. Chechulin, K. V. Kaurkov
project for Aeroflot building, 1934 (eventually
executed as RSFSR parliament building, 1981).
Shchusev Architecture Museum, Moscow

S. M. Polupanov
Uzbekistan Pavilion, All–Union Agricultural
Exhibition, 1939

I. A. Golosov, M. O. Barshch
Monument to the Defence of Moscow, 1941.
Shchusev Architecture Museum, Moscow

**A. N. Dushkin, N. D. Panchenko,
A. D. Khilkevich**
competition project for the Pantheon for the
Heroes of the Great Patriotic War, 1942–43.
Shchusev Architecture Museum, Moscow

N. Suyetin
Female figure,
1927.
Galerie
Gmurzynska,
Cologne

N. Suyetin
*Abstract
Composition*,
1932.
Galerie
Gmurzynska,
Cologne

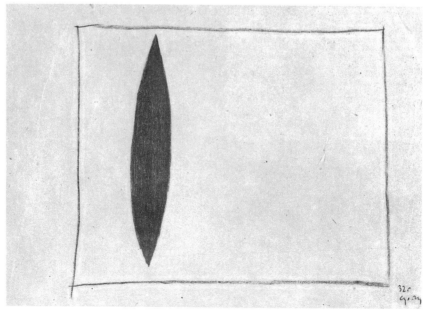

K. Malevich
Bearded Peasant, 1928–32.
State Russian Museum, St Petersburg
(not exhibited)

211

K. Rozhdestvensky
Man with Beard, 1929.
Galerie Gmurzynska, Cologne

K. Rozhdestvensky
New Still-life, 1935.
Galerie Gmurzynska, Cologne

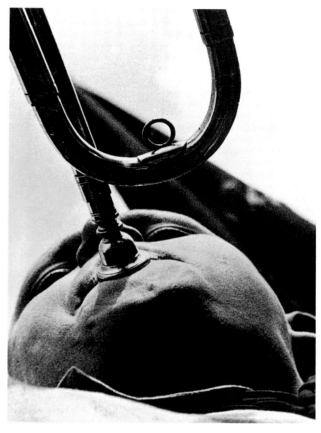

A. Rodchenko
Pioneer Girl, 1930.
Rodchenko and Stepanova Archive, Moscow

A. Rodchenko
Pioneer with a Trumpet, 1930.
Rodchenko and Stepanova Archive, Moscow

A. Rodchenko
Pioneer, 1930.
Rodchenko and
Stepanova
Archive, Moscow

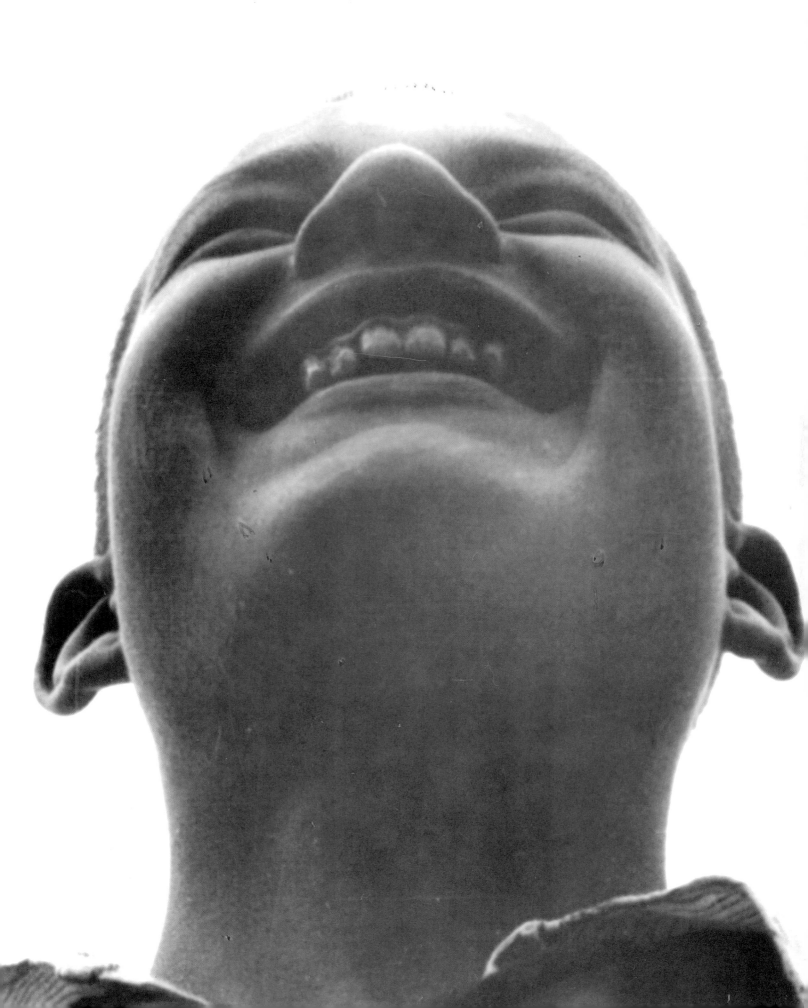

A. Rodchenko
The Installation 'Long live the Constitution', 1936.
Rodchenko and Stepanova Archive, Moscow

A. Rodchenko
The Wheel, 1936.
Rodchenko and Stepanova Archive, Moscow

A. Rodchenko
The Female Pyramid, 1936.
Rodchenko and Stepanova Archive, Moscow

G. Klucis
All of Moscow is Building the Metro, 1934.
Russian State Library, Moscow

G. Klucis
Cultured Life – Productive Work, 1932.
Russian State Library, Moscow

G. Klucis
Greetings to Those Who Have Completed the Dneprostroi, the Greatest Dam in the World, 1932.
Russian State Library, Moscow

G. Klucis
The Struggle for the Bolshevik Harvest is the Struggle for Socialism, 1931.
Russian State Library, Moscow

G. Klucis
Raise the banner of Marx, Engels, Lenin and Stalin! , 1937.
Russian State Library, Moscow

G. Klucis
Long Live the Stalinist Order of Heroes and Stakhanovites!, 1936.
Russian State Library, Moscow

G. Klucis
*Under the Banner
of Lenin for
Socialist
Construction*,
1940.
Russian State
Library, Moscow

221

V. V. Rozhdestvensky
Moscow Landscape. Construction, 1936.
State Tretyakov Gallery, Moscow

A. V. Lobanov
Training Cadres for Magnitostroi, 1932.
State Tretyakov Gallery, Moscow

S. Ya. Adlivankin
Voting to Expel the Kulak from the Collective Farm, 1931.
State Tretyakov Gallery, Moscow

A. A. Monin
Shock-Workers' Avenue, 1934.
State Tretyakov Gallery, Moscow

N. F. Denisovsky
Gold Mining. Prospectors Working a Mine,
1930.
State Tretyakov Gallery, Moscow

P. Filonov
Portrait of Stalin, 1936.
State Russian Museum, St Petersburg

P. Filonov
Two Male Figures, 1938.
State Russian Museum, St Petersburg

G. I. Rublëv
Portrait of Stalin, 1935.
State Tretyakov Gallery, Moscow

A. Rodchenko
The Juggler (No. 1) , 1935.
Rodchenko and Stepanova Archive

S. B. Nikritin
The People's Court, 1934.
State Tretyakov Gallery, Moscow

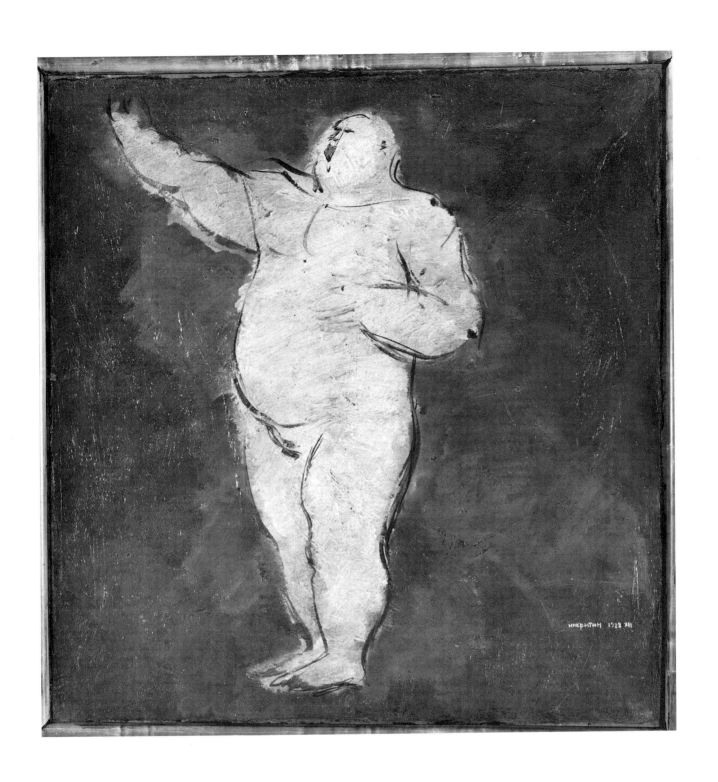

S. B. Nikritin
The Fat Man's Speech, 1928.
State Tretyakov Gallery, Moscow

A. Drevin
Outskirts, 1931.
State Tretyakov Gallery, Moscow

V. Lebedev
Stories, Songs, Riddles (text by S. Marshak) ,
1935.
Russian State Library, Moscow

T. G. Gaponenko
To Mother for the Next Feed, 1935.
State Tretyakov Gallery, Moscow

A. Samokhvalov
Kirov at the Sports Parade, 1935.
State Russian Museum, St Petersburg

A. Deineka
Berlin, 1945.
State Tretyakov Gallery, Moscow

A. Deineka
A Race, 1933.
State Russian Museum, St Petersburg
(not exhibited)

A. M. Gerasimov
Sketch for *Stalin's Speech at the 16th Congress of the Communist Party*.
State Tretyakov Gallery, Moscow

G. Shegal
*Leader, Teacher, Friend (Stalin at the Presidium
of the 2nd Congress of Collective Farm and
Shock Workers, February 1935)* , 1936–37.
State Russian Museum, St Petersburg

V. Mukhina
Industrial Worker and Collective Farm Girl (model for group installed at the International Exhibition, Paris 1937), 1935. State Russian Museum, St Petersburg

I. I. Brodsky
Portrait of Stalin, 1937.
State Russian Museum, St Petersburg

V. Kolyabin
Young People Everywhere Find a Way to Us!, 1951.
Russian State Library, Moscow

V. Govorkov
Citizens of the USSR have a Right to Recreation, 1936.
Russian State Library, Moscow

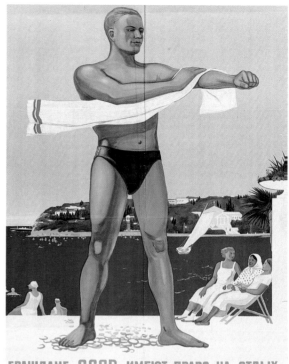

A. Deineka
We Demand Universal Compulsory Education, 1930.
Russian State Library, Moscow

L. Kaplan
Life Has Become Better, Comrades, 1936.
Russian State Library, Moscow

Unknown artist
Exhibition of Posters of Revolutionary Spain,
1937.
Russian State Library, Moscow

G. Klucis
*Long Live the USSR – Fatherland of Workers of
the World*, 1931.
Russian State Library, Moscow

G. Klucis
In the Storm of the Third Year of the Five Year Plan, 1930.
Russian State Library, Moscow

El Lissitzky
Send More Tanks, 1942.
Russian State Library, Moscow

WHEN STALIN MEETS HAUSSMANN

The Moscow Plan of 1935 *Jean-Louis Cohen*

1 *Generalnyi plan reconstruktsii goroda Moskvy* (Moscow, 1936); *Stroitel'svo Moskvy*, no. 7–8 (1935); *Arkhitektura SSSR*, no. 10–11, 1935.

2 Joseph Bradley, 'Moscow, from Big Village to Metropolis', in Michael F. Hamm, *The City in Late Imperial Russia* (Bloomington, Ind., 1986), 9–42.

3 Nina Smurova, 'Urbanistische Phantasien in der künstlerischen Kultur Rußlands Ende des 19., Anfang des 20. Jahrhunderts', in Selim Chan-Magomedov and Christian Schädlich, *Avantgarde 1 1900–1923: Russisch-Sowjetischer Architektur* (Stuttgart, 1991), 56–61.

4 On this see James von Geldern, *Bolshevik Festivals 1917–1920* (Berkeley, Los Angeles, and London, 1993), 175–207.

5 R. A. French, 'Moscow, the Socialist Metropolis', in Anthony Sutcliffe, ed., *Metropolis 1890–1940* (London, 1984), 355–80.

6 Manfredo Tafuri, 'Les premières hypothèses de planification urbaine dans la Russie Soviétique 1918–1925', *Archithèse*, no. 7 (1973), 34–41; Catherine Cooke, 'The Garden City Idea: the Russians', *Architectural Review*, no. 976 (June 1978), 353–62; Barbara Kreis, *Moskau 1917–1935. Vom Wohnungsbau zum Städtebau* (Munich, 1985), 11–31.

7 Jean-Louis Cohen, *Le Corbusier and the Mystique of the USSR: Theories and Projects for Moscow, 1928–1936* (Princeton, 1992).

8 Hugh D. Hudson, Jr, *Blueprints and Blood: the Stalinization of Soviet Architecture* (Princeton, 1994).

9 Vladimir Semënov, *Blagoustroistvo gorodov* (Moscow, 1912). On this urban planner, see Vladimir Belousov and Ol'ga Smirnova, *V. N. Semënov* (Moscow, 1980).

The signature of Joseph Stalin on the 'General Plan for the Reconstruction of the City of Moscow' adopted in 1935 testifies to the importance attached by the Soviet regime to a document that might have been expected to remain purely technical.[1] Presented by its authors as a radical break with the old shape of the city (which the incoming Soviets had reinstated as capital in 1918, two centuries after Peter the Great moved the seat of power into the northern marshes in 1712), this 1935 Plan was to determine the shape of Moscow for more than twenty years.

In the eighteenth century and thereafter, Moscow had remained the centre of commerce and the cradle of a conservative notion of Russian identity, as opposed to the 'Window on the West' opened by Peter in St Petersburg. After the fire of 1812, and later after the abolition of serfdom, Moscow had developed in a comparatively regular manner, its population rising to a million by the beginning of the twentieth century; but, unlike the other great cities of Europe, it had never had a comprehensive rebuilding programme.[2] Before 1914, initial attempts to create garden cities had met with little success; visions of a Moscow overrun with elevated railways, in the futuristic vein popular in American magazines, offered an alternative image based on a metropolitan level of population density.[3]

After the Revolution, the nationalization of land ownership – as called for by Social Democratic theory – gave the Soviets the opportunity to use land formerly owned by the Crown, the aristocracy and the Church, and also to define new uses for the city's individual districts. The landmarks called for in the plan of 'monumental propaganda' formulated by Lenin in 1918 began to appear in the urban space of the city. Artists and architects built temporary decorative structures and monuments in obedience to Vladimir Mayakovsky's 'Order of the Day to the Army of the Arts'. Though ephemeral, the practice of adorning the centre of Moscow with

emblems of Bolshevik culture for numerous festivals and processions served as a point of reference for the later planning of monumental focal features.[4]

In the years that followed the Revolution and the Civil War, there were repeated efforts to plan the development of the capital, whose population resumed its growth in 1921.[5] The resulting, often mutually contradictory proposals covered the whole spectrum of current European planning doctrines. Thus, shortly after 1917, Boris Sakulin's proposal for a network of towns outside Moscow was based on the idea of decentralization; Sergei Shestakov, for his part, suggested completely reorganizing the city by concentrating the system of production.[6]

The New Moscow (*Novaya Moskva*) plan, drawn up in 1923 under the direction of Aleksei Shchusev and Ivan Zholtovsky, was marked by the ideas of the Garden City movement: a number of realized projects, among them the Sokol garden city, embodied the principle of a low-density city clustered around industrial focal points. But migration to the capital became more and more intensive during the years of Lenin's mixed-economy New Economic Policy (NEP, 1920–27). In 1927, work started on drawing up a new plan to cope with the pressure of a population that had passed the two million mark one year earlier.

As the avant-garde architectural groups staked out their positions, the question of the shape of Moscow rapidly became one of their principal battlegrounds. Innovative projects included those of Nikolai Ladovsky and the 'Green City' of Mikhail Barshch and Moisei Ginzburg. Another radical proposal came from Le Corbusier in 1930: it was in response to a questionnaire drawn up by the Moscow Soviet that he formulated his concept of the 'Radiant City' (*Ville radieuse*), designed to obliterate and replace the existing city.[7] Denunciations of the respective 'utopias' of the Constructivist and 'Disurbanist' factions marked the turning points in a sometimes bitterly fought controversy,[8] which concerned

not only the shape of the city but the very notion of what a city was. Increasingly, the metropolis came to be seen as a great stage on which to affirm the values of the regime – but also as a productive force and a capital resource too valuable to waste.

The report presented by Lazar Kaganovich to the June 1931 plenum of the Central Committee of the Communist party inaugurated a new phase, in which a more conservative attitude to the existing urban fabric was combined with a profusion of monumental mega-projects. Cultural policy now emphasized the 'critical assimilation of the inheritance of the past', which became one of the touchstones of 'Socialist Realism'. This ruled out all doctrines based on total rejection of the existing city; as a result, the idea emerged of confirming the concentric network of the old streets while emphasizing the new centres of power and the egalitarianism proclaimed by the regime. Appointed by the party to supervise the development of Moscow, Kaganovich was the sponsor of the 1935 Plan.

Nevertheless, foreign architects were by no means excluded from the final round of consultations, which were held in 1932, concurrently with the Palace of the Soviets competition. Ernst May suggested applying the satellite principle (*Trabantenprinzip*), which he had used in Frankfurt in 1925–30, to transform the Moscow urban area into a vast archipelago of decentralized industrial-cum-residential 'ensembles'. Hannes Meyer, in a project no less radical than Le Corbusier's, proposed to replace the historic centre of the city with a totally new overall configuration. Gradually, the position of Vladimir Semënov, an architect who had worked in Britain before 1914, and who had introduced the methods of European urban planning and the American 'City Beautiful' to Russia,[9] became dominant. Semënov had been a member of the team headed by Shchusev and Zholtovsky, and in 1932 he became deputy head of the Directorate of

Architecture and Planning that was set up for Moscow. It was his vision of a dense and continuous city, based on a detailed reworking of the existing urban fabric, that ultimately prevailed.

Conceived in accordance with the emerging principles of Socialist Realism – never clearly defined until the Writers' Union conference of August 1934[10] – the city devised by Semënov 'assimilated' an 'inheritance' that was now conceived in different terms. Once considered as a legacy of the feudal or capitalist past, the concentric, radial shape of Moscow – dismissed by Le Corbusier as 'the old carcass of an Asiatic village' – became a treasure, something to be not only preserved but further developed: the new districts added to the city were mostly aligned with existing radial routes.

The 'assimilation' of the past took a particularly 'critical' form in the cases of religious buildings, and of a number of prominent urban landmarks. Just as the nineteenth-century rebuilding of Paris under Baron Haussmann had been based on land set free by the wholesale destruction of 'national assets', the transformation of Moscow entailed demolitions that frequently verged on sheer vandalism. The church of Christ the Saviour, built by Konstantin Ton in the nineteenth century, was demolished to make way for the Palace of the Soviets,[11] while the Strastnyi monastery was replaced by the *Izvestiya* complex. The Poultry and Game Market (Okhotnyi Ryad), the Red Gates and the Sukharev Tower (though long protected, and even taken as the inspiration of a 1930 project by Ivan Fomin), were flattened, along with countless lesser buildings – while much was made of the moving of a few houses in Tver' Street.

Though broadly based on Russian precedents, the General Plan for Moscow, adopted by a decree of the Central Committee and the Council of People's Commissars signed by Stalin and Molotov, nevertheless did not totally exclude Western influences. The almost unvarying density of the residential areas harked back to Otto Wagner's plan (1911) to turn Vienna into a boundless metropolis (*unbegrenzte Großstadt*) based on uniformity and repetition; and the transformation of the city's Garden Ring (Sadovoye Kol'tso) into a monumental thoroughfare is an echo of the earlier Ringstrasse in Vienna.

A reference of the same order to the urban configuration of Paris appears in the design of the major axis of the composition, oriented on Boris Iofan's projected Palace of the Soviets: this echoed the 'Triumphal Way' (*Voie triomphale*) from the Etoile to La Défense, for which a competition had been held in Paris in 1931. Again, Semënov based his new route structure for Moscow on designs formulated by Eugène Hénard in his *Etudes sur les transformations de Paris* (1903–09).[12] Finally, both the scale of the street blocks and the centralized focus of the plan echo the ideas of the City Beautiful movement, and above all the project for Chicago (1909) by Daniel Burnham and Edward Bennett: the Palace of the Soviets project by Iofan, Gel'freikh and Shchuko relates to the street layout in the same way as Civic Center Square in the Chicago plan.

It was envisaged that by 1960 Moscow would occupy an area of 60,000 hectares and house a population of 5 million (its population in 1935 was 3.6 million). Presented as the metropolis of a new social and cultural order that would eventually cover the whole planet, the Socialist city defined by the 1935 Plan aspired – like many other cities in the grip of strong political or technological forces – to become a *Gesamtkunstwerk*: a total work of art, based on a 'harmonious' interaction between urban composition, architecture, sculpture and the other arts.[13] The Plan laid great stress on the idea of the ensemble (*ansambl'*), based on classical, and especially Parisian, precedents such as the Place de la Concorde. Pierre Patte's eighteenth-century ideas on urban improvement were cited by many members of the working parties at the Academy of Architecture that formulated the ideological principles to accompany the Plan.

The layout proposed for Moscow combined big blocks (*kvartaly*) with big monumental thoroughfares (*magistraly*), in a system subsequently adopted in all the other cities of the Soviet Union. In contrast to the most abstract of the compositions devised in the 1920s by ASNOVA, or the machine concepts of OSA, the city was to be composed of clearly identified ensembles of buildings and open spaces, with monumental accents added through the use of a veneer of decor, combined with Realist sculpture. These blocks were treated like large

single buildings, often designed by a single architect, and incorporated shops, offices and dwellings within the envelope of an oversized *palazzo*. The streets were conceived as a succession of unexpected vistas and transverse sequences.[14] To coordinate the designs of the blocks, a specific design team was assigned to each *magistral*.

The most important of the *magistraly* was the one that set out from the Palace of the Soviets towards the southwest of Moscow, where a huge new district was to be developed. Of the other five major radial routes, one with an industrial emphasis led from the centre to the ZiS motor works in the southeast; another followed the line of Kirov (formerly Myasnitskaya) Street, northeast to Ismailovo Park. Under the overall supervision of Sergei Chernyshev, each of these routes was the subject of a planning project commissioned from one of the architectural offices of the Moscow Soviet. The first of them to be completed was Tver' or Gor'ky Street, which was widened to 40 metres.

Along these streets, there was a marked contrast between the perimeter of the blocks, which formed a continuous street wall, and the internal space. The new buildings on the outside served as a

10 Régine Robin, *Le réalisme socialiste, une esthétique impossible* (Paris, 1986).

11 Its expiatory reconstruction began in 1994.

12 Vladimir Semënov, 'Moskvu planirovat' i zastraivat' zanovo', *Stroitelstvo Moskvy*, no. 2 (1932), 2–6; Semënov, 'Kak planirovat' i zastraivat' Moskvu', *Stroitelstvo Moskvy*, no. 8–9 (1933), 8–11.

13 Boris Groys, *Gesamtkunstwerk Stalin. Die gespaltene Kultur in der Sowjetunion* (Munich, 1988).

14 Jean-Louis Cohen, Marco de Michelis and Manfredo Tafuri, *URSS 1917–1918, l'architecture, la ville* (Rome and Paris, 1979), 140–99. Vieri Quilici, ed., *Mosca, capitale dell'utopia* (Rome, 1991).

Lazar Kaganovich with the Moscow Plan, 1935

curtain or a piecrust that allowed the planners to conceal great tracts of waste land or tumbledown *izbi* (cottages). There is an echo here of the illusory canvas villages built for Catherine II by Count Potëmkin. But in this case the illusion of the façade – denounced by Adolf Loos in Vienna forty years previously – was compounded by the use of the entire on-street building itself to create the illusion of an imaginary city, concealing the prosaic substance that survived behind.

While the old radial lines were reinforced and widened, notably by the moving of a number of buildings, the ring roads (supplemented in accordance with Hénard's principles by new crosstown routes) were remodelled and punctuated by new landmarks. Under the direction of the former Rationalist, Nikolai Dokuchayev, the old Garden Ring became an astonishing array of symbolically charged buildings. This monumental line-up includes one outstandingly grotesque example of 'speaking architecture' (*architecture parlante*), in the shape of the Red Army Theatre, by that cynical bureaucrat Karo Alabyan: its overall plan, and the cross-section of its pillars, are in the shape of a five-pointed star.

While incorporating several elements of former Functionalist proposals, such as the plan for the Moskva River sports centre by Nikolai Ladovsky, the 1935 Plan rejects all rhetoric based on the exaltation of labour, choosing instead to enshrine a repertoire of forms borrowed from the Renaissance or derived, via a succession of 'enrichments', from a rather clumsy monumental Art Deco. The Moscow Metro (the first line was opened in 1935), on which both traditionalists and Modernists were given station platforms and entrances to design, clearly illustrates the very wide range of formal strategies that were currently available.[15]

Just as the ephemeral architecture of the first revolutionary pageants had blazed a trail for the experimentation of the Modernist architects, the parades staged for official festivals now gave rise to a triumphalist architecture, conceived as a backcloth for orderly mass processions. Kaganovich himself interpreted the concentric radial plan as a device whereby the masses, once duly organized, could be conducted towards the Kremlin: 'My aesthetic,' he declared, 'demands that the demonstration

processions from the six districts of Moscow should all pour into the Red Square at the same time.'[16]

The search for an 'assimilable' past – prescribed by Socialist Realism as the only way to make the city legible for the 'masses' – gave rise to a wide range of sometimes surprising architectural inventions (many of which remained on paper, as the pressures of impending war began to mount). And yet even this historicist frenzy did not put paid to all concern with modernization: work on industrialized building techniques led to schemes combining the planning conventions of the *kvartaly* with the use of prefabricated concrete panels – as in the buildings designed by Andrei Burov (a former Constructivist) and Boris Blokhin along the Leningradsky Prospekt in 1940.

The Second World War forced the regime into an ideological volte-face which restored a degree of visibility to Russian religion and Russian culture. Russian Revival forms, banished from the architectural repertoire of the 1930s, reappeared not only in single buildings but in whole planning schemes. Within the framework of the 1935 Plan, which remained in force, the Moscow skyline was transformed by the use of 'vertical buildings' – skyscrapers in all but name – as modern counterparts of the towers and spires of ancient churches.

In its eclectic formal dress, the new Moscow can thus be read as the close of a cycle initiated by Baron Haussmann in Paris eighty years before.[17] Of course, the land speculation so characteristic of the remodelling of Paris was eliminated by the regime, but it remains the case that a ruthless hierarchy of land use was applied, the city centre and the major street frontages being reserved for bureaucrats and for the official intelligentsia. The obliteration of the old pattern of land ownership, and of historic buildings, was quite as ruthless as in Paris; and the relationship between the unbroken tissue of residential development and the monumental points of focus was analogous – although the Moscow street blocks, with their gigantic internal courtyards, are very much larger.

Though it adopts some elements of modern technology, the 1935 Plan thus belongs in the context of the great urban plans of the late nineteenth century rather than of the regional plans that were under consideration for New York and for Paris

between 1920 and 1940. The urban modernization process carried through by Semënov – himself one of the reformers who had vainly tried to rationalize the city before the Revolution – thus ultimately led the 'Socialist' capital, reformed under the authority of Stalin, to drape itself in the monumental garb of a bourgeois metropolis.

Translated by David Britt

15 Nikolai Kolli and Sergei Kravets, *Arkhitektura moskovskogo Metro* (Moscow, 1936).

16 Quoted in Richard Stites, *Revolutionary Dreams; Utopian Vision and Experimental Life in the Russian Revolution* (New York and Oxford, 1989), 243.

17 Haussmann was denounced in terms that occasionally smack of the psychology of denial: see 'Sotsialisticheskaya Moskva', *Arkhitektura SSSR*, no. 10–11 (1935), 2.

Retouchers working on a photo-giant for Sverdlov Square, Moscow 1932

PHOTO-POWER

Painting and Iconicity in the First Five Year Plan *Brandon Taylor*

'It was the spring of 1932. The whole country was moving forward, was full of enthusiasm for the major construction sites of the Five Year Plan. Moscow was preparing to mark the international proletarian festival of workers – the First of May . . . We had the difficult but attractive task of trying to reflect in a decorative form the spirit and experiences of life out on our major sites of Socialist industry and energy.'[1]

The writer, an artist named G. S. Zamsky, is reminiscing about his participation in the building of three commemorative propaganda decorations for Sverdlov (formerly Teatral'naya) Square, just in front of the Bolshoi Theatre in Moscow. 'At out disposal', he goes on, 'was the central square of the capital, and we had to decorate it in a manner that was both ideological and artistic . . . We chose to feature the Dnieper Hydro-Electric Power Station [Dneprostroi], Magnitostroi, and the First Ball-Bearing Factory (in Moscow), as these three sites were the most inspiring and significant of the period.'

We learn from Zamsky's account that the ball-bearing factory was celebrated by a model of a magnified ball-bearing, some ten metres in diameter, placed in the public gardens in front of the Bolshoi. But it is one of the other schemes that interests us here. Zamsky tells us that 'the decoration for the Dnieper Power Station was in the form of a model of the dam, between whose piers were photographic displays of the new construction sites of the Five Year Plan, flanked at each end by . . . full-length portraits of Lenin and Stalin . . . 25 metres high and 10 metres wide. They were as tall as the Metropole Hotel.'[2]

The nature of such photographic representations is signficant, because they were so frequently used throughout the 1930s: decorations in Comintern Square in October 1932, for example, included three huge neon portraits, this time of Marx and Engels, Lenin, and again Stalin. It is my contention that there is a decisive link between such public propaganda photography and the official history

painting of the period – officially termed Socialist Realism at the 1934 Writers' Congress – and also between both and the traditional functions of the icon.

Of course, the very gigantism of the Sverdlov Square decorations, seen at night, formed an essential part of their propaganda function. From the mass-circulation journal *Proletarskoye foto* (Proletarian Photo) we learn that their size and complexity were seen as embodiments of quantitative aspects of the Five Year Plan itself. Stalin's close ally Lazar Kaganovich, and others, had already called for 'Magnitostroi of art', huge projects involving literary and artistic team-work on an ambitious and assertive scale.[3] Although Zamsky says despondently that 'the task [of decorating the square] was . . . was complicated by the fact that the artists had very little time or material at their disposal: there were pine boards, plywood, calico, photos and electric light bulbs, and that was all', nevertheless the scale of the Dnieper Dam decorations was impressive. Models of a blast furnace and other machinery occupied the centre of the public gardens, in front of the dam itself.[4] Running across

the top of the dam between the two photo-giants was Lenin's electrification slogan: 'Communism Equals Soviet Power Plus the Electrification of the Entire Country.'

The scheme was constructed in a spirit of supposedly rapid and enthusiastic team-work. Allegedly working round the clock, a total of 202 assorted negative handlers, enlargers, retouchers and glue- and wind-experts, working with a total of some 800 negatives taken from successive enlargements of images of the two leaders, pasted photo-panels measuring 50 by 60 cm onto larger rectangular boards, at which point teams of construction workers assembled them on towering scaffolds.[5]

Commissioned from no less a figure than Gustavs Klucis by Soyuzfoto and the First of May Commission of the Moscow Soviet, the medium and origins of the Sverdlov Square decorations are as important as their size in relation to the ways in which they are likely to have been seen. The image of Lenin derives from a series of still photographs taken by Pyotr Otsup, taken on 16 October 1918 (some seventeen days after the shooting incident

1 'Extracts from MS reminiscences of the artists G. S. Zamsky and N. A. Mutasov on their work for the May Day celebrations of 1932 in Moscow', in V. Tolstoy, I. Bibikova, C. Cooke, eds., *Street Art of the Revolution: Festivals and Celebrations in Russia, 1918–1933* (London, 1990), 209.

2 Ibid., 210

3 The phrase was first used in connection with literature, at the Fifth Plenum of the literary organization RAPP in the autumn of 1931. See my *Art and Literature under the Bolsheviks* (London, 1992), 2:157, 179, 185–86.

4 Details in L. Oginskaya, *Gustavs Klucis* (Moscow, 1981).

5 For the statistical data, see 'Biografiya fotogigantov', *Proletarskoye foto*, no. 6 (June 1932), 16–18, and 'Rozhdeniye fotogigantov', ibid., 19–20.

May Day decorations, Sverdlov Square, Moscow 1932

Izaak Brodsky,
*Lenin's Speech at
a Workers'
Meeting . . .*,
1927

6   A sequence of stills
from the film by A. F.
Vinkler and A. A.
Levitsky is published in
Lenin (Moscow, 1970).

7   See 'Lenin i
fotografiya', *Sovetskoye
foto*, no. 2/35 (15 January
1929), 33–35, and
Sovetskoye kino, no. 1–2
(1993), 10.

8   V. I. Lenin,
'Directives on the Film
Business', 17 January
1922, in Lenin, *Collected
Works*, vol. 42 (Moscow
and London, 1969),
388–89.

9   Note 446, in Lenin
(as note 8), 590–91.

10 'Deklaratsiya
Assotsiatsii
khudozhnikov
revolyutsionnoi Rossii',
1922, in I. Matsa et al.,
eds., *Sovetskoye iskusstvo
za 15 let* (Moscow and
Leningrad, 1933), 345,
and J. Bowlt, *Russian Art
of the Avant-Garde:
Theory and Criticism
1902–1934* (London,
1988), 265–67.

Lenin, 16 October
1918

Izaak Brodsky,
*Lenin in Front of
the Kremlin*, 1924

which almost proved fatal), which show the convalescent leader chatting outside his office in the Kremlin to V. D. Bonch-Bruyevich; there is a film-sequence, taken simultaneously, whose stills are also well-known.[6] The Stalin image appears, reversed, in Klucis's own poster of the first Five Year Plan, *The Feasibility of our Programme is the Real People, It's You and Me* (1931), in which Stalin appears marching alongside miners in pursuit of (presumably) unattainable targets. Now thoroughly abstracted by the retouchers from their original contexts, these two photos, 'as tall as the Metropole Hotel', prompt some pertinent questions about the cult of the leader, about propaganda, and about the modes of functioning of photography itself in Soviet reality and art.

Those modes turn out to be structured in some surprising ways. Lenin's own name was invoked by proletarian groups at the start of the Five Year Plan as having given an impetus to the photographic media, both still and moving. 'You must always remember that of all the arts the most important for us is the cinema,' Lenin had said in conversation to Lunacharsky.[7] In January 1922, in *Directives on the Film Business*, he had ordered that the People's Commissariat for Education should supervise the registration and screening of all film shows: both entertainment ('of course, without obscenity and counter-revolution') as well as films with a special propaganda message on themes of topical relevance. 'Besides films,' Lenin had gone on to insist, 'photographs of propaganda interest should be shown with appropriate subtitles.'[8] A month later, he had again insisted to Lunacharsky that the production of new films 'imbued with Communist ideas and reflecting Soviet

reality' should include newsreel, attached to 'worthless film . . . of a more or less usual type, to attract the public'.[9] It is the phrase 'imbued with Communist ideals and reflecting Soviet reality' that stands out; for it is this very double function, of film or photography – the documentary combined with the agitational – that lies at the foundation of the Socialist Realist aesthetic and informs the use of *both* painting and photography from the early 1920s through the 1930s and beyond.

For, strictly speaking, it is an impossible pair: the actual-as-actual of the documentary excludes the future; yet imag(in)ing the possible or theoretical future seems to exclude the here-and-now. In what terms then was that conjunction effected?

The paintings of Izaak Izrailevich Brodsky (1884–1939), or an important sub-set of them from around 1924 to 1937, might be taken as paradigmatic of mid-period Soviet culture, in so far as they displayed what was claimed to be a documentary and photographic reality. Brodsky had joined the group known as AKhRR (Association of Artists of Revolutionary Russia) in 1923, and in the following year had used Otsup's photo, already mentioned, for his own oil painting, reproduced so many times and in so many contexts thereafter, *Lenin in Front of the Kremlin*, together with its variants, in all of which Lenin appears in the same basic pose. It comes as no surprise to find that among groups devoted to painting it was AKhRR that used Lenin's double-formula first, in its *Declaration of 1922* which speaks of 'our

civic duty before mankind . . . to set down, artistically and documentarily, the revolutionary impulse of this great moment of history'; to depict in documentary form 'a true picture of events' or of what they call 'the present day'.[10]

By 1925, at the hands of Lunacharsky, the need for the documentary-cum-agitational picture had become a demand for 'the great social *kartina*' or thematic picture – 'the *kartina* understood as a social gesture'.[11] Brodsky's *kartina* painted in 1929, *Lenin's Speech at a Workers' Meeting at the Putilov Factory in May 1917*, provides an example; it was built up from photographs of Lenin, of individual workers, and of the factory site, so as to achieve a backward-looking contemporaneity that combines the vitality of the eyewitness account with a frankly tendentious appeal to the concept of a party leader of a certain kind. Here, shown only slightly elevated above the proletarian mass as first among equals, Lenin is a modest but enthusiastic leader or *vozhd'*, rendered in the illusionistic manner of a documentary photograph, yet magnified and transformed into the terms of oil paint on canvas.

Yet this was no ordinary transformation. As the debates which ensnared Rodchenko and the October Group in the later 1920s show, in the Five Year Plan period (nominally 1928–33), photography's original and most problematic claim – to be an index of the real – made it not only a potential rival to the easel painting but a subject of fervent debate concerning point of view, verisimilitude and – in conformity with the double formula – agitational value.[12] Indeed, by 1929 Brodsky had been marginalized with AKhRR – or AKhR, as it had become known in its new, proletarianized version – on the grounds that his paintings were 'too photographic' for the agitational programmes of the younger zealots and shock-workers of the Plan. The dogmatic and extreme proletarian radicalism of the early Plan years implied a denigration of the kind of easel picture that Brodsky had become celebrated for painting, notably *Lenin at Smol'nyi* (1930), which pictures Lenin in 1917 or early 1918 in his temporary headquarters at the convent girls' school in Petrograd.

Yet by the early part of 1932 the mood in the party was changing fast; a new compromise was being forged between the indexicality of the photo and its agitational use in public murals such as those in Sverdlov Square. In any case, the disputatious proletarian organizations had been summarily closed down by the Decision of 23 April 1932. And Brodsky himself was coming back into the fold as Stalin's favourite and Voroshilov's friend, as the dependable chronicler of the revolution and its history.

For students of Brodsky's method it should be recorded that it is V. K. Bulla's photograph of the artist drawing Lenin at the Third Comintern Congress of 1921 that is the source for *Lenin at Smol'nyi*, not the drawing in which Brodksy is here apparently engaged. Though capable of photographic drawing, Brodsky was more adept at reproducing the look and tone of the photographic surface in the painting itself. Thus the verisimilitude of *Lenin at Smol'nyi* is one that invades and is transformed by the moral framework of the fine-art easel picture, even as that framework welcomes the truth-effect of the photograph into its connotative structure. We might even deploy the terms of a much later analysis to point to the ways in which photographs generally commemorate the 'has-been-ness' of particular events, with a poignancy that speaks both of death and a paradoxical mode of survival.[13]

Over and above its literally commemorative function, then, Brodsky's painting serves to embrace the dead leader within a photographic image that memorializes even as it captures its ostensible subject. It is a function that Annette Michelson, following Ernst Kitzinger and W. Eugene Kleinbauer's analysis of the church icon, has called acheiropoietic or *nerukotvornyi*: not made by human hand but created by causal emanation from the sacred personage whose image it then comes to bear.[14] If so, then the result of the photographic effect within the painted surface was to lend it an icon-like presence and hence a transcendental meaning that elevated it beyond the here and now.

It was a formula that clearly appealed to the party. May 1932 was also the month in which *Literaturnaya Gazeta* demanded an art of 'honesty, truthfulness and a revolutionary, Socialist Realism in the representation of the proletarian revolution',[15] perhaps the first public use of the phrase which was to solidify into

doctrine at the Writers' Congress two years later, and which laconically formed the basis of so much subsequent Soviet aesthetics. By 1932, of course, the cult of Lenin that had begun in the power struggle following his death in 1924 had changed into something else, namely an aspect of the cult of Stalin. In the 1930s and after, Lenin's image is regularly combined with that of Stalin as a bonded and symbiotic pair. Either the two were paired, a political slogan running between them, or else photographs of Stalin in the company of Lenin were resurrected (or fabricated) which suggested relations between them to have been cordial – despite Lenin's dying recommendation to have Stalin removed from his post of general secretary of the party. In the case of the 1937 film *Lenin in October*, the role becomes advisory and avuncular, with Stalin (played by a handsome actor) paternally puffing on his pipe and counselling Lenin's every move.[16] In the openly hagiographical *Joseph Stalin: a Short Biography* of 1941, Stalin is fancifully reconstructed in the events of October 1917 as 'Lenin's right-hand man'.

It takes only a small step, then, to move from the openly photographic representational order of the two Sverdlov Square photo-giants and to see them as iconic, not only in the sense of picturing a referent but in the religious meaning of the icon as prescribed by Russian Orthodox traditional: to see them not only as powerful public images but as stimulating and re-evoking the presence of the two leaders who now stood before the public in relation of founder and successor respectively (we may have noticed that the Otsup-Brodsky image of Lenin after his wounding shows him, in effect, as risen from the dead). The direct

comparison is with the figures of SS. Peter and Paul, or more likely with the authors of the holy liturgy, SS. John Chrysostom and Basil, normally depicted facing inward towards each other and with the holy texts unfolding between them, as in a sixteenth-century Novgorod icon in the Russian Museum. The modern variant shows the two Soviet leader-saints, now both figuratively and literally in command of the Word, with the electrification liturgy running between them.[17]

And yet the making and erection of the photo-giants in the spring of 1932 marks the beginning of a secondary or degenerative phase in the relations between painting, photograph and reality in later Soviet culture. After that date, two developments become gradually evident. The first was that retouching – a technique available from at least the mid 1920s for the correction of illegibilities in the photographic print and for the removal of blemishes in countenance, clothing, posture and other details[18] – became sophisticated enough to enable (in conjunction with that Modernist technique, montage) a joining of disparate persons or events, or even the erasure of persons and events that party dogma could not at that point countenance. The

Brodsky drawing Lenin at the 3rd Comintern Congress, Moscow 1921

Izaak Brodsky, *Lenin at Smol'nyi*, 1930

11 A. V. Lunacharsky, opening remarks at the seventh AKhRR exhibition, 8 February 1925, in V. N. Perel'man, ed., *Bor'ba za Realizm: b izobrazitel'nom iskusstve, 20kh godov: materiali, dokumenti, vospominaniya* (Moscow, 1962), 124–129.

12 See M. Tupitsyn, 'Fragmentation versus Totality: the Politics of (De)framing', in exh. cat. *The Great Utopia, The Russian and Soviet Avant-Garde, 1915–1932* (New York, Solomon R. Guggenheim Museum, 1992), 483–496.

13 R. Barthes, *Camera Lucida* (London, 1984).

14 A. Michelson, 'The Kinetic Icon in the Work of Mourning: Prolegomena to the Analysis of a Textual System', *October*, no. 52 (Spring 1990), 16–51.

Follower of Dionisii, *St John Chrysostom and St Basil*, 16th century

15 *Literaturnaya gazeta*, May 1932.

16 For the Lenin cult, see N. Tumarkin, *Lenin Lives!* (Cambridge, Mass., 1983).

17 It would take a longer essay to detail the ways in which Brodsky and other artists emphasized Lenin as master or manipulator of the word: writing, reading, speech-writing, listening or advising others.

Izaak Brodsky, *Lenin Giving a Speech to Troops . . . on 5 May 1920*, 1933

Lenin addressing troops in Sverdlov Square, 5 May 1920

second development was that retouching – which can be described as painting or drawing on the image – now entered the domain of Socialist Realist painting with a vengeance.

Thus, when Brodsky painted his *Lenin Giving a Speech to Troops Departing for the Polish Front on 5 May 1920* in 1933, the still photographs used were probably versions of those by G. P. Goldstein showing Lenin straining to make his short speech heard in the high wind, with, to his left on the rostrum, the figures of Lev Kamenev and Leon Trotsky. Comparison of Brodsky's painting with the Goldstein photos, however, shows a scene if anything more significantly recomposed than in any of his paintings before. Adding banners to the crowd around the rostrum and a sea of portrait faces to the foreground and to left and right, he repositions Lenin in a theatrical posture that has him declaiming uncharacteristically with his hands, while – in common with doctored versions of Goldstein's photographs circulating at the time – he removes Trotsky and Kamenev from the scene. Trotsky's fate in the official documentary history of the Soviet state now became the abrupt opposite of Lenin's and Stalin's: just as they were constantly resurrected or immortalized in

the photo-surface, Trotsky's disappearance from that representational order was similarly and rigorously assured. The transposition of the false record into painting from the early 1930s onwards, in the hands of a master retoucher like Brodsky, becomes as flagrant and tragically familiar as the systematic attempts to rewrite substantial amounts of Soviet history itself.

Photo-reality – photography's indexical claim on the world it purports to capture and describe – thus slides into photo-unreality, as the propaganda machinery of the Soviet state discovers its true power in the dark days of the mid and later 1930s: the days in which – as in Katerina Clark's analysis of the Soviet novel – the distinction between fiction and fact became so blurred as to become impossible to define.[19] This was also the time in which, as Jeffrey Brooks has recently pointed out, the party organ *Pravda*, whose very title (Truth) carried a further claim to documentary authority, devoted an ever greater percentage of its copy to the mission of Soviet writers and artists to construct and document the new life, even as that construction became increasingly unhinged from actual events.[20]

Likewise, the claims of Socialist Realist painting to document living or historical actuality were vitiated by bathos and exaggeration as the decade wore on. Yet the *kartina* of society mediated by the photograph, published in poster and book reproduction on a vast and orchestrated scale, capitalized on that purported indexicality in spite of the amount of sheer historical error that it now embodied. It was the special and final conjuring trick of Socialist Realist doctrine that the double formula that began by claiming to combine the 'documentary' and the 'agitational' now discovered itself to be capable of virtually any version of reality providing it retained – in some of the elements of its style or address or making – the 'look' of the photo-document itself.

The short remainder of Brodsky's career after 1935 – he died in 1939, the first artist to be awarded the Order of Lenin – issued in a large number of portraits in lithograph and oil which skilfully iconized Soviet leaders in what had by now become his trademark, the adjusted or fabricated photographic style (p. 241). But a note may be added on the question of the religious icon and its

relation to the 'formalism' which Brodksy – as director of the prestigious Institute of Painting, Sculpture and Architecture of the All-Russian Academy of Fine Arts in Leningrad – became known for regularly purging in the later part of the decade.

In a recently published letter, written in 1930 by an icon-maker in Moscow to a friend, we find a predictable tone of lament that the traditional icon had been left to die out, that modern variants had become lacking in understanding of the true tradition of *acheiropoiesis* or simultaneous embodiment of the absence and presence of the divine. But what is even more remarkable about this letter – noticed only by church historians until now – is that the language developed to describe that true tradition reads, in its extraordinary emphasis on materiality, much like the terms of that arch exemplar of formalism, Cubism:

'All the media available to artists [of the icon] for the creation of the plastic image are part and parcel of that image in a material and non-abstract way. The surface of the panel is the material datum, the limited space in which the image incises itself . . . The action of the image . . . has a certain "shallow depth" . . . additional surfaces bring into the image those parts of the material body which the eye cannot see by the laws of visual perception . . . for instance, when a face is depicted front on, a surface is added which is simply the back of the head; or again, in a three-quarters portrait we see the missing quarter. Reversed perspective serves the same purpose. It prevents the viewer imagining a figure in depth and, to give greater fullness of impression, moves the object round by a law contrary to optical perspective.'

The icon-maker's purpose is naturally to 'create an image which with peace and assurance imports to the soul the real and inifinite integrity of true life, the mystery of another, heavenly world'.[21] Yet such a world, secularized, is also recognizable as the utopian programme of Bolshevism and its successor, Soviet Communism. It seems that what we may call Brodskyism – or photo-painting in general as the methodological centre of the Socialist Realist method – managed to invert the traditional icon method as part of its attack on formalism, while retaining something of that tradition's acheiropoietic function, its function as both mystification and power.

CONTEMPORARY VOICES *Compiled by John Willett*

A Moscow Diary, 1935 *Erwin Sinkó*

15 July 1935

Knowing that M had the day off, Steiner telephoned to ask if I felt like an outing. He proposed to collect us in his car and take us to meet a Soviet artist. There was something he wanted us to see, he added rather mysteriously, something that would speak for itself. Minutes later his car was at our door.

He told us nothing at all about where we were going. After a while he stopped outside a cemetery. Our path took us past tombs of which I have never seen the like. They provided disturbing evidence of how the reality of death leaves nothing for the Revolution to do but display sorrow. The more simply and silently it does this, the more human and dignified the effect. But in the first years of the October Revolution a radical attempt was made in Moscow to counter death with a new style of life. And this is a further proof that Lenin's October was animated by that naive and at the same time promethean-utopian drive without which, as Plato rightly said, neither belief nor disillusionment would be possible or worth while.

True enough, and although I cannot do more than recall that revolutionary impetus and its idealistic basis with respectful nostalgia, I must admit that here was a whole row of monumental sculptures from the first years of the Revolution, which were inspired by exactly the same driving spirit and high hopes, and now appeared like so many memorials to a grotesque distortion of human taste and human reason.

The first grave bore an iron framework representing a semaphore, the second a pair of compasses the height of a man, the third a hammer, the fourth a Cubist figure made up of iron rods: a whole long row of ultra-modern monuments proclaiming in a crude formal language – but none the less unmistakably – the radical concern of the first revolutionary years with the creation of a new world. Even the graveyards were to be pressed into proclaiming the triumph of the new subject matter, with its imperious call for new symbols.

The aim is unmistakable: the Bolsheviks wished death itself to be assimilated into their new world. Death, which didn't give a damn for the Revolution, and just went on practising its craft as it had done under the capitalists and the Tsars, back in ignoble prehistoric days. At the same time they wanted to re-train that impossibly stupid and awkward customer, Death, so as to celebrate the creativeness of Labour and Willpower by adopting a new language and new symbols.

As we walked on, we could see how, after the childish efforts of its early years, the Revolution promptly beat a retreat and withdrew beyond the cemetery walls. Realizing how things were, it admitted that there was nothing to be done about Death; that is to say, nothing new. From the start of the NEP in 1921 up to the present day, the monuments looked no different from those in an average municipal cemetery. They are like a desert of funerary slabs. On some you see a framed photograph of the deceased (now mouldering under the mound) in the prime of life. And here as elsewhere the inscriptions read as if the bereft were filling out a police report on their loved one. He gets described as soldier, doctor, engineer, worker, student, professor or former assistant director of a civil service department – as though the cosmic majesty of Death made it important to know what one was called and what position one held in that short interval between two non-existences which we love and suffer as Life.

As I was going along the ranks of the dead, deciphering the inscriptions and occasionally admiring the indifferent loveliness of some young tree growing among them, a gigantic white-bearded Orthodox priest loomed up. Without wasting a glance on us, he strode by as if we were not there. His attitude and gait conveyed the deeply majestic self-esteem of a personage who knew himself still to be unconquerable, at any rate in the graveyard.

I forgot to say that during our drive to the cemetery Steiner stopped the car at Tver' Street and picked up a middle-aged man who was waiting for us. Our new companion promptly introduced himself: Shadr. He spoke the name distinctly and, I felt, with a certain emphasis. But as this monosyllable conveyed nothing to me, I thought no more about it. He sat in the front beside our friend throughout the journey, while M and I sat in the back. Arrived at the cemetery, I even ceased to wonder about our friend's humorously mock-conspiratorial attitude. He had still not told us what sort of a surprise to expect. After we had been marching quite a while between the graves, which were now in military formation (leaving room for us too to be accommodated there), suddenly an armed militia man confronted us. 'It is forbidden to go further', he said. Steiner did his Mephisto act, a diplomatic Mephisto, as it were. His face gave nothing away. He looked serious, and acted as if he himself were unsure what to do next. Shadr put his hand in his pocket, fished out a *bumazhka* [a slip of paper] and exchanged a few words with the man in uniform, who then saluted and stood aside.

Shadr gestured to us, and on we went.

A moment or so later we were no longer among the graves, and had left our grassy path for an open clearing. Gravel crunched beneath our feet. Two other men in uniform came up. This time, however, it was not they who stopped us but Shadr, who was walking in front.

Vot!, he said (there you are!), and pointed to an isolated grave in the centre of the clearing. Shadr's blue eyes caught mine for a bare second; his gaze swept past me. Without a word, he became lost in a study of the sculpture. Steiner, with consummate tact, appeared anxious not to disturb our appreciation of this work of art. He stood a few paces away, with his panama hat in his hand, and seemed to be wholly absorbed in a thorough and prolonged study of the toes of his (as always) spotlessly polished shoes – much like Shadr's study of his own work.

M and I stood between them, and nothing was said. Shadr must have misinterpreted our silence, and decided that we were worthy to hear him describe his artistic concept. As we could see from the golden letters on the marble tomb, we were looking at the grave of Nadezhda Alliluyeva. This was Stalin's wife, who had killed herself a few years earlier. Shadr drew our attention not so much to the superb piece of marble as to the alarmingly lifelike pink rose that lay at the edge of the grave and was of marble too. This rose was his work. Lowering his voice, and without taking his eyes off his own achievement, he told us that he had been commissioned 'from the highest level' to prepare a design for her tomb. He had spent a long time wondering how he could prove himself worthy of this honour, an honour greater than any that had

Notes to Taylor, *Painting*, continued.

18 Cheap retouching pencils are advertised as 'necessary for every photographer and artist', for example in the opening pages of *Sovetskoye foto* for 1929 – and must have been available much earlier.

19 K. Clark, *The Soviet Novel* (Chicago, 1981).

20 J. Brooks, 'Socialist Realism in Pravda: Read All About It!', *Slavic Review*, 53, no. 4 (Winter 1994), 973–991.

21 'Icon, an Expression of Prayer and Sacrament', first published in *Messager de l'Exarchat Russe en Europe Occidentale*, 101/104 (January–December 1979), 85–93, and in English in G. Limouris, ed., *Icons: Windows on Eternity*, World Council of Churches Faith and Order Paper 147 (Geneva, 1990), 195–201.

previously come his way. (Steiner went on studying his toes with the same deadly solemnity. Probably he had already heard the story and no doubt had visited this *chef-d'oeuvre* in the company of the artist.)

Shadr explained to us that there were such things as moments of inspiration, one of which had given him the happy idea that this tomb called for a pink marble rose. Ordinary roses would fade, whereas the marble rose was not merely a thing of beauty but would last, thus symbolizing reliability. Nothing short of a marble rose could be worthy of the man who mourned Nadya Alliluyeva.

When he had finished talking, or rather declaiming, he put his head on one side, screwed up his eyes and slowly approached the marble rose, till the two armed guardians of the tomb blocked his way. With the masterful intensity of the self-possessed, he told them that he was the *khudozhnik* (artist), at which they stepped out of his path without asking for any proof in writing. I cannot forget how respectfully the two young men in uniform watched as the artist marched across the gravel to the tomb, bent down, picked up the marble rose and re-sited it some three centimetres further forward.

'It can be moved, just like a real rose,' he said as he rejoined us. 'But that has its drawbacks,' he added with some concern. 'The guard (mere amateurs!) will handle the rose, but can never put it back right. Each time I visit the grave I have to return the rose to the correct position.'

As he spoke he had put his head on one side, half-shut his eyes as if to check that he had found the adjustable marble rose the

I. D. Shadr, *Tombstone of Nadezhda Alliluyeva*, 1933, Novodevichie Cemetery, Moscow

best spot on Nadya Alliluyeva's tomb, the spot judged most propitious for both tomb and art work in the light of the highest aesthetic standards.

Evidently the artist so misinterpreted my silence and the astonished look in my wife's wide-open eyes, that he offered to show us round his studio on our way home. Our Mephisto, with his perfect manners, gave his approval with evident pleasure, and promptly offered to drive us there.

While he, Steiner, kept his back to us as he drove, Shadr turned round and talked incessantly. He asked if we had yet seen the huge naked figure in the Park of Culture. 'Yes', I told him, 'that figure made an impression on us when we first visited the Park.'

Quite true. That gigantic figure had indeed made an impression. It is supposed to radiate strength and happiness, but it is an abortion, a stony indication that the Muses must have kept well out of the way of the sculptor, who lacked even the most rudimentary skills of his craft. It was so painful to my eyes that I would willingly have covered it up or kept it hidden from the world, as my young ancestor Shem had once done to the nakedness of the drunken Noah, thereby in the words of the Bible qualifying for especial praise.

'That figure is by me', said Shadr.

At the studio we made sure our visit was a short one. Almost with one voice, M and I reminded Steiner that we had something important to do, which could not be put off. Our Mephisto pretended to be particularly interested in those figures and compositions which, in Shadr's words, were 'realistic, but monumental'. Before leaving, Shadr showed us a few drawings. Moreover, he had done the drawing for the certificates of the Soviet State Loan.

The worst of it was that nobody knew which way to look. Shadr's blue eyes took exact note of each twitch of an eyelash. Thanks to his total misapprehension, he alone enjoyed the impact of his monumental realist masterpieces, which left us simply at a loss for words. On top of that he showed us his trophies: photographs and hymns of praise to his works, published in *Pravda*, *Izvestiya* and the Soviet sculptors' journal on the occasion of his being given various official distinctions.

When we left his flat, Shadr took leave of us in the following words: 'When you get back to Europe you will be able to tell them that you have visited the Michelangelo of the present day in his studio.'

31 August 1935

For the last few days Pierre Vorms and his wife Mira have been in Moscow. I have pleasant memories of him from Paris, where he is a literary agent and has a gallery in the Rue de la Boétie. He is here to familiarize himself with Soviet art, and wants to hold a show of his Paris painters in Moscow and exhibit Soviet painters in his gallery.

He was invited to a lecture which a Soviet personality called Beskin was giving for Soviet painters on the subject of French painters and painting. Pierre had met Beskin in Paris at some reception or other at the Soviet Embassy. Beskin spoke in Russian, not realizing that Mira was Russian by birth and was giving her husband an instant translation of all he said. The unwitting comrade spoke as if he had been personally inspired by Goebbels; indeed he took the theory of 'degenerate art' a step further by sketching a portrait of the degenerate artist. He described him as living a life outside society, showing his indifference to the struggle of the masses, and being sick and decadent, in short rotten to the core.

Vorms was not at all amused. When Beskin's lecture as over, so Mira told me, Pierre went up to him and angrily demanded an explanation. He named a dozen French painters, personal friends of his, all of whom were Communists, active and self-sacrificing anti-Fascists with a good standing in the art world. Beskin, who speaks French well, was extremely taken aback. Drawing Pierre to one side, he assured him . . . that he himself did not believe one word of what he had been saying in the lecture. He had not gone quite crazy; he had had occasion to meet those painters in Paris; he regarded them and their work with admiration. *'Mais que voulez-vous, mon vieux?'* ['But what do you expect, old boy?'] And he finished, so Vorms himself told me, by giving an amiable, good-tempered laugh – without a vestige of guilt.

In any case, after Pierre had visited a number of studios – not excluding Shadr's – he abandoned all idea of showing the work of Soviet artists in Paris. Nor is there any enthusiasm here for the idea of holding an exhibition of French artists in Moscow. Even the proposal for a Masereel show was only accepted with reluctance.

From Erwin Sinkó, *Roman eines Romans: Moskauer Tagebuch* (Cologne: Verlag Wissenschaft und Politik, 1962), 189-94, 267-68.

Translated by John Willett

The Artist-Daubers, 1936 *from Pravda*

One of the darkest and cruellest criminal practices of the Middle Ages was the mutilation of children. The masters of this craft were called the *comprachicos* [literally, child-buyer/s]. Victor Hugo described them in his novel *L'homme qui rit*. The *comprachicos* maimed children, transforming their faces into monstrous masks. Revulsion from the tiny monsters and sympathy for them formed the basis of a profitable begging industry.

The *comprachicos* is a terrible grimace of the Middle Ages. But is it not strange, indeed preposterous, to see in our own times, in our own country, people who have made the mutilation of children their craft – on paper, of course, only on paper, only in drawings?

Here is a book which one peruses with revulsion, like a handbook of anatomical pathology. Here are all kinds of child monsters which could only be created by the imagination of a *comprachicos*: horrible rickety types on matchstick legs with swollen stomachs, children without eyes or noses, child-monkeys, feeble-minded children, savage and overgrown girls. Here the adults too are deformed and the animals are crippled. Here is a horrible cat arousing feelings of nausea and loathing. Here is something worse: flayed carrion, all that is left of a horse.

In this world of deformity, even plants seem to have passed through the hands of the *comprachicos*: trees are unhealthily distorted, with repulsive growths and lumps, vile palms, thorny shrubs, obviously lacking in scent. The sun never penetrated these dark jungles.

Even things, everyday things – tables, chairs, suitcases, lamps – have all been corrupted, broken, spoilt, deliberately given such an appearance that they are repellent to look at and impossible to use. It is as if an evil, ruthless *comprachicos*, with a deadly hatred for everything natural, simple, joyful, happy, wise and necessary, had passed through the whole book, spoiling and befouling everything, leaving his filthy mark everywhere. And, having done his disgusting deed, he contentedly signed his name: Drawings by V. Lebedev.

And instead of Latin inscriptions for all these nightmare images of deformity, we find the simple, kind, cheerful stories of S. Marshak.[1] Instead of the name of a medical publisher, the ornate colophon of Akademiya. Nothing is more striking than the contrast between the lively tone of Marshak's verse tales and this dark outburst of the distorted fantasy of Lebedev who, had he wished, could have provided skilful, understandable drawings. In the stories, all the words are simple, humorous, clear – this is why even small children love them. But everything in the drawings is deformed, distorted, totally humourless, incomprehensible, and completely unrelated to the text.

'Look, what a painted nasty,' said a young mother in one of Gogol's books, bringing a weeping child to a picture in which the blacksmith Vakula had depicted a horrible devil. That was rural education in the old days. But the artist Lebedev and his fellow *comprachicos* in art certainly do not paint their 'nasties' to frighten children. On the contrary, they wish to give children enjoyment. They even think that they are developing an aesthetic sensibility in children. Thus, certain adults think that children will understand them better if they say, 'Looky, diddums, how clever his dad-dad is!' Childish prattle is very appealing. When a child talks like this, he is trying to talk like a grown-up. He is learning. It is serious work. When an elderly, balding uncle produces childish prattle, it is stupid and repellent. There is neither art nor work in it.

Strangely enough, Marshak himself has not noticed this. His book includes a story about a 'Master Smasher'. How could he have allowed a master dauber on to the pages of his book?

Lebedev is not a solitary phenomenon. In children's books there is a school of *comprachicos*, master daubers all. Under the same Akademiya imprint, the artist Ts. Rozenfeld mutilated *Little Hunchback Horse*. The artist Konashevich ruined Chukovsky's stories. This was done not out of lack of talent, not out of illiteracy, but intentionally, in the style of a childish primitive. This is nothing but a stunt. This is 'art' whose principal aim is to have as little as possible in common with everyday reality.

In painting and sculpture, this 'art', used sometimes to be called progressive or 'left'. It was openly formalistic. Its bourgeois nature was betrayed by its passion for all kinds of deformity and distortion. This 'art' allowed the human form on to the canvas only on certain conditions. It was reconciled with nature only when nothing of nature remained. This formalism is not yet extinct. It has its 'masters' and advocates. It is sometimes disguised, by no means artlessly.

Nowhere does formalism reveal itself so openly as in drawings for children. It is here that its inner emptiness, morbidity, and decay are seen in their full colours. Daubings in children's books are deeply reactionary, since they are an open and complete denial of the whole of the real world of children. A healthy, happy, joyfully laughing Soviet child is hateful to the *comprachicos* artist, as is the everyday world of plants, flowers, objects and machines. Marshak's book of stories includes verses about the Dnieper Hydroelectric Project. What dark and messy illustrations Lebedev has produced for these verses! Instead of a crane, he gives us a smeared ink blot. But even his people are blots; his animals, his children – all blots. In this world of smeared ink there is, and can be, no room for laughter or sunshine. Obviously, the artist does not need them. Or rather, they are hateful to him because they are real, alive, speaking of health, strength

1 S. Marshak, *Skazki, pesni, zagadki* (Stories, songs and riddles). [Original note; see p. 233.]

V. Lebedev, cover for S. Marshak, *Tsirk* (1928)

and beauty. Formalism has a haughty, contemptuous attitude to the real world, to living colours and sounds. It rejects the integrity of the image in painting, as it denies melody and clear phrasing in music.

The formalist has a scornful attitude to the wider audience. Not only does he not want to be understood; he sees understanding as a humiliation for him. And if he can sometimes disguise this among adults, he gives himself away completely when he enters the world of children. Only a person who does not love Soviet children could depict a Pioneer campfire as it is on page 107 of Marshak's book.

When the artist set himself to produce his drawings, he was not thinking about children, the readers of the book, but only and exclusively about himself. Whether or not a drawing helps a child to understand and master the text of a story is a trifling matter, nothing at all to do with the task of art. The primary aim is to find a line which pleases the gaze of the artist himself. These are actually drawings for a small circle of aesthetes, tacked on to a children's book. Children will be repelled by the Formalists' daubs, but 'art lovers' will be pleased to place the book on the shelf reserved for publications in bad taste.

Deformity has its own history in art. For example, the gargoyles of Notre-Dame in Paris are well known. This is not the place to embark on an analysis of the sources of these dark images. Soviet masters have other sources of inspiration. In any case, we must mercilessly expel those who would decorate the walls of a Soviet children's home with sculpture in the style of the Parisian gargoyles. Whoever cannot or simply does not want to work gladly and lovingly for Soviet children, whoever hates the joyful sunny world of the Soviet child, whoever can only paint 'nasties' for his own pleasure – should keep away from children.

At a meeting on children's literature at the Central Committee of the Komsomol, Comrade A.A. Andreyev said: 'All this daubing which gives no real representation of reality, all distortions in this area must be mercilessly expunged from children's literature. Let such artists draw their pictures for themselves, for their own pleasure; we shall not allow this daubing to be presented to our children. To look at a children's book containing such daubs can be nauseating, sickening.'

Formalism has become deeply rooted in children's books, under the protection of publishing houses tinged with aestheticism.

Only a struggle with the Leftist deformity in painting will open the way to genuine and valid artistic design for Soviet children's books.

'O khudozhnikakh-pachkunakh', *Pravda*, 1 March 1936.

Translated by Roderick Riesco

Erwin Sinkó (1898–1967) joined the Hungarian revolutionary movement at the end of the First World War. He contributed to the Budapest magazines *Tett* and *Ma*, and took part in the Hungarian Soviet of 1919. He then went into exile in Austria, moving on to Yugoslavia, where he wrote a novel called *The Optimists*. Hunting round for a publisher in any country who would take that book, he turned eventually for help to Romain Rolland in Paris, who advised him to try Moscow. Unfortunately he arrived there in 1935 with his doctor wife (the M referred to above), just when Stalin's purges were making life dangerous for foreigners, including their patron the Hungarian Soviet leader Béla Kun, who was arrested and later executed. Coincidentally or not, it was a time of severe reaction in the arts, starting with Andrei Zhdanov's proclamation of Socialist Realism at the first Soviet Writers' Congress in 1934.

This Stalinist doctrine came to apply in all the arts, and in January 1936 an All-Union Committee on Art Affairs was formed under the chairmanship of P.M. Kerzhentsev. The signal that the new slogan was serious, and that the modern movement with its tendency to 'formalism' would not be tolerated much longer, was given around the same time by some editorial articles in *Pravda*, the Communist party paper, notably those attacking Dmitri Shostakovitch, Mikhail Bulgakov and Vsevolod Meyerhold. In among these came the article of 1 March which we cite, with its complaints against Vladimir Lebedev's children's book illustrations (those illustrated on p. 233). This was linked with an All-Union conference on children's books that had been held in mid-January and was addressed by Andreyev of the Central Committee secretariat. Lebedev, a Cubo-Futurist, had worked, like the late Vladimir Mayakovsky, on the ROSTA propaganda displays in the revolutionary years.

Ivan Dmitrevitch Shadr (1887–1941)

was a monumental sculptor, who made many portraits of Lenin and collaborated with Vera Mukhina on a huge statue of Gorky in Moscow; he was said to exemplify 'revolutionary romanticism', which was seen for a time as a legitimate alternative to Socialist Realism. Osip Beskin was an art critic and author of a book *O Formalizmu* – 'Formalism' – attacking an aesthetic theory of the early 1920s which for many years would be seen by the Party as the major art heresy.

Pierre Vorms was agent and publisher to Frans Masereel, the Flemish wood-engraver. Karlo Steiner (or Stajner), the Comintern official whom Sinkó likens to Mephisto, was to be banished for many years to Siberia. In April 1937 Sinkó returned to Paris with his wife, only to find that Moscow was advising the French Communists against publishing his work. When war came two and a half years later, the couple went back to Yugoslavia, where in due course they joined Tito's partisans. Sinkó eventually settled in Zagreb as a professor and academician, and saw his books published at last in Serbo-Croat and Hungarian.

GBI Berlin, Plan showing clearance and rebuilding schedules for the North-South Axis, 24 September 1941, Landesarchiv Berlin

NATIONAL SOCIALISM AND MODERNISM

Architecture *Iain Boyd Whyte*

1 Peter Gay, *Weimar Culture: The Insider as Outsider* (London, 1968), 144.

2 Walter Laqueur, *Weimar: A Cultural History 1918–33* (London, 1974), 270.

3 Wilhelm Hausenstein, *Ein Stadt auf nichts gebaut* (Berlin, 1984), 10; originally the chapter 'Berlin' in *Europäische Haupstädte* (Erlenbach, 1932).

4 Amédée Ozenfant, 'Weekend Berlin', *Der Querschitt*, no. 5 (1931), 297; quoted in Rolf-Peter Baacke, ed., *Berlin im 'Querschnitt'* (Berlin, 1990), 45.

The cultural history of Berlin in the 1930s still has to be written. The dozens of books and anthologies on the 'Golden Twenties' invariably end on a note of high pathos in January 1933. Peter Gay's *Weimar Culture*, for example, concludes: 'A few months later, Adolf Hitler was Chancellor of Germany, and the men of Weimar scattered, taking the spirit of Weimar with them, into the Aesopianism of internal emigration, into death in the extermination camps, into suicide.'[1] No hints of continuity or of enforced compromise were allowed to bridge the divide between the liberal and progressive culture of the Weimar years and the oppressive regime that followed. In Walter Laqueur's terse formulation: 'The Nazi era, needless to say, was the antithesis to everything Weimar stood for.'[2] The cultural history of Berlin has tended to stop on 30 January 1933, to be resumed in May 1945.

This does not mean, of course, that there is a lack of information about daily life or cultural production in the capital city during the 1930s and the war years. There are many distinguished memoirs and works of fiction describing Hitler's Berlin, and a large number of scholarly texts and exhibitions dealing with the relationship between National Socialism and specific areas of the visual arts and architecture, literature, theatre, cinema and music. These researches offer source material in great abundance. What is missing, however, is the synthesizing account that would illuminate the diverse relationships of dependence and interdependence, of location, political ideology, and artistic volition in 1930s Berlin. It is surprising – yet at the same time explicable, given the fraught nature of the material – that no general overview has been written of cultural life in Berlin in one of the most morbidly fascinating decades in its history.

In 1932 Wilhelm Hausenstein wrote of Berlin: 'It is as if it were grounded on nothing, but a nothing that is *the* nothing – a nothingness elevated into an essence . . . Think of Vienna, Paris, of the old cities in southern and western Germany, whose very essence and nature is their rootedness. Berlin has no provenance, as it were, no rootedness or history.'[3] Precisely this lack of roots or inertia, the dynamism and lust for novelty that has always marked the character of Berlin, made it the perfect laboratory for modernity during the 1920s, where the most recent developments in every

5 Julius Langbehn, *Rembrandt als Erzieher* (1890; 66th ed., Leipzig, 1925), 265.

conceivable aspect of human activity could be tested to destruction. Berlin in the 1920s was the Modernist city par excellence, the most American of the European capitals, the city that pointed the way forward, precisely away from the rootedness that marked Paris or Vienna. As the French painter and writer Amédée Ozenfant forecast in 1931, following a weekend in Berlin: 'Paul Morand describes Berlin as a failed New York. Who knows if in twenty years time New York will be seen as a failed Berlin! Say what you like: Berlin is European. Paris is still the ideal capital, but we have to advance.'[4]

The principal question that a cultural history of Berlin in the 1930s will have to address is the degree to which this progressive culture was totally eradicated over the decade, and what accommodations were made between Fascism and Modernism. In brief, was Nazi Berlin a Modernist city in the 1930s?

The Berlin Master Plan

Hitler was no great admirer of Berlin: nor was the city over-enamoured of Hitler and his party. In the elections of 5 March 1933, under 35 per cent of Berliners voted for the National Socialists. Seen from the sandy shores of Schleswig-Holstein or from the depths of the Thuringian Forest, Berlin meant asphalt, petrol fumes, morphine, sexual licence, and every possible form of decadence, depravity and delinquency. From the early days of the united Germany in the 1870s, Berlin was targeted by right-wing nationalists as an alien intrusion in the new state, an open sore in the body politic. A very typical view of the city can be found in Julius Langbehn's *Rembrandt als Erzieher* (Rembrandt as Educator), the gospel of the right-wing cultural pessimists, first published in 1890 and an influential voice right through the 1920s and 1930s. Like Ozenfant later, Langbehn saw close similarities between Berlin and New York, but he saw them in a strictly negative light. Both cities were identified as temples to greed and Mammon, unfruitful soil for traditional, 'organic' values: 'Until now, even this small drop of organic spirit has been missing in Berlin, as in North America, in the realm of the spirit and the arts.'[5] While he damned late nineteenth-century architecture as prosaic and unpoetical, the author of *Rembrandt als Erzieher* saw architecture itself as the great hope for the salvation of all the arts: 'Whoever understands the importance of a inner, spiritual sense of the architectonic will also know that this is the only way by which the German People and German art will achieve once again a great, solid, unified character.'[6]

As the last two quotations suggest, the 'Rembrandtdeutscher' and similar conservative thinkers were confronted by two conflicting positions. On the one hand, architecture – the supremely urbane art – was seen as the great regenerative force that would improve the condition not only of the other visual arts but of German society in general. On the other hand, however, the capital city was deeply distrusted as a cosmopolitan, Americanized, materialistic pile of bricks and stucco, quite devoid of the inner calm and monumental simplicity that characterized, they felt, the German soul.

The most extreme response to this problem was the suggestion that a new capital should be built on a virgin site, untainted by questionable Berlin mores. In 1919 Ludwig Finckh, an author of texts on race and genealogy that subsequently found favour with the National Socialists, insisted: 'We must draw a line between Berlin and ourselves, and leave it to its quarrels and its fate . . . The new nation must have a new capital . . . Somewhere in the heart of Germany, in a forest, on a heath, the new buildings should rise, in which a better national leadership will dwell. The spirit of the nation must renew itself.'[7]

Practicality, however, precluded this option, even after the Nazi seizure of power in 1933. The only alternative was to reshape Berlin in a form more congenial to the new regime; a task entrusted in January 1937 not to the established planning authorities, but to a new office, the General-bauinspektion (GBI), directed by a young and inexperienced architect, Albert Speer.

Working on the basis of guidelines and formal motifs devised by Hitler himself – the giant axis, the domed hall and the triumphal arch – Speer's vision for Berlin was both megalomaniac in its scale and very simple in its basic strategy. Two axes were to be established, running north-south and east-west. These would cross just to the south of a giant new square flanked by the existing Reichstag, a vast domed hall, the Führer's palace, and the Armed Forces High Command. At their extremities, the axes were planned to link with the outer autobahn ring, with a further four inner ring roads to provide concentric circulation.

Model of North-South Axis, as planned in 1938–39, seen from the north

6 Ibid., 104.

7 Ludwig Finckh, 'The Spirit of Berlin' (1919), in Anton Kaes, Martin Jay and Edward Dimendberg, eds, *The Weimar Republic Sourcebook* (Berkeley, 1994), 415.

The central section of the North-South Axis was conceived as a vast parade route, designed to house the principal public buildings, ministries, and commercial offices of the new Reich on a boulevard 5 kilometres long and 120 metres wide. Although large-scale demolition and site clearance was undertaken, little was actually built, and the North-South Axis remains a paper monument to the megalomania of the Hitler's Reich. In contrast, however, the East-West Axis, running along Unter den Linden, through the Brandenburg Gate and the Tiergarten and out into the western suburbs took on a more tangible form, still perceptible today. Ahead of Hitler's fiftieth birthday (1939), the nineteenth-century Siegessäule (Victory Column) was moved in 1938 from its original site in front of the Reichstag to a new site on the East-West axis. In the original scheme, the winged figure of Victory atop the column, celebrating the Prussian triumphs over Denmark (1864), Austria (1866) and France (1870–71), was to look westward, up the hill, to the Mussoliniplatz (now Theodor-Heuss-Platz), where her gaze would have been met by another giant figure, *Preparedness*, by the sculptor Arno Breker, set upon a columnar plinth designed by Speer. Although Breker made various versions of this work, including an 11 metre high plaster cast, and although Speer's columns were actually cut in a quarry near Stuttgart, the war intervened and nothing was built.

A similar fate overtook the University City, planned for an extension of the East-West axis near the Havelsee and Spandau, of which only fragments were built; after 1945 these were buried under one of Berlin's hills of bomb rubble, the Teufelsberg. The 1936 Olympic Stadium survives in the western suburbs as the only major element on either of the two major axes to be completed.

Rationalization and the Sublime

There is a general consensus that *Neues Bauen* – the white architecture of the 1920s, the architecture of the Bauhaus and of the great housing estates in Berlin and Frankfurt – had faltered around 1930, long before the National Socialist takeover in 1933. As Anna Teut noted in her pioneering book on Nazi architecture: 'Well before National Socialism was in a position to pass its guillotine sentence, *Neue Sachlichkeit* [the New Sobriety] as an official expression was dead, even if it survived as a small, vigorous branch.'[8]

8 Anna Teut, *Architektur im Dritten Reich 1933–45* (Frankfurt, 1967), 10.

9 Ludwig Sterneaux, 'Berlin hat die nackten Fassaden satt', *Der Montag*, supplement, 16 June 1930.

Goering and Speer (2nd from r.) with model of Victory Column as moved, 1938

Albert Speer, model of Mussoliniplatz with monument, 1939–40

The mass housing programmes in the cities, which had been the backbone of the Modernist architectural programme, were victims of the world economic crisis, and were formally abandoned by the Brüning government that watched helplessly as unemployment in Germany rose from 4,380,000 in December 1930 to 5,615,000 a year later: a tenth of the total population. In architecture as in every other aspect of German social and political life, the apparent certainties of the mid-1920s had ceased to be certainties, and the Modernist perspectives were already narrowing. Sensing a fundamental shift in taste, the popular press joined with the National Socialist ideologues to celebrate the passing of *Neues Bauen*. A typical headline from the summer of 1930, by the respected critic Ludwig Sterneaux, for example, insisted that 'Berlin is sick of naked façades!'[9]

Yet the 'small, vigorous branch' was by no means dead, and the support of the Modernist *Razionalismo* by the Fascist regime in Italy led to hopes that in Germany, too, political revolution could be identified with artistic modernism. The eminent art historian Wilhelm Pinder argued to the Kampfbund, for example, that the modern movement was essentially German; while in the summer of 1933 the National Socialist League of German Students condemned reactionary attitudes in the arts and proclaimed their support for the Expressionist art of Barlach, Heckel, Nolde and Schmidt-Rottluff.

These early hopes in the Modernist camp were fuelled by the ambiguous messages given out by the new regime in the months immediately following the Nazi accession to power in January 1933, and are represented in the exhibition by submissions for the 1934 Reichsbank competition, by Ludwig Mies van der Rohe, Walter Gropius and Hans Poelzig (pp. 288–89). The competition for the new Reichsbank headquarters was launched in February 1933, directly after the Nazi takeover, by the pro-Modernist ministerial director Martin Kiessling, who invited designers from all points in the architectural spectrum, from Mies at the Modernist end to Heinrich Tessenow and Wilhelm Kreis at the traditionalist end. Besides the quality of the entrants, the Reichsbank competition is noteworthy on several counts. It was the last great competition for a major public building in Berlin between 1933 and 1945. Thereafter, major commissions were awarded exclusively to members of the National Socialist inner circle. The brief is also interesting in that, with an unhappy prescience, it stipulated air-raid shelters in the basement.

In spite of conservative attempts to fix the jury, Ludwig Mies van der Rohe's winning scheme was resolutely Modernist in character. Unhappy with this outcome, Adolf Hitler personally intervened, divided the prize money among six of the entrants and awarded the commission to the chief architect of the Reichsbank, Heinrich Wolff, who produced a dull piece of conventional classicism, eminently suited to the building's subsequent use as the East German Ministry of Economics.

The end of open architectural competitions coincided with the rise of the Reichskulturkammer (Reich Chamber of Culture), the party organization responsible for all the arts. As Propaganda Minister Joseph Goebbels explained in November 1933: 'In future only those who are members of a Chamber are allowed to be productive in our cultural life. Membership is open only to those who fulfil the entrance condition. In this way all unwanted and damaging elements have been excluded.'[10] This intention became statute in the Architects' Law of October 1934, which specified that the title of architect could be used only by members of the Reichskammer der Bildenden Künste, the section responsible for architecture and the visual arts. Both the public nature of the profession and the experience of several years of unemployment during the recession of the early 1930s made the architects particularly vulnerable to this political pressure, and by 1935 the 15,000 architects represented the single largest group in the parent organization, the Reichskulturkammer.

In this climate of fear, the slightest suspicion of liberal sentiment exposed the architect to the risk of exclusion from the profession. Even before the National Socialists assumed control, the right-wing press delighted in denouncing the avant-garde as 'cultural bolshevists'. Hans Poelzig, for example, an entrant in the Reichsbank competition, had been attacked in the *Deutsche Tageszeitung* in December 1932 as 'the exponent of an artistically, culturally and ideologically radical left tendency', whose actions 'declared sympathy for bolshevism'.[11] Faced with an intensification of such attacks and the prospect of exclusion from the profession, many architects were all too eager to proclaim their support for the new leadership and to distance themselves as far as possible from any hint of cultural bolshevism, generously defined by the party ideologue Alfred Rosenberg as 'everything that National Socialism rejects'.[7]

Among the signatories of the pro-Nazi 'Aufruf der Kulturschaffenden' (Proclamation of the Creative Artists), published in the newspaper *Völkischer Beobachter* on 18 August 1934, for example, were the Expressionist artists Ernst Barlach and Erich Heckel and the Modernist architects Emil Fahrenkamp and Mies van der Rohe, the last director of the Bauhaus.[13]

With absolute power over the architectural profession focused at the centre, one would expect the emergence of a coherent design philosophy. That this was not the case reflects both the personality of Hitler himself and the structure of the National Socialist state.

The enormous difficulties experienced by historians in their attempts to establish coherent patterns in the National Socialist ideology are a reflection of the Nazi state itself, which, as William Carr has noted, 'was no monolith but a mosaic of conflicting authorities bearing more resemblance to a feudal state, where great vassals were engaged in a ruthless power struggle to capture the person of the king who in his turn maintained his authority by playing one great lord off against another'.[14]

In this context, conventional oppositions such as Modernist and traditionalist make little sense, as both tendencies were constantly present in the party ideology as essential counterweights in the balancing act performed by Hitler. As recent research has indicated, some of the leading figures in the party, such as Robert Ley, Fritz Todt and Albert Speer, were essentially modern in their thinking and in their policies, while others, such as Heinrich Himmler, Walther Darré or Alfred Rosenberg, had a mystical attachment to the German soil and to the whole apparatus of Blood and Soil. The technocrats had visions of a Modernist National Socialist state, almost American in its commitment to technology and industrial rationalization, while the anti-Modernists dreamed of rebuilding German greatness through the labours and ethics of the German peasant. In his necessarily ambiguous position in the centre, Hitler gave some encouragement to both groups but identified solely with neither. As in every other area of state policy, this nurtured ambivalence can be found in the Modernist/traditionalist debate as it affected architecture. In 1936, for example, Hitler's government warned against *Maschinenfeindlichkeit* (hostility to the machine) and advocated the rationalization of industrial production 'in order to utilize all the insights of economic progress in order to increase living standards'.[15] In a similar spirit, the quasi-official propaganda text on the new state architecture, Gerdy Troost's *Das Bauen im Dritten Reich*, proclaimed: 'Out of the very essence of technology, the power of a regulative world view [*Weltanschauung*] can develop

10 Joseph Goebbels, *Germania*, November 16, 1933; quoted in Peter Adams, *The Arts of the Third Reich* (London, 1992), 53.

11 Robert Scholz, 'Der "Fall" Poelzig', *Deutsche Tageszeitung*, 22 December 1932.

12 Quoted in Teut (as note 5), 21.

13 On Mies's relations with the National Socialist government, see Elaine S. Hochman, *Architects of Fortune: Mies van der Rohe and the Third Reich* (New York, 1989).

14 William Carr, 'Nazi Policy against the Jews', in Richard Bessel, ed., *Life in the Third Reich* (Oxford, 1987), 69.

15 Walter Waffenschmidt, 'Die gegenwärtigen Probleme der Rationalisierung in Deutschland', in *Soziale Praxis* 47 (1938), 1162.

analogous forms. Buildings are created that express measure and wonder, working through clear, economical lines to symbolize precise, exact work carried out within. With their freely exposed concrete, steel and glass they make a striking impression. How light, inventive and ambitious these technical buildings are! Here the artistic will to form has triumphed over matter.'[16]

Utterly contrasting ambitions, however, can be found in the speech on architecture delivered by Hitler at the party congress in 1937, in which he affirmed his intention to construct the greatest buildings ever seen in German history and insisted that 'only the great cultural documents of humanity made of granite and marble' offer stability and certainty in a world of change and transition.

In purely constructional terms, the lightweight structures praised by Gerdy Troost and Hitler's massive blocks of granite are poles apart. In terms of emotional response, however, monumental architecture and the power of industry and technology are linked by the aesthetics of the sublime, in that both offer images that overwhelm our perceptual or imaginative powers, making the scope of rational comprehension all the more exciting and vivid. In a telling passage in his memoirs, Speer pointed to the nature of Hitler's aesthetic sensibility, recalling that on walks in the Bavarian Alps,

16 Gerdy Troost, *Das Bauen im neuen Reich* (3rd ed., Bayreuth, 1941), 73. The author, an architect, was the widow of Paul Ludwig Troost.

17 Ibid., 47.

18 Adolf Hitler, 'Die Bauten des Dritten Reiches: Aus der Kulturrede des Führers auf dem Reichsparteitag 1937', quoted in Teut (as note 8), 190.

19 On the Nazi sublime see Iain Boyd Whyte, 'The Sublime', in Keith Hartley, ed., exh. cat. *The Romantic Spirit in German Art 1790–1990*, (Stuttgart, 1994), p.145.

Herbert Rimpl, Heinkel aircraft factory, Oranienburg

Emil Fahrenkamp, 'Chimneyless Power Station'

Hitler 'frequently admire[d] a beautiful view, but as a rule he was more affected by the awesomeness of the abysses than by the harmony of a landscape'.[17]

This preference for the vast, the fearsome and the potentially destructive points to the aesthetics of the sublime, a supposition confirmed by the conclusion of Hitler's 1937 party speech: 'These colossal works will, at the same time, represent the most sublime justification for the political might of the German nation. This state should not be a power without culture nor a strength without beauty. For the arming of a nation is only morally justified when it is the shield and sword of a higher mission. We do not aspire, therefore, to the naked force of a Ghengis Khan, but rather to a realm of power in the formation of a stronger, protected community as the bearer and guardian of a higher culture.'[18]

The aerial shots of the Nuremberg Rally Grounds in Leni Riefenstahl's film *Triumph of the Will* exactly capture the potent nexus of the mechanical and lithic sublime: the all-powerful machine confronting the massive stone edifice and countless ranks of the faithful.[19]

Even though 1937 is generally considered a turning point, when diversity in the visual arts was finally extinguished by the party, and firm distinctions drawn between official and 'degenerate' art, the flexible situation in architecture carried on as before. Particularly astonishing is Ludwig Hilberseimer's utterly Modernist proposal for the University City initiative, which offers a series of elegant slab blocks set in the green, in the best tradition of *Neues Bauen* and 1920s urban planning theory. The proposed site for the University City was set on an extension of Speer's East-West axis: and, as Wolfgang Schäche notes in his essay in this volume, the competition was conceived as a warm-up exercise for the great tasks ahead on the North-South Axis. Unsurprisingly, the more monumental schemes of architects like Gutschow and Distel (p. 286) won the day.

But the Modernists were by no means without work during the National Socialist years – particularly, but not exclusively, in the realm of high-technology industry. As Werner Durth's researches have revealed, Hans Dustmann – a former head of Walter Gropius's design office – became Reichsarchitekt of the Hitler Youth, responsible for a national chain of youth centres and sports facilities. Another Gropius associate, Ernst Neufert – who had been site architect for the Bauhaus building in Dessau – was in charge of standardization within Albert Speer's GBI, and produced norms for the German construction industry that survived long into the postwar era. Yet a third Gropius associate, Herbert Rimpl, led a team that designed the ultra-modern Heinkel aircraft factory in Oranienburg, to the north of Berlin, employing former assistants of Ernst May, the city architect of Frankfurt in the 1920s who had been responsible for the great housing schemes in that city.[20]

Significantly, Rimpl's office also designed traditional housing, with rustic shutters and high-pitched roofs, for the Heinkel factory workers. Consistent with the structures of the state and party hierarchies, the technological utopia of the machine – of flight and fire-power – was set side-by-side with the redemptive utopia of the cottage and the family hearth.

The North-South Axis, too, combined the ultra-modern with the ultra-historicist. The dominant language, of course, was the monumental classicism that in various guises found favour in Europe and North America in the 1930s as the architecture of authority. Set against the eternal values proposed by the gigantic architecture on the axis, however, is the Modernist insistence on mobility and transportation. The axis is anchored at its northern and southern ends by railway stations, and flanked on the south-east by the Tempelhofer Feld, which was now Tempelhof Airport. In this sense, Speer's general conception might be compared to the archetypical Modernist schemes for the dynamic city of the future, such as Antonio Sant'Elia's Città Nuova (1914) or Le Corbusier's Contemporary City for Three Million People (1922).

Clearly, Speer's own staff saw it as a thoroughly modern solution, measured to the demands of the twentieth-century city. As Rudolf Wolters, of one three staff chiefs in the GBI, wrote in 1941: 'The completion of the North-South Street, the commanding axis on which all new representative buildings important to the Reich will be set up . . . will, in addition to its exemplary purpose, result in a fundamental reordering of all technical, sociological, and economic city planning questions.'[21]

The mystical, symbolically framed ideal of party and state was married here with the apparent conviction that the solution was progressive and effective. The briefest glance at the general plan, however, in which the two inner ring roads crossed the main axis at ground level, suggest that the spectacle and parade were much more important than the solution of the city's traffic circulation problems. This is a fundamental difference, of course, between Speer's project for Berlin and the Modernist schemes of Sant'Elia and Le Corbusier, which were much more closely tied to

vehicular demands – substituting, perhaps, the democratic tyranny of the motor car for the autocratic tyranny of the parade ground.

The lasting contribution of National Socialism to the architectural history of Berlin was the simple, pared-down functionalist style, which had been evolved for public buildings at the end of the Weimar Republic and survived in the Nazi era as the favoured manner for low-ranking party, military and public buildings. Ernst Sagebiel's Tempelhof Airport is a very typical example of this Rohbau (or 'carcass') functionalism, in which the most modern structural frames were covered with smooth, rather bland façades that were neither classicist nor Modernist but nodded in both directions.

There is a parallel here between such silent, joyless façades, hung down in front of the steel skeleton, and the banners and decorations with which the main avenues in Berlin were bedecked on great public occasions like the 1936 Olympics or the visit of Benito Mussolini in 1937. The façades, like the flags, are impressive in their scale and repetition, but anonymous and inarticulate, masking rather than revealing. They deaden the city rather than articulate it, deprive it of its past and its history, and reduce it to a bland coulisse, with no cultural referents beyond those of the flag and the party.

Look, for example, at Unter den Linden dressed for the Mussolini visit, lined with columns and festooned with banners (p. 281). The result is a strange sense of emptiness, in which, as in Rohbau functionalism, the real fabric is masked, and the mask has nothing to proclaim beyond its own existence. Whereas in the best works of Neues Bauen the external form was derived from the articulation of the internal spaces, Rohbau functionalism is compromised and enfeebled by an

20 See Werner Durth, 'Architektur und Stadtplanung im Dritten Reich', in Michael Prinz and Rainer Zitelmann, eds., Nationalsozialismus und Modernisierung (Darmstadt, 1991), 151. On this theme see also Winfried Nerdinger, ed., Bauhaus-Moderne im Nationalsozialismus (Munich, 1993).

21 Rudolf Wolters, Neue Deutsche Baukunst (Berlin, 1941), 12.

Ernst Sagebiel, square outside Tempelhof Airport, Berlin, c. 1937

enforced symmetry, and by doomed attempts to achieve monumentality through repetition.

It would be a mistake, however, to look for Modernism in the architectural context merely in matters of style or materials. In his speech at the topping-out ceremony of the New Reich Chancellery, Hitler praised the building, erected to the design of Albert Speer in nine months, not only as an artistic masterpiece but also as a triumph of technology and logistics (pp. 264, 323). Building production in National Socialist Germany was, as already noted, highly rationalized. It differed significantly, however, from its counterparts in the European democracies or North America, in its use of slave labour. What Hitler did not mention in his speech at the Chancellery was that the stone that had appeared almost miraculously in such a short time had been cut in the concentration camp at Flossenbürg in Upper Bavaria (p. 27). Nor would he have mentioned the brick and tile works attached to the concentration camp at Sachsenhausen, just north of Berlin at Oranienburg, site of the Heinkel aircraft factory. The coexistence in the National Socialist realm of a Modernism based on instrumental reason and the animal barbarity of the concentration camps poses profound and still unanswered questions about the nature of the Modernist project.

22 Quoted in Magdalena Bushart, *Olympische Spiele in Berlin* (Berlin, 1991), 9.

23 Albert Speer, *Inside the Third Reich* (London, 1970), 80.

24 See Werner March, *Bauwerk Reichssportfeld* (Berlin, 1936), 24.

Albert Speer, New Reich Chancellery, Berlin, 1938–39

The Berlin Olympics

Had it not been for the First World War, the Olympic Games would have been held in Berlin in 1916. For this purpose, the Deutsches Stadion (German Stadium) was constructed to the design of Otto March in the Grunewald, the point at which the city meets the woods and lakes that dominate the western edge of the city. After the Olympic Committee agreed in 1930 to hold the 1936 Olympics in Berlin, Otto March's architect son, Werner March, was commissioned to redesign his father's old stadium for the purpose. When Hitler visited the site in October 1933, however, he was unimpressed by the comparative modesty of March's proposal, insisting that the German spirit demanded 'something gigantic'.[22] The Führer's wish was granted, with a complete redesign on the same site resulting in a complex that embraced the main stadium, a swimming pool, a large parade field, assorted smaller enclosures for tennis, hockey, and equestrianism, an open-air theatre, and a large sports institute. The stadium alone was designed to hold 100,000 spectators, who were delivered to the Olympic portals with brisk efficiency by the U-Bahn (underground) and S-Bahn (surface) railways, via stations located at the edges of the Olympic site.

Werner March's first design for the new stadium was strictly functional, with glazed partition walls and an exposed structural frame. As Albert Speer recounted in his memoirs, Hitler was outraged by this naked Modernism, saying that 'he would never set foot in a glass box like that'. Speer himself came up with the solution: 'Overnight I made a sketch showing how the steel skeleton already built could be clad in natural stone and have more massive cornices added. The glass partitions were eliminated, and Hitler was content.'[23]

None of this was reported, of course, in the official account of the stadium published under March's own name, in which the rather solitary, widely-spaced columns were compared to the pine trees in the sandy landscape around Berlin, which in turn were claimed as an inspiration for the great classical architects of Prussia: Schlüter, Knobelsdorff and Schinkel.[24] This contrived simile, invoking nature and culture to explain what appears to have been expediency, is characteristic of the Olympic enterprise in Berlin, which appealed to an extraordinary wide spectrum of references in order to send across the nation and around the globe specific messages about the National Socialist regime. In the Olympic arena, art and architecture were put to work squarely in the service of propaganda and power.

The overriding ambition behind the Nazi investment in the Games was the restitution of national pride following the defeat in the First World War and the humiliation of the Treaty of Versailles. The principal architectural device here was the axial configuration of the stadium, the Maifeld, and the Olympic bell-tower set on top of the Langemarck Halle. Through a 25 metre gap in the oval of the stadium, the axis led onto the Maifeld, a vast parade ground designed by Werner March to hold 250,000 troops 'from various formations of the movement: the SA, SS, DAF, Hitler Youth', in order to experience 'the great speech of the Führer from his position at the focal point of the entire complex under the bell tower.'[25] Set on the long axis of the stadium and framed by the twin towers of the Marathon Gate, the 76 metre high bell tower grew out of the Langemarck Halle, a monument to the volunteer army of 1914 and the raw recruits who were slain in their hundreds at Langemarck in December 1914 as they stormed the French machine-guns. The rhetoric of this ensemble, which lined up on one axis the bell-tower inscribed with memorials to the dead, a trough of soil from the cemetery at Langemarck, Hitler's dais, the parade ground and the stadium, made absolutely explicit the connection between sport and militarism. The German army might have been defeated in 1918, but the victories of the German sportsmen and sportswomen in the stadium not only expunged this disgrace, but also heralded military successes in the future.

The essential preconditions for such success are order and self-sacrifice, and these were high on the agenda both in the sculptural decoration of the complex and in the displays of mass gymnastics that accompanied the games. Josef Wackerle's matching pair of *Horse Leaders* – giant figures flanking the Marathon Portal on either side of the axis described above – make manifest the relationship between the resolved leader and the strong yet docile mass of the led. The sportsman as strong, single leader is the theme of several freestanding figures, most notably Josef Thorak's *Boxer*, modelled on the heavyweight champion Max Schmeling. Again, the contrast of strong leader and docile audience comes across in the kitsch of contemporary press photographs, which set the athlete against the bathing beauty (p. 266).

A further recurring pattern in the sculptural scheme is that of figures grouped in pairs – relay runners, discus throwers, comrades in sport – working together for ultimate victory. This leitmotiv of the renunciation of individual will and ambition for the sake of the wider

Josef Wackerle, *Horse Leader*, 1936, Olympic Stadium

25 Werner March, quoted in Hilmar Hoffmann, *Mythos Olympia: Autonomie und Unterwerfung von Sport und Kultur* (Berlin, 1993), 26.

Herbert Bayer, publicity photomontage, 1936

Werner March, Olympic Stadium, 1936, view from Führer's dais

community, the party or the state, was given its most striking expression in the gymnastics displays, in which hundreds of identical figures performed press-ups in perfect unison. These are illustrated in Leni Riefenstahl's volume of photographs *Schönheit im Olympischen Kampf* (Beauty in the Olympic Contest) under the improbable title 'Free exercises in the Stadium' (p. 279). Most apposite in this context is Walter Benjamin's observation, penned in the Olympic year 1936: 'Mankind, which in Homer's time was an object of contemplation for the Olympian gods, now is one for itself. Its self-alienation has reached such a

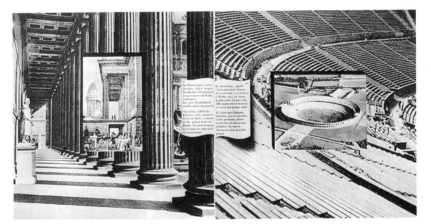

degree that it can experience its own destruction as an aesthetic pleasure of the first order. This is the situation of politics which Fascism is rendering aesthetic.'[26]

Pseudo-Homeric contemplation was also on offer, of course. Berlin had first been called 'Athens on the Spree' in a panegyric written during the reign of Frederick I of Prussia (1657–1713), and the epithet neatly summarized the prestige ambitions of the Prussian court from the late eighteenth century to the mid-nineteenth. Those buildings most closely associated with this powerful Hellenist tradition were tied to the Games and to the stadium physically by avenues of banners and improbable classical statuary, which turned the East-West Axis into a *via triumphalis* along which the Führer drove each day to the stadium. This invocation of classical authority and virtue was further reinforced by a whole series of events that stressed the Athens-Berlin axis. The opening ceremony of the International Olympic Committee was held in front of the Pergamon Altar; the Olympic torch was received in Berlin at a ceremony on the revamped Lustgarten in front of Schinkel's Altes Museum (see the essay 'Berlin, 1 May 1936' in this volume); there was an official Olympic Art Exhibition with medals for the winners, and two exhibitions of Hellenic art;[27] Handel's

opera *Heracles* was performed at the open-air theatre attached to the Olympic complex; and Aeschylus' *Oresteia* was staged in the city. Cultural enterprises such as these were intended to invest the parvenu National Socialist government with images of dignity, gravity and authority.

At the opposite end of the historicist spectrum, the German state used the Olympic Games to promote itself as modern, progressive, and technologically advanced. This was the theme of the exhibition entitled simply *Deutschland*, whose catalogue contrasted photographs of 'Bolshevik Street Terror' and 'Red Anarchy' with images of new bridges, autobahns, and enraptured workers listening to symphony concerts during their lunch interval – 'A pleasant interlude during factory work'.[28] Modernists were employed to sell the image of a modern Germany, and the exhibition installation was the work of the architect Emil Fahrenkamp and the graphic designer Herbert Bayer, whose double-page photomontage in the exhibition prospectus proposed a Prussian Classicism that embraced both Schinkel's Altes Museum and Werner March's Olympic Stadium (p. 265). Previously a master at the Dessau Bauhaus,[29] Bayer remained very influential in the design of National Socialist propaganda exhibitions until 1937.

Modernist typography was only one of the many techniques used by the government and the German Olympic Committee to promote the Games and manipulate both national and international opinion. Radio reports, film newsreels, and experimental television coverage were all employed to the greatest possible effect. Whereas the sporting triumphs at the classical Greek *agones* were celebrated in Pindaric odes, the victors in Berlin in 1936 were recorded for posterity on film, and in particular in Leni Riefenstahl's two films on the Olympics, *Fest der Völker* (Festival of Nations) and *Fest der Schönheit* (Festival of Beauty). The propagandistic link between Greece in 450 BC and twentieth-century Germany is made explicit in the prologue to *Fest der Völker*, which begins with misty shots of the Acropolis and the temple of Zeus at Olympia. The camera lingers on Myron's sculpture of the discus thrower, and the body in stone is dissolved into the living flesh of the German decathlete Erwin Huber: the Third Reich was the rightful heir to Athens and Sparta.

Yet a dark shadow hovers over this paean to physical beauty. As Thomas Wolfe recorded in his novel *You Can't Go Home Again*: 'The sheer pageantry of the occasion was overwhelming, so much so that he began to feel

26 Walter Benjamin, 'The Work of Art in the Age of Mechanical Reproduction', in Benjamin, *Illuminations* (New York, 1969), 242.

27 For details of the various exhibitions organized in Berlin to mark the Olympic Games, see *XI. Olympiade Berlin 1936: Amtlicher Bericht* (Berlin, 1937), 2:1106–28.

28 See Anon., *Germany: The Olympic Year 1936* (Berlin, 1936).

29 On Bayer's career in the Third Reich, see Ute Brüning, 'Bauhäusler zwischen Propaganda und Wirtschaftswerbung', in Winfried Nerdinger, ed., *Bauhaus-Moderne im Nationalsozialismus* (Munich, 1993), 24–47.

Josef Thorak, *Boxer*, 1936, press photograph

oppressed by it. There seemed to be something ominous in it. One sensed a stupendous concentration of effort, a tremendous drawing together and ordering in the vast collective power of the land. And the thing that made it seem ominous was that it so evidently went beyond what the games themselves demanded. The games were overshadowed . . . they became, day after day, an orderly and overwhelming demonstration in which the whole of Germany had been schooled and disciplined.'[30]

All of Germany, that is, except for those who for reasons of race, ideological conviction, or sexuality could not be considered *Volksgenossen* – members of the national community. By the time the Olympic Games opened on 1 August 1936, some 26,000 opponents of the regime had been incarcerated in the concentration camps. Millions were to follow. Hitler's words, quoted on the cover of the special Olympic issue of *Die Woche*, gave a chilling foretaste of what was to come: 'He who wishes to live must also fight, and he who will not strive in this world of struggle, does not deserve the gift of life.'[31]

Autobahn

No other Nazi invention was more potent as a generator of myths and fables than the autobahn. The idea of a network of high-speed roads was not, of course, original to the Nazi traffic planners. As early as 1913 a company was formed in Berlin to build a test stretch on the western side of the city, opened in 1921 as the AVUS (Automobilverkehrs- und Übungsstrasse), a dual carriageway running for nearly 10 kilometres

from Witzleben to Nikolassee without surface intersections. Towards the end of the 1920s several private companies were founded with the intention of constructing new roads on the AVUS model, with routes such as Hamburg-Frankfurt-Basel, Munich-Leipzig-Berlin, or Aachen-Cologne-Düsseldorf. These early plans foundered on grounds of economic and political orthodoxy: fast roads for the privileged few who could afford fast cars were not regarded as a high priority by the Brüning administration in the context of the world economic crisis of 1930–31. Yet a great deal of detailed research and planning was done at this time by the private companies, covering every aspect of autobahn construction and servicing. On this basis, the new Nazi government was quickly able to implement its vision of a national network of autobahns, with Adolf Hitler digging out the first shovelful of earth on 23 September 1933, less than eight months after his appointment as Chancellor.

While simple economic profit had motivated the private companies in the late 1920s, the Nazi motives for building the new roads were much more complicated. By linking and binding the far corners of the German Reich to the centre, the new roads gave concrete expression to the new unity of the People proclaimed by the Nazi revolution. As Fritz Todt – appointed Inspector-General of German Highways in June 1933 – insisted: 'The state autobahn, with its double ribbon stretching into the glinting distance, is a visible sign and simile of a new union of all the German provinces, or a new community of all Germans.'[32]

The road building programme symbolized not only physical unity and connection, but also the act of

30 Thomas Wolfe, *You Can't Go Home Again* (Garden City, NY, 1940), 625.

31 Adolf Hitler, quoted in *Die Woche*, special issue: 'Olympia 1936'.

32 Fritz Todt, preface to Erna Lendvai-Dircksen, *Reichsautobahn: Mensch und Werk* (Bayreuth, [1942]).

Erwin Huber as 'living statue'; Myron, *Discus Thrower*, c. 450 BC (Leni Riefenstahl, 1937)

Tischer and Tamms, viaduct near Rüdersdorf

Fritz Bayerlein, *Mauthäusl-strasse: the German Alpine Road, c.* 1936

working together as a nation on common goals for the common good. Emboldened by this great national programme, the German people would again be able to assert its claims among the nations. At the commencement of the work in September 1933, Hitler described the new roads as 'a milepost for the construction of the community of the German People [*Volksgemeinschaft*], a community which, both as nation and as state, will deliver to us what we are rightfully entitled to claim and demand in this world . . . German workers, on with the job!'[33]

If the first great narrative, in the propaganda campaign that was mounted with the same intensity as the road-building programme itself, was national unity, the second was work creation. Erna Lendvai-Dircksen's officially promoted book of photographs of the construction work shows sturdy German workers with massive pickaxes resting on their shoulders, welcoming the chance to work: 'After years of unemployment I am once again earning honest bread for seven sons and one daughter.'[34] This was the propaganda line that appeared in every book, article or film on the new road system: the autobahn meant work, economic stability, and an end to the fears of unemployment and inflation that had blighted the Weimar republic. The reality, of course, was less rosy. At its peak in 1936, the entire autobahn enterprise employed no more than 250,000 workers: half on the site, the other half in supply industries. Working conditions were unpleasant in the extreme, and the construction camps were filled with 'undependable' workers with Socialist or Communist backgrounds. Indeed, by 1938 it became necessary to pass labour conscription laws to halt the seepage of labour away from the autobahn programme. During the early war years this conscripted labour was augmented by prisoners of war.

When work stopped on the autobahns in 1942, some 3,870 kilometres had been completed. In practical terms the new roads had little impact, either on the economy or on strategic planning. Although promoted by the Nazi government through such programmes as the People's Car (Volkswagen), which appeared in prototype form in the late summer of 1936, car ownership in Germany was markedly lower than in comparable countries. In 1938, for example, there was one car for every 5 Americans, for every 27 British, and for every 44 Germans. Contrary to myth, the autobahns had limited strategic significance, as the concrete slabs were too thin to support the weight of heavy tanks or armoured vehicles. The war, furthermore, was fought elsewhere. Only after the war, with the economic development of the Federal Republic, did the level of car ownership justify the vast capital expenditure invested in the autobahns in the 1930s.

The lasting success of the programme, therefore, was propagandistic rather than tangible. The civil engineers, bridge-builders and architects who constructed the autobahns, and the painters, photographers and film-makers who sold the images, combined together to produce an extraordinarily powerful series of messages about the new regime and the Nazi revolution.

Compared at the time with the Great Wall of China, the Pyramids, the Acropolis, and the Gothic cathedrals, the autobahns were marketed not merely as works of technical expertise but as works of art. They were designed to achieve not the shortest but the 'noblest' route between two points. This blurring of criteria can be seen in many aspects of the programme. On one side there is a dominant theme of high technology, of steel, concrete, and minimalist precision; on the other historicist echoes of Roman aqueducts, massive arches of hand-cut masonry, and romantic vistas of the German countryside in its most medievalist, Blood and Soil guise.

At one extreme of the programme were the ultra-Modernist 'Frankfurt Model' filling stations, with flat, boomerang-shaped roofs in the best tradition of 1920s *Neues Bauen*; opposing such futuristic images were the autobahn works depots, which were disguised as farm buildings under high-pitched roofs and vernacular detailing. This division between the celebration of technology and its masking under traditional mores can also be seen in the painterly representation of the new roads and bridges. The drawings of the architects themselves and of painters like Fritz Jacobson stressed the technological triumph of material over nature with a cool, materialist objectivity that links back directly to the *Neue Sachlichkeit* painting of the 1920s.[35] In contrast, a whole genre of Romantic landscape painting flourished in the 1930s, with sublime images of Alpine peaks that might have been painted by Anton Koch in 1810, were it not for the ribbon of autobahn snaking round the mountainsides. The aesthetics of the sublime, which delighted in Alpine peaks and vistas of infinity, were reinforced by delight in the power of human invention and vigour.

In the mid nineteenth century, the German aesthetician Theodor Vischer stressed the positive and constructive aspect of the sublime in the response to nature: 'We feel ourselves elevated because we identify ourselves with the powers of nature, ascribing their vast impact to ourselves, because our fantasy rests on the wings of the storm as we roar into the heights and wander into the depths of infinity. Thus we ourselves expand into a boundless natural power.'[36] This sentiment might well be taken as the motto for Carl Theodor Protzen's painting of the autobahn bridge

over the Danube, near Leipheim, framed by terrifying imperatives: 'Clear the forest – dynamite the rock – conquer the valley – overcome distance – stretch the road through the German land.'

Yet the main thrust of the propaganda was one of reconciliation. As the first two texts in the Lendvai-Dircksen book claim: 'We are building the roads of the German Reich. / We are breaking open the eternal earth! Be of good cheer! We are healing fractures and wounds.'[37] Just as the building programme claimed the power to heal social and geographical divisions, so the aesthetic ambitions of the programme would heal the divisions in the battle between Modernist functionalism and conservative traditionalism. A bridge on the Berlin ring autobahn has a steel span supported on ashlar masonry piers, the ultra-modern resting on the ultra-traditional. Does this compromise indicate a Postmodernist sensibility, or simply irresolution in the face of the Modernist challenge?

33 Adolf Hitler, speech of 23 September 1933, quoted in Rainer Stommer, ed., *Reichsautobahnen: Pyramiden des Dritten Reichs* (Marburg, 1982), 12.

34 Lendvai-Dircksen (as note 1), n.p.

35 On this connection, see Adam C. Oellers, 'Zur Frage der Kontinuität von Neuer Sachlichkeit und nationalsozialistischer Kunst', *Kritische Berichte*, vol. 6, no. 6 (1978), 42–54.

36 Friedrich Theodor Vischer, *Über das Erhabene und Komische und andere Texte zur Ästhetik* (Frankfurt am Main, 1967), 155.

37 Lendvai-Dircksen (as note 1), n.p.

Fritz Jacobson, *Bridge in Construction near Siebenlehn, Saxony, c. 1935–36*

A LIFE-AND-DEATH STRUGGLE

Painting and Sculpture   *David Elliott*

1 Paul Schulze-Naumburg, *Kampf um die Kunst* (Munich, 1932), 5.

2 Ernst Jünger, *On the Marble Cliffs* (1939) (Harmondsworth, 1970), 80.

3 Cosmopolitanism was a code word that denoted 'harmful Jewish influence'. In this sense it was later taken over by Soviet ideologues in the purges of the 1940s and early 1950s.

4 The Nazis recycled for their own purposes a number of the strategies of committed left-wing artists; for example, the display techniques of the *Entartete Kunst* exhibition bore a striking resemblance to the German Dadaist exhibitions – in particular to the First International Dada Fair held in Berlin 1920 – which combined slogans with art works as a provocation.

5 Paul Schultze-Naumburg, *Das ABC des Bauens* (Munich, 1925). This contained a savage criticism of the rationalist, flat-roofed architecture of the Bauhaus.

6 Berthold Hinz, *Art in the Third Reich* (Oxford, 1980), 25–26.

'A life-and-death struggle is taking place in art, just as it is in the realm of politics. And the battle for art has to be fought with the same seriousness and determination as the battle for political power.' (Paul Schultze-Naumburg, 1932.)[1]

'Like all who hunger after power and mastery, he was led astray by his wild dreams into the realm of Utopias. It was his opinion that from the beginning of history there have been two races of men on this earth – the masters and the slaves – and that in the course of time the breeds had crossed.' (Ernst Jünger, 1939.)[2]

When Hitler assumed full dictatorial powers in Germany in the Enabling Act of March 1933, he set out to consolidate his authority and eliminate enemies as well as to establish a bureaucratic infrastructure by which education and culture could be brought into line with Party aims. Unlike in the USSR or Italy, artists were not actively involved in creating this framework, and cultural policy was forged out of a struggle within the ranks of the Nazi leadership. On one side was Joseph Goebbels, himself a collector of modern art, who believed, with such writers as Gottfried Benn, that Expressionism could be remodelled as a Nordic art movement which would be in keeping with the blood and soil ideologies of the party. The other, more conservative tendency was that encouraged by Alfred Rosenberg, party ideologue and editor since 1921 of its newspaper, *Völkischer Beobachter*, who in 1927 had founded the Kampfbund für Deutsche Kultur (Combat League for German Culture). Within this struggle Goebbels was to adopt many of Rosenberg's ideas, but he retained the political initiative and won control. Enemies were identified along ideological lines, and manifestations of 'cultural bolshevism', 'degeneracy' or 'cosmopolitanism' were ruthlessly suppressed.[3]

The Kampfbund criticized the fragmentation and confusion of modern life and culture, which it regarded as symptoms of a degeneracy which could only be counteracted by the dominance of a nordic Germanic race. One of Rosenberg's close associates at this time was the architect and cultural theorist Paul Schultze-Naumburg who, in one of the most chilling of books, *Kunst und Rasse* (Art and Race, 1928), compared photographs of deformed, diseased or disturbed people with examples of modern painting and sculpture, to

illustrate how the viewpoint of the modern artist was itself sick and degenerate (p. 330). Here, he argued, lay the source of Germany's misfortunes: in the discredited culture of the Weimar Republic. This was a jibe which, in the early days of the Republic, leftist artists such as George Grosz and Otto Dix had directed against the warmongering survivors of Wilhelmine Germany. In their paintings, militarists and profiteers alike were shown as syphilitic decadents whose features had been distorted by excess.[4]

In 1929 Schultze-Naumburg was put in charge of the Weimar Vereinigte Kunstlehranstalten (United Institutes of Art Instruction), in a move which anticipated Nazi cultural policy after 1933. The main art school was the building where, ten years previously, Walter Gropius had founded the Bauhaus; this still contained a mural by Oskar Schlemmer on its stairway. Schultze-Naumburg was a sworn enemy of everything the Bauhaus stood for; although the school had moved to Dessau in 1925, he ordered the mural painted over and all existing members of the Faculty dismissed.[5] This was the first official destruction of any public work of art by a member of the Nazi party, and the conservative, craft-based teaching policy which was now enforced completely negated the Bauhaus aim of the integration of art with technology.

Schultze-Naumburg had been appointed at the behest of Wilhelm Frick, a former head of the political police in Munich and a Nazi member of the Reichstag for the state of Thuringia. As Thuringian Minister for the Interior and Education, Frick now sought to replace most of his key officials with Nazi sympathizers. Left-wing works of art such as Eisenstein's films or Brecht's plays were banned in the state, and paintings and sculptures by a number of leading modern artists were removed from the walls of the Weimar Schlossmuseum on the grounds that they were inimical to 'the past life of the German soul and spirit'.[6]

Although Frick was dismissed from his post in April 1931, in 1933 he reappeared as Hitler's Reich Minister for the Interior and began to enact the same policies on a national scale. In March 1933 these were tabulated through the Führer's Council into a manifesto entitled 'What German Artists expect from the new Government'. This paper strongly emphasized the national, *völkisch* elements of German art and warned that art devoid of these characteristics would be destroyed, and that museum officials who showed or bought such work would be dismissed.[7]

Within the first year of Nazi power a large number of artists were dismissed from teaching posts or removed from the Academy, including Max Beckmann, Otto Dix, Paul Klee, Willi Baumeister, Max Liebermann and Carl Hofer.[8] A number of progressive provincial museum directors were also dismissed. Also from the spring of 1933, exhibitions which showed Modernism in a critical light started to be mounted in regional museums; these *Schreckenskammern der Kunst* (Chambers of Horrors of Art) or *Schandausstellungen* (Abomination Exhibitions) were forerunners of the *Entartete Kunst* (Degenerate Art) exhibition of 1937.[9]

In 1932 Schultze-Naumburg had published a new book, *Kampf um die Kunst* (The Battle for Art), which set out the lines of the campaign within the Nazi party for a spiritually regenerated, nationalist and *völkisch* art that would triumph over the cosmopolitan degeneracy of international Modernism. This view, however, represented only one tendency, and there was still a strong sympathy within the party for Modernism, which was supported by Goebbels. In June 1933 the National Socialist League of German Students organized a public demonstration in the Berlin Friedrich-Wilhelm University, entitled 'Youth Fights for German Art' which campaigned for the official adoption of Nordic Expressionism as Nazi art. Otto Andreas Schreiber, a member of this, and Goebbels's assistant, Hans Weidemann, founded a painters' group called Der Norden (The North) and supported the journal *Kunst der Nation* (Art of the Nation), which, until it was banned in 1935, provided a point of contact between modern art and literature and the Nazi party. In the summer of 1933 the group also organized an exhibition, *30 Deutsche Künstler*, at the Galerie Ferdinand Möller, which was immediately closed by Frick, working closely with Rosenberg. In the following year, the poet and short-term Nazi sympathizer Gottfried Benn published *Kunst und Macht* (Art and Power), a book which criticized Rosenberg's view and supported the idea of a Modernist culture.[10]

The battle which ensued within the party was not about art, style or aesthetics but about power. Goebbels set himself against Rosenberg in a bid for control over the whole realm of culture and propaganda. Although he was the eventual victor, in that the bureaucratic structure of the Reichskulturkammer – with six separate units for each art form – came under the direction of his Ministry of Public Enlightenment and Propaganda,

his public statements about art became increasingly conservative.[11] As in the USSR, membership of these units was obligatory for finding work, but the enforcement of party aims was more systematic. There were three levels of action which could be taken against an artist whose work was not felt to be in the correct spirit. The first was the withholding of the licence to teach; the second was the withholding of permission to exhibit; and the third, perhaps Goebbels's most imaginative invention, was the *Malverbot* – the withholding of permission to paint.

In common with the USSR, there had been no pre-existing party style. Throughout the 1920s and early 1930s a number of both avant-garde and more traditional artists had actively allied themselves to left front organizations, but very few had been affiliated to the Nazis.[12] In sculpture – as in architecture – a steroidally muscular classicism was the preferred form, and in painting the peasant realism practised in the late nineteenth century by Wilhelm Leibl and the Dachau School was strongly encouraged. The academic traditions of the Prussian Academy, as seen in the work of Arthur Kampf – a dedicated Nazi – were also adopted, as well as the more sensual approach of the Munich Secession in which Nazi painters such as Fritz Erler had been active members. Abstraction of any kind was not tolerated.

Hitler consolidated his political power in the so-called Night of the Long Knives in the summer of 1934, in which hundreds of SA (Brownshirt) leaders including Erich Röhm, its head, were murdered. President Hindenburg died at the beginning of August, and this moment represented the height of Hitler's power. At the party congress in autumn 1934, now as 'Reich Chancellor and Führer', Hitler announced the end of the German cultural revolution: stability had been achieved and the Thousand Year Reich could be proclaimed. He also promised to settle the divisions and conflicts which had beset the art world: he emphasized that all manifestations of modern art would be removed, but stressed that this did not mean that an old-fashioned German art, buried in *völkisch* Romantic fantasy, should be put in its place. The Rosenberg and Schultze-Naumburg predilection for ancient Nordic myth and folk culture was as much of a minority taste as the work of the Expressionists and Cubists. What had proved to be popular was the popular dislike of modern art, and this was to become the main feature of Nazi cultural policy.[13]

In November 1936, assiduously following the guidelines laid down by Hitler, Joseph Goebbels issued

7 Ibid., 27–28. The word *völkisch* means 'of the People' and implies a strong sense of national and ethnic unity.

8 See Stephanie Barron, ed., exh. cat. *'Degenerate Art'. The Fate of the Avant-Garde in Nazi Germany* (Los Angeles: Los Angeles County Museum of Art, and New York, 1991), 391–401.

9 Christoph Zuschlag, 'An "Educational Exhibition". The precursors of *Entartete Kunst* and its individual venues', in Barron (as note 10), 83–97.

10 Gottfried Benn, *Kunst und Macht* (Stuttgart and Berlin, 1934). Benn was subsequently engaged in a polemical battle with Nazi ideologue Wolfgang Willrich concerning his support for Modernism. Heinrich Himmler eventually intervened in Benn's favour. Correspondence reprinted in Joseph Wulf, *Literatur und Dichtung im Dritten Reich* (Frankfurt am Main, 1983), 140–44.

11 This new structure was announced at a ceremony held in Berlin on 15 November 1933. See Hinz (as note 8), 31. Rosenberg's importance within the party hierarchy was downgraded, and in 1934 the Kampfbund became the NS Cultural Association, which was then absorbed in Robert Ley's DAF (German Labour Front) in 1937. After 1936 his main position was as editor of the periodical *Kunst im Dritten Reich* (Art in the Third Reich).

12 Hans Schweitzer, who worked under the Old Norse name of Mjölnir (The Hammer), was an exception. He designed many posters for Nazi elections and events before 1933 and was a member of Ziegler's commission for the confiscation of art works in 1937. At the height of the Spanish Civil War, to condemn the Republican 'red murder gangs', the Nazis appropriated, under a false signature, an image originally entitled *Bread* which the anti-Nazi artist Käthe Kollwitz had originally made in 1924 in support of starving strikers.

the Decree Concerning Art Criticism, which forbade any writing on art independent of the party line. The new role of art editor was created in its place, whose work was to disseminate art rather than make any evaluation of its qualities.

The final act in establishing Nazi supremacy over the visual arts was played out in the following year, when virtually all Modernist works were confiscated from German museums by a specially appointed five-man commission headed by Adolf Ziegler.[14] Their fate was to be included in the large touring exhibition *Entartete Kunst* which opened in Munich in 1937, or to be sold off in Switzerland to foreign collectors; work which failed to find buyers was burnt. At the same time an earnest, 'improving', anodyne and banal exhibition of officially-approved art was held in the newly opened House of German Art. Not surprisingly, this attracted far fewer visitors than the work of the so-called degenerates. For the majority, then as now, it was more diverting to mock or dislike art than it was to take it seriously. The Nazi approach was chillingly efficient – within the space of five years modern art in Germany had officially ceased to exist.

'Degenerates' and their Fate

'Under the impact of the Imperialist War of 1914–18 the foundations of bourgeois culture and morality began to crumble one by one. Artists no longer kept abreast of events. The pencil was too slow and was overtaken by the lies spread by the bourgeois press. Revolutionary artists did not keep pace, but fell behind and failed to record each stage of the proletariat's struggle.' (Sergei Tretyakov on John Heartfield, 1936.)[15]

'While I wept along with the terrified children I was drawing, I really felt the burden I am bearing. I felt that I have no right to withdraw from the responsibility of being an advocate. It is my duty to voice the sufferings of humankind, the never-ending sufferings heaped mountain-high. This is my task.' (Käthe Kollwitz, 1920.)[16]

'I have been concerned to get over the talentless insanity of our times through intensive work. Everything will be so ludicrous and apathetic for the whole time that these political gangsters are in power that it should be best considered from the island of one's soul. But it is a beautiful thing when sometimes, from one's own private constellation, one can glimmer at others. And we hope that we will still often be able to do this.' (Max Beckmann, 1932.)[17]

In November 1931 John Heartfield, the most radical of German Communist affiliated artists, opened a large one-person exhibition in Moscow. There, at the height of the Soviet cultural revolution, his work was politely received but not universally acclaimed; in an important speech on 23 June 1931 Stalin had reformulated the relationship between technology and the labour force in a regimen which moved away from the importance of the machine to give a greater emphasis to the human element within Socialist reconstruction. This had an immediate impact on politics and economics but, within time, was also absorbed into the visual arts to support the proletarian ideology of class struggle. The spatial disjunctures upon which photomontage depended were seen as 'formalist' and dehumanizing – a greater emphasis had to be laid on the positive, 'organic' and 'heroic' role of the worker. Heartfield and the Latvian-Soviet artist Gustavs Klucis, with whom he had most in common were urged to modify the way they worked.[18]

Heartfield returned to Germany in the following year and, from the distance of Berlin, the ideological battle for art which had consumed the Soviet Union continued to be fought. But, in the streets and beer halls, there were more pressing battles – those against the rising power of the Nazi party. Artists of the left, who as well as Heartfield included Otto Dix, Otto Griebel (p. 291), Hans Grundig (p. 318), Käthe Kollwitz (p. 293) and Curt Querner, were members or associates of Asso (Association of German Revolutionary Visual Artists) which was sponsored by the Communist Party.[19] Griebel, Grundig and Querner were painters of proletarian life, and were in step with the militant tone of the new Moscow party line. Once

13 Hinz (as note 8), 35–36. Schultze-Naumburg received no official post from the Nazi government, and his role as rabid ideologue was, from 1936, taken over by Wolfgang Willrich, who in 1937 published *Säuberung des Kunsttempels: Eine kunstpolitische Kampfschrift zur Gesundung deutscher Kunst im Geist nordischer Art* (The Cleansing of the Temple of Art: an Art-Political Philippic on the Healing of German Art in the Nordic Spirit). He served on Ziegler's commission for the confiscation of art works and participated in the organization of the *Entartete Kunst* exhibition in Munich.

Catalogue cover, *Grosse Deutsche Kunstausstellung*, Munich 1937

Catalogue cover, *Entartete Kunst*, Munich 1937

the Nazis came to power all were actively persecuted, and both Griebel and Grundig were harassed by the Gestapo, Grundig spending four years in a concentration camp. Heartfield left the country.

In writing the history of German art of the 1930s and early 1940s a distinction has usually been made between those modern artists who decided to remain in Germany, and who therefore had to enter a state known as 'inner emigration', and those who went into exile.[20] The idea of inner emigration, rooted in the cultural polemics of the immediate postwar period, was an attempt to prove how those who stayed behind also had to 'emigrate' to preserve their integrity; today it seems a rather unsatisfactory description of the response of many modern artists to systematic persecution by the state. Those modern artists who made the painful decision to stay behind expressed, directly or symbolically – and as eloquently as any German artist abroad – their contempt for the situation in which they found themselves. In their work there was no emigration from the realities of life, and there was also no implication that under a different regime they would have wanted to make 'acceptable' art. Under the Nazi government's restrictions on teaching, exhibiting, or even working, only an unfailing and assertive belief in the autonomy of art gave them the strength to continue to work. What they produced took many different forms.

Ernst Barlach – a 'Blood and Soil' Expressionist sculptor, graphic artist and playwright – responded to being branded 'degenerate' by carving an eloquent standing figure which he simply entitled *The Bad Year* at the time of the Munich *Entartete Kunst* exhibition of 1937 (p. 292). He died in the following year, and his passing coincided with the most severe repression of artistic autonomy. The sculpture entitled *Grief* made at that time by Käthe Kollwitz, his close friend and associate, is typically a self-portrait, but it is an icon of desolation; her head is constricted by her hands which stifle her cry and black out her vision in grief. Like *The Tower of Mothers* (p. 293), it is also an expression of a more generalized suffering – that of the whole German people, and of women and mothers in particular, faced by tyranny and the threat of war.

Kollwitz worked in a block of studios at Klosterstrasse in Berlin which, towards the end of the 1930s, became a haven for sculptors and painters who felt out of step with the regime. Ludwig Kaspar worked there who, with more established sculptors such as Gerhard Marcks, Richard Scheibe and Georg Kolbe, represented the lyrical, Hellenistic, anti-Baroque tendency which had characterized sculpture in Berlin

since the first decade of the century. This work was in marked contrast to the oversized, cold, muscular classicism of such rising stars as Arno Breker or Josef Thorak, who received massive commissions from the Nazi party. Yet, because Kasper and the others combined classical style with modern subjects – particularly in figures of sportsmen and women – their work was easily confused with official art (pp. 298, 301, 335).

The simplified, classical paintings of Oskar Schlemmer, which also depicted sportsmen and sportswomen, similarly failed to attract official support; his mural at the former Weimar Bauhaus was the first work of art destroyed by the Nazis. In Italy his works were bought for the state; in Germany they were branded degenerate. Throughout the 1930s the subjects of figures in movement remained the same, but their mood became darker and more enclosed. During the War Schlemmer was able to survive by working in the laboratory of a commercial paint factory in Wuppertal with fellow artists Willi Baumeister, Georg Muche and Gerhard Marcks. In 1942 he painted a series of *Window Pictures* (*Fensterbilder*): watercolours and gouaches of the view through the windows of his flat on to the court and other apartments beyond (pp. 312–13). These small, delicate works proved to be his swansong.

14 Approximately 17,000 works by 1,000 artists were impounded by the state from museums prior to this exhibition. Werner Haftmann, *Banned and Persecuted. The Dictatorship of Art under Hitler* (Cologne, 1986), 124.

15 Sergei Tretyakov, *John Heartfield* (Moscow, 1936), 63.

16 Käthe Kollwitz, *Diaries and Letters* (Chicago, 1955).

17 Max Beckmann, 'Brief an Reinhard Piper, 18.2.1932', in Beckmann, *Die Realität der Träume in den Bildern* (Leipzig, 1987), 129.

18 See Hubertus Gassner, 'Heartfield's Moscow Apprenticeship 1931–32,' in P. Pachnicke and K. Honnef, eds., *John Heartfield* (New York, 1992), 258–89.

19 Asso was founded in 1928 and survived until the Nazis came to power. See exh. cat. *Revolution und Realismus: Revolutionäre Kunst in Deutschland 1917 bis 1933* (Berlin: Altes Museum, 1978) and *Icon and Revolution. Political and Social Themes in German Art 1918–1933* (Norwich: Sainsbury Centre for the Visual Arts, 1986). The former catalogue was a key document in the art historiography of the GDR.

20 The term 'inner emigration' was first used in 1945 by the writer Walter von Molo, in response to Thomas Mann's condemnation of those writers who had stayed behind in Germany under the Nazis. It has since been adopted as a term to describe the state of all modern artists under Nazism. Before unification, its use was confined to the Federal Republic; in the GDR more emphasis was laid on the idea of an art of (Communist) opposition. See *Revolution und Realismus* (as note 5) and Haftmann (as note 16), 217–22.

John Heartfield, *Bug Hunts Vermin*, cover of *AIZ* (Prague), 7 September 1933

Carl Hofer, who since 1920 had been based in Berlin, was known for his rather soft, classical-looking Modernist paintings and had been one of the most successful artists commercially. From the end of the 1920s onwards, he suffered from premonitions of disaster which increasingly figured in his work. The mood of his painting changed radically; it was no longer elegiac or balanced but showed figures in ruins, prisoners, a black room in which a naked man beats violently on a drum, ghostly figures on a vigil (p. 304) . . . He robustly denounced the Nazis and their policies, and in return was dismissed from his teaching post as degenerate. His first wife was arrested and died in a camp. Like other artists, he was able to make a meagre income by selling his work privately, though he was forbidden to exhibit in public.

Otto Dix had been scarred by his horrific experiences in the trenches in the First World War, and this was the central and recurring theme in his work. It was a topic which the Nazis identified with the defeatist spirit of the Treaty of Versailles, and this made him an immediate target for dismissal and denunciation once they came to power. Originally a Dadaist and then a leading painter of *Neue Sachlichkeit* (the New

Objectivity), his work became increasingly concerned with historical archetypes, and by the end of the 1920s he had embarked on an idiosyncratic research into the styles and allegories of such old German and Flemish masters as Albrecht Altdorfer, Hieronymus Bosch, Pieter Bruegel, Lucas Cranach, Hans Baldung Grien and Mathis Grünewald. In many ways this move anticipated the historicist and academic bent of Nazi cultural ideology, and a number of his landscapes of the late 1930s could almost seem like the official art of the time. Such appearances, however, were deceptive. In such large paintings as *The Seven Deadly Sins* (1933) or *The Triumph of Death* (1934), the evils and dangers of Nazism are clearly laid out, and throughout the whole period of Nazi rule he was regarded with suspicion. In 1939 he was arrested on the charge of being implicated in a plot on the Führer's life, but was later released.

In 1933 Willi Baumeister was dismissed from his teaching post at the Städel Institute in Frankfurt, and his work was removed from public collections soon after. In 1941 he was forbidden to exhibit in public. The abstracted human figures, often of sportsmen, which had characterized his work of the early 1930s, gave way to paintings which contained more fragmented, less specific, organic forms which approximated masks or stony landscapes. The mood of his paintings and drawings became increasingly sombre in a search for an archetypical or primitive spirit. These culminated in the series of *Reliefbilder*, the *Gilgamesh* cycle which referred to the epic of ancient Sumeria, both of 1941, and the *Metaphysical Landscapes* of 1944.

At the same time Baumeister indulged in a sarcastic and dangerous subversion of the stereotypes of Nazi art. His work had been represented in the degenerate art exhibition in Munich in 1937 and he had gone to see it there, at the same time visiting the exhibition of official Nazi painting. The following year he again visited Munich to see the second official exhibition and purchased a number of postcards, particularly of the work of Adolf Ziegler, Hitler's favourite painter and head of the Reichskunstkammer, who was also known, from his subject matter, as 'The Master of the German Pubic Hair'. These cards – and the work of Josef Thorak – provided the basis for a series of small collages which not only exposed the vapid eroticism, classicism and pomposity of official Nazi art (p. 309) but also, through the subversive weapon of humour, kept alive the oppositional and transgressive energy of the cultural avant-garde.[21]

A number of modern artists, however, occupied a more equivocal position in relation to official ideology.

21 Peter Chametzky, 'Marginal Comments, Oppositional Work: Willi Baumeister's Confrontation with Nazi Art', in exh. cat. *Willi Baumeister. Zeichnungen, Gouachen, Collagen* (Stuttgart: Staatsgalerie, 1989), 251–72.

Otto Dix, *The Seven Deadly Sins*, 1933, Staatliche Kunsthalle, Karlsruhe

The work of the Magic Realist, Georg Schrimpf, who had been influenced by the Italian artists of *Valori Plastici* in the 1920s, was included in the *Entartete Kunst* exhibition but then taken out on the instructions of Rudolf Hess. Schrimpf had been dismissed from his teaching post, and a number of his paintings had been removed from public collections; but, by the time he died in 1938, his work was no longer regarded as a prime example of degeneracy.

The sculptor Georg Kolbe consciously skipped along the fine line between official and personal art; his large bronze *Proclamation* was sited in the main hall of Speer's German Pavilion in the Paris International Exhibition of 1937 (p. 299). In the following year Heartfield in Prague pointed out in a photomontage that Kolbe had been commissioned to make monuments in honour of both Franco and Beethoven at the same time and might therefore be regarded as a Nazi artist. The caption imagined Kolbe talking to himself in a dream: 'Franco and Beethoven, can I create this nude? Perhaps it would be better if I made it like a centaur, half animal, half man.' Yet Kolbe never allied himself to the Nazis and in 1945 was to produce the small, hunched bronze figure of *The Liberated Man* – an anti-monumental image which was one of the most moving works of this time.

Other modern artists actively tried – and failed – to establish closer links with the Nazis. Bayer automatically came under suspicion because of his links with the Bauhaus where he had taught but, like a number of others with a similar background, he was able for a time to find work as a designer on official projects (p. 265).[22] In 1938, once it was clear that the Nazis would never support Modernism, he emigrated to New York.

Others decided to stay put. Magic Realist painter Franz Radziwill, formerly a member of the leftist November Group, had by 1933 joined the Nazi party and was given a temporary teaching post at the Düsseldorf Art Academy (it was a year when many vacancies occurred). In the end, however, his own work was judged to be degenerate, and in 1935 he was dismissed. Radziwill refused to compromise, and in 1938 he was expelled from the party and forbidden to exhibit; over fifty paintings were confiscated. From 1939 to 1942 he served in the army, and he then worked in an armaments factory and the Home Guard. His paintings of these years have a cold, Surrealistic foreboding; the recurrent motif of the single aeroplane in flight, which pervades all his work, is transformed into an instrument of war. Emil Nolde was the most established member of the generation of 'Blood and Soil' Expressionists who sympathized with the extreme nationalism of the Nazis. But this feeling was not reciprocated, and although for a time Goebbels supported his work as 'Nordic Expressionism', he was dismissed from the Prussian Academy of Arts in 1933. Over a thousand of his works were confiscated from museums. Nolde was also one of the most strongly featured artists in the *Entartete Kunst* exhibition of 1937, and in 1941 he was expelled from the Reichskunstkammer and forbidden to paint. This ban led to the creation of what have since been called the *Unpainted Pictures.* Made in the splendid isolation of the flatlands of Schleswig-Holstein where Nolde and his wife had constructed a house and studio, this series of obsessively worked watercolours continued, on a much smaller scale, the grotesque, mythological and personal themes he had initially explored in the large Berlin watercolours of 1931–35 (pp. 314–15). Like the *Fensterbilder* of Oscar Schlemmer, they are a retreat into an ageless and hermetic world.

Of the artists who emigrated, Heartfield left for Prague in 1933, on the night the SS broke into his apartment. There he continued working for the German-language picture paper *AIZ*, which published

22 See Winfried Nerdinger, ed., *Bauhaus-Moderne im Nationalsozialismus. Zwischen Anbiederung und Verfolgung* (Munich, 1993).

Georg Kolbe, *The Liberated Man*, 1945

his photomontages.[23] In 1938, just before the Nazi occupation of Czechoslovakia, he moved to London, where he stayed for the duration of the war.

The painter Oskar Kokoschka also chose to live in Prague in the mid-1930s and increasingly became involved in a number of anti-Fascist organizations based there. He moved to London at the same time as Heartfield, and there became a leading member of the Artists' International Association (AIA) and the Free German League of Culture. His *Self-Portrait as a Degenerate Artist* (1937, p. 303) was a direct response to his inclusion in the Munich degenerate art exhibition, and his work was also included in the émigré riposte to this which was organized by Oto Bihalji-Merin for the New Burlington Galleries in London in July 1938.[24] Kokoschka now began to cultivate an increasingly political and satirical strain in his work, referring back to Gillray, Rowlandson and Goya, which not only denounced the evils of Fascism but also the blindness of the Allies in confronting it (p. 302).

Since the late 1920s, Paul Klee had increasingly begun to withdraw into a remote and meditative frame of mind, and this change was remarked upon by his friends and associates. A common view of his later work is that it became increasingly hermetic – particularly from 1933, the period of his illness and exile in Switzerland. Yet Klee remained acutely aware of the changes that were taking place in Germany, and these are often expressed – although obliquely – in his work. In 1933, on being sacked from the Düsseldorf Art Academy, he emigrated to Bern and painted a blank and cancelled self-portrait entitled *Struck off the List*. As the decade drew to a close, images of fear, sorrow, stupidity, pride, death and fire became increasingly predominant, observed by the recurrent and haunting figure of the watchful angel. The title of a work in oil and tempera of 1939 (p. 310) is strangely prophetic: *from the Ether, 'And You Shall Eat Your Fill'*.

Max Beckmann led a similarly isolated and hermetic existence. Dismissed from the Städel Institute in Frankfurt in 1933, at the same time as Baumeister and Scheibe, he moved to Berlin to work. He had already started work on *Departure*, his first triptych, which in content harked back to the paintings and graphics he had produced at the time of the Spartacist uprising in Berlin during 1918 and 1919. Civilization was in retreat, and his work showed this unequivocally. In darkened rooms, people were being bound and tortured, while heralds and soldiers delivered cryptic messages; old forms of order were in disarray. Perhaps Beckmann overestimated the intelligence of the Nazi censors when he falsely described the panels of this triptych as 'decorative designs for plays by Shakespeare' on the reverse; but this indicates the intensity of his emotional response against the regime. Nearly 600 of his works were confiscated from museums and public collections, and he featured strongly as a maker of degenerate art in the Munich exhibition of 1937. At that time, he completed *Temptation*, his second triptych, and began to make a series of small bronze sculptures (p. 300) in which he expressed his thoughts more directly: a self-portrait mask; a figure of a man in the dark; a crawling woman; and a vast Adam and a small Eve after their expulsion from Paradise.

In 1937, the day after *Entartete Kunst* opened in Munich, Beckmann and his wife emigrated to Amsterdam, where they remained for the next ten years. The sinister figures derived from the *commedia dell'arte* which populated Beckmann's triptychs and large paintings often bore a disquieting likeness to the artist himself. He became absorbed in the themes of the Apocalypse and Faust, and images from both regularly surface in his work; acid allegories of death and torture predominate. *Carnival* (1942–43, pp. 316–17), a triptych completed at the height of the war, is one of the most desolate and lyrical of these paintings; it refers back to the story of Adam and Eve, as acted out by strolling players, and is a sardonic reminder not only of the artist's alienation but of his isolation from grace.

Hans Grundig, one of the founders of the Dresden group of Asso, had been arrested by the Gestapo on a number of occasions; his work was shown in the *Entartete Kunst* exhibition, and his wife Lea, who was Jewish, was forced to emigrate to Palestine. He stayed behind, was again arrested and was held in Sachsenhausen concentration camp for four years; his painting *The Victims of Fascism* (p. 318), made at the end of the war, directly chronicles his experience.

The Austrian-born painter Felix Nussbaum did not survive the camps. His paintings, which confront directly his own fate and that of Jewish people under the Nazis, combine the Magic Realism of Radziwill with the stark reality of the Holocaust (p. 305). Imprisoned in Saint-Cyprien in 1940 when the Germans occupied Belgium, he was deported to Bordeaux as an 'enemy alien'. He escaped and returned to Brussels, where friends sheltered him for four years; the Saint-Cyprien camp figured large in his work. In 1944 he was again arrested and was deported with his wife to Auschwitz, where they both perished.

23 From 1936 to 1938 this appeared under the modified title of *Volksillustrierte Zeitung* (People's Illustrated Newspaper).

24 The exhibition was entitled *Twentieth-Century German Art*; Max Beckmann attended and gave a public lecture. See also Peter Thoene (Oto Bihalji-Merin), *Modern German Art* (Harmondsworth, 1938).

CELLULOID LIES

Cinema   *Lutz Becker*

When sound film was introduced in 1929, German film, although it lost its international market, received a great creative boost. The cinema culture of the Weimar Republic had a final flowering with a number of intensely realistic films such as *Der Blaue Engel* by Josef von Sternberg, *M* by Fritz Lang, and *Kameradschaft* by Georg Wilhelm Pabst, which were seen by record audiences. This development was cut short by Hitler's election victory in January 1933. The Nazi party had prepared for the takeover of the German film industry; as early as 1930 it had established its own film organization, which provided the blueprint.[1]

Dr Joseph Goebbels, who became chief of party propaganda in Berlin in 1929, established his own Reich Ministry of Popular Enlightenment and Propaganda in March 1933. All information not produced and authorized by Goebbels was made illegal. One year after its foundation, the ministry employed 14,000 people. It concealed its propaganda function behind the illusion of factual reporting and representation.[2]

A special film administration was set up, the Filmkammer, which was in turn incorporated in the Reichskulturkammer, the body which controlled, through its membership, the employment of everyone in the media and arts. The Reich Film Legislation of 1934 gave extended powers to the film censor and transformed the entire production and distribution process.

All Jewish film people were expelled from the industry and driven into exile, an act which deprived the German cinema of a specific intelligence and flair. Although many non-Jewish artists and technicians remained in the industry and seriously tried to maintain their standards, the quality of the productions deteriorated. Devoid of fresh ideas, the industry gradually lost its international connections, and the German cinema declined into provincialism. As in literature and the fine arts, film too was undermined by narrow-minded ideological control and by the intellectual poverty of its new rulers. Fifty years after the end of the Second World War, the films of the period still fill us with a mixture of depression and awe. Sentimentalized nationalistic drama dominated feature film production, and documentaries mostly celebrated the Führer cult and the achievements of the Nazi party. Eugen Hadamowsky, later head of German radio (the Reichsrundfunk), declared in 1933: 'Having realized beyond doubt that the nation is the highest form of human existence, we have at once decided that our films should be judged from no other angle than that of national expediency.'[3]

Compared with the high attendance figures during the late Weimar Republic, cinema audiences dwindled, responding negatively to the diet of films with explicit political messages. Goebbels and his propaganda specialists quickly learned to create more sophisticated films and introduced more subtle programming and a more targeted distribution network. Cinemas showed a wider variety of material, mixing propaganda and entertainment in a more acceptable form. As fewer foreign films were allowed on German screens, audiences were obliged to rely on German productions specifically manufactured for them. One very convenient way to swell audience figures for 'politically valuable' films was the inauguration of mandatory screenings to 'invited' audiences from the party and mass organizations.

Goebbels maximized the impact of his productions through a series of massive investment initiatives. From 1935 onwards, he also enthusiastically promoted television, which made a popular breakthrough during the Berlin Olympics of 1936, when daily programmes were broadcast in Berlin and Munich.[4] Here, in television viewing rooms, he had a captive audience of 150,000 people.

These TV experiments, and the constant use of film to influence and direct the masses, were seen as part of a process of Social Darwinism. In 1936 Hans Hinkel, head of the film department at the Ministry of Propaganda, stated: 'Our great aim is to redirect the instincts of the people. What we need to achieve, through a living educational process, is that we shall make the German people accept the good, truly National Socialist film.'[5]

Aided by a compliant industry, the Ministry for Popular Enlightenment and Propaganda supervised and produced a constant flow of well crafted newsreels and thousands of documentaries which served a vast variety of propagandistic purposes. In its twelve years' existence, it produced 1,097 feature films.[6] Only 10 per cent of these carried overt political propaganda; the remaining 90 per cent, which were mainly escapist entertainment, were, nevertheless, of equal importance.

1 Curt Belling, *Der Film in Staat und Partei* (Berlin, 1936).

2 Z. A. B. Zeman, *Nazi Propaganda* (London, 1964).

3 Eugen Hadamowsky, *Propaganda und Nationale Macht* (Oldenburg, 1933).

4 Films on the development of television, Nazi style, at the Bundesarchiv, Koblenz, are *Das Auge der Welt* (1935); *Schreibendes Licht* (1936).

5 Hans Hinkel, *Rede des Reichskulturwarts in Dresden* 9.7.1936.

6 Gerd Albrecht, *Nationalsozialistische Filmpolitik. Eine soziologische Untersuchung der Spielfilme des Dritten Reiches* (Stuttgart, 1969).

They manipulated social expectations and helped to create a climate that made the masses susceptible to official propaganda. These films celebrated the Nazi state as the normal condition, disoriented morality and, often unobtrusively, instilled National Socialist attitudes, stereotypes and conventions. Propaganda films attuned the population to accepting the irrational: the state as a transcendental entity.

The pillar of the German film industry was UFA (Universum Film A.G.), which under the Weimar Republic had grown into one of Europe's most powerful studios. Now, under the direction of the nationalistic newspaper magnate Alfred Hugenberg, it produced films devoted to the image of Germany's militaristic and imperialistic mythology. Goebbels supported UFA above all other production companies and made it the centrepiece of his drive towards a centralized state film monopoly. The gradual nationalization of the German film industry continued throughout the war, as the Nazi film monopoly followed the advancing armies into the occupied territories. German films were shown in 27,000 cinemas throughout occupied Europe, enhancing the financial basis and the propagandistic power of UFA.[7]

The rigidity and megalomania with which the German film industry was run resulted in expensive productions of little artistic or intellectual merit. The erosion of the old ethos of style and quality lastingly undermined German film-making. Even after 1945, German films were unable to regain the quality and integrity of pre-1933 cinema.

The main themes prescribed by the regime centred around basic ideological concepts. The Führer Principle was demonstrated in a series of films on 'great

Germans'; the Blood and Soil myth was reflected in melodramas with Alpine or rural settings; racial propaganda was linked with the promotion of *Volksgemeinschaft* (the community of the People and the Nation). Films were to depict heroes fighting for the righteous cause of Germany at home or in the former colonies, in industry and on the farm, living heroic lives and dying sacrificial deaths at the war front, all in scenes of theatrical rhetoric and pathos. The leading directors were Veit Harlan (*Der Herrscher*, 1937; *Jud Süss*, 1940), Wolfgang Liebeneiner (*Bismarck*, 1940; *Ich klage an*, 1941), Karl Ritter (*Pour le Mérite*, 1938; *Stukas*, 1941), Hans Steinhoff (*Robert Koch*, 1939; *Ohm Kruger*, 1941). Leni Riefenstahl, in a special position, was possibly the only film-maker of the period fully able to express her enthusiasm for Hitler and his Utopia, in an intensely 'modern' genre of documentary film, which expanded the known boundaries of cinema. Her film on the Nazi party rally of 1934, *Triumph des Willens*, and her epic two-part work on the Berlin Olympics of 1936, *Olympia* (p. 279), provided prototypes for the future. A new kind of film propaganda was developed during the war in the newsreels of *Die Deutsche Wochenschau*, with its daring photography, dynamic editing and use of sound.

Goebbels and his helpers exploited an inherent ambiguity of cinema. They synthesized pictures and sounds to create convincing, captivating illusions that disconnected logic and suspended rational thinking. Thus they established a dependency on an omnipotent state and an infallible leadership.

Propaganda had helped the Nazis to come to power; constant and ever more sophisticated propaganda had to be employed to strengthen and to maintain that position. As early as 1934, Goebbels declared in a speech at the Nuremberg Rally: 'It may be sufficient to hold power that is based on guns; however, it is much more satisfactory and gratifying to win the heart of the nation and to keep it.'[8]

The mass media, press, radio and film were pliable propaganda instruments in the service of the Nazi state; they fed off each other in a circular arrangement, creating their own dynamics and a paranoid view of the outside world. They defined the new collective identity, in which the individual was nothing and the party was all. Propagandistic persuasion alternated with intimidation and the threat of violence.[9] Propaganda was a constituent part of an everyday reign of terror.

Nazi Germany was to some degree a creation of its film industry – 'a fantasy order which in equal measure was a dream machine and a death factory'.[10]

7 Wolfgang Becker, *Film und Herrschaft*, vol. 1: *Zur politischen Ökonomie des NS-Films* (Berlin, 1973).

8 This Goebbels speech is recorded in the film *Triumph des Willens* (*Triumph of the Will*, 1935), directed by Leni Riefenstahl.

9 'The Nazis knew that if they wanted their propaganda to be successful they had first to dominate the streets. Only then could it adopt the more respectable face of public and cultural life. Eugen Hadamowsky in 1933 [as note 3] was quite open about it: "Propaganda and the graduated use of violence have to be employed together in a skilful manner. They are never absolutely opposed to each other. The use of violence can be part of propaganda."' Karlheinz Schmeer, *Die Regie des öffentlichen Lebens im Dritten Reich* (Munich 1956).

10 Eric Rentschler, *Ministry of Illusion* (New York, 1994). Programme note of the Goethe-Institut, New York.

Hitler in Nuremberg, planning ceremonies with Leni Riefenstahl, 1930s

Free exercises in the Olympic Stadium (Leni Riefenstahl, 1936)

Light architecture
above the Olympic
Stadium, 1936,
conceived by
Albert Speer.
Private collection,
London

Unter den Linden, decorated for the visit of
Mussolini in September 1937 by the stage
designer Benno von Arent. Bildarchiv
Preussischer Kulturbesitz, Berlin

Adolf Hitler
design for a domed hall, c. 1925

Albert Speer
project for a Great Hall on the North-South
Axis, photographed in 1941.
Private Collection, London

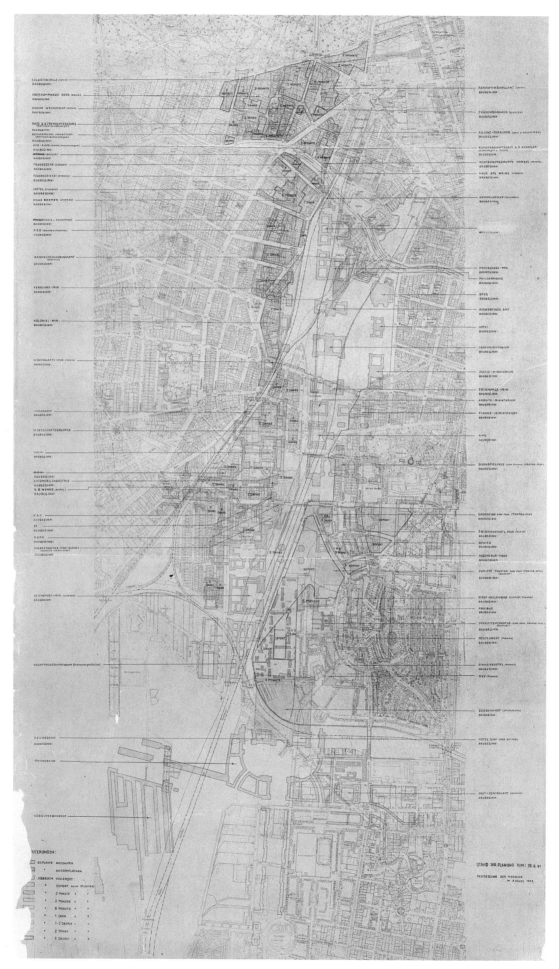

GBI plan of the
North-South Axis,
final version,
February 1942.
Wolfgang
Schäche, Berlin

GBI model of the
North-South Axis,
looking north
towards the Great
Hall, final version,
1942.
Wolfgang
Schäche, Berlin

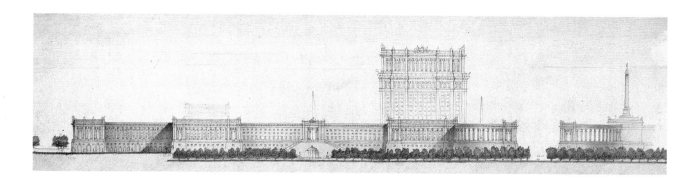

Cäsar Pinnau
government building and 3,000-bed hotel for
the North-South Axis, 1941–42.
Hamburgisches Architektenarchiv

Hermann Distel
project for the University Clinic in the University
City, 1941–42

Friedrich Tamms
autobahn bridge at Frankfurt/Oder, 1937.
Kunstbibliothek, Berlin

Ludwig Mies van der Rohe
competition project for the Reichsbank,
perspective from river front, Berlin 1933.
The Museum of Modern Art, New York

Walter Gropius
competition project for the Reichsbank, Berlin
1933.
Busch Reisinger Museum, Harvard University

Hans Poelzig
competition project for the Reichsbank, Berlin
1933.
Museum für Verkehr und Technik, Berlin

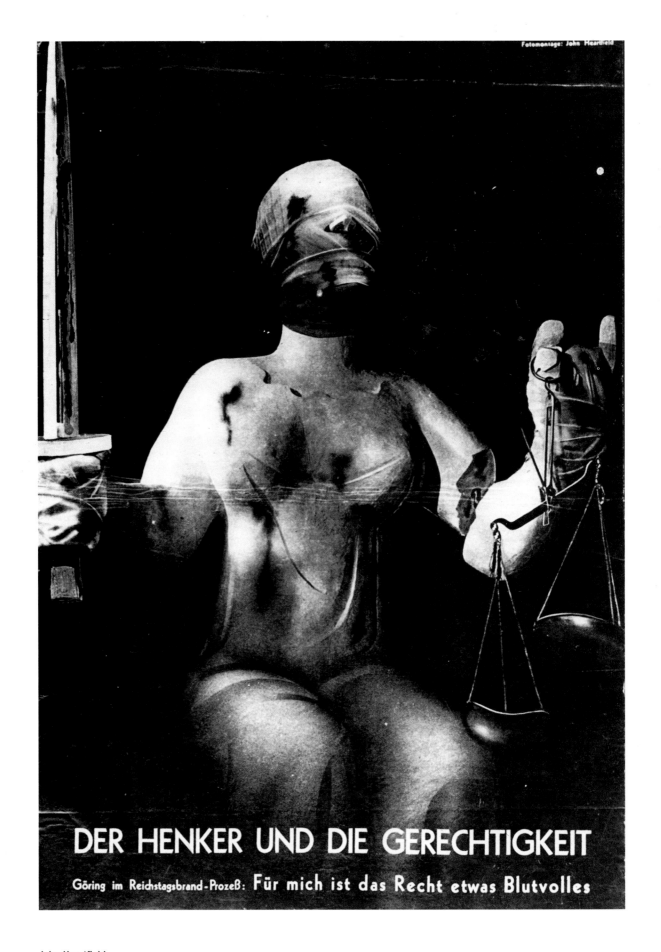

John Heartfield
Hangman and Justice, 1933.
Stiftung Archiv der Akademie der Künste, Berlin

Otto Griebel
The Internationale, 1928–30.
Deutsches Historisches Museum, Berlin

Ernst Barlach
Seated Old Woman, 1933.
Ernst Barlach Stiftung, Güstrow

Käthe Kollwitz
The Tower of Mothers, 1937–8.
Käthe-Kollwitz-Museum, Berlin

Arthur Kampf
Venus and Adonis, 1939.
Property of the Federal Republic of Germany

Heinrich Knirr
Portrait of Hitler, 1937.
Imperial War Museum, London

Adolf Ziegler
Female Nude.
Property of the Federal Republic of Germany

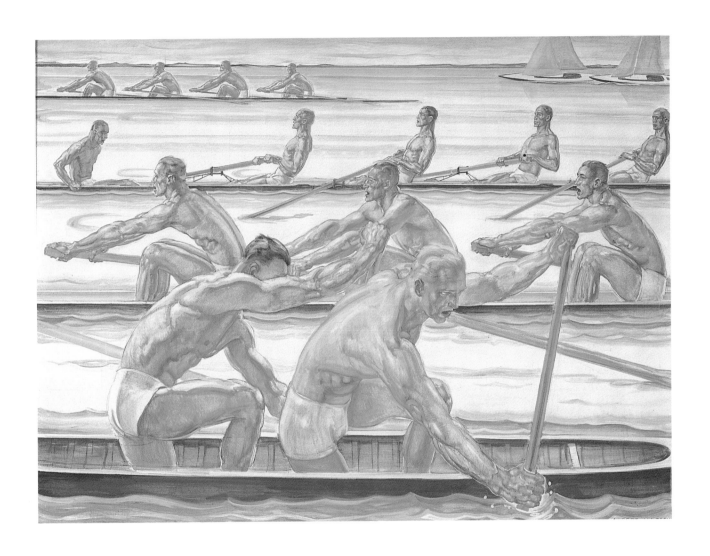

Albert Janesch
Water Sport, 1936.
Property of the Federal Republic of Germany

Richard Scheibe
Decathlete, 1937.
Städtische Galerie im Städelschen Kunstinstitut,
Frankfurt am Main

Georg Kolbe
Proclamation,
1937.
Berlinische
Galerie, Berlin

299

Max Beckmann
Man in the Dark, 1934.
Private collection

Max Beckmann
Crawling Woman, 1935.
Private Collection

Gerhard Marcks
Swimmer II, 1938.
Staatliche Museen zu Berlin, Nationalgalerie

Oskar Kokoschka
Anschluss – Alice in Wonderland, 1942.
Wiener Städtische Allgemeine Versicherung
Aktiengesellschaft, Vienna

Oskar Kokoschka
Self-Portrait as Degenerate Artist, 1937.
Private collection, on loan to the Scottish
National Gallery of Modern Art, Edinburgh

Carl Hofer
The Guardians, 1936.
Staatliche Museen zu Berlin, Nationalgalerie

Felix Nussbaum
The Secret, 1939.
Private collection

Oskar Schlemmer
Blue Group, 1935.
Leopold-Hoesch-Museum, Düren

Oskar Schlemmer
Dark Group, 1936.
Private collection, courtesy C. Raman
Schlemmer

Georg Schrimpf
Two Girls by the Window, 1937.
Staatliche Museen zu Berlin, Nationalgalerie

Willi Baumeister
Dripping Shapes, Relief-Picture, 1942.
Archiv Baumeister, Stuttgart

Willi Baumeister
*Arno Breker's "The Avenger" with Head drawn
by Willi Baumeister, c.* 1941.
Archiv Baumeister, Stuttgart

Paul Klee
Vigilant Angel, 1939.
Private collection, Switzerland

Paul Klee
Voice from the Ether, 'And You Shall Eat Your Fill', 1939.
Trustees of the Victoria & Albert Museum,
London

Paul Klee
Dancing with Fear, 1938.
Kunstmuseum Bern, Paul-Klee-Stiftung

Oskar Schlemmer
*Dinner at the Neighbour's House, Window
Picture I*, 1942.
Kunstmuseum Basel, Depositum Schlemmer

Oskar Schlemmer
Tripartite Window, Window Picture XVII, 1942.
Kunstmuseum Basel, Depositum Schlemmer

Oskar Schlemmer
Lit Kitchen with Woman, Window Picture X, 1942.
Kunstmuseum Basel, Depositum Schlemmer

Oskar Schlemmer
*Living Room with Working Woman, Window
Picture IV*, 1942.
Kunstmuseum Basel, Depositum Schlemmer

Emil Nolde
Old Man and Young Woman, 1938–45.
Stiftung Seebüll Ada und Emil Nolde

Emil Nolde
Ill-Suited Couple, 1938–45.
Stiftung Seebüll Ada und Emil Nolde

Max Beckmann
Carnival Triptych, 1942–43.
The University of Iowa Museum of Art, Iowa

Hans Grundig
Victims of Fascism, 1946.
Museum der Bildenden Künste, Leipzig

Felix Nussbaum
Crouching Prisoner in Saint-Cyprien, 1940.
Deutsches Historisches Museum, Berlin

Ludwig Hohlwein
League of German Girls in the Hitler Youth.
Kunstbibliothek, Berlin

Walter Riemer
13th Great German Radio Exhibition, 1936.
Kunstbibliothek, Berlin

Robert Zinner
Reich Autobahns in Germany.
Kunstbibliothek, Berlin

Mjölnir (Hans Schweitzer)
Our Last Hope: Hitler.
Imperial War Museum, London

Anonymous
German Youth Festival, 1934.
Imperial War Museum, London

A HIERARCHY OF STYLES

National Socialist Architecture Between Neoclassicism and Regionalism *Winfried Nerdinger*

In the exhibition *Wildwachsende Blumen* (*Wild Flowers*), at the Lenbachhaus in Munich in 1993,[1] Ian Hamilton Finlay suggested restoring the Nazi commemorative temples (*Ehrentempel*) on the Königsplatz, replacing the vanished 'Martyr Sarcophagi' either with bronze plaques recording the names of the wild flowers that have grown on the ruins since 1947 or with a pool to reflect the passing clouds as a symbol of eternity and transience. *Wild Flowers* forms part of *The Third Reich Revisited*, a project on which Finlay has been working for years, with the aim of 'denazifying Neoclassicism'. According to Finlay, it would be wrong 'to abandon a thousand years of architecture for the sake of a regime that lasted thirteen years'.[2] Finlay's installations and drawings caused as much distress as ever in Munich, even after nearly two decades of attempts to come to terms with Nazi Neoclassicism, or to rehabilitate Nazi architecture.

In the early decades after the Second World War, most architects in the West had great difficulty with the formal vocabulary of Neoclassicism. Columns and porticoes, axiality and symmetry, were taboo – Günter Eich wrote of 'involuntary laughter at the sight of columns' – not only because the Nazi period was still so close but also because, until the late 1950s, the Communist adversary beyond the Iron Curtain was using the same vocabulary. Even in 1973, in a rather grotesque polemic against John Summerson's *The Classical Language of Architecture*, Bruno Zevi wrote that symmetry, a constant of classicism, expressed a compulsive craving for security; since the schizophrenic type found the mobility and variety of life particularly hard to bear, classicism was thus the architecture of 'conformist schizophrenia' – or, in Freudian terms, of passivity and therefore of homosexuality.[3]

Numerous authors since the war have pointed out the relationship between Neoclassical architecture in Nazi Germany and contemporaneous buildings in other countries. By 1954 we find Hellmut Lehmann-Haupt, in his *Art under a Dictatorship*, comparing Nazi buildings by Paul Ludwig Troost and Albert Speer with prestige projects in the USSR, Italy and the USA. However, Lehmann-Haupt stressed the differences: in the 'imitative classicism'[4] of the Nazi architects he perceived exorbitant size, coarsened proportions and a sense of oppressive weight.

As for Speer, in his memoirs published in 1969 he asserted with lapidary clarity that Neoclassicism was not in the least confined to totalitarian states: 'Rather, it was characteristic of the era and left its impression upon Washington, London, and Paris as well as Rome, Moscow, and our plans for Berlin.'[5] In this he cited the authority of John Burchardt, Dean of Architecture at MIT in Boston, who in 1961 found little to choose between 'Fascist, Communist, and democratic taste'.[6]

Writing in 1970 and 1973, Karl Arndt was the first German art historian to argue that Neoclassicism was the 'contemporary style' of the period; but he stressed that it was 'a wider reaction against Modernist architecture', which 'found differing formulations in the work of individual artists and must therefore be seen, even within the wider framework of conservative thought, in terms of varying political contexts'.[7]

Arndt was still seeking to maintain scholarly distinctions; however, in the ensuing debate concerning Postmodern architecture and the random 'quotation' of historical forms as interchangeable set pieces, such distinctions and contextual factors largely went by the board.

Thus, the competition for the new Staatsgalerie in Stuttgart in 1977 brought the first public debate on the relationship between Neoclassicism and Fascism. An unsuccessful entrant, Günter Behnisch, called the circular form in James Stirling's design a 'Nazi form',[8] whereupon Stirling mockingly described the repetition of plazas in Behnisch's own design as 'fascistic'. Behnisch was still arguing from the postwar viewpoint of 'Moral Modernity'; Stirling mooted the open-ended, Postmodern interchangeability of historical set pieces – or, alternatively, the principle of topological design, based on geometric constants or historically invariant basic forms.

In the course of the Postmodern reclamation of past styles, not only was the Italian Rationalism of the 1930s vigorously championed by such architects as Aldo Rossi, Giorgio Grassi, Peter Eisenman and O. M. Ungers, but there were growing attempts to neutralize and even in some cases to ennoble Nazi Neoclassicism by absorbing it into an alleged international 1930s Neoclassicism. In architecture, National Socialism was being historicized years before the outbreak of the so-called Historians' Dispute on the subject in Germany. Once fitted into an international framework of comparison, the 'uniqueness' of Nazi architecture was obscured.

Revealingly enough, the historical debate was opened in 1978 by Speer himself, with a lavish publication of his architectural works. He himself laid down the principle that his work belonged to the category of buildings that commemorate the great figures of world history.[9] His own chosen historical position was within the tradition of Berlin Neoclassicism: the endpapers of the book show his Nuremberg Rally Ground – the Reichsparteitagsgelände – in the style of an engraving from Schinkel's works. In itself, this rendering exemplifies Speer's habit of falsification: in it, the Rally Ground, 17 square kilometres in area and 3 kilometres long, is distorted into a contemplative, green, Neoclassical idyll.

In the same volume, Lars Olof Larsson donned art-historical blinkers to follow Speer's line and presented 'Neoclassicism in Twentieth-Century Architecture'[10] in such a way that, on the strength of comparisons from Moscow,

1 Exh. cat. *Ian Hamilton Finlay. Wildwachsende Blumen* (Munich, 1993).

2 Exh. cat. *Ian Hamilton Finlay. Ideologische Äußerungen* (Frankfurt am Main, 1991).

3 Bruno Zevi, *The Modern Language of Architecture* (Seattle and London, 1978), 15. This absurd definition would imply that asymmetrical architecture must be heterosexual.

4 Hellmut Lehmann-Haupt, *Art under a Dictatorship* (New York, 1954), 117.

5 Albert Speer, *Inside the Third Reich* (London, 1970), 81.

6 John Burchardt, *The Architecture of America* (Washington D.C., 1961), as quoted by Speer (as note 5), 529.

7 Karl Arndt, *Baustelle Reichsparteitagsgelände 1938/39, Filmdokumente zur Zeitgeschichte* (Göttingen, 1973), 25; see also Arndt, 'Neoklassizistische Architektur im 20. Jahrhundert', *Neue Zürcher Zeitung*, 22 November 1970.

8 See Charles Jencks, *Die Postmoderne. Der neue Klassizismus in Kunst und Architektur* (Stuttgart, 1987), 324.

9 Albert Speer, *Architektur. Arbeiten 1933–1942* (Berlin, 1978).

Osbert Lancaster, 1950

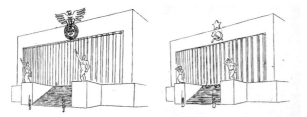

Washington, Helsinki and Rome, Speer emerged as an entirely normal case. In Léon Krier's subsequent Belgian edition (1985), Speer's oeuvre, totally depoliticized, was still further integrated into international Neoclassicism, and beyond that into the context of world architecture. Adopting the method of J. N. L. Durand's *Recueil et parallèle des édifices en tout genre anciens et modernes* (1800), Krier drew comparisons of typology and scale between Nazi work and the great monuments of world architecture, thus giving it a timeless status, and extolled Speer as the greatest architect since Karl Friedrich Schinkel.[11]

Since then there have been constant attempts to fit Speer into the 'continuities' of the twentieth century. In 1986 Franco Borsi produced his value-free compilation *L'ordine monumentale in Europa 1929–1939*;[12] and the 1989 exhibition *L'Europa dei razionalisti*[13] lumped together everything built or designed in the 1930s, from Le Corbusier to Marcello Piacentini and from Paul Schmitthenner to H. P. Berlage. This is the background to Hartmut Frank's preposterous but oft-repeated assertion that there are practically no discontinuities or caesuras in twentieth-century architecture: that the Blood and Soil vernacular was just a traditionalist subset of Modernism, and the New Reich Chancellery and Nuremberg Rally Ground merely extreme cases of a generalized international Neoclassicism – so that the very existence of such a thing as Nazi architecture was pure fiction.[14]

The first attempt at a comparative study of the architecture of twentieth-century totalitarian regimes came with the exhibition *Die Axt hat geblüht*, in Düsseldorf in 1987. Since the former Eastern Bloc was opened up, this seems to have become a particularly popular theme: the art and culture of the 1930s in Italy, Germany and the Soviet Union have formed the subjects of comparative exhibitions in Vienna in 1994[15] and now in London in 1995–96.

While Larsson, Krier and Frank see Nazi architecture scintillating in the reflected glow of international Neoclassicism, others take the view that in the night of totalitarianism all architecture is equally grey. In 1950 Osbert Lancaster wittily expressed this Cold War interpretation by juxtaposing identical architectural forms labelled 'Third Reich' and 'Marxism'.[16]

In purely formal terms, it is of course perfectly legitimate to compare buildings constructed under National Socialism with Neoclassical prestige buildings in other countries. But it is entirely untrue that – as Speer, Larsson and others alleged – the whole period inclined towards Neoclassicism: architecture in Switzerland, Holland, Czechoslovakia and also in Scandinavia took a totally different course.[17] In this case as in others, not everything can be compared with everything else: contextual factors such as building type, purpose and function must be taken into consideration, and – as Arndt pointed out back in 1973 – a sharp critical eye is needed.

Ultimately, too, it is a mistake to overestimate the expressive force of architecture. No one can analyse the Nazi system by looking at architectural forms alone. Monumentality is not in itself evil (as Peter Meyer first asserted in 1940, contradicting Peter Behrens). Individual architectural forms cannot convey a political programme; ultimately, the decisive factors are function, content and social relevance.[18]

Such distinctions are mostly neglected in current efforts to compare Nazi and other forms of Neoclassicism. Larsson, for instance, maintains that the courtyard of the Police Headquarters in Copenhagen, by Hack Kampmann (1924), with the 'regular ashlar of its walls and its heavy, smooth columns',[19] relates to the court of honour in Speer's New Reich Chancellery. Since the Copenhagen design was published in German journals, Larsson finds it 'not impossible' that Speer 'derived direct inspiration from Kampmann's building'. Since the Police HQ is 'entirely in the spirit of Christian Fredrik Hansen', the Chancellery stands forth in the light of the noble Danish Neoclassicism of the early nineteenth century. Larsson is likening the two-storey, rectangular, wholly enclosed Chancellery court, with its recessed giant order, to a circular, two-storey court with an open colonnade, coupled columns, cornices, balustrades and architrave mouldings. The comparison misfires on every single count.

The same applies, *mutatis mutandis*, to all Larsson's other parallels. For example, the Parliament Building in Helsinki, by Johan Sigfrid Sirén, stands in the nationalist tradition of Finnish Romantic

granite architecture; it is Sirén's own unaided invention, down to the details of capitals, cornices and entablatures. It is also the only building of its kind in the Finnish architecture of the 1920s and 1930s. To an art historian, Larsson's references to Ivar Tengbom's elegant concert hall and Gunnar Asplund's library and forest cemetery in Stockholm, in the context of Nazi architecture, are merely embarrassing. Again, the Neoclassical gesture of the Palais de Tokyo (p. 59), which opens out towards the Eiffel Tower, can perhaps be compared in terms of *type* with Bernini's colonnade at St Peter's, Rome, but not with the 'gestures of subordination and integration' of Nazi prestige buildings. In such comparisons the affinities boil down to the use of columns and a geometric structure, thus oversimplifying world architecture to the point at which Speer and Troost would fit in anywhere.

Even with columns, there are distinctions to be made: thus, the load-bearing, exposed concrete pillars on Auguste Perret's Musée des Travaux Publics in Paris belong to a different tectonic and structural context from the use by Troost, Piacentini or Speer of natural stone columns on a disguised, reinforced concrete skeleton. Again, the Red Doric of Ivan Fomin (also often adduced) was intended to ennoble proletarian dwellings in Moscow through an infusion of universal culture – whereas

10 Lars Olof Larsson, 'Klassizismus in der Architektur des 20. Jahrhunderts', in Speer (as note 9), 151–79. Larsson takes a more nuanced view of Nazi architecture – without, however, distancing himself from his wholesale use of Neoclassical analogies – in Larsson, 'Die Denkmalpflege und die Architektur des Nationalsozialismus', in Wilfried Lipp, ed., *Denkmal – Werte – Gesellschaft* (Frankfurt am Main and New York, 1993), 315–21.

11 Albert Speer, *Architecture 1932–1942*, ed. Léon Krier (Brussels, 1985); on this, see 'Klassik zum Völkermord', special issue of *Bauwelt*, no. 28–29 (1987).

12 Franco Borsi, *L'ordine monumentale in Europa 1929–1939* (Milan, 1986).

13 Exh. cat. *L'Europa dei razionalisti* (Milan, 1989).

14 Hartmut Frank, 'Welche Sprache sprechen Steine?', in Frank, ed., *Faschistische Architekturen. Planen und Bauen in Europa 1930–1945* (Hamburg, 1985), 7–21.

15 Jan Tabor, ed., exh. cat. *Kunst und Diktatur*, 2 vols (Vienna, 1994).

16 See Osbert Lancaster, *Homes Sweet Homes* (London, 1950).

17 See Isabelle Charolais and Bruno Marchand, eds., *Architecture de la raison: la Suisse des années vingt et trente* (Lausanne, 1991); exh. cat. *Tschechische Kunst der 20er und 30er Jahre* (Darmstadt, 1989).

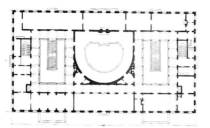

Paul Ludwig
Troost, Führerbau
(now Musikhoch-
schule), Munich,
1933–37:
plan, staircase,
elevation with
balcony

18 See Winfried
Nerdinger, ed., exh. cat.
*Bauen im
Nationalsozialismus –
Bayern 1933–1945*
(Munich, 1993), 12ff.

19 Larsson (as note 10),
156f.; also contains the
quotations that follow.

20 Robert Harbison,
'The Built, the Unbuilt,
and the Unbuildable', in
Harbison, *Pursuit of
Architectural Meaning*
(Cambridge, Mass.,
1991), 41ff.; see also
Larsson (as note 10),
174.

21 See Robin
Middleton, ed., *The
Beaux-Arts and
Nineteenth-Century
French Architecture*
(Cambridge, Mass.,
1982).

22 'Der Führer eröffnet
die "Große deutsche
Kunstausstellung 1937"',
*Die Kunst im Dritten
Reich* (1937), 54.

Paul Ludwig
Troost, Haus der
Deutschen Kunst,
Munich, 1933–37

John Russell
Pope, National
Gallery of Art,
Washington DC,
1937–41

in Germany such dignifying motifs were considered entirely inappropriate for the homes of the People.

Another often-cited analogy is between the National Gallery of Art in Washington, by John Russell Pope, and Troost's Haus der (Deutschen) Kunst in Munich – of which Robert Harbison, for instance, writes that it reminds an American visitor of Washington.[20] A reminder is often an inadequate basis for comparison. Anyone who takes a closer look at these two buildings – and comparisons are justified, since their functions are similar and their dates almost identical – will see that Pope has chosen the Ionic mode, common in the museum buildings of the previous 150 years (Glyptothek, Dulwich College Art Gallery, Altes Museum, British Museum, etc.), and that he has detailed it correctly, in accordance with the Beaux-Arts tradition pursued in almost all major public buildings in the USA since the Chicago World's Fair of 1893 and the

work of McKim, Mead & White. Troost's building, by contrast, displays (if anything) a Tuscan order: a mode that Vitruvian tradition assigns to the lowest category of buildings, such as market halls, prisons or custom houses.

This points to an important distinction. Pope and the American Neoclassicists stand in a line that runs from the Roman Revival of Thomas Jefferson's Capitol in Richmond to the architecture of the Beaux-Arts;[21] they can handle the Vitruvian formal apparatus. Troost's Haus der Kunst – praised by that architectural dilettante, Adolf Hitler, as the 'first beautiful building of the new Reich'[22] – stands right outside that tradition. Troost sought an austere architectural image that was later to be hailed as 'Germanic tectonics'.[23] He eclectically borrowed individual forms from buildings by Schinkel and by Leo von Klenze; but – in contrast to Beaux-Arts historical 'correctness' – Troost was a cabinetmaker, who planed all his profiles flat,[24] to achieve a hard, angular effect. In the process, he totally perverted his historical prototypes. He took over the Schinkel motif of the colonnaded façade, but in Schinkel's Altes Museum this is flanked by *antae*; Troost's rank of columns marches on into thin air. Again, in defiance of tectonic principle – and indeed of Neoclassicism itself – the whole supporting construction is concealed behind flat wall surfaces.

Since Troost set the tone for almost all Nazi public buildings, it is worth pursuing this antitraditional aspect – combined in Troost's case with architectural incompetence – in a further example. On the Königsplatz in Munich stand two large and externally almost identical buildings by Troost, each of which repeats the overall symmetry by having a pair of entrances facing directly onto the Königsplatz, the National Socialist Forum. The resulting pointless quadruplication of gigantic staircases shows that the architect has met the demand for symmetry with ineffectual reiteration. The plans reveal the true extent of his ineptitude. The gigantic vestibule of the so-called Führerbau stretches the whole length of the building and therefore lies at right angles to the direction of access, with the result that no one ever walks the length of it. Instead, the visitor, who is to be directed to Hitler's audience chamber, climbs the

stairs only to be confronted by a blank wall; he then has to be conducted around several twists and turns before reaching his goal. As the height of the top storey is reduced, the proportions of the staircase look totally wrong. Each of the two buildings has four 'Führer balconies', some of which, for reasons of symmetry, are placed between banks of toilets. Of course, a Nazi building cannot be judged on functional or structural grounds alone; but Troost's works are actually a failure as prestige buildings. I need hardly add that such references to their architectural shortcomings have no bearing on the historical significance of Nazi buildings as monuments.

Architectural incompetence is evident in many Nazi monumental designs. We have only to look at the access and staircase design of the Reichsmarschallamt planned for Goering; the totally inadequate access arrangements in Speer's domed Great Hall, its voids and its fourfold pilasters; the entrance to the Aviation Ministry; or the functional sequences in the SS Citadels or *Ordensburgen*, to realize what third-rate architects occupied the leading positions in Nazi public architecture.

I have concentrated on Nazi prestige projects and Neoclassicism; but here as elsewhere distinctions must be drawn. Nazi Neoclassicism, which might be better described as reductive or primitive classicism, is eclectic in itself. Not that its stylistic repertoire is particularly large: its allusions to Roman antiquity, the prototype of Nazi world conquest, have already been studied;[25] there are also Egyptian and Mesopotamian elements, allusions to Etienne-Louis Boullée and coarsened versions of Kaiser Wilhelm Neoclassicism. All are used as set pieces, stripped down and subordinated to the overriding imperatives of symmetry, size and monumentality.[26]

It is recognized that architecture under National Socialism observed a kind of stylistic hierarchy of genres.[27] But, in itself, the allocation of different programmes to different styles – primitive Neoclassical for public prestige projects; 'Blood and Soil' vernacular for housing developments, Hitler Youth hostels and schools; technoid-functionalist for utilitarian buildings – does not indicate stylistic pluralism, or even tolerance of differing approaches. It is all part of a cut-

and-dried hierarchic system. When Hitler denounced a museum design by Adolf Abel – in pointed contrast with Troost's Haus der Kunst – as a 'bath house' or a 'Saxon yarn mill',[28] or when he drew the distinction between classical Temples of the Party and glass-and-iron Temples of Labour, he was judging in genre terms; and this is a characteristic feature of historicist thinking, diametrically opposed to the primary Modernist principle that architecture must create a consistent and all-embracing expression of the age, couched in a new repertoire of forms and materials.

The stylistic hierarchy of National Socialism created no more than the illusion of diversity. In some categories – including social housing, Hitler Youth hostels, transportation and farmhouses – new buildings were officially required to adapt to the landscape, traditions and building materials of each region; but any architectural reference to Blood and Soil ideas was undermined by the imposition of type standardization and overridden by the hierarchy of styles.[29] Official show buildings existed to exemplify the adaptation of Hitler Youth hostels, *Autobahn* resthouses and officers' messes to regional traditions; and yet, wherever hostels, schools and farmhouses were actually built, they overwhelmingly conformed to a standard design. Regional elements were mostly decorative additions to a basic formula.

The purely artificial, applied character of Nazi regionalism is particularly evident in standardized mass housing, which was – at best – decorated with vernacular forms.[30] Even the 1936 Olympic Village in Berlin, a propaganda 'Village of Peace' that was said to reflect the shape of the German homeland in its very layout, contained only standardized buildings.[31]

What is more, the architects of the Stuttgart School and their successors were free to impose their own South German formulas all the way from Aachen to Königsberg, utterly regardless of local traditions – a practice that attracted criticism even in the 1930s.[32] The imposition of a shortlist of archetypally German (*urdeutsch*) regional traditions is particularly evident in the plans for the architectural 'Germanization' of the conquered East European territories. According to Speer, Hitler wanted the new German cities in the East to look like 'Regensburg, Augsburg, Weimar or

Regional patterns for Hitler Youth hostels

Barracks for Alpine troops, Berchtesgaden

Ainring airport, passenger building and hangar

Heidelberg'.[33] Hitler clearly regarded himself as the best judge of what was 'German architecture' and what was not.

Just how little the local vernacular counted for, in the land of Blood and Soil, is revealed by the absolute primacy of the hierarchy of genres. Thus, barracks for Alpine regiments sported Alpine dress; but, when it came to a prestige project like the *Ordensburg* at Sonthofen in the Allgäu, the architect Hermann Giesler chose a harsh ashlar construction utterly unrelated to the local tradition of plaster rendering.[34] At Ainring airport in Bavaria, the passenger building looks like an outsize Alpine farmhouse; but it is flanked by a hangar built in glass and iron.

In major prestige projects for areas of great natural beauty – as with the Hohe Schule beside the Chiemsee, or the Strength Through Joy seaside resort on Rügen – landscape and regional identity were ignored. Where local elements appeared at all, they did so as naive allusions such as the Renaissance motif of the Perlachturm on Giesler's Gauforum tower for Augsburg. In Roderich Fick's Neoclassical plan for Linz, the architect's

only concession to local colour was the leather shorts and dirndl skirts of the staffage figures.[35]

Regionalism in Nazi architecture was largely a decorative backdrop for the docile man of the People, who was expected to live in the same standardized shells all over Germany, and to be suitably impressed by the primitive Neoclassicism of the new public buildings.

Translated by David Britt

23 See Friedrich Tamms, 'Das Große in der Baukunst', *Die Kunst im Deutschen Reich* (1944), 547ff.

24 The phrase is Hans Eckstein's; see Paul Westheim, *Karton mit Säulen. Antifaschistische Kunstkritik* (Leipzig and Weimar, 1985), esp. 145ff.; on Troost's position see Karl Arndt, 'Die Münchner Architekturszene 1933/34 als ästhetisch-politisches Konfliktfeld', in *Bayern in der NS-Zeit* (Munich, 1980), 443–512.

25 See, most recently, Alex Scobie, *Hitler's State Architecture: The Impact of Classical Antiquity* (Pennsylvania University Park and London, 1990); review by Karl Arndt, *Gnomon*, vol. 65, no. 7 (1993), 631–34.

26 See Wolfgang Schäche, 'Nationalsozialistische Architektur und Antikenrezeption. Kritik der Neoklassizismus-These am Beispiel der Berliner Museumsplanung', in *Berlin und die Antike* 2 (Berlin, 1979): 557–570; see also W. Nerdinger and E. Mai, eds., *Wilhelm Kreis – Architekt zwischen Kaiserreich und Demokratie 1873–1955* (Munich, 1994).

27 See Gerhard Fehl, 'Die Moderne unterm Hakenkreuz', in Frank (as note 14), 88–122; Winfried Nerdinger, ed., *Bauhaus-Moderne im Nationalsozialismus* (Munich, 1993).

28 As note 22.

29 On the range of genres, see Nerdinger (as note 18).

30 Tilmann Harlander and Gerhard Fehl, *Hitlers sozialer Wohnungsbau 1940–1945* (Hamburg, 1986).

31 Hans Saalbach, ed., *Dorf des Friedens – Das olympische Dorf* (Berlin, 1936).

32 Wolfgang Voigt, 'Die "Stuttgarter Schule" und die Alltagsarchitektur im Dritten Reich', *arch+*, no. 68 (1983), 64–68.

33 Albert Speer, *Spandauer Tagebücher* (Frankfurt am Main, Berlin and Vienna, 1975), 337ff.; See also Gert Gröning and Joachim Wolschke-Bulmahn, *Die Liebe zur Landschaft – Der Drang nach Osten* (Munich, 1987).

34 See Nerdinger (as note 18), 141ff., 483ff.

35 'Der neue Brückenkopf in Linz an der Donau als Beginn der Neugestaltung der Stadt', *Die Kunst im Deutschen Reich* (1941), 87–107.

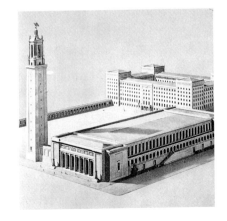

Hermann Giesler, model of new Gauforum for Augsburg

FROM BERLIN TO 'GERMANIA'

Architecture and Urban Planning   *Wolfgang Schäche*

In Berlin, as elsewhere, the new era that began on 30 January 1933 did not initially mark a clean break, either in administration or in policy. In organization, structure and allocation of responsibilities, the city building administration remained largely unchanged.[1] Stylistically – despite the Nazis' virulent witch-hunt against Modernism during the 'time of struggle' before their assumption of power – there were no overt sanctions. Drastic action was taken only in personnel matters.[2] All opposition was forcibly eliminated, and 'leftists and non-Aryans' in particular were 'removed' from the public service.[3]

Actual building had in any case practically come to a halt, as a result of the world economic crisis by which Germany, after its defeat in 1918, was particularly hard hit. Accordingly, the first thing that the city building administration did after the 'assumption of power' was to set in hand or reactivate a number of planning initiatives and building projects already envisaged before 1933. These works primarily served the political imperative of creating employment. They were governed by no particular planning objective; nor were they based on new urban or architectural ideas.

By contrast with these first, uncoordinated and almost exclusively employment-oriented projects, those that came in the years that followed, 1934–36, belonged within an overriding thematic context. With a view to the Olympic Games, which Berlin was due to stage in 1936, the Nazi city authorities sought above all to present foreign visitors with a coherently planned metropolis for the 'New Germany'. Accordingly, in a typical manifestation of Nazi ideas of organization and order, a number of squares and streets were scheduled for rebuilding, both in central Berlin and along the main axes of communication.[4]

Early in 1936 Hitler decided to take the future 'remodelling' (*Umgestaltung*) of the metropolis out of the hands of city government altogether. He chose to entrust the task to the young Albert Speer,[5] who had already been commissioned to lay out the site of the Nazi party rallies in Nuremberg. In the summer of 1936 – unbeknown to the city authorities[6] – Hitler instructed Speer to make plans for 'the remodelling of the Reich capital': 'With this City of Berlin we can get nothing done. From now on you make the design … When you have something ready, show it to me. You know I always have time for that.'[7]

The Nazis' declared aims – public demonstration of power and monumental self-advertisement – chimed perfectly with the construction industry's demand for long-term public projects. National Socialism demanded an appropriate architectural setting ('The Word in Stone'), and industry demanded a guaranteed profit. And so, not only for Berlin but in due course for Munich and Hamburg, and then for all the regional *Gau* capitals, 'remodelling' programmes were devised on a megalomaniac scale. All were based on the 'Law for the Remodelling of German Cities', enacted on 4 October 1937. Their execution guaranteed that the country's building capacity would be fully occupied for a long time to come.

In keeping with the new political assumptions of an expansionist foreign policy – and in anticipation, so to speak, of the warlike implementation of that policy – Berlin as the Reich capital was to be developed into a gigantic centre of power. To this end a new planning and executant authority was set up: that of the GBI (Inspector-General of Building for the Reich Capital of Berlin).[8]

Both the organization of the GBI and the plans that it produced for Berlin were copied in the lesser 'remodelled cities' elsewhere. It was characteristic of the new policy instituted by the GBI that the planned buildings themselves were largely devoid of practical usefulness – or, if they had any, this was a subordinate consideration. Their usefulness was to be a political and ideological one, as part of the technology of dominance, and an economic one, as manufactured assets. Architecture's social purpose had become non-existent; only the label of 'Art' could justify its cost, or conceal the vested interests involved in its making.

On 30 January 1933 Albert Speer was officially appointed Inspector-General of Building; the GBI office was given the authority of a government ministry directly responsible to the Führer. In the ten months since Hitler's informal instruction to him, Speer had produced initial plans and built up an organization that was now technically and organizationally ready to manage the future 'remodelling of the Reich capital'.[9] Organizationally, it patterned itself on the existing office of the Inspector-General of German Highways, headed by the civil engineer Fritz Todt.[10] The GBI was so organized that within the domain covered by 'remodelling' operations the planning responsibilities of the municipality, as well as of the Reich and Prussian governments, ceased to exist, and all legal authority – later still further extended – was vested in Speer. In the GBI's 'Areas of Interest Plan', drawn up on 1 August 1938,[11] those parts of the city in which no building work was to be undertaken without GBI approval covered well over half of its area. Additionally, any building activity unconnected with Speer's plans, especially in the private, commercial sphere, could be suspended 'by command of the Führer' in order to release materials and labour for the 'remodelling'.

The GBI's 'remodelling' plans were financed through an official budget that was set at 60 million RM (Reichsmark) per year until the year 1960. Additionally, from 1938 onwards the Berlin municipality had to find 70 million RM annually from its own resources for the purchase of land and buildings and for demolition work. The individual buildings in Speer's plan were to be financed by their respective future occupiers; it was understood, however, that the necessary labour and materials would be supplied as a result of the intended wars of conquest.

By the beginning of 1938 the planning had reached the point where design work could start on individual areas and buildings. The official media

1 See Frank Werner, *Stadtplanung Berlin* (Berlin,²1978), ch. 2-3, esp. 35, 38.

2 For a detailed account see Hans-Norbert Borkert, Klaus Matussek and Wolfgang Wippermann, '*Machtergreifung*'. *Berlin 1933* (Berlin, 1982).

3 The most prominent victim in the Berlin building authority was the city building commissioner, Martin Wagner. On 13 March 1933 he was '"suspended" from the post of city building commissioner, together with the Social Democrat members of the city council staff. Ludovica Scarpa, *Martin Wagner und Berlin* (Braunschweig and Wiesbaden, 1985), 148.

4 See Wolfgang Schäche, *Architektur und Städtebau in Berlin zwischen 1933 und 1945, Die Bauwerke und Kunstdenkmäler von Berlin*, Beiheft 17 (Berlin, 1991).

5 Speer's appointment as 'Architect to the Führer' in succession to Paul Ludwig Troost, who had died in 1934, was by no means a foregone conclusion, even at the end of 1935. It was only in the course of 1936 that Hitler took the decision to entrust Speer with the 'supreme task', the 'remodelling' of Berlin. See city council minute of a meeting in the Führer's office on 28 June 1935, on planned transport infrastructure works and the question of the future architect for Berlin (Bundesarchiv Koblenz [BAK], BA R 43 II/1181, 5 sheets).

6 See letter from State Commissar for the Capital City of Berlin, Julius Lippert, 'to the Führer and Reich Chancellor', dated 24 April 1936, on the timing of a meeting to finalize various plans (BAK, BA R 43 II/1182b, 3 sheets). Lippert's letter clearly shows that at that time the city administration knew nothing of Speer's appointment.

Albert Speer, axial layout for Berlin, 1938

reported on 'remodelling' in general terms, and there was publicity for a number of planning sectors and even for individual buildings; but the overall scope of the plans was deliberately kept from the public, to avoid raising questions about the enormous cost of the project at a time when the supply of consumer goods was already shrinking. Ultimately, such questions could not have been answered without revealing that its realization depended on the war plans implicit in the Nazis' second Four Year Plan, which was actually a mobilization programme.

Under the 'remodelling plan', the prime feature and also the backbone of the new city plan was to be a cross made up of two axes, north-south and east-west, intersecting at right angles in the vicinity of the Brandenburg Gate. The four ends of the cross formed interchange points on the ring autobahn which was planned to mark the new city limits of Berlin (and which has since been built). Four concentric inner rings completed the main framework, which was filled out with a large number of radial streets. The East-West Axis and the ring and radial thoroughfares partly followed existing street lines, which were to be widened or linked by clearances; but the North-South Axis (pp. 259, 284) was completely new. It was closely involved with the planned restructuring of the entire Berlin rail network. The functions of the existing termini were to be concentrated in two new main stations in the boroughs of Wedding and Tempelhof, which would mark the ends of the central section of the North-South Axis, designed as a 'grand avenue' some 7 kilometres long.

At the heart of the plan, this thoroughfare was to be lined by all those state and party buildings considered

relevant, by the prestigious headquarters of big business corporations, and by countless 'memorials and monuments'. This stretch was scheduled for completion in 1950 – when, on the occasion of a World Exhibition, the street and its buildings were to be inaugurated, and Berlin was to be 'solemnly renamed Germania'.

The realization of 'visions' of this kind was going to require some vigorous surgery on the obsolete urban structure. Dismissed as a symbol of social decline and moral decadence, the existing, nineteenth-century city was contrasted with the new, National Socialist city. Ruthlessly, some 4 per cent of the whole building stock of Berlin was singled out for destruction in the course of building Germania. For the 'grand avenue' section of the North-South Axis alone, it was calculated that more than 25,000 dwellings would have to be demolished, along with innumerable perfectly sound office and business premises, craft workshops, industrial buildings, cultural and social centres and churches. Over the whole area covered by the plan, more than 54,000 dwellings were to be sacrificed.

However, before the new axis of the longed-for world metropolis could be designed, the GBI needed to secure the services of capable 'master builders'. Late in 1937, by way of a dry run for the main project, a competition was held to design a 'University City'.[12] Its primary purpose was to recruit suitable 'remodelling architects'; and the competition brief offered an ideal basis for their selection. It incorporated all of the most important planning tasks that the GBI regarded as necessary for the future. It gave primacy to the longitudinal axis, the transverse axis and the monumental plaza, as well as the design and proportioning of large blocks as essential features of urban space. The programme also stipulated that 'construction and materials are so to be chosen that, now and in the future, the . . . buildings not only serve their immediate purpose but endure for centuries to come, as witnesses to a great past'.[13] The resulting designs (p. 286) duly brought forward a new aesthetic dimension, which was thenceforward to dominate the architecture of 'remodelling', with world hegemony in mind, on the eve of intended wars of conquest.[14]

Two views of North-South Axis model, 1941–42
Great Hall from the south; South Station and Triumphal Arch

Recruited and stage-managed by Albert Speer, whose planning section supplied the urban layout, the 'remodelling architects' now devised the decor for the North-South Axis, which was to be the climactic spectacle of the new city and the aesthetic embodiment of the Nazi state. Widened in its last version (1942) to 140 metres, its central stretch focused on a Great Plaza, on the bend in the River Spree, which was to form the new acropolis. Stone by stone, street block by street block, its axial architecture evoked imperial perspectives of future world hegemony.

This via *triumphalis* of human destruction began with a vast southern railway terminus. In front of this was a monstrous plaza, 800 metres long and 300 metres wide, bounded by a martial 'Avenue of Captured Weapons' to commemorate the victorious campaign against France. This southern plaza was to terminate in the Triumphal Arch (p. 328), more than 120 metres tall, based on sketches made by Hitler himself as far back as 1925. On the attic of the Arch would be carved the names of all those German soldiers who had fallen in the First World War, and who were thus to be converted *ex post facto* into victors.

7 Albert Speer, *Erinnerungen* (Frankfurt am Main, Berlin and Vienna, 1969), 87.

8 For a detailed account see Hans J. Reichardt and Wolfgang Schäche, *Von Berlin nach Germania. Über die Zerstörungen der Reichshauptstadt durch Albert Speers Neugestaltungsplanungen* (Berlin,²1985), and in particular the article 'Zu Geschichte und Aufbau des"Generalbauinspektors für die Reichshauptstadt Berlin" [GBI]', 35ff.

9 On the plans in general see Reichardt and Schäche (as note 8), as well as Lars Olof Larsson, *Die Neugestaltung der Reichshauptstadt. Albert Speers Generalbebauungsplan für Berlin* (Stuttgart, 1978).

10 See Franz W. Siedler, *Fritz Todt. Baumeister des Dritten Reiches* (Munich and Berlin, 1986).

11 Reichardt and Schäche (as note 8), 47ff.

12 For the competition brief see *Wettbewerb Hochschulstadt Berlin* (Berlin, 1937).

13 Ibid., 6.

Albert Speer (after Adolf Hitler), model of Triumphal Arch, 1939

14 On this see Wolfgang Schäche, 'Die Bedeutung der "Berliner Neugestaltungsmassnahmen" für die NS-Architekturproduktion. Dargestellt an der Funktion des "Generalbauinspektors für die Reichshauptstadt Berlin" [GBI]', in Berthold Hinz, Hans-Ernst Mittig, Wolfgang Schäche and Angela Schönberger, eds., *Die Dekoration der Gewalt. Kunst und Medien im Faschismus* (Giessen, 1979), 154ff.

15 Friedrich Tamms, 'Die Kriegerdenkmäler von Wilhelm Kreis', *Die Kunst im Deutschen Reich*, vol. 7, series 3, no. 3 (March 1943), 57.

16 Hans Stephan, *Die Baukunst im Dritten Reich. Insbesondere die Umgestaltung der Reichshauptstadt* (Berlin, 1939), 10.

Lined by close-packed, monumental buildings of inflated size – occupied by, among others, the Reich SS Command, the Gestapo, the German Labour Front, and a Reich Colonial Ministry – the grand avenue led to a circus, the Round Plaza, which was to be the cultural forum of the North-South Axis (with the House of Tourism, a big cinema, the Comradeship House of German Artists, the Thuringian House, and a Wehrmacht Officers' Mess).

North of the Round Plaza, and opposite Hermann Goering's office (the Reichsmarschallamt), would be the building known as the Soldiers' Hall, the hall of fame for the war heroes of the future. As part of the Army Supreme Command complex designed by Wilhelm Kreis, the Soldiers' Hall had exceptional iconographic significance for the self-image of the self-styled master race: 'The Soldiers' Hall . . . forms a contrast with all those military memorials that will mount guard throughout the freshly conquered *Lebensraum* [living space]. Its portico recalls the heritage of the West, though in a language that is all its own. Its vast internal barrel vault, with the light flooding in through the portico, is more expressive of the oath of the living than of the legacy of the dead. Only when one descends into the sepulchre, which runs as a crypt beneath the whole of the hall, does the massive weight of the vaulting invoke the admonitory presence of that spirit . . . And so, here in the Reich Capital as elsewhere, there will be a place for those who have made their sacrifice for the cause of homeland, national selfhood and *Lebensraum*. Here German people will find an awareness of the finitude of earthly life; it will be a place of reverence, admonition and homage, and therefore a shrine, hallowed by meaning and custom: a new, true, German cathedral, born of the sacrifice of those

who have laid down all that was dearest to them in order that the future might live.'[15]

The Soldiers' Hall represented a whole new dimension, unknown in any previous military memorial. In the past, people had revered or hero-worshipped the dead; but the Soldiers' Hall was planned as a 'shrine for heroes' *who had not yet been killed*. In the last resort, it was an open invitation to die a hero's death. The meaning of life was reduced to a ritual of sacrifice, thus distracting attention from the causes and the sufferings of war.

This was the principle that governed the conception and the architectural form of the North-South Axis: 'The basic stance of the new style is defined by the heroic basic stance of the National Socialist world-view. Simple, straightforward convictions call for simple, straightforward architectural expression. The organic articulation and rigorous order of the columns matches the organic rigor of the plan and elevations; the boldness and consistency of the political purpose is matched by the magnificence, boldness and consistency of the planning.'[16]

The massive pile of the Reichsmarschallamt formed a visually (though not functionally) necessary pendant to the Soldiers' Hall, and an effective introduction to the greenery of the Tiergarten, which in turn set off the distant prospect of the culminating feature of the North-South Axis: the Great Plaza, with its Great Hall, the largest building in the world (p. 283).

As recorded in final working drawings, the Great Hall was more than 300 metres square in plan. A whole district, the old Alsenviertel, together with the gentle bend in the Spree, would disappear beneath its rectilinear base block, 98 metres tall; above this, an immense dome would swell against the sky, and on its lantern an eagle would clutch the terrestrial globe in its aggressive talons. Some 320 metres in overall height, this monster was designed

to hold 180,000 people. In front of its massive portico, the wide but varied expanse of the former Königsplatz (renamed Platz der Republik in 1918) was to be paved with granite to form the Great Plaza, designed as a parade ground for a million people. The Spree would run through twin chambers beneath the Great Hall.

Enclosed and accessible only from the North-South Axis, the Great Plaza was to be lined with massive blocks of power architecture. On the west, on the site of the old Kroll amusement palace, would be the Führerpalast, a windowless pile with a single balcony, 15 metres up, over the heavy steel gates of its axial main entrance. Opposite this, and absurdly dwarfed by its surroundings, Paul Wallot's old Reichstag building (burnt out in 1933) would be restored, but only to serve as an archive, library and canteen building for its huge neighbour to the north, the new Great German Reichstag. The southern entrance to the Great Plaza, which could be blocked off with formidable wrought-iron grilles, was flanked by the new Reich Chancellery on the west, linked to the Führerpalast, and by the Wehrmacht Supreme Command on the east.

The Axis then swung northwest, where the Great Hall was mirrored in an artificial lake (the Great Basin), 1200 metres long and 400 metres wide; travellers emerging from the North Station would see its overwhelming bulk twice over. In front of the station, and at the edge of the lake, two tall, pylon-like structures crowned with eagles would define the ends of the station forecourt and simultaneously direct the eye towards the Great Hall. To the west of the Great Basin would be the Police Headquarters, the new City Hall, and the 'Technical City Hall'. To the east, precisely opposite the City Hall, would be the sprawling Naval Supreme Command (OKM) building. To the north of the OKM were to be areas of turf; to the south, the old Prussian Invalidenfriedhof (veterans' cemetery) would be left undisturbed. These open

Wilhelm Kreis, model of Soldatenhalle, 1939

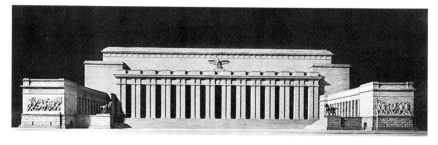

spaces were designed to enhance the effect of the OKM and to form an optical balance to the three vast buildings on the western side of the Great Basin.

In 1938 work began inside the bend of the River Spree on clearance work for the building of the Great Hall, which was scheduled to take twelve years in all. By the time all 'remodelling' works were finally halted in 1942, considerable sections of the Alsenviertel had already been demolished, street by street, or prepared for demolition. In 1937–39, all the 'heroic panoply' of German history on the old Königsplatz, including the Siegessäule (Victory Column) and the statues of Bismarck, Moltke and Roon, was moved along the East-West Axis to the expanded Grosser Stern intersection in the Tiergarten, to create a 'Forum of the Second Reich' (p. 260).

Extensive demolition also took place on the site of the Round Plaza and in the vicinity of the planned South Station. Though briefly interrupted on the outbreak of war in 1939, work here continued until late 1942.

At the end of November 1941, the GBI produced a detailed demolition and clearance plan (p. 257) for the whole central section of the North-South Axis. The first to lose their homes were Jewish citizens; to this end the GBI had a special 'Jewish dwellings' section. Their houses and apartments were 'freed' for use in a succession of wholesale eviction campaigns. Initially they were moved to emergency accommodation or allowed to take refuge with other Jews, but later the evictions were tied in with systematic mass deportations to the extermination camps.[17] Their savage fate was thus inseparably bound up with the 'remodelling' of Berlin.

If we now consider the architectural content of the 'remodelling' plans, the following emerges. Both the basic planning motif, that of the axial cross, which was applied even to the smallest

'Gau Capital', and the designs of the individual buildings along the 'grand avenue', were part of a formalistic game in which architecture and urban planning had degenerated into an additive arrangement of interchangeable components. Such features as the Round Plaza, the Great Plaza with its domed Great Hall, or the developments around the Great Basin, clearly show that functionality and fitness for purpose had lost all meaning as planning concepts. Architecture was enlisted to embellish the surfaces, and all that counted was the effect on the viewer.

The buildings were there to provide a setting for the public space that was regarded as necessary for constant spectacular assertions of the regime's claims to power and authority. The façades were debased into interchangeable set pieces, scenic flats slapped onto solid masses devoid of content; they were nothing but decor. The patterns of that decor were made up of stark, brutalized masses of stone, their artistic dimension supposedly derived from hand craftsmanship. The façade of a building was neither an expression nor a reflection of its content, but a scenic end in itself.

Architecture was envisaged as a 'World-View in Stone', with a commemorative aura of universality, timelessness, immovability, and immutability that would convey a message of overwhelming power. As a result, monumentality declined into vastness without scale; bigness coarsened into mass without dimensions. The buildings were intended as a dialectical pendant to the serried ranks and marching formations that would embody 'the tangible experience of the authority of the Fascist system'. They were to provide a disciplined framework for the 'Masses as Ornament' (Siegfried Kracauer), the end product of the rape of public space. 'Architecture' in this context was simply a backdrop for brute force.

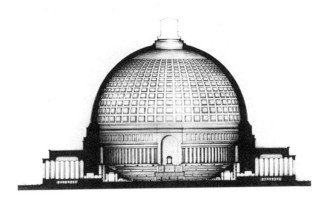

The Nazis' use of the 'architecture of remodelling' as an instrument of power was inseparably linked with rearmament and led seamlessly to war. In the synthesis of architecture, weaponry and war, borne along by the bloody elation of world conquest and the 'master race', it emerges as an aesthetic of horror. The domed Great Hall, as the emblem of desired world hegemony, is inseparable from the millions of war casualties; the Triumphal Arch, like every other block along the triumphal way, is inseparable from the destruction of cities, the deportation and annihilation of Jews, and the enslavement and murder of concentration camp prisoners.

In this connection, it was entirely appropriate that in 1942 Albert Speer was appointed Reich Minister of Armaments and War Production. He and the leading members of his GBI staff thenceforth managed the German machinery of war and destruction. 'Remodelling' had served its purpose. It found its logical conclusion in 'total war' and led straight to catastrophe.

Translated by David Britt

Albert Speer, interior of Great Hall showing speaker's dais, *c.* 1940

Great Basin, as planned in 1941, showing projected City Hall by Bestelmeyer

17 See Reichardt and Schäche (as note 8), 77.

Albert Speer, model of Reichsmar-schallamt, 1939–40

'DEGENERATE' AND 'AUTHENTIC'

Aspects of Art and Power in the Third Reich *Berthold Hinz*

The special alliance between Art and Power in Nazi Germany has a long ideological prehistory. In 1928 the Nazi party set up a supposedly nonpartisan Kampfbund or Combat League for German Culture, with the aim of politicizing the middle classes to its own advantage. In doing so, it appealed to the resentment that the triumphal progress of Modernism (in two stages, post-1900 and post-1918) had aroused, both in the conservative bourgeoisie and among the working class. Modern art was now declared to be synonymous with all manifestations of social 'degeneracy': notably with Bolshevism and Jewry, but also with speculative capitalism.

This makes it understandable that the Nazi state, after its birth in 1933, sought to manifest the incipient 'healing' of Germany by suppressing modern art. The art policy that was now inaugurated and spectacularly dramatized has been a major factor in earning the period of Nazi rule its reputation as something quintessentially 'barbaric'. It has been seen as particularly barbaric to have classified a large part – and for us today the most distinguished part – of twentieth-century art as 'degenerate art', which was then confiscated, exhibited with obloquy, and finally liquidated.

The word *barbaric* is also applied to the art and the taste that the Nazis put in place of 'degenerate art', once they had eliminated it: an art apparently calculated to appeal to the crude expectations of parvenus, military men and petits-bourgeois, and best defined by the one word *Kitsch*. It is easy – on both moral and aesthetic grounds – for us to dismiss and deride this Nazi art: and, for lack of other criteria, this has often enough been done. We also know that no contemporaries of any substance ever took it seriously.

But we ought not to shrug off the problem of 'barbarism' with quite such self-congratulatory ease. The fact is that the whole 'degenerate art' operation, and the installation of a Nazi art in its place, were essential components of a largely successful art and interior policy that played its part in consolidating both the *Führer* state and the *Volk* community, and thus materially contributed to the advent of the Second World War and to its associated crimes. So there is more to all this than a question of taste: there is a need to define political factors in the aesthetic domain.

By now, a great deal is known about the ways in which hostility to minorities is engineered and used: if the blame for generally perceived evils can be attributed to a particular, more or less clearly identifiable group, the majority will feel exonerated from all responsibility for those evils. This mechanism depends for its effect principally on clarity of presentation: minority and majority must be furnished with a clearly defined visual image – based on vague characteristics, but extending far beyond them – which gives aesthetic expression to an unequivocal value judgment.

In Germany, the showdown in the much-publicized confrontation between ('unvalued') minority and ('valued') majority was staged on the terrain of art. In Munich, in the summer of 1937, two exhibitions were mounted simultaneously, with a view to creating a spectacular contrast. These were *Entartete Kunst* (Degenerate Art), in the gallery wing of the Hofarkaden, and the first *Grosse*

Deutsche Kunstausstellung (Great German Art Exhibition), the opening show of the Haus der Deutschen Kunst in Prinzregentenstrasse, the first of Hitler's prestigious public buildings, built as a 'temple of German Art'.

The confrontation in 1937 was carefully timed. Though the Nazis had been whipping up hostility to 'degenerate art' ever since 1933, they seem to have decided not to crush it too quickly (by some such direct action as the book-burning and subsequent book-banning of 1933). Instead, the art conflict was strung out and kept going for four long years until its adroitly staged denouement. The cover illustrations of both exhibition catalogues (p. 272) were designed as unequivocal signals of the nature of the confrontation: on one side Otto Freundlich's *New Man*, derisively taken at its word, and on the other the work that

Page from *Entartete Kunst* catalogue, Munich 1937

Spread from Paul Schulze-Naumburg, *Kunst und Rasse* (1928)

Poster of *Entartete Kunst* exhibition, Hamburg 1938

was henceforth to be the emblem of 'German Art', a would-be-classical head of Pallas Athene by the Nazi party's chief designer, Richard Klein. It is no accident that both works show human faces and heads: they are physiognomical emblems of opposing kinds of art. For the Hamburg showing of the *Entartete Kunst* exhibition in 1938, 'degenerate art' was personified on the cover of the brochure not by Freundlich's *New Man* (a Late Expressionist 'Negro Sculpture') but by a typical caricature of a Jew.

This – so to speak – synoptic confrontation had been well rehearsed. In the very first years of the Nazis' 'art struggle', long before they took power in 1933, the party had pursued political polarization by polarizing – comparing and contrasting – images. The most consistent exponent of this technique was Paul Schultze-Naumburg (once a distinguished architect), whose speciality was juxtaposing clinical photographs of deformities with recent works of art (by Emil Nolde, Ernst Barlach, Erich Heckel, Karl Hofer and E. L. Kirchner, among others) and thus defining the art as pathological. In this he took his cue from treatises on ethnology and race theory, in which illustrations of somatic and above all facial types were used to demonstrate ethnic characteristics – often with an implied value judgment. In these, too, works of art were occasionally called in evidence, where there was a particularly apt point to be made. The use of clinical photographs in direct comparison with modern works of art was intended to supply quasi-scientific confirmation of the contention that the art was itself pathological. Schultze-Naumburg summarized his 'findings' in his book *Kunst und Rasse* (Art and Race), first published in Munich in 1928.

The ground was thus prepared, well before 1933, for the method that was perfected in the course of the 'degenerate art' operation. The works in question were not condemned as works of art 'in themselves', using the techniques of art criticism: they were deemed to be mirrors of reality and condemned as such. The accusation of 'degeneracy' and 'pathology' was almost always directed at the subjects of the paintings and sculptures (with a passing mention for the mental states of their creators). Whenever (as in Hitler's speeches) the enemy had to be listed, no contemporary 'ism' was left out, and

nonrepresentational art appeared alongside the rest; but in the specimen collections presented in publications and in exhibitions – in the propaganda material itself, that is – stylistic and art-historical criteria played no part whatever. Instead, figures predominated, categorized according to subject matter. In the printed guide to the Munich *Entartete Kunst* exhibition, figurative images account for fifty-two out of a total of fifty-six illustrations; and – with minimal exceptions – the same was true of the exhibition itself.

Clearly, it was hardly considered worth while to denounce works of a nonrepresentational, abstract or mainly quasi-abstract kind: the chosen targets were those that were thematically close enough to empirical reality to attract attention on a social rather than an artistic level. The figurative imagery of Expressionism, and of the 'Verism' exemplified by George Grosz and Otto Dix, lent itself particularly well to this approach. These were the two 'isms' singled out for particular denunciation in Nazi propaganda, which thus latched onto the *depictive* function of works of art. The *thing depicted* became the criterion of argument and judgment, just as if it had been a social or pathological reality. This is confirmed by most of the published texts and illustrations. Thus, the page headings in the *Entartete Kunst* exhibition guide (1937–38) are mostly about social and political themes – themes regarded by the regime as particularly strong in propaganda appeal:

'"Art" Preaches Class Conflict!'
'Painted Military Sabotage'
'The Harlot Is Held Up as a Moral Ideal!'
'"Revelations of German Religious Feeling"'

The visual image of the inferior being was self-evident and memorable: more so than verbal propaganda. The image served to channel aggressive feelings away from the real situation, and towards the individuals and groups perceived as the instigators, wire-pullers and agents of political and social evils. In the 'degenerate art' context, the enemy was not so much the art itself as the 'degenerate' human being whom it seemed to embody – and whose elimination was prompted, anticipated or accompanied by the operation against 'degenerate art'.

In this context, 'Third Reich art' can

be regarded as a programme for the visual manifestation of the authentic or 'pure-bred' alternative. Racial discrimination – i.e., exclusion – always implies inclusion: the inclusion of those who do the discriminating. Just as the objects of discrimination are given a negative image, the discriminators give themselves a positive one. Negative and positive art policies are thus inseparable.

And so, with Pallas Athene as its trademark, 'Third Reich art' elected to visualize the 'authentic' being (human or animal) in terms of its 'biological optimum forms' (F. A. Kauffmann, 1941). For this purpose, traditional forms of painting and sculpture, whether naturalistic or idealistic, commended themselves. It has been clear for some time now that 1933 brought no sudden emergence of a new, genuinely National Socialist art with an unmistakable profile: on an artistic and a personal level, existing traditions were reactivated. It is noticeable that the Nazi veterans of the 'years of struggle', such exponents of ultranationalist art as Fidus (alias Hugo Höppener), Franz Stassen, Hans Adolf Bühler and Paul Schultze-Naumburg – men who had seen themselves as the arbiters of future art policy – did not come to the fore. What was wanted was not proven ideological soundness (Emil Nolde was a case in point!) but a form that could provide a convincing counter-image to set against the phenomena of 'degeneracy'.

Both of the artistic traditions named above – naturalistic and idealistic – were entirely compatible with the techniques of *Neue Sachlichkeit*: simplification, smoothing, harmonizing. And so the unmistakable style of Nazi realism gradually emerged. Though the 1937 exhibition was not exactly a resounding

Richard Klein, *Awakening*, 1937

success in this respect, it established trends that gradually took shape over the following years. A pioneer example of the 'New Man' as seen from a racial and Nazi viewpoint – and another counter-image to Freundlich's eponymous head – is Klein's *Awakening* (p. 331), the keynote image of the *Grosse Deutsche Kunstausstellung* of 1937. Its title and its physical presence made it the emblem of the 'national body', now cleansed of its impurities.

Equally crucial were the small and initially inconspicuous changes through which themes, forms, and formats were brought into line, and which led to the emergence of a striking, 'positive' counter-image to 'degenerate art' (and particularly to its images of 'degenerate' nature and 'degenerate' humanity). In the career of an artist like Georg Kolbe, who in 1933 was already well established, with a clearly defined personal style, we trace a marked tendency not only to work on a larger scale but to move from the subjective to the exemplary. Kolbe's earlier work (see *Night*, 1930) shows mobility and dynamic balance, together with apparently chance irregularities in both anatomy and technique. Later, all this is eliminated: the attitude becomes a pose; stability triumphs; the surface changes from an artistic texture into a smooth, encasing, body-sheathing skin (see *The Protectress*, 1938). The image of the contemporary sportsman and sportswoman begins to dominate.

The same rounded forms and fully modelled physiques found their way into paintings and came to dominate their structure. Here the prime example is that of Adolf Ziegler, whose sole subject, the female nude, dispenses with all but the minimum of thematic justification and comes to stand for a purely external,

physical presence. In all this, Ziegler, who also held office for a time as president of the Reich Chamber of Fine Arts and took charge of the 'degenerate art' operation, was followed by numerous younger artists, who turned his kind of modelling into a standardized technique. Here there is certainly a link with the painting of *Neue Sachlichkeit*, which Hitler expressly denounced, but which found its way into the art shows of the Nazi State on a broad front, shielded from criticism by neatness of technique and unexceptionable subject matter. In the process, both figures and objects lost the authentically 'sober' (*sachlich*) introversion of *Neue Sachlichkeit* and turned into exemplary embodiments, models of prototypes.

No area of subject matter remained unaffected by this development, as can be seen from the landscapes, portraits and technological, industrial and military scenes of the period. But, in the wake of Klein and Ziegler, the central image of Nazi art was the human figure. In painting, this was almost exclusively female; in sculpture, the sexes were better balanced. Visitors to art exhibitions found themselves inspecting serried ranks of idealized but visibly *physical* and *contemporary* bodies, which nevertheless showed a marked tendency to sport outfits, names and titles from classical mythology. There was no sign of the Germanic and Nordic themes that Nazi ideology might have led one to expect; no doubt this was because Teutonic mythology lacked a developed visual imagery of characters and bodies that might have served as recognizable prototypes. (In literature, with no visual imagery, Nordic and Germanic themes predominated, as ideology dictated.)

These formal and motivic tendencies emerged in the absence of any overt state control; and a study of the available illustration material reveals how this was able to happen. Reproductions were published in vast quantities, throughout the mass-circulation press, and even on the front pages of daily newspapers (principally in response to the annual *Grosse Deutsche Kunstausstellung*, held in Munich from 1937 to 1944). Additionally, some works were reproduced again and again: after the initial wave of topical appearances in the press and newsreels, they turned up as the favourites of writers and editors and were marketed by public bodies and commercial interests alike, in

brochures, colour prints, books, postcards and elsewhere. These selection and dissemination processes frequently began with purchases made by leading State and party figures ('Acquired by the Führer/Reichsmarschall'), which were then confirmed through the prompt involvement of market forces. There was thus no need of any official *Diktat* to create the specific trends that resulted in something like a specific artistic profile of National Socialism. It seems, in fact, that the very process by which the work made its way into the public domain helped to define its distinctive imagery and formal idiom.

It has frequently been observed that 'Third Reich art', both painting and sculpture, looks like a photograph; but this comment has most often been based on knowledge not of the original but of a reproduction. The originals themselves confound our expectations. They surprise us by their unexpectedly large dimensions; and yet their linear layout, precise outlines and even, poster-like application of colour makes them look rather dull and flat. These are precisely the characteristics required for successful reproduction; and, when reproduced, they look like a quasi-photographic representation of nature. The artist seems to have anticipated the requirements of technology; the handling looks like a calculated response to the requirements of reproduction and mass publication.

Over and above these technological, not to say technocratic aspects, the media alliance inevitably also influenced the artistic and formal outcome. However, the experience of Pop Art and Photorealism should warn us against too readily dismissing the resulting 'facsimile appeal' as the triumph of crass and vulgar taste. Modern advertising techniques might suggest a way to gain a more critical understanding of the artistic principles that we see in operation under the Third Reich: by which I mean the suggestive, almost physical sense of self-identification which is vital to successful advertising – and which springs from imagery designed in this way.

Such was the authentic art of Nazism; and it followed a course first set by the prototypical twentieth-century art of illusion, the cinema. The key event in this aesthetic context was staging of the Olympic Games in Berlin in 1936, which afforded a perfect opportunity to turn

Georg Kolbe, *Night*, 1930

Georg Kolbe, *The Protectress*, 1938

physical culture and physical beauty – the propaganda value of which had now been discovered – into a subject for media presentation. The decisive breakthrough came with Leni Riefenstahl's film of the 1936 Olympics, *Olympia: Fest der Völker – Fest der Schönheit*, which shifted Hitler's traditionally rather prudish 'Movement' away from its old, defensive posture. The key sequence comes at the start of the film, when, by way of overture, images of famous antique statues, male and female, are illusionistically crossfaded to shots of men and women posing naked in the same poses: this is a naturalization of the ideal, and simultaneously an idealization of nature (p. 267).

The art-nature relationship, thus presented by Riefenstahl as a seamless metamorphosis, subsequently became a sanctioned partnership in art publishing: the photograph and the artwork side by side. Picture books werepublished, in which identical motifs were juxtaposed in painted and photographed form; and the resulting artistic perceptions led to a close formal and motivic affinity between photography and fine art. A method first explored as a negative ploy – that of presenting 'degenerate' art side by side with photographs of 'degenerate' (because 'racially alien' or pathological) persons, with a view to discrediting both – could now be used to juxtapose exemplary images in art with those in nature (photography). The two techniques of presentation served to authenticate each other: the painted or sculptured representation of a person certified by racial doctrine as the 'optimum biological form' sought photographic confirmation from reality. Conversely, his or her photographic representation needed art to confirm its credentials as an expression of the ideal. There could thus be a visible concordance between the real, as exemplified by photography and film, and the ideal, as vouched for by art.

In accordance with a universally valid principle of modern (visual) advertising, namely that the consumer is recruited into a specific image group, the imagery of National Socialism (which of course was a monopoly, unlike the imagery of the marketplace) aimed to ensure that the members of the *Volk* would belong and (at least subliminally) adhere to the 'race community'. Once the 'degenerate' (artworks and people) had been excluded, the 'pure-bred' or 'authentic' (artworks

and people) could be *in*cluded. Just as the ugly image of the common foe served as a dump for all inner and social conflict (and was ultimately liquidated), the visualized racial ideal could visibly reflect the 'body of the nation', cleansed of inner conflict: beyond all social boundaries and conflicts, the nation had been *aesthetically* 'socialized'.

Translated by David Britt

Literature
General:
Hans-Ernst Mittig, 'Kunst und Propaganda im NS-System', in *Funkkolleg Moderne Kunst, Studienbegleitbrief 9* (Weinheim/Basel, 1990),
11-48.
Art and politics: Hildegard Brenner, *Die Kunstpolitik des Nationalsozialismus* (Reinbek bei Hamburg, 1963); Otto Thomas, *Die Propaganda-Maschinerie. Bildende Kunst und Öffentlichkeit im Dritten Reich* (Berlin, 1978).
Painting: Berthold Hinz, *Die Malerei im deutschen Faschismus. Kunst und Konterrevolution* (Munich, 1974).
Sculpture: Klaus Wolbert, *Die Nackten und die Toten des 'Dritten Reichs'. Folgen einer politischen Geschichte des Körpers in der Plastik des deutschen Faschismus* (Giessen, 1982); exh. cat. *Skulptur und Macht. Figurative Plastik im Deutschland der 30er und 40er Jahre* (Berlin: Akademie der Künste, 1983).
'Degenerate Art': exh. cat. *Die Kunststadt München 1937. Nationalsozialismus und 'Entartete Kunst'*, Munich: Staatsgalerie moderner Kunst, 1987; Peter-Klaus Schuster, ed., *Ergänzungsband: Dokumentation zum nationalsozialistischen Bildersturm am Bestand der Staatsgalerie moderner Kunst in München* (Munich,1987); Review of the above by Hans-Ernst Mittig, *Kritische Blätter 16* (1988), no. 2, 76-88; Kathrin Hoffmann-Curtius, "Entartete Kunst". Die Nationalsozialisten und die moderne Kunst', in *Funkkolleg Moderne Kunst, Studienbegleitbrief 9* (Weinheim/Basel, 1990), 49-88; exh. cat. *'Degenerate Art': The Fate of the Avant-Garde in Nazi Germany* (Los Angeles: Los Angeles County Museum of Art, 1991; Berlin; Altes Museum, 1992).
Art and media: Berthold Hinz, Hans-Ernst Mittig, Wolfgang Schäche, Angela Schönberger, eds., *Die Dekoration der Gewalt. Kunst und Medien im Faschismus* (Giessen, 1979)
History of research: Berthold Hinz, '1933/45: Ein Kapitel kunstgeschichtlicher Forschung seit 1945', *Kritische Berichte 14* (1986), no. 4, 18-33.

Images from H. W. Fischer, *Menschenschönheit* (1935): Wilhelm Leibl (1844–1900), *Dachau Woman*; photograph by Retzlaff

Julius Engelhardt, *Bathing in a Mountain Lake*, 1944; Bather, photograph from W. Burghardt, *Sieg der Körperfreude* (1940)

Spread from magazine *Kunst im deutschen Reich* (1941), showing work by Alfred Zschorsch, Adolf Abel, Adolf Wamper

TECTONIC SCULPTURE

Autonomous and political sculpture in Germany *Bernd Nicolai*

'"Of course," he thought, "it could only be about this figure." Gregor could well understand why the others did not want to let the young man go on sitting and reading. Anyone who sat reading like that was a menace.

Knudsen, too, looked at the figure. "That thing there?" he asked in amazement. "What's that supposed to represent?"

"The figure is called *Monastery Schoolboy, Reading*," explained Helander.' (Alfred Andersch, *Sansibar oder der letzte Grund*, 1957.)[1]

'The commitment to the laws of architecture and the experience of the supra-individual substance of the political message of our era has extended Breker's will-to-form to monumental dimensions . . . Every last feature of the artistic style represents a total fusion of form and content.' (Robert Scholz on Arno Breker, 1942.)[2]

The triumphal progress of abstract sculpture since 1945 has tended to make us forget the diversity of figurative sculpture in the preceding decades. Under the respective headings 'tectonic' and 'architectonic', the opposing polarities of autonomous sculpture, on the one hand, and sculpture intended for a particular setting on the other, dominated the artistic and art-historical debate in this field from the beginning of the twentieth century onward. Under the National Socialist regime in Germany, these differences became manifest. Sculptures that looked comparatively similar could be evaluated quite differently, in ideological terms, on the basis of their 'inner conception'. The question at issue was this: to what degree could sculpture be politically instrumentalized? On one side stood political, racially determined sculpture, conceived in close collaboration with architecture; on the other the autonomous, timeless figure, sufficient unto itself.

Our attempts to clarify the criteria involved are complicated by the fact that both categories of sculpture are ultimately based on a conception of antiquity – or rather on two very different conceptions of antiquity, which are too often lumped together. If we free ourselves from the categories of abstract and realist sculpture, then 'a work by Kasper (or by Marcks or Blumenthal) stands infinitely closer, intellectually, to the so-called "abstract" sculpture of, say, Brancusi than to the sculptural muscle men that paraded in front of the buildings of the Third Reich'.[3] Why this should be the case will be explained in this essay, by reference to individual sculptors from the National Socialist era. But first a brief summary of the 'tectonic' debate.

In the context of architecture the word *tectonic* has been used since the Neoclassical era to describe the clearly articulated, formally and symmetrically composed structures represented in Germany by the works of Friedrich Gilly and Karl Friedrich Schinkel. The term was first appropriated for sculpture by Adolf von Hildebrand in his polemical text *Das Problem der Form in der bildenden Kunst* (1893), in which he described 'the architectonic', or 'the inner construction', as a constituent quality that goes beyond the merely 'imitative' and transforms the work of sculpture into an 'independent whole, able to assert itself beside and against nature'.[4] This interpretation, based on the theories of Hans von Marées, led Hildebrand to produce sculpture intended to be viewed – like a relief – from one side only. The figure was to emerge out of the plane and be comprehensible at a glance.

This theory was opposed by a model derived from the classical Greek principle of free-standing sculpture. As Aristide Maillol put it: 'I seek architecture and corporeal volumes. Sculpture is architecture, equipoise of masses, tasteful composition.'[5] And, according to Julius Meier-Graefe, it was Maillol who instilled 'a more rigorous attitude' into 'lyrical' sculptors such as the young Georg Kolbe or Karl Albiker. Hermann Haller worked variations on this theme; others, such as René Sintenis or Ernesto de Fiori, found a tradition already established for them.[6]

After the First World War, Neoclassicists and the avant-garde converged towards the notion of the 'simple plastic constellation'. Eventually, writing in 1923, Paul Westheim united archaic Greek and modern sculpture in a way that emphasized the autonomous character of art. The Hera of Samos, he wrote, 'can appear in no other way than as the brilliant realization of a discipline, the discipline of spiritual consciousness. This Hera is a construction, if you will, with the logical consistency of a modern bridge structure; one that has not become an intellectualized abstraction but has sought to project a Poussinesque or Cézannesque spirit into the realm of the expressive and the sensuous. This process of construction —which at the same time is a process of forming – this incarnation of sculptural energy is to be understood as the architectonics of the plastic art.'[7]

For Westheim, monumentality lay in substance and in the 'inner dimension', rather than in scale. He thus established a theoretical basis for the approach to archaic Greek sculpture, which could accommodate autonomous and abstracting elements with equal ease. This was in contrast to the approach based on the classical canon of Polyclitus, which had been a constant component of the Berlin sculptural tradition ever since Schadow and Raich, but which had been installed afresh in Munich through the influence of Hildebrand. In this respect, modern sculptors like Kolbe, Scheibe, Marcks, and even Thorak were tied to a form of naturalism that imprisoned their work in a time-specific, almost modish aspect.

Under National Socialism, alongside the general deprivation of social rights, and the persecution of such diverse ethnic groups as Jews and Gypsies, artistic freedom was curtailed in a surely unique manner. Following an initial period of a few years in which no coherent cultural policies were apparent, the 1936 Olympic Games were followed by the exhibition *Entartete Kunst* (Degenerate Art), held in Munich in 1937, and the anathematization of the avant-garde (including those elements of it which were thoroughly nationalistic). Concurrently, in the parallel *Grosse Deutsche Kunstausstellung* (Great German Art Exhibition), Hitler proclaimed a new,

1 Alfred Andersch, *Sansibar oder der letzte Grund* (Zürich, 1970 [first edition 1957]), in reference to a fictional sculpture by Ernst Barlach during the 'Degenerate Art' campaign in Germany, 1937.

2 Robert Scholz, 'Die Sendung der neuen deutschen Plastik: Zur Arno Breker-Kollektivausstellung in Paris', *Kunst im Deutschen Reich*, no. 6 (1942), 172.

3 Werner Haftmann, *Der Bildhauer Ludwig Kasper* (Munich, 1978), 25.

4 Adolf von Hildebrand, *Das Problem der Form in der bildenden Künste* (Munich, 1893; 10th ed., Baden-Baden and Strasbourg, 1961). Included in Harry Mallgrave and Eleftherios Ikonomou, ed. and tr., *Empathy, Form, and Space; Problems in German Aesthetics 1873–1893* (Santa Monica, 1994), 227ff.

5 Quoted by Eduard Trier, *Bildhauertheorien des 20. Jahrhunderts* (Berlin, 1971), 53.

6 Julius Meier-Graefe, *Die Entwicklungsgeschichte der modernen Kunst*, 2nd ed. (Munich, 1927), 3:547–51.

7 Paul Westheim, *Architektonik des Plastischen* (Berlin, 1923), 9f.

8 Adolf Hitler, speech at the opening of the House of German Art, Munich, 1937, quoted in German and in English in Stephanie Barron, ed., exh. cat. 'Degenerate Art', (Los Angeles, 1991), 384. Quoted here in the translation made by John Willett for the present volume.

racially motivated, classicizing ideal of the body, which was to be imposed as the new norm:

'Never was Mankind closer than now to Antiquity in its appearance and its sensibilities. Sport, contests and competition are hardening millions of youthful bodies, displaying them to us more and more in a form and temper that they have neither manifested nor been thought to possess for perhaps a thousand years . . . This human type, which we saw appearing before the whole world last year at the Olympic Games in its proud, radiant physical power and fitness, this human type (O you prehistoric art stutterers!) is the type of the New Age.'[8]

Hitler thus laid down an official, and utterly superficial, definition of the ideal sculptural image. Works of sculpture were to be symbols of the new society, one that admitted only the healthy and the racially pure. In this respect, the sculptural modelling of the outer surface of the skin – the external limits of the body – played an absolutely critical role. At the same time, there was a total rejection of those 'reflections on reality' (Wahrbilder) that took as their theme the inner condition of man.

The identity crisis of the Weimar Republic had found clear expression before 1933 in the controversy over the war memorial made by Ernst Barlach for Magdeburg in 1928–29. This was a fundamental confrontation between reactionary and liberal forces about the way in which the First World War should be remembered: it was all about avenging humiliation on one side, all about grief and understanding on the other. With his memorial, Barlach broke a taboo by allegorically representing the horrors of the poison-gas war, of death and despair. These soldiers were not radiant victors but men marked down to die. Barlach had created a 'reflection' of the reality of war, and thus a 'pure expression', which denied any ulterior purpose or instrumentalization.

As soon as the work was unveiled, the three soldiers were reviled as 'cross-eyed, half-witted Territorials', who stood side by side looking 'dull and imbecilic'. In 1934 the memorial was taken down and sent to the auction of 'degenerate' art held in 1938 at Lucerne, where it was bought by Barlach's sponsors Hetsch and Böhmer and in this way preserved.[9] In its weight and gravity, Barlach's sculpture can be compared with that of Käthe Kollwitz. Yet Kollwitz had a greater didactic intention and invested her work with an a priori social function.

The absolute opposite might be said of Beckmann's figures. These are private allegories of the forlornness of exile. Man in the Dark and Adam and Eve go back to existential or archetypical themes. In the case of Beckmann, one can see in the recourse to historical formats – as in the triptychs and self-portraits – a specific imagery of exile, which in his sculptures runs counter to every tradition. Beckmann's pessimism leads to a primitivism that might be compared – if with anything – with the figures of Ernst Ludwig Kirchner.[10]

These works of Beckmann's represent an unequivocal rejection of the human type demanded by the National Socialist authorities; sculptors like Toni Stadler or Ludwig Kasper continued to make classicizing references, but strictly as formal experiments. In their archetypical stylization, the resulting works are definitely not 'expressive figures' but rather meditative focuses. As Werner Haftmann wrote in 1939, in a monograph on Kasper that was banned by the regime: 'This sculpture is intentionally impersonal. It is neither impressionistic nor expressionistic. It stands outside the general realm of human receptivity and expressivity. The object and the impression it makes are important, insofar as within this object the imaginary figure is able to develop the inner logic of its own beauty. It is inexpressive, in that it is not the vehicle of an emotional experience but rather creates a new, self-sufficient existence.'[11]

This quality is manifest even in a public sculpture like Kasper's Spear Carrier, made in 1938 as a commission for a Luftwaffe base. Through its reference to the classical kouros, the figure remains hermetically closed.[12] It is not an expressive figure in an affirmative sense – as are, for example, Kolbe's war memorial in Stralsund (1933–35) or his Great Guardian for the anti-aircraft barracks in Lüdenscheid (1936–37). In addition to Kasper and Stadler, Joachim Karsch and, in particular, Hermann Blumenthal belong to the group of sculptors that doggedly worked on in the 'Berlin exile' of their shared studio in Klosterstrasse. In his Roman Man (1935) and Stargazer (1936), Blumenthal created two of the

9 Kristine Pollack and Bernd Nicolai, 'Kriegsdenkmale, Denkmäler für den Krieg?', in exh. cat. Skulptur und Macht, (Berlin, 1983), p. 68, cat. no. 3.23; Ernst Piper, Nationalsozialistische Kunstpolitik: Ernst Barlach und die 'entartete Kunst' (Frankfurt am Main, 1987), documents 5–19.

10 See Cornelia Stabenow, 'Metaphern der Ohnmacht: Zu den Plastiken Max Beckmanns', in exh. cat. Max Beckmann Retrospektive (Munich, 1984), 140ff.

11 Haftmann (as note 3), 8. For a critique of Haftmann's book and of Kaspar's art, see Deutscher Wochendienst, 15 January 1943, quoted in Otto Thomae, Die Propagandamaschinerie des 3. Reichs (Berlin, 1978), 494. Deutscher Wochendienst complained that the 'anonymity and generality of the object . . . is taken too far'.

12 See exh. cat. Archaik und Moderne: Statuarische Plastik im 20. Jahrhundert (Berlin, 1982); Bruno E. Werner, Deutsche Plastik der Gegenwart (Berlin, 1940), 126, 129–31.

Ludwig Kasper, *Spear Carrier*, 1938

Ernst Barlach, *War Memorial*, Magdeburg Cathedral, 1938

13 Concept from Bruno Kroll, 'Tektonische Plastik: Neue Arbeiten von Ludwig Kaspar', *Kunst für Alle* 54 (1938–39), 99–105.

14 Max Sauerlandt, *Deutsche Bildhauer um 1900 von Hildebrand bis Lehmbruck* (Königstein im Taunus and Leipzig, 1925). See Alfred Hentzen, *Deutsche Bildhauer der Gegenwart* (Berlin, 1934), p. 7. Like Werner Haftmann's book on Kaspar, this book was banned shortly after publication because it covered the ostracized sculptors in detail. See Magdalena Bushart, 'Bauplastik im Dritten Reich', in Bushart, Bernd Nicolai et al., *Architektur, Bildhauerei und ihre Instrumentalisierung 1920 bis 1960* (Berlin, 1985), 104–13.

15 Kurt Lothar Tank, *Deutsche Plastik unserer Zeit* (Munich, 1942), 103, 105.

Josef Thorak, *Monumental Group*, German Pavilion, Paris 1937

principal works of this classicizing tendency.

Such cerebral images mark, if indirectly, an insistence on the private sphere, and the attempt to escape from the external world of total control. In their timeless, archetypical form, they do nothing to confront the naked embodiment of the racist ideal; and yet they could never be exploited or put to use by the National Socialist authorities.

Josef Thorak, *Monumental Group*, Security Monument, Ankara 1934–36

While 'tectonic sculpture'[13] in one sense had affirmed the autonomy and modernity of sculpture, a second tendency interpreted tectonics primarily in terms of the nexus of architecture and sculpture. The critics Sauerlandt and Hentzen had already characterized sculpture as a 'not entirely free art', which they felt was at its most effective in conjunction with architecture.[14]

In 1942 Kurt Lothar Tank celebrated Josef Thorak as a 'master of architectonic sculpture': this in order to argue that 'The new German man, the warrior as portrayed by Thorak, is produced by a mighty spiritual movement. For this reason, massive dimensions are not a danger to Thorak; we must imagine them set in the context of the new state architecture.'[15]

Even before the enormous state commissions that began in 1937, Thorak was working 'architectonically': as in *Penthesilea*, a terracotta high-relief figure for the Kleist School in Berlin (1928–29), and in the Security Monument, erected in Ankara (1934–36) for the new Turkey of Kemal Atatürk. In the latter project, Thorak worked out in the greatest detail some figure groupings that were subsequently to make him famous. In contrast to Anton Hanak's bronze figures on the front side of the monument, Thorak's muscular figures of Atatürk's attendants are more strongly stylized and reduced to essentials, without losing their terse expressiveness. They recall the classical motif of armour in the form of a muscular torso, as revived in 1906 by Louis Tuaillon's equestrian statue of Kaiser Friedrich III in Bremen. Thorak took this a step further – as did his colleague and rival Arno Breker – by fusing together the classical armour and the surface of the skin to create an armoured body.

This inflated the athlete into the warrior, the emblem of personal and ideological invulnerability.[16] This became the hallmark of political sculpture in Germany during the 1930s.[17] It was the pair of figures on the left-hand side that formed the prototype of the group *Comradeship*, which in 1937, augmented by a third figure, flanked the German Pavilion at the International Exhibition in Paris. However, in Germany itself Thorak never again tied his figures to architectural form.

The sculptures made for the Olympic

Karl Albiker, *Discus Throwers*, Olympic Stadium, Berlin 1936

Games site in 1936 – such as Karl Albiker's *Discus Throwers* or Josef Wackerle's *Horse Leaders* (p. 265) at the Marathon Portal – represented the last attempt to build limestone figures into architectural structures. The classical norms proclaimed by Hitler demanded the abandonment of the tectonic stone sculptural tradition that had flourished in Germany since 1905 or so. After 1937, giant bronze sculptures had to be produced to stand in front of architecture. In formal terms, these works followed Hildebrand's notion of a single viewing point. As a result, they complemented their architectural backgrounds almost like reliefs. The example of the German Pavilion at the International Exhibition in Paris makes clear the new function of sculpture: the clumsily assembled groups of three figures were intended to emphasize the architectural form of the pavilion.

The question was thus posed: how substantial could such sculptures actually be? In them, apart from generalities like power, strength, health, and vehement gesture, there are very few specific qualities to be discerned: only formal elements. The sculptures of Breker and Thorak drew their significance from specific ideological usage rather than from their function as images.

Until 1933, Arno Breker had been influenced by a quite different sculptural tradition, derived from Rodin and Despiau; he radically changed his conception of sculpture in response to the new opportunities afforded by the National Socialist regime: 'He had heard the call of the Reich as an inner appeal, and this appeal – which struck his will – also changed his style.'[18] Setting out from his still very archaic-looking figures of the (female) *Winner* and the *Decathlete* in the House of German Sport on the 1936 Olympic Games site, Breker embarked, with the allegories of *The Party* and *The Wehrmacht* for the New Reich Chancellery in Berlin, on a series of figures that could be described as political. Central to these works is the fact that, for Breker, artistic and political conviction were one and the same: 'An "uncompromising embodiment of a new artistic will" can be recognized in these works – a concept of beauty in which, "besides Nordic racial feeling, the substance is visibly penetrated by the inward emanation of a significant will".'[19]

For the benefit of those engaged in 'art reporting' – art criticism was not allowed – Goebbels stressed the inseparability of political patronage and artistic form. Breker accordingly turned out his sculpture on an industrial scale at the factory premises of 'Steinbildhauer Werkstätten Arno Breker GmbH' (Arno Breker Statue Workshop Ltd), at Wriezen, which came under state ownership in 1941 under the aegis of Albert Speer's General Building Inspectorate (see Wolfgang Schäche's essay, above). The actual content of its products was so non-specific that a figure like *Preparedness* was earmarked for a total of three different sites. Even individual body parts, such as heads and limbs, were interchangeable.[20]

In formal terms, the classical references and gestural language of Breker's sculptural figures are quite different to those of works by Kolbe and

Arno Breker, *Vocation*, 1940; *Harbinger*, 1941, both seen at Eberswalde

Scheibe. *Contrapposto* is a motif, rather than a compositional device designed to pay homage to the antique. The torsos of Breker's figures, beginning with *The Party* and *The Wehrmacht* and moving on via *Preparedness* to *Harbinger* and *Vocation*, are markedly frontal in alignment, and convey an impression of rigidness and inflexibility – the image of the armoured breastplate. Horizontal hip and shoulder lines emphasize the rigidity of the composition. The gestures turn the always naked figures into shells for an ideological function.

The sculptures extract their specific meaning exclusively from the architectural or propagandistic space in which they are located: *The Party* and *The Wehrmacht* in the courtyard of the New Reich Chancellery; *Vocation* on the fountain in the square in front of the Great Hall; *Preparedness* as the crowning element of the proposed Mussoliniplatz in Berlin (p. 260), or else on the parade ground in Nuremberg. (Yet they contain contemporary elements as well: the haircuts are generally fashionable ones for the period, and it is not difficult to date them to the 1930s or 1940s.)

As Magdalena Bushart has shown, as soon as these figures are removed from their intended site and located in a different context – for example, on the Soviet Army sports arena in Eberswalde – they entirely lose their original significance.[21] In defiance of the National Socialist propaganda purpose that loaded these works with meaning and ideological imperatives, the forms themselves turn out to be extraordinarily devoid of content, amounting to no more than the

cliché of a combative sporting figure. This emptiness was, of course, necessary for the initial 'loading' of the figures with political meaning.

When compared with such works as these, the ostensibly 'inexpressive', autonomous, archaic figures of a sculptor like Kasper, with their avoidance of the accidental or contingent, take on a distinctly subversive weight of meaning.

Translated by Iain Boyd Whyte

16 On the equestrian statue in Bremen, see Gert-Dieter Ulferts, *Louis Tuaillon* (Berlin, 1933), 99f., cat. no. 22; on the body as armour see Klaus Theweleit, *Männerphantasien* (Reinbek, 1980); on the Security Monument, built under the direction of Clemens Holzmeister to mark the entrance to the government quarter in Ankara, see Hermann Neumann, 'Der Bildhauer Josef Thorak', doctoral dissertation, T.U. Munich, 1989, 592–94; and Bernd Nicolai, 'Moderne und Exil: Deutschsprachige Architekten in der Türkei 1925–1955', professorial dissertation, T.U. Berlin, 1995, 39ff.

17 See Pollack and Nicolai (as note 9), 61–92, cat. no. 3.10.

18 Tank (as note 15), 113.

19 Werner Rittich, 'Zu einigen neueren Werken des Bildhauers Arno Breker', *Kunst im Deutschen Reich* 7 (1943): 236.

20 See Magdalena Bushart, 'Arno Breker: Kunstproduzent im Dienst der Macht', in *Skulptur und Macht* (as note 9), 179–82.

21 Magdalena Bushart, 'Überraschende Begegnungen mit alten Bekannten: Arno Brekers NS-Plastik in neuer Umgebung', *Kritische Berichte*, 17 (1989): 31–50.

Arno Breker, *The Party*, New Reich Chancellery, Berlin 1939

CONTEMPORARY VOICES *Compiled by John Willett*

Peroration of Speech at the Great German Art Exhibition, 1937 *Adolf Hitler*

Any artist who counts on being exhibited in this House, or making any sort of future appearance in Germany, must have a certain competence. His will to do so can surely be assumed from the start! For it would be beyond all bounds for anybody to force his works on his fellow-citizens unless they embodied Will. But when these mountebanks try to make their works seem palatable by offering them as expressions of a New Age, then they have to be informed that it is not Art that creates New Ages, but the ordinary life of a People that adopts new forms and accordingly often seeks a new expression. It is only those who spoke of New Art in the Germany of recent years that failed to understand Germany's New Age. For it is not writers but fighters that shape a new epoch: i.e. the truly formative Leaders of Peoples, the figures who thereby make History. This is something to which those wretched muddled dabblers and scribblers would hardly lay claim. Moreover it is either an outrageous impertinence or a barely comprehensible stupidity to offer our present Age works that might have been made by Stone Age Man some ten or twenty thousand years ago.

They talk about Art being Primitive, quite forgetting that it is not the task of Art to distance itself regressively from the development of a People; on the contrary, its task can only be to symbolize this living development.

Today's New Age is at work on a new type of Mankind. Enormous efforts are bearing fruit in countless departments of Life so as to elevate the People, making our men, boys and youths, or girls and women, healthier and thereby stronger and more beautiful. And from this power and this beauty flows a new sense of Life, a new joy of Living.

Never was Mankind closer than now to Antiquity in its appearance and its sensibilities. Sport, contests and competition are hardening millions of youthful bodies, displaying them to us more and more in a form and temper that they have neither manifested nor been thought to possess for perhaps a thousand years. A radiantly beautiful human type is growing up, the most intensive of whose work achievements do honour to that fine old phrase: 'Weeks of sweat, days of joy.'

This human type, which we saw appearing before the whole world last year at the Olympic Games in its proud, radiant physical power and fitness, this human type (O you prehistoric art stutterers!) is the type of the New Age. Meanwhile, what are you manufacturing? Deformed cripples and cretins, women who look merely loathsome, men who resemble beasts rather than humans, children that if encountered in real life would be viewed as a curse of God. And this is what our horrible amateurs nowadays have the effrontery to put forward as the Art of our Age: i.e. as the expression of what is being created under the stamp of the present day.

Never let it be said that these artists see things this way. Among the pictures submitted here I have observed several works where one can indeed only conclude that some people's eyes do not see things as they are, i.e. that there truly are those who see our People as nothing but total cretins, who feel (or they would say 'experience') blue fields, green skies, sulphur-yellow clouds etc. I am not going to get involved in an argument as to whether those concerned really do or do not see and feel everything this way, but I would like in the name of the German People simply to forbid such unfortunates, who are clearly having trouble with their vision, from thrusting their erroneous observations on the rest of us as Reality, even putting them forward as 'Art'.

No, there are only two possibilities. Either these so-called 'Artists' really do see things that way, and therefore believe what they are depicting – in which case their defective vision must be due to mechanical factors or to heredity. The one being a profound tragedy for the unhappy offenders, the other a matter for the Reich Ministry of the Interior, which would have to tackle the question of how to prevent the hereditary transmission of such frightful defects in future. Alternatively, they may not actually believe in the reality of such impressions but have other motives for imposing their humbug on the Nation – in which case their action renders them liable to criminal prosecution. Anyway, this House was neither planned nor built for works by such incompetents and abusers of Art.

Nor, above all, did it take four and a half years' work, demanding the maximum

productivity from a thousand workers, in order to exhibit the products of persons so corrupt as to spend five hours daubing a canvas in the hope and belief that its risky accolade as the brilliant offspring of a genius of that kind would make the required impression and justify its acceptance. No, the sweat expended by the builder of this House, along with the sweat of his fellow-workers, has to be matched by the sweat of whoever wishes to be shown in it. Nor am I in the least bit interested as to whether these pseudo-artists cluck mutual approval of the eggs they hatch or not!

For the artist creates not for artists but, exactly like everybody else, for the People!

And we shall be concerned to see that henceforward the People is called upon to be the judge of its Art.

For do not let it be said that the People lacks real understanding for the truly worthwhile enrichment of its cultural life. Long before the critics justly appreciated the genius of a Richard Wagner, the People were with him. In recent years, by contrast, the People had absolutely no more use for the so-called modern art that was put in front of them. They had no kind of relationship with it. The broad masses would pass through our art exhibitions without showing the least interest, or simply stay away. Their healthy reaction was to see all such rubbish as it was, as a monstrosity born of shameless and impertinent pretensions or else of an alarming inadequacy. Millions of our people were instinctively convinced that the art chatter of these last decades, corresponding as it did to the clumsy achievements of untalented children between eight and ten, is in no way to be adjudged an expression of our present Age, let alone the Future of Germany.

If today we know that every single human being repeats in a few decades within himself our evolution over millions of years, then we can see the proof that an artistic output no better than the achievements of a child of eight is not 'modern' or 'forward-looking' but on the contrary very old-fashioned. For it lies right back beyond the period when Stone Age Man used to scratch what he observed of his surroundings on the wall of his cave. So these bunglers are by no means modern but lamentable hangovers from prehistory, and

338

there is no place for them in this modern Age.

As a result, I know that when the German People now walks round these galleries it will acknowledge me here too as its spokesman and adviser, because it will observe that for the first time for decades it is not an artistic confidence trick but honest artistic achievement that is being celebrated.

And just as it has given approval to our buildings today, so it will be inwardly relieved to express its joyful agreement with the cleansing of our Art.

Which is conclusive. For an Art which cannot count on the most joyful and inward approval of the healthy Popular Masses but is supported only by little cliques – part sophisticated, part financially interested – is intolerable. It sets out to confuse the sane, instinctively confident feeling of a People instead of supporting it with joy.

For all it creates is trouble and depression, so there is no excuse for those pathetic wretches to claim that even the greatest Masters of the past were equally misunderstood in their own day. No, on the contrary. It was only the petty critics – in other words, once again literary men – who stood apart from their People and tortured and tormented the geniuses in question. We however are convinced that the German People will once more display a full and joyful understanding of the truly great German artists that are to come. Above all, however, it must once more value decent labour and honest effort, and take pains to serve and repay our People from all the profundity of the German Heart. And this too is a task for our artists. They cannot stand aside from their People if they are not very soon to find themselves isolated.

In short, today's Exhibition is a beginning. The necessary and wholly hopeful beginning, I am convinced, which can bring about the same blissful change in this sphere as we have managed to achieve in so many others. Let nobody get wrong ideas about this. National Socialism has now set itself the task of freeing the German Reich – and with it our People and its Life – from all those influences that might be noxious to our Being. And even if this cleansing cannot be completed in a single day, let no element which contributes to that noxiousness be in any doubt that sooner or later the hour for its elimination will strike.

The opening of this Exhibition marks the end of German art craziness and therefore of the destruction of our culture.

From now on we shall wage a relentless war to clean up the last elements of our cultural demoralization. Should these include anyone who still believes he is destined for higher things, then he has already had four years in which to prove it. But the same four years have been enough for us to reach a final verdict. From now on, let me assure you, all those mutually supportive and thereby still surviving cliques of chatterers, dilettanti and art fakers will be picked out and eliminated. Let those prehistoric cultural cave dwellers and art stutterers creep back into their ancestors' caverns and fill them with their primitive international scrawls.

The House of German Art in Munich stands on its own as having been built by the German People for its German Art.

Today to my great joy I can see that new Masters are arising among our Youth to join the many decent, hitherto terrorized and oppressed, but still at bottom stubbornly German, older Artists. A walk through the Exhibition will allow you to find much that once again strikes you as beautiful, and above all decent, and that you will consider good. In particular the graphic works submitted reached on the whole an exceptionally high, and thus satisfactory standard.

Many of our young artists will recognize in what they find here the Way that they must henceforth follow. Perhaps they will also get new impulses from the greatness of the Age in which we are all living, and above all acquire the Courage needed for a truly devoted, and ultimately competent piece of work.

And once a holy conscientiousness regains its proper place in this domain, then I have no doubt that the Almighty will once again take individuals from among the mass of these decent creators and raise them to the eternal starry heaven of the immortal, divinely inspired artists of our greatest Ages. For we do not believe that the Age of the creative power of divinely inspired individuals came to an end with the great men of past centuries, only to yield in future to that of a puddingy mass collectivity! No! We believe that it is precisely today, when the highest individual achievements are proving themselves in so many domains, that the highest value of Personality will once more emerge victorious in the realm of Art.

Therefore the only wish I can express at this moment is that it may be given to this new House to be able to reveal to the German People many works by great Artists

in its halls during the centuries to come, thereby contributing not only to the fame of this true City of Art but to the honour and standing of the German Nation as a whole.

I hereby declare the Munich Great German Art Exhibition of 1937 open!

'Hitler's Rede zur Eröffnung der "Großen Deutschen Kunstausstellung"', in Peter-Klaus Schuster, ed., *Nazionalsozialismus und 'Entartete Kunst'* (Munich: Prestel-Verlag, 1987), 250-52.

Translated by John Willett

Hitler wished Munich, scene of the failed Nazi failed coup in 1923, to be not only the 'Capital City of the Movement' but also the 'City of Art'. Its old Glaspalast, the venue for what was perhaps the country's most important annual art exhibition, having been destroyed by fire, the Führer had a Neoclassical 'temple of art' designed by his favourite architect, Paul Ludwig Troost, who died in 1934 soon after the foundation stone had been laid. On 18 July 1937 this scheme came to fruition, when the first new-style *Grosse Deutsche Kunstausstellung* (Great German Art Exhibition) was opened, Hitler himself having weeded out a few residually modern works from the hanging committee's selection. Across the gardens in the Archaeological Institute, an exhibition of *Entartete Kunst* (Degenerate Art) was opened by Adolf Ziegler (president of Goebbels's Kunstkammer) on the following day. Wolf Willrich, a painter who had helped put this together, published his polemical work *Säuberung des Kunsttempels* (or 'Cleansing the Temple of Art') before the end of the year. All this was the product of a genuine obsession with traditional German (and specifically Bavarian) art, felt by a number of leading Nazis such as Darré and Rosenberg, but above all by Hitler himself.

Hitler delivers the above speech, Munich 18 July 1937

The Isle of Man Internees' Exhibition, 1940 *Richard Friedenthal*

The day of the great art exhibition was approaching. The former art dealer Marke Rüsselsheimer had first mooted the idea in the Künstlercafé, and from then on all arrangements had been left in his experienced hands. A hanging committee was formed to decide matters of admission and space allocation. The artists called for the selection to be strict.

'No amateurs!' they said. 'No outsiders or dabblers! All schools to be included, of course. But the whole thing must be representative.'

Architect Zatzelmann had come and submitted his comprehensive plan for a modern redevelopment of the entire waterfront, with tower blocks and enormous car parks. It was turned down. That was something for the polytechnic, they said. That was where he had given his lectures, declaring that the ethos of the new architecture spurned the idea of having pictures on its austere smooth walls.

'If he's got no use for our pictures,' said one of the painters, 'then we've no use for his plans.'

A whole lot of sketches and drawings, linocuts and woodcarvings were submitted by amateurs and thrown out. Marke Rüsselsheimer however pulled a carefully painted oil-on-card number out of the pile and put it in the light: 'This should go in, gentlemen. We must have a real Sunday painter to be complete.'

The picture gave a bird's-eye view of Huddlestone Square, meticulously drawn, with the tight gables of the yellow brick buildings, the barbed-wire fence and the 'sluice'. The tiny black figures of the internees stood on the green grass. Their doll-like faces were tilted stiffly upwards, as if to scan the grey skies.

'This fellow has got something,' said Marke. 'Moreover, in civil life he's in the post office, like our unforgettable August Stramm. Don't miss the boat, gentlemen. There are amateur Sunday painters and there are professional Sunday painters. This is one of us. He's called Minkwitz. You'll be hearing his name again.'

'I ca-can see you b-buying up a few hundred Min-Minkwitzes,' stammered Lichtenberger, agonizedly screwing up his white face, 'and then flogging them off.'

'Roll up, roll up,' said the dealer, 'too bad the man's still alive; I'd sign up his widow right now. Then put the Estate stamp on the back of the card, and watch them going at eight hundred marks apiece. This picture of the camp has atmosphere, of course we should show it. I've a title for it already: "Waiting for release"!'

There were arguments about the hanging. Erich Grimme wanted an entire wall for his large coloured sketches with their jagged shapes that ran off the canvas. The sculptor Thumann had one evening simply uprooted the big cement plinth with his powerful arms from the middle of the grass and carried it up the stairs, a superhuman effort that baffled everyone. He dumped the grey block at the hall entrance, and set the larger-than-lifesize clay maquette of his *Childbirth* on top of it. One night too, without consulting his fellow-artists, he had wrenched two mahogany doors off a cupboard in House 47, and carved wild African reliefs on these. He fixed them to the wall with one-inch nails.

Everybody grumbled. Three of his colleagues combined to try and shift the block on to its side. It wouldn't budge. Finding an iron bar protruding from its base, Thumann had jammed it into the floor . . .

Everybody wanted to come. Tickets for the opening, in the presence of the Commandant, were the subject of heated disputes. The camp hierarchy of course had a right to be there, but the remaining tickets had to be drawn out of a hat. There were disappointed faces. Rüsselsheimer's solution was to call the opening 'Private View' and issue a whole lot of new tickets for the following day, marked 'Grand Opening'. This had a calming effect.

The Commandant arrived at eleven sharp. He was met at the barbed-wire barrier by an official committee composed of Rüsselsheimer, Gärtner and Groterjahn representing the artists. After Major Hicks came a large retinue: the Medical Officer, Intelligence Officer, Camp Administrative Officer and Sergeant Monihan. Rüsselsheimer had arranged for a small table to be placed at the entrance to the show, with an official programme on special paper and a bottle of sherry and some glasses.

Hicks nodded benevolently, raised his glass, waited for the members of his staff to fill theirs, then gave a toast to the King:

'The King!'

'The King!' replied his retinue. They drained their glasses. Hicks turned to the committee and the others: 'Delighted to have this opportunity, your enterprise does you credit, shows the right spirit, good way of raising morale among the prisoners, I mean the internees; wish your show every success.'

'Thank you very much, sir,' said Rüsselsheimer. He had actually been intending to make his own introductory speech, not without some misgivings about how to adjust his highly ironic thought processes to the Major's receptivity. Agreeably warmed by the sherry, however, Hicks was already setting off to do the rounds. Rüsselsheimer hurried ahead in the hope of steering the Major's eye towards those items which might please him. In the centre, Thumann's massive group was at least quantitatively impressive, having clearly called for great strength; it earned a nod from the distinguished visitor, who had fortunately failed to grasp its theme. Erich Grimme's wall-sized sketches, with their limbs rampaging in wild elephantiasis, admittedly met with a certain disfavour and provoked some doubt as to whether they showed 'the right spirit'.

'That fellow doesn't know how to draw', said the Major to the doctor. 'Or has he something wrong with his eyes? You should have him tested. Doesn't he realize that himself?'

Baby Bitter's *Speech Sculpture* of course said nothing to him. Rüsselsheimer tried to stave off the Major's mounting resentment by such phrases as 'a very modern artist, sir, experimental, you know'.

'Experimental? Well, I must say . . .'

At this point luckily the Major's glance fell on Groterjahn's *Girl with a Jug*. His expression cleared. He looked at it from all sides, closed his eyes and opened them again, started to smile and was drawn to feel the nude figure's charming curves with his hand, which he quickly took away. He viewed it from behind, and found that equally satisfactory. For quite a while he chatted to Groterjahn, who had for once given himself a careful shave for the occasion, and stood there without embarrassment making conversation with the Commandant.

'All that effort must be encouraged,' said

the Major, pointing at the curves. 'That's the spirit we want to cultivate.' He took Groterjahn aside for a moment and asked 'How about animals? D'you model horses, for instance?' Groterjahn explained that they were not his strong point, and in any case he needed a live model to work from.

'Pity', said Hicks. 'Then that's out. How's one to get hold of a decent horse in this place? All they've got is ponies for the milk-carts, or else miserable carthorses, worn out nags with no breeding, no fire in them. A proper Arab, y'know, a thoroughbred mare . . . Oh, forget it. It's no use.' He stared ahead with his malarial eyes in their wrinkled yellow pouches.

'What about sport?' he went on. 'Not cricket, of course, that's something your lot wouldn't have. But football, how about that?'

Groterjahn shook his head.

'Or golf? Ever watched it played?'

Groterjahn nodded; he had been an occasional guest at the Hamburg golf club.

'Well done, good show,' said Hicks. He proposed that the sculptor should model him a statuette of a lady golfer, 'not too big, I'd want to have it on my desk with all my other stuff; no clothes of course; like your girl here. Know how to grip a club?'

Groterjahn gave a cautious bow in affirmation.

'I'll send my set of clubs down to the studio for you,' said Hicks. 'Pick one for yourself. That can be your model. The pose: like this!' He gave a pirouette to convey a drive. His crumpled boy's face lit up.

'If there's anything else you want, say so. Sergeant Monihan will see to it. It's been a great pleasure, Mr Grootjohn, really a great pleasure.'

He walked away with a swing.

Sergeant Monihan stayed behind. With a sign to Gärtner, he in turn conducted a short inspection, paying little attention to the works of art on show; the Major had approved them, good enough. However, his sharp NCO's eye instantly spotted Thumann's cupboard doors.

'From House 47, eh?' he said. 'Those two big mahogany cupboards on the top landing. The owners are going to kick up hell when they get their house back and find Indians and bloody niggers carved all over their doors. Can't really have that'.

But he left it at 'really', having been impressed by the power with which Thumann had worked the hard wood and polished it till it shone. Then, however, he took exception to the strong iron hooks with which the sculptor had secured the doors against any attempt to change their position.

'The bugger's destroying our whole wall. He'll never get those hooks out without making a hole as big as my hand. See he plasters and paints those holes till they're good as new!'

He inspected Thumann's block of concrete. 'How did you lot get that up the stairs?' Gärtner tried to explain that Thumann had dragged the huge lump up to the hall all by himself one night; admittedly the action was not wholly according to the book.

'By himself?' asked Monihan. 'Good God, the man must be strong.' He put his arms round the block and tried to shift it. It was as if the plinth had been welded in place. The sergeant went red in the face, and put all his energy into another attempt. Then he gave up as if the matter were below his dignity, lightly rubbed his hands and straightened his tunic. He gave a last surprisingly amiable look round the hall:

'That's a good job you done here. Just those pieces of paper' – he indicated Erich Grimme's sketches, which had been rather inadequately secured with drawing pins and come adrift at one corner – 'need to be fixed better if they're to last more than a day. And mind you see Thumann gets them holes properly plastered. I'm counting on you people.'

He took his companion aside for a moment, and said: 'Mustn't let it get you down, it won't last for ever. I heard some talk of releases. Don't pass that on, or I'll have a lot of nutcases on my hands. Just see that plinth gets put back properly, and the bugger doesn't smash up our whole staircase in the process. He can't possibly have done that all on his own.'

'He did,' said Gärtner. 'And thank you very much. I won't tell anyone.'

Monihan left, after helping himself to a second glass of sherry.

The Grand Opening for the general public was introduced by Rüsselsheimer, who used the phrase 'roll up, roll up,' as had been expected. But the dealer abandoned his normal ironic manner. He was touched. He kept saying that of all the many exhibitions he had opened, this was the finest, the most moving experience of a rich life. He started to stammer:

'Art, gentlemen, art and artists, even here behind the wire . . . the war . . . painting, drawing and sculpture go on as in the great days . . . classicism, Expressionism, Surrealism, even a Sunday painter: we've got it all here . . . it's magnificent, unforgettable, they go on painting and carving as if there was no such thing as submarines and air raids, art goes on, nothing can stop the development of modern art . . .

He suddenly broke off, and quietly said:

'I herewith declare the 1940 Exhibition of the Huddlestone Camp Artists' Association open!'

Richard Friedenthal, *Die Welt in der Nußschale* (Munich: Piper, 1956), 312–23.

Translated by John Willett

Three years on from Hitler's speech, after the fall of France, a group of anti-Nazi refugee artists interned in Hutchinson Camp in the Isle of Man held the exhibition described in Richard Friedenthal's good-humoured novel. His 'Baby Bitter' was of course Kurt Schwitters, four of whose pictures had been among the 'Degenerate "Art"' works in Munich. Other participants appear to have been the sculptors Georg Ehrlich and Siegfried Charoux, and the delicate draughtsman Fritz Kraemer. The preternaturally strong sculptor must have been Ernst Blenzdorf, the architect-planner Bruno Ahrends. Erich Kahn (who figures as Grimme) and Fred Uhlman were there too, as were Max Reinhardt's stage designer Ernst Stern and the Berlin Expressionist Ludwig Meidner, though he kept apart from such activities. The Commandant was Major O. H. Daniel, and his guide to the exhibition was Klaus Hinrichsen, who gave his own account in *Immigrants and Minorities*, vol 2, no. 3 (November 1992), 188–209.

Inside Hutchinson internment camp, Douglas, Isle of Man, c. 1940

AFTERWORD

Landscape After the Battle   *Neal Ascherson*

After a war, men and women at last have leisure to wash the filth off themselves.

My friend Georgia, who is no longer alive, was eighteen when she was marched out of Ravensbrück with thousands of other bald skeletons who had once looked like women. The SS guards soon abandoned them and ran away. Some of the prisoners were killed by Russian shells as they lay in a wood, and more died when Russian tankmen unwisely gave them rich food to eat – real bread and sausage. But the survivors made their way to the nearest German village. There they found a woman SS guard trying to hide; they clawed her to the ground and stamped and trod until nothing recognizable was left. Then they went into the clean little German houses with their white, sweet-smelling bolsters, and they ravaged, fouled and filthied those houses in many imaginative ways.

After that, the women were very tired and there was nothing left to do. It was over: the war, the camp, the screaming voices and the gunfire, the revenge, the liberation. So they began to wash themselves. The weather was still cold, but the water in the village pumps was pure and in some of the houses the women had found hoarded cakes of prewar soap. The street became quiet except for the jingle of the pumps and the splashing.

Everything requires to be washed at such a time. In 1945, after six years of war and a generation of totalitarianism, human brains were nearly as clogged and dirty as human skins. Culture itself had to be taken to the bath-house to be shaved, deloused and scrubbed. This was easier in some countries than in others. It was easier in nations that had been crushed, like Germany, or that – like Poland, France or Italy – had emerged from the war physically and mentally shattered by the experience of defeat and occupation. It was more difficult for the British and the Americans to sense the cultural accretions of wartime mobilization. The Soviet Union admitted to no need for renewal at all.

First came the cleansing of language. Poets, above all, took language down to the river and scraped at it and pounded it until it broke up into basic, primary pebbles of meaning. All the coagulations and aggregations and compoundings into political reinforced concrete were split up and thrown away. In Germany, the Nazi vocabulary with its inimitable, indispensable items like *Einsatzbereitschaft* (readiness-to-take-action), or *Gebärfreudigkeit* (female joy-in-giving-birth), or *Opferbereitschaft* (readiness-to-sacrifice-oneself), fell apart and was washed downstream.

The German poet Günter Eich made his poem 'Inventory' out of pebbles:

This is my cap,
this is my greatcoat,
and here's my shaving kit
in its linen bag.

A can of meat:
my plate, my mug,
into its tin
I've scratched my name . . .

(Translated by Michael Hamburger)

Looking a little more widely across the landscape after the battle, at themes of art and power, the Polish poet Tadeusz Rózewicz wrote:

After the end of the world
after death
I found myself in the midst of life
creating myself
building life
people animals landscapes

this is a table I said
this is a table
there is bread and a knife on the table
knife serves to cut bread
people are nourished by bread

man must be loved
I learn by night and day
what must one love
I would reply man.

(Translated by Adam Czerniawski)

The same idea – that power could somehow be rinsed out of art – was strong in the visual arts well before the final defeat of Fascism. Power in its most malignant forms, it was reasoned, had mobilized and then debased the artist in the service of propaganda. Those who would not submit to the demands of totalitarian politics were, it went without saying, suppressed or chased into exile. This was plainly true about Hitler's Germany, and in a rather different way about Mussolini's Italy. However, it was also largely true about the Soviet Union. Majestic works of real integrity could still emerge from Soviet cinema, stage production and literature, but the enslavement of the visual arts was little better than in the Third Reich.

The argument for an art without power, or a culture insulated against politics, was therefore never a left-wing one. For a Marxist the problem about Nazi art was not that it had been politicized but that it had been politicized by the wrong politics. Moderate Socialists might point out the difference between a regimented art and an art aware of the social and political dimensions of its time. But all could agree that the idea of a culture which could isolate itself from politics altogether was absurd. It was in the liberal-conservative world, and especially in the United States, that the notion not just of 'art for art's sake' but of 'art for nobody' took shape.

The outcome was the stampede away from the figurative and representational which seized the West – or at least many of its gallery owners and curators – in the first postwar decades. It came to be supposed that figurative art lent itself to political manipulation, whereas the abstract offered some guarantee for the independence of the artist. Willi Baumeister, who managed to survive the Third Reich in obscurity, followed this path to abstraction. He wrote afterwards that 'art has progressed along the path from dependence to independence, from the commission which is given to personal responsibility. The free autonomous artist receives his commission from himself.' A new line was drawn between abstraction as the 'art of liberty' and representational art, perceived in the West as 'accident-prone' – easy to subvert in the cause of totalitarian propaganda. Like all dogmas, this was eventually pushed to absurdity, at the point at which West German galleries would refuse to contemplate figurative work on the grounds that the artist might be a Communist or have Communist sympathies.

It was true that the dictators had used a 'literalist' representation of the human body to suggest favourite values like collective violence, credulity, and all the variants of *Einsatz- und Opferbereitschaft*. But there were limits to what could be deduced from that. In the first place, it is hard to define what is the 'literal' imaging of an object as Protean and variable as the human body. Secondly, the Nazi regime hesitated in the 1930s before choosing its preferred style in the arts, and might well have opted for a cleaned-up version of German Expressionism as the 'art of the national revolution'. Expressionism certainly carried the rebellious, elemental, iconoclastic vigour which the Nazis claimed.

Washing the visual arts clean, then, turned out to be a more difficult, incomplete operation than washing language. But the first impressions collected by an imaginary survivor standing on a hill to inspect the landscape after the battle would not be of statues, still less of words. They would be of ruins. Architecture, in its relationship with totalitarian power, had a great deal to explain away.

At the same time, a ruined Europe had to raise houses to shelter in and halls to meet in. This could not be done without architects but, because the need was so overwhelming and the private sector so comprehensively broke, neither could it be done without the state. Here, inescapably, was a new relationship between art and power.

The response of architects, often enough, was to disguise the nature of that relationship. The official architecture of the 1930s had made statements: I am strong, I am merciless, I am an act of will. Postwar architecture in the West, by contrast, affected a rueful modesty, utility and austerity. Pilasters, which for some reason had become the single feature most often used to evoke State arrogance, vanished entirely. Doors or windows were here or there because of the inhabitant's need and convenience, not because of the architect's impulse. Building design was put under the pressure hose, and a great deal of the intimidating, meretricious visual language of the 1930s was washed off.

At the same time, however, the underlying relationships between this particular art and power survived more or less undisturbed. It was not hard for Speer to persuade Hitler that the servant's designs merely distilled the vaster visions of his master. In consequence, not long after 1945 architects throughout Europe, but especially in the West, were once again making statements through buildings and reciprocating State patronage with designs proclaimed to express the 'spirit' of the regime of the day.

But there was something salutary in that recidivism. The bond between architecture and authority shows that there is a limit to what can be washed off after war and dictatorship. It is true that the worst of propaganda rhetoric, verbal and visual, can be scrubbed away, and the joy and liberation when that is done is very real. At the same time, words and signs are not really like pebbles, not even the monosyllabic nouns of Eich and Rózewicz or the designs of Baumeister and Mark Rothko. They retain their radiation, artefacts glowing with allusion and memory. They belong to a wider culture which includes politics, and the notion of an art immune to power is only a myth. As far as culture is concerned, the landscape after the battle is only the landscape before the next one.

CATALOGUE LISTINGS

Items in the Paris 1937 section of the exhibition are listed under their countries of origin.

SPAIN

Architecture

1.1 Francisco Cabrero Torres-Quevedo
design for a monumental cross for the Valley of the Fallen: drawing of the façade, 1941–42
63.5 × 49.5 cm
Private collection, Madrid

1.2 Francisco Cabrero Torres-Quevedo
design for a monumental cross for the Valley of the Fallen: perspective drawing, 1941–42
46.2 × 38.5 cm
Private collection, Madrid

1.3 Josep Lluís Sert, Luis Lacasa
Spanish Pavilion, International Exhibition, Paris 1937 (model 1987)
wood and plastic, 140 × 230 × 101 cm
Museo Nacional Centro de Arte Reina Sofía, Madrid (Reg. No. 11702)

Art

1.4 Emiliano Barral
Portrait of Luis Quintanilla (Retrato de Luis Quintanilla), 1925
bronze, 42 × 24.5 × 25 cm
Museu Nacional d'Art de Catalunya, Barcelona (MNAC/MAM 113992)

1.5 Joan Borràs Casanova
Old Spain (Vella Espanya), 1937
oil on canvas, 84 × 64 cm
Museu Nacional d'Art de Catalunya, Barcelona (MNAC/MAM 145153)

1.6 Salvador Dalí
Soft Construction with Boiled Beans – Premonition of Civil War, 1936
oil on canvas, 100 × 99 cm
Philadelphia Museum of Art, The Louise and Walter Arensberg Collection

1.7 Horacio Ferrer
Madrid 1937 (Black Aeroplanes) (Madrid 1937 [Los aviones negros]), 1937
oil on canvas, 148 × 128.5 cm
Carmen Ferrer, Adán Ferrer, Horacio Ferrer, Madrid

1.8 Julio González
The Front (El front), c. 1934–36
bronze, 9 × 14 × 5.5 cm
Museu Nacional d'Art de Catalunya, Barcelona (MNAC/MAM 113402)

1.9 Julio González
Cowled Head (El capirot), 1935–36
bronze, 15 × 22.8 × 20 cm
Museu Nacional d'Art de Catalunya, Barcelona (MNAC/MAM 113415)

1.10 Julio González
Woman Before a Mirror (Mujer ante el espejo), c. 1936–37
iron, 203.8 × 60 × 46 cm
IVAM. Instituto Valenciano de Arte Moderno – Generalitat Valenciana, Valencia

1.11 Julio González
Imploring Figure (Personatge implorant), 1937
pen and ink on paper, 32.3 × 25.1 cm
Museu Nacional d'Art de Catalunya, Barcelona (MNAC/GDG 113465-D)

1.12 Julio González
La Montserrat, 1937
iron, 165 × 45 × 45 cm
Stedelijk Museum, Amsterdam

1.13 Julio González
Aggressivity (Agressivitat), 1938
pen and ink on paper, 32.7 × 25.1 cm
Museu Nacional d'Art de Catalunya, Barcelona (MNAC/GDG 113462-D)

1.14 John Heartfield
Madrid 1936 – They Shall Not Pass! We Shall Pass! (Madrid 1936 – No pasarán! Pasaremos!), 1936
p. 240 in VI, no. 15, 25/11/1936, 38 × 28 cm

1.15 José Antonio
Soldier (Soldat), 1937
bronze, 30.7 × 30 × 23.5 cm
Museu Nacional d'Art de Catalunya, Barcelona (MNAC/MAM 113994)

1.16 Nicolàs de Lekuona
Untitled, c. 1934
collage, 23.5 × 32 cm
IVAM. Instituto Valenciano de Arte Moderno – Generalitat Valenciana, Valencia (1992.11)

1.17 Francisco Mateos
Law (La Ley), 1937
No. 5 in series: ¡Salamanca!
etching, 32.7 × 24.7 cm
Museu Nacional d'Art de Catalunya, Barcelona (MNAC/GDG 28105-G)

1.18 Francisco Mateos
Hope to God that Franco Wins (Quiera Dios que gane Franco), 1937
No. 6 in series: ¡Salamanca!
etching, 32.5 × 24.6 cm
Museu Nacional d'Art de Catalunya, Barcelona (MNAC/GDG 28106-G)1015

1.19 Francisco Mateos
The Generalísimo is Receiving Today (¡Hoy recibe el Generalísimo!), 1937
No. 8 in series: ¡Salamanca!
etching, 32.5 × 24.6 cm
Museu Nacional d'Art de Catalunya, Barcelona (MNAC/GDG 28108-G)

1.20 Francisco Mateos
Legionaires (Los legionarios), 1937
No. 2 in series: El sitio de Madrid
lithograph, 66.5 × 44.5 cm
Museu Nacional d'Art de Catalunya, Barcelona (MNAC/GDG 28111-G)

1.21 Francisco Mateos
Prussian Chiefs (Los jefes prusianos), 1937
No. 6 in series: El sitio de Madrid
lithograph, 67 × 48.5 cm
Museu Nacional d'Art de Catalunya, Barcelona (MNAC/GDG 28115G)

1.22 Francisco Mateos
The Vaticanists (Los Vaticanistas), 1937
No. 9 in series: El sitio de Madrid
lithograph, 68 × 46.5 cm
Museu Nacional d'Art de Catalunya, Barcelona (MNAC/GDG 28118-G)

1.23 Francisco Mateos
Italian Music (Música italiana), 1937
No. 10 in series: El sitio de Madrid
lithograph, 65.6 × 47.7 cm
Museu Nacional d'Art de Catalunya, Barcelona (MNAC/GDG 28119-G)

1.24 Joan Miró
Aidez l'Espagne, 1937
stencil print, 31.2 × 24 cm
Imperial War Museum, London (15319)

1.25 Joan Miró
Head of a Man, 1937
gouache and india ink on black paper, 64.8 × 49.5 cm
Richard S. Zeisler Collection, New York

1.26 Joan Miró
Still Life with Old Shoe, 1937
oil on canvas, 81.3 × 116.8 cm
The Museum of Modern Art, New York, Gift of James Thrall Soby, 1969

1.27 Francisco Pérez Mateo
Bear (Oso blanco), 1931
Colmenar stone, 57 × 83 × 46 cm
Museo Nacional Centro de Arte Reina Sofía, Madrid (Reg. No. 1882)

1.28 Santiago Pelegrín
Bomb in Tetuán, Madrid (Bomba en Tetuán, Madrid), 1937
oil on canvas, 124 × 103 cm
Museu Nacional d'Art de Catalunya, Barcelona (MNAC/MAM 145193)

1.29 Pablo Picasso
Woman's Head (Boisgeloup) (Tête de Femme [Boisgeloup]), 1932
bronze, 64.3 × 42.5 × 22 cm
Musée Picasso, Paris (MP. 1980–111)

1.30 Pablo Picasso
Dream and Lie of Franco 1 and 2 (Sueño y mentira de Franco), 1937, no. 1: 38.8 × 57 cm; no. 2: 38.9 × 57.1 cm
British Museum, London (1980–11–8–10 (1 and 2))

1.31 Pablo Picasso
Head of Crying Woman with Handkerchief (Cabeza de mujer llorando con pañuelo) III, 1937
oil on canvas, 92 × 73 cm
Museo Nacional Centro de Arte Reina Sofía, Madrid (R. DE-0106)

1.32 Pablo Picasso
Mother with Dead Child (Madre con niño muerto) II, 1937
oil on canvas, 130 × 195 cm
Museo Nacional Centro de Arte Reina Sofía, Madrid (R. DE-0104)

1.33 Josep Renau
The Path of Bourgeois Democracy (El camino de la democracia burguesa), 1932
Page from Orto, no. 9, 1932, 23.5 × 15.3 cm
IVAM. Instituto Valenciano de Arte Moderno – Generalitat Valenciana, Valencia

1.34 Josep Renau
Nueva Cultura. 4 volumes: June to July 1935; October 1935; January 1936; July 1936
IVAM. Instituto Valenciano de Arte Moderno – Generalitat Valenciana, Valencia

1.35 Josep Renau
Industry of War (Industria de guerra), 1936
photomontage, 47.5 × 33.5 cm
IVAM. Instituto Valenciano de Arte Moderno –

Generalitat Valenciana, Valencia

1.36 Josep Renau
The Commissioner at the Nerve Centre of our Popular Army (El Comisario, nervio de nuestro ejército popular), 1936
photomontage, 35.1 × 51.7 cm
IVAM. Instituto Valenciano de Arte Moderno – Generalitat Valenciana, Valencia

1.37 Josep Renau
Middle Ages: Illicit Love (Medioevo: amor en la ilegalidad), 1936
sheet inserted between pages 16 and 17 of Estudios, no. 149, January 1936, 18.5 × 12.8 cm
IVAM. Instituto Valenciano de Arte Moderno – Generalitat Valenciana, Valencia

1.38 Josep Renau
19 Years of the Soviet Union and of Fighting for Liberty and World-Wide Peace (19 años de Unión Sovietica y de lucha por la libertad y la paz mundial), 1936
poster, 99 × 67 cm
Biblioteca Nacional, Madrid (BA Cart-337)

1.39 Josep Renau
Strengthen the Ranks of the PSU of Catalonia, Workers, Peasants, Soldiers, Intellectuals! (Reforceu els rengles del Partit Socialista Unificat de Catalunya: obrers, camperols, soldats, intel·lectuals), 1936
poster, 73 × 107 cm
Biblioteca Nacional, Madrid (BA Cart-211)

1.40 Josep Renau
Negrín's 13 Points (Los 13 puntos de Negrín), 1938
silver prints, 22 × 15 cm
IVAM. Instituto Valenciano de Arte Moderno – Generalitat Valenciana, Valencia

1.41 Josep Renau
Victory: Today More Than Ever (Victoria: hoy más que nunca), 1938
poster, 100 × 136 cm
Biblioteca Nacional, Madrid (BA Cart-398)

1.42 Josep Renau
Stalingrad. The New Star of Freedom (Stalingrado. Nueva estrella de la libertad), 1942
photomontage and ink on card, 44.7 × 32.1 cm
IVAM. Instituto Valenciano de Arte Moderno –

Generalitat Valenciana, Valencia

1.43 Josep Renau
Happy New Year 1943 (Feliz Año 1943)
photomontage and ink on card, 44.8 × 32 cm
IVAM. Instituto Valenciano de Arte Moderno – Generalitat Valenciana, Valencia

1.44 Carlos Sáenz de Tejada, Agustín de Foxa
Canción de la Falange, 1939
Published by Ediciones Españoles, S.A., Sevilla, 31.5 × 42.5 cm
Biblioteca de Catalunya, Barcelona (R. 192.054)

1.45 Alberto Sánchez Pérez
Sign of a Country Woman, on a Road, in the Rain (Signo de mujer rural, en un camino, lloviendo), 1927–30
bronze, 62 × 16.5 × 6.5 cm
Colección Escultórica Eduardo Capa, Madrid

1.46 Alberto Sánchez Pérez
The Spanish People Have a Path that Leads to a Star (El pueblo español tiene un camino que conduce a una estrella), 1937
plaster, 185.5 × 33 × 33 cm
On loan to Museo de Santa Cruz, Toledo

1.47 José María Sert
The Intercession of St Teresa in the Spanish Civil War (La intercesión de Santa Teresa en la guerra civil española), 1937
Known at the 1937 Paris Exhibition as 'St Teresa, Ambassadress of Divine Love to Spain, Offers to Our Lord the Spanish Martyrs of 1936'
oil and gold on canvas, approx. 600 × 300 cm
Museu Nacional d'Art de Catalunya, Barcelona (MNAC/MAM 42115)

1.48 José Gutiérrez Solana
The Procession of Death (La procesión de la muerte), 1930
oil on canvas, 209 × 123 cm
Museo Nacional Centro de Arte Reina Sofía, Madrid (Reg. No. 871)

1.49 Various authors and illustrators
Laureados de España, 1940
Ediciones Fermina Bonilla, Madrid, 27.5 × 21 cm
Biblioteca de Catalunya, Barcelona (R. 195.571)

Posters

1.50 Anonymous
Madrid. The 'Military' Practice of the Rebels
67 × 49.3 cm
Imperial War Museum, London (PST 15348 (2))

1.51 Anonymous
Los Nacionales
International Brigade Archive, Marx Memorial Library, London

1.52 Anonymous
What Are You Doing to Prevent This?
39.4 × 27.4 cm
Imperial War Museum, London (PST 4622)

1.53 Anonymous
Bolshevism, Social Injustice, Corrupt Politicians, Freemasons, Separatism, F.A.I. (Bolchevismo, injusticia social, politicastros, masones, separatismo, F.A.I.), 1938?
119 × 84 cm
Biblioteca Nacional, Madrid (BA Cart-493)

1.54 Anonymous
Spain is the Spiritual Leader of the World (España orientadora espiritual del mundo), c. 1939
100 × 70 cm
Biblioteca Nacional, Madrid (BA Cart-489)

1.55 Anonymous
¡¡Franco!!, 1939
90 × 60 cm
Biblioteca Nacional, Madrid (BA Cart-491)

1.56 Anonymous
Generalísimo Franco: Victorious Soldier of Glorious Spain (Generalísimo Franco: victor miles Hispaniae gloriosae), 1939
100 × 71 cm
Biblioteca Nacional, Madrid (BA Cart-485)

1.57 Anonymous
Never Again (Jamás), c. 1939
90 × 60 cm
Biblioteca Nacional, Madrid (BA Cart-490)

1.58 Anonymous
Spain Resurrects (España resuscita), 1939
126 × 90 cm
Biblioteca Nacional, Madrid (BA Cart-494)

1.59 Augusto
The People of Madrid Demand the Laureada for Their Heroic Defender, General Miaja (El pueblo de Madrid pide la Laureada para su heroico defensor General Miaja)
99.2 × 69 cm
Imperial War Museum, London (PST 4622)

1.60 Arturo Ballester
Praise the Heroes! (¡Loor a los heros!)
100 × 71 cm
Imperial War Museum, London (PST 8048)

1.61 Pere Català i Pic
Let's Squash Fascism (Aixafem el feixisme), 1936 (reissued 1981)
104 × 73 cm
IVAM. Instituto Valenciano de Arte Moderno – Generalitat Valenciana, Valencia (1992.15)

1.62 Coves
We Shall Win for the Good of the World's Proletariat (Vencerem pel bé del proletariat mundial), 1936
100 × 70 cm
Biblioteca Nacional, Madrid (BA Cart-103)

1.63 L. Goni
Your Brothers at the Front Await You (Els teus germans del front t'esperen)
100 × 70 cm
Imperial War Museum, London (PST 15937 (4))

1.64 Lleó
Assassins!, 1936–39
100 × 71 cm
Biblioteca Nacional, Madrid (BA Cart-246)

1.65 Moneny
Citizens, Join in Homage to the USSR on its Twentieth Anniversary (Ciutadans adheriu-vos a l'homenatge a la URSS: en el seu XXo aniversary), 1937
89 × 65 cm
Biblioteca Nacional, Madrid (BA Cart-336)

1.66 Monleón
Syndicalist Party (Partido Sindicalista)
88 × 65 cm
Imperial War Museum, London (PST 8046)

1.67 Morell
Spain Has Arrived (Ha llegado España), 1939
125 × 90 cm Biblioteca Nacional, Madrid (BA Cart-495)

1.68 Oliver
Attack is Victory (Atacar es vencer)
100 × 71.5 cm
Imperial War Museum, London (PST 9053)

1.69 Rafel Tana
Squash Fascism (Per a aixafar el feixisme)
100 × 70 cm
Imperial War Museum, London (PST 16082)

1.70 Toledo
Foreign Fascist Hordes Try to Invade Our Territory (Las hordas fascistas extranjeras pretenden invadir nuestro territorio)
100 × 71.5 cm
Imperial War Museum, London (PST 8050)

ROME

Architecture

2.1 Anonymous
Statue of Augustus in Armour (Statua loricata di Augusto), 1937
plaster, approx. 150 cm
Museo della Civiltà Romana, Rome (M.C.R. n. 14)

2.2 Anonymous
coloured poster/map print, 99 × 72 cm
Archivio Centrale dello Stato, Rome (EUR)

2.3 Anonymous
Via Imperiale, plan from the Lido to central Rome
ink on paper, 38 × 126 cm
Archivio Centrale dello Stato, Rome (EUR S 6 – 7)

2.4 Enrico del Debbio
Redevelopment of the Augusteo, view from corso Umberto, 1927
crayon and pencil on paper, 57 × 46 cm
Archivio Del Debbio, Rome

2.5 Enrico del Debbio
Redevelopment of the Augusteo, view from via Tomacelli, 1927
crayon and pencil on paper, 60 × 42 cm
Archivio Del Debbio, Rome

2.6 Enrico del Debbio
Accademia di Educazione Fisica, perspective from river, 1928
tempera on card, 80 × 175 cm
Archivio Del Debbio, Rome

2.7 Enrico del Debbio
Foro Mussolini, bird's-eye view perspective of intermediate plan, 1930
charcoal and crayon on paper, 135 × 230 cm
Archivio Del Debbio, Rome

2.8 Enrico del Debbio
Casa della Balilla Madre, perspective, 1933
tempera on board, 65 × 104 cm
Archivio Del Debbio, Rome

2.9 Enrico del Debbio
Barrack stores (Magazzini di casermaggio), perspective, 1933
tempera on board, 48 × 72 cm
Archivio Del Debbio, Rome

2.10 Enrico del Debbio
Palazzo Littorio, Foro Mussolini, perspective view, 1938–40
pencil on paper
Archivio Del Debbio, Rome

2.11 Enrico del Debbio
Foresteria Sud, perspective from river
coloured tempera, 32.5 × 95 cm
Archivio Del Debbio, Rome

2.12 Enrico del Debbio
Olympic Stadium, perspective
crayon and pencil on paper, 50 × 67 cm
Archivio Del Debbio, Rome

2.13 Achille Funi
Head of the Goddess Roma (Testa della Dea Roma)
black and coloured chalk on paper, 115 × 79 cm
Archivio Centrale dello Stato, Rome

2.14 Giris
Reconstruction of a Lictor from Trajan's Time (Littore dell'età di Trajano, ricostruzione), 1937
plaster, approx. 150 cm
Museo della Civiltà Romana, Rome

2.15 Ernesto Bruno Lapadula
Palazzo della Civiltà Italiana, EUR, preliminary sketch, CI sketch A/1, 1937
pencil on paper, 17 × 18 cm
Archivio Lapadula, Rome

2.16 Ernesto Bruno Lapadula
Palazzo della Civiltà Italiana, EUR, preliminary sketch, CI sketch B/2, 1937
pencil on paper, 18 × 23 cm
Archivio Lapadula, Rome

2.17 Ernesto Bruno Lapadula
Palazzo della Civiltà Italiana, EUR, preliminary sketch, CI sketch B/3, 1937
pencil on paper, 22 × 28 cm
Archivio Lapadula, Rome

2.18 Ernesto Bruno Lapadula
Palazzo della Civiltà Italiana, EUR, preliminary sketch, CI sketch XXVI, 1937
pencil on paper, 28 × 14 cm
Archivio Lapadula, Rome

2.19 Ernesto Bruno Lapadula
Palazzo della Civiltà Italiana, EUR, interior perspective, Foundation of the Church, 1939
pencil on paper, 22 × 29 cm
Archivio Lapadula, Rome

2.20 Ernesto Bruno Lapadula
Palazzo della Civiltà Italiana, EUR, interior perspective, attic storey with Dea Romana, 1939
pencil on paper, 29 × 22 cm
Archivio Lapadula, Rome

2.21 Ernesto Bruno Lapadula
Palazzo della Civiltà Italiana, EUR, interior perspective, Sala dell'Impero, 1939
pencil on paper, 22 × 29 cm
Archivio Lapadula, Rome

2.22 Ernesto Bruno Lapadula
Palazzo della Civiltà Italiana, EUR, interior perspective showing plan of Rome at the far end, 1939
pencil on paper, 22 × 29 cm
Archivio Lapadula, Rome

2.23 Bice Lazzari
Mostra del Tessile, sketch for the wall decorations, 1937
tempera on card, 34.7 × 24.6 cm
Archivio Lazzari, Rome

2.24 Bice Lazzari
Mostra del Minerale: Asbestos 4, 1938
coloured chalk and pencil on cardboard, 32.5 × 50 cm
Lazzari Archive, Rome

2.25 Adalberto Libera
Post office on the Aventine (Palazzo Postale all'Aventino), Rome, 1933–34
Model in wood, 30 × 100 × 120 cm
Museo d'Arte Moderna e Contemporanea di Trento e Rovereto, Trento

2.26 Angiolo Mazzoni
Roma Termini railway station, façade towards the square, 1932–38
pencil on tracing paper, 36 × 123 cm
Museo d'Arte Moderna e Contemporanea di Trento e Rovereto, Trento (46/D)

2.27 Angiolo Mazzoni
Roma Termini railway station, general perspective towards the Severan walls, 1936
charcoal on tracing paper, 64 × 200 cm
Museo d'Arte Moderna e Contemporanea di Trento e Rovereto, Trento (5/T)

2.28 Minucci and others
Palazzo degli Uffici, interiors: Ufficio del Presidente
coloured chalk on paper, 65 × 78 cm
Archivio Centrale dello Stato, Rome (EUR S 14 – 10 G)

2.29 Minucci and others
Palazzo degli Uffici, interiors: Ufficio del Sovrintendente dell'Architettura
coloured chalk on paper, 65 × 78 cm
Archivio Centrale dello Stato, Rome (EUR S 14 – 10 G)

2.30 Luigi Moretti
competition project for Palazzo del Littorio (perspective sketch of design from corner towards Colosseum), c. 1934
pencil and charcoal on card, 34 × 46.8 cm
Archivio Centrale dello Stato, Rome (Archivio Moretti)

2.31 Luigi Moretti
competition project for Palazzo del Littorio, Project A? (interior perspective of staircase), c. 1934
charcoal on paper
Archivio Centrale dello Stato, Rome (Archivio Moretti)

2.32 Luigi Moretti
competition project for Palazzo del Littorio on the Aventine, 2nd competition (perspective), 1937
tempera on wood, 82.9 × 122.4 cm
Archivio Centrale dello Stato, Rome (Archivio Moretti)

2.33 Luigi Moretti
Villa for Ettore Muti on the island of Brioni (perspective), 1942
pencil on paper, 50 × 70 cm
Archivio Centrale dello Stato, Rome (Archivio Moretti)

2.34 Luigi Moretti
Interior design of apartment for Ettore Muti, over Porta San Sebastiano in the Aurelian walls
pen on paper
Archivio Centrale dello Stato, Rome (Archivio Moretti)

2.35 Luigi Moretti
Interior design of apartment for Ettore Muti, over Porta San Sebastiano in the Aurelian walls (interior perspective)
ink on paper
Archivio Centrale dello Stato, Rome (Archivio Moretti)

2.36 Luigi Moretti
Interior design of apartment for Ettore Muti, over Porta San Sebastiano in the Aurelian walls (interior perspective)
ink on paper
Archivio Centrale dello Stato, Rome (Archivio Moretti)

2.37 Luigi Moretti
Piazzale Imperiale, plan, 1:200
ink on paper, 69.9 × 154.3 cm
Archivio Centrale dello Stato, Rome (Archivio Moretti)

2.38 Luigi Moretti
Piazzale Imperiale, plan of mosaic (1/2 disk)
ink on paper, 56.6 × 89 cm
Archivio Centrale dello Stato, Rome (Archivio Moretti)

2.39 Luigi Moretti
Piazzale Imperiale, plan of mosaic (1/2 disk)
ink on paper, 56.6 × 89 cm
Archivio Centrale dello Stato, Rome (Archivio Moretti)

2.40 Luigi Moretti
Theatre, EUR, plan and sketches of variants
pencil on paper
Archivio Centrale dello Stato, Rome (Archivio Moretti)

2.41 Luigi Moretti
Theatre, EUR, preliminary design, elevation
pencil on paper, 46.5 × 86.5 cm
Archivio Centrale dello Stato, Rome (Archivio Moretti)

2.42 Luigi Moretti
Villa for Ettore Muti on the island of Brioni (perspective)
coloured print on paper
Archivio Centrale dello Stato, Rome (Archivio Moretti)

2.43 Giulio Pediconi
Porta Imperiale, entrance to EUR from the North (perspective of Modernist variant)
charcoal on paper, approx. 80 × 80 cm
Pediconi Archive, Rome

2.44 Marcello Piacentini
Via Imperiale (perspective towards Piazza Imperiale with the Marconi obelisk), 1939
ink on paper, 73 × 101 cm
Archivio Centrale dello Stato, Rome (EUR S 10 – 6a)

2.45 G. Tripodi
Model of the Ara Pacis reconstructed (Ara Pacis, plastico ricostruttivo), 1:20, 1937
plaster
Museo della Civiltà Romana, Rome (M.C.R. n. 226)

2.46 Luigi Vieti
Sketch Plans for EUR, 1938–39
Vietti Archive, Milan

Art

2.47 Ambrosi
Portrait of Benito Mussolini with View of Rome Behind (Ritratto di Benito Mussolini con sfondo di Roma), 1930
oil on canvas, 124 × 124 cm
Private collection, Rome

2.48 Corrado Cagli
View of Rome (Veduta di Roma), 1937
tempera and encaustic on panel, 2 panels, each 240 × 200 cm
Private collection, Rome

2.49 Carlo Carrà
Resting Athletes (Gli atleti in riposo)
oil on canvas
Private collection, Milan

2.50 Tullio Crali
Nose-Diving on the City (Il tuffo sulla città), 1939
oil on canvas, 130 × 155 cm
Private collection, Milan

2.51 Giorgio de Chirico
Gladiators (I gladiatori), 1928–29
oil on canvas, 90 × 117 cm
Civico Museo d'Arte Contemporanea, Milan

2.52 Giorgio de Chirico
Visit to the Mysterious Baths (Visita ai bagni misteriosi), 1935
oil on canvas, 38 × 46 cm
Private collection, Verona

2.53 Gerardo Dottori
Portrait of the Duce (Ritratto del Duce), 1933
oil on canvas, 101 × 106 cm
Civiche Raccolte d'Arte, Milan

2.54 Lucio Fontana
Female Bust (Busto Femminile), 1931
coloured terracotta, 29.5 cm
Civico Museo d'Arte Contemporanea, Milan

2.55 Lucio Fontana
The Harpoonist (Il Fiocinatore), 1933–34
bronze, 173 cm
Civico Museo d'Arte Contemporanea, Milano

2.56 Lucio Fontana
Abstract Sculpture (Scultura astratta), 1934
coloured plaster, 41 × 25 cm
Collection Giorgio Marconi, Milan

2.57 Lucio Fontana
Abstract Sculpture (Scultura astratta), 1934
(autograph reconstruction made in the 1950s)
painted iron, 63.5 × 41 × 7 cm
Galleria Civica d'Arte Moderna e Contemporanea, Turin

2.58 Lucio Fontana
Relief (Rilievo), 1934
coloured plaster, 27 × 28 cm
IVAM. Instituto Valenciano de Arte Moderno, Valencia

2.59 Achille Funi
Publius Horatius Kills His Sister (Orazio che uccide la sorella), 1932
oil on canvas, 230 × 200 cm
Staatliche Museen zu Berlin, Nationalgalerie (A II 790)

2.60 Renato Guttuso
Flight from Mount Etna (Fuga dall'Etna), 1940
oil on canvas, 144 × 254 cm
Galleria Nazionale d'Arte Moderna, Rome

2.61 Osvaldo Licini
Joke (Scherzo), 1933
oil on canvas, 18.5 × 26 cm
Museo d'Arte Contemporanea di Villa Croce, Genoa

2.62 Osvaldo Licini
Rhythm (Ritmo), 1933
oil on canvas, mounted on board, 21 × 29 cm
Museo d'Arte Contemporanea di Villa Croce, Genoa

2.63 Baldassarre Longoni
The Golden Lands of Italy (Tèrre dorate d'Italia), 1940
oil on canvas, 130 × 160 cm
Banca Popolare di Cremona, Cremona

2.64 Giacomo Manzù
Crucifixion (Crocifissione), 1939
bronze, 53 × 33 cm
Galleria Nazionale d'Arte Moderna, Rome

2.65 Marino Marini
Boxer (Pugile), 1933
bronze, 82 × 50 × 64 cm
Museo d'Arte Moderna e Contemporanea di Trento e Rovereto, Trento (M.P.A. 667)

2.66 Arturo Martini
The She-Wolf (La lupa), 1930–31
bronze, 86 × 135 × 60 cm
Courtesy Gian Ferrari Arte Moderna, Milan

2.67 Arturo Martini
Athena (Atena), 1934–35
bronze, 125 × 57 × 29 cm
Galleria Nazionale d'Arte Moderna, Rome

2.68 Arturo Martini
model for the Palazzo della Giustizia relief, Milan, c. 1935
100 × 100 × 16 cm
Collection Daniela Balzaretti, Milan

2.69 Fausto Melotti
Sculpture No. 23 (Scultura n. 23), 1935
plaster, 90 × 90 cm
Museo d'Arte Moderna e Contemporanea di Trento e Rovereto, Trento (M.P.A. 196)

2.70 Fausto Melotti
Sculpture No. 24 (Scultura n. 24), 1935
plaster and metal, 90 × 90 cm
Fondo Rivetti per l'Arte, Turin

2.71 Fausto Melotti
Mother and Child, 1939
plaster, 260 × 150 × 100 cm
Private collection, Carrara

2.72 Giorgio Morandi
Landscape (Paese), 1935
oil on canvas, 60 × 71 cm
Galleria Civica d'Arte Moderna e Contemporanea, Turin

2.73 Giorgio Morandi
Large Still-Life (Natura Morta grande), 1935
Oil on canvas, 50 × 50 cm
Private collection

2.74 Giorgio Morandi
Still-Life (Natura Morta), 1941
Oil on canvas, 63 × 41.5 cm
Private collection, Switzerland

2.75 Arturo Nathan
Figure on the Beach (Figura sulla spiaggia)
Oil on canvas, 80 × 100 cm
Private collection, Trieste

2.76 Fausto Pirandello
The Bath (Il bagno)
oil on canvas
Private collection, Rome

2.77 Alberto Savinio
The God of Armies (Le dieu des armées), 1931–32
tempera on canvas, 55 × 46 cm
Courtesy Gian Ferrari Arte Moderna, Milan

2.78 Scipione (Gino Bonichi)
Piazza Navona, 1929
oil on canvas, 34 × 41 cm
Private collection, Rome

2.79 Scipione (Gino Bonichi)
The Roman Courtesan (La Cortigiana Romana)
oil on canvas
Private collection, Switzerland

2.80 Mario Sironi
Shepherd (Pastore), 1932
oil on canvas, 90 × 80 cm
Civico Museo Revoltella, Trieste

2.81 Mario Sironi
Works and Days (Le opere e i giorni), 1932
tempera on paper, 199 × 241 cm
Crediop Spa, Rome

2.82 Mario Sironi
The Builders (I costruttori), 1933
oil on canvas, 110 × 90 cm
Private collection, Bagnatica

2.83 Mario Sironi
Hospitality (Woman with Dog) (L'ospitalità [Donna con cane]), 1936
mixed media on paper, mounted on canvas, 317 × 241 cm
Arco Farnese, Rome

2.84 Mario Sironi
study for the mosaic 'L'Italia Corporativa', 1936
mixed media on paper, mounted on canvas, 209 × 277 cm
Arco Farnese, Rome

2.85 Alberto Ziveri
The Fight (La rissa), 1937–38
oil on canvas, 210 × 260 cm
Galleria Nazionale d'Arte Moderna, Rome

Posters

2.86 Anonymous
Division San Marco (San Marco Division)
lithographic poster, 100 × 70.5 cm
Imperial War Museum, London (8084)

2.87 Anonymous
The Glory of the Army (Gloria della milizia)
lithographic poster, 70 × 50.5 cm
Imperial War Museum, London (4995)

2.88 Anonymous
The Voice (Mussolini) (La voce [Mussolini])
lithographic poster, 100 × 70 cm
Imperial War Museum, London (4990)

2.89 Gino Boccasile
Women of Italy (Donne d'Italia), c. 1943
poster, 100 × 70 cm
The Mitchell Wolfson Jr. Collection, Genoa (GD 1994.6.1)

2.90 Nico Edel
Vercelli and its Province from Roman Times to Fascism (Vercelli e la sua provincia dalla romanità al fascismo), 1939
poster, 138.5 × 100 cm
The Mitchell Wolfson Jr. Collection, Genoa (GD 1995.116)

2.91 Mancioli
We Shall Return . . . Fascist Italian Africa Institute (Ritorneremo . . . Istituto Fascista Africa Italiana)
lithographic poster
Imperial War Museum, London (4989)

2.92 Retrosi
Rome (Roma)
lithographic poster, 100 × 63 cm
Imperial War Museum, London (15883)

2.93 Rosa Salva
. . . in Time of War Sport is a Duty (. . . in tempo di guerra lo sport è un dovere), 1940
poster, 100 × 70 cm
The Mitchell Wolfson Jr. Collection, Genoa (GD 1995.117)

2.94 Rosa Salva
Victory! Royal Rowing Federation (Vincere! Reale Federazione di Canotaggio), 1941
poster, 100 × 70 cm
The Mitchell Wolfson Jr. Collection, Genoa (GD 1995.118)

MOSCOW

Architecture

3.1 B. M. Iofan, M. V. Adrianov, A. I. Baransky, S. A. Gel'fel'd, Yu. P. Zenkevich, D. M. Iofan, Ya. F. Popov, V. B. Polyatsky, D. M. Tsiperovich
competition project for USSR Pavilion at the 1937 International Exhibition, Paris (perspective), 1936 (built)
pastel, pencil, carbon on paper, 134 × 206 cm
Shchusev State Museum of Architecture, Moscow (R1a 10665/62)

General Plan for Moscow and Public Buildings

3.2 V. N. Semënov, S. E. Chernyshev, Moscow City Council Studio
General Plan for the Reconstruction of Moscow, 1935
ink, gouache and pencil on paper, 149 × 188 cm
Shchusev State Museum of Architecture, Moscow (R1a 11918)

3.3 Construction of Smolenskaya and Rostovskaya Embankments in Moscow (perspective), 1934
pencil, white pigment and bronze powder on paper, 149 × 248.7 cm
Shchusev State Museum of Architecture, Moscow (R1a 5582)

3.4 A. V. Shchusev, A. K. Rostkovsky, A. V. Kurovsky
Construction of Rostovskaya Embankment in Moscow (perspective), 1934–35 (partially built)
ink, pencil and watercolour on paper, 68 × 96.5 cm
Shchusev State Museum of Architecture, Moscow (R1a 3569)

3.5 A. N. Dushkin, V. S. Belyavasky, N. S. Knyazev
competition project for Great Academic Film Theatre of the USSR, Moscow (perspective with view of the Kremlin, detail), 1936
watercolour, ink and pencil on paper, 119.5 × 98.5 cm
Shchusev State Museum of Architecture, Moscow (R1a 4177)

3.6 I. A. Golosov, P. I. Antonov, A. S. Zhuravlev
competition project for House of the Book, Moscow (perspective), 1934
ink and white pigment on paper, 145 × 196.5 cm
Shchusev State Museum of Architecture, Moscow (R1a 4815)

3.7 I. A. Fomin, P. V. Abrosimov, M. A. Minkus
competition project for People's Commissariat for Heavy Industry, Red Square, Moscow (perspective from Theatre Square), 1934
ink, gouache, white pigment on paper, 97.8 × 148.2 cm
Shchusev State Museum of Architecture, Moscow (R1a 3491)

3.8 A. G. Mordvinov
competition project for People's Commissariat for Heavy Industry, Moscow (perspective from Red Square), 1935
ink and watercolour on paper, 65 × 129.5 cm
Shchusev State Museum of Architecture, Moscow (R1a 3693)

3.9 A. A. Vesnin, V. A. Vesnin
competition project for People's Commissariat for Heavy Industry (perspective), 1934
pencil and watercolour on paper, 47 × 111.5 cm
Shchusev State Museum of Architecture, Moscow (R1a 6594/41)

3.10 A. A. Vesnin, V. A. Vesnin
competition project for People's Commissariat for Heavy Industry (perspective from Red Square), 1934
pencil and charcoal on paper, 122.3 × 250.1 cm
Shchusev State Museum of Architecture, Moscow (R1a 3753)

3.11 K. S. Mel'nikov
competition project for People's Commissariat for Heavy Industry, Moscow (perspective from the Kremlin), 1934
ink, watercolour and pencil on paper, 148.3 × 150.1 cm
Shchusev State Museum of Architecture, Moscow (R1a 3731)

3.12 L. I. Savel'ev, O. A. Stapran
Hotel Moskva (perspective), 1933
pencil, watercolour, pastel and charcoal on paper, 113.5 × 256 cm
Shchusev State Museum of Architecture, Moscow (R1a 211)

3.13 I. P. Lobov and others
Reconstruction of Zamoskvorech'e, Moscow (bird's eye view), 1935
pencil on paper, 109.5 × 198.1 cm
Shchusev State Museum of Architecture, Moscow (R1a 4707)

3.14 B. M. Iofan, V. G. Gel'freykh, Ya. B. Belopol'sky, V. V. Pelevin and others
Palace of the Soviets (variant, perspective from River Moskva), 1946
pencil, watercolour and white pigment on paper, 88 × 124 cm
Shchusev State Museum of Architecture, Moscow (R1a 11290/3)

3.15 A. V. Shchusev
Academy of Sciences of the USSR, Moscow (perspective), 1939
watercolour and pencil on paper, 88.4 × 198.3 cm
Shchusev State Museum of Architecture, Moscow (R1a 7459/2)

3.16 A. V. Samoilov, B. V. Yefimovich; consultants G. B. Barkhin, V. I. Obraztsov
competition project for Palace of Engineering, Moscow (perspective)
watercolour and pencil on paper, 98.7 × 149.3 cm
Shchusev State Museum of Architecture, Moscow (R1a 2915)

3.17 I. A. Golosov
Academy of Communal Economy, Moscow (perspective), 1935
watercolour and ink on paper, 94 × 246.5 cm
Shchusev State Museum of Architecture, Moscow (R1a 4813)

3.18 Kh. Kh. Solomonov
Central Anti-Religion Museum, Moscow (perspective), 1935
watercolour and ink on paper, 62.1 × 82.1 cm
Shchusev State Museum of Architecture, Moscow (R1a 4603)

3.19 D. N. Chechulin, K. V. Kaurkov
Aeroflot Offices, Moscow (perspective), 1934
gouache and white pigment on paper, 196 × 244.5 cm
Shchusev State Museum of Architecture, Moscow (R1a 5157)

The Moscow Metro

3.20 I. A. Fomin, A. F. Denishchenko (engineer)
competition project for Krasnye Vorota Station (interior perspective, platform hall), 1934–5 (built)
pencil, gouache, watercolour and white pigment on paper, 58.1 × 81.5 cm
Shchusev State Museum of Architecture, Moscow (R1a 3497)

3.21 N. Ya. Kolli, F. I. Zammer, A. F. Denishchenko (engineer)
competition project for Myasnitskaya (subsequently Kirovskaya) Station (interior perspective, platform hall), 1934–35 (built)
pencil, watercolour and white pigment on paper, 59.7 × 83 cm
Shchusev State Museum of Architecture, Moscow (R1a 4002)

3.22 B. S. Vilensky, L. D. Fishbein, M. G. Manizer (sculptor), S. G. Mel'nitsky (engineer)
Izmailovskaya Station (interior perspective, ground-level pavilion), 1936–44 (built)
pencil, watercolour and coloured ink on paper, 78.1 × 60.5 cm
Shchusev State Museum of Architecture, Moscow (R1a 7256/1)

3.23 B. M. Iofan, Yu. P. Zenkevich, V. V. Pelevin, B. V. Greits (engineer), B. M. Prikot
Spartakovskaya (Baumanskaya) Station (ground-level hall, perspective, detail, variant), 1938–44 (built)
pastel and charcoal on tracing paper, 117.5 × 96 cm
Shchusev State Museum of Architecture, Moscow (R1a 7243)

3.24 V. S. Andreyev
Sokol'niki Station (perspective, interior of platform hall)
pencil and watercolour on paper, 77 × 136.6 cm
Shchusev State Museum of Architecture, Moscow (R1a 4010)

3.25 D. F. Fridman
Dzerzhinsky Square Station (façade), 1934
pencil, ink, watercolour, powdered silver and white pigment on paper, 87 × 138 cm
Shchusev State Museum of Architecture, Moscow (R1a 4012)

Military Buildings

3.26 L. V. Rudnev, V. O. Munts
competition project for Frunze Military Academy (perspective), 1931 (built)
pencil, watercolour and gouache on paper, 67 × 155.5 cm
Shchusev State Museum of Architecture, Moscow (R1a 5133)

3.27 M. A. Minkus
competition project for Frunze Military Academy (perspective, plans, façades, variants), 1931
pencil on tracing paper, 34.7 × 43.6 cm
Shchusev State Museum of Architecture, Moscow (R1a 11852/2)

3.28 M. A. Minkus
competition project for Frunze Military Academy (axonometric projection), 1931
pencil on photograph, 33.4 × 28.6 cm
Shchusev State Museum of Architecture, Moscow (R1a 7138/1)

3.29 K. S. Mel'nikov
competition project for Frunze Military Academy (façade), 1931
ink and watercolour on paper, 31.6 × 161 cm
Shchusev State Museum of Architecture, Moscow (R1a 4910)

3.30 K. S. Alabyan, V. N. Simbirtsev
Red Army Theatre, Moscow (perspective)
pencil, watercolour and ink on paper, 119.5 × 172.1 cm
Shchusev State Museum of Architecture, Moscow (R1a 4795)

3.31 L. V. Rudnev
People's Commissariat for Defence, Moscow (Arbat Square) (perspective), 1932–38 (partially built)
pencil and watercolour on paper, 95.5 × 200.3 cm
Shchusev State Museum of Architecture, Moscow (R1a 4900)

All-Union Agricultural Exhibition

3.32 Yu. P. Zenkevich
Square in front of main entrance to VSKHV (All-Union Agricultural Exhibition) (perspective), 1939
pencil, watercolour and ink on paper, 51.5 × 73.2 cm
Shchusev State Museum of Architecture, Moscow (R1a 4885)

3.33 R. B. Barkhin, M. G. Barkhin
Main Pavilion of VSKHV (façade), 1935–36
pencil, ink and wash on paper, 75 × 158 cm
Shchusev State Museum of Architecture, Moscow (R1a 4580)

3.34 A. A. Vesnin, V. A. Vesnin
Grain Farming Pavilion of VSKHV (perspective), 1936
pencil and charcoal on paper, 64 × 88 cm
Shchusev State Museum of Architecture, Moscow (R1a 6621/2)

3.35 S. N. Polupanov
competition project for Uzbek SSR Pavilion at VSKHV (perspective), 1937 (built)
ink, watercolour and pencil on paper, 58.1 × 79.1 cm
Shchusev State Museum of Architecture, Moscow (R1a 4888)

Monuments and Military Memorials

3.36 I. A. Golosov
Museum and Monument to the Defence of Moscow (perspective), 1941
ink and watercolour on paper, 54.7 × 99.5 cm
Shchusev State Museum of Architecture, Moscow (R1a 5122/2)

3.37 A. N. Dushkin, N. D. Panchenko, A. D. Khil'kevich
competition project for Pantheon for the Heroes of the Great Patriotic War, Moscow (façade), 1942–43
pencil, ink and watercolour on paper
Shchusev State Museum of Architecture, Moscow (R1a 5128)

Art

3.38 Samuil Adlivankin
Voting to Expel the Kulak from the Collective Farm, 1931
oil on canvas, 95 × 139 cm
State Tretyakov Gallery, Moscow (ZhS-694)

3.39 Pavel Bazmanov
At Haymaking, 1932
watercolour and gouache on paper, 25.2 × 32.8 cm
State Tretyakov Gallery, Moscow (10569)

3.40 Pavel Bazmanov
An Outing with the Children, 1933
watercolour on paper, 16 × 20.6 cm
State Tretyakov Gallery, Moscow (RS-2409)

3.41 Pavel Bazmanov
A Holiday Outing, 1934
watercolour on paper, 16.3 × 21.6 cm
State Tretyakov Gallery, Moscow (RS-2408)

3.42 Konstantin Bogayevsky
Oil Fields, 1931
oil on canvas, 108 × 206.5 cm
State Russian Museum, St Petersburg (Zh-2337)

3.43 Izaak Brodsky
Demonstration on 25 October Prospect, 1934
oil on canvas, 258 × 200 cm
State Tretyakov Gallery, Moscow (15145)

3.44 Izaak Brodsky
Portrait of Stalin, 1937
oil on canvas, 210 × 143 cm
State Russian Museum, St Petersburg (Zh-4381)

3.45 Iosif Chaikov
Portrait of V. V. Mayakovsky, 1940
black granite, 65 cm
State Tretyakov Gallery, Moscow (27458)

3.46 Aleksandr Deineka
Landscape with Herd, 1934
watercolour and gouache on paper, 41.5 × 34.6 cm
State Tretyakov Gallery, Moscow (RS-2339)

3.47 Aleksandr Deineka
Torpedo Boat, Sebastopol, 1934
watercolour and tempera on paper, 29.6 × 49.3 cm
State Tretyakov Gallery, Moscow (13598)

3.48 Aleksandr Deineka
Black Youth, 1935
oil on canvas, 75 × 51.5 cm
State Russian Museum, St Petersburg (ZhB-1814)

3.49 Aleksandr Deineka
Future Pilot, 1938
oil on canvas, 131 × 161 cm
State Tretyakov Gallery, Moscow (27654)

3.50 Aleksandr Deineka
Berlin: Ruined Buildings, 1945
watercolour, tempera and pencil on paper, 47.8 × 35.9 cm
State Tretyakov Gallery, Moscow (RS-561)

3.51 Aleksandr Deineka
The Day of the Signing of the Declaration, 1945
watercolour and tempera on paper
State Tretyakov Gallery, Moscow (26861)

3.52 Aleksandr Deineka
On the Outskirts of Berlin, 1945
watercolour and tempera on paper, 39 × 49 cm
State Tretyakov Gallery, Moscow (26863)

3.53 Nikolai Denisovsky
Gold Mining. Prospectors Working a Mine, 1930
oil on canvas, 99 × 124 cm
State Tretyakov Gallery, Moscow (ZhS-3133)

3.54 Aleksandr Drevin
Outskirts, 1931
oil on canvas, 68 × 71.5 cm
State Tretyakov Gallery, Moscow (ZhS-1376)

3.55 Pavel Filonov
Portrait of Stalin, 1936
oil on canvas, 99 × 67 cm
State Russian Museum, St Petersburg (Zh-9590)

3.56 Pavel Filonov
Head II, c. 1936
oil on paper, 74 × 64 cm
State Russian Museum, St Petersburg (Zh-9617)

3.57 Pavel Filonov
Two Male Figures, 1938
oil on paper, 84 × 64 cm
State Russian Museum, St Petersburg (Zh-9615)

3.58 Pavel Filonov
Raid, 1938
oil on paper, 70.5 × 86.5 cm
State Russian Museum, St Petersburg (Zh-9603)

3.59 Taras Gaponenko
To Mother for the Next Feed, 1935
oil on canvas, 105 × 155 cm
State Tretyakov Gallery, Moscow (22510)

3.60 Aleksandr Gerasimov
Sketch for 'Stalin's Speech at the 16th Congress of the Communist Party'
oil on canvas, 99.5 × 128 cm
State Tretyakov Gallery, Moscow (15141)

3.61 Boris Golopolosov
At Dneprostroi, 1932–3
oil on canvas, 160 × 104 cm
State Tretyakov Gallery, Moscow (ZhS-3576)

3.62 Gustavs Klucis
In the Storm of the Third Year of the Five Year Plan, 1930
autotype, 103 × 74.5 cm
Russian State Library, Moscow (16314-38)

3.63 Gustavs Klucis
We Shall Complete the Plan of Great Works, 1930
offset lithograph, 124 × 87.5 cm
Russian State Library, Moscow (30-85457/30-85458)

3.64 Gustavs Klucis
Long Live the USSR – Fatherland of Workers of the World, 1931
2 mezzotints, 74.5 × 103.5 cm
Russian State Library, Moscow (31-85333, 31-127684)

3.65 Gustavs Klucis
The Struggle for the Bolshevik Harvest is the Struggle for Socialism, 1931
autotype and chromolithograph, 142 × 101 cm
Russian State Library, Moscow (32283-55)

3.66 Gustavs Klucis
Cultured Life – Productive Work, 1932
chromolithograph and autotype, 146 × 101.5 cm
Russian State Library, Moscow (32-75835/32-75838)

3.67 Gustavs Klucis
Greetings to Those Who Have Completed the Dneprostroi, the Greatest Dam in the World, 1932
offset lithograph, 143.5 × 101 cm
Russian State Library, Moscow (32-23374)

3.68 Gustavs Klucis
Youth to the Aircraft. Moscow-Leningrad, 1934
chromolithograph, 141.5 × 98 cm
Russian State Library, Moscow (34-58384)

3.69 Gustavs Klucis
All of Moscow is Building the Metro, 1934
chromolithograph, 141 × 96.1 cm
Russian State Library, Moscow (34-38906)

3.70 Gustavs Klucis
Long Live the Stalinist Order of Heroes and Stakhanovites!, 1936
offset lithograph, 79.5 × 101.4 cm
Russian State Library, Moscow (36-68692)

3.71 Gustavs Klucis
Raise the Banner of Marx, Engels, Lenin and Stalin!, 1937
mezzotint, 50 × 94 cm
Russian State Library, Moscow (36-75885)

3.72 Gustavs Klucis
Under the Banner of Lenin for Socialist Construction, 1940
offset lithograph, 97.5 × 72 cm
Russian State Library, Moscow (38-13872)

3.73 Aleksandr Labas
Flight to the Moon, 1935
watercolour and tempera on paper, 23.7 × 23.5 cm
State Tretyakov Gallery, Moscow (RS-5114)

3.74 Aleksandr Labas
The Coast at Batum, 1936
gouache on paper, 29.4 × 45.8 cm
State Tretyakov Gallery, Moscow (RS-4210)

3.75 Aleksandr Labas
In the Metro in Wartime, 1941
watercolour on paper, 42.3 × 31.6 cm
State Tretyakov Gallery, Moscow (RS-2267)

3.76 Aleksandr Labas
Portrait of Tatlin, 1946
on paper, 36.5 × 25.2 cm
State Tretyakov Gallery, Moscow (RS-2268)

3.77 Vladimir Lebedev
Stories, Songs, Riddles (text by S. Ya. Marshak), 1935
illustrated book
Russian State Library, Moscow

3.78 Sarra Lebedeva
Portrait of Aviator V. P. Chkalov, 1936
bronze with labradorite base, 37 cm
State Tretyakov Gallery, Moscow (27398)

3.79 Sarra Lebedeva
Miner (Large Figure for Socialist Industry), 1937
bronze, 200 cm
State Tretyakov Gallery, Moscow (SKS 415)

3.80 Sarra Lebedeva
Kalmyk Woman, 1938
bronze, 37 cm
State Tretyakov Gallery, Moscow (SKS 531)

3.81 El Lissitzky
The Baltic Deputy, 1941
film script cover – watercolour on toning paper, 18.1 × 13.3 cm

State Tretyakov Gallery, Moscow (RS-1835)

3.82 El Lissitzky
Bluebeard's Eighth Wife, 1941
film script cover – gouache on paper, 18.2 × 13.4 cm
State Tretyakov Gallery, Moscow (RS-1838)

3.83 El Lissitzky
Chkalov, 1941
film script cover – watercolour and gouache on paper, 18.2 × 13.5 cm
State Tretyakov Gallery, Moscow (RS-1836)

3.84 El Lissitzky
Lenin in October, 1941
film script cover – gouache on paper (variant), 18 × 13.7 cm
State Tretyakov Gallery, Moscow (RS-1831)

3.85 El Lissitzky
Lenin in October, 1941
film script cover – gouache on paper (variant), 18.2 × 13.3 cm
State Tretyakov Gallery, Moscow (RS-1832)

3.86 El Lissitzky
Send more Tanks, 1942
autotype, 90 × 59.2 cm
Russian State Library, Moscow (42-65940)

3.87 El Lissitzky
The Great Waltz, 1947
film script cover (sketch) – pencil on paper
State Tretyakov Gallery, Moscow (RS-1837)

3.88 A. V. Lobanov
Training Cadres for Magnitostroi, 1932
oil on canvas, 90 × 121 cm
State Tretyakov Gallery, Moscow (ZhS-1008)

3.89 Kazimir Malevich
Primitive (Cobbler), c. 1930
pencil on paper, 14.7 × 13.4 cm
Museum Ludwig, Cologne

3.90 Kazimir Malevich
Portrait of the Advanced Worker, 1932
oil on canvas, 64 × 55 cm
State Russian Museum, St Petersburg (9402)

3.91 Kazimir Malevich
Peasant Woman Praying, 1933
pencil on paper, 28.8 × 17.6 cm
Museum Ludwig, Cologne

3.92 Kazimir Malevich
The Smith, 1933
oil on canvas, 64 × 56 cm
State Russian Museum, St Petersburg (9466)

3.93 Matvei Manizer
Worker: Figure for planned Monument to the Victims of 9 January 1905, for Leningrad, 1930
bronze, 70 cm
State Tretyakov Gallery, Moscow (59038)

3.94 Matvei Manizer
Head of a Young Man (Metro study), 1939
bronze, 54 cm
State Tretyakov Gallery, Moscow (26915)

3.95 Aleksandr Matveyev
Maquette for a monument, 1931
bronze, 75 × 81 × 55 cm
State Russian Museum, St Petersburg (SO-770)

3.96 Aleksandr Matveyev
Self-portrait, 1939–41
bronze with labradorite base, 43 cm
State Tretyakov Gallery, Moscow (SKS 461)

3.97 Aleksandr Monin
Shock-Workers' Avenue, 1934
oil on canvas, 47 × 160 cm
State Tretyakov Gallery, Moscow (ZhS-4907)

3.98 Vera Mukhina
Industrial Worker and Collective Farm Girl (model of group installed at Paris International Exhibition 1937), 1935
bronze, 158.5 × 106 × 112 cm
State Russian Museum, St Petersburg (SO-724)

3.99 Vera Mukhina
Flyer (project for planned monument 'The Saving of the Chelyuskintsy'), 1938
bronze, 61.8 cm
State Tretyakov Gallery, Moscow (SKS 243)

3.100 Vera Mukhina
North Wind/Boreas (project for planned monument 'The Saving of the Chelyuskintsy' for Moscow), 1938
bronze, 35 cm
State Tretyakov Gallery, Moscow (SKS 233)

3.101 Vera Mukhina
Female Partisan, 1942
bronze, 46 cm
State Tretyakov Gallery, Moscow (30673)

3.102 Dimitri Nalbandian
At the Yalta Conference, 1945
oil on canvas, 74.5 × 120 cm
State Russian Museum, St Petersburg (Zh-5962)

3.103 Mikhail Nesterov
Portrait of the Surgeon S. S. Yudin, 1935
oil on canvas, 80 × 97 cm
State Tretyakov Gallery, Moscow (15720)

3.104 Solomon Nikritin
The Fat Man's Speech, 1928
oil on plywood, 41 × 41 cm
State Tretyakov Gallery, Moscow (ZhS-1124)

3.105 Solomon Nikritin
Composition, 1930
oil on canvas, 68 × 58 cm

State Russian Museum, St Petersburg (Zh-9252)

3.106 Solomon Nikritin
Composition, 1930
oil on canvas, 58 × 68 cm
State Tretyakov Gallery, Moscow (P.46976)

3.107 Solomon Nikritin
Discussion (sketch for painting), 1930
gouache and watercolour on paper
State Tretyakov Gallery, Moscow (RS-4909)

3.108 Solomon Nikritin
The People's Court, 1934
oil on plywood (sketch), 36 × 36 cm
State Tretyakov Gallery, Moscow (ZhS-1125)

3.109 Solomon Nikritin
Sketch for 'The People's Court', 1934?
oil on paper, 11 × 11 cm
State Tretyakov Gallery, Moscow (RS-4910)

3.110 Yuri Pimenov
City Children, 1930
oil on canvas, 139.7 × 73.7 cm
Museum Ludwig, Cologne

3.111 Aleksandr Rodchenko
Pioneer, 1930
photograph (vintage print), 29.5 × 23.6 cm
The Rodchenko and Stepanova Archive, Moscow

3.112 Aleksandr Rodchenko
Pioneer Girl, 1930
photograph (vintage print), 30 × 23.3 cm
The Rodchenko and Stepanova Archive, Moscow

3.113 Aleksandr Rodchenko
Pioneer with a Trumpet, 1930
photograph (late print), 33 × 28 cm
The Rodchenko and Stepanova Archive, Moscow

3.114 Aleksandr Rodchenko
First Cavalry, 1935
photo-album
The Rodchenko and Stepanova Archive, Moscow

3.115 Aleksandr Rodchenko
The Juggler (No. 1), 1935
oil on board, 106 × 65 cm
The Rodchenko and Stepanova Archive, Moscow

3.116 Aleksandr Rodchenko
The Female Pyramid, 1936
photograph (vintage print), 40 × 29.5 cm
The Rodchenko and Stepanova Archive, Moscow

3.117 Aleksandr Rodchenko
The Wheel, 1936
photograph (vintage print),

47 × 30 cm
The Rodchenko and Stepanova Archive, Moscow

3.118 Aleksandr Rodchenko
The Installation 'Long Live the Constitution', 1936
photograph (vintage print), 47 × 29.8 cm
The Rodchenko and Stepanova Archive, Moscow

3.119 Aleksandr Rodchenko
Soviet Uzbekistan photo-album
The Rodchenko and Stepanova Archive, Moscow

3.120 Konstantin Rozhdestvensky
Man with Beard, 1929
oil on canvas, 54 × 49 cm
Galerie Gmurzynska, Cologne

3.121 Konstantin Rozhdestvensky
New Still-Life, 1935
oil on canvas, 36.4 × 54 cm
Galerie Gmurzynska, Cologne

3.122 Konstantin Rozhdestvensky
Suprematist Architectural Landscape, 1935
pencil on paper, 15 × 20.2 cm
Galerie Gmurzynska, Cologne

3.123 Vasily Rozhdestvensky
Moscow Landscape. Construction, 1936
oil on canvas, 75.5 × 104 cm
State Tretyakov Gallery, Moscow (ZhS-1177)

3.124 Boris Rybchenkov
Outskirts. Bright Evening, 1933
oil on canvas, 59 × 69 cm
State Tretyakov Gallery, Moscow (ZhS-1847)

3.125 Georgi Rublëv
Portrait of Stalin, 1935
oil on canvas, 152 × 152 cm
Private Collection, Courtesy State Tretyakov Gallery, Moscow

3.126 Aleksandr Samokhvalov
Kirov at the Sports Parade, 1935
oil on canvas, 305 × 372.5 cm
State Russian Museum, St Petersburg (ZhB-1962)

3.127 Ivan Shadr
Girl with Torch (design for sculpture for Soviet Pavilion at 1939 New York World Exhibition), 1937
bronze, 156 cm
State Tretyakov Gallery, Moscow (27543)

3.128 Ivan Shadr
Young Man with Star and Banner (design for sculpture for Soviet pavilion at 1939

348

New York World Exhibition), 1937
bronze, 119 cm
State Tretyakov Gallery, Moscow (27544)

3.129 **Ivan Shadr**
'Stormy Petrel' (Head of Gorky), 1939
bronze, 98 × 85 × 89 cm
State Russian Museum, St Petersburg (SO-29)

3.130 **Grigory Shegal**
Leader, Teacher, Friend (Stalin at the Presidium of the 2nd Congress of Collective Farm and Shock Workers, February 1935), 1936–37
oil on canvas, 340 × 260 cm
State Russian Museum, St Petersburg (Zh-5613)

3.131 **Pavel Sokolov-Skalya**
Grief at the Tomb of S. M. Kirov, 1934
oil on canvas, 89 × 70 cm
State Tretyakov Gallery, Moscow (22704)

3.132 **Nikolai Suyetin**
Female Figure, 1927
pencil on paper, 41.2 × 31.8 cm
Galerie Gmurzynska, Cologne

3.133 **Nikolai Suyetin**
Suprematist City, 1931
pencil on cardboard, 49.4 × 50.5 cm
Galerie Gmurzynska, Cologne

3.134 **Nikolai Suyetin**
Abstract Composition, 1932
pencil on paper, 21 × 30.5 cm
Galerie Gmurzynska, Cologne

3.135 **Vladimir Tatlin**
Branches, 1946
oil on canvas, 82 × 65 cm
State Russian Museum, St Petersburg (Zh-8348)

3.136 **Vladimir Tatlin**
Poplars, 1946
oil on canvas and plywood, 49.5 × 39.5 cm
State Russian Museum, St Petersburg (Zh-8374)

3.137 **Nikolai Tomsky**
S. M. Kirov (maquette for the monument in Leningrad), 1935
bronze, 47 × 27 × 21 cm
State Tretyakov Gallery, Moscow (30931)

3.138 **Aleksandr Tyshler**
Young Red Army Soldiers Reading the Newspaper, 1936
oil on canvas, 56 × 65 cm
State Russian Museum, St Petersburg

3.139 **Konstantin Vialov**
The Red Brotherhood, 1932
oil on canvas, 125.8 × 99.8 cm
Museum Ludwig, Cologne

3.140 **Vera Yermolayeva**
'The Bubbles' by E. Shvarts design for book cover, watercolour, white pigment and pencil on paper, 26.8 × 20 cm
State Tretyakov Gallery, Moscow (RS-1838)

3.141 **Vera Yermolayeva**
'Bubbles in the Sky', from 'The Bubbles' by E. Shvarts
book illustration, watercolour and gouache on paper, 27 × 20.1 cm
State Tretyakov Gallery, Moscow (RS-4869)

3.142 **Vera Yermolayeva**
'The Bubbles Flown Away', from 'The Bubbles' by E. Shvarts
book illustration, watercolour and gouache on paper, 27 × 20.5 cm
State Tretyakov Gallery, Moscow (RS-4870)

3.143 **Vera Yermolayeva**
'Car and Carriage' and 'Piglet and Wagon' from 'The Unlucky Coachman'
book illustration, watercolour, white pigment and pencil on paper, 23.3 × 18.7 cm
State Tretyakov Gallery, Moscow (RS-4864)

3.144 **Vera Yermolayeva**
'Horse and Beetle' and 'Steamer and Boat' from 'The Unlucky Coachman'
book illustration, watercolour, white pigment and pencil on paper, 22.9 × 18 cm
State Tretyakov Gallery, Moscow (RS-4865)

3.145 **Nikolai Yevgrafov**
The New Life, 1932
oil on canvas, 124 × 87 cm
State Russian Museum, St Petersburg (Zh-9001)

Posters

3.146 **Anonymous**
Exhibition of Posters of Revolutionary Spain, 1937
chromolithograph, 93.5 × 65 cm
Russian State Library, Moscow (37-76938)

3.147 **Aleksandr Deineka**
Collective Farm Worker, Become an Athlete, 1930
chromolithograph, 73.8 × 104.5 cm
Russian State Library, Moscow (31-5309)

3.148 **Aleksandr Deineka**
We Demand Universal Compulsory Education, 1930
chromolithograph, 106 × 72.2 cm
Russian State Library, Moscow (55-13970)

3.149 **V. Deni**
GPU. Revolutionary Lightning (author of text D.

Bednyi), 1930
chromolithograph, 104 × 74.3 cm
Russian State Library, Moscow (31-10166)

3.150 **V. Deni and N. Dolgorukov**
Our Army and Our Country are Strengthened with the Spirit of Stalin!, 1939
mezzotint, 92 × 61 cm
Russian State Library, Moscow (40-87389)

3.151 **V. Govorkov**
Citizens of the USSR have a Right to Recreation, 1936
chromolithograph, 108 × 69.5 cm
Russian State Library, Moscow (36-74829)

3.152 **V. Govorkov**
Stalin in the Kremlin Cares for Each of Us, 1940
chromolithograph, 90.1 × 59.1 cm
Russian State Library, Moscow

3.153 **D. Grinets**
Thanks to the Party, Thanks to Dear Stalin for a Happy, Joyful Childhood, 1937
chromolithograph, 107.2 × 61 cm
Russian State Library, Moscow (38-66329)

3.154 **L. Kaplan**
Life has Become Better, Comrades . . . , 1936
chromolithograph, 90.5 × 59.5 cm
Russian State Library, Moscow (36-68381)

3.155 **A. Kokorekin**
We Shall Kill the Fascist German Aggressors in Their Den, 1944
chromolithograph, 58 × 84 cm
Russian State Library, Moscow (45-2769)

3.156 **V. Kolyabin**
Young People Everywhere Find a Way to Us!, 1951
offset, 81 × 57 cm
Russian State Library, Moscow (Arch.4940)

3.157 **V. Koretsky**
Europe Shall Be Free, 1944
lithograph, 61 × 41.2 cm
Russian State Library, Moscow (44-4875)

3.158 **A. Koil'**
Glory to the Conquerors of the Air!, 1936
chromolithograph, 67 × 98 cm
Russian State Library, Moscow (36-73038)

3.159 **Kukryniksy**
The Brother Nations Have Called a Meeting over the Enemy's City. With each Handshake Fascist Germany Trembles (text by S. Marshak), 1941
chromolithograph, 90 ×

59.3 cm
Russian State Library, Moscow (41-97512)

3.160 **Leonov**
Long Live the First of May – Military Inspection of the Revolutionary Forces of the International Proletariat, 1935
mezzotint, 180.5 × 62.5 cm
Russian State Library, Moscow (38-29794)

3.161 **B. Prorokov**
Fascism Is the Enemy of Culture, 1939
chromolithograph, 42 × 57.5 cm
Russian State Library, Moscow (39-72683)

3.162 **Pavel Sokolov-Skalya**
The Train Goes from the Station of Socialism to the Station of Communism, 1939
chromolithograph, 103.5 × 70.3 cm
Russian State Library, Moscow (39-73106)

3.163 **N. Vatolina**
Thanks to Dear Stalin for a Happy Childhood!, 1939
offset lithograph, 59.6 × 88.2 cm
Russian State Library, Moscow (39-75389)

BERLIN

Architecture

4.1 **Anonymous**
site plan of SS barracks and concentration camp at Sachsenhausen, 1:20,000, 20 January 1941
print, 85 × 105 cm
Landesarchiv Berlin

4.2 **Paul Bonatz**
autobahn bridge over the River Elbe, 1938
watercolour, 101 × 59.5 cm
Family Estate Paul Bonatz

4.3 **Paul Bonatz**
Headquarters of the Navy, 1939
inverted blueprint with white highlights, 98 × 200 cm
Family Estate Paul Bonatz

4.4 **Paul Bonatz and Kurt Dübbers**
Police Headquarters, Central Block, 1941
pencil on transparency paper, 116 × 183 cm
Family Estate Paul Bonatz

4.5 **Generalbauinspektion**
Construction of the Great Hall, 1:600
3 prints on parchment paper, each 82 × 42 cm
Landesarchiv Berlin (GBI 10)

4.6 **Walter Gropius**
competition project for the

Reichsbank, Berlin (perspective from the water), 1933
print with gouache, 37.8 × 78.1 cm
Busch-Reisinger Museum, Harvard University Art Museums, Gift of Walter Gropius (BRMGA 70.2)

4.7 **Konstanty Gutschow**
project for the University City, Berlin (perspective view from the west), 24 August 1938
blueprint on paper, 48 × 106 cm
Staatsarchiv Hamburg (621-2 Konstanty Gutschow, Architekt, A 251/1)

4.8 **Ludwig Hilberseimer**
project for the University City, Berlin (perspective view of Heerstrasse and Berlin University), 1937
ink on paper, 36.2 × 50.8 cm
The Art Institute of Chicago (1983.995.1)

4.9 **Wilhelm Kreis**
Soldatenhalle (side elevation facing Tiergarten), 1:100
print, 84 × 140 cm
Landesarchiv Berlin

4.10 **Gotthold Nestler**
Agfa Building (administration building for IG Farben), section of main façade facing North-South Axis, 1:20
coloured print, 188 × 92 cm
Landesarchiv Berlin (GBI 178)

4.11 **Cäsar Pinnau**
project for government building and 3000-bed hotel, 1:500
sepia blueprint, coloured, 55 × 149 cm
Hamburgisches Architekturarchiv, Collection Cäsar Pinnau, Private collection (GM 378/1)

4.12 **Cäsar Pinnau**
project for a hotel II, 1:200, 1942
pencil on transparency paper, 91 × 138 cm
Hamburgisches Architekturarchiv, Collection Cäsar Pinnau, Private collection (GM 378/2)

4.13 **Hans Poelzig**
competition project for the Reichsbank, Berlin, 1933
charcoal on parchment paper, 70 × 82.7 cm
Museum für Verkehr und Technik, Berlin

4.14 **Ernst Sagebiel**
Tempelhof Airport photograph of model, showing north (entrance) front
Staatliche Museen zu Berlin, Kunstbibliothek

4.15 **Ernst Sagebiel**
Tempelhof Airport photograph during construction, showing cantilever roof
Staatliche Museen zu Berlin, Kunstbibliothek

4.16 **Ernst Sagebiel**
Tempelhof Airport, main building, sectional drawing blueprint, 71 × 497 cm
Staatliche Museen zu Berlin, Kunstbibliothek

4.17 **Albert Speer**
Great Hall, section west-east (right half), with view of interior, 1:300
brown print with crayon additions, 168 × 90 cm
Landesarchiv Berlin (GBI 19)

4.18 **Albert Speer**
Triumphal Arch, section north-south, 1:500
print, 75 × 52 cm
Landesarchiv Berlin (GBI 210)

4.19 **Friedrich Tamms**
autobahn bridge at Frankfurt/Oder
watercolour
Staatliche Museen zu Berlin, Kunstbibliothek

4.20 **Friedrich Tamms**
bridge on the South Axis, section through the bridge (planned viaduct over the Teltow Canal and Dresden railway), 1:200, c. 1941
105 × 320 cm
Landesarchiv Berlin (GBI 203)

Art

4.21 **Ernst Barlach**
Seated Old Woman (Die sitzende Alte), 1933
bronze, 82 × 31.5 × 45 cm
Ernst Barlach Stiftung, Güstrow

4.22 **Ernst Barlach**
The Terrible Year of 1937, or The Bad Year (Das schlimme Jahr 1937), 1937
wood, 87.2 cm
Scottish National Gallery of Modern Art, Edinburgh (GMA 3036)

4.23 **Willi Baumeister**
Man with Pointed Beard (Mann mit Spitzbart), c. 1941
postcard, 14.7 × 10.5 cm
Archiv Baumeister, Stuttgart

4.24 **Willi Baumeister**
Man with Pointed Beard II (Mann mit Spitzbart II), c. 1941
postcard, 14.7 × 10.5 cm
Archiv Baumeister, Stuttgart

4.25 **Willi Baumeister**
Arno Breker's 'The Avenger' with Head drawn by Willi Baumeister (Arno Brekers 'Der Rächer' mit Kopf von Willi Baumeister), c. 1941
postcard, 26 × 18.5 cm
Archiv Baumeister, Stuttgart

4.26 Willi Baumeister
Dripping Shapes, Relief-Picture (Tropfende Formen, Reliefbild), 1942
oil on board, 65 × 45 cm
Archiv Baumeister, Stuttgart

4.27 Willi Baumeister
Drumbeat (Trommelschlag), 1942
oil on board, 53 × 45.5 cm
Archiv Baumeister, Stuttgart

4.28 Max Beckmann
Man in the Dark (Mann im Dunkeln), 1934
bronze, 56 cm
Private collection

4.29 Max Beckmann
Crawling Woman (Kriechende Frau), 1935
bronze, 30 × 57.5 × 20 cm
Private collection

4.30 Max Beckmann
Adam and Eve (Adam und Eva), 1936
bronze, 85 cm
Städelsches Kunstinstitut, Frankfurt am Main, on loan from the Deutsche Bank AG, Frankfurt am Main

4.31 Max Beckmann
Self-Portrait (Selbstporträt), 1936
bronze, 35.5 cm
Galerie Pels Leusden, Berlin

4.32 Max Beckmann
Apocalypse (Apokalypse), 1941–42
book with 27 lithographs
Sprengel Museum, Hannover (Gr. 1965, 217)

4.33 Max Beckmann
Carnival Triptych (Karneval), 1942–43
oil on canvas, 190.5 × 296.5 cm
The University of Iowa Museum of Art, Iowa

4.34 Arno Breker
Prometheus, 1937
bronze, 300 × 110 × 100 cm
Dr.-Hanns-Simon-Stiftung, Bitburg

4.35 Richard Gessner
Fuel Refineries under Construction (Treibstoffwerk im Bau)
oil on canvas, 101 × 151 cm
Property of the Federal Republic of Germany

4.36 Anna Griebel-Zietlow (copy after Otto Griebel)
The Internationale (Die Internationale), 1989 (1928–30)
oil on canvas, 125 × 185 cm
Deutsches Historisches Museum, Berlin

4.37 Hans Grundig
Day Labourers' Colony in Pomerania (Tagelöhnersiedlung in Pommern), 1934

oil on canvas, 88.5 × 98.5 cm
Deutsches Historisches Museum, Berlin (Kg 62/092)

4.38 Hans Grundig
Victims of Fascism (Opfer des Faschismus), 1946
oil on hardboard, 110 × 200 cm
Museum der Bildenden Künste, Leipzig (1431)

4.39 John Heartfield
The Face of Fascism – Italy in Chains (Das Gesicht des Faschismus – Italien in Ketten), 1928
print on paper, 38 × 27 cm
Stiftung Archiv der Akademie der Künste, Berlin

4.40 John Heartfield
The Meaning of Geneva (Der Sinn von Genf), 1932
print on paper, 38 × 27 cm
Stiftung Archiv der Akademie der Künste, Berlin

4.41 John Heartfield
Bug Hunts Vermin (Die Wanze als Kammerjäger), 1933
photomontage, 45.2 × 32.5 cm
Stiftung Archiv der Akademie der Künste, Berlin

4.42 John Heartfield
Bug Hunts Vermin (Die Wanze als Kammerjäger), 1933
print on paper, 38 × 27 cm
Stiftung Archiv der Akademie der Künste, Berlin

4.43 John Heartfield
Everything in Perfect Order! (Alles in schönster Ordnung!), 1933
print on paper, 38 × 27 cm
Stiftung Archiv der Akademie der Künste, Berlin

4.44 John Heartfield
Hangman and Justice (Der Henker und die Gerechtigkeit), 1933
print on paper, 38 × 27 cm
Stiftung Archiv der Akademie der Künste, Berlin

4.45 John Heartfield
Hitler's Programme (Hitlers Programm), 1933
photomontage, 43.9 × 32.2 cm
Stiftung Archiv der Akademie der Künste, Berlin

4.46 John Heartfield
Hitler's Programme (Hitlers Programm), 1933
print on paper, 38 × 27 cm
Stiftung Archiv der Akademie der Künste, Berlin

4.47 John Heartfield
New Chair at German Universities (Neuer Lehrstuhl an deutschen Universitäten), 1933
photomontage, 46 × 33 cm
Stiftung Archiv der Akademie der Künste, Berlin

4.48 John Heartfield
New Chair at German Universities (Neuer Lehrstuhl an deutschen Universitäten), 1933
print on paper, 38 × 27 cm
Stiftung Archiv der Akademie der Künste, Berlin

4.49 John Heartfield
The Thousand-Year Reich (Das tausendjährige Reich), 1934
print on paper, 38 × 27 cm
Stiftung Archiv der Akademie der Künste, Berlin

4.50 John Heartfield
Hurra! The Butter's All Gone! (Hurra! Die Butter ist alle!), 1935
print on paper, 38 × 27 cm
Stiftung Archiv der Akademie der Künste, Berlin

4.51 John Heartfield
Normalization (Normalisierung), 1936
print on paper, 38 × 27 cm
Stiftung Archiv der Akademie der Künste, Berlin

4.52 John Heartfield
Brown Artist's Dream (Brauner Künstlertraum), 1938
print on paper, 38 × 27 cm
Stiftung Archiv der Akademie der Künste, Berlin

4.53 John Heartfield
This is the Salvation They Bring us! (Das ist das Heil, das sie bringen!), 1938
print on paper, 38 × 27 cm
Stiftung Archiv der Akademie der Künste, Berlin

4.54 Sepp Hilz
The Red Necklace (Die rote Halskette)
oil on canvas, 30 × 28 cm
Property of the Federal Republic of Germany

4.55 Carl Hofer
The Guardians (Die Wächter), 1936
oil on canvas, 152 × 127 cm
Staatliche Museen zu Berlin, Nationalgalerie (A IV 411)

4.56 Albert Janesch
Water Sport (Wassersport), 1936
oil on canvas, 153 × 135 cm
Property of the Federal Republic of Germany

4.57 Arthur Kampf
Venus and Adonis (Venus und Adonis), 1939
oil on canvas, 183 × 158 cm
Property of the Federal Republic of Germany

4.58 Ludwig Kasper
Standing Girl (Stehendes Mädchen), 1931–32
cast stone, 163.5 cm
Wilhelm-Lehmbruck-Museum, Duisburg

4.59 Paul Klee
Dancing with Fear (Tänze vor Angst), 1938
watercolour on paper, mounted on cardboard, 48 × 31.4 cm
Kunstmuseum Bern, Paul-Klee-Stiftung (F 122)

4.60 Paul Klee
Voice from the Ether, 'And You Shall Eat Your Fill!' (Stimme aus dem Äther, "und du wirst dich satt essen"!), 1939
oil and tempera on wrapping paper, 50 × 38 cm
Victoria & Albert Museum, London (P4-1965)

4.61 Paul Klee
Another Angel of the Cross (anderer Engel vom Kreuz), 1939
zulu pencil on paper, 45.7 × 30.2 cm
Kunstmuseum Bern (Z 1974)

4.62 Paul Klee
Let It Roll! (Lass rollen!), 1939
pencil on paper, 29.7 × 20.9 cm
Kunstmuseum Bern (Z 1692)

4.63 Paul Klee
Outbreak of Fear (Angstausbruch), 1939
pen and ink on paper, mounted on cardboard, 27.1 × 21.5 cm
Kunstmuseum Bern (Z 1413)

4.64 Paul Klee
Outbreak of Fear III (Angstausbruch III), 1939
watercolour on paper, mounted on cardboard, 63.5 × 48.1 cm
Kunstmuseum Bern, Paul-Klee-Stiftung (F 127)

4.65 Paul Klee
S.O.S. Last Signal (S.O.S. letztes Zeichen), 1939
pencil on paper, 20.9 × 29.6 cm
Kunstmuseum Bern (Z 1769)

4.66 Paul Klee
Vigilant Angel (Wachsamer Engel), 1939
tempera and pencil on newspaper, mounted on cardboard, 48.8 × 32.9 cm
Private collection, Switzerland

4.67 Paul Klee
A Warning (Eine Warnung), 1939
pencil on paper, 20.9 × 29.6 cm
Kunstmuseum Bern (Z 1763)

4.68 Paul Klee
Monument to a Tooth (Denkmal einem Zahn), 1940
pencil on paper, 29.7 × 21 cm
Kunstmuseum Bern

4.69 Paul Klee
Silly Question from a Child (Dumme Frage eines Kindes), 1940
zulu pencil on paper, 29.6 × 21 cm
Kunstmuseum Bern (Z 2193)

4.70 Heinrich Knirr
Portrait of Hitler (Bildnis Adolf Hitler), 1937
oil on canvas, 127 × 76 cm
Imperial War Museum, London

4.71 Oskar Kokoschka
Self-Portrait as Degenerate Artist (Selbstporträt als entarteter Künstler), 1937
oil on canvas, 110 × 85 cm
Private collection, on loan to the Scottish National Gallery of Modern Art, Edinburgh (GML 285)

4.72 Oskar Kokoschka
Anschluss – Alice in Wonderland (Anschluss – Alice im Wunderland), 1942
oil on canvas, 63.5 × 73.6 cm
Wiener Städtische Allgemeine Versicherung Aktiengesellschaft, Austria

4.73 Oskar Kokoschka
Portrait of Ivan Maisky (Bildnis Ivan Maisky), 1942–43
oil on canvas, 102 × 77 cm
Tate Gallery, presented by Dr Henry Dreyfuss 1943.

4.74 Georg Kolbe
Proclamation (Verkündung), 1934–35
bronze, approx. 350 cm (including pedestal)
Land Berlin

4.75 Georg Kolbe
Couple (Menschenpaar), 1936
bronze, 113 × 50 × 38.5 cm
Georg-Kolbe-Museum, Berlin

4.76 Georg Kolbe
Proclamation (Verkündung), 1937
bronze, approx. 160 cm
Berlinische Galerie, Berlin

4.77 Georg Kolbe
The Liberated Man (Der Befreite), 1945
bronze, 34 × 21 × 29 cm
Georg-Kolbe-Museum, Berlin

4.78 Käthe Kollwitz
Death Holding a Young Girl on His Knees (Der Tod hält ein junges Mädchen auf seinen Knien), 1934
lithograph on paper, 59 × 46.1 cm
Käthe-Kollwitz-Museum, Berlin

4.79 Käthe Kollwitz
Self-Portrait (Selbstporträt), 1934
lithograph on paper, 24.7 × 21.1 cm
Käthe-Kollwitz-Museum, Berlin

4.80 Käthe Kollwitz
The Call of Death (Der Ruf des Todes), 1934–35
lithograph on paper, 64.7 × 53.9 cm
Käthe-Kollwitz-Museum, Berlin

4.81 Käthe Kollwitz
Death Recognized as Friend (Der Tod als Freund erkannt), 1934–35
lithograph on paper, 64.8 × 53.9 cm
Käthe-Kollwitz-Museum, Berlin

4.82 Käthe Kollwitz
Pietà (Mother with Dead Son) (Pieta [Mutter mit totem Sohn]), 1937–38
bronze, 38 × 27 × 39 cm
Staatliche Museen zu Berlin, Nationalgalerie (B II 23)

4.83 Käthe Kollwitz
The Tower of Mothers (Der Turm der Mütter), 1937–38
bronze, 27 × 27.5 × 28 cm
Käthe-Kollwitz-Museum, Berlin

4.84 Gerhard Marcks
Swimmer II (Schwimmerin II), 1938
bronze, 163 × 40 × 43 cm
Staatliche Museen zu Berlin, Nationalgalerie (B III 44)

4.85 Gerhard Marcks
Ver Sacrum, 1943
bronze, 126.5 cm
Gerhard-Marcks-Stiftung, Bremen

4.86 Erich Mercker
Granite Quarries at Flossenbürg (Granitbrüche Flossenbürg)
oil on canvas, 120 × 120 cm
Property of the Federal Republic of Germany

4.87 Erich Mercker
Voss Street (Voßstrasse)
oil on canvas, 122 × 150 cm
US Army Center of Military History, Washington DC (1.4803.47)

4.88 Bodo Meyner
Relocation of the Victory Column on the Great Star in 1938 (Umsetzung der Siegessäule auf den Grossen Stern 1938), 1941
oil on canvas, mounted on hardboard, 80 × 68 cm
Stadtmuseum Berlin, Berlin

4.89 Berthold Müller
Autumn Landscape, Harvest (Herbstlandschaft, Ernte)
oil on canvas, 170 × 154 cm
Property of the Federal Republic of Germany

4.90 Emil Nolde
Children and Grey Ghost (Kinder und graue Spukgestalt), 1931–35
watercolour, 60.5 × 45 cm
Stiftung Seebüll Ada und Emil Nolde

4.91 Emil Nolde
Two Old Men (Zwei alte Männer), 1931–35
watercolour, 53.3 × 37 cm
Stiftung Seebüll Ada und Emil Nolde

4.92 Emil Nolde
Chinese in Front of a Burning Town (Chinese vor brennender Stadt), 1938–45
watercolour, 23 × 17.3 cm
Stiftung Seebüll Ada und Emil Nolde

4.93 Emil Nolde
Couple under Red Blossom (Liebespaar unter roter Blüte), 1938–45
watercolour, 18.2 × 17.4 cm
Stiftung Seebüll Ada und Emil Nolde

4.94 Emil Nolde
Crouching Nude (with Violet Ribbons) (Hockender Akt [mit violetten Bändern]), 1938–45
watercolour, 15.4 × 19.1 cm
Stiftung Seebüll Ada und Emil Nolde

4.95 Emil Nolde
Dispute (Streitgespräch), 1938–45
watercolour, 23.3 × 18 cm
Stiftung Seebüll Ada und Emil Nolde

4.96 Emil Nolde
Flower-Lover (Blumenfreundin), 1938–45
watercolour, 23 × 17.1 cm
Stiftung Seebüll Ada und Emil Nolde

4.97 Emil Nolde
Group of People I (Menschengruppe I), 1938–45
watercolour, 15.2 × 24.3 cm
Stiftung Seebüll Ada und Emil Nolde

4.98 Emil Nolde
Group of People II (Menschengruppe II), 1938–45
watercolour, 18.4 × 24 cm
Stiftung Seebüll Ada und Emil Nolde

4.99 Emil Nolde
Ill-Suited Couple (Ungleiches Paar), 1938–45
watercolour, 19.5 × 18.9 cm
Stiftung Seebüll Ada und Emil Nolde

4.100 Emil Nolde
'The Joy of Dancing' ('Tanzfreude', 1938–45
watercolour, 18.3 × 15.6 cm
Stiftung Seebüll Ada und Emil Nolde

4.101 Emil Nolde
Men and Women (Männer und Frauen), 1938–45
watercolour, 17.8 × 24 cm
Stiftung Seebüll Ada und Emil Nolde

4.102 Emil Nolde
Old Man and Young Woman (Alter Mann und junge Frau), 1938–45
watercolour, 24 × 18.9 cm
Stiftung Seebüll Ada und Emil Nolde

4.103 Emil Nolde
The Redhead (Die Rothaarige), 1938–45
watercolour, 24.9 × 17.4 cm
Stiftung Seebüll Ada und Emil Nolde

4.104 Emil Nolde
Spanish Woman (Spanierin), 1938–45
watercolour, 21.8 × 16.8 cm
Stiftung Seebüll Ada und Emil Nolde

4.105 Emil Nolde
Two Couples (in the Park) (Zwei Paare [im Park]), 1938–45
watercolour, 24.3 × 17.3 cm
Stiftung Seebüll Ada und Emil Nolde

4.106 Emil Nolde
Two Girls (Zwei Mädchen), 1938–45
watercolour, 13.1 × 23.5 cm
Stiftung Seebüll Ada und Emil Nolde

4.107 Emil Nolde
Woman and Two Children (Frau und zwei Kinder), 1938–45
watercolour, 23.9 × 15 cm
Stiftung Seebüll Ada und Emil Nolde

4.108 Felix Nussbaum
The Secret (Das Geheimnis), 1939
oil on canvas, 61 × 74.5 cm
Private collection

4.109 Felix Nussbaum
Crouching Prisoner in Saint-Cyprien (Kauernder Gefangener in St. Cyprien), 1940
oil on canvas, 47 × 42.5 cm
Deutsches Historisches Museum, Berlin

4.110 Felix Nussbaum
Saint-Cyprien, 1942
oil on canvas, 68 × 138 cm
Kulturgeschichtliches Museum, Osnabrück

4.111 Felix Nussbaum
Organ-Grinder (Orgelmann), 1943
oil on canvas, 102 × 83 cm
Kulturgeschichtliches Museum, Osnabrück

4.112 Carl Theodor Protzen
The Highways of the Führer (Die Strassen des Führers)
oil on canvas with painted frame, 169 × 257 cm
Property of the Federal Republic of Germany

4.113 Curt Querner
Demonstration, 1930
oil on canvas, 87 × 66 cm
Staatliche Museen zu Berlin, Nationalgalerie (A IV 78)

4.114 Franz Radziwill
Where to Go in This World (Wohin in dieser Welt), 1940
oil on canvas, mounted on plywood, 119 × 170 cm
Staatliche Museen zu Berlin, Nationalgalerie, on loan from Private collection

4.115 Paul Roloff
Portrait of Professor Paul Ludwig Troost
oil on canvas, 140 × 111 cm
US Army Center of Military History, Washington DC (1.5851.47)

4.116 Ivo Saliger
Diana's Rest (Die Rast der Diana), 1939–40
oil on canvas, 200 × 190 cm
Property of the Federal Republic of Germany

4.117 Richard Scheibe
Decathlete (Zehnkämpfer), 1937
bronze, approx. 200 cm
Städtische Galerie im Städelschen Kunstinstitut, Frankfurt am Main (SGP 112)

4.118 Oskar Schlemmer
Blue Group (Blaue Gruppe), 1935
oil on oil paper, 65 × 50 cm
Leopold-Hoesch-Museum, Düren

4.119 Oskar Schlemmer
Dark Group (Dunkle Gruppe), 1936
oil on oil paper, mounted on board, 65.3 × 45.5 cm
Private collection, courtesy C. Raman Schlemmer

4.120 Oskar Schlemmer
Interior I (Interieur I), 1942
oil on oil paper, 17.9 × 10 cm
The Oskar Schlemmer Archive and Family Estate

4.121 Oskar Schlemmer
Dinner at the Neighbour's House, Window Picture I (Abendessen im Nachbarhaus, Fensterbild I), 1942
oil, watercolour and pen on card, 31.9x 18.1 cm
Kunstmuseum Basel, Depositum Schlemmer

4.122 Oskar Schlemmer
Living Room with Woman Working, Window Picture IV (Wohnraum mit arbeitender Frau, Fensterbild IV), 1942
oil over pencil and gouache on card, 32.3 × 19.7 cm
Kunstmuseum Basel, Depositum Schlemmer

4.123 Oskar Schlemmer
Lit Kitchen with Woman, Window Picture × (Beleuchtete Küche mit Frau, Fensterbild X), 1942
oil over pencil and pen on card, 31.9 × 22.2 cm
Kunstmuseum Basel, Depositum Schlemmer

4.124 Oskar Schlemmer
Tripartite Window, Window Picture XVII (Dreigeteiltes Fenster, Fensterbild XVII), 1942
oil over pencil and gouache on card, 29 × 22.8 cm
Kunstmuseum Basel, Depositum Schlemmer

4.125 Kurt Schmid-Ehmen
Eagle from the Reich Chancellery, 1938
bronze, 165 × 287 × 48 cm
Imperial War Museum, London

4.126 Georg Schrimpf
Two Girls by the Window (Zwei Mädchen am Fenster), 1937
oil on canvas, 78.5 × 73 cm
Staatliche Museen zu Berlin, Nationalgalerie (A IV 92)

4.127 Josef Thorak
Young Nude Siegfried or Walking Boy (Jünglingsakt Siegfried oder Schreitender Jüngling), before 1935
bronze, 170 × 49 × 42 cm
Wohnstift Rathsberg, Erlangen

4.128 Adolf Ziegler
Female Nude (Weiblicher Akt)
oil on canvas, 105 × 80 cm
Property of the Federal Republic of Germany

4.129 Adolf Ziegler
The Goddess of Art (Göttin der Kunst)
postcard, 14.7 × 10.5 cm
Archiv Baumeister, Stuttgart

Posters

4.130 Anonymous
The Whole Nation Says Yes on 10 April (Das ganze Volk sagt ja am 10. April)
lithographic poster, 83 × 58.5 cm
Imperial War Museum, London (3183)

4.131 Anonymous
German Youth Festival (Deutsches Jugendfest), 1934
poster, 80 × 58.5 cm

4.132 Anonymous
Hitler
poster, 84.5 × 57.5 cm
Staatliche Museen zu Berlin, Kunstbibliothek (II D kl)

4.133 Axster-Heudtlass
Berlin Motor Show, 15 February – 1 March (Autoschau Berlin, 15. Februar – 1. März), 1936
poster, 102 × 63 cm
Staatliche Museen zu Berlin, Kunstbibliothek (II D gr)

4.134 Axster-Heudtlass
Reich Competitions of the SA (Reichswettkämpfe der SA), 1937
poster, 84 × 59.5 cm
Staatliche Museen zu Berlin, Kunstbibliothek (II D kl)

4.135 Herbert Bayer
Exhibition German People and German Work (Ausstellung Deutsches Volk und Deutsche Arbeit)
poster, 95 × 69 cm
Staatliche Museen zu Berlin, Kunstbibliothek (II D gr)

4.136 Herbert Bayer
Teutoburg Forest (Teutoburger Wald)
poster, 84 × 59 cm
Staatliche Museen zu Berlin, Kunstbibliothek (II D kl)

4.137 Leo Bothas
International Exhibition Paris 1937 (The German Pavilion) (Internationale Ausstellung Paris 1937 (Das Deutsche Haus))
poster, 110 × 63 cm
Staatliche Museen zu Berlin, Kunstbibliothek (II D gr)

4.138 Engelhard
SA Man Brand, a Portrait of Our Time (SA-Mann Brand, ein Lebensbild aus unseren Tagen), 1933
poster, 141 × 92.5 cm
Staatliche Museen zu Berlin, Kunstbibliothek (II D gr)

4.139 Hermann Grah
Work Wins (Arbeit siegt)
poster, 171.2 × 117.2 cm
Staatliche Museen zu Berlin, Kunstbibliothek (II D gr)

4.140 Ludwig Hohlwein
Air Raid Protection (Luftschutz)
poster, 83 × 58.8 cm
Staatliche Museen zu Berlin, Kunstbibliothek (Deutschl. kl)

4.141 Ludwig Hohlwein
League of German Girls in the Hitler Youth (Bund deutscher Madel in der Hitlerjugend)
poster, 120 × 83 cm
Staatliche Museen zu Berlin, Kunstbibliothek (II D gr)

4.142 Ludwig Hohlwein
Reich Sports Day of the League of German Girls, 13 September 1934 (Reichssporttag des BDM 13. September 1934), 1934
poster, 119 × 84 cm
Staatliche Museen zu Berlin, Kunstbibliothek (II D)

4.143 Richard Klein
Germany (Deutschland), 1937
poster, 102 × 63 cm
Staatliche Museen zu Berlin, Kunstbibliothek (II D gr)

4.144 Mjölnir (Hans Schweitzer)
Our Last Hope: Hitler (Unsere letzte Hoffnung: Hitler)
lithographic poster, 85 × 56 cm
Imperial War Museum, London (3181)

4.145 Mjölnir (Hans Schweitzer)
Waffen SS: Join on Reaching the Age of 17 (Waffen SS Eintritt mit vollendetem 17. Lebensjahr)
poster, 83 × 59 cm
Staatliche Museen zu Berlin, Kunstbibliothek (II D kl)

4.146 Walter Riemer
13th Great German Radio Exhibition (13. Grosse Deutsche Rundfunkausstellung), 1936
poster, 118 × 83.5 cm
Staatliche Museen zu Berlin, Kunstbibliothek (II D gr)

4.147 F. Spindel
Give us Radio Sets (Gebt uns Rundfunkgeräte)
poster, 84 × 59 cm
Staatliche Museen zu Berlin, Kunstbibliothek (II D kl)

4.148 Robert Zinner
Reich Autobahns in Germany (Reichsautobahnen in Deutschland)
poster, 101 × 63 cm
Staatliche Museen zu Berlin, Kunstbibliothek (II D gr)

BIOGRAPHIES

Artists and Architects 1930–1945 *Ines Schlenker*

Abbreviations
EUR   *Esposizione Universale di Roma* (Rome Universal Exhibition), scheduled for 1942
GDK   *Grosse Deutsche Kunstausstellung* (Great German Art Exhibition), Haus der Deutschen Kunst, Munich, 1937–44
MJP   Musée du Jeu de Paume, Paris
MOMA   The Museum of Modern Art, New York
MPI   Moscow Polygraphic Institute
MRF   *Mostra della Rivoluzione Fascista*, Rome, 1932
ODAII   *Origines et développement de l'art international indépendant*, Paris, 1937
PAK   Preussische Akademie der Künste (Prussian Academy of Arts), Berlin
IEP   International Exhibition (Exposition Internationale), Paris 1937
VSKK   Vereinigte Staatsschulen für Kunst und Kunstgewerbe (Unified State Schools for Art and Crafts), Berlin

Grigory Borisovich Barkhin
Architect
1880, Perm – 1969, Moscow
1928–30 editor-in-chief of Annuals of the Moscow Architectural Society
1928–41 works in Mossoviet planning department
1930 teaches at Institute of Architecture, Moscow

Mikhail Grigorievich Barkhin
Architect, theorist, author
1906, Bobruisk – 1986, Moscow
1930 onward teaches at Institute of Architecture, Moscow
1932 onward teaches at Military Academy, Moscow
Major works in conjunction with his father, G. B. Barkhin:
1931 Sverdlovsk Theatre (competition project)
1932 Palace of Labour, Moscow (competition project)
1934 Minsk Theatre (competition project)
1937 Main Pavilion, All-Union Agricultural Exhibition, Moscow (project)
1937–39 circus with 2,500 seats (project)

Ernst Barlach
Sculptor, graphic artist, dramatist
1870, Wedel – 1938, Rostock
1930 solo exhibition PAK; Venice Biennale; signs contract with Alfred Flechtheim
1933 member of order *Pour le mérite*; protests against expulsion of Kollwitz and Heinrich Mann from PAK; forced to give up house in Güstrow.
1933 mail is censored, police watch his home.
1934 war memorial in Magdeburg Cathedral moved to basement of the Nationalgalerie, Berlin
1935 performances of his drama *Die echten Sedemunds* forbidden

1936 works removed from exhibition, PAK; volume of his drawings, ready for distribution, confiscated
1937 war memorial in Güstrow Cathedral dismantled; 381 works removed from museums and churches; included in *Entartete Kunst*, Munich
1937 forbidden to exhibit
1938 dies of a heart attack; permission to place memorial plaque on birthplace denied; death notices in newspapers limited to ten lines of factual material; work shown in *Twentieth-Century German Art*, New Burlington Galleries, London

Willi Baumeister
Painter, graphic designer, stage designer, theorist
1889, Stuttgart – 1955, Stuttgart
1930 member of *Cercle et Carré*
1931–33 exhibits in *Abstraction–Création*
1932 exhibition Kunstverein Frankfurt (with Schlemmer); exhibits in *Deutsche Kunstausstellung*, Galerie Cassirer, Berlin
1933 dismissed as professor at Städtische Kunstgewerbeschule, Frankfurt; returns to Stuttgart; works as commercial graphic designer; included in exhibition *Kulturbolschewistische Bilder*, Mannheim and Munich
1935 solo exhibition Galleria del Milione, Milan
1937 51 works confiscated from German public institutions; included in *Entartete Kunst*, Munich; exhibits in ODAII, MJP
1938 moves some works to Kunsthalle Basel for safe keeping; exhibits in *Twentieth-Century German Art*, New Burlington Galleries, London
1938 works at Kurt Herbert's paint factory, Wuppertal; collaborating with Schlemmer on book *Anfänge der Malerei* (published 1941 without authors' names)
1939 exhibition Galerie Jeanne Bucher, Paris; press asked not to review exhibition to avoid negative repercussions for Baumeister in Germany; shows at Salon des Réalités Nouvelles, Paris
1943 home damaged in bombing; moves to Urach, Lake Constance; begins his theoretical work *Das Unbekannte in der Kunst* (published 1947)
1945 returns to Stuttgart

Herbert Bayer
Graphic designer, painter, typographer, photographer, poster and exhibition designer
1900, Haag, Austria – 1985, Montecito, California
1928–38 director of Dorland Studio, Berlin
1930 co-designs German section of *Exposition de la Société des artistes décorateurs*, Grand Palais, Paris; group exhibition, Harvard Society for Contemporary Art, Cambridge, Mass.
1931 co-designs Building Trades Union Exhibition, Berlin, and German Cork Industry exhibition, Berlin; solo exhibition, Bauhaus, Dessau; First Prize in inaugural international exhibition of advertising photography
1931–34 exhibits in group shows, Julien

Levy Gallery, New York
1933 prospectus for Chicago World Fair
1934 develops style and direction for structure and graphic design for factory exhibitions.
1935 designs travelling exhibitions and municipal exhibition, Berlin; advertisements for Adrianol-Emulsion; publicity brochure, *Das Wunder des Lebens*
1936 designs travelling exhibition for German wallpaper industry, Hamburg; solo exhibition Kunstverein, Salzburg; medal of the City of Salzburg; exhibits in *Fantastic Art, Dada and Surrealism* and *Cubism and Abstract Art*, MOMA
1937 designs gas and water exhibition, Leipzig; solo exhibition London Gallery, London; three works removed from German museums; included in *Entartete Kunst*, Munich
1938 moves to New York; co-designs exhibition *Bauhaus 1919–1928*, MOMA
1939 designs displays for State of Pennsylvania's exhibition, New York World Fair; solo exhibitions P. M. Gallery, New York, and Black Mountain College, North Carolina
1940–42 graphic designs for drug companies, magazines, department stores and industrial corporations
1942 designs exhibition *Road to Victory*, MOMA
1943 designs exhibition *Airways to Peace*, MOMA

Banfi, Belgiojoso, Peressutti and Rogers (BBPR)
Architects, industrial designers
1932 Partnership BBPR established in Milan by:
Gian Luigi Banfi (1910, Milan – 1945, Mauthausen concentration camp)
Ludovico Barbiano Belgiojoso (1909, Milan –)
Enrico Peressutti (1908, Udine – 1976, Milan)
Ernesto Nathan Rogers (1909, Trieste – 1969, Gardone)
1932 Grillo Bar; master plan for Pavia
1933 Weekend House for a Married Couple (*Casa del Sabato per gli Sposi*), Milan Triennale (exhibition project with Fontana)
1934 Palazzo del Littorio, Rome (competition project); Exhibition Hall, *Mostra dell'Aeronautica*, Milan
1935 Casa Feltrinelli; Exhibition Halls, *Mostra dello Sport*, Milan (with Guttuso, Melotti); Pavilion, Brussels World Fair; Exhibition Halls, *Mostra del mare*, Trieste
1936 Bozzi & Crippa Pavilion, *Fiera Campionaria*, Milan; Pavilion, Milan Triennale (with Melotti)
1936–37 master plan for Val d'Aosta
1937 Italian Marine Pavilion, IEP (with Fontana), *Mostra del Teatro Italiano*, Como; First Prize, Ente Nazionale Risi di Lombardia e Piedmonte; Exhibition Halls, Leonardo da Vinci exhibition, Milan 1937–38
Heliotherapy Clinic, Legnano
1939 formation of anti-Fascist group; Children's Holiday and Health Centre, Milan; Terni Pavilion, *Fiera Campionaria*, Milan

1940 Belsana Paper Mills, Genoa; Spiga and Corrente Galleries, Milan; Central Office Building, EUR Quarter
1941 Rural Casa del Fascio (competition project)
1944 Belsana Building, Milan
1945 master plan for Milan (project)

Max Beckmann
Painter
1884, Leipzig – 1950, New York
1930 City of Frankfurt extends teaching contract at Städelschule for 5 years; monograph by Heinrich Simon published, Berlin and Leipzig; solo exhibitions Kunsthalle Basel, Kunsthaus Zürich; Venice Biennale
1931 solo exhibition Galerie de la Renaissance, Paris; exhibits in *German Art of the 20th Century*, MOMA
1933 dismissed from Städelschule; Beckmann room in Kronprinzenpalais museum, Berlin, closed; works included in a hostile exhibition, Stuttgart; scheduled exhibition in Erfurt banned
1935 works withdrawn from exhibition *Berliner Kunst in München*, Neue Pinakothek, Munich
1937 590 works confiscated from German public institutions; included in *Entartete Kunst*, Munich; emigrates to Amsterdam
1938 makes speech at opening of *Twentieth-Century German Art*, New Burlington Galleries, London
1939 First Prize, *Golden Gate International Exhibition of Contemporary Art*, San Francisco
1940 when Germany invades Holland, destroys his diaries (1925–40)
1942 solo exhibition Arts Club of Chicago
1944 solo exhibition Museum of Art, Santa Barbara

Paul Bonatz
Architect
1877, Solgne – 1956, Stuttgart
1929–36 Consultant to Neckar Canal Authority
1930 Cathedral Plaza, Cologne (project)
1931 Hotel Graf Zeppelin, Stuttgart
1933 houses in Cologne and Stuttgart; Flag Tower, Gymnastic Festival, Stuttgart; exhibits at Kochenhof Estate, Stuttgart (project)
1935 Stumm Company Building, Düsseldorf; Water Tower, Kornwestheim
1935–40 Consultant to Inspector-General of German Highway Construction
1935–41 Autobahn bridges
1936 Locks, bridges and weirs on the Neckar Canal; Memorial Chapel to the War Dead, Heilbronn; Kunstmuseum Basel
1939–42 Main Railway Station, Munich (project)
1939–43 Naval High Command, Berlin (project)
1941 suspension bridges at Cologne and Hamburg
1943 Stuttgart Corporation Buildings (project)

Arno Breker
Sculptor
1900, Elberfeld – 1991, Düsseldorf
1933 Prix de Rome; spends year at Villa Massimo, Rome
1935 exhibits at Galerie Vömel, Düsseldorf; exhibits in Berlin Secession
1936 exhibits in *Olympische Kunstausstellung*, Berlin; Olympic Silver Medal for Art; bas-reliefs, Nordstern Building, Berlin; exhibits in *Malerei und Plastik in Deutschland*; exhibition Kunstverein Hamburg
1937 exhibits at Kunsthalle Hamburg; statues for German Pavilion, IEP
1937 onward exhibits in GDK
1938 commissions for sculptures, Yugoslav embassy, Museum Island, Berlin; exhibits at Kunsthalle Hamburg
1938–45 professor at Staatliche Hochschule für bildende Künste, Berlin; sculptor-in-chief to the Third Reich. Collaboration with Albert Speer leads to numerous government commissions: Triumphal Arch, Great Round Fountain (projects); sculptures and reliefs, New Reich Chancellery, Berlin; sculptures for buildings in several German cities
1939 study trip to Italy
1940 member of PAK; awarded Grand Prix d'Italie; accompanies Hitler to Paris
1942 solo exhibition Orangerie, Paris; monograph by Charles Despiau published, Paris; exhibits in *Deutsche Plastik der Gegenwart*, Warsaw and Zagreb
1943 solo exhibition Haus der Rheinischen Heimat, Cologne

Izaak Izrailevich Brodsky
Painter, graphic artist
1884, Sofiyevka – 1939, Leningrad
1930 President of Kuindzhi Society
1932 Honoured Art Worker of the RSFSR; Venice Biennale; exhibits in *Artists of the RSFSR over 15 Years*, Russian Museum, Leningrad
1934 first artist to be awarded Order of Lenin
1934–39 director of All-Russian Academy of Arts, Leningrad
1937 Grand Prix, IEP
1939 Doctorate of Art History; dies in Leningrad

Carlo Carrà
Painter, graphic artist, author, muralist
1881, Quargnento – 1966, Milan
1922–1939 art critic, *L'Ambrosiano*
1930 solo exhibition Galleria Bardi, Milan
1931 own room at Rome Quadriennale; Second Prize for Painting, Rome Quadriennale
1932 travels to Germany, Austria, Czechoslovakia; solo exhibition Umelecka Beseda, Prague; publishes essay *Pittori romantici lombardi*, Bergamo; Venice Biennale
1933 signs Sironi's *Manifesto della pittura murale*; murals, Milan Triennale
1935 solo exhibition Galleria del Milione, Milan
1936 Milan Triennale
1938–9 murals, Palace of Justice, Milan
1940 exhibits in *La Nazione*, Florence (with Mafai, Sironi)
1941 gives series of lectures on 20th-century European art in Zürich, Lugano, Lausanne, Geneva; is offered post as professor of painting, Accademia di Brera, Milan
1942 solo exhibition Accademia di Brera, Milan; after political attacks, Fascist

authorities cover murals at the Palace of Justice
1943 evacuation to Corenno Plinio, Lake Como; publishes autobiography

Iosif Moisevich Chaikov
Sculptor, graphic artist
1888, Kiev – 1986
1930 Venice Biennale; exhibits in Berlin and Vienna
1931 exhibits with Association of Russian Sculptors
1934 exhibits in Venice and Istanbul
1935 exhibits in Moscow (with Mukhina)
1936 writes articles on sculpture for Soviet magazines
1937 monumental sculptures for propylaea of Soviet Pavilion, IEP
1939 exhibits in New York

Dimitri Nikolayevich Chechulin
Architect
1901–1984 (or 1981?)
1930s and 1940s builds mostly in Moscow; receives prestigious commissions and prime sites
1940 Tchaikovsky Concert Hall, Moscow
1945–49 chief architect of Moscow

Tullio Crali
Painter
1910, Igalo –
1930–35 exhibits in all important *Aeropittura* exhibitions (Turin, Milan, Trieste, Paris, Brussels, Venice)
1934 Venice Biennale
1935 Rome Quadriennale
1936 Venice Biennale, exhibits in *Olympische Kunstausstellung*, Berlin
1938 Venice Biennale; lives in Rome
1939 Rome Quadriennale
1940 own room, Venice Biennale
1942 Venice Biennale; writes *Manifesto dell'illusionismo plastico* with F. T. Marinetti
1943 Rome Quadriennale; writes *Manifesto delle parole musicali* with Marinetti

Salvador Dalí
Painter, graphic artist
1904, Figueras – 1989, Figueras
1930 publishes *La femme visible*; paintings slashed at Paris premiere of Luis Buñuel's film *L'Age d'or*, which is eventually banned
1931 solo exhibition Galerie Pierre Colle, Paris; exhibits at Wadsworth Atheneum, Hartford (Conn.)
1932 solo exhibition Galerie Pierre Colle, Paris; exhibits at Julien Levy Gallery, New York
1933 exhibitions Galerie Pierre Colle, Paris; solo exhibition, Julien Levy Gallery, New York; lectures accompanying exhibition in Barcelona end in brawls
1934 expulsion from official Surrealist movement due to 'counter-revolutionary offences' and 'glorification of Hitler Fascism'; trip to USA; solo exhibitions Galerie Bonjean, Paris; Zwemmer Gallery, London; Julien Levy Gallery, New York; Wadsworth Atheneum, Hartford; prize, Carnegie Institute, Pittsburgh
1936 exhibits in *International Surrealist Exhibition*, New Burlington Galleries, London; *Fantastic Art, Dada and Surrealism*, MOMA
1937 takes part in Spanish radio programme on a Picasso exhibition; exhibits in ODAII, MJP; trip to Italy
1938 exhibits in Surrealist exhibition, Galerie des Beaux-Arts, Paris; meets Sigmund Freud in London
1939 trip to USA; solo exhibition, Julien

Levy Gallery, New York; arrested for breaking shop-window; New York World Fair
1940 moves to USA
1941 solo exhibition MOMA
1942 publishes *The Secret Life of Salvador Dalí*, New York
1945 decorations for Alfred Hitchcock's *Spellbound*

Giorgio de Chirico
Painter, stage designer, muralist
1888, Volos, Greece – 1978, Rome
1930 exhibits in *Prima Mostra di pittori italiani a Parigi*, Galleria del Milione, Milan
1931 solo exhibition Galleria Barbaroux, Milan
1933 included in room of Italian artists at Kronprinzenpalais, Berlin (opened by Hermann Goering); Nazis confiscate paintings from museums in Essen and Zwickau; mural *The Culture of Our Time*, Milan Triennale; sets and costumes for *I puritani*, Florence
1935 own room at Rome Quadriennale; solo exhibition Pierre Matisse Gallery, New York
1935–37 in USA
1936 exhibits in *Fantastic Art, Dada and Surrealism*, MOMA
1937 exhibition Zwemmer Gallery, London (with Picasso)
1944 after a few years spent in Florence settles in Rome

Aleksandr Aleksandrovich Deineka
Painter, graphic artist, sculptor, poster designer
1899, Kursk – 1969, Moscow
1928–1934 teaches at MPI
1930 exhibits with October group, Moscow
1930–34 works primarily as poster designer
1931 member of Russian Association of Proletarian Artists
1932 First Prize, Carnegie Institute, Pittsburgh; Venice Biennale; exhibits in *Artists of the RSFSR over 15 Years*, Russian Museum, Leningrad
1934 designs murals for cinema, Gorky Park, Moscow, and People's Commissariat of Agriculture, Moscow
1934 teaches at Surkov State Art Institute, Moscow
1935 travels to USA, France, Italy; solo exhibition, Moscow
1937 mural, Soviet Pavilion, IEP
1938 panels for exhibition in Minsk; works on mosaic cycle *24 Hours of the Soviet Country*, Metro station Mayakovskaya, Moscow
1939 murals, gymnasium, House of the Red Army, Minsk, Red Army Theatre, Moscow, and Far East Pavilion, All-Union Agricultural Exhibition, Moscow
1940 designs mosaics for Metro station Paveletskaya, Moscow (realized in Metro station Novokuznetskaya in 1943); becomes professor of monumental painting
1942 visits the battle front; heads poster studio of political administration of Moscow Military District
1943 exhibits in Tretyakov Gallery, Moscow (with Mukhina)
1945 director of Academy of Applied and Decorative Arts, Moscow; Honoured Art Worker of the RSFSR

Enrico del Debbio
Architect
1891, Carrara – 1973, Rome
1930 general plan and several buildings for sports complex, Foro Mussolini, Rome
1930–32 Olympic Stadium, Rome
1934 Heliotherapeutic Colony, Foro Mussolini, Rome

Mario de Renzi
Architect
Rome, 1897 – Rome, 1967
1932 Apartment and Movie House, Rome; German Cultural Centre (interior reorganization), Villa Sciarra, Rome; Palazzo delle Esposizioni (temporary facade with Libera), MRF; Pontifical School, Rome
1933 Post Office building, Rome (with Libera); Italian Pavilion, Chicago World Fair (with Libera)
1935 Italian Pavilion, Brussels World Fair (with Libera); Auditorium, Rome (competition project with Libera)
1936 Police Magistrates' Office complex, Rome (competition project)
1937 *Colonie estive* exhibition, Rome (with Libera); Palazzo del Littorio, Rome (competition project with Libera)
1939–42 Palace of Armed Forces, EUR
1940 INCIS quarter Rome (project with Libera)

Aleksandr Davidovich Drevin
Painter
1889, Venden, Latvia – 1938, in exile, Altai region
1927–32 member of Society of Moscow Artists; contributes to exhibitions
1930 visits Kazakhstan and Altai region
1931 exhibits with Thirteen group, Moscow
1931–35 Vice-President, International Bureau of Revolutionary Artists
1932 Venice Biennale; exhibits in *Artists of the RSFSR over 15 Years*, Russian Museum, Leningrad
1933 travels in Armenia
1934 exhibits in State Cultural and Historical Museum, Erevan; journal *Tvorchestvo*, Moscow, publishes interview with Drevin on his methods of work and principles of painting
1938 arrested and shot

Aleksei Nikolayevich Dushkin
Architect
1903 (1904?) – 1977
1932 Palace of Soviets, Moscow (competition project)
1933 member of project team, Palace of Soviets, Moscow
1935 Metro station Dvorets Sovetov (Palace of Soviets), Moscow
1937 Metro station Ploshchad' Revolyutsii (Revolution Square), Moscow
1938 Metro station Mayakovskaya, Moscow
1940 Metro station Avtozavodskaya, Moscow
1941 Stalin Prize

Ermolaeva, see Yermolayeva

Horacio Ferrer Morgado
Painter
1894, Córdoba – 1978, Madrid
1932 exhibits with *Artistas en Acción* group
1934 exhibits at Escuela Nacional de Bellas Artes; goes to Florence on scholarship from Junta de Ampliación de Estudios
1935 professor of mural painting; returns to Madrid

353

1936 exhibits in *Exposición nacional de Bellas Artes*, Madrid, nominated for Second Prize (not awarded; exhibition closes at outbreak of civil war)
1936–39 exhibits with Comité de Defensa de los Intelectuales
1937 exhibits *Madrid 1937*, Spanish Pavilion, IEP
1938 exhibits in *Exposición Trimestral de Artes Plásticas*, Barcelona
1939 onward works as picture restorer; decorates several churches in Madrid, member of Círculo de Bellas Artes

Pavel Nikolayevich Filonov
Painter, graphic artist, composer, theorist, illustrator
1883, Moscow – 1941, Leningrad
1929–30 solo exhibition installed but never opened, Russian Museum, Leningrad
1930 main theoretical work *The Ideology of Analytical Art* published in *Pavel Filonov: Catalogue of Works in the Russian Museum*, Leningrad
1931–33 illustrates Finnish epic *Kalevala* with students
1932 Collective of Masters of Analytical Art (Filonov School) closed; exhibits in *Artists of the RSFSR over 15 Years*, Russian Museum, Leningrad
1933 exhibits in *Paintings of the Leningrad District Artist's House*, House of Culture, Leningrad, *Works by Artist Tourists*, Scholars' House, Leningrad
1934 onward not represented at any official exhibition
1941 exhibits in *Painting and Sculpture by the Leningrad City Committee of Artists*, Stanislavsky House of Arts, Leningrad; dies of pneumonia in the Leningrad blockade

Lucio Fontana
Painter, sculptor
1899, Rosario de Santa Fe, Argentina – 1986, Comabbio
1930 solo exhibition Galleria del Milione, Milan; Venice Biennale
1931, 1932 solo exhibitions Galleria del Milione, Milan
1933 Casa del Sabato per gli Sposi, Milan Triennale (exhibition project; see BBPR)
1934 solo exhibition Galleria del Milione, Milan; Premio Nazionale Tantardini, *Mostra del Sindacato interprovinciale di Lombardia*, Milan
1935 co-founder Gruppo del Milione, Milan (with Melotti); joins Abstraction-Création, Paris; signs manifesto of *Prima mostra collettiva d'arte astratta italiana*; exhibits in *Gruppo del Milione*, Galleria del Milione, Milan; Rome Quadriennale; exhibits in *Prima mostra collettiva di arte astratta italiana*, Turin
1936 Milan Triennale; monument to General Júlio Roca, Buenos Aires (competition project)
1937 works at Sèvres factory, Paris; bas-relief, Palace of Justice, Milan; solo exhibitions Galerie Jeanne Bucher, Paris, Galleria del Milione, Milan; Italian Marine Pavilion, IEP (with BBPR); Silver Medal, IEP
1938 Ceramics Award, Spotorno; Victory Monument, Milan (project, Third Prize); solo exhibitions Galleria del Milione, Milan; Galerie Zach, Paris
1939 Rome Quadriennale; exhibits in *II. Mostra di Corrente*, Galleria Grande, Milan
1940 settles in Argentina; honorary diploma, Milan Triennale
1941 group of sculptures for project of

Palace of Water and Light, EUR
1941 onward several prizes, Salón Nacional de Bellas Artes, Buenos Aires
1942 solo exhibition Museo Municipal de Bellas Artes, Santa Fé

Vladimir Georgevich Gel'freikh
Architect
1885, St Petersburg – 1967, Moscow
1928–52 Lenin Library, Moscow (at first with Shchuko)
1930–36 Gorky Theatre, Rostov-on-Don (with Shchuko)
1932–33 Palace of Soviets, Moscow (competition project with Shchuko)
1934–39 Palace of Soviets, Moscow (project with Iofan, Shchuko)
1937–39 Main Pavilion, All-Union Agricultural Exhibition, Moscow (with Shchuko)
1938 Great Stone Bridge, Moscow (with Minkus, Shchuko)
1940s several Metro stations, Moscow

Aleksandr Mikhailovich Gerasimov
Painter, stage designer
1881, Kozlov – 1963, Moscow
1930s Stalin's court painter
1932 exhibits in *Artists of the RSFSR over 15 Years*, Russian Museum, Leningrad
1934 co-founder and co-director of M. B. Grekov Studio of Military Painting
1936 Honoured Art Worker of the RSFSR
1937–39 chairman of Moscow Artists' Union
1939–43 chairman of organizing committee of Union of Soviet Artists
1941 Stalin Prize for *Stalin and Voroshilov in the Kremlin* (1938)
1943 Stalin Prize for *A Hymn to October*
1945 Stalin Prize for *Group Portrait of the Oldest Artists*

Ilya Aleksandrovich Golosov
Architect
1883, Moscow – 1945, Moscow
1931 Communal Building, Ivanovo-Voznesensk; Palace of Soviets, Moscow (competition project)
1933 onward heads studio at Mossoviet for redevelopment of Moscow, responsible for numerous public buildings and housing schemes
1934 Theatre, Minsk; workers' housing, Moscow Academy of Military Engineering; collective housing, Yausky Boulevard, Moscow
1936–40 Hydro-Electric Station, Gorky
1940s builds several mausoleums and memorials
1945 dies in Moscow

Julio González
Sculptor
1876, Barcelona – 1942, Arcueil
1930 solo exhibition Galerie de France, Paris
1928–31 collaborates with Picasso
1930–32 associated with Cercle et Carré, Abstraction-Création groups
1931 solo exhibition Galerie Le Centaure, Brussels
1931–34 exhibits in Salon des Surindépendants, Paris
1934 exhibition Galerie Percier, Paris (with Picasso, Miró); solo exhibition Galerie des Cahiers d'Art, Paris; exhibits at Kunsthaus Zürich; monograph by Ricardo Pérez Alfonseca published, Madrid
1935 solo exhibition Galerie des Cahiers d'Art, Paris; exhibits in Maurice Raynal's *Exposition-Manifeste*

1936 group exhibition Galerie des Cahiers d'Art, Paris; exhibits in *Cubism and Abstract Art*, MOMA; declines invitation to become Secretary of Prado, Madrid
1937 solo exhibition Galerie Pierre, Paris; exhibits *Montserrat*, Spanish Pavilion, IEP; exhibits in ODAII, MJP; takes part in Spanish radio programme on a Picasso exhibition
1939 exhibits in *Art in our Time*, MOMA
1940 moves to the Lot
1941 returns to Arcueil
1942 solo exhibition Galerías de Arte Libros, Barcelona; begins works on a second *Montserrat*; dies of a heart attack

José Gutiérrez Solana
Painter, graphic artist, author
1886, Madrid – 1945, Madrid
1932 own room, Venice Biennale
1933 solo exhibition Agrupación Castro Gil, Madrid
1935 solo exhibition Salón Ruiz Vernacci, Madrid
1937 exhibits 15 oil paintings at Spanish Pavilion, IEP; exhibits in Carnegie Institute, Pittsburgh
1938 solo exhibition Gazette des Beaux-Arts, Paris
1940, 1942 Venice Biennale
1943 solo exhibitions Galería Estilo, Madrid, Sala Argos, Barcelona, Sala Vilches, Madrid
1945 prize, *Exposición Nacional de Bellas Artes*, Madrid; exhibits in *Salón de los Once*, Madrid; dies in Madrid

Renato Guttuso
Painter, sculptor, graphic designer
1911, Bagheria – 1987, Rome
1931 Rome Quadriennale
1932 works as picture restorer for Galleria Perugia and Galleria Borghese, Rome; exhibits with Gruppo di pittori siciliani, Galleria del Milione, Milan
1934 exhibition Galleria del Milione, Milan; co-founder Gruppo dei Quattro
1935 Exhibition Halls, *Mostra dello Sport*, Milan (with BBPR, Melotti)
1935–36 military service, Milan
1937 exhibits in *Cinque Artisti Siciliani*, Galleria Mediterranea, Palermo; his studio is meeting-place of several intellectuals critical of the regime
1938 solo exhibition Galleria della Cometa, Rome
1940 joins the clandestine Italian Communist party; writes articles for *Primato*, *Il Selvaggio*, *Le Arti* and *Meridiano di Roma*; joins *Corrente*
1941 paints *Crucifixion*; its implicit criticism of Fascist regime provokes fierce reaction from Church and government (awarded Second Prize at 6th Premio Bergamo)
1943 leaves Rome for political reasons
1944 returns from Genoa; joins Resistance; exhibits in *L'arte contro la barbaria*, sponsored by the Communist paper *L'Unità*; drawings subsequently published in album *Gott mit Uns*, 1945

John Heartfield
Graphic artist, photomontage artist, designer
1891, Berlin – 1968, East Berlin
1929–33 photomontages for left-wing journal *AIZ (Arbeiter-Illustrierte-Zeitung)*; book covers for Malik-Verlag, Berlin
1930 exhibition in Moscow
1931–32 travels in Russia
1933 numerous works destroyed by SA;

flight to Prague; continues working there for *AIZ* and Malik-Verlag
1934 deprived of German nationality; exhibition at Mánes Gallery, Prague, causes diplomatic friction between Czechoslovakia and Germany
1936 monograph by Sergei Tretyakov published, Moscow; some works removed from *International Photo Exhibition* at Mánes Gallery, Prague, when Germany threatens to break off diplomatic relations with Czechoslovakia
1937 member of Oskar Kokoschka League, Prague; studios in Prague and Germany seized
1938 Hitler regime demands Heartfield's extradition; flight to London; exhibition, Pat Henry Club, New York
1939 exhibition *One Man's War against Hitler*, Arcade Gallery, London; illegal exhibition in Basel; involved in Artists' International Association and Free German League of Culture
1940 interned for a time in three camps as enemy alien
1941 Free German League of Culture honours Heartfield's fiftieth birthday with an exhibition of his book covers and photomontages
1942 exhibits in *Allies Inside (Nazi) Germany*, London
1942 onward book covers and illustrations for publishers Lindsay Drummond, Penguin Books, Dennis Dobson
1943 is given permission to work as freelance cartoonist
1944 exhibits in *Kämpfende Kunst*, Basel
1945 Konrad Farner publishes *John Heartfield: Photomontagen zur Zeitgeschichte*, Zürich

Ludwig Hohlwein
Architect, painter, graphic artist, poster designer
1874, Wiesbaden – 1949, Berchtesgaden
1930s and early 1940s designs propaganda posters for the Nazi party
1936 exhibits in *Olympische Kunstausstellung*, Berlin
1937 onward exhibits at GDK most years
1944 Munich studio destroyed by bombs; moves to Berchtesgaden

Boris Mikhailovich Iofan
Architect
1891, Odessa – 1976, Moscow
1927–31 Timiryazev Agricultural Academy
1928–31 Housing and amenities complex for Communist party officials, Serafimovich Street, Moscow
1929–33 Sanatorium, Barvikha
1931 Government housing complex, Bersenev Quay, Moscow
1931–39 winning project for Palace of Soviets, Moscow (with Shchuko, Gel'freikh)
1937 Gold Medal for Soviet Pavilion, IEP
1939 Soviet Pavilion, New York World Fair; Honorary Citizen of New York
1939–44 Metro station Baumanskaya, Moscow

Arthur Kampf
Painter, graphic artist
1864, Aachen – 1950, Castrop-Rauxel
1939 exhibits in GDK
1942–43 executes three big paintings for a planned ministry building
1944 moves to Oberlangenau, Silesia
1945 moves to Berchtesgaden

Ludwig Kasper
Sculptor
1893, Gurten, Austria – 1945,
Mauerkirchen, Austria
1930–43 exhibits at PAK
1933 moves to Berlin
1936 PAK bursary, travels in Greece for six
months; solo exhibition Wilhelm-
Lehmbruck-Museum, Duisburg
1937 exhibits in *Junge Bildhauerkunst*,
Galerie Buchholz, Berlin: solo exhibition
Verein Berliner Künstler, Berlin
1939 solo exhibition Galerie Buchholz,
Berlin; Villa Massimo Prize of the PAK,
spends a year in Rome
1941 solo exhibition Galerie Buchholz,
Berlin
1943 teaches at Kunstschule,
Braunschweig
1944 moves to Austria after destruction of
Kunstschule
1945 dies of kidney failure

Paul Klee
Painter, graphic artist
1879, Münchenbuchsee – 1940, Muralto-
Locarno
1930 exhibition MOMA
1931 contract with Bauhaus finishes;
professor of painting at Kunstakademie
Düsseldorf
1933 house in Dessau searched by Nazis;
letters temporarily confiscated; dismissed
from Kunstakademie; signs contract with
Daniel-Henry Kahnweiler; emigrates to
Bern
1934 exhibitions Mayor Gallery, London,
Galerie Simon, Paris
1935 exhibitions Kunsthalle Bern,
Kunsthalle Basel; Nazis confiscate Will
Grohmann's book on Klee's drawings
1937 102 works confiscated from German
public institutions; included in *Entartete
Kunst*, Munich; exhibits in *Twentieth-Century German
Art*, New Burlington Galleries, London;
Freie Deutsche Kunst, Maison de la Culture,
Paris; *Bauhaus 1919–1928*, MOMA
1938–40 applies in vain for Swiss
citizenship
1940 exhibitions Kunsthaus Zürich,
Kunsthalle Bern, MOMA; dies in
Sant'Agnese hospital, Muralto-Locarno
1941 exhibition Kunsthalle Basel

**Gustavs Klucis (Gustav Gustavovich
Klutsis)**
Painter, sculptor, graphic artist, designer
1895, Ruiena, Latvia – c. 1944, in exile,
Central Asia
1928–36 sent on study tours to various
cities of Soviet Union
1929–32 member of Association of
Revolutionary Placard Painters
1930 exhibits with October, Moscow;
member of photography section of
October; teaches at MPI
1932–33 interior and graphic designer for
Soviet exhibitions in USA, France, Spain,
Brazil
1933–34 exhibits in poster exhibitions in
Belgium, Italy, Britain
1937 co-designer of interior and head of
installation, Soviet Pavilion, IEP
1938 arrest and deportation
1944 dies in labour camp (probably
executed)

Oskar Kokoschka
Painter, graphic artist, dramatist
1886, Pöchlarn, Austria – 1980, Montreux,
Switzerland

1930 member of PAK
1931 exhibition Galerie Bonjean, Paris;
solo exhibitions Kunsthalle Mannheim,
Galerie Georges Petit, Paris; exhibits in
Modern German Painting and Sculpture,
MOMA,
Vom Abbild zum Sinnbild, Städel, Frankfurt
1932 Venice Biennale
1933 exhibition at Galerie Fiegl, Prague;
exhibits at Carnegie Institute, Pittsburgh
1934 emigrates to Prague
1935 exhibits at Kunsthaus Zürich; paints
portrait of Czechoslovak President
Thomas Masaryk; volume of drawings
published in Germany by Ernst Rathenau
seized
1936 attends Peace Conference in Brussels
as member of Czechoslovak delegation
1937 solo exhibition at Österreichisches
Museum für Kunst und Industrie, Vienna;
417 works confiscated from German public
institutions; included in *Entartete Kunst*,
Munich; émigré artists establish Oskar
Kokoschka League, Prague (OK does not
join)
1938 expelled from PAK; solo exhibition
Buchholz Gallery, New York; emigrates to
England; active in émigré organizations;
co-founder of Free German League of
Culture; exhibits in *Twentieth-Century
German Art*, New Burlington Galleries,
London
1940 solo exhibition Saint Etienne Gallery,
New York
1941 solo exhibition Arts Club of Chicago;
becomes President of Free German
League of Culture; joins Free Austrian
Movement
1942 publishes essay *The Truth is Indivisible*
in periodical *Freie Deutsche Kunst – German
Anti-Nazi Monthly* of the Free German
League of Culture
1943 donation for care of Russian and
German soldiers wounded in Stalingrad
1945 poster *Christ Helps the Starving
Children*, 5,000 copies displayed in London
Underground stations; donation for Czech
war orphans

Georg Kolbe
Sculptor, graphic artist
1877, Waldheim – 1947, Berlin
1931 group exhibition Kunsthaus Zürich;
monograph by Ludwig Justi published
1932 First Prize in competition for Heine
monument, Düsseldorf; travels to Moscow
and Leningrad
1933 prohibition of exhibition in
Chemnitz reversed instantly; declines
directorship at Kunstakademie Düsseldorf;
Heine monument in Frankfurt destroyed;
monograph by Rudolf Binding published;
covert investigation of Kolbe's ancestry
1935 chairman of *Deutscher Künstlerbund*;
inauguration of monument at Stralsund
1936 exhibition of *Deutscher Künstlerbund*
at Hamburger Kunstverein closed; Goethe
Prize, Frankfurt; sculptures for Olympic
Stadium, Berlin
1937 own room in exhibition at PAK;
Honorary Member of Akademie der
Bildenden Künste, Munich; IEP;
monograph by Wilhelm Pinder published
1937 onward exhibits in GDK
1938 City of Frankfurt commissions
Beethoven monument; travels to Spain
(paints portrait of Franco); exhibits in
Twentieth-Century German Art, New
Burlington Galleries, London
1940 several bronzes melted down
1941 exhibition Galerie Günther Franke,
Munich

1942 receives Goethe Medal for Art and
Science
1944 leaves Berlin after bomb damage to
house and studio
1945 returns to Berlin

Nikolai Iakovlevich Kolli
Architect
1894, Moscow – 1966, Moscow
1929–30 Dnieper Dam and Hydro-
Electric Station (Dneprostroi; with Vesnin
brothers)
1928–36 works on design for
Headquarters of Trade Unions in Le
Corbusier's Paris studio; site architect,
Kirov Street, Moscow
1930 Housing Estates, Zaporozhe
1935 Metro station Kirovskaya, Moscow
1944–49 Paveletsky Ring Road, Moscow

Adalberto Libera
Architect
1903, Trento – 1963, Rome
1930 interior design Casa Elettrica, Monza
Triennale
1931 exhibition of Italian architecture,
Berlin
1932 Nicoletti House, Rome; Palazzo delle
Esposizioni (temporary façade with De
Renzi), MRF
1933 Post Office Building, Rome (with De
Renzi); Italian Pavilion, Chicago World
Fair (with De Renzi)
1934 Palazzo del Littorio, Rome
(competition project)
1935 Houses for Tirrena Society, Rome;
Italian Pavilion, Brussels World Fair (with
De Renzi); Auditorium, Rome
(competition project with De Renzi)
1936 master plan for Aprilia, Latina
(competition project); Pavilion, Milan
Triennale
1937 *Colonie estive* exhibition, Rome (with
De Renzi); Palazzo del Littorio, Rome
(competition project with De Renzi)
1937–40 symbolic arch for EUR (project)
1937–42 Reception and Congress
Building, EUR
1939 Palace of Water and Light, EUR
(competition project)
1940 INCIS quarter, Rome (project with
De Renzi); railway station, Sofia, Bulgaria
(competition project)
1940–41 Ministerial complex, Bratislava,
Slovakia (competition project); apartment
building, Rome
1942 *First Exhibition of Race*, Rome
(project); Atatürk Memorial, Ankara,
Turkey (competition project)

El Lissitzky (Lazar Markovich Lisitsky)
Painter, graphic artist, architect, theorist,
interior and stage designer
1890, Polchinok – 1941, Moscow
1927–30 architectural designs and model
set for *I Want a Child*, Meyerhold Theatre
1930 designs for a *Pravda* complex and for
a House of Heavy Industry; exhibits with
October, Moscow; exhibition designer,
Soviet section, International Hygiene
Exhibition, Dresden, and International Fur
Trade Exhibition, Leipzig; publishes
architectural theories in book *Russland: Die
Rekonstruktion der Architektur in der
Sowjetunion*, Vienna
1931 onward leading artist-architect,
Gorky Park, Moscow
1932 designs book of Mayakovsky's poems,
For the Voice, Berlin; publishes portfolio
Victory over the Sun, Hanover; exhibits in
Contemporary Russian Art, Philadelphia;
solo exhibition, Hanover

1932 onward art editor of periodical *SSSR
na stroike* (published in English as *USSR in
Construction*)
1934 designs covers for periodical
Arkhitektura SSSR
1935 works on All-Union Agricultural
Exhibition
1941 dies of tuberculosis in Moscow

Mario Mafai
Painter, author
1902, Rome – 1965, Rome
1930 travels to Paris and London; exhibits
in *II. Mostra del Sindacato delle Belle Arti del
Lazio*, Rome; exhibition Galleria di Roma,
Rome (with Scipione)
1931 Rome Quadriennale; exhibits at
Baltimore Museum of Art
1932 exhibits in *III. Mostra del Sindacato
regionale fascista delle Belle Arti del Lazio*,
Rome; Venice Biennale
1934 Venice Biennale
1935 exhibits in *Contemporary Italian
Painting*, Museum of the American Legion
of Honor, San Franscico; prize, Rome
Quadriennale
1936 exhibits in *VI. Mostra del Sindacato
fascista delle Belle Arti del Lazio*, Rome;
Venice Biennale
1937 solo exhibition Galleria della
Cometa, Rome; exhibits in *VII. Mostra del
Sindacato fascista delle Belle Arti del Lazio*,
Rome; exhibits in *Mostra di 16 artisti*,
Salone del Cinema Acquario, Rome, and
Anthology of Contemporary Italian Painting,
Cometa Art Gallery, New York
1938 Venice Biennale; exhibits at Galleria
Lazecca, Turin, and in *60 artisti italiani*,
Galleria Mediterranea, Palazzo De Seta,
Palermo
1939 Rome Quadriennale; is called up for
army; solo exhibition Galleria Arcobaleno,
Venice; exhibits in *II. Mostra di Corrente*,
Galleria Grande, Milan
1940 solo exhibition Galleria Barbaroux,
Milan; exhibits in *IX. Mostra del Sindacato
interprovinciale fascista delle Belle Arti del
Lazio*, Rome; exhibits in *La Nazione*,
Florence (with Carrà, Sironi); exhibits at
Galleria Barbaroux, Milan; prize at 2nd
Premio Bergamo; spends the year in
Genoa
1941 solo exhibition Galleria Genova,
Genoa; exhibits at Galleria di Roma, Rome
1942 exhibits in *X. Mostra del Sindacato
interprovinciale fascista delle Belle Arti del
Lazio*, Rome

Kazimir Severinovich Malevich
Painter, graphic artist, stage designer,
theorist
1878, Kiev region – 1935, Leningrad
1930 solo exhibition in Moscow and Kiev,
closed after short time; gives course on
painting theory at House of Art,
Leningrad; exhibits in *Sowjetmalerei*,
Berlin, *Russische Kunst von heute*, Vienna.
Arrested and detained for questioning;
friends burn number of manuscripts as
precautionary measure
1931 murals, Red Theatre, Leningrad
1932 heads experimental laboratory at
Russian Museum, Leningrad; exhibits in
Artists of the RSFSR over 15 Years, Russian
Museum, Leningrad; exhibits in exhibition
of contemporary Russian art, Philadelphia
1935 exhibits in exhibition of Leningrad
artists, Leningrad; dies in Leningrad; City
Council of Leningrad pays for his public
funeral in view of his contribution to art
world; Russian Museum buys several works
and awards pension to his family

Matvei Genrikhovich Manizer
Sculptor, author
1891, St Petersburg – 1966, Moscow
1931 *Monument to the Victims of 9 January 1905*, Leningrad
1932 monument to V. I. Chapayev, Kuibyshev
1935 monument to Taras G. Shevchenko, Kharkov
1935–41 teaches at All-Russian Academy of Arts
1936–39 figures for Metro station Ploshchad' Revolyutsii (Revolution Square), Moscow
1937–41 chairman of Leningrad Section of the Union of Soviet Artsts
1940 monument to Lenin, Ulyanovsk
1941 Stalin Prize for monument to Lenin, Ulyanovsk
1942 monument to Zoya Kosmodemyanskaya
1943 Stalin Prize for monument to Zoya Kosmodemyanskaya

Giacomo Manzù
Sculptor, painter, graphic artist
1908, Bergamo – 1991, Bergamo
1931 exhibits at Galleria Tre Arti, Milan
1932 decoration of chapel, Catholic University, Milan; exhibits in group show, Galleria del Milione, Milan; monograph by Giovanni Scheiwiller published
1933 Milan Triennale; solo exhibition Galleria del Milione, Milan; exhibition Galleria Tre Arti, Milan
1934 solo exhibitions St Gallen and Galleria Tre Arti, Milan
1936 Venice Biennale; exhibits in Budapest
1937 solo exhibition Galleria della Cometa, Rome; several friends are arrested, his house is searched; Gold Medal, Milan Triennale; exhibits in Musée National d'Art Moderne, as part of IEP
1938 causes scandal at Venice Biennale with *The Crucifixions*; exhibition Galleria Genova, Genoa
1939 exhibits with *Corrente*, Milan; exhibits in *Italian Art, Ancient and Modern*, San Francisco Museum of Art
1940 solo exhibition, Zürich
1941 professor of sculpture, Accademia di Brera, Milan (including courses at the Turin Academy); solo exhibition Galleria Barbaroux, Milan
1942 *The Crucifixions* denounced by Church and State at exhibition at Galleria Barbaroux, Milan; gives up teaching in Turin; moves to Clusone
1943 Grand Prize for Sculpture, Rome Quadriennale
1944 ordered out of Clusone by Germans; moves to Bergamo; solo exhibition Galleria Galatea, Turin
1945 settles in Milan

Werner March
Architect
1894, Berlin – 1976, West Berlin
1930 professor in Berlin
1933–36 stadium, grounds, and ancillary buildings on the Reichssportfeld in Berlin for the Olympic Games
1937 commission for museum in Bagdad; Grand Prix, IEP
1938 urban plan for Breslau; Elbe riverbank development, Hamburg; Yugoslav Legation, Berlin
1939 design of a stadium for Belgrade; master plan for Silesian cities of Beuthen, Gleiwitz and Hindenburg

Gerhard Marcks
Sculptor, graphic artist
1889, Berlin – 1981, Burgbrohl
1932 commission for completion of figures by Ernst Barlach, church of St Catherine, Lübeck
1933 defends colleague Marguerite Friedländer-Wildenhain, dismissed for being Jewish; dismissed from National Art School, Giebichenstein; proposed appointment to Kunstakademie Düsseldorf prevented
1935 Villa Massimo Prize
1936 exhibits in *Olympische Kunstausstellung*, Berlin
1937 works confiscated from German public institutions; included in *Entartete Kunst*, Munich; planned solo exhibition Galerie Buchholz, Berlin, prohibited from opening; attempts to have him elected to PAK fail
1937 onward several galleries continue to show single works in larger exhibitions
1943–45 some works destroyed in bombing of Galerie Buchholz and bronze foundries in Berlin; house and studio levelled by bombs

Arturo Martini
Sculptor, painter
1889, Treviso – 1947, Milan
1931 First Prize for sculpture, Rome Quadriennale
1932 exhibition Galleria di Palazzo Ferroni, Florence; own room at Venice Biennale
1933 monument to Duke of Aosta, Turin
1934 *Victory in the Air*, Post Office, Naples
1935 Rome Quadriennale; *Athena*, University of Rome
1937 bas-relief *Corporate Justice*, Palace of Justice, Milan; solo exhibition Galleria del Milione, Milan; wall sculpture, *Victory in the Air*, Italian Pavilion, IEP
1938–39 bas-relief *The Sforzas*, Ospedale Maggiore, Milan
1939 Rome Quadriennale
1940 solo exhibition Galleria Barbaroux, Milan
1942 Venice Biennale; *Titus Livius*, Padua University; teaches at Accademia di Belle Arti, Venice
1945 publishes book *La Scultura lingua morta*, Venice

Aleksandr Terentievich Matveyev
Sculptor, ceramic artist
1878, Saratov – 1960, Moscow
1918–48 teaches at Petrograd Academy of Arts (later Repin Academy of Painting, Sculpture and Architecture of the Soviet Academy of Arts, Leningrad)
1930s designs monuments to Lenin, Gorky, Chekhov, Lermontov and Yermolova
1931 *Monument to the Fallen Soldiers of the Far Eastern Army in Dauria*, Russian Museum, Leningrad
1932 exhibits in *Artists of the RSFSR over 15 Years*, Russian Museum, Leningrad
1932–35 director of Institute of Painting, Sculpture and Architecture, Leningrad
1932–48 teaches at All-Russian Academy of Arts, Leningrad
1940 member of Communist party
1940–48 teaches at Surikov State Art Institute, Moscow

Konstantin Stepanovich Mel'nikov
Architect, designer
1890, Moscow – 1974, Moscow
1930 Moscow Chamber Theatre (reconstruction); Frunze Military Academy,

Moscow (competition project); *Green City*, suburbs of Moscow (competition project)
1930s chief architect of Mossoviet studio for replanning of Moscow
1931–32 Palace of Soviets, Moscow (competition project, ignored by jury)
1933 Milan Triennale; teaches at Institute of Architecture, Moscow
1934 Intourist Garage, Moscow; Heavy Industry Commissariat, Moscow (competition project)
1936 Soviet Pavilion, IEP (competition project); dismissed from Institute of Architecture, Moscow
1937 denounced as an impractical individualist and stripped of professional title at First Congress of Soviet Architects; forbidden to teach or practise architecture; dismissed from Mossoviet studio
1944 teaches again at Institute of Architecture, Moscow

Fausto Melotti
Sculptor
1901, Rovereto – 1986, Milan
1930, 1933 Milan Triennale
1934 solo exhibition Galleria del Milione, Milan
1935 co-founder Gruppo del Milione, Milan (with Fontana); joins Abstraction-Création group, Paris; signs manifesto of *Prima mostra collettiva d'arte astratta italiana*; solo exhibition and exhibits in *Gruppo del Milione*, Galleria del Milione, Milan; exhibits in *Prima mostra collettiva di arte italiana*, Turin; Exhibition Halls, *Mostra dello Sport*, Milan (with BBPR, Guttuso)
1936 Pavilion, Milan Triennale (with BBPR)
1937 Premio Internazionale, La Sarraz
1937–39 bas-reliefs, Palace of Justice, Milan
1941–43 lives in Rome, works on monumental figure groups for inclusion in EUR
1943 many works destroyed by bombing raid on Milan; Rome Quadriennale
1944 Giovanni Scheiwiller publishes volume of Melotti's poems *Il triste Minotauro*

Erich Mercker
Painter
1891, Zabern (Saverne) –
1937 Great Gold Medal, IEP
1937 onward exhibits at GDK

Mikhail Adolfovich Minkus
Architect
1905, Odessa – 1963, Turku, Finland
1930 Theatre, Kharkov (competition project)
1931 various projects for bus and car garages, Moscow; Military Academy, Moscow (competition project)
1933 onward works in Mossoviet architecture studio, Moscow
1934 Heavy Industry commissariat, Moscow (competition project)
1938 Great Stone Bridge, Moscow (with Shchuko, Gel'freikh)

Joan Miró
Painter, sculptor
1893, Barcelona – 1983, Mallorca
1930 solo exhibitions Galerie Pierre, Paris, Valentine Gallery, New York; paintings slashed at premiere of Buñuel's *L'Age d'Or*, Paris
1931 solo exhibitions Arts Club of Chicago, Galerie Pierre, Paris

1932 designs sets and costumes for *Jeux d'enfants*, Monte Carlo; solo exhibitions Pierre Matisse Gallery, New York; Galerie Pierre Colle, Paris
1933 exhibits in Salon des Surindépendants, Paris; solo exhibitions Mayor Gallery, London; Galerie Bernheim, Paris; Pierre Matisse Gallery, New York
1934 exhibition Galerie Percier, Paris (with Picasso, González); exhibits at Kunsthaus Zürich; solo exhibitions Arts Club of Chicago, Galerie des Cahiers d'Art, Paris; Christian Zervos devotes special issue of *Cahiers d'Art* to Miró
1935 solo exhibition Pierre Matisse, New York
1936 group exhibition Galerie des Cahiers d'Art, Paris; exhibits in *L'Art Espagnol contemporain*, MJP; *International Surrealist Exhibition*, New Burlington Galleries, London; *Fantastic Art, Dada and Surrealism* and *Cubism and Abstract Art*, MOMA; solo exhibition Pierre Matisse Gallery, New York; monograph by Shuzo Takiguchi published (in Japanese); moves to Paris
1937 takes part in Spanish radio programme on a Picasso exhibition; solo exhibitions Zwemmer Gallery, London; Galerie Pierre, Paris; exhibits in ODAII, MJP; designs poster *Aidez l'Espagne* for Spanish Loyalists; paints mural *Le Faucheur (El Segador, The Harvester)*, otherwise known as *Catalan Peasant in Revolt*) for Spanish Pavilion, IEP
1938 solo exhibitions Pierre Matisse Gallery, New York; Mayor Gallery, London; Galerie Pierre, Paris
1939 solo exhibitions Galerie Pierre, Paris; Pierre Matisse Gallery, New York
1940 solo exhibitions Pierre Matisse Gallery, New York; returns to Spain
1941 solo exhibitions Pierre Matisse Gallery, New York, MOMA; monograph by James Johnson Sweeney published
1943 solo exhibitions Arts Club of Chicago, Galerie Jeanne Bucher, Paris
1945 solo exhibitions Pierre Matisse Gallery, New York

Giorgio Morandi
Painter, graphic designer
1890, Bologna – 1964, Bologna
1930 Venice Biennale; exhibits in Carnegie Institute, Pittsburgh, and in exhibition of engravings, Bibliothèque Nationale, Paris
1930–65 professor of printmaking, Accademia di Belle Arti, Bologna
1931 member of jury, inclusion of several works and prize, Rome Quadriennale; whole edition of *L'Italiano* dedicated to Morandi
1932 exhibits in *Mostra dell'incisione italiana moderna*, Florence
1933 exhibits in *Moderne Italienische Kunst*, Künstlerhaus, Vienna; exhibits in Carnegie Institute, Pittsburgh
1934 Venice Biennale; exhibits in *Mostra d'Arte Italiana*, USA; trip to USA
1935 included in Roberto Longhi's *Momenti della pittura bolognese*; member of jury and inclusion of several works, Rome Quadriennale; exhibits in *Ancient and Modern Italian Art*, MJP
1936 exhibits in Carnegie Institute, Pittsburgh
1937 IEP; exhibits in Berlin
1938 exhibits at Kunsthalle Bern
1939 exhibits in *Golden Gate International Exhibition of Contemporary Art*, San Francisco; own room at Rome Quadriennale; Second Prize for Painting,

Rome Quadriennale, causes public uproar; monograph by Arnaldo Beccaria published, Milan
1940 exhibits in Italian Art exhibition, Kunsthaus Zürich
1941 First Prize, *Collectionist Exhibition*, Cortina d'Ampezzo
1945 solo exhibitions Galleria del Fiore, Florence, Galleria La Palma, Rome

Luigi Moretti
Architect
1907, Rome – 1973, Isola di Capraia
1932 city redevelopment plans, Perugia and Verona (competition projects with Paniconi, Pediconi)
1933 House for a Scholar, Milan Triennale (with Paniconi, Pediconi); Youth Centre, Rome
1934 Young Women's Centre, Piacenza; *Arte Sacra*, exhibition layouts, Rome; Palazzo del Littorio, Rome (competition project); Casa delle Armi, Foro Mussolini, Rome
1935 pavilion, *Colonie estive* exhibition, Rome
1936 Fencing Academy, Foro Mussolini, Rome; Film Academy, Grand Hall, Italian-German Friendship Building, Esplanade, Foro Italico, Rome; Church of San Basilio and San Nicolò da Tolentino, Rome; exhibits in *Olympische Kunstausstellung*, Berlin
1937 Olympic Stadium, Rome; Co-operative Buildings, Rome; State Employees' Housing Complex, Rome; Foro Italico, redevelopment plan I, Rome; Piazza dell'Impero, Rome
1938 Ministry of External Affairs Building, Rome (competition project); Piazza Imperiale, EUR
1939 Foro Italico, redevelopment plan II, Rome
1940 Palazzo del Littorio, Rome (competition project); Military Police Headquarters and zone redevelopment plan, Rome; monumental fountain, Foro Italico, Rome (project)
1941 College of Higher Classical Education (project), Foresteria Nord Building, various gardens, Foro Italico, Rome; Sports and Youth Centre, exhibition layouts, Florence; School of Horsemanship, The Forum, Rome; Trajan's Markets, Rome; *Gioventù italiana*, exhibition layouts, EUR; Villa Blanc, EUR Quarter

Vera Ignatievna Mukhina
Sculptor, graphic artist, stage and textile designer
1889, Riga – 1953, Moscow
1930 member of Russian Academy of Arts; moves to Voronezh
1930s produces dress designs
1932 exhibits in *Artists of the RSFSR over 15 Years*, Russian Museum, Leningrad; returns to Moscow
1933 member of Arts Council, Moscow House of Clothing Design
1935 exhibits in Moscow (with Chaikov)
1937 colossal *Industrial Worker and Collective Farm Girl*, Soviet Pavilion, IEP
1941 Stalin Prize for IEP work
1943 exhibits in Tretyakov Gallery, Moscow (with Deineka); Stalin Prize for portraits of Khizhnyak and Yusupov

Solomon Borisovich Nikritin
Painter, graphic artist, stage designer, museologist, theorist
1898, Chernigov – 1965, Moscow

1929–30 teaches at Art Teacher Training Technical School
1930s director of Polytechnic Museum, Moscow; designs museum interiors and exhibitions
1931 member of *Izobrigada*
1936–41 leading designer of All-Union Agricultural Exhibition

Emil Nolde (Emil Hansen)
Painter, graphic artist
1867, Nolde – 1956, Seebüll
1930 solo exhibitions Galerie Ferdinand Möller, Berlin, Kunsthaus Schaller, Stuttgart; exhibits in *Deutsche Kunstausstellung*, Glaspalast, Munich; exhibits in Carnegie Institute, Pittsburgh
1931 member of PAK; exhibits in *Modern German Painting and Sculpture*, MOMA, *Vom Abbild zum Sinnbild*, Städel, Frankfurt; first volume of autobiography, *Das eigene Leben*, published
1933 only still-lifes and landscapes shown at Kronprinzenpalais, Berlin; exhibits in Carnegie Institute, Pittsburgh; supported by National Socialist League of German Students; rejected as President of VSKK, and as member of Kampfbund für deutsche Kultur (Combat League for German Culture)
1934 joins North Schleswig National Socialist Workers' Cooperative (absorbed into Nazi party 1935); solo exhibition Kestner-Gesellschaft, Hanover; second volume of autobiography, *Jahre der Kämpfe*, published; soon afterwards his books are banned; exhibitions that are closed by Himmler and Rosenberg are reopened by Goebbels or Rust; exhibits in *Neue deutsche Malerei*, Kunsthaus Zürich, *Das Bild der Landschaft*, Kunsthalle Hamburg
1935 solo exhibition Kunstverein, Cologne; works withdrawn from *Berliner Kunst in München*, Neue Pinakothek, Munich
1936 exhibits in *Malerei und Plastik in Deutschland*, Kunstverein Hamburg
1937 1052 works confiscated from German museums; included in *Entartete Kunst*, Munich; solo exhibition Galerie Ferdinand Möller, Berlin; solo exhibition at Kunsthaus, Mannheim, closed after three days
1938 exhibits in *Twentieth-Century German Art*, New Burlington Galleries, London
1938–45 paints his *Unpainted Pictures* at Seebüll
1939 solo exhibition Buchholz Gallery, New York; exhibits in *Art in our Time*, MOMA, *Contemporary German Art*, Institute of Modern Art, Boston
1940 solo exhibition Katharine Kuh Galleries, Chicago
1941 expulsion from the Reich Chamber of Visual Arts; forbidden to paint
1943 exhibits in *Ausländische Kunst in Zürich*, Kunsthaus Zürich
1944 exhibits in *Rohlfs und andere Maler*, Kunsthalle Basel

Mario Paniconi
Architect

Guilio Pediconi
Architect
Major works by Paniconi and Pediconi:
1932 city redevelopment plans, Perugia and Verona (competition projects with Moretti)
1933 House for a Scholar, Milan Triennale (with Moretti)
1938–39 Porta Imperiale, EUR (project)

Francisco Pérez Mateo
Sculptor
1903, Barcelona – 1936, Madrid
1931 signs *Manifiesto dirigido a la opinión y a los poderes públicos*; exhibits at Museo de Arte Moderno; Lyceum Club; Sociedad de Artistas Ibéricos, San Sebastián; *Escultura Nueva*, Ateneo, Madrid; exhibition of Spanish art, Oslo
1932 Third Prize, *Exposición Nacional de Bellas Artes*
1933 exhibits in *I. Exposición de Arte Revolucionario*, Ateneo, Madrid; goes to Villanueva y Geltrú as teacher
1935 goes to art school at Manresa
1936 exhibits in *L'Art Espagnol Contemporain*, Paris; joins Alianza de Intelectuales Antifascistas; joins the Fifth Regiment, goes to the front; dies in Madrid
1937 Spanish Pavilion, IEP

Marcello Piacentini
Architect, author
1881, Rome – 1961, Rome
1930s principal architect to Mussolini
1930 publishes book *L'Architettura d'oggi*, Rome; Cinema-Theatre, Barberini, Rome; Piazza Missori, Milan; Cassa Nazionale delle Assicurazioni Sociali, Milan
1931 Ministry of Corporations, Rome; master plan for Rome
1932 City Center, Via della Conciliazione, Via Regina Elena, International Temple of Peace, Rome; Memorial Arch, Genoa
1932–33 master plan, University of Rome (chief architect)
1932–40 Palace of Justice, Milan
1934 Church of Cristo Re, Rome
1935 Gold Medal, City of Turin
1936 Banca Nazionale del Lavoro, Headquarters, Rome; Rectorate, University City, Rome; General Insurance Building, Jerusalem; *Architettura attuale e la tradizione italiana*, exhibition layouts, Rome
1937 Italian Pavilion, IEP
1937–42 EUR (supervising architect, with Vietti)
1938 Via Roma, Turin
1940 exhibition layouts, Milan Triennale
1942 master plan for EUR district; Piazza della Vittoria, Genoa; master plan for University City, Rio de Janeiro

Pablo Picasso
Painter, sculptor, graphic artist
1881, Málaga – 1973, Mougins
1928–31 collaborates with González
1930 First Prize, Carnegie Institute, Pittsburgh; solo exhibition, Arts Club of Chicago
1931 *Thirty Years of Pablo Picasso*, Alex Reid and Lefèvre Gallery, London
1932 solo exhibitions Galerie Georges Petit, Paris, Kunsthaus Zürich; exhibition Kestner-Gesellschaft, Hanover (with Schlemmer); first volume of Christian Zervos's catalogue raisonné of paintings and drawings published
1933 Bernard Geiser's catalogue raisonné of engravings and lithographs published
1934 exhibition Galerie Percier, Paris (with González, Miró)
1936 takes part in group exhibition at Galerie des Cahiers d'Art, Paris; appointed director of Prado, Madrid; committed to Republican cause during Spanish Civil War; sells works to raise funds; exhibits in *Fantastic Art, Dada and Surrealism* and *Cubism and Abstract Art*, MOMA
1937 exhibits *Guernica*, Spanish Pavilion, IEP; exhibition Zwemmer Gallery,

London (with De Chirico); exhibits in ODAII, MJP; exhibits in *Les Maîtres de l'Art indépendant*, Petit Palais, Paris; *20 Years in the Evolution of Picasso*, Seligmann Gallery, New York; MOMA buys *Les Demoiselles d'Avignon*; works in German museums confiscated
1938 solo exhibition New Burlington Galleries, London (including *Guernica*, also seen at the Whitechapel Art Gallery)
1939 *Picasso, Forty Years of his Art*, MOMA; *Guernica* shown in solo exhibitions at Valentine Gallery, New York; Stendahl Art Galleries, Los Angeles; Museum of Fine Arts, San Francisco; Arts Club of Chicago
1940–44 spends occupation years in Paris
1941 solo exhibition MOMA; *Guernica* shown in solo exhibition at Fogg Museum of Art, Cambridge, Mass.; Gallery of Fine Arts, Columbus, Ohio
1944 joins Communist party; exhibits in *Salon d'Automne*, Paris

Fausto Pirandello
Painter, author
1899, Rome – 1975, Rome
1930 trip to Berlin; solo exhibition Galerie Bakum, Vienna
1931 returns to Rome; solo exhibition Galleria di Roma, Rome
1932 Venice Biennale; exhibits in *III. Mostra del Sindacato regionale fascista delle Belle Arti del Lazio*, Rome
1933 solo exhibition Galleria Milano, Milan
1934 Venice Biennale
1935 prize, Carnegie Institute, Pittsburgh; prize, Rome Quadriennale
1936 exhibits in *VI. Mostra del Sindacato fascista delle Belle Arti del Lazio*, Rome; Venice Biennale; exhibits in exhibition of Italian art, Budapest
1937 exhibits at Galleria della Cometa, Rome; exhibits in *Anthology of Contemporary Italian Painting*, Cometa Art Gallery, New York, and *VII. Mostra del Sindacato fascista delle Belle Arti del Lazio*, Rome
1938 solo exhibition Galleria della Cometa, Rome; exhibits in *VII. Mostra del Sindacato fascista delle Belle Arti del Lazio*, Rome
1939 exhibits with Corrente group, Milan; prize, Rome Quadriennale; exhibits at Carnegie Institute, Pittsburgh
1940 Venice Biennale; exhibits in *IX. Mostra del Sindacato interprovinciale fascista delle Belle Arti del Lazio*, Rome
1941 solo exhibition Galleria delle Terme, Rome; exhibits in *III. Mostra del Sindacato Nazionale fascista delle Belle Arti*, Palazzo dell'Arte, Milan
1942 solo exhibition Galleria Gian Ferrari, Milan; exhibits in *X. Mostra del Sindacato interprovinciale fascista delle Belle Arti del Lazio*, Rome; Venice Biennale
1943 Rome Quadriennale
1944 solo exhibition Galleria del Secolo, Rome

Josep Renau Berenguer
Photomontage artist, muralist, graphic designer, poster designer
1907, Valencia – 1982, Berlin
1930 exhibits in *Exposición nacional de Bellas Artes*, Madrid
1931 member of Communist party
1932 co-founder Unión de Escritores y Artistas Proletarios; prize, poster competition for *Exposición Nacional de Bellas Artes*
1932–34 Graphic director of magazine *Orto*, Valencia

1932–36 teaches at Escuela de Bellas Artes de San Carlos
1933 works for magazine *Nuestro Cine*; mural for trade union, Valencia (destroyed after civil war); exhibits in *I. Exposición de Arte Revolucionario*, Ateneo, Madrid; First Prize, poster competition for Instituto Nacional del Vino
1934 member of jury, *Exposición Regional de Bellas Artes*, Valencia; photomontages for magazine *Crónica*
1934–35 designs covers for magazine *La Revista Blanca*
1935 exhibits in *Exposición Nacional de Bellas Artes*, Madrid; First Prize, poster competition for *Ferias y Fiestas de Valencia*; exhibits in *Concurso Asociación de la Prensa*
1935–37 founder and director of magazine *Nueva Cultura*
1936 named Director General of Fine Arts, in charge of safeguarding the national artistic heritage during the Civil War; designs posters for Spanish Communist party
1936 onward co-director of newspaper *Verdad*
1937 publishes book *La Función social del cartel publicitario*; co-organizes Spanish Pavilion, IEP; commissions Picasso to paint mural for Spanish Pavilion
1938 named director of graphic propaganda to the General Staff; series of photomontages commissioned by Republican government for New York World Fair
1939 New York World Fair; is exiled; travels to France; settles in Mexico
1940 becomes Mexican citizen; exhibits in *Pintura Española en el exilio*, Casa de la Junta de Cultura Española, Mexico
1942 first prize, United Hemisphere International Poster Competition, MOMA

Aleksandr Mikhailovich Rodchenko
Painter, sculptor, graphic artist, designer, photographer, theorist
1891, St Petersburg – 1956, Moscow
1930 co-founder, photography section of October group; exhibits with October group, Moscow; co-producer, educational film *Chemistry in the Forest*; anti-militarist photomontages and covers for periodical *Za Rubezhom*; exhibits in *Das Lichtbild*, Munich
1930–35 photo-album *White Sea Canal*
1931 expelled from October; exhibits in *Fotomontage*, Berlin; stage design for *One-Sixth of the World*, Music Hall, Moscow
1932 exhibits in *Artists of the RSFSR over 15 Years*, Russian Museum, Leningrad
1932 teaches photography at MPI; stage and costume designs for *The Army of the World*, Zavadsky Theatre, Moscow
1933–40 photo-journalist for periodical *SSSR na stroike (USSR in Construction)*; designs more than ten issues
1935 exhibits in *Masters of Soviet Photography*, Moscow
1936 attacked for formalism at discussion on naturalism and formalism in photography, House of Cinema, Moscow; designs book *Film in the USSR* (editions in different languages for foreign markets)
1937 photo-album *The First Cavalry*; typographical work exhibited in Soviet Pavilion, IEP
1938 photo-album *The Red Army*
1938–40 photo-album *The Soviet State Farm*
1939 exhibition, Writers Club, Moscow; publications exhibited in Soviet Pavilion, New York World Fair; photo-album *Soviet Aviation*

1940 photo-album *Mayakovsky*
1941 is evacuated from Moscow
1941–42 produces propaganda posters, photographic reportage for newspaper *Stalinskii udarnik*
1942 returns to Moscow
1942–45 photo-album *From Moscow to Stalingrad* (not published); organizes exhibitions for *Sovinform*
1943 co-organizes exhibition *History of the Party*, Museum of Revolution
1944 Artistic director, House of Technology, Moscow

Lev Vladimirovich Rudnev
Architect, painter, graphic artist, sculptor
1885, Novgorod – 1956, Moscow
1925–32 Head of Architecture Committee, Municipal Economic Division, Leningrad
1930 Government Building, Minsk (project)
1931 Palace of Culture, Moscow (competition project)
1933 heads team working on People's Commissariat of Defence, Moscow
1931–37 Frunze Military Academy, Moscow
1934–55 Ministry of Defence, Moscow

Alberto Sánchez Pérez
Sculptor, stage designer
1895, Toledo – 1962, Moscow
1930 exhibits in Ateneo in Madrid; receives prize for maquette of the monument to Góngora at national competition, organized by the Ministry of Education
1931 exhibits in *Grupo de Arte Constructivo*
1932 designs sets for Lope de Vega's *Fuenteovejuna* for the theatre group La Barraca; becomes professor at Instituto de Segunda Enseñanza, El Escorial
1936 last solo exhibition, Madrid; joins the Fifth Regiment, goes to the front
1937 part of his work and house destroyed; exhibits *El pueblo español tiene un camino que conduce a una estrella (The Spanish People Have a Path that Leads to a Star)*, Spanish Pavilion, IEP; goes to Valencia; professor at Instituto Obrero, Valencia
1938 sent to Moscow by Republican government to teach evacuated Spanish children
1940 decorations and figurines for Tolstoy's *The Devil's Bridge*, Kamerni Theatre
1941 set decorations and figurines for *La zapatera prodigiosa* and *La gitanilla* by Cervantes, Gitano Theatre, Moscow
1943 set decorations for Lorca's *Bodas de sangre*, Gitano Theatre, Moscow

Oskar Schlemmer
Painter, sculptor, stage designer
1888, Stuttgart – 1943, Baden-Baden
1929–32 teaches at Kunstakademie Breslau
1930 murals at Weimar Bauhaus effaced
1931 exhibition Galerie Flechtheim, Berlin
1932 Kunstakademie Breslau closed; exhibition Kunstverein Frankfurt (with Baumeister); organizes and opens exhibition of *Schlesischer Künstlerbund*; appointed to VSKK; Bronze Medal, International Dance Contest, Paris; exhibition Kestner-Gesellschaft, Hanover (with Picasso)
1933 murals removed Museum Folkwang, Essen; dismissed from VSKK; moves to Switzerland; solo exhibition Württembergischer Kunstverein, Stuttgart, closed day after opening
1934 works removed from view, Museum Folkwang, Essen
1936 exhibits in *Malerei und Plastik in Deutschland*, Kunstverein Hamburg

1937 solo exhibitions Galerie Ferdinand Möller, Berlin; Galerie Valentin, Stuttgart; London Gallery, London; 51 works confiscated from German public institutions; included in *Entartete Kunst*, Munich, *Bolschewismus ohne Maske*, Kroll-Oper, Berlin
1938 exhibits in *Twentieth-Century German Art*, New Burlington Galleries, London; exhibits in *Bauhaus 1919–1928*, MOMA
1939 works as house painter, camouflages military units
1940 works at Kurt Herbert's paint factory in Wuppertal; collaborating with Baumeister on book *Anfänge der Malerei* (published in 1941 without authors' names)
1943 dies of complications from diabetes

Scipione (Gino Bonichi)
Painter, poet
1904, Macerata – 1933, Arco
1930 exhibition Galleria di Roma, Rome (with Mafai); illustrates book covers for editions of Eugenio Montale, Bruno Barilli and Vincenzo Cardarelli
1930 onward literary vignettes and parodies regularly feature in cultural journal *L'Italia Letteraria*
1931 Rome Quadriennale; co-planning of new literary and artistic journal *Fronte*
1932 exhibits in *22 Artistes italiens modernes*, Galerie Bernheim, Paris
1933 dies in Arco; *L'Italia Letteraria* devotes special issue to Scipione's memory
1935 solo exhibition, Rome Quadriennale
1938 first edition of Scipione's poetry, *Le civette gridano*, published by Giovanni Scheiwiller
1941 solo exhibition Accademia di Brera, Milan
1943 Einaudi publishes Scipione's collection *Carte segrete*

José María Sert
Painter, muralist
1874, Barcelona – 1945, Barcelona
1930 paintings for dining room, Baron Becker's residence, Brussels
1931–32 solo exhibition Wildenstein Galleries, New York
1931–33 decorations, Hotel Waldorf Astoria, New York
1932 wins competition for decoration of reception hall of Rockefeller Center, New York; five ceilings for Palacio Perreda, Buenos Aires; commission from French government for series of cartoons for tapestries for the Gobelins factory near Paris; 75 square metres of paintings in chapel of convent San Telmo, San Sebastián
1935 donation of painting *La Barca de Catalunya* to council of Palamós; paintings for San Gregorio, Venice
1936 mural paintings in Vic cathedral destroyed by arson; paintings for League of Nations, Geneva
1937 second commission for Rockefeller Center; altarpiece for Vatican Pavilion, IEP; intervenes actively for salvation of artistic heritage of Spanish State
1941 third commission for Rockefeller Center (ceiling, staircase, balustrade); begins restoration of decorations in Vic Cathedral
1943 triptych for chapel, Spanish Embassy, Paris; solo exhibition, Ministry of Foreign Affairs, Madrid
1944 music room for Palacio March, Palma de Mallorca
1945 inauguration of second set of mural paintings for Vic Cathedral; dies in Barcelona

Ivan Dmitrevich Shadr
Sculptor
1887, Shadrinsk – 1941, Moscow
1924 onward works on numerous Lenin portraits
1938 full-length portrait of Gorky
1939 monument to Nemirovich-Danchenko, Novodevichy Cemetery, Moscow; full-length portrait of Pushkin
1941 dies in Moscow

Vladimir Alekseyevich Shchuko
Architect, stage designer, graphic artist
1878, Berlin – 1939, Moscow
1928–39 Lenin Library, Moscow (with Gel'freikh)
1930s stage designer, Bolshoi Theatre, Moscow
1930 Metro station Elektrozavodskaya, Moscow
1930–36 Gorky Theatre, Rostov-on-Don (with Gel'freikh)
1932 leading figure, Union of Architects
1932–33 Palace of Soviets, Moscow (competition project with Gel'freikh)
1934–39 Palace of Soviets, Moscow (project with Iofan, Gel' freikh)
1934–39 Main Pavilion, All-Union Agricultural Exhibition, Moscow (with Gel'freikh)
1938 Great Stone Bridge, Moscow (with Gel'freikh, Minkus)
1939 dies in Moscow

Mario Sironi
Painter, stage and exhibition designer, caricaturist, muralist, critic
1885, Sassari – 1961, Milan
1927–33 art critic, *Il Popolo d'Italia*
1930 co-organizes Monza Triennale; Venice Biennale; exhibits in *Novecento* exhibition, Buenos Aires; monograph by Giovanni Scheiwiller published
1931 Second Prize, Carnegie Institute, Pittsburgh; Rome Quadriennale
1932 stained-glass window, *Work*, Palazzo dell'Industria, Rome; rooms for MRF; exhibits in *Novecento* exhibition, Oslo; Brera and Venice Biennale; exhibits in *22 Artistes italiens modernes*, Galerie Bernheim, Paris
1933 co-organization and mural *Works and Days*, Milan Triennale; publishes *Manifesto della pittura murale* with definition of Fascist style; stage sets for *Lucrezia Borgia*, Florence
1934 solo exhibition Galleria Milano, Milan; Palazzo del Littorio, Rome (competition project with Vietti)
1934–39 art critic, *La Rivista illustrata del Popolo d'Italia*
1935 mural *Italy Between the Arts and Sciences*, University of Rome
1936 co-organizes Milan Triennale; mural *Law Between Justice and Strength*, Palace of Justice, Milan
1937 co-organizes Italian Pavilion, IEP
1939–41 bas-reliefs *The People of Italy*, Palazzo dei Giornali, Milan
1940 co-organizes Milan Triennale; exhibits at Kunsthaus Zürich; exhibits in *La Nazione*, Florence (with Carrà, Mafai)
1941 designs for EUR; exhibits at Galleria del Milione, Milan
1942 exhibits at Accademia di Brera, Milan
1943 solo exhibition Galleria del Milione, Milan; supports the Republic of Salò; exhibits in *Ausländische Kunst in Zürich*, Kunsthaus Zürich

Albert Speer
Architect, Minister of Armaments and War
Production
1905, Mannheim – 1981, London
1928–32 Adolf Hitler House
(remodelling), Nazi party business offices
(remodelling), Berlin
1931 joins the Nazi party
1932 Nazi party headquarters renovation,
Berlin
1933 Reich Chancellery (remodelling of
interior), Ministry of Propaganda interiors,
Berlin; temporary buildings for Party
Congress, Nuremberg (permanent from
1934)
1933–45 Adolf Hitler's chief architect;
responsible for design and organization of
party rallies
1936 Thorak sculpture studio, Baldham;
Speer studio, Obersalzberg; Stadium of the
Four Hundred Thousand, Nuremberg
(project)
1937 German Pavilion, IEP; Grand Prix
for projects for Nuremberg Stadium and
Gold Medal for Pavilion, IEP
1937–45 Inspector-General of Building,
responsible for rebuilding Berlin and other
German cities
1938 Reichsmarschallamt and Great Hall,
Berlin (projects); becomes Prussian State
Councillor; receives Nazi Golden Party
Badge of Honour
1938–39 New Reich Chancellery (Neue
Reichskanzlei), Berlin
1939 Oberkommando der Wehrmacht,
Führerpalais and Central Station, Berlin
(projects); urban development plan for
Berlin
1941 elected to represent the constituency
of Berlin West in the Reichstag
1942 member of Central Planning Office;
Minister of Armaments and War
Production; General Inspector of Water
and Energy; heads the Nazi party's main
office for technology
1945 resists Hitler's destruction orders

Vladimir Yevgrafovich Tatlin
Painter, sculptor, graphic artist, designer,
architect
1885, Moscow – 1953, Moscow
1929–33 heads experimental workshop,
Novodevichy Monastery, Moscow
1930 designs catafalque for Mayakovsky's
funeral; presents model of tower,
Monument to the Third International, at *War
and Art*, Russian Museum, Leningrad
1930s works at Moscow Textile Institute
1931 Honoured Art Worker of the RSFSR
1931–33 supervises Research Laboratory
for Plastic Arts, People's Commissariat for
Public Enlightenment
1932 presents *Letatlin*, Writers Club,
Moscow; solo exhibition, Pushkin
Museum, Moscow; exhibits in *Artists of the
RSFSR over 15 Years*, Russian Museum,
Leningrad
1934 visits White Sea Canal construction
site
1938 co-designer All-Union Agricultural
Exhibition, Moscow; murals for Cattle-
Breeding Pavilion denounced and
destroyed
1939 exhibits in exhibition of Theatre
Artists, Moscow; designs for Khlebnikov's
Unpublished Works
1941–43 is evacuated to Sverdlovsk
1943 designs for plays on war, *The Blue
Cloth* and *Missing*
1945 exhibits at conference *Theatre
Productions of Moscow Artists*

Josef Thorak
Sculptor
1889, Salzburg – 1952 Hartmannsberg
1934 death mask of President Hindenburg
1935 bust of Kemal Atatürk
1936 Hitler bust for Olympic Stadium,
Berlin; exhibits in *Olympische
Kunstausstellung*, Berlin
1937 sculpture *Kameradschaft* for German
Pavilion, IEP; Grand Prix, IEP
1937 onward teaches at Munich Academy;
works in his monumental studio in
Baldham near Munich; sculpts bust of
Mussolini, produces monumental figures
for the new Reich Chancellery in Berlin,
Autobahn sculptures and numerous war
memorials; exhibits at GDK

Nikolai Vasilevich Tomsky
Sculptor
1900, Ramuschev – 1984, Moscow
1933 co-designer of monument to Lenin,
Mogiliov
1935 exhibits in exhibition of Leningrad
artists, Leningrad
1935–38 Kirov monument, Leningrad; 11
monuments are erected in several cities of
the Soviet Union after this design
1937 Soviet Pavilion, IEP
1939 New York World Fair; exhibits in
All-Union Exhibition *The Industry of
Socialism*
1940 Lenin statue, Voronezh;
commissioned for Lenin
monuments in Erevan, Perm and Kursk
1941 Stalin Prize for Kirov monument,
Leningrad; joins group of sculptors to
work on satirical bas-relief *Hitler and
Napoleon*
1942 moves to Moscow
1943 two monumental sculptures of Soviet
soldiers erected in Moscow

Aleksandr Aleksandrovich Vesnin
Architect, painter, stage designer, graphic
designer
1883, Yurevets – 1959, Moscow
1930s teaches at Institute of Architecture,
Moscow
1933 onward heads Mossoviet design
studio
1939 member of Moscow Academy

Viktor Aleksandrovich Vesnin
Architect, theorist
1882, Yurevets – 1950, Moscow
1932 elected to Board of Association of
Soviet Architects
1933 heads Mossoviet design studio
1937–49 Secretary, Association of Soviet
Architects
1939–49 first President, All-Union
Academy of Architecture

Major works by the Vesnin brothers:
1929–30 Dnieper Dam and Hydro-
Electric Station (Dneprostroi; with Kolli)
1929–34 Club for Former Political
Prisoners of the Tsars, Moscow
1930 urban plans of Stalingrad and
Kuznetsk
1931 Kharkov State Theatre
1931–33 Palace of Soviets, Moscow
(competition projects)
1931–34 Film Actors' Club, Moscow
1931–37 Palace of Culture, Moscow
1933 Nemirovich-Danchenko Theatre
(project)
1934 Heavy Industry Commissariat,
Moscow (competition project)
1935 interior design, Metro station
Paveletskaya, Moscow

Luigi Vietti
Architect
1934 Palazzo del Littorio, Rome
(competition project with Sironi)
1937 site plan for EUR (with Piacentini)

Ernst Vollbehr
Painter, graphic artist, author
1876, Kiel –
1930 travels to the Philippines
1932–33 travels to China, Japan and
California
1933 commissioned to make an artistic
record of the achievements of the Third
Reich (new buildings, marches, Autobahn
construction)
1934 moves to Berlin
1935 publishes autobiography *Bunte,
leuchtende Welt*, Berlin
1940 solo exhibition Kunstverein, Munich
1941 receives Goethe Medal for Art and
Science

Vera Mikhailovna Yermolayeva
Painter, illustrator, graphic artist, stage and
costume designer
1893, Petrovsk – 1938, in exile, Siberia
From mid-1920s illustrates children's
books; works on editions of Krylov's fables
1925–34 works at State Children's Book
Publishing House
1932 exhibits in *Artists of the RSFSR over
15 Years*, Russian Museum, Leningrad
1934 arrested and exiled because of her
brother's involvement with Mensheviks
1936 serious illness causes progressive
amputation of her legs
1938 dies in a Siberian camp

Adolf Ziegler
Painter
1892, Bremen – 1959, Varnhalt
1933 professor at the Munich Academy;
becomes foremost official painter of the
Third Reich
1936 appointed President of the Reich
Chamber of Visual Arts
1937 authorized to strip all galleries and
museums in the Reich of so-called
'degenerate' art; organizes *Entartete Kunst*;
exhibits in *Arts graphiques et plastiques*, IEP,
and is awarded Grand Prix
1937 onward exhibits at GDK most years

£120

CREDITS

Exhibition Videos

Produced and compiled by Lutz Becker in conjunction with Flashback Television Ltd, Taylor Downing and Jonathan Lubert.

1 International Exhibition, Paris 1937

2 The Spanish civil war: the defence of Madrid

3 New Moscow

4 A Metro for Moscow

5 Sports parade on Red Square, 1937

6 Competition for the Palace of the Soviets: the monumental work of Sergei Merkorov and Vera Mukhina

7 Foro Mussolini, Rome

8 *Antichità*: via dell'Impero

9 Ten Years of Fascist Revolution, 1932

10 New cities: Sabaudia, Littoria, EUR

11 Albert Speer's new Berlin

12 Olympic Games, Berlin 1936

13 *Entartete Kunst*, Munich 1937

14 The Hitler cult and monumentalism: the work of Josef Thorak and Arno Breker

Film archives:
Archives du Film de la Cinématographie (CNC). Bois-d'Arcy: British Pathé News Ltd. London; Cineart Film- und Fernsehproduktion GmbH, Munich; Creswell Research Services, Leighton Buzzard; Educational & Television Films Ltd (ETV), London; Gosfilmofond of Russia, Belye Stolby; Imperial War Museum, London; Istituto LUCE, Rome; Library of Congress, Washington DC; National Film and Television Archive (NFTVA), London; Philips Lighting Ltd, London; Russian Central State Archive for Film and Photographic Documents, Krasnagorsk
Video editors: Colin Barratt, Marck Budzynski
Video Displays: Video Power Ltd, Perivale
Laser Disks: Pioneer High Fidelity (GB) Ltd, Slough

The producer wishes to express his gratitude for help and advice received throughout from Clyde Jeavons, Anne Fleming, Jane Hockings and Orwen Terris of the NFTVA, London; Roger Smithers, Jane Fish and Paul Sargent of the Imperial War Museum, London; Michelle Aubert and Eric Le Roy of CNC, Bois-d'Arcy; Stanley Forman and Betty Baker of ETV, London.

Copyright bylines

© ADAGP, Paris, and DACS, London 1995: Julio González 74, 75; Joan Miró 80, 81, 82, 83
© Ernst und Hans Barlach Lizenzverwaltung Ratzeburg 1995; Ernst Barlach 292, 335
© Archiv Baumeister 1995; Willi Baumeister 308, 309
© Atelier Breker (Düsseldorf) & Museum Europäische Kunst (Nörvenich) 1995; Arno Breker 337(3)
© IVAM Centre Julio González, Valencia 1995; Pere Català i Pic 97
© The Artist 1995; Tullio Crali 153
© DACS 1995: Herbert Bayer 265; Max Beckmann 300, 316; Giorgio de Chirico 166, 167; Otto Dix 27; Hans Grundig 318; José Gutiérrez Solana 87; Renato Guttuso 176; John Heartfield 273, 290; Ludwig Hohlwein 320; Paul Klee 310(2), 311(2); Richard Klein 331; Heinrich Knirr 295; Oskar Kokoschka 302, 303; Georg Kolbe 299, 332(2); Käthe Kollwitz 293; Marino Marini 158; Pablo Picasso 76, 77, 78, 79; Alberto Sánchez Pérez 72, 73, 112(2), 114(2); Alberto Savinio 164; José María Sert 100, 101
© DEMART PRO ARTE BV/DACS 1995: Salvador Dalí 103
© Archivio G. del Debbio 1995: Enrico del Debbio 147
© Carmen Ferrer, Adán Ferrer, Horacio Ferrer 1995: Horacio Ferrer Morgado 85
Courtesy of US Army Center of Military History, Washington DC: Rudolf Hengstenberg 44
© The Art Institute of Chicago 1995: Ludwig Hilberseimer 47
© Landesarchiv Berlin 1995: Wilhelm Kreis 328; Albert Speer 281, 283
© Estate of Lapadula Archive 1995: Ernesto Bruno Lapadula 148
© Banca Popolare di Cremona 1995: Baldassarre Longoni 174
© Estate of the Artist 1995: Gerhard Marcks 301
© Estate of the Artist 1995: Arturo Martini 53, 159, 160, 161
© Estate of Fausto Melotti Archives 1995: Fausto Melotti 172
© Nolde-Stiftung Seebüll 1995: Emil Nolde 314, 315
© Hamburgisches Architekturarchiv, Collection Cäsar Pinnau, 1995: Cäsar Pinnau 286
© Museum für Verkehr und Technik, Berlin 1995: Hans Poelzig 289
© Fundación Renau, Valencia 1995: Josep Renau 92(4), 93, 94(2), 95(2), 98
© Estate of the Artist 1995: Josef Thorak 266, 366(2)

Additional photo credits for plate sections

Jörg P. Anders, Berlin; Arxiu Fotogràfic, Barcelona; Tim Benton; Studio Fotografico Lucca Carrà, Milan; Ursula Edelmann, Frankfurt am Main; R. Friedrich, Berlin; Klaus Göken, Berlin; Foto Hauk-Werbestudios, Mannheim; Hart, Trento; Heartfield-Archiv, Berlin; Image + Communication, Turin; Foto Cine Luchetti, Cremona; Museum für angewandte Kunst, Vienna; Museo Nacional d'Art de Catalunya (Barcelona), Servei fotogràfic del MNAC (Calveras/Sagrista); Gasparo Neva, Trieste; Opticon GmbH, Stuttgart; Foto Otto, Vienna; Maura Parodi, Genoa; Wolfgang Pulfer, Munich; Foto Saporetti, Milan; G. Schiavinotto, Rome; A. Sergeyeva and V. Popkova, Moscow; Foto Strenger, Osnabrück; John Webb, London; Julius Wilcke.

Text illustration credits

Additional picture research by Georgina Bruckner

Accademia di San Luca, Rome, Fondo De Renzi 42, 125
Akademie der Künste, Berlin 49, Photo Roman März 273
AKG London 14, 18b, 20
Archives Nationales, Paris 51, 59(3), 65, 66, 67, 109
Archivio Centrale dello Stato, Rome, Archivio Moretti, Photo Vasari 127
Arkhitektura SSSR 10–11 (1935) 247
Art Institute of Chicago 47
Associated Press 2, 26
Lutz Becker Collection 22b, 24, 30, 139, 195
Tim Benton 37, 38, 40, 126
Berlin Museum 441
Biblioteca Nacional, Madrid 111
British Film Institute 29, 199, 200
Camera Press 24r, 29
Central Museum of V. I. Lenin, Moscow 250, 251 m, 252
Civiche Raccolte d'Arte, Milan 53
Farabollafoto, Rome 121
Fotociclo, Rome 122t
George-Kolbe-Museum, Berlin 275
Berthold Hinz, Berlin 330(3), 331, 332(2), 333(3)
Imperial War Museum, London, P. Daniel Collection 341
Istituto LUCE, Rome 138
David King Collection, London 21, 22b, 27t

F. Kollar © Association française pour la diffusion du Patrimoine photographique; Ministère de la Culture – France 69, 70
L'Illustration, Paris 57
Landesbildstelle, Berlin 43, 264
Museo Nacional Centro de Arte Reina Sofía, Madrid 114(2)
Winfried Nerdinger, Munich 323(2), 324(3), 325(4)
Bernd Nicolai, Kassel 336, 337
Novosti 250 b
Osbert Lancaster, *Façades and Faces* (London: John Murray, 1950) 322
Preussischer Kulturbesitz, Berlin: Bildarchiv 260t, 266; Archiv Nationalgalerie 183
Rassegna 41t
Roger-Viollet (© Harlingue-Viollet) 12, 129
Russian Academy of Art, St Petersburg 251t
Bildbestand Wolfgang Schäche, Berlin 257, 259, 262t, 327, 328(2), 329(2)
Shchusev State Museum of Architecture, Moscow 185, 191, 192(2), 193, 194
Staatliche Museen zu Berlin, Kunstbibliothek 260b
Staatliche Kunsthalle, Karlsruhe 274
Städelsches Kunstinstitut, Frankfurt am Main 45
State Russian Museum, St Petersburg 251 b
US Army Center for Military History, Washington, DC 44 r, 48
Wiener Library, London 25, 28

Literary credits

Amédée Ozenfant, 'Notes d'un touriste à l'Exposition', *Cahiers d'Art* 12 (1937) 242ff. (slightly abridged): 115

Giuseppe Bottai, 'L'arte moderna', *Critica Fascista*, 1 December 1938: 181

Kurt Craemer, *Mein Panoptikum*, ed. Rudolf Hagelstange (Hamburg: Hoffmann und Campe, 1965), 124–25, 128–32, 132–34, 233–36; 182

Erwin Sinkó, *Roman eines Romans: Moskauer Tagebuch* (Cologne: Verlag Wissenschaft und Politik, 1962), 189–94, 267–68; 253

Richard Friedenthal, *Die Welt in der Nußschale* (Munich: Piper, 1956), 312–23; 340

Tadeusz Rózewiez, 'In the Midst of Life', from *The Burning Forest: Modern Polish Poetry*, tr. Adam Czerniawski (London: Bloodaxe Books, 1988): 342

Günter Eich, 'Inventory' (extract), from Eich, *Pigeons and Moles: Selected Writings*. tr. Michael Hamburger (London: Skoob Books, 1991): 342